Warwick the Kingmaker

Warwick the Kingmaker as patron of Tewkesbury Abbey, from the Tewkesbury Abbey Chronicle *(Bodleian Library, Oxford, MS Top.Glouc.d.2, f.36v).*

Warwick the Kingmaker

Michael Hicks

Blackwell Publishers

Editorial Offices:
108 Cowley Road, Oxford OX4 1JF, UK
    Tel: +44 (0)1865 791100
350 Main Street, Malden, MA 02148-5018, USA
    Tel: +1 781 388 8250

The right of Michael Hicks to be identified as the Author of this Work has been asserted in accordance with the UK Copyright, Designs and Patents Act 1988.

First published 1998 by Blackwell Publishers Ltd, a Blackwell Publishing company
First published in paperback 2002

Transferred to digital print 2006

Library of Congress Cataloging-in-Publication Data

Hicks, M. A. (Michael A.)
    Warwick the Kingmaker / Michael Hicks.
        p. cm.
    Includes bibliographical references (p. 314) and index.
    ISBN 0–631–16259–3 (hb : alk. paper)—ISBN 0–631–23593–0 (pb. : alk. paper)
    1. Warwick, Richard Neville, Earl of, 1428–1471.   2. Great Britain—
History—Wars of the Roses, 1455–1485.   3. Great Britain—Politics and
government—1399–1485.   4. Great Britain—Kings and rulers—
succession.   5. Nobility—Great Britain—Biography.
I. Title.
DA247.W25H53   1998
942.04'4'092—dc21
[B]   98-9225
                                                                                              CIP

A catalogue record for this title is available from the British Library.

Set in 10 on 11.5 Ehrhardt
by G & G Editorial, Brighton
Printed and bound in Great Britain by Marston Book Services Limited, Oxford

For further information on Blackwell Publishers, visit our website:
www.blackwellpublishers.co.uk

Contents

Plates   vii

Genealogical Tables   ix

Preface   x

Abbreviations   xiii

1   The Legend of Warwick the Kingmaker   1

2   The Formative Years   7
    2.1   Pedigree and Patrimony   7
    2.2   Northern Roots   17
    2.3   Shaping the Future   22

3   Earl of Warwick   31
    3.1   Warwick Inheritance Update   31
    3.2   Gathering the Spoils   36
    3.3   Effectively Earl   48
    3.4   The Warwick Traditions   53

4   The Polarization of Politics 1449–54   64
    4.1   The Ascendancy of the Opposition   64
    4.2   The Royalist Reaction 1451–3   75
    4.3   Time for Decision   85

5   Partisan Politics 1454–6   94
    5.1   York's First Protectorate 1454–5   94
    5.2   The First Battle of St Albans 1455   112
    5.3   York's Second Protectorate 1455–6   119

6 Countdown to Civil War 1456–9   126
   6.1 Towards Reconciliation   126
   6.2 Captain of Calais and Keeper of the Seas   138
   6.3 The Opportunity Missed   148
   6.4 Rout   159

7 Fortune's First Wheel 1459–61   168
   7.1 *Reculer pour mieux sauter*   168
   7.2 Warwick's Triumph   177
   7.3 The Ideology of Reform   191
   7.4 From Abyss to Victory   210

8 The Rule of the Nevilles 1461–7   220
   8.1 The First Family   220
   8.2 The Pacification of the North   234
   8.3 Changing Priorities   248

9 Dropping the Pilot 1467–9   255
   9.1 Growing Apart   255
   9.2 Rising Tensions 1467–9   263
   9.3 Warwick's First Coup 1469   271

10 Fortune's Second Wheel 1470–1   279
   10.1 Warwick's Second Coup 1470   279
   10.2 Warwick as Kingmaker   286
   10.3 From Triumph to Disaster 1470–1   296

11 Terminus   311

Select Bibliography   314

Index   326

Plates

1   The Neville matriarch Joan Beaufort Countess of
    Westmorland and daughters at prayer   101

2   Warwick's parents Richard Neville and Alice Montagu
    as Earl and Countess of Salisbury   101

3   Richmond Castle   102

4   Bear and ragged staff from a gold ring supposedly taken
    from Warwick's body at Barnet   103

5   The Neville screen, Durham Cathedral   103

6   The south-west corner of Guyscliff Chapel   104

7   Guy's Tower, Warwick Castle   105

8   Warwick as a mourner from the monument of his
    father-in-law Richard Beauchamp Earl of Warwick
    at the Beauchamp Chapel, Warwick   106

9   Muzzled bears and ragged staves from the entrance to
    the Beauchamp Chapel, Warwick   107

10 Warwick's seal as Lord of Glamorgan   108

11 Two cheap lead badges of the type distributed wholesale
    to Warwick's retainers   108

12 Cardiff, the principal town of Warwick's lordship of
    Glamorgan, from the early seventeenth-century map
    of John Speed   201

13 Henry VI sits in triumph whilst the future Edward IV
   and other Yorkist lords embark for Calais, 1459   201

14 The east end of Tewkesbury Abbey   202

15 A court scene   203

16 Bisham Priory   204

17 Reconstruction of Middleham Castle   204

18 Warwick and the Countess Anne from John Rous's Roll
   of the Earls of Warwick   205

19 Warwick's sole surviving book   206

20 King Louis XI of France   207

21 Signed letter of 12 February 1471 in French from
   Warwick to Louis XI   207

22 The Battle of Barnet: Edward IV leads the royal army
   to victory and Warwick's men flee to the right   208

Genealogical Tables

2.1	The Hollands	8
2.2	The Montagus	9
2.3	The Neville Family in the 1430s and 1440s	14
3.1	The Beauchamp and Despenser Inheritances	38
3.2	Title to the Lordship of Abergavenny	41
5.1	The Royal Family and the Protectorate 1454	95
7.1	The House of York's Title to the Crown 1460–1	188
8.1	The Salisbury Celebrations at Bisham 1463	229
8.2	The Nevilles in the North in the 1460s	231
10.1	Title to the Crown and the Succession 1470–1	283

Preface

Warwick the Kingmaker played a central role in all England's political crises between 1450 and 1471. He ranged across the islands of Britain and its nearest neighbours. He was a family-man, a great nobleman, statesman, rebel, general, admiral and subaltern, patron, benefactor and much else besides. If his own records are largely lost, he crops up in many other archives and chronicles in many different languages. No historian, certainly not this one, can consult everything or be expert in all these areas. I gratefully acknowledge both the work of my contemporaries and also of the centuries of researchers, editors, writers and archivists who have brought us to our present state of knowledge and understanding. All historians of the reigns of Henry VI and Edward IV must start and finish with the monumental studies of Professor Ralph Griffiths and Miss Cora L. Scofield. Though the late K. B. McFarlane now conditions all studies of late medieval English politics, it is Professor R. L. Storey's pioneering *End of the House of Lancaster* and Professor J. R. Lander's classic articles that are most influential in interpreting the reigns respectively of Henry VI and Edward IV. Many earlier writers are cited in the Bibliography, amongst whom for their guidance on particular areas I thank especially the late Mr John Armstrong, Dr Gerald Harriss, Dr Paul Johnson, Professor Tony Pollard, Professor Colin Richmond, the late Professor Charles Ross, Mr T. B. Pugh, Dr Livia Visser-Fuchs, and the editors of *John Vale's Book*. Mr Adrian Ailes, Dr Anne Curry and Dr Michael K. Jones supplied useful references and advice, the latter many times. Dr John Cherry and Mr Geoffrey Wheeler helped with the illustrations. Whilst I hope that they are all happy with the use I have made of their help, the responsibility for what appears here is mine.

Inevitably this book departs from existing works at many points. Any fresh look from a different angle, particularly from the vantage of a particular individual – for everyone's history is different – forces the historian or biographer to reassess and revise in search of the best fit of evidence to interpretation. Narratives, arguments and analyses that appear to work well do so no longer when approached from a different point of view. Even accounts of the same events by the same author with reference to different individuals vary by more than mere perspective. I have tried to return to the evidence and not merely to repeat my own earlier work or that of others. At several points where others have seemed certain, I have not been so sure and freely admit that I do not know the answer. What is written here constitutes my current synthesis. It is not the last word on the subject nor, probably, my own last word. Much still remains to be learnt and doubtless to be much better understood. It is staggering how far we have come in the last hundred, fifty, and twenty years.

Biography is the study of an individual. It requires the presentation of the past in relation to that person and ideally through the eyes of that person. A taxing and ultimately impossible task. That does not mean that the biographer must take his subject's side, must ignore the views or decry the motives of others, or abandon objectivity. If I have sought to understand Warwick's actions, I have also, I believe, pointed out how unjustifiable, unreasonable or perverse they often were. I have not called Warwick great. He was certainly remarkable and demands some admiration. We do not have to like him. Can modern historians like any of the kings, politicians and magnates of late medieval England? But we should note that many people who lived in the fifteenth century definitely did admire Warwick.

Many years of reading, researching, travel, discussion, reflection and writing have gone into this book. They would not have been possible without the support and tolerance of my long-suffering family, especially my wife Cynthia to whom I dedicate this book, to her late mother who read all my books, and to my History colleagues at King Alfred's College, Winchester. The College kindly awarded me study leave in 1989 and has supported my attendance at conferences and in other ways. St John's College, Oxford, awarded me a scholarship in the summer vacation of 1994 to study in Oxford. I have benefited from membership of research seminars of the Institute of Historical Research and of the Wessex Medieval Centre at Southampton and from attendance at a dozen fifteenth-century colloquia. I am indebted to a host of librarians and archivists in many repositories over nearly thirty years. The notes I made on George Duke of Clarence as a research student have proved impressively full and unexpectedly useful. I acknowledge the contributions of John Armstrong, T. B. Pugh, and Charles Ross in that context too.

At a more technical level, efforts have been made – I hope with complete success – to avoid confusion in the early chapters between two Richard Nevilles, two Richard Beauchamps, two Richards Earl of Warwick, two Anne Beauchamps Countesses of Warwick, and four George Nevilles! Quotations in foreign languages have been silently translated; middle English has been retained, the runic thorn being replaced by the modern 'th'. In Middle English 'v' and 'u' are often interchangeable; so are 'i' and 'j'. Unless otherwise indicated, all manuscripts are at the Public Record Office and all works cited were published in London. Prices in marks and ecus have been translated into modern British pounds and new pence without regard for inflation over 500 years.

September 1997
Winchester

Abbreviations

Manuscripts in the Public Record Office (PRO) are cited by callmark only.

Annales	'Annales Rerum Anglicarum', *The Wars of the English in France*, ed. J. Stevenson (Rolls Series, 4 vols, 1864), ii(2).
Anstis	*Register of the Most Noble Order of the Garter*, ed. J. Anstis, 2 vols, 1724.
Benet's Chron.	'John Benet's Chronicle for the years 1400 to 1462', ed. G. L. and M. A. Harriss (*Camden Miscellany* xxiv, Camden 4th ser. ix, 1972).
BIHR	*Bulletin of the Institute of Historical Research.*
BL	British Library.
Bodl	Bodleian Library.
Carpenter, *Locality*	M. C. Carpenter, *Locality and Polity: A Study of Warwickshire Landed Society 1401–99* (Cambridge, 1992).
CCR	*Calendar of the Close Rolls.*
CChR	*Calendar of Charter Rolls 1427–1516.*
CFR	*Calendar of the Fine Rolls.*
CPL	*Calendar of the Papal Letters.*
CPR	*Calendar of the Patent Rolls.*
CSPM	*Calendar of State Papers Milanese.*
Davies Chron.	*An English Chronicle*, ed. J. S. Davies (Camden Soc. lxiv, 1856).
DKR	*Reports of the Deputy Keeper of the Public Records.*
EETS	Early English Text Society.
EHD	*English Historical Documents*, iv, *1327–1485*, ed. A. R. Myers (1969).

EHR	*English Historical Review.*
Ellis, *Original Letters*	*Original Letters Illustrative of English History*, ed. H. Ellis, 3 ser. 1824–46.
Foedera	*Foedera, Conventiones, et cujuscunque Acta Publica*, ed. T. Rymer (The Hague, 10 vols, 1745; 20 vols, 1704–35).
GEC	G. E. C[okayne], *Complete Peerage*, ed. H. V. Gibbs (13 vols, 1910–59).
Gregory's Chron.	*Historical Collections of a Citizen of London*, ed. J. Gairdner (Camden Society, new series xvii, 1876).
Griffiths, *Henry VI*	R. A. Griffiths, *The Reign of King Henry VI 1422–61* (1981).
Griffiths, *King & Country*	R. A. Griffiths, *King and Country: England and Wales in the Fifteenth Century* (London, 1991).
Hicks, *Clarence*	M. A. Hicks, *False, Fleeting, Perjur'd Clarence: George Duke of Clarence 1449–78* (rev. edn Bangor, 1992).
Hicks, *Richard III*	M. A. Hicks, *Richard III and his Rivals: Magnates and their Motives during the Wars of the Roses* (1991).
HMC	Historical Manuscripts Commission.
HR	*Historical Research.*
JMH	*Journal of Medieval History.*
Johnson, *York*	P. A. Johnson, *Duke Richard of York 1411–60* (Oxford, 1988).
Kendall, *Warwick*	P. M. Kendall, *Warwick the Kingmaker* (London, 1957).
'Neville Pedigree'	R. H. C. FitzHerbert, 'Original Pedigree of Taylboys and Neville', *The Genealogist*, new ser. iii (1886), 31–5, 107–11.
NMS	*Nottingham Medieval Studies.*
PL	*The Paston Letters AD 1422–1509*, ed. J. Gairdner (6 vols, London, 1904).
Paston L & P	*Paston Letters and Papers of the Fifteenth Century*, ed. N. Davis (2 vols, Oxford, 1971–6).
Plumpton L & P	*The Plumpton Letters and Papers*, ed. J. Kirby (Camden 5th ser. iv, 1997).
POPC	*Proceedings & Ordinances of the Privy Council.*
RO	Record Office.
Rous Roll	*The Rous Roll*, ed. W. H. Courthope (London, 1859).
RP	*Rotuli Parliamentorum*, Record Commission, 6 vols, 1767–83.
Scofield	C. L. Scofield, *The Life and Reign of Edward IV* (2 vols, London, 1923).
SHF	Société de l'Histoire de France.

Stevenson	*Letters and Papers illustrative of the Wars of the English in France*, ed. J. Stevenson, 3 vols in 2, Rolls Series, 1864.
Stone's Chron.	*The Chronicle of John Stone*, ed. W. G. Searle (Cambridge Antiquarian Society, octavo series xxiv, 1902).
Storey, *Lancaster*	R. L. Storey, *The End of the House of Lancaster* (2nd edn, 1986).
TCWAS	*Transactions of the Cumberland & Westmorland Archaeological Society.*
Three 15th-Cent. Chrons.	*Three Fifteenth-Century Chronicles*, ed. J. Gairdner (Camden Society, new series xxviii, 1880).
TRHS	*Transactions of the Royal Historical Society.*
Vale's Bk	*The Politics of Fifteenth-Century England: John Vale's Book*, ed. M. L. Kekewich, C. F. Richmond, A. Sutton, L. Visser-Fuchs, and J. Watts (Stroud, 1995).
Warkworth's Chron.	J. Warkworth, *Chronicle of the First Thirteen Years of the Reign of King Edward the Fourth*, ed. J. O. Halliwell (Camden Society vi, 1839).
Watts, *Henry VI*	J. L. Watts, *Henry VI and the Politics of Kingship* (Cambridge, 1996).
Waurin	*Receuil des Anciennes Chroniques par Waurin*, ed. W. and E. L. C. P. Hardy (5 vols Rolls Series, 1864–91), vol. v.
Waurin-Dupont	*Anciennes Chroniques de l'Engleterre*, ed. E. L. M. E. Dupont, 3 vols, Société de l'Histoire de France, 1858–63.
Whetehamstede	*Registrum Abbatiae Johannis Whetehamstede, Abbatis Monasterii Sancti Albani*, ed. H. T. Riley (2 vols, Rolls Series, 1872–3).

1

The Legend of Warwick the Kingmaker

Warwick the Kingmaker dominated the first half of the Wars of the Roses (1455–71). Traditions of service and royal blood destined him to be the loyal subject of the last Lancastrian King Henry VI and the natural opponent of his critic Richard Duke of York. He had realigned himself by 1454. In 1455, for the first battle of St Albans, he was a dashing Yorkist. In 1459–60 he was York's most formidable champion. Following the duke's death, he masterminded the victory over Lancaster of York's son and his usurpation as Edward IV. At first Warwick and his brothers ruled, whilst Edward merely reigned. Parting company acrimoniously, Warwick became Edward's fiercest critic. In 1470 Edward was dethroned in favour of Henry VI until, finally, in 1471 Warwick himself fell in battle. Had he lived, perhaps King Henry could have retained his throne. Such a central figure has attracted biographers: Thomas Gainford's *Unmatchable Life and Death of Richard Nevill Earle of Warwicke in his tyme the darling and favorite of kings* of 1618 × 1624 and more recently the lives by Sir Charles Oman (1909), K. H. Francis (1916), and Paul Murray Kendall (1957). More material and new insights demand a more coherent and complete treatment.

Warwick is a household name. For those of a certain age who learnt the whole of English history by rote, he is forever the 'wicked baron' to whom contenders for the crown submitted application forms that specified their preferred means of death.[1] Yet no household name is so little known.[2] Like other late medieval politicians Warwick was depicted by Shakespeare. Following the *Mirror for Magistrates* he was 'thou plucker down and setter up of kings', but only in the *Henry VI* trilogy, hardly the playwright's most memorable or most frequently performed plays. Fortunately perhaps, since Shakespeare merged our Warwick

---

1   W. C. Sellar and R. J. Yeatman, *1066 and All That* (1930), 47–8.
2   Kendall, *Warwick*, 7.

with an earlier earl, his father-in-law and war hero, and made him the proposer of York's usurpation rather than its obstacle.[3]

Scarcely anybody in the past ninety years has favoured Warwick, observes Professor Richmond. A reassessment is perhaps overdue? In the way stands 'Warwick's amorality: he seems to have been the first of the serial killers of the Wars of the Roses'.[4] Even for Kendall, Warwick was 'a gigantic failure . . . because he poisoned his character . . . [and] sold what he was for what he ought to be'.[5] Kendall refers here to Warwick's deposition of Edward, which to a modern audience involved the overturning of his whole career and hence identified him with egotism and selfishness. This late *bouleversement* (reversal) has become the touchstone of his whole career.

If Warwick is controversial now, it is in part because he was controversial in his own day. Victory for York and maritime renown were earned at the expense of Lancastrians and Burgundians. It is one of the Lancastrians' misfortunes that their point of view was not preserved. Burgundian writers did however record their hatred of Warwick, a bogeyman akin to Talbot, and celebrated his death in verse and prose. For them, summarizes Livia Visser-Fuchs:

> he was proud, a trickster and a coward who was a hero in his own thoughts and a child in his actions; a poor idiot whose hands were unable to hold all that he tried to grasp; a fool and a traitor rushing towards his end; and as a crowning insult he is made to say of himself that we must not regard him as one of the Nine Worthies, but rather as a character from Boccaccio, a conceited but helpless victim of Fortune's wheel. . . . Warwick's fall . . . was another instance of how men and cities, through their *oultrecuidance*, their excessive pride, could not but come to grief in the end and serve as a warning to others.[6]

There is a savage vindictiveness to the assessments of Georges Chastellain and Thomas Basin. Such French and Burgundian testimony was concealed from centuries of English historians in distant manuscripts in foreign languages.

Warwick was fortunate that there was no alternative view to the hero of the English, Yorkist, sources. Surely no other English medieval magnate attracted such acclaim during his life and since? His break with Edward was generally attributed to Edward's foolish marriage; Warwick was not at fault. It was not Warwick who was inconsistent. He was justified in feeling slighted by the king's match. His honour was unjustifiably impugned when he was required to answer smears of treason by Edward, who overlooked how much he owed the earl. Warwick's change of allegiance, his defeat and death did not prevent generally

---

3   W. Shakespeare, *Henry VI Part II*, Act I sc. i; *Part III*, I.i, II.iii, III.vi.
4   *Vale's Bk.* 49.
5   Kendall, *Warwick*, 8.
6   L. Visser-Fuchs, 'Edward IV's *Memoir on Paper* to Charles, Duke of Burgundy: The so-called "Short Version of the *Arrivall*"', *NMS* xxxvi (1992), 170; see also A. Gransden, *Historical Writing in England c.1307 to the Early Sixteenth Century* (1982), 485–7.

favourable interpretations. 'Thow froward fortune hym deceuyd at his ende', wrote his chaplain John Rous, he remained always:

> A famus knyght and excellent gretly spoken of thorow the moste parte of christendam . . . He had all England at his ledyng and was dred and dowhyted thorow many landis. And thow froward fort[u]ne hym deceuyd at his ende yot his knyghtly acts had be so excellent that his noble and famous name could neuer be put owt of laudable memory.[7]

'I was no hippocrite,' the earl is made to say in *The Mirror for Magistrates* (1559).

> I never did nor sayd, save what I mente,
> The common weale was still my chiefest care,
> To priuate gayne or glory I was not bent . . .
> Which whan the people playnly vnderstoode,
> Bycause they sawe me mind the common weale
> They still endeuored how to do me good,
> Ready to spend their substaunce, life, and blud,
> In any cause wherto I did them move
> For suer they wer it was for their behove.

Hence Warwick's opposition to the abuses under Henry VI.

> But whan king Edward sinful prankes stil vsed,
> And would not mend, I likewise him refused:
> And holpe vp Henry the better of the twayne
> And in his quarel (iust I thinke) was slayne.

'Sure', observed the *Mirror*, 'I thinke the Erle of Warwike although he wer a glorious man, hath sayd no more of him selfe than what is true.'[8] When Warwick turned against Edward IV, the latter commissioned new histories hostile to the earl, but these reposed in manuscript until Victoria's reign[9] and thus missed the publicity given to Warwick's own manifestos that were printed in the *Annales of England* of the Elizabethan John Stow. For four centuries of historians it was the earlier, Yorkist, Warwick that was praised.

'Of him, it was said that he made kings and at his pleasure cast them down', wrote the Scot John Major (1521), when first dubbing him the kingmaker in Latin (*regum creator*).[10] The English translation was first deployed by the

---

7   *Rous Roll*, nos 56, 57.
8   *The Mirror for Magistrates*, ed. L. B. Campbell (1938), 208, 211.
9   'The Chronicle of the Rebellion in Lincolnshire', ed. J. G. Nichols (Camden Misc. i, 1847); *Historie of The Arrivall of Edward IV*, ed. J. Bruce (Camden Soc. i, 1838).
10   *John Major's History of Greater Britain* (Scottish Hist. Soc., 1892), 390–1; J. Major, *Historia Maioris Britanniae* (Lodoco Badia, 1521), f. cxlv.

Elizabethan Samuel Daniel and achieved currency only in the eighteenth century with David Hume;[11] during the interim 'the great', 'the stout earl of Warwick' and 'Warwick make-king' were preferred.[12] It was Warwick's glory to have made and unmade kings. To his first biographer, he deserved the surname

> Great, by reason of his hospitality, riches, possessions, popular love, comelynes of gesture, gracefulnes of person, industrious valour, indefatigable paynstaking and all the signatures of a royal mynde and generous spirite.[13]

For Thomas Carte (1750) Warwick was 'the most popular man of the age, universally beloved and esteemed. He was undoubtedly the greatest subject in England for power and estate and deserved all the popularity he enjoyed'.[14] For Warwick's fellow northerner James Raine the Elder (1834), the earl was:

> 'the greatest subject that ever lived. . . . His marriage with the heiress of the Beauchamps added to the splendour of his inheritance and his valour and extraordinary energy, combined with his profuse liberality and fascinating manners, rendered him the idol of the multitude. He was, in good truth, the setter up and putter down of kings.

He was 'King Edward's father' who 'trained him up', 'the Soul of Edward's Army', even worthy of the crown itself. He stood for the public good.[15] He was a romantic or heroic subject to nineteenth century-painters. Those cited above are merely the most extravagant of many tributes.

Such hero-worshipping historians were themselves the products of an age of aristocracy. They still understood and respected the lineage, magnificence, largesse, hospitality, committed retainers, ruthless justice, courage, boldness and frankness that they perceived in Warwick. They praised him for his virtues and for his popularity with the people, which they attributed to his eloquence, to his generosity and hospitality, and to his good lordship, and illustrated always with the same examples from *Fabyan's Chronicle* and Commines's *Mémoires*. 'Warwicke had their hartes', said Daniel.[16] 'The common people,' wrote Edward Hall, 'iudged hym able to do all thynges, and that without hym, nothyng to be

---

11   S. Daniel, *The Ciuill Wares betweene ye howses of Lancaster and York* (1609), 146; D. Hume, *History of England* (8 vols, Oxford, 1826), iii. 160.

12   E.g. F. Biondi, *A History of the Ciuill Warres of England* (1641), esp. 39; W. Dugdale, *Baronage of England* (2 vols, 1675), i. 304; P. Rapin de Thoyras, *History of England*, ed. N. Tindall (2nd edn, 1732), i. 579; Bodl. MS Wood F24, p. 7.

13   BL Add. MS 34352, p. 8 [Gainford's *Life*].

14   T. Carte, *General History of England* (1750), ii. 741.

15   *Testamenta Eboracensia*, ed. J. Raine (Surtees Soc. xxx, 1834), ii. 242n; Dugdale, *Baronage*, i. 305; Rapin, *History*, i. 579; Bodl. MS Wood F12, f. 136; Campbell, *Mirror*, 209.

16   Daniel, *Ciuill Warres*, 185.

well done'.[17] 'Send his soul rest', asked the *Mirror*, 'for sure his bodye never had any.'[18]

An absence of rest can be translated into unruliness and disorder. So thought Thomas Habington, who saw Warwick's 'mighty spirite . . . consumed in his own fire'.[19] 'Nothing more glorious could be said of a private man', observed Rapin de Thoyras in 1732, 'if true glory consists in excess of power'.[20] The values that Warwick stood for became antique and out of date: pride of lineage was trans-muted into haughty arrogance, liberality into extravagance, and his exceptional ruthlessness was ruthlessly exposed. His generalship, his abilities and his char-acter were considered more critically. Historians more overtly biased towards kings and towards progress took no pride in those who opposed such desirable ends. The Scot David Hume categorized Warwick into 'the greatest, as well as the last, of those mighty barons who formerly overawed the crown, and rendered the people incapable of any regular system of civil government'.[21] For Sharon Turner in 1823, he was a poor general, irascible and splenetic, ambitious and rest-less, 'too powerful to be a peaceful subject to any sovereign, yet compelled always to remain one' and hence better off dead.[22] Lord Lytton's three-volume novel *The Last of the Barons* presented Warwick as the end of his type, 'the old Norman chivalry',[23] at which the new critical and scientific historians rejoiced. 'He comes hardly within the ken of constitutional history', Stubbs opined.[24] 'He was the last great feudal nobleman who ever made himself dangerous to the reigning king', denounced Gairdner. 'His policy throughout seems to have been selfish and treacherous and his removal was an unquestionable blessing to his country.'[25]

Most of Gairdner's twentieth-century successors have followed his lead. Integrating the hostile testimony of Yorkist and Burgundian propaganda and Milanese despatches into balanced assessments has inevitably diluted and detracted from the English eulogies. Warwick became a diplomat subservient and inferior to Kendall's real hero, the French King Louis XI.[26] Thanks to K. B. McFarlane, modern historians are more sympathetic to English magnates and have rediscovered the material bases of aristocratic power that earlier generations

17 *Hall's Chronicle*, ed. H. Ellis (1809), 232, derived from P. Vergil, *Historia Angliae 1555* (1972 edn), 503; *Three Books of Polydore Vergil's English History*, ed. H. Ellis (Camden Soc. xxix, 1844), 95.
18 *Mirror*, 211.
19 T. Habington, *A Survey of Worcestershire*, ed. J. Amphlett (2 vols, Worcs. Hist. Soc. i, ii, 1895–9), ii. 111; see also his son William's *Historie of Edward the Fovrth King of England* (1640), esp. 85.
20 Rapin, *History*, i. 613.
21 Hume, *History*, iii. 160–1.
22 S. Turner, *History of England during the Middle Ages* (1823), iii. 290, 337.
23 E. G. E. L. Bulwer-Lytton, *The Last of the Barons* (3 vols, London, 1843), esp. i. 8.
24 W. Stubbs, *Constitutional History of England in the Middle Ages* (3 vols, Oxford, 1878), iii. 212.
25 J. Gairdner, *The Houses of Lancaster and York* (1874), 186.
26 Kendall, *Warwick*; *Louis XI* (1971).

of historians took for granted. Rediscovering the ambience and values is more difficult. Modern researchers cannot be content with the mere assertion that Warwick had good qualities and was popular as their predecessors had been, but the sources are lacking to reconstitute these qualities. A full biography is impossible. A fuller one is my attainable end.

This book avoids judging Warwick's whole career by the *bouleversement* of his last years. It tries to identify the influences that formed him, his actions, and motives at each stage of his career. For any biographer, still more one of a man who died 500 years ago, this is a challenging task. We lack almost all the materials of a modern life and most of those desired by medievalists. Warwick must always be seen through the eyes of others, always partisan, often mistaken or misled by his own propaganda, or deduced from actions capable of more than one interpretation. Though much seems clear enough, his total character is beyond recall.

Though still only forty-two when he died, Warwick is a big subject for a biographer. He was the greatest nobleman of his age, the heir to four great families, their estates, connections and traditions. He was the wealthiest and the most wide-ranging in interests. Bursting full-grown and unexpectedly on to the national scene in 1449, he constantly added geographical interests, new activities, and responsibilities to his portfolio. He ceded none to others. His relentless attention to business demanded an extraordinary energy that we can only marvel at. His ceaseless journeys took place over unmade-up roads, on horseback and sailing ships, and in English weather conditions. He was apparently never ill and never flagged. He is the model rather of the medieval nobility of service and of the all-encompassing chief minister of the future. Pragmatism and ruthlessness went hand in hand with honour. He was a daring subaltern, the boldest and most brilliant of strategists, a consummate logistician, and a pioneer in the tactical use of seapower, combined operations, and field artillery; flawed solely (but fatally) as a battlefield tactician. There was nothing Warwick would not attempt and no obstacle that he would not overcome. He was indomitable, never surrendered, and never failed to recover until the very end. For twenty years he shaped events, his own career, and indeed history itself. An underlying strength of will and determination and an intolerance of opposition and viciousness towards opponents needs to be set against the charm that cajoled, persuaded and won over men of whatever standing. It was this indefinable popularity that made him so much more than the greatest of subjects.

2

The Formative Years

2.1 Pedigree and Patrimony

Richard Neville, the future Warwick the Kingmaker, was born on St Cecilia's day (Monday, 22 November) 1428.[1] At birth he had nothing whatsoever to do with Warwick. That connection came later with his marriage. Until he became Warwick he will be referred to here as Richard, the baptismal name that he shares with his father. Richard was the eldest son and the third out of the eleven children of Sir Richard Neville and his wife Alice Montagu, who were to be recognized as Earl and Countess of Salisbury in Alice's right on 7 May 1429.[2] From the moment of his birth there was mapped out for him a political and military career as the head of one of the dozen leading English families. Yet only half a dozen facts are recorded about the first twenty years of his life. Very little, in particular, can be known about the upbringing that prepared him for his remarkable career, though we may presume it followed the conventional course sketched out for others of his class. Much more is known about the influences around him that constrained and shaped his subsequent career. It is with these, therefore, that we must commence.

Richard's mother was the only surviving daughter of Thomas Montagu, Earl of Salisbury, by his first wife Eleanor, one of the six sisters and ultimately four heiresses of Edmund (d. 1408), the last Holland Earl of Kent. From the thirteenth century the Montagus had been outstanding servants of the crown. Several had been stewards of the royal household. William, first Earl of Salisbury (d. 1344), had helped Edward III to overthrow Isabella and Mortimer and had

---

1 *Rous Roll*, no. 57. Unless otherwise stated, genealogical information in this chapter is from *GEC passim*.
2 *POPC* iii. 324–5.

been rewarded with the Isle of Man, subsequently alienated, the castle, honour, borough and hundred of Christchurch Twynham, and other lands in Hampshire, Wiltshire, Somerset and Dorset. John (d. 1400), the poet and third earl, had committed himself to Richard II even beyond his deposition and died a traitor to Henry IV in consequence. His forfeiture for treason was reversed in favour of his son, but the actual sentence of condemnation was revoked by parliament only in 1461 at Richard's request. Several Montagus were soldiers of renown and knights of the Garter. Thomas himself was a distinguished general, the best of the

Table 2.1   The Hollands

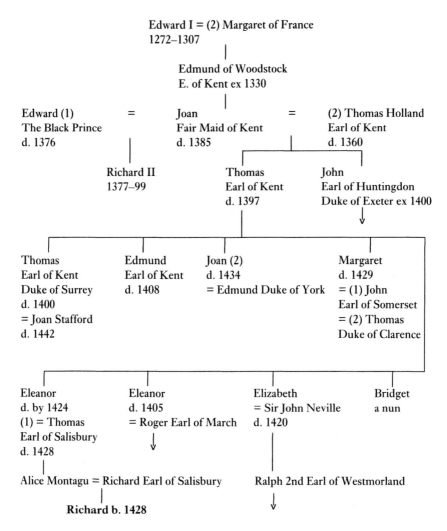

English commanders in France after Henry V's death, and his death in 1428 was a grievous blow to the English. The Montagus had been earls for almost a century, barons somewhat longer, and had built up a proud tradition of royal service.

The Montagu lineage is celebrated in the Salisbury Rolls of Arms, which consist of a succession of pairs of stylized portraits of husbands and wives. Two versions now survive: the earlier tentatively dated to 1463 and attributed to Richard and a second one more definitely commissioned for his son-in-law

Table 2.2 The Montagus

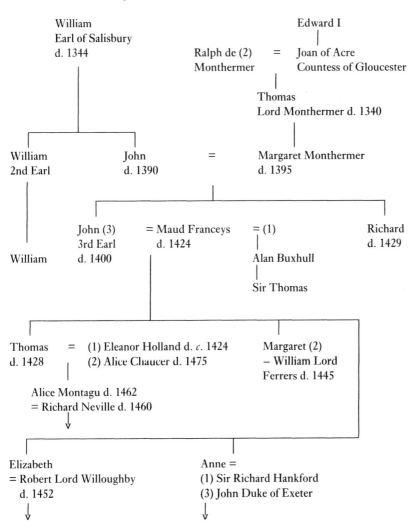

King Richard III.[3] Although late, each records traditions apparently preserved and elaborated by Richard and his parents and apparently transmitted to them by earlier rolls that have been lost. They reveal how the Montagu and Neville earls perceived themselves: their self-image, which Richard shared and promulgated.

Clues to what these earlier versions comprised can be detected in those that survive. Both surviving rolls are preoccupied with the family's royal descent and noble in-laws. Though the Montagus were not themselves royal nor even descended from earlier earls of Salisbury, both rolls include William Longespée, Earl of Salisbury, bastard son of Henry II; interestingly the arms of Longespée were included by the Kingmaker on his seal. Unlike other earlier earls, also unrelated to the Montagus and hence omitted, William was royal. Instead of tracing the Montagus to their origins, the rolls start only with Simon Montagu, heir to Affrica Lady of the Isle of Man. They highlight the first earl's foundation of the Augustinian priory of Holy Trinity Bisham (Berks.), the spiritual home of the family, where subsequent Montagus and Nevilles – including Richard – were buried. There is an illumination of the priory church. The Montagu line proceeds side by side with that of the Monthermers whose first ancestor, Ralph Earl of Gloucester (d. 1325) and his wife Joan of Acre (d. 1307), daughter of King Edward I and Queen Eleanor of Castile, feature on the roll. The union of the two lines in 1340 on the wedding of John Montagu, father of the third Earl, to Margaret Monthermer, which brought royal blood to their descendants, could have prompted the preparation of a first roll; particularly as the second Earl subsequently alienated the Isle of Man. In the next generation Earl John was to marry the widowed Maud Franceys, daughter of a London alderman: a plebeian marriage that has been made much of by modern historians. This connection is acknowledged but not stressed in later rolls.

A second updated version of the roll may have been prepared by Earl Thomas about 1420. The earliest surviving version records his first wife Eleanor, not the second married by 2 November 1424, and it includes the marriage contracted by 1421 of his daughter Alice to [Richard Neville] 'son of the Earl of Westmorland', who died in 1425, but none of their offspring. Strangely it ignored the royal descent both of the Countess Eleanor from Edward I and of the Nevilles from Edward III. Much is made of kin relevant in the 1420s, notably Earl Thomas's siblings Margaret Lady Ferrers of Chartley, Elizabeth Lady Willoughby, and the much married Anne, eventually Duchess of Exeter. Earl Thomas's kin were also those of his daughter, his son-in-law Richard Neville Earl of Salisbury, and their son, Richard. Salisbury had dealings with Maud Franceys's elder son Sir Alan Buxhull, who served under him in France in 1436, acquired land from Buxhull's son Thomas, and was guardian of Maud's Hankford grand-daughters in 1431.[4]

---

3   A. Payne, 'The Salisbury Roll of Arms, c. 1463', *England in the Fifteenth Century*, ed. D. Williams (Woodbridge, 1987), 187–98, esp. 181–91; BL MS Loan 90, ff. 176–225. These are the source of the next two paras.
4   *CCR 1422–9*, 116; E 326/ B5455, B9266; Devon RO Chanter MS 722 f. 2.

Some collateral lines, such as the Willoughbys, were updated for the 1463 version. If he had no other kin but the Montagus, therefore, Richard inherited a lineage and pride of lineage that was long-standing, noble, and royal, and kinship with many of the leading English families.

Richard's maternal grandmother Eleanor Holland hailed from a family as noble, royal, and much better endowed than his own. Her grandmother, the Fair Maid of Kent, grand-daughter of Edward I, had married the Black Prince and her father was therefore stepbrother of Richard II, who had briefly made dukes of both his half-brothers. Eleanor's own brothers both died prematurely without legitimate offspring, but three of her sisters married the dukes of York and Clarence, the Earl of Somerset, and the Earl of Westmorland's eldest son John Neville. The Holland connection also brought Earl Thomas and hence Richard an extensive kindred among the highest nobility.

Eleanor also brought Earl Thomas a fifth share of the Holland inheritance; other portions later accrued to Alice on the deaths of Holland dowagers and a childless aunt. Together her quarter share of the Holland inheritance was worth more than what remained of Thomas's own patrimony.[5] But Eleanor bore Earl Thomas no son to continue the Montagu line, only two daughters: Joanna, who died young, and Alice, who was married to Sir Richard Neville before 12 February 1421, when the bridegroom carved before Queen Katherine of France at her coronation and the bride was also in attendance.[6] Following Eleanor's death, Earl Thomas remarried at once to the widowed heiress Alice Chaucer, grand-daughter of the poet Geoffrey Chaucer, with a view to producing a son to continue the Montagu line and, inevitably, to cut his daughter and new son-in-law out of the Montagu inheritance. This match was barren. Had Earl Thomas survived Orleans and borne a son, the careers of both Richard Nevilles would have been very different. When Earl Thomas died, Alice and Richard succeeded at once to the Holland lands of his first wife and to those lands he had held in fee simple and in tail general. After the death of Thomas's elderly uncle Sir Richard Montagu in 1429, Richard and Alice were recognized by Henry VI's minority council as earl and countess of Salisbury: a decision perhaps influenced by Neville's royal lineage and confirmed by Henry VI in 1443. Finally and with doubtful legality, in 1461, Alice secured all Thomas's tail male lands too. Only very much later, in 1475, long after the deaths of the earl and countess of Salisbury and even of Richard too, did Alice Chaucer's West Country jointure finally return to the main line. In 1429 she had settled for complete manors and a pension in lieu of her legal entitlement to scattered thirds of everything. On 10 December 1436 Salisbury also agreed with her new husband to share the proceeds and costs of any of Earl Thomas's property recovered in France. This husband was William de la Pole, Earl of

---

5   Hicks, *Richard III*, 357.
6   *The Brut or The Chronicles of England*, ed. F. W. D. Brie (Early English Text Soc. cxxxvi, 1908), ii. 445-6. Clavering (Essex) was apparently part of their jointure, see SC 6/839/16 rot. 1 m. 2, but see also E 315/32/92; E 315/36/53.

Suffolk and steward of the royal household, later to be Duke of Suffolk and Henry VI's most trusted councillor, a kinsman with whom Salisbury was to have future dealings. Mediation was provided by Henry Cardinal Beaufort, kinsman of both parties.[7]

Sir Richard Neville – or *Salisbury* as we shall henceforth call him – was himself of royal and noble (if somewhat more ambiguous) ancestry. The Nevilles were already significant northern barons in the twelfth century and their fifteenth-century members justifiably believed themselves on the strength of their (largely fictional) family genealogies to have originated with the Norman Conquest. Geoffrey, the earliest Neville, was supposedly William I's admiral; Ribald, first Lord of Middleham (Yorks.), was bastard brother of Alan the Red of Brittany, the Conqueror's Earl of Richmond; and Ansketill de Bulmer was first lord of Sheriff Hutton (Yorks.). The Nevilles, however, were not content merely to be associated with the victorious invaders, but claimed descent also from the vanquished Anglo-Saxons. A fourth line was derived from Ughtred son of Earl Waltheof and in some rolls was extended back to King Ethelred II the Unready. These four lines intermarried into one by 1320 that derived from Ughtred, but which adopted the Neville surname. Their four castles of Raby, Brancepeth (Dur.), Sheriff Hutton and Middleham (Yorks.) were first united in the hands of Ralph Lord Neville of Raby (d. 1367). The barons Neville of Raby were wealthier than many an earl and were well able to support the earldom of Westmorland created for Salisbury's father in 1397.

The Nevilles were distinguished by much more than the length of their pedigree. Successive heirs married well: when not to heiresses, to other notable northern families. There had been two Percy matches before Salisbury's sister Eleanor married the second Earl of Northumberland. Moreover the Nevilles were a prolific breed who produced half a dozen younger sons and daughters with each generation. They spawned several cadet branches and a whole series of successful churchmen. There was supposedly a Thomas, archdeacon of Durham, before Alexander (d. 1388) Archbishop of York, whose brother was elected, but never consecrated, as Bishop of Ely. Robert (d. 1457) was to be bishop of Durham and George (d. 1476) was another archbishop. As befitted such a great house, the Nevilles patronized the church, founding the Premonstratensian house at Swaynby (later Coverham Abbey), the Franciscan friary of Richmond, a hospital at Welle, chantries at Sheriff Hutton and Durham Cathedral, and presumably the many other churches in which their arms of *gules a saltire argent* were reportedly displayed. The saltire (St Andrew's cross) appears prominently on the tomb in Durham cathedral of John Lord Neville (d. 1388), the donor of the Neville screen there. Probably they also shared in the distinc-

---

7   Hicks, *Richard III*, 356; *Catalogue of Ancient Deeds* iv. A6166. The rest of this section is based on 'Neville Pedigree'; J. R. Lander, 'Marriage and Politics in the Fifteenth Century: The Nevilles and the Wydevilles', *Crown and Nobility 1450–1509* (London, 1976), 95–7; M. A. Hicks, 'Cement or Solvent? Kinship and Politics in Late Medieval England: The Case of the Nevilles', *History* 83 (1998), 31–46.

tive enthusiasms of the late medieval archdiocese, patronizing hermits like their FitzHugh and Scrope neighbours did. Two of Earl Ralph's daughters were to join that most enclosed order of nuns, the minoresses. In 1442 Pope Eugenius IV agreed to exempt from residence any of the eight chaplains serving in Salisbury's household chapel holding cures of souls.[8]

The Nevilles were major players in the Scottish wars, in which Robert 'Peacock of the North' was killed and his brother Ralph (d. 1367) was captured, which Ralph shared in the victory at Neville's Cross in 1346 when King David Bruce was captured. The next Baron Neville, John (d. 1388), moved beyond his purely northern context. This 'magnanimous knight and famous baron' was a knight of the Garter, who distinguished himself in France and was lieutenant of Gascony. It was his son Ralph (d. 1425), that 'illustrious and most famous of princes', who was created Earl of Westmorland in 1397 and who was briefly earl marshal. The attendance of attorneys of Westmorland and his cousin Northumberland are registered at Yorkshire parliamentary elections. It is this Ralph who is the culmination – the hero – of the Neville genealogies. Yet although Ralph had a national profile, it is clear that he also saw himself and his family in their local context and in terms of local traditions. He sought to advance himself locally, founding a college at Staindrop near Raby in County Durham, and marrying his offspring into such baronial houses as the Mauleys, Lumleys and Dacres. The senior Neville line, represented by Ralph's eldest son John, who predeceased him, and the latter's son Ralph second Earl of Westmorland (d. 1484), remained of regional rather than national importance.

In this context Salisbury was very much a younger son: one of at least twenty-one children of Ralph. There were also two elder half-sisters from his mother's first marriage. The excellent marriages that they all made, the most remarkable sequence of the fifteenth century, are celebrated in the *Neville Book of Hours*, which shows the earl, countess and their children all kneeling in prayer and identifiable by Robert's mitre and their coats of arms. No distinction is made in the *Book* between the issue of Westmorland's first and second consorts. Yet a distinction needs to be made, for it was the earl's second family – his offspring by Joan Beaufort – who married best and who constituted Richard's closest relations. In this case the step really mattered.

Amongst Ralph's second brood, Salisbury was the most senior. He and his siblings of the whole blood were to have a very different, indeed national, destiny. Not only were they more numerous thirteen at the last count! – but they married into the noblest houses in England. Thus Katherine married a Duke of Norfolk, Anne a Duke of Buckingham, Eleanor in turn to Lord Despenser and the Earl of Northumberland, and the youngest, Cecily, to Richard Duke of York. Salisbury, as we have seen, married Alice Montagu and his brothers William, Thomas, George and Edward wed the Fauconberg, St Maur, Beauchamp of Bergavenny, and Beauchamp/Lisle heiresses. Moreover Ralph secured the modest Latimer barony for George and a sixth son Robert rose to

8   *CPL 1434–47*, 34; see also J. Hughes, *Pastors & Visionaries* (1988), 16.

become bishop of Salisbury and then, in 1437, bishop of Durham. Only Thomas St Maur died prematurely. During the 1450s, five brothers – Salisbury, Fauconberg, Latimer, Bergavenny and Durham – sat in the house of Lords in company with four brothers-in-law. Similarly Salisbury and Fauconberg, both distinguished soldiers, met with their brothers-in-law the Dukes of York and Buckingham and the Earl of Northumberland at chapters of the most noble order of the Garter.

This remarkable transformation resulted partly from Ralph's good service to the house of Lancaster, but mostly from his match with Joan Beaufort, one of the four legitimated bastards of John of Gaunt, Duke of Lancaster (d. 1399), son of

Table 2.3 The Neville Family in the 1430s and 1440s

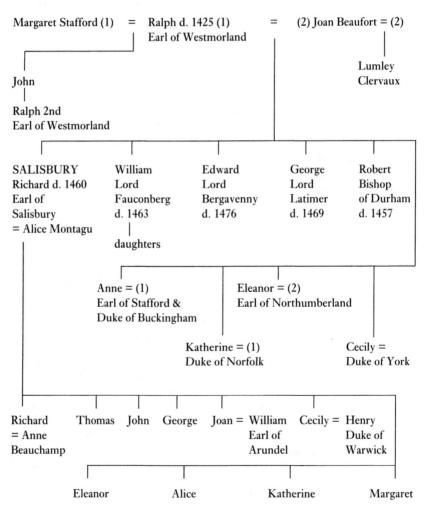

Edward III, by his mistress and eventual third wife Katherine Swinford. Westmorland and his brother-in-law John Beaufort were both made earls in 1397, when Richard II was promoting other members of the royal family and created six royal dukes, the duketti. After King Richard's deposition and death the Countess Joan was half-sister of King Henry IV, aunt of Henry V, and great-aunt of Henry VI. Letters patent of Henry IV describe the Earl Ralph as 'the king's brother'.[9] The de luxe royal genealogies mass-produced in London in the 1430s and 1440s treat the offspring of Ralph and Joan, especially Salisbury and Bishop Robert, as members of the royal house; another such roll, dating from 1455–6, included young Richard, his brothers and sisters.[10] The fifteenth century was a time, as treason and sumptuary laws make clear, when royalty was rising in status and in privilege. Such royal connections, which were not shared by the senior Neville line, more than counteracted any inferiority arising from the fact that the junior house of Neville was a cadet line. Both Salisbury and his son Warwick displayed on their seals the arms of Neville with a label, signifying cadetship, throughout their lives. Salisbury, his brothers and sons prided themselves on their birth and certainly did not regard themselves as parvenus. The Countess Joan's three Beaufort brothers rose to be earl of Somerset, duke of Exeter, and cardinal-bishop of Winchester respectively. Later Beaufort dukes of Somerset and Lady Margaret Beaufort were cousins. Royal and Beaufort kinship was to be of great practical value to Salisbury and Warwick and in particular assisted them at court and in council in their various inheritance disputes.

Ralph reinforced these links, as his family genealogy makes plain, by quashing the Percy uprisings against Henry IV in 1403 and 1405. He thus earned his place in the king's 'most secret counsel'.[11] He was rewarded with the title of earl marshal, the honour of Richmond for life, the lordship of Penrith (Cumb.) in tail, gifts of forfeited estates, the grant of valuable wardships on favourable terms, and a host of other favours. He was committed inextricably to the Lancastrian king. It was logical for successive Lancastrian kings to entrust him with the wardship and marriage of the heirs of such former traitors as the earls of Norfolk, Cambridge and Gloucester, thus ensuring that the youngsters grew up into loyal members of the royal house. It was equally logical for the heirs of such other erstwhile traitors who wanted to rehabilitate themselves politically to marry Ralph's daughters and thus into the royal family. Ralph not only helped his new son-in-law Northumberland to recover his family inheritance in 1416; he surrendered those forfeited lands in Cumbria that had been granted to himself, and acted as his feoffee (trustee). Similarly he surrendered the title of earl marshal to John Mowbray when he married his daughter Katherine. It was because Ralph and Joan were brokers of royal favour that they were able to match their offspring so

9   CPR 1401–5, 227.
10   Handbook to the Maude Roll, ed. A. Wall (Auckland, 1919); BL Harley Roll T12; Lansdowne Roll 2; MS Sloane 2722A.
11   'Neville Pedigree', 109.

successfully. Salisbury and Richard continued Ralph's matrimonial strategy on behalf of their own children with very similar success.

Salisbury, as we have seen, had married well and secured Alice Montagu's earldom and estates. Additionally Ralph had seen in him, rather than his eldest son by his first marriage, his natural successor as the great northern magnate and guardian of the northern borders. Salisbury also saw himself primarily as a northern rather than a West Country magnate. Some royal grants made specifically to Earl Ralph and his second countess and the heirs of both their bodies were to devolve on Salisbury, who was also associated with his father as warden of the West March in his last years. More important yet were those Neville possessions that Ralph transferred to the children of his second marriage from the senior line with the consent, strangely, of his eldest son John.

It was John's son Ralph, second Earl of Westmorland (d. 1484), who took less kindly to this resettlement. He and his family were alienated from the Salisbury line. They disliked the occupation of much of their inheritance by the Countess Joan even in her own lifetime, objected forcibly in the 1430s, and after her death in 1440 sought to right their wrongs by violent means. Always, however, they were at a disadvantage, both because Salisbury had better connections with the court as royal kinsman and councillor and because he offered much better service both in the borders and in France, where Westmorland never went. The reality of their loss had eventually to be recognized and a compromise was reached in 1443 that left Salisbury in possession of almost everything. Undoubtedly latent ill-feeling persisted – the senior and junior Nevilles were to fight on opposite sides in 1461 – perhaps until 1478, when the Westmorland line was recognized as residual heir to the former Neville lands should the junior line expire.[12] This dispute was not, however, everything and did not shape all relations between the two lines on every topic. Westmorland and Salisbury co-operated peaceably enough when sharing out instalments of the Holland inheritance in 1434 and 1442. When resettling two properties in 1449, Salisbury and his whole brothers included a contingent remainder to their half-brother Ralph Neville of Ousley. Sir Thomas Neville of Raby supported the junior line in the Percy–Neville feud in 1453–4, when the royal council feared that Westmorland himself might help the Neville side. It was this Thomas, not Salisbury's son, who was Bishop Robert's justice of assize in 1448.[13]

Under the unequal compromise of 1443, the earls of Westmorland had received less of the family patrimony than that enjoyed by the fourteenth-century barons Neville of Raby, though they were spared from actual poverty by the fortunate marriage of Ralph's eldest son John to yet another of the Holland heiresses. Westmorland kept Raby and Brancepeth in County Durham, whilst Salisbury retained the much more valuable lordships of Middleham, Sheriff Hutton and Penrith. Salisbury's share was much more lucrative – Middleham alone was worth more than a thousand pounds a year – and was more valuable

---

12   Storey, *Lancaster*, 113–14; CP 25(1)/281/164/32.
13   Hicks, *Richard III*, 357; *CPR 1446–52*, 281; Griffiths, *King & Country*, 342–3; *DKR* 34 (1873), 192.

than Alice's southern inheritance. He succeeded also to Ralph's powerful local connection of gentry, to his regional hegemony, commitments and aspirations. This was ultimately his son Richard's inheritance too.

Richard was heir to several lines: the Montagus, Monthermers, Hollands, who feature surprisingly little, and the Nevilles. The Salisbury Roll of 1463 records Richard and Alice, Countess of Salisbury, with their banners: the fusils of Montagu and the eagle of Monthermer quarterly and the Neville saltire with a label of cadency. This was also the arrangement on Salisbury's seal. As a younger son, Salisbury gave priority to his wife's arms, Montagu and Monthermer, in quarters 1 and 4, reserving 2 and 3 for the arms of Neville, which, noticeably, are quartered with those of no other family. Yet, as we shall see, it was the northern Neville associations that shaped Salisbury's career.

2.2 Northern Roots

The Neville–Neville dispute, as it has been called, was settled in 1443 and assured Salisbury's family of their patrimony and influence in northern England. Perhaps it was for the ceremonies of settlement or the more private celebrations of Salisbury's family that genealogies of the Nevilles were prepared. There had been earlier ones: an outline pedigree up to the early fourteenth century belonged to the abbey of St Mary York.[14] Indeed it is hard to see how so much data could have been preserved without previous exemplars. There are two mid-fifteenth-century versions: one recording all four lines from the Norman Conquest and including no collaterals, and another that focuses merely on the direct line.[15] The direct version contains a Latin commentary that reads as though written at Coverham Abbey and certainly uses records from Coverham; significantly perhaps it omits grants to nearby Jervaulx. Monasteries were expected to keep records of coats of arms and family histories. The commentary focuses on Middleham and the junior house of Neville, includes the death of Countess Joan, and ends with the expectation of future praises for Salisbury. The inclusion of Joan's death in 1440 and the omission of the elevation of two daughters to duchess in 1444 (Buckingham) and 1445 (Warwick) dates the commentary to 1440 x 1444. It appropriates to the junior house of Neville all the achievements of the Nevilles since the Norman Conquest. Two additional paragraphs added to this version, of particular interest to Coverham Abbey,[16] are included in the four-line version too. The earliest exemplar belonged to Sir Henry Neville of Latimer, killed at Edgecote in 1469. A Clervaux variant may be even earlier.[17] Thereafter the basic

14 W. Dugdale, *Monasticon Anglicanum*, ed. W. Dunstable (6 vols, 1821), vi. 921; see also Hughes, *Pastors & Visionaries*, 15–18.
15 'Neville Pedigree', *passim*; *Visitations of the North 1480–1500*, ed. C. H. H. Blair (Surtees Soc. xli, 1930), 23–9.
16 'Neville Pedigree', *passim*; *Visitations of the North*, 26–7.
17 BL MS Harley 2096, f. 261 [which had lately belonged to John Ld. Latimer of Snape (d. 1577)].

material was updated, selected from, and elaborated by different lines, so that the Tudor and Stuart heralds recorded many alternatives, most obviously with Westmorland, Latimer and Abergavenny preoccupations.

If not quite the greatest in title, wealth, or power, Richard's family was acknowledged to be of the blood royal and enjoyed the favour of king and council that royal cousinage conferred. The dukes of Gloucester, Suffolk and Somerset, in turn most influential with the king, were his relatives. His kinship network was excessively extensive and defies diagrammatic delineation as a whole: he was related directly or indirectly to almost every contemporary nobleman, to some several times over. Westmorland was his cousin twice over, through the Neville and Holland lines; his uncles Latimer and Bergavenny were also his brothers-in-law; and his future brother-in-law John Earl of Shrewsbury (d. 1453) had been stepson to his own great-great-uncle Thomas Lord Furnival (d. 1407). Since noblemen were formally instructed in their pedigrees, Richard should have known of and acknowledged these ties, as indeed he did, which is not to say that all or even most were significant politically or otherwise. On the Neville side, his great-grandfather, grandfather and father had made themselves national figures and royal councillors. Yet his roots were local. Salisbury remained primarily a northerner who sought to maintain and reinforce his family as predominantly a northern dynasty. Only Northumberland rivalled him as a northern landholder and there was no John of Gaunt to take priority. Yet Salisbury never possessed northern lands as extensive as either his father or his son nor did he ever exercise undisputed sway throughout the region. His was never 'a comprehensive influence in the North approaching that of Richard of Gloucester in the 1470s'.[18]

Salisbury's principal seat at Middleham in Wensleydale consisted of a substantial Norman keep that had been extended across the centuries into a square castle of two wards. The inner curtain wall, towers and chapel date from the thirteenth century, the machicolated gatehouse from the fourteenth, and in the fifteenth century stone offices and lodgings were added on every side, so that scarcely any courtyard remained. On to a relatively small site, the residential requirements of the greatest magnate had been packed. The raising of the keep, to create a two-storeyed hall and great chamber lit by huge windows from above, created the most modern and imposing accommodation out of the ancient fabric. Whose work it was – Salisbury's, Warwick's or Gloucester's – we unfortunately cannot tell. To the castle and borough at Middleham, a later fifteenth-century lord was to add a college and fairs.

Middleham can only ever have been a small market town, with a population of hundreds, and is no more than a village today. Richmondshire was dominated by Richmond. Richmond castle, with its massive Norman keep and two wards, high on a cliff over the River Swale, was the caput of Richmond honour. Richmond was also the principal town. If no metropolis, Richmond – unlike Middleham –

18   The pedigree in BL MS Add. 5530 terminates with the Clervaux–Vavasour marriage of 1442.

is clearly a town, and still has an impressive market-place. Richmond honour itself extended to Lincolnshire, East Anglia and elsewhere. Supposedly the honour was granted to Earl Alan the Red by William I; fifteenth-century copies of the honorial register depict the apocryphal presentation of the sealed charter to Earl Alan by King William with an audience of knights behind. Another illumination depicts the earl and his knightly tenants. The register records the Breton earls of Richmond down to 1341, extracts from Domesday, Kirkby's Quest and other information about knights fees, the charter of liberties, and castleguard obligations. A third illumination of the castle itself indicates these. The latest item is an account of the feodary of the honour in 1410–11 when Earl Ralph was lord: it is not unreasonable to suggest that the register in its present form was composed on his behalf.[19] No Neville copy exists, although a future lord had access to some of the material, but two copies survive. That such material remained useful indicates that the honour remained a reality unusually late.

By the fifteenth century five noblemen held substantial estates in Richmondshire – the Nevilles themselves, assessed at £1,903 in 1436, and four barons: FitzHugh of Ravensworth (£484), Latimer of Snape and Welle (£175), Scrope of Bolton (£557) and Scrope of Masham. There were besides many gentry, ranging from those of county-wide to purely parochial importance. All were tenants of the honour, directly or indirectly, and shared in its history. The major mesne tenants traced their tenure from the Norman Conquest. Others beside the Nevilles could resort to family pedigrees or chronicles: there survives a FitzHugh chronicle and genealogy, a Clervaux genealogy, and several monastic accounts of the Scropes. Supposedly the FitzHughs were descended from Bardolf, bastard brother of Earl Alan, the first Scrope came with John Gant, and Sir Hamo de Clervaux was another of the Conqueror's army.[20] The Nevilles claimed descent from Earl Alan's brother Ribald. They thought that Earl Alan had granted him Middleham, Earl Stephen had confirmed it, and Earl Conan had added the forest of Wensleydale.[21] The shared obligations of honorial tenants and their common history were a further source of honorial unity. Professor Pollard has noted how inward-looking the local aristocracy were, intermarrying with one another rather than with elsewhere even within Yorkshire. 'In the later fifteenth century', observes Professor Pollard, 'a member of the gentry of Richmondshire could count practically all the gentry of the district among his cousins.'[22] Such ties help

---

19   *Registrum Honoris de Richmond*, ed. R. Gale (1722), which reprints BL MS Cotton Faustina BVII. Gale did not print it exactly as the original, which was rearranged by Sir Robert Cotton, *Summary Catalogue of the Lyell Manuscripts*, ed. A. de la Mare (1971); Bodl. MS Lyell 22.

20   Hughes, *Pastors & Visionaries*, 17; BL Cotton Ch. xiii, no. 32; C 47/9/13; BL Add. MS 6046, f. 75.

21   'Neville Pedigree', 31–2.

22   A. J. Pollard, 'The Richmondshire Community of Gentry during the Wars of the Roses', *Patronage, Pedigree and Power in Later Medieval England*, ed. C. D. Ross (Gloucester, 1979), 37–59, esp. 48; 'Lord FitzHugh's Rising in 1470', *BIHR* lii (1979), 171–5.

explain why, from the reign of John to Henry IV, from the Wars of the Roses to the Pilgrimage of Grace, the Richmondshire tenantry formed such a cohesive and politically potent connection.

The political beneficiaries of Richmondshire's distinctive cohesion in the fifteenth century were the Nevilles. Ralph's sisters married a Lumley and a Scrope, his own daughters were wed to Lords Maulay, Dacre and Scrope of Bolton, and two sons held Yorkshire baronies by marriage. Through them he was connected to the Scropes of Masham, FitzHughs and Greystokes. Looking ahead to the 1450s and 1460s, Ralph's three Fauconberg grand-daughters, three of his Salisbury grand-daughters, and Warwick's own bastard daughter married into leading local families. Latimer and Clervaux were probably not alone in cherishing Neville genealogies culminating in themselves. Yet it was only from the late fourteenth century, if then, that the Nevilles emerge as the predominant family. Was it as earl of Richmond that John of Gaunt had first recruited the future Earl Ralph into his service? After the restoration of the Breton earl in 1372 and a further forfeiture, it was to Lord FitzHugh that Queen Anne granted the custody of the honour; her executors could lease only the reversion to Earl Ralph, who secured FitzHugh's surrender in 1396, and in 1399 secured a grant from Henry IV of the whole honour for life. In 1413 he was granted the manor of Bainbridge in tail.[23] If Ralph hoped to make his life estate hereditary, he was disappointed, for in 1414 Henry V granted the reversion to his brother John Duke of Bedford.[24] All was not lost, however, for Salisbury remained steward and master forester to the duke, continued in office after Bedford's death in 1435 and skilfully exchanged dubious trifles with the crown for the Yorkshire rights and possessions of the honour. Bedford's young widow Jacquetta retained her third share throughout. In 1445 the advowson and one acre at Ringwood (Hants), of little value to him, were granted to Henry VI's new college at Eton in return for the sheriff's tourns, other liberties, the bailiwick of Hang West wapentake, two-thirds of Richmond feefarm, of three manors and the knights fees, and the reversion of the remaining thirds on Jacquetta's death. Again in 1449 two manors (which were immediately leased back), some annuities and reversions were exchanged for all the liberties in Yorkshire and the four Richmond wapentakes.[25] The 1445 properties were to be held of the Montagu inheritance and those of 1449 of the Neville patrimony, a discrepancy which could have created problems later; in the short run what mattered was that the title was hereditary. If never earl of Richmond, nor indeed holder of all its possessions in Yorkshire, Salisbury was no longer a mere mesne tenant, but effectively lord and could thus use honorial authority to reinforce his effective predominance in Richmondshire.

Whereas fourteenth-century Nevilles fought the Scots as subordinates, Ralph was the first to be warden of the West March just as his cousin Northumberland

---

23   *CPR 1391–4*, 492; *1392–6*, 586; *1396–9*, 13; *1399–1401*, 24; *1408–13*, 407; 'Neville Pedigree', 121.
24   *CPR 1413–16*, 259–60.
25   *CPR 1429–36*, 510; *1436–41*, 96; *1441–6*, 409, 429; *1446–52*, 281–2.

became the first Percy warden of the East March.[26] If the simultaneous elevation of both families recognized their growing estates and wealth, it was achieved initially as the trusted instruments of the house of Lancaster. It was thirty years or more after the Lancastrian succession before its connection ceased to be a force and that the Percies and Nevilles could emerge fully from its shadow. Westmorland's wardenship, the West March, constituted that part of the Scottish borders in Cumberland and Westmorland. As warden he was expected to defend the march, raising sufficient troops at his own expense, to command the local levies against the Scots, and to exercise marcher law over the English borders. For this he was paid a substantial annual salary, larger in war than peace. The wardenship could be a source of profit and of influence. As Salisbury was lord only of Penrith, he had to draw on manpower from Yorkshire and Durham, but his office enabled him to dominate such better endowed families as the Percys of Cockermouth and the Cliffords of Brougham. He was constable of Carlisle, military commander of the march, and exercised martial law within it. Ralph and subsequent wardens sought to monopolize royal possessions in Cumbria, leasing fisheries, closes within Inglewood and even the forest itself. Salisbury drew annuities of £70 from the barony of Kendal after Bedford's death, to which he added in 1443–5 the stewardship, the farm of two-thirds of the land, and the reversion of the rest on the death of the dowager-duchess.[27] The logical culmination was the palatinate created in 1483.

Salisbury had succeeded his father as warden in his own lifetime, but surrendered the office in 1435 on a plea of poverty. It seems unlikely that he was genuinely poor: whilst certainly he had not been paid all he was owed, the full salary considerably exceeded the normal peacetime costs. His resignation freed him to serve in France and thus assert a moral advantage over his nephew Westmorland. Northumberland did likewise, surrendering the East March in 1434. One wonders whether both earls relinquished office in the hope of driving a tougher bargain with the crown for continuing? If so, the ploy failed in the short term, for in 1436 Marmaduke Lumley, Bishop of Carlisle, the cadet of a northern baronial family, took on the West March at lower wages. Salisbury's dissatisfaction with this new arrangement resulted in his successful bid in 1439 for the reversion of the wardenship from 1443 for yet lower wages, £983 6s. 8d., admittedly now securely assigned on local revenues; he was also appointed chief justice of the northern forests and of Inglewood. Northumberland also resumed office in 1440, but on less favourable terms. That Salisbury saw the permanent tenure of the wardenship as an essential component of his family power-base is suggested by a further grant in 1445 of the reversion jointly to himself and his son Richard; he also sought to keep the wardenship of the northern forests, which he held in tail male.[28]

The Neville kinship network was densest at local level and inclined its

26 R. L. Storey, 'The Wardens of the Marches of England towards Scotland 1377–1489', *EHR* lxxii (1957), 593–605; for this para., see also Storey, *Lancaster*, ch. 7.
27 *CPR 1441–6*, 540.
28 Storey, 'Wardens', 604–5, 613; *CPR 1446–52*, 566.

members to serve the lord of Middleham. Many of the Neville marriages can be seen as extending the earl's influence, including those of his daughters to the northern barons FitzHugh, Stanley and Harrington; so too several contracts sought to bind to him important individuals of rank or domicile naturally beyond his ambit, such as those with Ralph Lord Greystoke, who was freed from Barnard Castle (1447), Sir Thomas Dacre (1435), and the Cumbrian knights Henry Threlkeld (1431) and Walter Strickland (1448). Two lawyers were formally retained of counsel, Thomas Stokdale from Pishiobury (Herts.) and John Hotoft from Ware (Herts.) in 1429. Stokdale in particular features as mainpernor, feoffee and trusted man of business in many contexts along with John Quyxley, William Frank, John Tunstall, Thomas Witham, from 1435 Thomas Colt, Robert Danby, Richard Weltden and John Middleton. Somewhat higher in rank were such leading gentry as Sir Christopher Conyers, Sir James Strangways, Sir Robert Constable and Richard Musgrave, who acted as receivers, Boyntons, Scargills, Vavasours, Rouclifs and Fulthorps. In 1459 Salisbury's executors included three senior retainers in Conyers, Strangways and Danby, by then a royal justice, and three lesser officials in Witham, Middleton and John Ireland. How inadequate such evidence of association and service can be emerges from the glimpse of reality afforded by the surviving fragment of the Middleham account of 1456–9, when 20 per cent of the lordship's revenues was spent on fees and annuities.[29] The same may be true of other northern lordships then and, indeed, earlier; the southern estates were reservoirs of cash.[30] Many of these men, whether powerful gentry or professional officials, also served his son, sometimes from his succession to the earldom of Warwick in 1449, more often after Salisbury's own death in 1460.

2.3 Shaping the Future

These were the families and the traditions to which Richard was the culmination. He was heir to them all and the long-term future rested with him. He was particularly valuable to his parents as their eldest son and stood out amongst his siblings as their eldest brother. He was the key to continuity for his kindred, dependants and neighbours. What this meant in practice can only be guessed, for there is

---

29   E 159/207 rec. Trin. 9 Hen. VI m. 1; E 159/227 brevia Easter 28 Hen. VI m. 7; brevia Mich. 28 Hen. VI m. 8d; E 159/230 brevia Mich. 32 Hen. VI m. 17; E 326/B9374; T. Madox, *Formulare Anglicanum* (Oxford, 1702), 144, 331; Ellis, *Original Letters*, ii. i. 116–17; *CPR 1429–36*, 122–3; *Testamenta Eboracensia* ii, ed. J. Raine (Surtees Soc. xxx, 1855), 246; F. W. Bragg, 'An Indenture in English', *TCWAS* n.s. ix (1909), 283–4; A. J. Pollard, 'The Northern Retainers of Richard Nevill, Earl of Salisbury', *Northern History* xi (1976), 52–69; Pollard, 'Richmondshire Gentry', 45; 'Private Contracts for Life Service in Peace and War 1278–1476', ed. M. Jones and S. Walker, *Camden Miscellany* 5th ser. iii (1994), 126–7, 147, 150–1, 156–8, 162–3. Hotoft's indenture (no. 117) is dated at Ware (Herts.) not Warwick, E 315/40/154.
30   Hicks, *Richard III*, 357–8.

almost nothing to illuminate his early life and all the more promising lines of inquiry have produced only blanks. There is no conclusive evidence that he was one of the noble heirs who was brought up with the somewhat older King Henry VI as the minority council had decreed. It is likeliest that he resided with his parents in the North, encountering and familiarizing himself with his father's household, his neighbours and retainers. Richard ought to have been well-acquainted with the three northern cathedral cities: Durham, his uncle Robert's see, where Salisbury was confrater from 1431; Carlisle; and York, where in 1461 he was to be joint founder of a college for the minister's chantry priests. We are probably right to envisage him living in his father's draughty northern castles, albeit substantially modernized (Middleham) or recently constructed (Penrith), where the halls were thronged with people, the walls hung with tapestries, and plate and jewels were prominently displayed. Maybe he also visited London, residing at the Neville mansion of le Erber whilst Salisbury attended parliament or council. Perhaps he accompanied the earl as a toddler to France in 1431 for Henry VI's coronation in Paris, when Salisbury dined several times with Richard's future father-in-law Richard Beauchamp, Earl of Warwick;[31] as a boy on the campaign of 1436; or perhaps later was an unrecorded esquire or knight in somebody else's retinue. Most probably, though unrecorded, he joined his parents at Rouen in 1445 to receive the new Queen Margaret of Anjou.[32] He was still only sixteen. It would be nice if he already knew the French realm, language and people before they bulked so large in his later life. He may be one of the few major political figures in the 1450s who was wholly without direct experience of the war in France. By then his high promise and abilities were already apparent. Richard's later accomplishments do permit us to presume with confidence that he enjoyed a conventional aristocratic education in horsemanship and arms, in heraldry and genealogy, letters and the faith. But again there is and can be no direct evidence.

What we can discern through the Neville genealogies is the slow evolution of Richard's family.[33] Three of his four grandparents died before he was born: the fourth, the Neville matriarch Joan Beaufort, potentially so influential, lived on until 1440, when Richard was twelve, apparently mainly at Raby and Sheriff Hutton, where her Bergavenny grandchildren and Richard's cousins were born[34] and where the Middleham Nevilles could easily have visited her. Perhaps wisely in view of the Neville–Neville dispute, Joan chose not to be buried with Ralph at Staindrop College, but beside her mother in Lincoln Cathedral. Perhaps Richard was at the funeral. Although Richard's parents had married in or by 1421, their children and especially the sons they desired were initially slow in

31 M. V. Clin-Meyes, 'Le Registre des Comptes de Richard Beauchamp Conte de Warwick 14 Mars 1431–15 Mars 1432' (unpub. diploma at Warwickshire RO), 188, 244 quoting Warwicks. RO CR 1618/W1915.
32 See below p. 29.
33 This section is based on 'Neville Pedigree', 110–11.
34 BL Add. MS Harl. 1807, f. 75v; but see proof of age of George Neville locating birth and baptism at Guildford (Surrey) C 139/162/17/2.

coming. Thereafter they came thick and fast. Eventually there were twelve. The first was born before 2 November 1424.[35] Probably it was Joan. Certainly the two eldest were daughters, Joan and Cecily, most probably named after their grandmother Joan Beaufort and their aunt Cecily, the so-called 'Rose of Raby' and Duchess of York. Both were presumably toddlers at the birth of Richard, the eldest son, in 1428; unless of course Cecily took her name from her day of birth and was his twin. Richard took his father's name. Then followed in rapid succession three further sons – Thomas, John and George – making four boys no more than four years apart. Their co-operation later in life suggests that they were close as children and that Richard was always the leader to whom the others deferred. By 14 May 1431 Salisbury had three sons and two daughters.[36] George, the fourth son to reach maturity, was born in 1432; John Wessington, prior of Durham, was a godfather.[37] Thomas and John were always destined for secular careers; George, perhaps godson of Salisbury's brother George Lord Latimer, was dedicated by 1442, if not before, to a career in the Church.[38] By then, or at least by the earliest surviving genealogy, there were a further three daughters – Alice, Eleanor and Katherine – and two shortlived sons, Ralph and Robert, buried respectively (and presumably born) at Sheriff Hutton and Middleham.[39] Finally Margaret completed the brood.

The family did not merely grow, of course: it also ebbed as marriage carried its members away, perhaps even before all of Salisbury's own brothers had been bestowed. The first to marry were Cecily and Richard himself, who married another pair of brothers and sisters, Henry and Anne Beauchamp, respectively the son and heir and the youngest daughter of Richard Beauchamp, Earl of Warwick. That was in 1436. Probably Cecily took up residence with her father-in-law and husband at once. Although the eldest of Salisbury's children, Joan was the third to marry, after 17 August 1438, when Salisbury bought the marriage of her bridegroom William Earl of Arundel from the king:[39] Joan does not seem to have had many further dealings with Richard. There was then a long delay, as the famed Neville matrimonial machine faltered in the provision of heirs and heiresses for child brides and grooms. Actually it was George, the youngest surviving son, who was next to be financially independent, accumulating a succession of lucrative livings including the golden prebend of Masham in Richmondshire, and who was next to leave home, moving about 1448 to Balliol College, Oxford, to study and to feast.[40] It was fifteen years from Joan's wedding to the next one: until 1453, when Richard's next brother Thomas, a knight already in his twenties, married the young widow and heiress Maud Stanhope,

35   *CCR 1422–9*, 159.
36   *CPR 1429–36*, 123.
37   G. I. Keir, 'The Ecclesiastical Career of George Neville 1432–76', Oxford BLitt (1970), 6; R. B. Dobson, *Church and Society in the Medieval North of England* (1996), 7n.
38   *Biographical Register of the University of Oxford to* AD *1500*, ed. A. B. Emden (3 vols, Oxford, 1957–9), ii. 1347.
39   *CPR 1436–41*, 194, 224.
40   Emden, *Biographical Register*, ii. 1347; Keir, 'George Neville', 26–7.

Lady Willoughby. Eleanor probably married Thomas, the future Lord Stanley, about 17 December 1454, when Hawarden Castle in Flintshire was resettled. John had to wait until April 1457 for Isabel Ingoldsthorpe. Whether Alice and Katherine had to wait even longer or were already contracted to Lords FitzHugh and Harrington we cannot be sure.[41] A respectable collection of matches, if not comparable to those celebrated in the *Neville Hours*, and perhaps a harking back to the earlier era when the Nevilles had operated within the more restricted northern marriage market.

Such an impression would be mistaken, for these later marriages offered more than appears at first sight. Already modest heiresses, both Maud Stanhope and Isabel Ingoldsthorpe promised much more, Maud as one of the two coheiresses of the wealthy Lord Cromwell in 1456 and Isabel as potential heiress to the Tiptoft earldom of Worcester, which eventually materialized for her daughters.[42] No mere northern baron, Stanley was already set to dominate Lancashire and Cheshire, and Harrington's modest northern estate was set to merge with his grandfather's West Country Bonville barony. Such matches were carefully calculated with an eye to the future.

Yet Salisbury would surely have preferred to match his offspring earlier to spouses already endowed with title and fortune rather than speculating on uncertain futures. Why had he not? It was surely because he sought not respectable and advantageous matches but great ones and they, as always, were in short supply. The very success of earlier Neville marriages left few potential spouses not related within the prohibited degrees. Such problems were obstacles to be overcome by papal dispensations rather than insuperable barriers. More significant, perhaps, were the other priorities of the greatest magnates of the 1440s. Whereas the Nevilles were unquestionably of royal blood, it was derived through a junior, female, and illegitimate route that offered no title to the crown. The matches contracted between the royal dukes of York, Exeter, Somerset and Buckingham, Professor Griffiths has persuasively argued, were designed to tie them ever closer to whichever of them made good his title to the crown should the house of Lancaster end with Henry VI.[43] In that context, Salisbury had nothing to offer. His status as king's kinsman and councillor carried less influence with Henry VI himself and therefore with others than his father had enjoyed thirty years before. After 1438 Salisbury won no plum wardships: nothing comparable to those of Anne Beauchamp and Margaret Beaufort awarded to the king's favourite Suffolk in the 1440s and to his half-brother Edmund Tudor in the 1450s. Salisbury qualified for no higher precedence and remained well down the list of earls, though he did successfully deflect a suit from his brother-in-law

---

41 For Thomas and John, see below pp.87–8, 130–1; for Eleanor, see *Calendar of Deeds & Documents*, iii, *The Hawarden Deeds*, ed. F. Green (Aberystwyth, 1931), 14, 16. All were married or contracted by 10 May 1459, *Testamenta Eboracensia* ii. 243–4.

42 M. A. Hicks, 'What Might Have Been: George Neville, Duke of Bedford', in *Richard III*, 292, 296.

43 R. A. Griffiths, 'The Sense of Dynasty in the Reign of Henry VI', *King & Country*, 89–93.

Northumberland.[44] Even Cardinal Beaufort bequeathed the escheated Montagu manor of Canford (Dors.) not to Salisbury, who coveted it, but to another nephew Edmund Beaufort, Duke of Somerset.[45] As the kinship ties with the Beauforts and Lancastrian kings widened with the generations, from the king's brother to second cousin, so Salisbury became merely one of many magnates whose influence depended on good service rather than royal blood. The same evidently applied to our Richard.

After Richard's birth, the next important event known about his life is the marriage mentioned above. It is difficult to be absolutely sure of the date. The two earls received a papal dispensation for the marriage of their unnamed children in 1434 and the Tewkesbury Chronicle baldly states 1434,[46] which is too early; many of the chronicle's dates are wrong. The marriage was agreed by 9 March 1436 but not yet concluded. The account of Thomas Porthaleyn, keeper of Warwick's household, actually precedes both the possible dates for the wedding, but records £152 in expenses of the earl, countess, Henry and Anne riding to [Leic]ester to conclude the marriage contract and a further £40 for the marriage itself at Abergavenny. Whilst the wedding could have been in late July/August, when other transactions at Abergavenny were recorded, it seems to be somewhat earlier, on or about 4 May 1436, when Warwick himself was at Abergavenny. After the marriage, the account states, the Earl of Warwick proceeded from Abergavenny to Warwick, where he spent twelve days recruiting his retinue of war for the relief of Calais,[47] where he campaigned under Humphrey Duke of Gloucester in late July and August. Salisbury, who is not explicitly mentioned in the account, sailed in May with Richard Duke of York to Normandy and was campaigning in Caux until at least August. Hence May 1436 seems the more likely.

We cannot tell whether Richard was married in the castle chapel or, more probably, in the church of the Benedictine priory, formerly a cell of St Vincent Abbey at Le Mans and now the parish church, where the furnishings of the choir are substantially unchanged. Porthaleyn's expenses suggest a modest affair. It is understandable that Richard later preferred to call himself lord of Abergavenny rather than of any of his other lordships and fought to hang on to the lordship with such vigour. Holding the wedding at Abergavenny was convenient to Richard Beauchamp, Earl of Warwick. The lordship had been held by William Beauchamp, Lord Bergavenny (d. 1411) and then by his long-lived wife Joan until her death on 14 November 1435. It then devolved under an entail by William of 1395 on the male heirs of the comital Beauchamp line, which was represented in 1435 by Warwick himself. However it was contested by Salisbury's brother Edward Neville, who had married William and Joan's granddaughter Elizabeth. Henceforth Edward used the title Lord Bergavenny. He

44   M. W. Warner and K. Lacey, 'Neville vs. Percy: a Precedence Dispute *circa* 1442', *HR* lxix (1996), 211–17.
45   Hicks, Richard III, 359.
46   *Monasticon*, ii. 63; *CPL 1431–47*, 251, 508.
47   *CPR 1429–36*, 516; BL Egerton Roll 8775 m. 8; Griffiths, *Henry VI*, 204.

later claimed to have entered the lordship and to have been put out.[48] Warwick's visit and the marriage was an assertion of Warwick's control. It was the occasion for Warwick to discomfort Salisbury's brother and young Richard's uncle. It is unfortunate that Porthaleyn's account does not reveal whether Richard accompanied his new father-in-law to Warwick Castle, Hanslope Castle (Bucks.), Salwarpe (Worcs.) and Cardiff Castle during the next five months. Probably he went at least to Warwick: stayed at the castle, saw the town, and offered at the college and at Guyscliff.

Since these were matches between four children, the oldest at most 13 and the youngest, our Richard, aged 7, we need not ponder about romantic love. These were marriages arranged by the two fathers primarily in their own interests. The partners were Richard, his elder sister Cecily, and Warwick's two children by his second marriage to Isabel Despenser: his heir Henry Lord Despenser (b. 1425) and his youngest daughter Anne (b. 1426). Warwick also had three elder daughters by his first marriage: indeed it had been to obtain a male heir to continue the line of Beauchamp and Warwick title that he (like Earl Thomas Montagu) had remarried. The eldest daughter, Margaret, was wife of John Lord Talbot; the second, Eleanor, was married in turn to Thomas Lord Roos (d. 1430) and to Edmund Beaufort, Count of Mortain; and Elizabeth, the youngest, aged 22 and more in 1439, was wed to Salisbury's brother and Richard's uncle, George Lord Latimer. George and Elizabeth's wedding cannot be dated precisely: surely it had preceded that of his nephew and her younger sister in 1436; most probably it had happened a decade before. The Countess Isabel had also been married previously, to another Richard Beauchamp, Earl of Worcester (d. 1422), and had a daughter, another Elizabeth Beauchamp, who had been married by 1424 to Salisbury's youngest brother Edward Lord Bergavenny.[49] The double marriage of 1436 was thus an alliance between close kindred, certainly within the prohibited degrees: hence the papal dispensation of 1434.

In 1436 Warwick was assessed for tax on £3,116, far above the corresponding figures for Salisbury (£1,238) and the Countess Joan (£667) combined. If Salisbury still had expectations, so too had Beauchamp, whose anticipated income in a valor of his last years was £5,471.[50] Scattered across England and Wales, from Elvell in Powys to Barnard Castle, Warwick's estates were concentrated in the Midlands, especially in Worcestershire and Warwickshire, where he exercised a regional hegemony.[51] By his second marriage to Isabel Despenser, which added the marcher lordships of Ewyas Lacy and Glamorgan to those of Elvell and Abergavenny, he was also a principal lord in the marches

---

48   *CFR 1430–7*, 267; C 81/76/9107.
49   *Wills and Inventories of the Northern Counties of England* (Surtees Soc. ii, 1835), ii. 71–2; *GEC* i. 27.
50   *Glamorgan County History* iii, ed. T. B. Pugh (1971), 190; H. L. Gray, 'Incomes from Land in England in 1436', *EHR* xlix (1936), 614–15; C. D. Ross, *The Estates and Finances of Richard Beauchamp, Earl of Warwick* (Dugdale Soc. occas. paper xii, 1956), 17.
51   M. C. Carpenter, 'The Beauchamp Affinity: A Study of Bastard Feudalism at work', *EHR* xcv (1980), 514–32.

of South Wales and Gloucestershire. Barring the Lisle inheritance of his first wife and elder daughters, the whole was scheduled to pass to Beauchamp's only son Henry, his heir presumptive. It was that inheritance that Salisbury secured for his daughter and her issue as he presumably intended. We do not know what jointure was settled on Henry and Cecily. The second match, between Richard Neville and Anne Beauchamp, gave Richard a spouse of appropriate status, but not the heiress he could doubtless have secured elsewhere and which Neville heirs traditionally espoused. Richard was the most attractive bridegroom among Salisbury's four sons. Should Henry die prematurely or without issue, Richard would acquire a stake in Henry's inheritances. This, Salisbury must have calculated, as Warwick himself anticipated in his wills of 1437 and 1439,[52] would comprise a quarter share of the Beauchamp inheritance when split four ways between Warwick's four daughters and half of the Despenser inheritance shared between Isabel's two. Perhaps Salisbury discounted the possibility that further sons would be born to the ageing earl as the latter still hoped in his will. Richard and Anne's share should then have been worth over fifteen hundred pounds a year – more than either the Montagu or Neville inheritances – and might well have included the Beauchamp lordship of Barnard Castle in County Durham that Salisbury leased and coveted. Salisbury cannot have overlooked such contingencies, but in 1436, when the marriages were contracted, Cecily rather than Richard was the intended beneficiary.

Ostensibly these transactions were attractive to both parties and had been, as the papal dispensation shows, under consideration for several years. The marriage of one's daughter to the other's heir was an excellent match. There was little need, one might suppose, for a marriage portion. Actually, however, Salisbury agreed to pay Warwick 4,700 marks ($£3,233.66$):[53] one of the largest portions known. Evidently Salisbury wanted the matches more than Warwick and the portion was what persuaded Warwick to comply. Surely Warwick did not object to the marriage of Anne to Richard: a more advantageous match than any arranged for his elder daughters? It follows, therefore, that it was the second pairing that was so expensive: Henry Beauchamp, the greatest heir of his time, could have done much better, married an heiress as his father himself had twice done, and forged new ties rather than merely reinforcing the old. Hence it seems the portion was what persuaded Warwick to eschew an heiress. That, in turn, implies that Warwick wanted the money, which is understandable: the crown owed him substantial sums for earlier service in France, some of which he remitted for immediate payment of $£1,000$ in 1437, when taking up the lieutenant-generalship and governorship of Normandy and France.[54] Though Professor Ross interprets the deficits of $£2,643$ in 1420–1 and $£1,672$ as mere book-keeping errors, Porthaleyn's account of 1435–6 also points to chronic over-

---

52   Earl Richard's deathbed will of 1439 (DL 26/5) differs only in omitting Lord Cromwell from the executors: it was never proved.
53   W. Dugdale, *Antiquities of Warwickshire*, ed. W. Thomas (1730), i. 410–11, 414.
54   Ross, *Estates*, 16–17; BL Egerton Roll 8775 m. 7.

spending.[55] Warwick really needed the money in 1436: hence the marriage.

Salisbury had agreed in parliament in December 1435 to serve in France with Warwick on conditions that the royal council acceded to on 7–11 March 1436. Warwick consented to accept in part payment and the crown agreed to pay £700 due to Salisbury as the down-payment 'on the day of the espousals of their children'. Probably the balance was secured by instalments from the enfeoffed Montagu lands. Shortly beforehand Salisbury gave up his wardenship. Salisbury's departure was calculated in other ways: the council intervened in the Neville–Neville dispute, binding his nephew Westmorland with sureties and curtailing his aggression, and it guaranteed Salisbury immediate admission to his Neville inheritance should his mother Joan Beaufort die during his absence abroad. He was also licensed to do what he had already done in 1431, to settle substantial Montagu lands on feoffees. War itself was not without risk and the tide had turned against the English. Should Salisbury be killed, he had already arranged an advantageous match for young Richard, who would be spared the matrimonial whims of crown or grantees; that most of his lands would be immune from waste because enfeoffed or held by his countess in her own right, jointure and dower; and that resources were available to fulfil his will. Young Richard's marriage, in short, was an element in the strategic planning of Salisbury in the mid-1430s and of Warwick also, who had similar concerns.

In case our Richard died without inheriting and to provide for his wife and any offspring, jointure was settled on Richard and Anne in 1436: only the outlying manor of Swainstown, Isle of Wight, which was de-enfeoffed, can be identified.[56] It was surely not until the mid-1440s that Richard and Anne started to live together as man and wife and their first child was not born until 1451. We do not know whether they lived with Salisbury or had a separate establishment: they were certainly not living at Swainstown! Richard was already a knight by 6 August 1445: as his parents met Queen Margaret at Rouen on 22 March, he was most probably dubbed at her coronation on 22 April.[57] We do not know what were the intimate services that he had rendered that were referred to in a grant of 1449.[58]

Salisbury planned for young Richard's succession to his Neville lands, royal offices, and influence in the North. Thus in 1446 he secured the reversion for a further twenty years of the wardenship of the West March from the end of his current ten-year term (in 1453) for Richard and himself jointly; in 1445 he had also the master forestership of Blackburn and Bowland (Lancs.) and the steward-ship of the Duchy of Lancaster lordship of Pontefract (Yorks.) regranted to himself, Richard and Thomas jointly.[59] Allegedly Richard had rendered good

55   *CPR 1429–36*, 516.
56   *CPR 1429–36*, 598.
57   *GEC* xii. ii. 385; *Chronique de Mathieu d'Escouchy*, ed. G. du Fresne de Beaucourt, i (SHF cxviii, 1863), 86–7.
58   *CPR 1446–52*, 235.
59   Storey, 'Wardens', 605–6, 614; R. Somerville, *History of the Duchy of Lancaster*, i (1953), 507, 513–14, 518.

service at his own expense in the Scottish war of 1448–9,[60] when a Percy defeat in the West March was reversed by Salisbury himself. He received his first royal grant on 5 April 1449, when he was leased the manor of Deighton in Yorkshire and a third of the lordship of Egremont in Cumberland, which Salisbury had just surrendered for further concessions in Richmondshire.[61] The Nevilles had no intention of actually giving up anything that they had once held! His sureties were two promising northerners, both Neville clients, both probably lawyers, and both with distinguished careers in royal service under the Yorkists lying ahead: Thomas Colt of Middleham, past escheator and current JP for Cumberland and future MP of Carlisle; and Henry Sotehill of Sotehill (Yorks.). Now Richard was almost of age and the succession of an adult heir was virtually assured, he could be more useful to his father, and his career as a northern magnate could commence.

On 3 June 1449,[62] however, his niece Anne Beauchamp died. Within a week Richard was an earl, not of Salisbury, but of Warwick. Henceforth he was Warwick to contemporaries and will be called *Warwick* in this book. His succession to the earldom fundamentally changed his life and diverted his career into channels quite different from that which Salisbury had planned. For the next twelve years, for the rest of Salisbury's life and beyond, Warwick was interested in the borders and the Nevilles' northern affairs, but he was not directly involved. Instead his attention moved to the Midlands and Wales, to Calais and the keeping of the seas: all areas that had concerned neither Salisbury nor any previous Neville. He became a major figure in national politics in his own right and even overshadowed his own father. Moreover the Warwick Inheritance, as it can be collectively called, embroiled the Nevilles in national politics, provoked a rift with the Lancastrian house with which they had hitherto identified, and determined the stance that they all adopted during the Wars of the Roses.

60   *CPR 1446–52*, 225; H. Summerson, *Medieval Carlisle* (2 vols, Cumberland & Westmorland Arch. Soc. extra ser. xxv, 1993), ii. 434–5. The sack of Dumfries, if it occurred, cannot have been in June 1449, when Salisbury was at parliament.
61   *CPR 1446–52*, 281–2; *CFR 1445–52*, 131.
62   Dugdale's date of 3 January, *Baronage*, i. 248, followed by *GEC*, is a mistranscription of the inquisitions, C 139/135, which are unanimous about 3 June.

3

Earl of Warwick

3.1 Warwick Inheritance Update

At the time of the two Beauchamp–Neville marriages in 1436, Earl Richard
Beauchamp was in his mid-fifties and, by contemporary standards, well-
advanced in years. His death in 1439 was no surprise. Though twenty years
younger, his countess was also in ill health and died the following December.
Their son Henry succeeded them, duly came of age, served in France, and was
elevated first to premier earl in 1444 and then to duke of Warwick in 1445. He
was a close friend of the king. Duke Henry liked honours: his signet letters
dubbed him 'Prime Count of England', which conferred precedence over other
earls and the right to wear a gold circlet; as duke he had a precedence dispute
with the Duke of Buckingham.[1] Grants were made in reversion to enlarge his
inheritance with: the Channel Isles; the forest of Feckenham (Worcs.); and the
castle of St Briavels and the forest of Dean (Gloucs.), which complemented and
connected his possessions in Gloucestershire and his Welsh marcher lordships.
In 1444 he was even granted in tail male the principal offices in the king's
Lancaster honours of Tutbury (Staffs.) and Duffield and lordship of High Peak
(Derbys.) on the death of Buckingham, the current holder.[2] On St Valentine's
Day (14 February) 1444 there was born to Henry and Cecily a daughter, another
Anne Beauchamp.[3] More children, especially sons, were confidently expected –
indeed the duchess thought herself pregnant again[4] – when Duke Henry died,
on 11 June 1446.

1 Oxfordshire RO Dil II/b/6 attached bill; *CChR 1427–1516*, 41, 50; *Reports on the
Dignity of a Peer*, v. 242; *Rous Roll*, no. 54. Allegedly he was also 'king of the Isle of Wight',
Monasticon, ii. 63–4.
2 *CPR 1441–6*, 400–1; *Rous Roll*, no. 54.
3 *Monasticon*, ii. 63; *Rous Roll*, no. 55.
4 *CPR 1441–6*, 437.

The infant Anne, now countess of Warwick, was the greatest heiress of her day. Her wardship and marriage, first granted to the queen, was soon diverted to the most powerful man about the king: William de la Pole, husband of Alice Chaucer, shortly to be duke of Suffolk. He designated young Anne as spouse for his own heir.[5] Her death on 3 June 1449 frustrated his hopes; whilst some surprise to the Nevilles – for the death of so young an heiress cannot have been a wholly unforeseen eventuality! – it occurred at a moment particularly fortunate for the prospects of young Richard Neville.

Though Earl Richard Beauchamp had died in debt, he left an elaborate will that took over forty years to execute. The costs of building the Beauchamp Chapel at Warwick College, at Guyscliff, and of chantries at Warwick and Tewkesbury Abbey were borne from lands worth £325 a year earmarked for the purpose.[6] In contrast the wills of his countess and son were relatively modest and easy to execute. Countess Isabel Despenser had already constructed her chapel at Tewkesbury Abbey and had interred her first husband in it. Its endowment, the priory of Goldcliff, was conveyed to it in 1442. The resettlement of most of her lands on trustees should have enabled her executors to clear any debts quite quickly. Her son Duke Henry had little time to build up debts. Though no will survives, he too ordered the Despenser trustees to found a chantry for him at Tewkesbury, which was endowed in 1450. There was no separate chapel. The original objectives of the Despenser trust therefore seem to have been fulfilled by 1450.

There had been other changes in the identity and status of the Warwick heirs since 1436. The three elder sisters duly succeeded to their mother's Lisle estate in 1439[7] and continued the Berkeley–Lisle dispute with James Lord Berkeley. Margaret's eldest son John Talbot (III) assumed the style of Lord Lisle. Margaret's husband John Talbot (I) had been created earl of Shrewsbury in 1442; *his* heir was not Lisle, but another John Talbot (II), his eldest son by his first wife. Eleanor was now a duchess, following the creation of her husband Edmund Beaufort as duke of Somerset in 1448; her heir was her son by her first marriage Thomas Lord Roos. In the longer term, it was greatly to our Richard's advantage that only the current earl of Shrewsbury and current duke of Somerset had an interest in the Beauchamp inheritance.

Isabel Despenser's other daughter Elizabeth Lady Bergavenny had died by 1448, leaving her husband Edward Neville a widower and her son George a minor. The Duchess Cecily remarried soon after 3 April 1449 to John Lord Tiptoft,[8] who was shortly advanced to the earldom of Worcester. And finally Richard's wife Anne Beauchamp was elevated from being the youngest daughter of Earl Richard Beauchamp and Countess Isabel to being the sole sister of the whole-blood – *whole sister* – of Duke Henry and arguably there-

---

5   Ibid. 436; *1446–52*, 1; RP v. 182.
6   Hicks, *Richard III*, 337–51.
7   M. A. Hicks, 'Between Majorities: The "Beauchamp Interregnum" 1439–49', *HR*, lxxii (1999), 31.
8   *CPR 1446–52*, 242; *CPL 1447–55*, 438.

fore the senior sister: a quite crucial alteration.

The Beauchamp and Despenser heirs were fortunate that their inheritance was in such good order. An inheritance that had suffered two minorities in the past decade might well be expected to be in disorder: exploited and wasted by the crown and other predators. It has also been argued that the West Midlands hegemony of Earl Richard Beauchamp had been eroded and overthrown by rivals, most notably Humphrey Stafford, Duke of Buckingham, and that its shattered ruins needed to be reconstituted. This view is mistaken.[9]

As usual, it was not the high-ranking executors of Earl Richard Beauchamp who fulfilled his will, but more humble administrators and councillors: John Throckmorton of Coughton Court (Worcs.), Nicholas Rody (d. 1458), Master William Berkeswell (d. 1470) and Thomas Hugford of Emscote (Warw.), the last survivor, who died in 1469. All were local men with twenty years' service: Throckmorton and Hugford followed in their fathers' footsteps. Throckmorton was Earl Richard's undersheriff of Worcestershire in 1416–17 and later Warwick chamberlain of the exchequer. Rody, the son of a Warwick goldsmith, was master of the household of the Countess Isabel in 1431–2 and undersheriff of Worcestershire in 1437–8. By 1423 Berkeswell was already in the service of the earl, who presented him in turn to the chantry at Guyscliff in 1430, to St Michael's hospital at Warwick in 1435, and to a prebend at Warwick College in 1438. Hugford was the earl's councillor by 1417, receiver-general from 1432, undersheriff in 1435, and was receiver and steward of Glamorgan at the earl's death.[10] All except Throckmorton, who died in 1445, continued to serve Duke Henry, his duchess and daughter and Earl Richard Neville. These executors and Hugford's son exercised this trust for almost fifty years.[11]

When the earl died in 1439, King Henry felt grateful to his erstwhile tutor and succumbed to the blandishments of the countess on her deathbed. What Beauchamp lands had not been enfeoffed by the earl in his own life were granted on 18 June 1439 to eight custodians chosen by the countess. They were headed by the Duke of York, Earl of Salisbury, Warwick's extremely distant cousin Sir John (later Lord) Beauchamp of Powicke and Sir William ap Thomas, father of William Herbert and lord of Raglan Castle in the marcher lordship of Usk. There were four trusted retainers and administrators: Throckmorton and Hugford, whom we have already encountered, John Norris and John Vampage.[12] Rival claims were fended off. Salisbury quickly rebuffed the designs of his brother Robert Bishop of Durham as overlord on Barnard Castle, which local ministers resisted by force.[13] Another of Salisbury's brothers Edward Lord Bergavenny

9   By Carpenter, *Locality*, ch. 11, esp. 400–1, 403–6, 410–12, 418–19, 422, 434, as corrected in Hicks, 'Between Majorities'.

10   *Ministers' Accounts of the Collegiate Church of St Mary Warwick 1432–85*, ed. D. Styles (Dugdale Soc. xxvi, 1969), 16n, 17n; Carpenter, *Locality*, 687–9; *List of Sheriffs* (PRO Lists & Indexes ix), 158; Warwicks. RO 1618/W1915.

11   Hicks, *Richard III*, 337–51.

12   *CPR 1436–41*, 279; F. Devon, *Issues of the Exchequer* (1840), 445, 455.

13   M. A. Hicks, 'The Forfeiture of Barnard Castle to the Bishop of Durham in 1459', *Northern History* xxx (1997), 225.

seized Abergavenny itself. One of the Beauchamp custodians, Richard Duke of York, was commissioned to put the occupiers out: they were ordered to desist on their allegiance on pain of being reputed as rebels. This was by signet letter dated 15 October, probably in 1443 or 1444. York was later pardoned as occupier and Bergavenny later admitted to being forcibly excluded.[14] During Duke Henry's minority the custodians answered for the revenues to the exchequer and then to the king's uncle Humphrey Duke of Gloucester.

Before her own death in December 1439, Isabel was allowed to settle most of her own lands 'at the king's command' on her own eight feoffees for the fulfilment of her will. Five were already Beauchamp custodians and four administered the trust until at least 1457. These latter included two rising courtiers – Ralph, the future Lord Sudeley, and John, later Lord Beauchamp of Powicke – and two estate administrators, Norris and the Cornishman John Nanfan.[15] Nanfan was particularly close to the late earl, whom he served in France and attended at his deathbed; already in his service by 1427, when he was undersheriff of Worcestershire, he was master forester of Glamorgan to Isabel and subsequently served her son, grand-daughter, and son-in-law Earl Richard Neville.[16]

Of all Earl Richard Beauchamp's lands, therefore, only the Lisle lands were lost and only a handful of Despenser properties passed to the crown. When Duke Henry came of age, he entered only into those lands that had not been enfeoffed or were held by the Beauchamp custodians. He made a host of new appointments and grants of annuities.[17] The feoffees of the Beauchamp and Despenser trusts accepted him as the beneficiary and residual heir. They deferred to his wishes over appointments, presentations to church livings, and payment of bills.[18] Some lands were even conveyed to him in fee simple (e.g. Mereworth in Kent) and a Warwickshire manor was exchanged for lands in Cornwall.[19] In 1450 the Despenser feoffees conveyed the advowson of Sherston (Wilts.) to Tewkesbury Abbey for a chantry in fulfilment of his will.[20] Short though his majority was, it was crucial for the future succession of his whole sister Anne.

At his premature death Henry was seised of the Beauchamp lands held by custodians in 1439–45, which were thus threatened with wardship and with exploitation by a host of predatory royal servants. Much was assigned in dower to the Duchess Cecily, who was committed to her daughter's interests; another,

14   E 159/232 brevia Mich. 34 Hen. VI m. 19; *Excerpta Historica*, ed. S. Bentley (1833), 6–7. The undated original, C 81/1370/56, is in a file that spans 21–36 Hen. VI. The king's presence at Windsor on 15 October does not fix the year. In 1445 York ceased to be a custodian. The commission was never enrolled.

15   *Monasticon*, ii. 63; *CPR 1436–41*, 359–60.

16   Habington, *Survey of Worcestershire*, i. 120–1; DL 26/65; BL Roy. MS 17 BXLVII f. 165v; SC 12/18/45 f. 13; *List of Sheriffs*, 158.

17   Hicks, 'Between Majorities'.

18   E.g. Oxfordshire RO Dil II/b/8 m. 6; II/b/6 att. bill.

19   Deduced, E 368/220 m. 120; Exeter MS Chanter 722 ff. 3, 9v.

20   E 28/79/31.

older dowager, Salisbury's sister Eleanor Countess of Northumberland, widow of Isabel's brother Richard Lord Despenser (d. 1414), wisely had her dower re-assigned.[21] What came into royal hands was land valued at a little over £800 a year: a very substantial amount, more than enough to endow an earl, but a mere fraction, perhaps a quarter or a fifth, of the total inheritance.

At this point Lord Beauchamp of Powicke claimed the whole Beauchamp inheritance as heir general of Earl William (d. 1298), first of the Beauchamp earls.[22] As almost everything had been resettled in tail on the heirs of subsequent earls, it is not surprising that he was unsuccessful, despite his excellent connections at court. Once again it appears that Edward Lord Bergavenny claimed the lordship of Abergavenny from which his title derived and Mereworth in Kent. Mereworth had been settled by William Lord Bergavenny (d. 1411) in jointure on his son Richard Beauchamp Earl of Worcester and Isabel Despenser and should have reverted to their daughter Elizabeth Lady Bergavenny rather than her son Duke Henry. The marcher lordship of Abergavenny, as we have already seen, was entailed by William on his heirs male, who died out in 1421, on the heirs male of the Warwick line, who died out in 1446, and Edward felt that they should then revert to his wife Elizabeth, William's grand-daughter, rather than on his great-great-niece. Without the original entail, we cannot tell whether he was right. Anyway his claim was again rejected. Bergavenny resorted to self-help, perhaps by seizing Abergavenny and certainly by presenting to a living there in his wife's right.[23] Even without these lordships, Bergavenny was a formidable opponent, for through her grand-mother Joan Lord Bergavenny (d. 1435) his first wife was one of the three and ultimately two heirs general of Thomas Earl of Arundel and Warenne (d. 1417). Hence his income of £667 in 1436. Hence perhaps the twenty-one annuities totalling £111 13s. 4d. paid out from Abergavenny by the custodians to twenty-one gentry in 1446–7, the largest single fee being the 20 marks (£13 6s. 8d.) paid to Sir Walter Devereux.[24]

With two claims to dower of the Duchess Cecily and Countess Eleanor, Bergavenny's designs on Abergavenny, and a horde of courtiers seizing what they could get, the integrity of the inheritance was certainly at risk. Not all contenders carried equal standing at court, where a disproportionate and indeed over-whelming influence was exercised by the king's favourites and above all by Suffolk. On 16 September 1446, two such courtiers who were also trusted Beauchamp feoffees, Sudeley and Beauchamp of Powicke, respectively Lord Treasurer and steward of the royal household, joined with Suffolk and Salisbury, who as the young countess of Warwick's grandfather 'would therefore be more

21 *CPR 1446–52*, 37–8, 87; see also Hicks, 'Between Majorities'. Eleanor had probably remitted her third-share for an annuity, Pugh, *Glamorgan County History*, iii. 186.
22 C 81/1546/14; Hicks, 'Between Majorities'.
23 *GEC* i. 28 9, 30n; C 139/96/1/15; C 81/761/9607. The original entail of Abergavenny is lost, but see R. I. Jack, 'Entail & Descent: The Hastings Inheritance 1370–1436', *BIHR* xxxviii (1965), 11.
24 E 368/220 m. 120.

friendly and favourable to Anne than any other person'.[25] Salisbury was also father of the dowager duchess, father of Richard and brother of Lords Latimer and Bergavenny, who were husbands of three of the next heiresses should the infant Anne die. Given that he was no longer part of the inner court circle and hence lacked much say nationally – he attended only 3 out of 57 meetings of the much weakened royal council in 1447–9[26] – Salisbury was fortunate to have such a say. Suffolk secured the young countess's wardship and marriage and all four shared the administration of her estates. Most of the royal patentees were dismissed. Suffolk, Salisbury, Sudeley and Beauchamp of Powicke controlled the estate and its archive, running it from London with the collaboration of the family administrators in Warwick.[27] Also Earl Richard Beauchamp's executors acted for the new custodians,[28] as they were later to do for young Richard as the new earl. There was no interruption of estate administration. Fees and annuities continued to be paid to retainers. The Beauchamp retinue remained intact and continued to dominate the region unchallenged by Buckingham or anyone else. A going concern was available for the next heirs: Richard was fortunate that his father and his kinsman Suffolk were those running it.

3.2   Gathering the Spoils

Fourteen forty-nine was the year of crisis that ushered in the tense decade culminating in the Wars of the Roses. The French war that Henry V and Bedford had conducted so successfully had turned into a stubborn defence of English conquests until, in 1444, a breathing space was offered by the truce of Tours. Garrisons were immediately run down and expenditure was reduced to more acceptable peacetime levels. Apart from conceding Henry VI's hand in marriage, the English surrendered Anjou and Maine, thus exposing Normandy itself to future attack. This followed when an English force attacked Fougères on 24 March 1449, as it now appears on the instructions of the home government and in order to pressurize Brittany. English protests that their *coup de main* was not a breach of truce were rejected and offered the French a pretext for a full-scale invasion of Normandy, to which the English offered only very ineffective defence. Charges of negligence and even treachery were later laid against the English commander, Warwick's brother-in-law Edmund Beaufort Duke of Somerset by his uncle Richard Duke of York. On 9 May Pont L'Arche fell and Salisbury's brother Lord Fauconberg was captured. Rouen itself capitulated in November. Among those engaged in the Norman campaign were several directly interested in the Beauchamp and Despenser inheritances: Shrewsbury, husband of Margaret, the eldest Beauchamp sister; Somerset, husband of Eleanor, the second sister, and Roos, her son and heir by her first husband; and Salisbury's

25   *CPR 1446–52*, 1.
26   R. Virgoe, 'The Composition of the King's Council 1437–61', *BIHR* xliii (1970), 158.
27   *CPR 1446–52*, 1.
28   Hicks, 'Between Majorities'.

brother Bergavenny, widower of the other Despenser heir, and his son George Neville. Young George, Roos and Shrewsbury were among those surrendered as hostages on terms that were not kept and thus had to be ransomed, which took some years and great expense.[29] Salisbury's brothers Fauconberg and Bergavenny had grounds for resentment: against Somerset?

Hence Shrewsbury, Somerset, Roos, Bergavenny and his son were removed from the English political scene at the crucial moment when the fate of the Warwick inheritance was decided, in June 1449: Shrewsbury until after his release as a hostage on 11 July 1450 and actually until 20 December 1450; Somerset until late July 1450;[30] and George into the 1460s. However, this was less of a disadvantage than might be supposed: all parties, as we shall see, secured royal patents favourable to their claims within a few weeks of young Anne's death and were able to obtain others at intervals. After the initial moves in June 1449, it may actually have been to the advantage of the Beauchamp sisters that their husbands were together and thus able to act in concert: something that they were already accustomed to in the Berkeley–Lisle dispute. Strangely, perhaps, they did not make common cause with Bergavenny against their common enemy, the new earl. Influence at court proved to be very different from power in the localities. The Beauchamp sisters found it more difficult to obtain favourable verdicts in inquisitions than to secure royal licences and still more so to achieve actual possession of disputed lands. Here the absence of their husbands may have been decisive.

The resumption of hostilities in France, as yet not particularly serious, was the backcloth to the third session of the 1449 parliament at Winchester from 16 June to 16 July 1449. Somerset, Roos, Shrewsbury and Bergavenny, as we have seen, were absent; Suffolk, Salisbury and his son Richard, Tiptoft, Sudeley and Beauchamp of Powicke were all there. Anne Beauchamp died on 3 June 1449 at Ewelme, Suffolk's Oxfordshire seat.[31] The news was brought to Winchester at once: the very next day, 4 June, writs of *diem clausit extremum* were issued ordering inquisitions *post mortem* in London and other counties. Only a week after her death, on 10 June 1449, Dowager-Duchess Cecily and her new husband Tiptoft were granted the custody of George Neville's Despenser lands during his minority even though his father Bergavenny was alive. It was perhaps because he controlled the duchess's substantial dower and half the Despenser inheritance that Tiptoft was now created earl of Worcester. Eleanor Countess of Northumberland as dowager-lady Despenser wisely secured the reassignment of her dower on 19 July.[32] Already the division of the Despenser inheritance

29 *The Brut*, 515; *Chronique de Mathieu d'Escouchy*, ed. G. Du Fresne de Beaucourt (SHF, 1874), iii. 360–1; BL MS Harley 807 f. 75v; A. J. Pollard, *John Talbot and the War in France 1427–53* (1983), 65. For Fauconberg's ransom, see D. Rowland, *Genealogical Account of the Most Noble House of Neville* (1830), 85–6; *CPR 1446–52*, 496.

30 Watts, *Henry VI*, 284n; Pollard, *Talbot*, 65–6.

31 See above p. 30. The Tewkesbury Chronicle states Harpenden, very close to Ewelme, and that she was buried at Reading Abbey, *Monasticon*, ii. 64.

32 *CFR 1446–52*, 111; *CPR 1446–52*, 87.

between the representatives of the Countess Isabel's two daughters had been
agreed: a principle that was enshrined in the later inquisitions *post mortem* and
which was initially accepted by the founder's chronicle of the Despenser abbey
of Tewkesbury. Had the same principle been accepted for the Beauchamp inheritance, as the three elder sisters wished, there would have been no dispute at
all. Richard Neville first sought the earldom and Warwick itself as well as his
share and subsequently all the rest as well: with complete legal justification, it
must be stressed.

Table 3.1 The Beauchamp and Despenser Inheritances

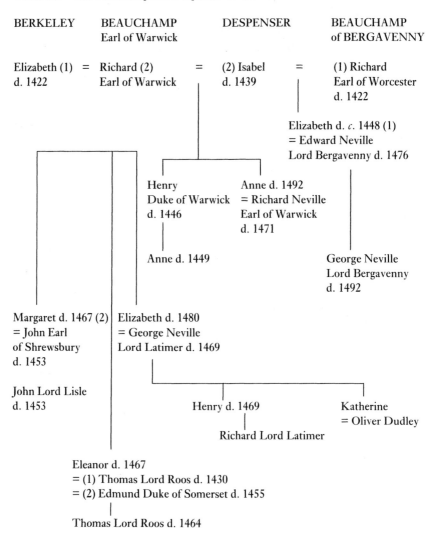

BERKELEY	BEAUCHAMP Earl of Warwick	DESPENSER	BEAUCHAMP of BERGAVENNY
Elizabeth (1) = d. 1422	Richard (2) Earl of Warwick	= (2) Isabel d. 1439	= (1) Richard Earl of Worcester d. 1422

Elizabeth d. *c*. 1448 (1)
= Edward Neville
Lord Bergavenny d. 1476

Henry
Duke of Warwick
d. 1446

Anne d. 1492
= Richard Neville
Earl of Warwick
d. 1471

Anne d. 1449

George Neville
Lord Bergavenny
d. 1492

Margaret d. 1467 (2)
= John Earl
of Shrewsbury
d. 1453

Elizabeth d. 1480
= George Neville
Lord Latimer d. 1469

John Lord Lisle
d. 1453

Henry d. 1469

Richard Lord Latimer

Katherine
= Oliver Dudley

Eleanor d. 1467
= (1) Thomas Lord Roos d. 1430
= (2) Edmund Duke of Somerset d. 1455

Thomas Lord Roos d. 1464

Young Anne Beauchamp died on 3 June, Worcester secured the Despenser custody on 10 June, and on 19 June, only three days into the parliamentary session, Richard Neville attended the Lords as earl of Warwick in right of his wife Anne.[33] The letter patent that formalized Richard's recognition as earl of Warwick is dated only to 23 July. In support of his promotion it refers to his kinship and intimate service to the king and to his good service against the king's enemies the Scots at his own costs:[34] service that all his brothers-in-law could certainly have matched and capped! Had they been present, more might have been made of the fact noted in the patent that Richard was a minor, who would not come of age until November; his wife Anne was at least 22 years of age. For the youngest sister of four to be given preference can only have been because she was the only *whole* sister of the late Duke Henry: it implies the application of the common law principle that 'possession of the brother in the whole blood makes the sister heir'. For the moment the exclusion of the half-blood was applied only to the earldom. There was no licence issued to Richard and Anne alone to enter any of the lands of the earldom. Indeed no such licence was ever issued.

What the new earl and countess of Warwick thought this meant is revealed by the lawsuit that they immediately initiated on the quindene of Trinity (22 June) against Thomas Colt and Henry Sotehill, both Neville servants from the North, with a view to a final concord resettling their share of the lands on themselves jointly and their heirs. Had Anne died prematurely and without offspring, this might have given our Richard a life-estate in her inheritance. A fine to agree was paid at once in the exchequer by Colt, probably as Warwick chamberlain of the exchequer, though actually the final concord was not executed at this time. The draft concord settled Warwick and seven other Warwickshire properties – the heartlands of the earldom – and quarters of many other properties and reversions in thirteen other counties, Wales and the Channel Isles on Richard and Anne and her heirs.[35] It invites three immediate observations. Firstly, the list of lands was incomplete and paid no attention to the entails by which the lands had hitherto been held, to whether they were held in dower by the Duchess Cecily, or to the titles that were to be recognized by the infant Anne's inquisitions *post mortem*. The grant of the earldom was also defective. The claim to the lands and the fine was evidently initiated well before even Richard, whose father was one of those in control of the Beauchamp archives, could carry out the necessary research and seek the appropriate legal opinion; as we shall also see, the other sisters also lacked access to this information. Secondly, the reservation of the Warwickshire lands implies the application of the whole-blood principle that operated with the earldom to those lands and only those lands: a distinction that made no legal sense. Thirdly, the quarters show that the

---

33 Griffiths, *King & Country*, 261.
34 *CPR 1446–52*, 235–6; C 81/1454/38.
35 *Warwickshire Feet of Fines*, iii, ed. L. Drucker (Dugdale Soc. xviii, 1943), no. 2683 quoting CP 25(1)/294/74/41. Although the action was initiated and £40 was paid by Colt for a licence to agree (E 401/821), it was deferred and suspended (CP 40/758 rot. 285-d; CP 40/760 rot. 356d), and was only completed in 1466. No draft fine now survives.

rights of all four sisters as coheirs were acknowledged at this stage.

It is astonishing how rapidly such controversial decisions affecting so many important noblemen were reached and implemented. It indicates that Richard (or more probably Salisbury) and Worcester exploited the absence of potential rivals in France. To achieve it, they surely required the assistance of Suffolk and also perhaps of Sudeley, now steward of the royal household. This time, in contrast to 1446, rigid control was exercised and only a couple of royal grants were made to suppliant courtiers.[36] Yet the verdict was not that Richard and Anne received everything, but a compromise, whereby they obtained half the Despenser inheritance, a quarter of the Beauchamp lands, plus the earldom and Warwick itself. If Anne were to die childless, everything would remain to her sisters except Warwick, Sutton Coldfield, and Brailes (Warw.), which would revert to Margaret Countess of Shrewsbury as senior sister, the heirs of her body, and, failing them, to the right heirs of Earl Richard Beauchamp. So runs the final text of the fine in 1466: whilst we cannot be certain of intentions in 1449, it is striking that similar remainders were applied to the earldom itself in 1450.[37] Since the draft fine was voluntary and not forced on Richard and Anne, it suggests that they were happy to settle with this compromise: a position that they later changed. Some concessions *could* have been forced on Richard and Anne by parliament. That, however, would have taken time, as arbitration typically involved full consideration of the cases and evidence of all parties that clearly did not happen, as the issue was decided almost at once. More probably, therefore, the compromise enshrined in the draft fine and the division of the Despenser inheritance was proposed from Richard's side and accepted by parliament as unexceptional.

That is not to say that it actually was unexceptional. The elder sisters had been accustomed for thirty years to the notion that they would inherit equally in default of male heirs both before and after Henry's birth. This was to be their position from 1449 to 1466–7, when they were obliged to settle for very much less.[38] They claimed throughout to be daughters and coheirs of Earl Richard Beauchamp: a case that could have prevailed had Duke Henry never taken seisin. It could have been supported orally, though not mentioned in their surviving patents, that almost all the Beauchamp lands had been entailed in tail male by earls Thomas I (d. 1369) and II (d. 1401) with remainder to their right heirs, which all four daughters could claim to be. At this period, whenever there were several coheiresses and sufficient income to support the title after partition of the lands, the senior could commonly expect to secure that title and the principal seat. Hence the hope of Margaret's husband Shrewsbury in his will of 1452 'that any tyme hereafter Y may atteyne to the name and lordeship of Warewik as *right wolle*'.[39] This was their position as early as 5 July 1449, only a fortnight after

36   E.g. *CPR 1446–52*, 274; E 28/79/37; C 81/1454/27.
37   *Warwicks. Fines*, no. 2683; *CPR 1446–52*, 451.
38   Hicks, *Richard III*, 324.
39   A. F. J. Sinclair, 'The Beauchamp Earls of Warwick in the Later Middle Ages' (London Univ. PhD thesis, 1987), 387.

Table 3.2   Title to the Lordship of Abergavenny

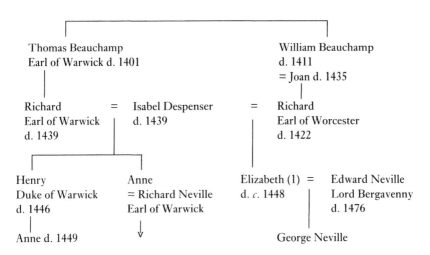

Richard's recognition as earl, when the three elder sisters petitioned for a licence authorizing all four of them to enter the Beauchamp lands in England and Wales entailed on them as daughters and coheirs general of Earl Richard Beauchamp. Specifically excluded was property held in fee simple, of which there was little if any; property inherited from Duke Henry, most notably the Channel Isles; and estates settled jointly on Richard and Isabel, many of which were actually subject to earlier entails.[40] This licence could thus have given the new earl and countess of Warwick a larger share than their sisters, though ironically Warwick itself and other lands they assigned to themselves in their fine would not have been reserved for them. It could have initiated a process whereby the lands were allocated according to the titles derived from earlier title deeds; this did not actually happen. It seems the Beauchamp sisters were no better informed than Richard and Anne. Whilst their licence purported to represent all four sisters, clearly it was initiated solely on Anne's half-sisters' behalf: a feature that was to recur repeatedly over the next few years.

Apart from the Despenser and Beauchamp estates, there was a third element to be considered: Abergavenny and Mereworth. An esquire of the body Thomas Danyell was appointed steward, receiver, constable and master forester of Abergavenny on 6 June 1449.[41] From the start the new earl of Warwick included the style *dominus de Bergavenny* among his titles.[42] Alleging earlier entries to

---

40   C 81/761/9098, which is misrepresented in *CPR 1446–52*, 262–3.
41   C 81/1454/27. Although signed by Henry VI and delivered to chancery on 6 June, it was not enrolled and presumably not implemented.
42   6 Dec. 1450, E 159/230 rec. Hil. 32 Hen. VI m.4.

Abergavenny on the death of Joan Lady Bergavenny in 1435 and after the deaths of previous lords in 1439 and 1446, on each occasion to be put out again by force or by inquisitions, Edward Lord Bergavenny petitioned once again for a licence to enter the lordship, which he secured on 14 July 1449. Mereworth followed in 1454.[43] As one would expect, Bergavenny also sought to maximize his son's share of the Despenser inheritance. He never secured the wardship of his own son George or custody of his Despenser purparty.

What the grants to the Beauchamp coheirs and Bergavenny demonstrate is their easy access to royal favour even when abroad. At court they were formidable opponents for the new earl of Warwick. Their patents, which actually preceded the formal creation of Warwick as earl, were incompatible with it. Whereas Warwick's was warranted by the king himself, theirs were under the privy seal: which may or may not be significant. All three demonstrate yet again the weakness of Henry VI's government: his incapacity to reach a decision, to stick to it, and to avoid making contradictory grants. Henry was to continue issuing them for several years yet. That these were quarrels within the family, amongst rivals related several times over in each case, did not mean that 'there do not seem to have been any serious repercussions'.[44] The disputes were to be pursued at court and in the provinces, by influence on the king and by force in the localities. In this battle, our Richard had four crucial advantages: his initial recognition as earl; his rivals' continued absence abroad; divisions among his rivals; and his control of the localities. In the longer term they scarcely sufficed against the dominance of Somerset at court after 1450.

Warwick's strategy was not purely defensive, but offensive. The inquisitions *post mortem* on Anne Beauchamp were a vital element. Several writs had been issued on 4 June and the very first inquisition was held at Hereford on 20 September 1449. The jurors reported that the infant Anne held in fee simple by inheritance from Duke Henry and his father the lordships of Abergavenny, Pains Castle in Elvell, Ewyas Lacy and other properties and that Warwick's wife Anne was sole sister and heiress of Duke Henry. It was a crucial verdict in several different ways. It accepted the principle that Warwick's countess was the sole Beauchamp heiress – a significant change from the Trinity term fine. Warwick had now rejected the original compromise, perhaps because of the opposition of the Beauchamp coheirs, and was seeking the whole inheritance to their total exclusion. It applied the same principle without any further comment to the Despenser lordship of Ewyas Lacy in defiance of the partition with George Neville anticipated in the grant of custody to the Earl of Worcester. Finally, and more parochially, it rejected Bergavenny's claim to Abergavenny, which itself had been recognized only on 14 July.[45] The jurors thus found for Richard and Anne on each issue and against her Beauchamp sisters, George Neville's Despenser claim, and Bergavenny's claim to Abergavenny. It is likely that the

43   *CPR 1446–52*, 264–5; C 81/761/9107; C 81/1462/3, printed in Rowland, *Neville*, 137–8; see also *CPR 1452–61*, 107. Additional oral explanation must be presumed.
44   Storey, *Lancaster*, 237.
45   C 139/135/5/11.

jury was overawed. The new earl of Warwick was at Abergavenny the previous day (19 September 1449) in company with Sir Humphrey Stafford of Grafton and doubtless other important Beauchamp retainers.[46] He was there, we may be confident, not just to revisit the place where he was married, but also to reinforce his hold on the disputed lordship. Bergavenny had been ousted on his last visit, in 1436. On this occasion also, absent in Normandy, he was in no position to resist. But he did not give up.

The Hereford inquisition was delivered to chancery only on 12 October,[47] but Warwick – who had been there – already knew the verdict. With such a satisfactory ruling behind him, we may suppose that it was he who initiated the issue of further writs on 6 October 1449. For some shires there are no inquisitions extant, probably because none were held. Where returns do survive, all the result of inquests between March and December 1450, they all without exception found Anne to be sole heir of the Beauchamp lands as sole sister of her brother Henry: as at Hereford, they rejected the claims of her elder Beauchamp sisters. The juries made no distinction between Beauchamp lands formerly entailed on the male line, in tail general, or in fee simple. Whatever their influence even *in absentia* at court which had secured them the licence to enter, the three Beauchamp sisters were unable to prevail against Warwick at provincial inquests.

However, highly significantly and in contrast to the Herefordshire verdict, all these juries also found Anne to be merely coheir with her cousin George Neville to the Despenser properties.[48] This is very surprising since the justification was the entail of 1290 resulting from the resettlement by Earl Gilbert de Clare on the issue of himself and his wife, in tail general. With the demise of the male line in 1446, was not the title of Beauchamp and Despenser lines identical? Should not Richard's wife Anne have succeeded as whole sister of Duke Henry everywhere? No wonder that several historians have been mystified why the principle of the exclusion of the half-blood was found to be inapplicable to the Despenser lands. This conclusion differed from the Herefordshire verdict and was obviously very much to Warwick's disadvantage. Why should Warwick reject the Beauchamp claims and concede the Despenser ones? How could he simultaneously in a succession of inquests get his way over one set of lands and not over another? The explanation lies not in legal titles, which were indeed identical, but in the effective use of influence to modify the verdicts early in 1450 by the agents of Lord Bergavenny, who was the obvious beneficiary.

Apparently Warwick spent much of the autumn in Glamorgan and Christmas at Warwick, proceeding after 1 January 1450 to Westminster for the parliamentary session that opened on the 22nd.[49] With the coheirs embroiled in the loss of

46 BL Add. Roll 74169 m. 2d.
47 C 139/135/5/11.
48 C 139/135/5 *passim*.
49 Warwick CRO WCM 49; W. Rees, 'Accounts of the Rectory of Cardiff and other Possessions of the Abbey of Tewkesbury in Glamorgan 1449–50', *South Wales & Monmouth Rec. Soc.* ii (1950), 179.

Normandy, he was without rivals at court and in parliament and was able to use 1450 to consolidate his hold on all the inheritances. Given the disasters in France, this was inevitably a stormy session of recriminations, retribution and retrenchment. Attacks on the government focused on William Duke of Suffolk himself, its front man, who was impeached and destroyed. On 17 March Warwick was among the forty-six peers present in the chamber over the cloister at Westminster Abbey at which the king exonerated the duke and nevertheless exiled him for five years to France.[50] It was whilst leaving by sea that Suffolk was intercepted and executed. On 2 March Warwick had surrendered his 1449 patent of creation as earl of Warwick – to the ancient, immemorial, earldom of the Beauchamps and Beaumonts – for recognition instead as earl of Warwick, as Duke Henry had been after 1444. Now he was premier earl in England; he took precedence after dukes and marquises over all other earls in parliament and elsewhere; he could wear a distinguishing circlet on all public occasions; and his heir if he had one – and he still had no issue – would take precedence over sons of all other earls. We may presume that Warwick wanted this enhanced dignity and exercised it. The reversion in default of issue was granted to the Countess Margaret even though it derived from her half-brother and not her father.[51] From this grant we may also deduce that Warwick saw himself as heir to his wife's brother Henry Duke of Warwick. We should expect him to seek the latter's title of duke, lands and offices whenever opportunity offered.

Following the king's verdict on Suffolk on 17 March, Warwick's father Salisbury went to France. Warwick himself proceeded to Warwick (21 March) and perhaps to Cardiff, the headquarters of his marcher lordship of Glamorgan. Thereafter he proceeded to the parliament at Leicester, which opened on 29 April, arriving on 5 May with an entourage of 400 men 'and moo' including some sent by the Midland baron William Lord Ferrers of Chartley, whose attendance 'did me right thonkful seruice and Right grete worship'. This may have been with a view to service abroad, perhaps with his father, perhaps at Calais.[52] This time he was not accompanied by Stafford of Grafton, who arrived separately after attacking Warwick's future estates steward Sir Robert Harcourt on 10 May at Stanton Harcourt in Oxfordshire in pursuance of their private blood feud. It was at this session that the Commons forced on the king an act of resumption, designed both to provide resources for the French war and to punish those favourites and courtiers who were seen as feathering their nests at the king's and the public's expense. All royal grants since 1422 were to be resumed. The effects were greatly reduced by provisos of exemption, some general and some particular. Thus Warwick's title as earl – and his father's as earl of Salisbury – were protected by a general proviso covering titles of honour. More specifically, Warwick was allowed another proviso covering lands granted to Duke Henry. These comprised the Channel Isles, the forest of Feckenham, and several re-

---

50   *RP* v. 182–3.
51   *Dignity of a Peer* v. 244.
52   *Paston L & P* ii. 37; Bloom, 'Letter of the "Kingmaker"', 120.

versions yet to fall in. Tutbury was not included. Salisbury retained his rights in Richmondshire and Cumbria. Their main estates were exempt anyway, since they were held of inheritance rather than royal grant. Those who were absent, such as Somerset and Shrewsbury, lost more heavily.

The Leicester parliament adjourned on 6 June amidst alarming rumours of the impending Kentish rebellion of Jack Cade, which the earl transmitted to Ferrers on Monday 8 June from Warwick. The king, he reported:

> hath desired and charged me to be with hymm at Saynt Albones on Saturday next comyng [13 June] accompaigned with suche a feliship as that I may . . . [to ensure that] we schal be of power to withstand ther malice and evil wil. Wherefor I pray you with al my hert with suche personnes as ye nowe arrays and secure ye wel send to me at Warrewyk ther to be on Wednesday [10 June] at nyght next commyng as semblable wyse wol and shal do to you suche tyme ye desire me for your worship. . . .[53]

As Ferrers died next day, his men may not have been despatched, but the earl presumably followed his own timetable and accompanied the king thereafter. It was his retainer Stafford who pressed Cade too closely and was defeated and killed at Tonbridge. Finding the rebels too strong and his own forces too unreliable, the king withdrew on 25 June, first to Berkhamsted (Herts.) and then to Kenilworth (Warw.), probably with Warwick in attendance. Cade was captured on 10 July and died on the 12th. The Countess of Warwick was at Coventry in July. Warwick himself was at Warwick on 1 August, at Cardiff later in the month, and returned to Warwick by 1 October.[54] Presumably, therefore, he missed the celebrated meeting in late September or early October of the Duke of York with the king at Westminster.

As we have seen, Warwick had secured a favourable inquisition in Herefordshire on 20 September 1449. Someone, however, was dissatisfied and made representations directly to the king: this someone, we may deduce from the results, was Bergavenny. Accordingly Henry VI ordered a new inquisition for Herefordshire by signet letter dated at Eltham Palace in Kent on 26 September 1449, only a week after the previous one. Nothing happened: the writs issued on 6 October did not include Herefordshire.[55] Presumably the warrant was intercepted before a writ could be issued. It was probably in consequence, therefore, that stronger action was taken. On 3 March new inquisitions were ordered to be taken by special commissioners. This was a procedure highly favourable to the applicant, who named the commissioners: in the Herefordshire case those who acted were Henry Griffith and Thomas FitzHarry esquire, neither of whom were among those feed from Abergavenny in 1447–8. Their return of 15 April 1450 confirmed Anne as sole heiress of the Beauchamp

53   Ibid.
54   Rees, 'Cardiff Rectory Accounts', 182–3.
55   C 81/1371/16; C 139/135/5.

lordships, but differed in two other vital particulars from its predecessors. Abergavenny was altogether omitted – it had not been held by Anne Beauchamp at all[56] – a result so highly favourable to Lord Bergavenny and to nobody else that it indicates that he was behind the application for new inquisitions. This may explain why on 5 September 1450 Lord Bergavenny was summoned to parliament: at last, for he had long used the title and had ample means from his late wife's other inheritances. Secondly, Ewyas Lacy was returned on this occasion not as heritable by the Countess Anne alone, as in September, but as a Despenser property to be shared equally between her and George Neville. The principle of the inheritance by the half-blood was not accepted in this case. The two commissioners responsible were immediately granted the farm of Ewyas Lacy.[57] If Bergavenny was behind the new inquisition, he was also seeking to maximize his son's share of the Despenser inheritance. Warwick's possessions in the Welsh marches could be halved or worse. One of his two main areas of regional hegemony would be removed.

The partition of the Despenser inheritance was also a feature of an inquisition held by the Gloucestershire escheator on 10 March 1450 at Gloucester, which found Glamorgan to be heritable by both Anne and George, but returned nothing about any other property in the county. This had been preceded by the issue of yet another special commission on 25 February, headed by Lord Berkeley and again including FitzHarry, which sat on 24 April 1450, not at Gloucester, but at Berkeley Castle: a location where the commissioners could evidently exercise maximum pressure on the jurors. The verdict again found Glamorgan to be the inheritance of both Anne and George. What was new about it, however, and different from its predecessor, was that it found Tewkesbury and Sodbury also to be heritable jointly.[58] These were properties of the Despenser feoffees, who were still in occupation and whose title was not mentioned. The inquisition, in short, threatened Warwick's hold on those Despenser lands that were otherwise spared immediate division by the trust.

Several conclusions follow from this. Bergavenny was behind the verdicts of all subsequent juries that the Despenser lands were to be divided between Anne and George. He actually wanted more, to end the Despenser trust and to divide its lands in the same way, but this he was unable to achieve in any other county. Obviously untrue, it apparently required a special commission to achieve such verdicts, and no more were issued. Secondly, such commissions were used in Herefordshire and Gloucestershire, where the Berkeleys were Bergavenny's allies. This is highly significant since they were the enemies of the elder Beauchamp sisters: the Berkeley–Lisle feud flared up again in September 1450, when the Berkeleys sacked Wotton-under-Edge, house of the Countess Margaret and her son Lord Lisle. The latter secured a special commission of oyer and terminer against the Berkeleys on 28 September 1450, which was headed by Lisle

56   C 139/135/5/13, 16; *CFR 1446–52*, 155, 162.
57   *CPR 1446–52*, 432–3.
58   C 139/135/5/16.

and Warwick himself.[59] It seems that Bergavenny was not making common cause with the Beauchamp sisters, but was pursuing only the claims of himself and his son. That was how it was possible for Warwick to get his way in inquisition after inquisition over the Beauchamp lands, but not over the Despenser ones. At this stage Bergavenny was more successful in influencing juries than the Beauchamp sisters. In contrast to what happened only a little later, when feuds escalated and gelled as participants saw allies in their enemy's enemy, at this stage their disagreements did not force Bergavenny and the Beauchamp sisters together against Warwick as common enemy and did not prevent Warwick and Lisle, otherwise rivals, from co-operating against Berkeley. Moreover, as we shall see, Berkeley was to be the loser.

If there was a considerable gap between a licence to enter and an inquest verdict in one's favour, there was a still larger gulf between such a verdict and actual possession of the land. The inquisitions confirmed Warwick's right to the Beauchamp lands that he already held. He did not accept George's title to the rest. The Gloucestershire verdict did not yet affect the control of the Despenser feoffees over Tewkesbury; nor probably in practice was Warwick dislodged from Abergavenny. The verdicts did imply that Ewyas Lacy, Glamorgan, and a few other Despenser properties held in chief should be divided. George's share had been farmed by the earl of Worcester; new farmers were found for Ewyas Lacy. In theory. Actually an inquisition reveals that up to April 1450 all the issues from Glamorgan were taken by John Nanfan, the receiver appointed by Duke Henry, and Thomas Butler. Warwick was at Cardiff in the autumn of 1449, when he was accepted unambiguously as lord by the receiver of Tewkesbury Abbey estate. Writs were issued from the Cardiff chancery in March and May in Warwick's name alone. Thus Warwick probably held the whole lordship even ahead of 20 May 1450, when Worcester surrendered the custody with royal consent to Warwick.[60] This concession may merely have recognized reality; it may indicate Worcester's sympathy for his wife's brother; and most probably, in view of Worcester's later track record, it was made for some substantial inducement. It meant that in practice Warwick could keep hold of Glamorgan until he could find some means of re-establishing his title to be sole Despenser heir.

Warwick's sister the Duchess Cecily died on 26 July 1450,[61] when her Beauchamp and Despenser dower should have reverted to the right heirs. Several grants from them were made by the crown, including the under-shrievalty of Worcester on 19 August to John Brome in lieu of Thomas Hugford.[62] Several of the inquisitions on Anne Beauchamp also covered the duchess. They found the countess of Warwick to be sole heir of the Beauchamp lands and she and George Neville to be coheirs of the Despenser lands.[63] It is probable that Warwick

59   *CPR 1446–52*, 432–3.
60   The mainpernors were Witham and Colt, *CFR 1445–52*, 157–8. The patent was exemplified at Leicester on 21 May 1450, PSO 1/18/938.
61   C 139/135/5/16.
62   *CFR 1445–52*, 144, 181, 182.
63   C 139/135/5/4; *CPR 1446–52*, 309; see also E 149/189 m. 1.

immediately took possession of all of them. Admittedly the exchequer leased out Cherhill (Wilts.) and Flamstead (Herts.) in December.

Another exceptional property was the Warwick chamberlainship of the exchequer, an appurtenance of the former Mauduit and Beauchamp manor of Hanslope (Bucks.), for which the earl secured a royal patent of recognition on 6 December and another notifying the exchequer on 7 December.[64] The deputy chamberlain was John Brome of Baddesley Clinton (Warw.), who claimed to have been appointed by Duke Henry on 4 July 1445 after the death of John Throckmorton: if so, Duke Henry had also granted the office to John Nanfan. Brome however had himself confirmed for life or for forty years by the king himself, quite irregularly, on 5 November 1449.[65] On 7 December Warwick took possession of the keys and coffers, dismissed Brome, and installed Thomas Colt as Warwick chamberlain.[66] Warwick had established his right. The chamberlainship seems to complete his control of the whole of Anne Beauchamp's estate held in chief, whether Beauchamp or Despenser.

3.3   Effectively Earl

It is the contradictory letters patent that indicate that the inheritances were disputed. There is little such evidence in the localities. The inquisitions are unanimous in what they say; the elaborate recital of the Despenser title in particular indicates that they were orchestrated. From the Home Counties to the Welsh Marches and the Midlands heartlands, where juries might perhaps have been overawed, to peripheral areas, where the earl was a minor figure, Warwick's will prevailed, his rivals apparently powerless or inactive and unrepresented. We have to deduce in the absence of direct evidence. There seems little reason to doubt that Warwick *did* secure the Beauchamp lands in the summer of 1449 – they were, after all, already being administered by sympathetic custodians. He did hold half or more probably all of Glamorgan, again in their custody, from the same date, by March 1450, and certainly by May 1450.[67] If there was an interlude, the estate was again in sympathetic hands that represented continuity, those of his sister Cecily and her new husband. And when Cecily herself died and her dower reverted to the heirs, the inquisitions and Warwick's recognition as chamberlain indicate that he again took possession.

There is little more direct evidence. As we have seen, Warwick proceeded in force almost at once in September 1449 to Abergavenny, where there may have been an intruder, presumably to oust him and to restore order. Although Bergavenny obtained several further licences to enter Abergavenny, he was never

64   *CPR 1446–52*, 409; E 159/227 rec. Hil. 29 Hen. VI m. 9d.
65   E 28/79/37. Brome did not receive livery as chamberlain in 1447–50, E 101/409/18.
66   E 159/227 rec. Hil. 29 Hen. VI m. 9d, 149d; E 159/230 rec. Hil. 32 Hen. VI m. 4. Colt's deputies were John Otter (usher), Thomas Stokdale, Thomas Witham and Ralph Ingoldsby (clerks), E 403/793 m. 4.
67   C 139/135/5/16: not the royal grantees of 2 Aug. 1449, *CPR 1446–52*, 274.

to do so again. Warwick visited Cardiff – headquarters of Glamorgan – on several occasions, first perhaps sometime or sometimes between 8 September and Christmas 1449, when his men apparently appropriated 16 quarters of corn and 15 quarters of oats from Cardiff rectory without licence. By then his estates steward was William Herbert of Raglan – future earl of Pembroke and son of the Despenser feoffee William ap Thomas – who claimed expenses from Tewkesbury Abbey's grange of Llanwit. Hence the abbey receiver composed a petition to Warwick with the help of a clerk of the Cardiff chancery. Warwick pardoned the expenses under his small seal in October, presumably 1449. Subsequently the receiver spent four days at Cardiff in August 1450 putting the abbey's case over Llanwit to the earl and his council. Warwick's bailiffs were also oppressively collecting fees and other dues from the estates of the Cistercian abbey of Margam, as Abbot Thomas Franklin complained, so on 24 March 1450 Warwick issued a writ of protection for Margam to the sheriff of Glamorgan, perhaps already his younger brother Sir Thomas Neville. From at least then charters and writs were being issued from the Cardiff chancery on Warwick's behalf under the style of Lord Despenser, Glamorgan and Morgannok.[68] A new charter that he granted to Cardiff borough on 12 March 1451 was witnessed by the three most prominent churchmen in the lordship, the bishop of Llandaff, abbots of Neath and Margam, by his brother Thomas and the prominent local gentleman Sir Edward Stradling of St Donats, and by his trusted servants Nanfan, Colt and Porthaleyn.[69] If perhaps his hold was less secure in the Welsh marches – hence the despatch of war-horses there for the use of his men from Warwick in January 1452[70] – he was nevertheless able to enforce his will and assert control.

On the way to Abergavenny in the summer of 1449, again over Christmas 1449, in January, March, June, August and October 1450, the earl was at Warwick; his countess was at Coventry in July and at Warwick in August and on 5 September 1451, when their eldest daughter Isabel was born.[71] Their itinerary indicates that he treated Warwick as his principal seat and resided there. The account of Henry Somerlane as bailiff of Warwick in 1451–2 confirms this impression and enables us to reach back into Warwick's earliest years. There was continuity among the officers and beneficial tenants at Warwick, many of whom were recorded there in 1446–7 and some of whom were appointed in the 1420s or 1430s. Just as Duke Henry made changes and filled vacancies on his majority, so too did Earl Richard Neville. Geoffrey Lovelace, the warrener, was appointed by the new earl on 20 December 1449, Richard Messenger, the messor, on 1 January 1450, and

68 Rees, 'Cardiff Rectory Accounts', 179, 182–3; C 56/30 no. 8; Birch, *Margam Abbey*, 346; G. T. Clark, *Cartae et alia munimenta quae ad Glamorgancie pertinent*, (Cardiff, 1910) iv. 1618–19, 1621–5, 1631–2; W. de Gray Birch, *History of Margam Abbey* (1897), 346.

69 *Records of the County Borough of Cardiff*, ed. J. H. Matthews (6 vols, Cardiff, 1898–1911), i. 138–41.

70 Warwicks. RO WCM 491 m. 5.

71 Warwicks. RO WCM 491 mm. 5–6, 4d; BRL 168023 m. 3; *Stratford Gild Accounts* (1912), 31; *Rous Roll*, no. 58. For what follows, see Warwick RO WCM 491 mm. 5, 6.

Helne Wode as one of the parkers of Wedgenock Park on 21 March following; also in 1450 Warwick confirmed or granted annuities to William Pleasance, Margaret Raven and Janet Cokefield. Three cottages in Warwick had been leased, one to Margaret Raven rent-free by the countess on 30 August 1451. Payments were made for grain, bread, and sheep supplied to the separate households of earl and countess; household servants were paid their wages. Many of these are recorded by name: the steward of the earl's household was John Duffield and the *custos* was William Crosse. Horses were driven to Cardiff for the use of the earl's men and the bailiff attended on Thomas Hugford and others of the earl's council in London. Hugford was among those reimbursed on authority of warrants under the earl's signet or from Crosse, twenty-one of whose bills were filed in the audit house at Warwick, where all the estate's accounts were traditionally audited, digested into valors, and stored. Such items are the everyday routine of a resident lord. Moreover we know of other annuities and appointments at this time, at Berkeswell, Moreton Morell, Brailes (Warw.), Yardley and Elmeley Castle (Worcs.), and at Walsall (Staffs.), and of new ones granted at this time to Sir Humphrey Stafford and Thomas Burdet of Arrow (Warw.).[72]

Warwick was accepted as rightful lord in right of his wife by those officers and retainers who mattered. Direct evidence of what they thought comes somewhat later: the roll of that native of Warwickshire John Rous, who does not question the Countess Anne's right *vis à vis* her sisters; and in the *Black Book of Warwick*, which states that the countess was 'procreated sister and heir of [Duke] Henry in the whole blood.'[73] That was written after 1471 and hence not by Dean Berkeswell, who died in 1470. Of indirect evidence there is plenty. All three of Earl Richard Beauchamp's executors continued to serve the new earl: Thomas Hugford, appointed constable of Warwick and supervisor of the Warwickshire estates by Duke Henry, was his councillor; William Berkeswell, whom the earl made dean of Warwick in 1454 and who made the college's records available to him and his countess; and the somewhat older Nicholas Rody who died in 1458, and bequeathed his property in Warwick to the earl.[74] As executors of Earl Richard Beauchamp they deferred to the new earl, paying bills, making appointments to office and presentations to livings at his request.[75] They never acted thus for the elder Beauchamp sisters. Since Richard and Anne succeeded to the lands in fee, the feoffees accepted them also as heirs to the lands in trust, whatever the sisters themselves on the strength of their father's will may have asserted.

So, too, it seems with the less well-documented Despenser trust. Though only

---

72   *CPR 1452–61*, 587; J. M. W. Bean, *From Lord to Patron* (Manchester, 1989), 185; SC 6/1038/2 m. 2; BRL 168023 m. 2; BL Egerton Roll 8541 m. 3; Worcs. RO 989/113.
73   *Rous Roll*, no. 56; Warwicks. RO CR 26/4, p. 28.
74   WRO WCM 491 mm. 5, 6; Exeter MS Chanter 722, f. 7; Warwicks. RO CR 26/4, p. 128.
75   P. B. Chatwin, 'Documents of "Warwick the Kingmaker" in Possession of St Mary's Church, Warwick', *Trans. Birmingham Arch. Soc.* lix (1935), 3, 4; Warwicks. RO CR 1886/EM2.

one of two coheirs to the lands in fee, Anne was treated as sole heir and her husband as lord in the few surviving acts of the feoffees. Though most date to the mid-1450s, it was as early as 24 March 1450 that Warwick was approached regarding the conveyance to Tewkesbury Abbey of the advowson of Sherston (Wilts.) in fulfilment of Duke Henry's will.[76] As the wishes of Isabel and Henry had been fulfilled, the income from the trust was available for Isabel's heirs to enjoy. Good reason for Warwick and his countess to perpetuate an arrangement that gave them more than their strict legal entitlements under the inquisitions. Sudeley, Beauchamp, Nanfan and Norris all served Warwick in other capacities. One of these committed feoffees was Sir William Mountford, who is wrongly supposed to have deserted Warwick for the service of Humphrey Duke of Buckingham.

For Warwick's tenure of his wife's midland estates was not uncontested. He had rivals in her Beauchamp half-sisters, who found at least some limited support among the family retinue. John Brome of Baddesley Clinton, the pretender to the Warwick chamberlainship of the exchequer, was apparently one such. Certainly a retainer of Duke Henry, he apparently committed himself to the Countess Margaret and was an executor of her husband Shrewsbury in 1452. Brome was ousted from the chamberlainship. His Warwickshire properties were attacked in July and August 1450 by the men of Warwick and apparently the earl's stable headed by Robert Commander, the town bailiff, and Richard Clapham, almost certainly, as Dr Carpenter has argued, at Warwick's behest. Brome's property was raided twice more in 1451. It was not until 16 July 1453, when Somerset was supreme, that a commission was issued against the offenders, to no effect.[77]

It is not this dispute that has caused modern commentators to question the effectiveness of Warwick's takeover of his father-in-law's hegemony, but the dispute that supposedly set him against Humphrey Duke of Buckingham. Warwick was strong in the south of Warwickshire, Buckinghamshire in the north, and a struggle for supremacy occurred. So runs the argument.[78] Actually the only direct evidence for disagreement between Buckingham and Warwick, the latter's failure to pay rents due in 1450–8 from Drayton Basset (Staffs.), arises because Warwick did not hold it: it had already been seized by his sister-in-law and rival Margaret Countess of Shrewsbury.[79] Warwickshire was

76   E.g. BL Add. Ch. 72684; *CPR 1476–85*, 97; E 28/79/31; *CPL 1447–55*, 593; *Monasticon* ii. 64; E 28/79/31.
77   Carpenter, *Locality*, 189–90, 458.
78   Carpenter, *Locality*, chs 11 and 12; S. M. Wright, *The Derbyshire Gentry in the Fifteenth Century* (Derbys. Rec. Soc. viii, 1983), 74; I. Rowney, 'Government and Patronage in the Fifteenth-Century: Staffordshire 1439–59', *Midland History* viii (1983), 49–69, esp. 55–6, 65–6.
79   K. B. McFarlane, *Nobility of Later Medieval England* (Oxford, 1973), 223; C. Rawcliffe, *The Staffords, Earls of Stafford and Dukes of Buckingham 1394–1521* (Cambridge, 1978), 150; *Sir Christopher Hatton's Book of Seals*, ed. L. C. Loyd and D. M. Stenton (Northants. Rec. Soc. xv, 1950), no. 229.

not a county in which violent feuding demanded royal attention. Its supposed divisions and this so-called dispute alike arise from a rather perverse reading of the evidence.

Of course there were quarrels among the landholders and gentry as there were everywhere, that resulted in riots and lawsuits in the common law courts, but nothing directly implicates either magnate. Inevitably members of Warwick's connection, such as Beauchamp of Powicke and Sudeley, enjoyed direct relations with Buckingham, but there is no evidence that the duke suborned them from their service to Warwick on which their local standing principally depended. Duke and earl co-existed peaccably: they had no cause for friction, since Warwick looked south from Warwick and Buckingham north from Maxstoke. Warwick has recently been shown not to have been involved in Derbyshire affairs;[80] he appears equally uninterested in Staffordshire and north Warwickshire. His axis was Warwick–Tewkesbury–Cardiff. Duke and earl co-operated in restraining potentially disruptive quarrels among the gentry. When the Warwick retainer Sir Thomas Malory went off the rails and indulged in the attacks on Buckingham and Combe Abbey that are still inexplicable, those aggrieved associated the earl with the duke as commissioners of arrest. The commission was actually executed by Buckingham, whose sixty Staffordshire men sufficed to deal with Malory (but hardly with Warwick), and Malory was indicted at Nuneaton and imprisoned at Coleshill, not the more usual Warwick. Such facts do not demonstrate Malory's conduct to be part of a Stafford–Neville feud. Warwick was in Wales. He was willing to leave matters to Buckingham and to Mountford, a sheriff who was both his retainer and a Despenser feoffee. Mountford's decision to transfer his estates from his elder son Baldwin to his younger son Edmund and to make Buckingham a feoffee may well have preceded Warwick's succession. That Warwick feed Baldwin need not demonstrate a breach with William and Edmund or their desertion of his service for that of Buckingham. An arbitration award that was surely imposed during the first protectorate with Warwick's assent actually divided the estates between the two brothers; it is more likely that Baldwin and his son Simon rather than Edmund broke it. Warwick's reactions are unknown. Warwick cannot be shown to have intervened in the Stafford–Harcourt dispute or to have backed the Harcourts; the reverse is more probable. Buckingham did indeed take Edmund Mountford's side from 1456, but evidence that he and Warwick were at loggerheads dates only from 1459.[81]

Warwick's effective control is best measured by its fruits. Before his succession, as we have seen, the new earl had no significant estates or resources of his own. He is not recorded as attending parliament, council or anywhere else with a significant entourage. Thereafter his impressive company was frequently

80   H. Castor, '"Walter Blount was gone to serve Traitours": The Sack of Elvaston and the Politics of the North Midlands in 1454', *Midland History* xix (1994), 21–3, 32.
81   This section reinterprets the material in Carpenter, 'Sir Thomas Malory and 15th-century Local Politics', *BIHR* liii (1980), 31–43; *Locality*, ch. 12; Griffiths, *King & Country*, 366–71.

remarked: presumably it originated from his estates. The single surviving bailiff's account for Warwick in 1451–2 reveals how substantial were the households both of himself and his countess. Repeatedly he called out his West Midlanders and Welshmen arrayed for war. The men of Stafford of Grafton and Ferrers of Chartley served alongside his own. The company that he took to Abergavenny in 1449 probably imposed order there. Armed men were maintained in Glamorgan. The 400 men 'and moo' from the West Midlands and probably Wales that he took to the Leicester parliament in 1450 may have been earmarked for foreign service. The West Midlands retinue turned out again against Jack Cade in June, late in November to overawe parliament, to parade through London on 3 December, when he and the Duke of Buckingham together led 3,000 men, and to suppress York's uprising at Dartford early in 1452. Warwick was able to mobilize the resources of the earldom. The comments of observers and royal gratitude imply that his success was already remarkable. Warwick already perceived the political and moral advantages of an impressive turnout and display of force: not just in battle, but to cow opponents and earn royal gratitude. The resources for this came from his wife's inheritance: which therefore he had to keep intact and protect against rivals. The aggression he brought with him.

After paying expenses, which included the dower of the Countess Eleanor and annuities to retainers, the Beauchamp custodians accounted for a surplus of £828 in 1448. This was considerably more than the qualifying income for an earl. Warwick held these lands and revenues. Additionally he controlled the income of the Beauchamp trust and may have enjoyed the use of it; there, as on the Despenser trust, he exercised both the patronage and political influence. The reversion of the dower of his sister Cecily in 1450 substantially augmented both income and West Midlands estates. Only an approximation of his income can be calculated. Taking McFarlane's calculations as a base, his income may have been £3,900; after deducting the Countess Eleanor's dower and rent due from George Neville's half share of the Despenser estate, a total of £3,000 a year seems possible.[82] Whilst this was well short of two uncles, the dukes of York and Buckingham, it compared with his father and his uncle of Northumberland, and comfortably outstripped such minor earls as Devon, Wiltshire and the king's Tudor half-brothers.

3.4 The Warwick Traditions

Very extensive, spread across twenty counties, Warwick's estate was concentrated in the West Midlands and the Welsh marches, far from his Neville and Montagu origins. It was a source of revenue, of manpower, and hence of power,

---

82   This rough total deducts the Lisle estate, Wickwane, Mereworth, the Countess Eleanor's dower, and a half share of Glamorgan from McFarlane's estimate of Earl Richard Beauchamp's income, *Nobility*, 199.

both locally and on the national stage. As great landholder and lord of retainers, Earl Richard Beauchamp had been the dominant figure in the West Midlands, in Warwickshire and probably Worcestershire too, where he had most lands and the hereditary office of sheriff. Such attributes had also made the de Clare Earls of Gloucester, the Despensers, and their heirs the most powerful marcher lords of southern Wales. Yet this was no mere assembly of disparate possessions, but two estates of comital importance united and shaped over many generations by the two ancient families of Beauchamp and Despenser and only recently combined. What cemented the Warwick inheritance together was not merely the accident of common tenure, but long association over time, traditions and loyalties that were inherited and shared, and which magnified the more material benefits several times over. As substantial and pervasive, perhaps more so, as the Montagu, Neville and Richmondshire traditions with which Warwick was imbued as he grew up, the Beauchamp, Warwick and Despenser histories and legends demanded Warwick's respect and were his to exploit: although an outsider, he was – through his wife – the heir and representative to lands, connection, loyalties and traditions, and had the most pressing reasons to foster and maintain them.

The earldom of Warwick created by William the Conqueror for Henry de Beaumont in 1088 passed via his descendants (the Newburghs) and Walter Mauduit to the Beauchamps of Elmeley Castle (Worcs.) in 1268. The six Beauchamp earls added to the original core the estates of the Mauduits, the Beauchamps and d'Abitots, the Tosnys, the Bassets of Drayton, and ultimately the Despensers. The earls and their ancestors had been founders of monasteries as far away as Shouldham Priory in Suffolk and Westacre Priory in Norfolk and had patronized Markyate Priory and Oseney Abbey (Oxon.). Thus they were founders of Warmington nunnery in Warwickshire, the Worcester Greyfriars, and the chantry college in their castle of Elmeley (Worcs.), and benefactors of Coleshill Priory and Bordesley Abbey, where Earl Guy (d. 1315) lay buried. They had many residences on their estates: apart from the castles of Warwick, Hanley and Elmeley (Worcs.), Barnard, and in the Welsh marches, they maintained residences or lodges in at least eight other places in Staffordshire, Warwickshire, Gloucestershire, Berkshire and Buckinghamshire.[83]

The centre of the earldom – its *caput* – was Warwick itself. This was a town of moderate size, with a population only of about 2,000 even in the early sixteenth century, and unfavourably situated by an unnavigable river, the Avon, off all the principal routes. It was overshadowed commercially by its near neighbour Coventry, eight miles up the road, which was several times as large, the seat of a bishop and a cathedral priory, a walled city and from 1451 a county borough.

---

83   *Rous Roll, passim*; *Pageant of the Birth, Life and Death of Richard Beauchamp, Earl of Warwick*, ed. H. Dillon and W. H. St John Hope (1914); W. Worcestre, *Itineraries*, ed. J. H. Harvey (1969), 209–11. Unless otherwise stated, this section is based on these sources *passim*.

Warwick stood on a hill-top site and its streets were constrained by the surrounding ditch and rampart, surmounted in part by walls, which were pierced by three gates, those to east and west with chapels on top, each with its extra-mural suburb. There was a market, a booth hall, and, to the south, a bridge across the Avon maintained by the gild of the Trinity and the Virgin. Although after 1367 there were only two parish churches, St Nicholas and the collegiate church of St Mary, there were additionally St Sepulchre's Priory of canons regular, a house of Dominican friars, the three hospitals of St Michael, St John and St Lawrence, a hermitage on the site of the former Templar house, and, to the north by the Avon, the hermitage, chapel and chantry of Guyscliff. Warwick, in short, had many of the distinguishing features of a much larger centre, which it owed to its lords the earls of Warwick, whose principal seat was Warwick Castle and whose revenues were largely disbursed within the town. Although merely a seig-neurial borough, subject to the earl's direction and generally returning his men to parliament, Warwick was also the county town: control of Warwick could bestow a disproportionate local influence.

The antiquary John Rous and indeed the earls themselves saw Warwick as *their* town and fostered its interests, as disinterested 'good lords' and as potential bene-ficiaries of any commercial success. Rous noted carefully their efforts to improve town, castle and church. Warwick Castle stood on a cliff above the River Avon and the town. The ancient motte and shell keep remained at the west end, but the east, south and then the north sides were remodelled along the latest lines. The fourteenth-century work has a decidedly French appearance. The walls and gates, according to Rous, were the handiwork of Thomas I. Certainly it was he who erected Caesar's Tower at the south-east corner above the river. Immensely lofty, 147 feet tall, it is encircled by a machicolated wall-walk one storey below the crenellated top. A formidable gatehouse with barbican in front connects on the north-east corner with Guy's Tower. Twelve-sided, 128 feet tall, vaulted on each floor and with two spiral staircases, Guy's Tower cost Earl Thomas II £394 5s. 2d. Though out of proportion to any potential military threat, it compared not unfavourably with Kenilworth Castle five miles to the north: a massive concentric castle with elaborate water defences that was being re-furbished with little regard for cost about the same time by the richest medieval English nobleman, John of Gaunt. At Warwick self-contained luxury to the highest contemporary standards was provided by the suites of one large and two small chambers each with fireplaces and separate access on each floor of Guy's Tower; the gatehouse and Caesar's Tower were also residential. If this vertical arrangement was inconvenient, it may be that better-connected accommodation was provided on the south side when Earl Richard Beauchamp 'rebuilt the south side . . . with a splendid new tower and various domestic offices'. Embedded in the modern house are the medieval hall, chamber-blocks, undercrofts and the chapel of All Saints, once scheduled to become collegiate. To the north side the Clarence and Bear Towers, it is generally agreed, are the unfinished corner turrets of another massive tower, perhaps begun by Earl Richard Neville, certainly under construction by his son-in-law Clarence, possibly briefly continued by Richard III. Somewhere there was the treasury or audit where records were filed and audited and Earl Richard Beauchamp's splendid 'stable of great size' costing 500 marks (£333 13s. 4d.) for the destriers that were bred at the Warwick stud. There was hunting at Wedgenock Park and at other parks at Claverdon, six miles westwards, at Sutton Coldfield, eight miles north-west, and at Berkeswell, where there were lodges that Earl Richard rebuilt almost from scratch.[84] By 1449 Warwick was both a palatial residence worthy of the greatest of noblemen and far more than a purely decorative fortress.

The Beauchamp earls had also improved the town. Thomas I erected the booth hall, Thomas II set up the Trinity gild, Richard St Bartholomew's fair, and Henry planned a larger common and new maces for the bailiffs. Richard, indeed, had more far-reaching plans for the town's commercial development, intending, so Rous tells us, to wall the town, channel the river, widen the bridge arches, and clear mills from the river as far as Tewkesbury, with a view to making the Avon navigable and fostering trade from Warwick via Tewkesbury as far as Bristol and the sea. Had it been undertaken, this would have been a river improvement worthy of two centuries later and a strain even for the deepest purse. Tewkesbury belonged to his wife. In patronizing her foundations, building at her houses, and fostering Tewkesbury's trade, the earl anticipated the permanent union of their inheritances.

Warwick was also the spiritual home of the earldom. The Beauchamp earls and their families were religious, some exceptionally so. Thomas II, Rous tells us, was a great almsgiver, who visited the bedridden in person, and Richard was inspired in his patronage by the advice received and sought from Dame Emma Raughton, anchoress of North Street, York. In 1421 his receiver accounted for the costs of fetching a recluse from Winchester to London by William (? Berkeswell) chaplain of Guyscliff. Allegedly his daughter Margaret tolerated no blasphemy in her household and his son Henry confessed and recited the psalter daily and forbade oppression by his staff. Warwick's religious houses, hospitals and churches were tangible evidence of their piety. Pensions were paid annually to some religious institutions. Pride of place belongs to the college of St Mary's, originally founded by the Beaumont earls for a dean and canons, whose livings remained amongst the most attractive in the gift of later earls. St Mary's Church stood in a precinct then much larger than the present churchyard that also contained a chapter house, treasury, deanery, houses for the canons and a hall for the vicars choral. Large and cruciform with a western tower, St Mary's was a low-lying Norman structure, of which only the crypt now survives. Whereas Earl Guy was buried at Bordesley Abbey (Warw.) in 1315, his son Thomas I selected St Mary's for his burial place. He was responsible for discontinuing divine service in all churches in Warwick except St Mary's and St Nicholas's, to which henceforth all residents were to resort, and it was he who began the building of the choir in a loftier, more delicate, and altogether more fashionable style. His table tomb stands in the

84   Worcestre, *Itineraries*, 209–11. For Brewster, see also M. Lowry, 'John Rous and the Survival of the Neville Circle', *Viator* 19 (1988), 101. For the cottage, see Devon RO MS Chanter 722 f. 6.

centre. His son Thomas II, who finished the choir, is commemorated by a splendid brass. It was the latter's son Richard who commissioned the three-bay Beauchamp Chapel to the south, on the site of the old deanery, which cost £2,200 over nearly fifty years to erect and equip. Walls, vaults and stained glass are covered with coats of arms, muzzled bears, and family portraits. In the centre stands his own splendid alabaster tomb with his brass effigy. Richard and Anne are among the miniature brazen mourners along the sides. There also lie Sir Henry Neville of Latimer and Oliver Dudley, killed at Edgecote on the Kingmaker's behalf in 1469.

An inventory of 1465 records the great store of vestments, service books, and plate accumulated by the college, some given by past earls and countesses, but much also by prebendaries, by such Warwick retainers as Watkin Power, by residents and tenants of Warwick, like William father of John Rous. Items had been given by Earl Thomas II and his Countess Margaret Ferrers of Groby (hence the intertwined initials T and M) and by Earl Richard and Countess Isabel. Hence the plethora of bears and ragged staves, the arms of Warwick, Beauchamp, Elmeley Castle, Ferrers and Spencer. Our Richard's consort Anne 'now countess of Warwick' had given two rich copes, the orfrais set with her father's arms, the body of purple velvet and cloth of gold, with a hood of fine embroidered work set with a little scutcheon of the Despenser arms.[85] More, doubtless, would follow on their deaths. Earl Richard Neville had borrowed a fine mass book from the sacrist – just as his consort had earlier borrowed her parents' dispensation from the college archives: both were returned.[86] The college was no mere resting place of the comital family, where they were assured of prayers, it was also the religious centre of the town where dependants of all kinds worshipped and adorned. It was also a conspicuous testimony to their rank, wealth and power that nobody present at the services could overlook. And if the college commemorated earls, the Beauchamp Chapel was nothing short of princely.

Important though their regional base was to them, the Beauchamps were no mere provincial notables. They had played their full part in national and even international affairs: as Lords Ordainer and Lords Appellant, as knights of the Garter, as crusaders, conquerors of Gower from the Welsh, and in foreign and civil war. None more so than Richard, a hero and a legend in his own lifetime. Knight, jouster, diplomat, statesman, general and tutor of the young Henry VI, who attended the General Council of the Church at Constance and visited the Holy Land, he was dubbed by the Emperor Sigismund father of courtesy, 'ffor and all curtsy were lost . . . hyt myght haue be found in his person'. Yet amidst all this glory, he remembered his roots, jousting with a lord of Germany first in the arms of Warwick, secondly in those of Elmeley Castle (Worcs.), and thirdly as baron of Hanslope (Bucks.). The arms of Tosny also featured. His crest was invariably the bear and ragged staff. Always, however, he was the local magnate who fostered the interests of his town of Warwick.

85   E 154/1/46.
86   Warwicks. RO CR 26/4 p. 110; E 154/1/46.

The well-known eulogies of about 1483 in the rolls of John Rous cantarist of Guyscliff and in the anonymous *Pageant of Richard Beauchamp Earl of Warwick* are prefigured in the lost reminiscences of his own receiver-general John Brewster. Besides his master's achievements in war and peace, Brewster recorded his building works at Warwick, at Hanley and Elmeley Castles (Worcs.), at Drayton Basset (Staffs.), Baginton, Sutton Coldfield and Berkeswell (Warw.), at Caversham (Berks.) and at Hanslope (Bucks.). Brewster's son was still living in his father's rent-free cottage at Warwick in 1449, presumably with John Brewster's book. There survive love poems attributed to Earl Richard and a description supposedly of his funeral service. The *Rous Roll* presumes the existence of such raw material. For earlier earls, too, Rous needed other sources: perhaps genealogies like those of the Nevilles, Montagus or FitzHughs. And it is no accident that accounts of Richard's funeral and executors were preserved locally for several centuries.

The Beauchamps, perhaps especially Earl Richard, were proud of their lineage, their name and their title: the *Rous Roll* and the Beauchamp Chapel proudly record their quarterings. At least three earls on four occasions sought to preserve their line, name and title. When remarrying Earl Richard refounded the chapel at Guyscliff near Warwick on the advice of a York recluse 'that he might have eyres male'; later he enjoined his son Duke Henry never to change his title from Warwick.

Many legends of the Beauchamp's ancestors were already current in the fourteenth century. The thirteenth-century Tosnys traced their line from the Swan knight; the ceremonial gold cup of the Swan passed via their Beauchamp descendants to Earl Richard Neville and beyond. The famous badge of the bear and ragged staff brought together the Beauchamp bear, probably derived from Urse d'Abitot, and the ragged staff of Sir Guy of Warwick. Guy was a legendary giant, whose story was recounted in a romance that Mason dates to the Warwick–Oilly marriage of 1205 which was greatly elaborated by Rous. 'The flour and honour of knyghthode' and heroic conqueror of Colbrond at Winchester, Guy retired to live as a hermit in the cave of Guyscliff by Warwick and was supposedly ancestor to future earls of Warwick. Hence when Earl William Beauchamp inherited the earldom, he identified with Guy, giving the name to his son and successor. A new tower was called Guy's Tower and Earl Thomas I named two of his own sons Guy and Reinbrun after the giant and his son. 'In changing their patterns of nomenclature, the Beauchamps indicated that they truly identified with the honour to which they had fortuitously succeeded': a model followed by our Warwick and his sons-in-law Clarence and Gloucester. Earl Thomas I also acquired the cave from St Sepulchre's priory, and 'new bylt hit the mansion undre the chapell and namyd hit Gyclif in memory of sir Gy'. Perhaps it was also he who hewed the eight-foot statue of Guy from the rock. Inspired by the anchoress Emma Raughton, Earl Richard replaced the hermit with a chantry for two priests, 'which in process of time' (observed an over-optimistic eulogist!) 'shall growe to a place of great worship oon of the best made in England'. The two-aisled chapel was physically reconstructed and partly carved out of the rock by his executors. It was at Guyscliff that Dean Berkeswell was cantarist before becoming dean of Warwick College and that Rous himself served out his life.[87] The fan-vaulted tower was erected by the executors in 1449–50, Richard Neville's first year as earl of Warwick.

The Despensers can also be traced back to the thirteenth century, but the core of their inheritance – Glamorgan and Tewkesbury – goes back much further, to Robert FitzHamo. Around 1100 he refounded Tewkesbury Abbey, to which he gave the rectory of St Mary's at his new borough of Cardiff. His daughter Mabel carried them first to Henry I's bastard Robert of Gloucester and thence to the de Clare Earls of Gloucester and Hertford. A second royal line was introduced by the marriage of Earl Gilbert to Edward I's daughter Joan of Acre, whose second family by Ralph Monthermer were ancestors of the Montagu earls of Salisbury. Following the death of the last de Clare earl at Bannockburn in 1314, the inheritance was divided among their three daughters, among them Eleanor wife of Edward II's favourite Hugh Despenser the Younger. Despenser's share included the lordship of Glamorgan in the marches of South Wales. Hard though he tried, he was unable to recreate the earldom of Gloucester, which was held only briefly in 1397–9 by his great-grandson Thomas. Even alone, Glamorgan was the greatest and most valuable of all the marcher lordships.

If Wales was no longer a war zone, the Welsh were not altogether subdued: witness the prolonged rebellion of Owen Glendower, that had caused damage even in Cardiff. The marcher lords retained their privileged status, free from royal interference and entitled to their own sheriffs, chancellors and exchequers. None had a tradition of independence greater than the lords of Glamorgan. Hence too the host of castles that were maintained in defensible condition: Caerphilly, with its concentric tower-studded walls and water-defences, rivalled both Edward I's North Welsh castles and John of Gaunt's Kenilworth. There were several seigneurial boroughs – Neath, Kenfig, Cowbridge and Cardiff itself; a cathedral at Llandaff; and the two Cistercian abbeys of Neath and Margam.

The largest town in Glamorgan, perhaps in Wales, was the port of Cardiff. Walled, with several gates and towers, Cardiff may have had a thousand inhabitants in the early sixteenth century and had probably changed little by the time of Speed's map of 1611. Cardiff stood on the right bank of, and partly encircled by, the River Taff (since diverted), over which there was a strategically important bridge. The parish church at the south end of the broad main street was appropriated to Tewkesbury Abbey; the tithes were farmed by Thomas Porthaleyn. At the north end stood the stone-built castle. Twelfth century in origin, with a large motte surmounted by a shell keep and encircled by a ditch, it had two wards and included the surviving lofty tower constructed by Earl Richard Beauchamp. Cardiff Castle was the seat of seigneurial government, of the chancery and exchequer; it was where Warwick himself resided. The constable was also mayor of Cardiff: the aldermen and officers swore oaths to him. Apparently the citizens had only just finished the town wall, gates and

87   E. Mason, 'Legends of the Beauchamps' Ancestors: the Use of Baronial Propaganda in Medieval England', *Journal of Medieval History* 10 (1984), 25–40, esp. 28, 31, 33, 35.

towers at great cost to themselves and allegedly to the service of the new earl on 12 March 1451, when Warwick confirmed their existing liberties and granted them new privileges. Henceforth all cases except felonies wherever committed by residents of Cardiff could be tried only in the constable's hundred court.[88] Warwick also granted new charters to the borough of Cowbridge and to the abbeys of Margam, Neath and Tewkesbury.[89] He acted like previous lords, operated within traditional expectations, and was accepted as such: hence the impressive lists of witnesses to his charters.

Tewkesbury Abbey, seven miles north of Gloucester at a strategically important crossing of the Severn, was the spiritual home of the de Clares and the Despensers. It was via Tewkesbury that Warwick regularly proceeded from Warwick to Abergavenny, Cardiff and back. Tewkesbury was perhaps the most important Benedictine house not in royal patronage; its abbot was the last to be summoned to the House of Lords after the patronage passed to the crown. The nave retains the colossal Norman columns of the original design, but the choir was lavishly remodelled in the Decorated style by the Younger Despenser and his wife. Their models were apparently Westminster Abbey and Hailes Abbey (Gloucs.), the masterpieces of Henry III and his brother Richard King of the Romans, and apparently Despenser's intention was to create a mausoleum to outshine theirs. 'Though lacking blue-blood and the title of Gloucester, Despenser was the peer (and more) of any nobleman living or deceased, and the rightful successor of his forerunners at Tewkesbury.' The vault of the whole church traces the life of Christ from his birth in the west to his heavenly glory in the east, where the Despenser mausoleum is to be found. The eastern apse, with its chevet of chapels, includes one dedicated to St Margaret of Scotland, significantly an ancestress of the Despensers. Seven clerestorey windows were glazed soon after 1340 with imposing portraits of armoured men identifiable by their surcoats as, among others, Despensers, de Clares, Robert of Gloucester and the founder Robert FitzHamo. Long after FitzHamo's death, in 1397, his body was transferred by Abbot Parkares to a chantry chapel of the stone cage type in the north choir arcade. His de Clare successors lie beneath the choir floor before the altar. The Younger Despenser himself rests immediately south of the altar, his son Hugh (d. 1349) immediately to the north, and the kneeling effigy of his grandson Edward (d. 1375) prays atop his chantry chapel to the south. The opposite bay on the north side was appropriated for the most splendid chantry of all: that of Richard Earl of Worcester (d. 1422), completed in 1438, which his countess chose as her own resting place in preference to her second husband's college at Warwick. Three empty niches may once have contained figures of herself and her two husbands.[90] Her son Duke Henry, formerly Lord Despenser,

88 *Boroughs of Medieval Wales*, ed. R. A. Griffiths (Cardiff, 1978), ch. 5, esp. 110, 124.
89 Clark, *Cartae*, v. 1631–2; L. J. Hopkin-James, *Old Cowbridge (1922)*, 46–7; W. De Gray Birch, *History of Neath Abbey* (Neath, 1902), 138–9; idem, *Margam*, 346; see above nn. 68–9.
90 R. K. Morris, 'Tewkesbury Abbey – the Despenser Mausoleum', *Trans. Bristol & Gloucs. Arch. Soc.*, xciii (1987), 142–55.

lies buried somewhere at Tewkesbury, and her grand daughter Isabel the Duchess and her husband George the Duke of Clarence selected a site behind the altar for their sepulchre. In Tewkesbury, Richard and Anne were as much parts of an ongoing tradition as at Warwick.

The monks of Tewkesbury continued their founders' chronicle down to the death in 1476 of Isabel Duchess of Clarence. It records the history of the family, not very accurately, itemizes births and christenings, confirmations, marriages and deaths. It reports how the earls of Gloucester built Tewkesbury bridge, endowed it with tolls, and otherwise patronized the town just like the Beauchamps at Warwick. The priory of Goldcliff that Robert FitzHamo had also founded was granted by Henry VI to Duke Henry, who conveyed it in 1442 to the abbey as endowment for his mother's chantry. The chronicle was continued on several occasions. It treats the Countess Anne and George Neville first as coheirs; and then, presumably after 1461, Anne as sole heir. It is decorated with illuminations of the coats of arms of successive patrons down to those of Warwick's two sons-in-law after 1471 and contains stylized illuminations of many of them. The Countess Isabel lies on her deathbed. Our Warwick is portrayed as a stout, bearded man, who holds his sword point uppermost and rests his left hand on the scabbard; his shield of many quarterings appears below.[91]

These were traditions to which Warwick found himself heir: a spiritual or moral cement that enhanced the whole. They were traditions of which he was a part: the Swan cup and Guy's armour remained in his castle at Warwick. The swan crest and the muzzled bear appear on his seals. Warwick used the badge of bear and ragged staff from at least 1452; in 1450 his retainers were issued with badges of ragged staves; and Warwick died wearing a ring engraved with a bear. He features as a mourner on his father-in-law's tomb in the Beauchamp Chapel, as a drawing and a life in the *Rous Roll*, as a roundel in the pedigree of the *Beauchamp Pageant*, and as an illumination in the Tewkesbury Abbey Chronicle. He saw value in Rous's historical researches: when the antiquary found material on legendary earls of Warwick at St Albans Abbey in the *Gesta Abbatum* of Matthew Paris, he sent a copy to the earl.[92]

It is not improbable, though not susceptible of proof, that he was among the 'many lordes & ladyes and other worshipfull people there beyng present' at his father-in-law's funeral at St Mary's Warwick on 4 October 1439 or that of his mother-in-law at Tewkesbury in 1439–40. Such traditions were worth fostering even at some material cost. In 1450–1 he confirmed the charter of Robert FitzHamo to Tewkesbury Abbey, the charters of his Despenser and Beauchamp predecessors to Cardiff and to Margam Abbey, and in 1452 secured royal confirmation of charters to both Margam and Tewkesbury. Several times

91 Bodl. MS Top. Glouc. d. 2 [Chronica de Theokesburie], pp. 31–2, 36; see also P. B. Pepin, '*Monasticon Anglicanum* and the History of Tewkesbury Abbey', *Trans. Bristol & Gloucs. Arch. Soc.* xcviii (1981), 95–7.
92 A. Gransden, *Historical Writing in the Middle Ages*, ii (1982), 311.

he secured the necessary royal licence to alienate in mortmain for his wife's ancestors' foundations. He gave land to enlarge the churchyard at Warwick College. He helped feoffees to endow Duke Henry's chantry at Tewkesbury and Earl Richard Beauchamp's executors to endow the Beauchamp Chapel.[93] Several of his most trusted officers spent all their adult lives and almost all his own life carrying out his father-in-law's wishes and had still not finished at his own death. Among the three hospitals at Warwick, there was no almshouse for retired servants: a highly fashionable and expensive concept, to be found at Edward IV's Windsor, Suffolk's Ewelme, and Cardinal Beaufort's St Cross, which was to be his model. Warwick therefore determined to construct Guyscliff more solidly and endow it better, as his father-in-law had wished, and to enhance it with such an almshouse. Rous indeed claims that Warwick came to prefer the Warwick traditions to those to which he was born. Instead of following the example of his parents, brother and maternal ancestors, he intended rejecting the Montagu mausoleum of Bisham, claims Rous somewhat improbably, in favour of the Beauchamp Chapel of his father-in-law.[94]

Warwick was thus part of vibrant traditions and legends that offered guidance on how he should behave. He chose to live within these traditions and indeed to model his conduct to fit them. He chose also to rely on the trusted servants of his Beauchamp and Despenser predecessors. He was wise to do so. He had much more to gain than lose by accepting them and much more to lose than gain by rejecting them. Those administrators and retainers still on the payroll could have become mere employees or, worse still, have identified themselves with his rivals the Beauchamp and Despenser coheirs. By fulfilling his hereditary role as earl of Warwick and lord Despenser, by behaving as they expected, he was able to draw on their devoted service and was able to trust them. No doubt Berkeswell, Hugford, Rody, Nanfan and Porthaleyn were good administrators, but he could not have trusted them as much as he did, witnessed both by what they did and by what additional rewards they received, if they had not been devoted to his cause. He would then have needed to import servants devoted to his family, the Nevilles, on a much larger scale than he actually did and would have risked alienating those to whom he was the natural lord.

Many Beauchamp officers and annuitants remained on the payroll in 1449. Our Warwick was an outsider, who had not expected to succeed and can have known little of the estate or of its key personalities before 1449. Understandably he brought with him some trusted personnel from his northern origins: his brother Sir Thomas Neville; Colt, Sotehill and Stokdale, who acted as mainpernors; Richard Clapham, Thomas and John Otter; and later William Kelsy.[95] The Warwick inheritance was no windfall to be plundered to patronize northerners, as the earl's son-in-law Richard III was later accused of doing to the

---

93 CPL 1455–64, 593; Monasticon, ii. 64; Hicks, Richard III, 342–3, 345; Birch, Margam, 347; Birch, Neath, 138–9; Matthews, Cardiff Recs. i. 38–40, 42; C 56/30 no. 8.
94 Rous Roll, no. 57.
95 Warwicks. Fines, no. 2683; Carpenter, Locality, 126n; CFR 1445–52, 158.

South from 1483. There was continuity of personnel at all levels: among the lesser ministers of Warwick – the bailiff, parkers, rent-collector; among the leading estate officers; and among the retainers. Moreover, from the moment of his succession, Warwick – like any other lord – tried to strengthen his retinue. Some received new rewards, like Hugford, who was feed from Brailes; others were feed anew, like Stafford and Burdet, whose families had long associations with the earldom: and Lord Ferrers of Chartley, far from being the rival to Warwick that has been suggested, accepted the earl's lordship and his retinue was included in the earl's. If Ferrers died almost at once, his heir Walter Devereux already enjoyed the largest fee from Warwick's lordship of Abergavenny. That Warwick was a resident lord who modelled his conduct on earlier lords reinforced the claim to hereditary service and loyalty that emanated from his countess's acceptance as the rightful sole heiress. The birth of their daughter in 1451 promised the continuance of the line into the next generation. By then he had succeeded to the hegemony that his father-in-law had enjoyed.

4

The Polarization of
Politics 1449–54

4.1 The Ascendancy of the Opposition

Warwick came of age and into politics at a time of escalating political crisis. Military defeat led first to the collapse of Suffolk's regime, then to a decade of political instability that culminated in 1461 in a dynastic revolution. The disasters of 1449–50 are traditionally regarded as inescapable. From 'May 1448 . . . the loss of Normandy was already inevitable'.[1] Similarly Suffolk's narrow faction, self-interested and corrupt both nationally and in the localities, was widely hated and feared, isolated, and hence doomed to destruction once the political nation reasserted itself. It is evidence of his weakness that in 1447 he sought to destroy his principal critic, the king's uncle Humphrey of Gloucester, and that Richard Duke of York, Gloucester's successor as heir presumptive, was exiled to Ireland. Suffolk's regime could not abide criticism or co-operate with 'the ancient royal blood of the realm'. When disasters came, there was no fund of goodwill among the commons, who demanded reform, or even amongst the aristocracy. Suffolk 'so distrusted his fellow peers', notes Professor Griffiths, 'that he refrained from appealing to them for judgement, as was his right, in accordance with Magna Carta'.[2] Though relinquishing Suffolk's services, King Henry governed on through his almost equally discredited colleagues, strove to withstand the irresistible tide of reform, and thus lost the chance of a fresh start. There was no new administration broadly based enough to attract the confidence necessary for effective prosecution of the war abroad and government at home. Instead polit-

1   T. B. Pugh, 'Richard Plantagenet (1411–60), Duke of York, as the King's Lieutenant in France and Ireland', *Aspects of Late Medieval Government & Society*, ed. J. G. Rowe (Toronto, 1986), 126.
2   Griffiths, *Henry VI*, 684.

ical divisions persisted, the regime remained on the defensive, and the possibility of reform at home or recovery abroad passed away.

That several of the principal statesmen of the late 1440s paid for their failure with their lives testifies to the passions aroused against them and their regime early in 1450. It was *after* the failure of their policies that enemies penned the articles of impeachment of Suffolk, the manifestos of Jack Cade, and the savagely satirical verses. Such charges have been substantiated with evidence contemporary to the regime itself. The Paston letters, for instance, are damning about the Tuddenham and Heydon gang, Suffolk's East Anglian allies. Jack Cade's revolt has been traced back through to origins in the 1430s.[3] It is from such vivid testimony that the notoriety of the regime has been established.

Well-documented and sanctioned by time though this orthodoxy is, it relies overwhelmingly on partisan and retrospective evidence. All the principal witnesses are hostile. The Pastons, though strictly contemporary, were partisans. Suffolk's men were their personal enemies and they themselves were their victims. As so often happens when a government collapses, the fact of its fall, the desire of its enemies to complete its destruction, and the opportunities thereby afforded brought many grievances to light that might otherwise have been overlooked. The articles of impeachment and Cade's manifestos are valuable evidence that can often be substantiated in detail, but they may be less remarkable than they at first appear. Suffolk's sins compare with those of other administrations at other times that did not fall.

Many of the counts against Suffolk are absurd, untrue or unproven; others apply equally to other ministers or relate to matters authorized by the king. That some can be substantiated tells us that the relevant events or the discreditable conduct did indeed occur. It does not necessarily mean that they threatened the continuance of the regime or brought it down. So, too, with the polemical poetry. It was *because* of the loss of Normandy that criticism arose and proliferated, that charges were framed, that verses were composed, sharpened and circulated. If there was already disquiet before 1450, it was in retrospect that the fall of 'good Duke Humphrey' acquired its new, symbolic, significance. The chorus of hostility and the dirt that was dug does not demonstrate the gradual decay of the regime. The tide of criticism flowed the stronger *because* the disastrous policy enjoyed general support almost to the end. There was a consensus among the magnates in support of the treaty of Tours, the surrender of Maine, and the arrest of Gloucester.[4] But for the seizure of Fougères, the truce could have continued into 1450, might have been further extended, and the loss of Normandy could have been postponed or even averted. Perhaps we are right with hindsight to see Suffolk's policy towards France as doomed, though even the French did not foresee so easy a victory, but we cannot be certain. It was defeat that has caused modern historians to condemn the policy and that prompted the political crisis at home that generated the vitriol by which the regime is judged. If Normandy

3   I. M. W. Harvey, *Jack Cade's Rebellion of 1450* (Oxford, 1991), ch. 2.
4   Watts, *Henry VI*, 222–36.

had not been lost, would Suffolk's regime have attracted the notoriety with which this chapter began?

The immediate background to Warwick's majority was quiet and peaceful. Spectacular victory in France had given way to an apparently unending war of attrition, that no longer offered successes to justify the financial strain. It was a relief when warfare ceased and Henry VI married Margaret of Anjou. Regarded at the time as a diplomatic coup for Suffolk, the match was widely welcomed and celebrated, and was expected to lead in due course to a lasting peace. As late as June 1449 the Lords in Parliament approved François de Surienne's seizure of Fougères.[5] Peace relieved much of the pressure on the English government. Garrisons could be reduced and military expenditure curtailed. With the most divisive issues of policy – peace or war? – resolved and with expenses greatly reduced, domestic government could revert to a peacetime footing: there was no call for parliamentary taxation and a chance for Lord Treasurer Lumley to retrench.[6] If attendance at the royal council declined and few magnates attended, this was as much because there were few matters of moment to decide or initiatives to take as because power was monopolized by those immediately attendant on the king. Everyday politics, once again, was about patronage rather than policy.

None of this was unusual. It was the normal, if unfamiliar, peacetime situation, when routine administration replaced crisis management and when decisions were implemented rather than made. The great retired to their estates, content to leave government to the king, ministers and courtiers. It was the mark of a government confident in the support of the political nation that a formal parliamentary trial was staged early in 1447 for the king's uncle and heir Humphrey of Gloucester, the resolute opponent of the accepted peace policy and hence, by extension, of the popular peace itself. Had it taken place, Gloucester's trial could have been as carefully orchestrated and as apparently unanimous as that of Clarence thirty years later. Even a king like Henry VI, who lacked much inclination or capacity for government, was capable of occasional decisive action and secured obedient compliance from the political nation when he took it. On an everyday level, as always in medieval governments, it was those in favour and those around the king who shared the fruits of royal patronage, among them those arising from Gloucester's fall and the Beauchamp minorities. Ministerial and household offices revolved within a small group among whom Suffolk, in succession to Cardinal Beaufort, was the leader. Such dominance at court had repercussions locally, where it was the clients of those in power who were best placed to secure royal favour, to lord it over their neighbours, and, indeed, to corrupt the administration of justice.

Whilst Henry VI was notoriously generous and susceptible to the influence of

5   M. H. Keen and M. J. Daniel, 'English Diplomacy and the Sack of Fougères in 1449', *History* lix (1974), 383.
6   G. L. Harriss, 'Marmaduke Lumley and the Exchequer Crisis of 1446–9', *Aspects of Late Medieval Government & Society*, 147, 149, 152–71.

those about him, it is questionable how accurate this overall interpretation is. Was the king really as extravagant and was his regime really as narrow as they have been portrayed? Existing enfeoffments to fulfil his predecessors' wills meant that the king had only limited access to the duchy of Lancaster. It was with difficulty that he endowed his queen at a decidedly parsimonious level. His new colleges of Eton and King's could proceed only slowly.[7] There were relatively few big escheats or wardships and some at least of these, like the Beauchamp inheritance, were farmed and brought in revenue. Nobody was raised from the dust to opulence by royal patronage alone. Serious efforts were made to retrench. If the crown remained impoverished, this was due to accumulated debts and declining customs revenues rather than profligate grants. The call for the resumption of royal grants in and after 1449 was not the financial panacea that was predicted. Even sustained exploitation of an enlarged crown estate in time of peace after 1461 was to take twenty years to clear accumulated debts of £350,000.

The 1440s were remarkable for the number of elevations to the peerage and promotions within it, including the creation of six new dukes, which benefited most of the leading families. Considerations of royal blood prompted the promotion to dukedoms of two Beaufort Dukes of Somerset, John Holland Duke of Exeter, and Henry Stafford Duke of Buckingham. Conspicuous among them was the king's friend Henry Beauchamp, Duke of Warwick, who patronized such royal favourites as James Fiennes, later Lord Say and Lord Treasurer. If the Warwick inheritance was run through two minorities by royal courtiers, it was because Duke Henry and indeed the whole Warwick affinity were part of the ruling elite. The most influential of the Despenser feoffees were Sir Ralph Boteler and Sir John Beauchamp, former councillors of the Regent Bedford, who were created lords Sudeley and Beauchamp of Powicke and who were appointed to ministerial and household offices. Salisbury, father-in-law of Duke Henry and lessee of his lordship of Barnard, may not have attended the royal council much, but, as we have seen, he obtained what he wanted from the government: the confirmation of his earldom, the permanent tenure of Richmond honour and the West March, more favourable assignments than his brother-in-law Northumberland, an effective share in the custody of Anne Beauchamp's estates, and, in 1449, the earldom of Warwick for his son. Even his ostensibly impoverished brother-in-law York was granted an extensive appanage in Normandy, part of it earmarked for his younger son, the lordships of the Isle of Wight and Hadleigh (Essex), the elevation of two sons into earls, royal backing in his quest for a French princess to marry his heir, and the lieutenantcies in turn of France and of Ireland, where he was the greatest lord, with unparalleled powers and the option of withdrawal at will.[8] There are no grounds before 1449 for depicting York at odds with Suffolk or his government. The benefits of Suffolk's regime

---

7   A. R. Myers, 'The Household of Queen Margaret of Anjou 1452–3', *Crown, Household and Parliament in Fifteenth Century England* (1983), 137–9; B. P. Wolffe, *Henry VI* (1981), 141.

8   M. K. Jones, 'Somerset, York, and the Wars of the Roses', *EHR* civ (1989), 289–90.

were broadly spread. The Nevilles had no obvious cause to move from their favoured position within the royal family into opposition.

Of course, all was not well. If Henry VI's promise to surrender Maine was the necessary price for a truce, it was nevertheless a mistake and difficult to implement, and the French exploited each diplomatic opportunity. The attack on Fougères caused the resumption of hostilities that led to decisive defeat. Even financial retrenchment necessitated defence cuts that proved disastrous. All this is obvious with hindsight; not at the time. Our Warwick's first parliamentary session, in June 1449, received reports on Fougères and approved the government's course of action.[9] The defeats that followed, including the capitulation of Rouen, aroused strong criticism of the regime – even denunciations of treason against Suffolk! – and demands for reform, but did not create a political crisis. Suffolk still enjoyed the confidence of the king and, probably, the House of Lords, who rejected as unsubstantiated the first articles of impeachment proposed by the Commons.[10] Other charges followed. To counts of treason derived from his foreign policy, which Suffolk cunningly showed to have been shared with many others, were added more specific allegations of abuse of power in England. Without conceding the duke's guilt, the king stopped his trial and exiled him: Suffolk was murdered on his journey abroad.

That was in March 1450. In June Cade's rebellion followed, starting in Kent, spreading as far west as Wiltshire, and attracting the sympathy not only of rustics and townsmen, but also local elites. This was a rising of people who saw themselves as loyal subjects, who posed no threat to the king or the monarchical system of government, but who were highly critical of the failings of Henry's administration and its personnel: its ministers, household officials and courtiers, and councillors, especially bishops. The original grievances related to specific abuses of power in Kent by members of the royal government and household, who were denounced as traitors and indicted as such by terrified commissioners overawed by the rebels, and whose arrest and trial was even demanded by the retainers assembled by magnates to suppress the insurrection. The complaints were then codified in Cade's second manifesto into a more general denunciation of the regime itself. The king

> hath hadde ffalse counsayle, ffor his londez ern lost, his marchundize is lost, his comyns destroyed, the see is lost, ffraunse is lost, hymself so pore that he may not [pay] for his mete nor drynk; he oweth more than evur dyd kynge in Inglond, and zit dayly his traytours that beene abowte hyme waytethe whereevur thynge shudde coome to hyme by his law, and they aske hit from hyme.

In particular the household was accused of securing exemptions to the act of resumption; resumption of royal grants, rather than taxation, was the cure to

---

9   Keen and Daniel, 383.
10   Griffiths, *Henry VI*, 677.

the king's poverty. What was required was a broader government headed by the ancient royal blood of the realm, in particular York himself.[11]

Following Suffolk's fall and Cade's rebellion, the king made new appointments to replace the murdered ministers. Cardinal Kemp took over as chancellor and Lord Beauchamp became treasurer. A welcome reinforcement was Somerset, the defeated commander in France, who returned in July/August, apparently convinced his critics of his good conduct in France, and immediately took his seat in the royal council. In somewhat ironic recognition of his military expertise, Somerset was appointed constable of England and started trying the recent rebels. The government's priorities, as declared to parliament in November, were the defence of the realm and Acquitaine, the keeping of the seas, and the restoration of public order.[12] Such a programme proved insufficiently radical. The treasonable nature of Cade's rebellion, its defeat and his own death did not discredit demands for reform and for vengeance on the so-called traitors from the populace, from the parliamentary Commons, and even apparently among the Lords, who both in 1450 and 1453 found that Somerset had a case to answer. Unapologetic about Cade's revolt, the Kentish jurors returned indictments in August against county officials for offences denounced in the rebel manifestos and against royal officers for oppressions arising from its suppression.[13] Unpaid and defeated soldiery, who felt betrayed both by their commanders and the government, were a destabilizing influence easily manipulated by critics of the regime. Emboldened by York's support, the Commons in the new parliament elected his chamberlain Sir William Oldhall as their Speaker and took up the call for resumption, reform and revenge.

At this point York himself took the centre of the political stage that he was to dominate for the next decade. For nearly twenty years he had pursued the conventional career of a great nobleman, commanding both in France and Ireland, without identifying a discernible role separate from the elite as a whole. Absent in Ireland as lieutenant from June 1449 to September 1450, York escaped direct implication in the political and military disasters of those months, and returned much changed. Henceforth, as we shall see, he was not merely one of the ancient royal blood of the realm, but *the* ancient royal blood, who demanded consideration by the king as an individual not as one among many noblemen, expected answers to his questions, refused to accept the king's decisions as final, and conducted discussions and negotiations in the full glare of publicity. He identified himself with public criticism of the regime and repeatedly invoked public opinion on his side. He had his sword borne point uppermost ahead of him at his arrival at London on 23 November 1450.[14] The nearest English medieval parallel before Warwick himself was Thomas of Lancaster under

11 Harvey, *Jack Cade's Rebellion*, 186–91, at 189.
12 *RP* v. 210.
13 Johnson, *York*, 91n; R. Virgoe, 'Some Ancient Indictments in the King's Bench referring to Kent 1450–2', *Kent Records: Documents Illustrative of Medieval Kentish Society*, ed. F. R. H. Du Boulay (Kent Rec. Soc. 18, 1964), *passim*.
14 Johnson, *York*, 88.

Edward II, also the greatest nobleman of his time and a prince of the blood royal.

York's extensive lands in Ireland, Wales and England made him marginally richer, though always indebted, than the greatest of his peers. He was the premier duke. He was a prince of the blood royal of Europe as well as England who cherished hopes of a Spanish crown and of marrying his heir to a French princess. Together with an elevated sense of honour and objection to slurs on it, his pride had brought him into conflict with Bishop Moleyns, caused him now to denounce ministers 'broughte up of noughte', and was shortly to feed his feud with Somerset himself.[15] York's descent in the female line via the Mortimers from Edward III's second son Lionel gave him a claim to the throne perhaps superior to the king himself, but it could not be published without provoking a confrontation that York could not win. The duke was identified in genealogies as a supporter of the house of Lancaster. *His* claim to be next heir to the king after the death of Gloucester in 1447 surely arose through his grandfather Edmund, fourth son of Edward III and younger brother of John of Gaunt. This gave him precedence over descendants of the fifth son Thomas, grandfather of Buckingham and the Bourchiers. He was heir male of the king himself, unless the legitimized Beaufort line was admissible. His maturity advantaged him over Henry Holland, Duke of Exeter and Margaret Beaufort, two alternative Lancastrian candidates who had their advocates.

Hence it was that York was apparently identified as heir presumptive by several groups of rebels in 1449–50: by the mariners who murdered Bishop Moleyns at Portsmouth in January; by Jack Cade, who used the already significant *alias* of Mortimer and who called for York's involvement in government; and, perhaps most significantly, 'by divers fals pepyll . . . in divers of *your* tounes'.[16] Next year the Commons were to demand York's recognition as heir presumptive through the mouth of the Bristol MP Thomas Young, a client of the duke who was surely acting in his master's interests. In the highly disturbed conditions of 1450, it is no wonder that 'diverse langage' was uttered to the king 'which shoulde sounde to my [York's] dishonour and reproch', that spies were posted at ports to intercept any communications between the rebels and the duke, that the king ordered his officials in North Wales to obstruct York's return, sent messengers to discover his intentions, and closed Chester and Shrewsbury to him. As Henry himself put it, they feared that he intended taking upon himself what he ought not, presumably the crown.[17] Hence, no doubt, the arrival of some of the so-called traitors to seek his protection: there would have been no point if York was not to be in a position of power! York denied these suspicions in a series of bills and protested his loyalty, which the king accepted. His actions indicate political intentions that the regime if not the king were right to fear.

It is improbable that York was directly involved in any of the disturbances of

15   *Vale's Bk.* 180–2, 187–8; Jones, 'Somerset, York', 305–6.
16   Johnson, *York*, 79–81; R. A. Griffiths, 'Duke Richard of York's Intentions in 1450 and the Origins of the Wars of the Roses', *King & Country*, 301. Vale's book says 'our' towns, *Vale's Bk.* 186.
17   Griffiths, *King & Country*, 299, 301.

the first half of the year. Surely he cannot have foreseen in advance how formidable Cade's rebellion was to become! On 12 June, when the king's vanguard against Cade reached London, York was still preoccupied with the non-payment of his own salary as lieutenant of Ireland and threatened to abandon his charge in consequence.[18] That he did indeed return to England in September was not for this reason, which is mentioned in none of his subsequent bills. Nor does it appear to be because of the return of Somerset, his hostility for whom emerged later. Between 15 June and 22 August, York heard that he was implicated in the rebellion and petitioned the king for exoneration, offering – if need be – to appear in person to confront his accuser. That, apparently, was before unfounded rumours reached him that he had actually been indicted of treason, which was most probably his real reason for returning to England. Departing about 28 August, he was obstructed by royal agents at Beaumaris, Chester and Shrewsbury. Proceeding slowly westwards, to Denbigh (7 September), via Shrewsbury (12 September), Stony Stratford and St Albans to London (27 September), he presented a fuller bill with appropriate humility to the king in person and received in response an interim royal letter of exculpation as a loyal and obedient subject which promised a fuller explanation later. Having failed to stop York, Henry sought to remove him from the list of potential opponents. He failed. Combined with intelligence received and promises of support, the king's answer enabled York to take the strong political line that, perhaps, he had already intended.

York's first bill, the king's reply, and York's second bill all date between 27 September and 6 October. Describing himself as the king's humble liegeman and declaring his commitment to his safety and prosperity and to the welfare of the realm, York adopted the language of reform and aligned himself firmly with opponents of the regime. It was generally accepted, he pronounced, that the law was not properly administered. In particular, those royal servants indicted as traitors by the rebels – in the king's eyes, surely improperly indicted – were not punished. York demanded that they should be, offering his 'devoir' to this end, and requested the king to instruct his officers to arrest them, so that they could be imprisoned and subjected to due process of the law. Presentation of this bill may have been backed by a display of force, 'the grete bobaunce and inordinate people . . . harneised and arraide in manere of werre' subsequently alleged. Henry reserved his response for due consideration and replied in writing. Had York's bill been granted, he could have purged all those most unpopular in the country from the royal government and household.

That was not acceptable to the king. Whilst recognizing York's commitment to the common good, it was not appropriate to allow such power to any single

18 *Calendar of the Carew Manuscripts*, ed. J. S. Brewer and W. Bullen, v (1873), 258; Griffiths, *King & Country*, 299; M. A. Hicks, 'From Megaphone to Microscope: The Correspondence of Richard Duke of York with Henry VI, 1450', *JMH*. The next 4 paras are based on ibid.; Griffiths, *King & Country*, 277–304, Johnson, *York*, 83–8; *RP* v. 347. Apparently Lord Rivers and Lord Scales accompanied York at the presentation of one of his bills, Griffiths, *Henry VI*, 707 at n. 108.

individual. Instead he set up 'a sadde and substancial counselle' including York to handle this and other pressing matters and instructed the chancellor to summon the lords so that it could begin work straight away. What Henry expected of the council was doubtless less than York's desires, but nevertheless the offer should have disarmed the duke. It did not. Instead it was perhaps at this time that York published his second bill, which was probably widely disseminated in London by 6 October, in an overt appeal to popular sentiment and an effort to bring pressure on the king and the new council. The king's response was to publish the text of their exchange of letters to show that appropriate remedies were offered to York's complaints. It presumably preceded York's final bill which, given his known movements, must surely have been presented after his departure for East Anglia on 9 October.

York's next bill addressed to the king and to the lords of this new council took a much more drastic line. Whereas his previous bill had attacked only those already indicted of treason (and therefore specifically excluded Somerset), this bill encompassed not only those involved in treasons, extortions and subversion of the law, but also those who had lost French conquests by treaty or in war: those 'unlawfully embassiators and by other weyes' behind 'the losses of his glorious reaume of Fraunce, his commodious duchie of Normandie, his keyes of his diffensable duchie of Aungoye and his counte of Mayne and that caused his liege men to here utterest destruccion withouten reason or defence'. Without mentioning names, but to remove any doubts, he attributed such misconduct to 'highe astates', 'beyng aboute the kinges personne', and 'broughte up of noughte'. It brought in not merely those indicted in 1450, but also councillors, ambassadors, and commanders involved in royal policy, negotiations, and warfare with France as far back as the treaty of Tours. Not merely Suffolk, Moleyns, Aiscough and Say, not merely Somerset, but current royal ministers, councillors, and officials were implicated. This time the remedy lay not with himself, but in 'the trewe lordes of the counsele and speciali the lordes of the mighti blood roiall' and 'honorable knightes and juges undefouled'. The scarcely veiled implication was that there were untrue councillors and discredited knights and judges, who should be excluded. 'Alas,' York lamented, that the true lords of the council allowed such things to happen! The bill is highly rhetorical. It appeals to the public weal, muses philosophically on the necessity for observation of law, dwells both on the king's oath at his coronation to keep the law and the councillors' own oaths to offer 'trewe counseile without feare', and was clearly designed for a wider audience.[19] This bill leaves us in no doubt that York's objective was to root out the whole of the existing regime and to destroy its principal members: mere reform and punishment of abuses by a 'sadde and substancial counsele' was not enough.

Just as York had tried to coerce the king into agreement by a display of force and by enlisting public support for his second bill, so now he coerced the council – even those, perhaps, implicated in the actions he denounced – with a bill that

19   *Vale's Bk.* 187–8.

appealed to popular support. No reply is recorded to this bill, which presumably antedated the meeting of parliament, and no known action was taken on it. Certainly it must have been unacceptable to the king and his ministers. Coercion by parliament came next. The rejection or shelving of York's proposals led to York's alliance with the Duke of Norfolk, who was with him at Bury St Edmunds on 15–16 October, where they agreed on candidates as knights of the shire for Suffolk. York then progressed through his estates, from East Anglia via Fotheringhay (Northants) on 17 October to Ludlow (5 November). Assemblies later indicted as treasonable were held on other properties.

York's men had also made attacks on the servants and properties of the Duke of Somerset,[20] who was to be the focus for attack in parliament. For several chroniclers in retrospect the session was dominated by the quarrel of York and Somerset. This was a quarrel that was to keep recurring until Somerset's death in battle at St Albans. For several chroniclers and some recent historians it stemmed from differences arising from their careers in France. In particular Somerset had replaced York as commander in France at some damage to his *amour propre* and even honour.[21] He had yielded to the French much more easily than York imagined he would have done and in the process had lost York valuable seigneuries that he could ill afford. Yet these grievances are absent from York's earlier bills. It is improbable that Somerset's arrival prompted York's return from Ireland and York's first three bills did not touch him. By November 1450 York had identified Somerset as the principal obstacle in his way. Maybe Henry would have conceded the demands in York's last two bills, but for the stiffening provided by Somerset himself. If Somerset could be removed, by trial for the treasonable loss of France, or by murder, perhaps York's drastic purge and the Commons' demands for reform might yet be achieved? Had York identified Somerset's military failure as the weak point on which to concentrate if the duke was to be removed? That would explain why parliament's petition to exclude 29 named individuals from court was concerned with 28 implicated in domestic abuses and only one, Somerset, for offences committed abroad. Not 'a clumsy composite', the bill recognized how crucial it was for Somerset to be removed. His military failings were his weakest point. And when York dwelt on these, as he repeatedly did, sympathetic chroniclers accepted his explanation for the quarrel.

That York and Norfolk delayed their attendance at parliament until a fortnight into the session demonstrates their confidence in the critical temper of the Commons, especially with Oldhall as Speaker. York made his ceremonial entry on 23 November, followed next day by Norfolk. Both brought large and threatening retinues. The London mob was mobilized to put pressure on parliament itself. On 30 November a great shout was raised against the false traitors in Westminster Hall and vengeance was demanded against them. Next day an attempt was even made to lynch Somerset, who escaped only narrowly from Blackfriars by water. Though the credit for his escape was later attributed to

20   Jones, 'Somerset, York', 288.
21   Ibid. 288, 290–1, 304–6.

York, it seems most likely that he instigated it.[22] York needed him removed too much to care about the means. Shortly afterwards Somerset was confined in the Tower. Demands were made for the exclusion of those 'mysbehaving' about the king and for a further act of resumption. It was only reluctantly that the Commons recognized the financial necessity arising from the unsuccessful war, voting an experimental tax that inevitably raised less than was needed, and surrounded it with conditions for payment and audit that symbolized their lack of trust for the regime.

The new earl of Warwick was present at this parliament also and rode 'thurgh the citee with a mighti people arraied for the werre'.[23] As anarchy threatened, so on 3 December Warwick, Salisbury and many other noblemen accompanied the king in parading their forces nearby, which even York had to join. Salisbury condemned one rioter who was executed as a deterrent. It was three days after this parade, perhaps as reward, that Warwick was recognized as chamberlain of the exchequer.

Warwick, indeed, had attended many of the principal events of this turbulent year, always well-accompanied and always loyal. Whilst York might be proposed as the king's heir, nobody was yet presenting him as an alternative. Where Warwick stood politically – for or against the regime – is more difficult to fathom. Indeed there are only three clues. Suffolk's fall had resulted from his impeachment, which was only made possible by divisions within the government. Attributing a murderous attack on himself at Westminster in November 1449 by the duke's client William Tailbois to the duke himself, Ralph Lord Cromwell initiated the attack on Suffolk. According to the chronicler pseudo-Worcestre, it was he who inspired the impeachment,[24] which, with a longer perspective, encouraged Cade to revolt, York to intervene, and initiated the divisions that followed. This interpretation makes sense of Warwick's otherwise puzzling accusation after the first battle of St Albans in 1455 that Cromwell was responsible for all the troubles.[25] Warwick's later judgement *suggests* that in 1450 his own preference was to back the government, as indeed his own interests so obviously dictated. Perhaps this is also what should also be read into the one direct reference to him, typically laconic and opaque, in the topical verse of the time:

> The Bere is bound that was so wild,
> Ffor he hath lost his ragged staff.[26]

To read ineffectiveness and lack of military force appears inappropriate. Far from leading the attack, it appears that Warwick was bound to and supported

---

22 *Six Town Chronicles*, ed. R. Flenley (1909), 137; Johnson, *York*, 91; Jones, 'Somerset, York', 287. I doubt if York was concerned that his rival should survive.
23 *Six Town Chronicles*, 137.
24 *Annales*, 766.
25 *PL* iii. 44.
26 *A Collection of Political Poems and Songs*, ed. T. Wright (Rolls Series, 2 vols, 1859–61), ii. 222.

the government. Indeed, he had good cause to, when two Despenser feoffees were royal ministers (Sudeley and Beauchamp). Yet other close connections were denounced as traitors: the Despenser feoffee John Norris and the Beauchamp retainers Say, Daniel and Vampage. If Warwick and Salisbury were ever prepared to back York's programme, as a German source suggests,[27] there is no supporting evidence at this stage and nothing came of it.

4.2 The Royalist Reaction 1451–3

The year 1450 ended with the ruling regime apparently in retreat on all fronts. Somerset himself was imprisoned in the Tower. The Commons were baying for his trial and for that of his allies as traitors, for the posthumous condemnation of Suffolk, and for a further resumption of their grants. So, too, with the Warwick inheritance, where Warwick's capture of the chamberlainship sealed his victory over Somerset and his Beauchamp sisters-in-law. York calculated that pressure from his unruly retinue, the Commons, and popular unrest would force Henry to give way over Somerset just as he had over Suffolk.

York miscalculated badly. However apparently pliable and lacking in political judgement, King Henry was secure on his throne and possessed an inner strength that enabled him to ride out the storm. As early as 25 January 1451 he revoked his earlier concession to his council of some control over grants: this was to be no collective government! Henry would not discredit the peace policy that he himself had formulated, or his agents who had carried it through. He declined to surrender any power to York. He refused to dismiss Somerset, his other ministers and favourites. Whilst eventually accepting the Commons petition and removing some courtiers, he emasculated it with exceptions for peers and those customarily attending on him. York could not exploit his apparently overwhelming advantage. Whilst public opinion, carefully nurtured, remained hostile to the court and accepted York's assessment of himself as saviour of the commonweal, from early 1451 to mid-1453 it was the king's men who had the advantage and Somerset, not York, who held the political initiative.

The session of parliament that reconvened on 20 January 1451 was unsatisfactory for the reformers and was hamstrung by the priority that the king gave to judicial sessions in Kent: in which York had no choice, but to participate. Warwick was among those commissioned to hear and determine offences in Kent and also to try Thomas Hoo, late treasurer of Normandy, who was acquitted.[28] The king rejected the bill against Suffolk. There were acquittals of Suffolk's duchess by the Lords and of other lesser men when their cases came to trial. Royal influence was exerted to achieve these results, but no stretching of the rules could bring the king's councillors and courtiers within the *legal* definition of treason! As one chronicler put it, nothing came of it.[29] An attempt to increase York's

27 Griffiths, *Henry VI*, 707 at n. 108.
28 *CPR 1446–52*, 437–9.
29 *Annales*, 770.

leverage, his nomination by Young as heir presumptive, was firmly quashed. Somerset, far from condemned, was released, appointed to commissions, conducted the king's progress, and in April was appointed captain of Calais. By the summer, foreign ambassadors recognized him as the dominant influence in government.[30]

Loyal though the Nevilles had been and were to be again in 1452, the revival of the king's party and the recovery of Somerset proved as unfortunate for them as it was for York and the cause of reform. Proud though the Nevilles were of their royal Beaufort and Lancastrian lineage, Somerset was to sever them too from the court and was to drive them into the arms of York. Neither Salisbury nor Warwick were members of King Henry's inner circle of advisers. Each attended only two of the fifty recorded meetings of the royal council between 1450 and 1453; though even Somerset attended only twenty.[31] They received no significant expressions of royal patronage between 1450 and 1453. The act of resumption that was Henry's only genuine concession to his critics inevitably injured a family so successful in exploiting his patronage. Neither Warwick nor Salisbury secured provisos. Effective from Lady Day 1451, the act revoked all grants made since 1422, this time including the exchanges by which Salisbury had accrued royal rights and possessions in Richmondshire and the West March. His Carlisle feefarm was actually regranted to Henry Percy, Lord Poynings. Warwick lost two grants originally made to Duke Henry. He had held only the reversion of the forest of Feckenham, but the loss of the Channel Isles was more serious. He was still in possession on 18 January 1452. Potentially most serious of all was the cancellation of his custody of George Neville's half of the Despenser inheritance.[32] The Nevilles were not among the host who secured renewals of leases in advance of the sheriffs' inquisitions or thereafter in the latter half of the year.

If these losses arose from the drive for reform rather than any malicious intent by the government, the absence of any confirmations suggests disfavour, and Somerset's involvement in the Warwick inheritance was deliberately hostile. For the next two years Warwick was in retreat, striving to maintain his hold on those parts of his wife's inheritances to which he no longer had the right, playing for time and ignoring successive royal mandates. Fortunately more pressing matters preoccupied his opponents until the early summer of 1453.

Somerset was the second husband of Eleanor, the second of the three Beauchamp sisters, and he really needed her inheritance to compensate for the inadequacies of his own endowment. It was helpful to him on all fronts that in December Shrewsbury returned to England from the pilgrimage to Rome that was a condition of his release from France. Shrewsbury's military reputation was unassailable. He had been Somerset's closest ally and associate in Normandy and

30   Jones, 'Somerset, York', 286.
31   Virgoe, 'King's Council', 158.
32   B. P. Wolffe, *Royal Demesne in English History* (1973), 259; *Henry VI* (1981), 246; *CPR 1446–52*, 57. They remained in possession until the inquisitions were returned.

did not agree that Henry VI's other realm had been 'sold' to the French. He was, moreover, Somerset's brother-in-law, the husband of Margaret, the eldest of the Beauchamp coheirs, believed himself to be rightly earl of Warwick, and was committed to making the most of her Beauchamp and Berkeley inheritances.

On 26 December 1450, only six days after parliament was prorogued, all four Beauchamp sisters were granted the custody of the Duchess Cecily's dowerlands of which they were heiresses (the Beauchamp not the Despenser lands) at a farm to be agreed by midsummer.[33] This suspended Warwick's title, contradicted several inquisitions, and signalled a sustained attack on the earl's tenure of the whole Beauchamp inheritance. An immediate effect was that the earl lost his latest acquisition, the chamberlainship of the exchequer. Objections were raised at the exchequer, perhaps by the other chamberlain Lord Cromwell, who was also chamberlain of the king's household. Colt was suspended from the office, which was exercised jointly pending adjudication by Cromwell and Beauchamp of Powicke, the treasurer. Warwick, the king declared on 24 January, had acted improperly and even illegally by not obtaining exchequer consent for his actions and in 'grete derogacion of our right'. This was nonsense, for Warwick had royal authority for his action, a patent under the great seal with a *non obstante* (notwithstanding) clause, which had both been registered by the exchequer. But the pretext sufficed. The king pronounced the chamberlainship as properly the inheritance of all four sisters. Warwick was excluded and Brome was reinstated as Warwick chamberlain.[34]

The evidence is better for the chamberlainship than for other properties, but it seems that custody was exercised over at least some properties by all four sisters. On 6 June 1451 Thomas Throckmorton was appointed steward of Cecily's Worcestershire dowerlands by Somerset, Warwick, Shrewsbury and Latimer jointly: the patent bears all their seals, including the bear-and-ragged-staff emblem of Warwick himself.[35] Four days later, on 10 June 1451, the king licensed all four sisters to enter those of the Duchess Cecily's dowerlands of which all four were heirs. There is no evidence that any of the other Beauchamp lands held by the infant Anne in 1449 passed to the three elder half-sisters at this time.

Nor was Warwick's only setback in the Warwick inheritance dispute. On 5 May 1452 a Gloucestershire inquisition found the manor of Wickwane to belong not to his countess, but to their distant cousin Beauchamp of Powicke as heir general of Earl William (d. 1298).[36] Beauchamp remained Warwick's trusted ally in other respects. Beauchamp, Sudeley, Norris and Nanfan continued to operate as surviving Despenser feoffees despite the unfavourable Gloucestershire inquisition of 1450 that found Tewkesbury and Sodbury to be

33   *CFR 1445–52*, 184.
34   E 404/67/226; E 159/227 brevia Hil. 29 Hen. VI m. 33, which is discussed by Johnson, *York*, 93n.
35   Warwicks. RO CR 1886/59/8. For what follows, see *CPR 1446–52*, 451.
36   E 149/189/3 m. 3.

held in chief. The exchequer moved slowly and it was not until 4 April 1453 that George's moiety of Ewyas Lacy was leased out, to Warwick himself. It was a recognition of reality that on 28 May the feoffees appointed John Throckmorton parker of Tewkesbury park at the request of the earl and countess,[37] clear evidence of their intention to maintain the trust to Warwick's advantage for as long as possible regardless of the inquisition verdict. Repeated royal licenses to Bergavenny to enter Abergavenny took no effect.

Whilst these were significant setbacks to Warwick, who certainly did not accept them as final, they do not seem to have had any immediate effect on his tenure of his estates. Glamorgan remained in his hands, as husband of his countess and custodian for George Neville, and the inquisition that found Tewkesbury not to be enfeoffed was simply ignored. Even the Beauchamp licence was of limited value, for it neither specified what lands were involved nor how they were to be divided. Whilst Margaret and Eleanor seem to have known very well what was involved, their desires were not confirmed by inquisitions, all of which recorded Anne as sole heir. It is probably because of their weakness locally where Warwick was so strong that no new inquisitions were sought. Moreover on 11 June 1451, one day after the Beauchamp sisters' licence to enter, the king granted Warwick's father Salisbury the custody on grounds of idiocy of the person and lands of his brother George Lord Latimer, husband of the youngest sister Elizabeth.[38] This countermeasure surely prevented Margaret and Eleanor from acting effectively? The Countess of Warwick was now no longer the sole dissenting voice. No attempt was made at this stage to revive the sisters' claims to those parts of the Beauchamp inheritance that Cecily had not held in dower. The various licences were unenforceable and the disputes hung fire for nearly two years.

This was possible only because Warwick's opponents had other priorities. The disorders of 1450, which York had nurtured, caused the king to progress through southern and central England through much of 1451–3. He was accompanied by Somerset, by three senior magnates in Buckingham, Salisbury and Shrewsbury, and by the royal judges. His progress was punctuated by sessions of parliament and the great council. Somerset had his hands full defending himself and directing policy. Shrewsbury was appointed first to keep the seas in March 1451 and then, in September 1452, he was despatched to recover Acquitaine. As Lord Berkeley had already resorted to violence, Shrewsbury gave priority to settling that feud ahead of his dispute with Warwick. Already on 15 June 1451 Lady Berkeley warned her husband against Shrewsbury, who was soon recruiting retainers for the prosecution of private war. On 6 September 1451 in a surprise attack Lisle seized the Berkeleys within their castle. Next month at Chipping Norton (Oxon.) a judicial commission found against Lord Berkeley and imposed

37 *CFR 1452–61*, 28; BL Add. Ch. 72684. On 22–3 May Salisbury was at Westminster at the council and treating with the Scots, E 28/83/9; *Rot. Scot.* ii. 368.
38 *CPR 1446–52*, 430, 451. This had already been conceded in December 1449, Watts, *Henry VI*, 258.

draconian penalties.[39] Meantime Shrewsbury and Salisbury were ordered by the king to quell the Courtenay–Bonville dispute in the West Country, but were fore-stalled by York himself, who was anxious to save the Earl of Devon from punishment. Devon's opponents, the Earl of Wiltshire and Lord Bonville, were imprisoned at the king's command.

Yet these are almost York's only recorded actions in the latter half of 1451. As English Gascony collapsed into French hands, a process completed in August, and as Calais and the south coast were threatened, so the case for reform, if anything, was strengthened. Yet the king had rejected most of York's demands. He had declared his confidence in Somerset and thus, in his eyes at least, the question of treason was closed. To the king the quarrel between York and Somerset, a continuing source of political instability, was a private matter, to be settled as such private matters normally were, by arbitration. That, apparently, was one objective of the great council he held at Coventry in September 1451,[40] to which York and Devon were summoned, but did not come. The duke saw no point in attending meetings which he could not influence at places where he could bring no power to bear. Evidently he did not accept the king's pardoning of Somerset nor was he inclined to the sort of compromise that commonly emerged from arbitration. He determined instead to force his will upon the king: to oust Somerset; to take over direction of the war, which he certainly thought he could do much better; to purge the government and household; and pre-sumably also to take on the direction himself. He appears impatient with Henry VI at the helm of affairs a great deal sooner than the other magnates.

There are remarkable parallels between York's coercion of the king in 1450 and his attempted coup d'état in 1452. Again, the plan had been prepared several months earlier, perhaps in November. Once again, there were the widespread distribution of manifestos, disturbances on his estates, the raising of what was hoped to be overwhelming force, and the enlisting on his side of London. Once again, on 9 January 1452, he began by declaring his loyalty. His oath on the sacra-ments was witnessed at his invitation by two lords with court contacts: Shrewsbury, still his most expensive annuitant, and the courtier Bishop Boulers of Hereford. That was the context for what followed. Letters dated 3 February 1452 appealed for popular support: nothing had been done about reform; fail-ures in Normandy and now Gascony were linked to imminent disaster at Calais and on the south coast; Somerset – again a 'traitor' – was denounced as the cause; York himself as humble liegeman was again to provide the cure; and violence was to be eschewed. With a large force, he marched on London and, failing to secure entry, sought to raise Kent once again.

---

39 Pollard, *Talbot*, 132–3; Griffiths, *Henry VI*, 573. *Pace* Johnson, York may well have conveyed Berkeley to prison. Such disputes had not yet determined local alignments. Shrewsbury was York's annuitant, T. B. Pugh, 'The Magnates, Knights and Gentry', *Fifteenth-Century England 1399–1509*, ed. S. B. Chrimes, C. D. Ross and R. A. Griffiths (1972), 108.

40 *Annales*, 770–1.

However, 1452 was not like 1450. Henry VI and Somerset had matters under control and were well-informed of York's movements, both because his letters crossed their own summonses to a great council at Coventry and because recipients forwarded his missives to the king. Whatever York may have believed – or sought to transmit through his overt declarations of loyalty – there was an enormous difference between constitutional action in parliament albeit backed by force and an insurrection that like all rebellions was treasonable. For Warwick and almost all other magnates, allegiance came first. Whatever the case for reform, King Henry could count on support from the magnates and from urban oligarchies. Most noblemen obeyed his summons, only Devon and Cobham overtly supporting York, London shut its gates and Kent failed to rise. York was pinned down at Dartford, admittedly in a strong position if he wished to fight. Of course, he did not and probably could not, for Henry was the undisputed king and to fight him was unquestionably treason.

Fortunately for York, his opponents also wished to avoid extremes. Twice during his southward journey negotiations had taken place, though without conceding the duke's demands. Even now Henry spared York's life and property, agreed not to treat his campaign as either a rebellion or treason, in return for his capitulation and his formal, public, oath of allegiance. This was particularly solemn, sworn on 10 March 1452 on the Gospels, the True Cross and the consecrated host at St Paul's Cathedral, and included his formal recognition that any breaches would result in degradation from 'all maner worship, astate or dignite'. The conditions were remorselessly comprehensive. York swore to bear the king 'feithe and trouthe' and to withstand any treasons that came to his knowledge. He promised to attend whenever the king commanded. More specifically,

> I shall never here after take upon me to gader any riottys or make any assemble of your people withoute your commandement or lycence or my leful defence,

such lawful defence being reported to the king and the Lords. He would not take 'the weye of feete' – resort to violent self-help against any subject – but would submit any grievances 'to your highnesse and procede aftir the cours of your lawes', nor would he 'atempte by weye of feete or otherwise ageinste your roiall astate'.[41] Humiliating though it was, York's oath was an extremely light penalty for what could have been regarded as a treasonable conspiracy and could thus have destroyed the duke utterly. That York was treated so much more gently than Devon and Cobham, who were imprisoned, and than lesser men who suffered forfeiture, is ironic evidence that he was receiving the more favourable treatment appropriate for a duke and heir presumptive that he had been demanding! His articles against Somerset were ignored. Naturally. If he could not obtain his way from positions of strength, in the earlier negotiations, what

41 *Vale's Bk.* 193–4.

hope had he when boxed into a corner? His disagreements with Somerset were once again treated as private matters, to be settled by arbitration by arbiters appointed on 13 March, who were to report almost at once, or, failing their award, by the king. That no award was made is no surprise: there was too little time. That none was made by the king was an unfortunate oversight. Perhaps nobody saw the need, since York was discredited and Somerset in the saddle. Why should Somerset compromise and make the inevitable concessions to his defeated opponent?

York chose not to recognize how generously he was treated. Against all the obvious evidence, he continued to believe that he had observed his allegiance and that he had acted honourably. He regarded the whole affair and the indictment of Devon as slurs on his honour and secured the acknowledgement of his loyalty at the first available opportunities by the great council in November 1453 and by parliament the following February. He considered his oath to have been extracted by duress, seeking papal release from it which he had allegedly obtained by 1460. Hence, perhaps, his refusal to attend councils and probably parliament too up until November 1453. He considered that he had been deceived by the negotiators, whom he believed had promised him Somerset's trial, and harked back to it in 1455. And, very obviously, he considered the curious notion of self-defence displayed in 1452 and the 'weye of feete' to be perfectly legitimate for him (but not, of course, for anyone else) at the first battle of St Albans in 1455 and again in 1459.

Salisbury had been in attendance on the king for much of 1451 up to and including York's Dartford demonstration, but his son was not. Warwick was at Cardiff on 12 March and at Warwick itself on the 29th and was back at Cardiff in June. On 12–13 July he received incompatible commissions: one requiring his action in the Channel Isles, the other instructing him and his uncle Buckingham to arrest Sir Thomas Malory and take sureties of him not to do harm to the Axholme charterhouse and to appear at council around Michaelmas; Buckingham it was who acted. Perhaps Warwick attended the September great council at Coventry, since his daughter was born that month at Warwick. He himself was at Warwick on 2 October, 20 November, and shortly before 14 January 1452, when he proceeded once again to Cardiff. Recalled by the king's urgent summons, he joined him with a substantial force, some at least wearing the eighty-one yards of red-and-white cloth for arm-bands that cost the Warwick bailiff £6 12s. 10d.; doubtless this was also 'the right grete necessite' for which he was lent £9 6s. 8d.[42] Warwick and Salisbury were among the six ambassadors who negotiated the armistice at Dartford on 1–2 March, an indication of their acceptability both to duke and king; Salisbury was one of the arbiters. Warwick was in London on 10 March, when he granted an annuity to Thomas Middleton, presumably at York's oath-taking at St Paul's, on 14 March, and probably for a

42 *Cardiff Recs.* i. 38–41; BRL 168023 m. 3; *CPR 1452–61*, 476; *1494–1509*, 99; *Ministers' Accounts of the Warwickshire Estates of the Duke of Clarence*, ed. R. H. Hilton (Dugdale Soc. xxii, 1952), 21; Warwicks. RO Warwick Castle MS 491 m. 4–d; *Rous Roll*, no. 58.

fortnight after. It was on 17 March that Salisbury ordered Richard Musgrave, his receiver of the south parts, to pay £2 debts of his household in London from January and February. Warwick may have returned to Cardiff by 4 May, was certainly at Warwick on 5 and 18 July and 30 August. He passed through Stratford on 14 September on his way to Wales and was at Tewkesbury, presumably returning, on 20 October.[43] Most likely he attended the knighting of the king's two brothers on 5 January 1453, when his own brothers Thomas and John were also dubbed.[44]

Both Neville earls were well rewarded for their 'faithful and diligent service' at Dartford. Warwick was paid £300. He and his countess were pardoned for entries without licence to her inheritance and custodies; so were her Beauchamp sisters. He secured royal confirmations of charters for Welsh tenants. On 7 May he was appointed to the commission of the peace for Warwickshire for the first time and on 28 June to the commission of oyer and terminer to try some of York's offending adherents. On 26 March 1452 both earls were rewarded by the renewal of leases at increased rents of their Yorkshire and Cumbrian properties and, most crucially, of George Neville's half of the Despenser inheritance.[45] Warwick did not recover the Channel Isles, for which John Nanfan remained governor for the king,[46] nor the reversion of Feckenham.

The Nevilles did suffer from Henry VI's decision to recognize his two Tudor half-brothers, the sons of his late mother Queen Katherine of France by Owen Tudor, and to promote them earls: the very least that he could do. Actually the king had considerable difficulty in endowing them each with the 1,000 marks (£666 13s. 4d.) that was the minimum for an earl. Jasper's earldom and lordship of Pembroke had been resumed from the young duke of Suffolk, whose betrothal to the heiress Margaret Beaufort was broken off to permit her marriage to Edmund. Other properties were resumed from York. Edmund Tudor was created earl of Richmond and received the castle, honour, overlordship of feudal tenants, and feefarm that the Nevilles had so long coveted and that Salisbury had thought he had secured by exchange in 1449. Salisbury was permitted to keep other grants to him from the honour made before 1422. Apparently the new earl appointed Salisbury to some at least of the key offices, for in 1459 he was bailiff of the wapentakes of Hang East and Hang West, but it was still a substantial blow and likely to be permanent. Though Edmund died in 1456, there was a posthumous son Henry to succeed him. Edmund was also granted the lordship of Kendal (Cumb.), for which he retained Salisbury as steward.[47]

For Warwick, as premier earl, there was another blow, for the newcomers were granted precedence over any other earls and indeed marquises too. Warwick as

43   BRL 168023 m. 3; Ellis, *Original Letters*, i.i. 14, ii.i. 116–17; Warwicks. RO Warwick Castle MS 491 m. 4; *Stratford Gild Accounts*, 33.

44   *Annales*, 770; Griffiths, *Henry VI*, 698–9.

45   E 159/228 recorda Easter 30 Hen. VI m. 3; C 81/1458/10; *CPR 1446–52*, 523–4, 580–1, 596; *CFR 1445–52*, 268–9; see above pp. 76.

46   *DKR* 48 (1887), 392.

47   *CPR 1452–61*, 544, 574.

premier earl now ranked third: an undated attendance list of the House of Lords from 1453–4 shows Warwick seated after the two Tudor earls. It was no compensation that Warwick was nominated to the Garter by Viscount Bourchier at the Garter chapter held on 7 May in the king's bedchamber at Westminster but not elected.[48] He must also have been worried about the ill-health and childbearing that on 7 July prompted a papal licence for his countess to eat meat and eggs during Lent.[49]

The parliament that opened at Reading in March 1453 and sat at Westminster from April to July was the first at which Warwick was a trier of petitions.[50] It also, in Professor Griffiths' words, 'marked the zenith of recovery' for the king.[51] Shrewsbury had achieved victories abroad to match the discomfiture of York at home. The king's constant progresses, assiduous attendance at judicial sessions and executions, and his firm punishment of even favoured magnates involved in violent feuding had proved his genuine commitment to the restoration of order. The anarchic public disorders of 1450 were past. No more attempts were made to murder ministers and courtiers. The only two violent quarrels among magnates, the Berkeley–Lisle and Courtenay–Bonville feuds, had been firmly (if somewhat partially) quelled and the principal offenders were in prison. The king had even held judicial sessions in August 1452 at York's heartland of Ludlow to punish participants in the Dartford disaster. Somerset, as the man behind the throne, was as vigorous in enforcing law and order as York had been in demanding it. Further royal judicial progresses were promised on 2 July 1453, the last day of the second session, though Henry cannot have appreciated the scale of the disturbances to be encountered. At once he demonstrated his resolve by salutary (if brief) imprisonment of Lord Cromwell, Lord Grey of Ruthin, and the Duke of Exeter, the three principal contestants in the Ampthill dispute. Even elder statesmen and dukes were subject to royal discipline. The policy that the king enforced was that no 'escalation of private feuds' was allowed.[52]

Understandably impressed, the Commons now elected in Thomas Thorpe a reliable exchequer official as Speaker and voted a substantial tax towards the war in Gascony. Now at last Henry had the parliament to attaint Jack Cade, to revoke the indictments of 1450 against courtiers, and to repeal the act excluding favourites from his company. Grants to those with York at Dartford were resumed and Sir William Oldhall, the former Speaker and York's right-hand man, was attainted. The creation of the king's brothers was confirmed, to the loss of Salisbury and York. It must already have been apparent that Queen Margaret was to provide him with an heir of his own body. The king's triumph sealed York's defeat: it was at this point that he lost the two important offices of lieu-

---

48   *RP* v. 250–3; Anstis, i. 150.
49   *CPL 1447–55*, 151.
50   *RP* v. 227.
51   Griffiths, *Henry VI*, 699.
52   S. J. Payling, 'The Ampthill Dispute: A Study of Aristocratic Lawlessness and the Breakdown of Lancastrian Government', *EHR* civ (1989), 892–3; for the quotation, see Storey, *Lancaster*, 27.

tenant of Ireland and chief justice of the southern forests. The lieutenantcy went to the Earl of Wiltshire. Unable to protect his servants and bereft of the most important, York had been politically invisible for a year and had little future politically beyond the normal role of a great magnate, sulking on his estates, unless Somerset overstepped himself. Now supremely confident, it was Somerset himself who took the chief justiciarship of southern forests from York on 2 July 1453,[53] the last day of the second session. It was also on Somerset that on 15 June the custody of George Neville's half of Glamorgan was bestowed. Warwick's territorial position had also been threatened in April by two licences to enter Abergavenny and Mereworth to Bergavenny and by the farming of Ewyas Lacy by the exchequer.

It was Somerset's intention to make the division of the Despenser inheritance into a reality. Perhaps he hoped to raise the stakes in his own Beauchamp dispute. Perhaps he wished to build up his power in an area where he had a long-standing interest as steward of the adjoining Lancaster lordships of Kidwelly to the west and Monmouth and Three Castles to the north-east. Warwick's tactic, as before, was to ignore such patents and hold on to what he had. But this was no mere court-based paper exercise. Somerset was now ready to make his title good, by force if necessary, and was backed by the authority of the crown. Presumably an initial peaceful approach from Somerset was rebuffed. Next, in force and anticipating resistance, Somerset's men entered the lordship and were resisted. Reports reached the royal council by 19 July, when the sheriff of Glamorgan William Herbert and eight others were summoned to explain themselves. On 21 July both Somerset and Warwick were cited to appear, Somerset being present at the time. Perhaps it was now that Warwick intervened in person: recording as passing through Coventry from Warwick towards Wales in July, he was at Ross on Wye on 2 August:[54] coming or going? By 27 July 'diverse variances and controversies' had reached the council's ears at Westminster.

> the which caused diverse in the countrys ther grete gatherynges congregacions & assembles unlaweful & the towne of Cardieff withe the Castele & towne of Coubryge kept with grete strength as it were in land of war [to] our grete displeasure and grete trouble. . . .

Cowbridge, in west Glamorgan, was close to Kidwelly. By 'the feythe & liegeaunce that ye owe unto us', Warwick was ordered to desist from such manoeuvrings, to disband any assemblies already assembled, and to surrender the castles to the courtier Lord Dudley pending the council's decision on the rule and governance.[55] It is surely evidence of the council's alarm (and perhaps Somerset's too) that Glamorgan was confided first to a third party, even if the

53 Johnson, *York*, 121.
54 E 28/83; Pugh, *Glamorgan County History*, 196; *Stratford Gild Accounts*, 33; BL Egerton Roll 8536 mm. 2–3.
55 E 28/83/41–2.

duke, who was present at the meeting, expected the ultimate decision to be in his favour. Removing Warwick's grasp from Glamorgan was a victory for Somerset and half the battle won.

This same poorly attended meeting of council wrote equally vigorously to Warwick's father Salisbury and Northumberland and commanded them to suspend their feuding in Yorkshire.[56] That same day King Henry left Westminster on judicial progress, first stop Clarendon in Wiltshire,[57] that was obviously destined to take him to Wales ahead of the North. Warwick could not resist the king. Perhaps reinforcements from Somerset arrived at Cowbridge first. At Tewkesbury on 20 August, Warwick was at Cardiff on the 24th.[58] But the threat to Warwick's allegiance did not happen, for King Henry proceeded no further; Somerset stayed at court; Warwick did not surrender Glamorgan to Dudley and indeed crushed his opponents with the aid of a contingent from Staffordshire. Fulk Stafford of Clent (Staffs.), who was feed from Walsall, was paid for his costs and expenses on divers occasions whilst at Cardiff at the time of the rebellion there by authority of a signet warrant of the lord earl dated at Cardiff on 24 August. Henry Flaxhale, some relative of Warwick's bailiff at Walsall, was granted an annuity of £2 and he and his fellows were paid £5 in expenses for riding from Walsall to Cardiff to the earl at the time of the aforesaid rebellion, staying there, and returning. Evidently they had returned by 6 September, the date of the earl's warrant. By then Warwick was again at Tewkesbury,[59] and could turn his attention to other matters. His control was not to be endangered again.

4.3　Time for Decision

Many issues, public and private, served to divide the peerage in 1450–3, even when apparently most united against York's Dartford *putsch*, but they had not caused any firm taking of sides. The Nevilles suffered the advancement of the Tudor brothers and did not come to blows with other contenders for the Warwick inheritance. In the summer of 1453, that changed. Actions against their interests by the court placed them logically in the opposition and the fortuitous madness of the king made York into the avenue for them to achieve their aims. There is no need to postulate a conversion to notions of reform for the common good. It was self-interest that drove them to ally with York. It was an alliance that was to last and to shape Warwick's whole subsequent career.

As parliament dispersed on 2 July 1453, three violent quarrels among noblemen demanded royal attention: Somerset's attempted takeover in Glamorgan; Exeter v. Cromwell over Ampthill (Beds.); and the Percy–Neville

56　E 28/83/76.
57　Johnson, *York*, 122.
58　BL Egerton Roll 8536 m. 2.
59　Ibid. 8536 m. 2; 8541 m. 7.

feud in Yorkshire. All involved Warwick or his family and became interlocked.

Like so many noble quarrels, the Percy–Neville feud took place within the family. The second Earl of Northumberland, the head of the Percies, was married to Salisbury's sister Eleanor and the offspring of both earls were therefore first cousins. Northumberland had owed his restoration in 1416 to Salisbury's father and the two families had co-operated amicably over the years, for example in the Scottish war of 1448–9, and had stood aside from one another's quarrels. The situation was stable. Neville aggrandizement had ceased: indeed ground had been lost through resumption and the creation of a potential rival in both their principal domains in Edmund Tudor, Earl of Richmond, lord of Kendal and Wyresdale. It is not at all obvious that 'without any shadow of doubt by 1453 the Nevilles were the stronger and their strength was still growing'.[60] They had reached and perhaps passed their peak. The marriages that Salisbury was to arrange for his daughters with other northern noblemen, whilst worthy enough, signal a retreat from the national stage, where dilute Beaufort blood no longer worked wonders, to the provincial pattern that had prevailed before Earl Ralph's second brood.

The feud, therefore, was not a long-standing dispute: it seems to have arisen abruptly in the summer of 1453.[61] Nor was it an inheritance dispute. Perhaps, therefore, as modern historians have argued, it arose from local rivalries. The respective domains of the two families were different: Richmondshire, Barnard Castle, Cumbria and the West March for the Nevilles, the East Riding, Craven, Northumberland and the East March for the Percies. Nothing was changing here. Admittedly their spheres overlapped in Cumbria, whence Northumberland's son Thomas Lord Egremont took his title and where another son William was newly Bishop of Carlisle. Near Thirsk in the North Riding only a few miles separated the Percies' Topcliffe and the Nevilles' Sowerby. Their interests also coincided at York, the provincial capital. It is unclear how significant was the geography. Certainly the Egremont title was irrelevant, for it was Northumberland, not his son, who held only one-third of the lordship as a coheir of the Multons, and Egremont had no estate anywhere of his own. Neither earl was much in favour at court and each was having difficulty in providing for his younger children, especially the younger sons, who took the lead in this quarrel. Ties of kinship did not cause holds to be barred, as the Percies sought to murder and the Nevilles to bankrupt their cousins. Possibly competitive power-seeking was the cause; perhaps rivalry between their younger sons, who took the lead, and for whom cousinage understandably counted for less than ties between siblings. The records of the prosecution of the Percies by allies of the Nevilles the following year provide copious data about events, but regrettably little explanation. It is far from obvious that the Percies were at fault.[62]

---

60   A. J. Pollard, *North-Eastern England during the Wars of the Roses* (Oxford, 1990), 249.
61   Ibid. 248, here preferred to Summerson, *Carlisle*, 440.
62   Unless otherwise stated, this section is based on Storey, *Lancaster*, 105–32; Griffiths, *King & Country*, 321–64.

What first reached the ears of the royal council were the actions of Northumberland's son Egremont before 8 June 1453, when he was summoned to answer before them. He did not appear and indeed persisted in his behaviour, provoking further summonses on 26 June and 7 July, when he was urged to serve in Gascony.[63] Whatever he was doing was omitted from the later indictments. Evidently it offended Salisbury's son Sir John Neville, who was summoned on 26 June and who on the 29th attacked the Percy castle of Topcliffe, only to find Egremont was not there.[64] Probably it was the news of this that prompted the issuing of an authoritative commission of oyer and terminer on 12 July for the North Riding alone on which both earls, three other peers, and thirteen others were named. Griffiths describes this as biased towards the Nevilles and certainly Salisbury was attending council, as he had not for three years, up to 22 July.[65] On 25 July the commission was reissued: then apparently rescinded, perhaps as the council realized that the principal offenders were not acting independently of their fathers, that they could not sit together, and that disturbances were more widespread. On 27 July more drastic action was taken. The two earls were urged to control their sons, rioters were identified and ordered to submit, and a new commission was appointed to inquire into riots, routs and congregations throughout the northern counties and to take security from offenders. Gone were the magnates, to be replaced by the councillor Sir William Lucy and three judges.[66] That nine Percy retainers summoned on 10 August were from the West March reveals that the feud had developed, either into Cumbria or more probably by the importation of Cumbrian manpower into a Yorkshire dispute.[67] And on 24 August, in a further escalation, there was a skirmish at Heworth just outside York, where Egremont, allegedly with 5,000 men (710 known by name), encountered a Neville cavalcade apparently en route for Sheriff Hutton that included Salisbury himself and his countess, their sons Thomas and John, and Thomas's wife. There was little bloodshed.

The Nevilles' presence at Heworth is explained by the chronicler pseudo-Worcestre:

In the month of August Thomas Nevyle, the son of the Earl of Salisbury, married [Maud Stanhope Lady Willoughby] the niece of Lord Cromwell at Tateshale in the county of Lincoln. And after the wedding when returning home there was a very great division between Thomas Percy Lord Egremont and the said earl near York. This was the beginning of the greatest sorrow in England.[68]

63   E 28/83/15, 19A, 21.
64   E 28/83/43.
65   E 28/83/39; *CPR 1452–61*, 122.
66   *CPR 1452–61*, 122–3, E 28/83/43, 45.
67   E 28/83/46.
68   *Annales*, 770.

Probably the Nevilles were heading for Salisbury's castle of Sheriff Hutton. Henry VI had licensed the match on 1 May.[69] As the youthful widow of a wealthy baron, as the coheiress with her sister Joan of their late brother Henry Stanhope's modest Nottinghamshire estates, and as coheiress of the veteran statesman Lord Cromwell himself, Maud offered her husband the glittering prospect of an estate of genuinely comital proportions. Cromwell's bonds to various Nevilles probably assured them that the inheritance would actually materialize.[70] It was his new castle at Tattershall that was the venue. Cromwell wanted this match – and that of his other coheiress to a younger son of Viscount Bourchier and nephew of York – to provide his nieces and successors with husbands of royal lineage and the connections to defend his somewhat dubiously-acquired wealth after his death. It is hard to see how a Neville alliance could have helped Cromwell in his feud with the Duke of Exeter either at court or in the East Midlands.

Reading into chronicler's comments that the marriage was the cause both of the Percy–Neville feud itself and the subsequent civil wars, modern historians have searched for reasons why the Percies should have objected so violently to the match and have found them. Cromwell held the East Riding lordship of Wressle and Burwell (Lincs.), formerly Percy possessions forfeited and still coveted by the family, which by this match could have passed on Cromwell's death to Maud and thus to the Nevilles, supposedly their arch-rivals. 'This particular match was obnoxious to the earl of Northumberland', writes Professor Griffiths. 'Resentment at Neville aggrandisement was second nature to him, but it was heightened by the connection with Lord Cromwell.' So, too, for Professor Pollard. 'This was the first time that Neville was to gain directly at the expense of Percy.' Why had 'Sir Thomas Nevill's profitable match . . . inevitably aroused the jealousy and resentment of his Percy cousins, the two landless younger sons'?[71] Unless of course they were rivals for Maud's hand, of which there is no evidence whatsoever! These are original notions, but too speculative. Why should Maud, rather than her sister, inherit these particular properties? They were not settled on her marriage, for in 1454 Cromwell enfeoffed them to use for the performance of his will, that might take a long time yet. There were disturbances at neither place. And why should Egremont initiate a feud in Yorkshire to thwart an event years ahead that might never happen? Besides the antecedents demonstrate that the quarrel, whatever its nature, *preceded* the marriage and originated with Egremont and Sir John Neville in Yorkshire and focused for some mysterious reason on Topcliffe. The marriage was not the cause of the feud, but the occasion for the skirmish at Heworth. If anything, the chronicler indicates that Salisbury was the target. It was his son John, not Thomas, with whom Egremont had already crossed swords. Neville-inspired indictments are the sole source that Egremont was the aggressor at Heworth.

69   *CPR 1452–61*, 64.
70   Griffiths, *Henry VI*, 604.
71   Griffiths, *King & Country*, 325; T. B. Pugh, 'Richard, Duke of York, and the Rebellion of Henry, Duke of Exeter, in May 1454', *HR* lxiii (1990), 251–2.

In retrospect, Heworth was the beginning not the end, as the feud escalated. There were unsuccessful attempts to mediate in late September, first by the mayor of York and then by Archbishop Bothe, Salisbury's brother Bishop Neville, and the second Earl of Westmorland. The trio may not have been impartial, for on 8 October the council told them not to assist the Nevilles. It also complained to both earls of their continuing 'grettest assemblees of our liegemen', urging them to settle their differences peacefully rather than violently as parliament had provided, and instructing them to submit on pain of degradation. The crisis was reached on 20 October when the two parties at full strength were only four miles apart: at Topcliffe the earl of Northumberland, his sons Lord Poynings and Egremont, and lord Clifford; at Sandhutton Salisbury, Warwick and his other sons, FitzHugh and Scrope of Bolton. They did not fight. A truce of some kind was arranged, that enabled Northumberland to return to Leconfield and Warwick and Salisbury to leave at once for London.

Whatever the original cause of the Neville–Percy feud, by 20 October it had become a contest for regional hegemony. Witness the participation of other Yorkshire noblemen. Witness the presence of Percy retainers from Northumberland and Cumberland and of Northumberland himself, who was at Petworth (Sussex) at the time of Heworth.[72] Witness, especially, Warwick. Both sides mobilized all their resources. Warwick had been absent from his home country since his unexpected promotion in 1449 and did not return even when he joined his father Salisbury as joint-warden of the West March in December. With pressing business in Cardiff on 24 August, nevertheless he proceeded via Tewkesbury on 6 September, when his countess was at Grafton, via Stratford to Berkeswell (Warw.) on 12 September, Lichfield (Staffs.) on the morrow, and thence via Middleham to Sandhutton on 20 October.[73] For Warwick it was a turning point in his career. Immersed in the affairs of his new inheritance, commuting between Warwickshire and South Wales, he had encountered his father Salisbury only on major political occasions, at parliaments, councils and at Dartford, and had surely escaped paternal direction in politics. He had not even attended his brother's wedding at Tattershall. Not only did Warwick engage himself in the Nevilles' northern affairs, in October 1453 – surely in response to his father's urgent summons? – but in national politics, in which henceforth the two Neville earls were to be both active and inseparable.

Nor was this the only escalation. If Cromwell was the Nevilles' ally, was not Cromwell's enemy that of the Nevilles too? Hence perhaps Exeter's support for the Percies – and the Percies' support for Exeter – next year. Significantly it was at the house of Maud Dowager-Lady Stanhope at Tuxforth in Nottinghamshire that Egremont and Exeter 'ben sworne togeder' in January.[74] Three separate feuds were becoming entangled and two sides were emerging. And, as we shall

72   Carlisle RO Cockermouth Castle MS D/Lec 29/3 m. 2d.
73   BL Egerton Roll 8536 m. 3; Bodl. MS Dugdale 13, f. 434.
74   *Paston L & P* ii. 295–9.

see, the Nevilles became aligned with York, permanently. No wonder pseudo-Worcestre saw Heworth as the beginning of the sorrows!

The greatest danger, which actually materialized, was that one side should be the king's and the other, therefore, opposed to him. It was a king's task to prevent this by imposing order rigorously on the parties as Henry VI, to his credit, had recently done. Even-handed justice, whilst desirable, was inessential. King Henry's council tried to appear impartial, but was probably not in practice. Already there were indications of royal favour to the Percies. Whatever its initial stance, the council inclined increasingly towards the Percies. Since Sir William Lucy and Judge Portington actually took the Percy side, it seems the second commission of 27 July had a distinctly pro-Percy bias. It was against co-operation with the Nevilles that the council warned in October. Whilst Salisbury reappeared in the royal council after a three-year absence on 18 and 22 July 1453, it is striking that he saw no advantage in remaining even though the council was prosecuting his sons. Somerset and the other councillors could not dissociate Neville defiance in the North and in South Wales. The full authority of the crown was deployed in favour of Somerset and the Percies and against the Nevilles. And yet that authority was ineffective in both venues, defied not just by the Nevilles, but by the Percies too. Warwick in South Wales risked the threatened rupture in his allegiance and the two northern earls ignored the threat of degradation, which had never before happened and which doubtless they disbelieved. They were right to do so: both Neville earls resumed their council seats. To back up its threats, effective action was needed by the king, doubtless again manipulated by Somerset. Somerset could not do it by himself. And so it could not be done at all, for the king was mad. And the first fruit of that madness was an immediate escalation of the feuds that had been so effectively stifled in the previous two years.

It is not quite clear when King Henry's madness began. Certainly later than 7 July, the date offered by *Giles's Chronicle*; later probably than 27 July, when he set off for Clarendon. Perhaps he was overset by the news of Châtillon: the disastrous defeat and death in Acquitaine of Shrewsbury and Lisle, and hence, shortly, the loss of Bordeaux (19 October) and Gascony itself. The government fetched him back to Windsor. Somerset and his ministers continued acting as though he was sane, striving to regulate feuds with his authority, yet tied to court, unable to proceed to the provinces to repress disorders. They must have hoped, even expected, the king to get better. But they could not continue once his illness was established. Already, no doubt, news had leaked out, though the fiction of his authority was maintained. The birth of an heir apparent in Prince Edward on 13 October 1453 offered some inkling of where authority might lie. Parliamentary authority would be required, but parliament needed management. Parliament, due to resume at Reading on 12 November, was to be prorogued until February, pending agreement amongst themselves by the great, who were summoned to a great council in November supposedly 'to sette rest and union betwixt the lords of this lande'.[75] That, we may presume, was decided by those hostile to York,

75   *POPC* vi. 163–4.

who was not summoned, for on 23 October he was invited at a meeting of nine councillors not including Somerset, the chancellor (Cardinal Kemp), or the treasurer (Wiltshire). No realistic consensus could be achieved without him. And perhaps because he would not come otherwise, as perhaps he had failed to attend councils and parliament since Dartford, they added that the great council would consider the 'variance betwixt hym and sum othre of the lordes'.[76] As Johnson observes, this must mean Somerset. In Henry's absence, those who were not York's satellites were prepared to revive a quarrel that the king had thought to have quashed. They did not want Somerset, whose rule would cause the realm to perish, and they saw in York the only credible alternative.

That applied also to Warwick and his father Salisbury. It was at this point that they committed themselves to York and for these selfish reasons – not from a public-spirited commitment to the commonweal and reform. Henceforth Salisbury, after a gap of ten years, and Warwick were to immerse themselves in national politics, an involvement that lasted for the rest of their lives. It was at this point that Warwick, still only 25 years old, became a political figure of the front rank.

York and a small entourage arrived early for the great council on 12 November. He was in no conciliatory mood, determined to avenge former injuries rather than to heal wounds, perhaps more interested in destruction than good rule, and confident that circumstances now favoured him. The king was no longer available to make decisions and he no longer had the dubious status of heir presumptive. Now that a constitutional avenue had opened to him, it was possible to repair fences with former allies like Norfolk who had baulked at his attempted coup in 1452, and with those penalized for that attempt. Salisbury, Warwick and Cromwell attended all known sessions of the council in the Star Chamber at Westminster, latterly with Salisbury's brother Fauconberg, captured in Normandy and recently ransomed, his retainers FitzHugh and Scrope of Bolton, and Cromwell's ally Grey of Ruthin. Conspicuous absentees were their adversaries Northumberland, Poynings, Egremont, Clifford and Exeter, who failed to appreciate, it seems, that the affairs of the North and Ampthill might be decided at Westminster. The assembly thus offered hope to the Nevilles whom, we may safely assume, had no desire to legitimize and reinforce the authority of their rival Somerset.

At least half of those eventually attending were late and thus missed the opening session on 21 November, which York hijacked. The minute records him rehearsing at length, once again, his loyalty, his commitment 'to all that sholde or might be to the welfare of the king and of his subgettes', before embarking on the business for which, he pointed out, he had been summoned. Apart from approval for his 'moderate' request to have his banned councillors back, the Earl of Devon was freed from the incarceration he had suffered since Dartford, and an appeal of treason was made by Norfolk of Somerset, who two days later was consigned to the Tower. The session on 30 November, attended by 52 peers and

76 Johnson, *York*, 124.

councillors, was much less controversial.[77] Who could object to an oath to keep order and to enforce the lawful instructions of the council to keep the peace?

Much more difficult was what form the government should take, which was considered by only twenty-three peers on 5 December, again in the Star Chamber. Those who absented themselves included not only the inexperienced, non-councillors and most of the barons, but such recent ministers as Sudeley and Beauchamp, and partisans on both sides with causes to champion. Salisbury's brothers Bishop Neville and Fauconberg were absent; so, too, his retainers, FitzHugh and Scrope of Bolton. So varied a group was not excluded; they absented themselves to avoid commitment and responsibility. Warwick, Salisbury and the others present were self-selecting. It was a lively debate, we may deduce, that reached the lame conclusion that the royal council could take decisions during the king's infirmity, but only on matters that could not be put off: 'in estuinge irreparable inconvynyentees ... as must of nessessyte be entended unto and by the whch yf the[y] wer not forsene grete inconveyence wer lyeke to ensue' . . . Even that result was subscribed by only fourteen peers – a bare majority of those present: only the bishops and an abbot, surely immune from future penalties, and the three dukes, two Neville earls, and York's brother-in-law Viscount Bourchier among the lay magnates dared subscribe. Some sort of government must continue. The Earl of Worcester, now Lord Treasurer, did not; neither did Bishop Waynflete, the earls of Pembroke and Wiltshire, too close perhaps to the king to concede his power; nor the barons, Cromwell among them. Far from demanding power, even the subscribers were frightened of responsibility, fearful of taking on royal prerogatives, and formally protested that they did only what was essential until parliament had specified their powers.[78] What if the king recovered? What, moreover, if parliament held them accountable for what was going wrong? For the same reason, fuller minutes of decisions were taken, so that authority and especially responsibility could be shared.[79] It was probably to place his loyalty on record rather than to justify the restoration of his councillors that York had the council minute of 23 November formally exemplified next day, on 6 December.[80] It showed that he had kept his oath at St Paul's.

Scarcely any decisions were taken over the Christmas period and there are no surviving council records until February 1454, when parliament was to resume. However, there was plenty of political activity and preparations were afoot nearly a month beforehand to locate parliament amidst an armed camp. The unfolding crisis is documented by the newsletter of 19 January 1454 of John Stodeley. The king's incapacity had been confirmed. Far from accepting defeat, the regime had been planning for the future and making the most of its control of the machinery of government and household. Anticipating a potential coup involving the

77 CPR 1452–61, 143–4; R. A. Griffiths, 'The King's Council and the First Protectorate of the Duke of York 1450–1454', King & Country, 315–17.
78 Griffiths, King & Country, 316–17.
79 Ibid. 307.
80 CPR 1452–61, 143–4.

seizure of the person of the king, it was proposed that a guard should be set about him. Even imprisoned, Somerset was the mind behind the regime, a potent and, to Stodeley's mind, a malign influence, whose spies were everywhere. Letters were being intercepted and Norfolk should watch out for ambush. As Somerset's continued rule was apparently unattainable, rule by the queen, enhanced in status as mother to the heir, was being advocated. Five articles were proposed that would have given her 'the hole reule of this land', control over appointments to royal and ecclesiastical office, and sufficient resources to support the king, prince and herself. Nothing was to be left to chance. An armed retinue attended Cardinal Kemp, the chancellor. All the lodgings by the Tower had been taken for the retainers of Somerset, who was thus assured against the repetition of Lord Say's seizure or his own attempted lynching in 1450. Prominent magnates were coming in force: the courtier Viscount Beaumont; the treasurer Wiltshire and Bonville were recruiting men at Taunton at 6*d.* a day; the northerners Lord Clifford and the Percy brothers Poynings and Egremont, fresh from his alliance with Exeter at Tuxforth. Reportedly Buckingham had prepared 2,000 Stafford bands with knots – his livery badge – 'to what entent men may construe as their wittes wole yeve them'. Bills supporting the king and prince had been posted by courtiers, determined this time to get public opinion on their side, and York himself was to be discredited if not destroyed. Articles against him had been prepared by the Speaker himself, Thomas Thorpe, for this was the same Reading parliament that had been so accommodating to the court and so condemnatory of Dartford and Oldhall. Moreover the royal council had written to Norfolk and doubtless other disaffected lords directing them not to bring large forces with them. The government was to be strongest and the stronger party was to prevail.

From such a coalition, York and the Nevilles had much to fear. They were not daunted and were no less advanced in their preparations. 'A feliship of gode men' had been sent in advance of the duke, who was bringing his household fully equipped for war, and was to be accompanied by the two Tudor brothers and Warwick himself. 'And natheles therle of Warwyk wole haue M [a thousand] men awaityng on hym beside the feliship that cometh with him, as ferre as I can knowe.' Salisbury was due on Monday with 140 knights and squires, 'beside other meynee'. Stodeley's master should bring as many men as he could make and explain that he needed it for his own security.[81] Conflict loomed. And Warwick and Salisbury were agreed that this time they would fight on the side of the Duke of York.

---

81 *Paston L & P* ii. 295–9.

5

Partisan Politics 1454–6

5.1 York's First Protectorate 1454–5

The climax that Stodeley foresaw did not happen. Or did not happen yet. For several reasons. Whilst prepared for violence, the magnates did not want it, and avoided precipitating it. York's allies brought weapons, not to hand but in carts,[1] because they hoped not to use them. The Nevilles and Percies had alike declined the opportunity for battle both at Heworth and at Sand Hutton. Whatever Stodeley's impression on 19 January, Exeter and the Percies did not actually come to parliament. Stodeley misunderstood their intentions. Maybe Bonville and Wiltshire were more interested in their quarrels with Devon. Perhaps Exeter and Egremont rated their disputes with Cromwell and the Nevilles higher than the fate of the government. It is subsequent historians who have read two sides into Stodeley's report, which may not have been meant. Perhaps he really did not know to what end Buckingham ordered his knots? Surely there were at least three sides: the court, represented by the queen, cardinal and Somerset; York and the Neville earls; and Exeter and the Percies. For the latter, the enemy was not just the Yorkists, but also the court. As grandson of Henry IV's whole sister Elizabeth, Exeter saw himself as the legitimate heir of the house of Lancaster and of the duchy of Lancaster too. His father-in-law York, the queen and the Beauforts could all be expected to oppose his claim in parliament. Therefore it was not worth attending. Though the Nevilles had turned to York against Somerset, the Percies did not yet perceive Somerset as their natural ally against the Nevilles. Rather than fight a hopeless battle at court, was it not better for Exeter and the Percies to assert their authority in the North, where the duchy of Lancaster was so strong, against the Nevilles and subsequently to pressurize

---

1 *PL* ii. 298.

Table 5.1 The Royal Family and the Protectorate 1454

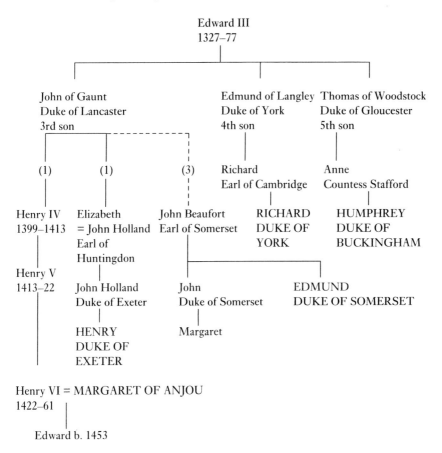

the government? Their behaviour towards officially constituted authority was similar to York's the previous year.

Avoiding meetings dominated by opponents, where crucial decisions had to be taken, or where responsibility had to be accepted was already the practice of many of the lords. *Pace* K. B. McFarlane, there was already plenty of that cravenness that he observed in 1485. More than half the nobility failed to appear. Whilst personal animosities ran deep, all of those present did recognize the need for a caretaker government, to maintain order at home and defend against French attacks.

And yet they went to the wire. Warwick attended a council meeting on 4 February but even on 6 February, five days before parliament was resumed, there was no agreement on who should open it: ostensibly an empty but symbolic role, but one that involved another delegation of 'the kinges power'. Council prorogued the session for another three days. The Lords met in the great council chamber at Westminster on 13 February to decide. Perhaps more were present, but again relatively few subscribed, twenty-nine in all: less than half the peerage, less than half the bishops or secular lords, including no dukes, abbots or viscounts. Warwick and Salisbury were there, as they were to be on all important occasions during the session, and signed their names. Council nominated York to preside as king's lieutenant and, greatly daring, 'to do all thyng that shalbe necessarie therfore to any of the premisses'.[2] Did this ambiguous sentence authorize him to exercise the royal assent? It is surely not coincidental that only two days later, on 15 February, Warwick secured a definitive judgement in his favour over the Warwick chamberlainship of the exchequer.

That Buckingham was simultaneously appointed to the highly prestigious but largely honorific stewardship of England identifies him as an alternative lieutenant. Buckingham also was a great-grandson of Edward III, the grandson of that king's youngest son Thomas of Woodstock, another descendant of Edward I through his daughter Joan of Acre, and allied by marriage to the Beauforts. He was as royal a duke as York, Somerset and Exeter. His compliance or co-operation had to be secured. A steward was needed to acquit Devon. Did York also hope, unrealistically, that Buckingham would be needed to sentence Somerset? Buckingham presided over the Garter chapter at Windsor on 11 May.[3]

This parliament had been highly favourable to the king and Somerset the previous year and had not altogether changed. The Commons were critical and the Lords decidedly cautious. No agreement could be reached on major issues for the first six weeks of the session. York and his allies were in the ascendant, however, and exploited the possibly temporary opportunity to their factional advantage whilst they could. Some of their rivals had unwisely absented themselves from the parliament, others had legitimate reasons for absence such as attendance on the king, and the majority of the lords merely absented themselves to avoid commitment. York, once the voice of public opinion, had already taken the offensive against Thorpe, securing his imprisonment during the vacation and thus deflecting the promised charges. Now he defied the Commons by rejecting their complaint and directing the election of a replacement. The new Speaker was the Middlesex knight Thomas Charlton, who saw some career advantage in the post; he features on the Salisbury Roll as grandson of Maud Franceys, Warwick's great-grandmother. On 14 March the charges of treason against Devon arising from the Dartford affair were revoked, York taking the opportunity once again to affirm his loyalty.

York's supporters also took the offensive. Cromwell petitioned against Exeter and the Nevilles against the Percies. The Nevilles roundly condemned Egremont and his brother Richard Percy; they wisely omitted Northumberland and Poynings. Both bills passed. Exeter was required to surrender Ampthill by Whitsun on pain of £10,000 and the Percies on pain of forfeiture and outlawry

---

2   J. F. Baldwin, *The King's Council in the Middle Ages* (1913), 197n.
3   Anstis, i. 151–2; *Benet's Chron.* 211.

were to attend on the chancellor: their opponent Salisbury! The November oath to obey conciliar commands became a statute backed by forfeiture.[4]

The Warwick inheritance dispute proceeded more surreptitiously. Warwick was already in possession of the chamberlainship on 13 February, when the Lords inspected the coffers and keys in pursuit of fraud, and was confirmed in possession on the 23rd, when he was also granted backpay from 6 December 1450 totalling £1 6s. There could be no opposition. With Latimer insane in Salisbury's custody and Somerset in prison, there was only the Countess Margaret to oppose: her husband and son had fallen at Châtillon; the new earl of Shrewsbury, her stepson, was no friend of hers as she added the Talbot–Talbot dispute to her other feuds. Lord Treasurer Worcester, Warwick's erstwhile brother-in-law, who presided at the exchequer, had found in Warwick's favour once before. This decision implies Warwick's entitlement to the whole of the Duchess Cecily's dower. Partial Somerset may have been, but not like this.

On 15 March 1454 Henry's infant son was recognized as Prince of Wales by the Lords, including Warwick and Salisbury.[5] The young prince's rights were reserved in what followed. Much needed to be done: to defend the realm, protect Calais, improve the administration of justice, and establish an effective form of government. No money was forthcoming; appropriate what you have, recommended the Commons, which York at least was willing to do. The sticking point was the form of the executive. Where was that 'sadde and a wyse counsaill' promised at Reading, asked the Commons? 'They have noo knoweleche as yit.' To this the chancellor promised 'good and comfortable aunswere, without eny grete delay or tariyng'. That was on 19 March.[6] Perhaps, it has been suggested, it was the chancellor himself, Cardinal Kemp, who was obstructive.[7] Certainly it was his death on 22 March that removed the obstacle. That, however, may have been because decisions had to be taken, if even routine matters were legitimately to pass under the great seal. The appointment of a chancellor was no part of a council's normal competence. It was only with utmost caution, after another visit had established that the king was *really* incapacitated, that royal prerogatives were vested in a protector, a chancellor and a council. And even the protector, as in 1422, was to be merely a chief counsellor with powers to defend the land against enemies within and without, not 'no name that shall emporte auctorite of governance of the lande', saving the rights of Prince Edward.[8] That protector was agreed to be Richard Duke of York.

Yet York was not the only candidate. The queen, though young, inexperienced and French, had presented her case. She stood for continuity. What of the princes of the blood? Somerset, whether alone or *éminence grise* to the queen, was blamed for the recently extended run of foreign defeats, not credited with recent

4   Payling, 'Ampthill Dispute', 899; Griffiths, *King & Country*, 341–2.
5   *RP* v. 249.
6   *RP* v. 240.
7   Johnson, *York*, 133–4.
8   *RP* v. 242.

achievements, and had personal enemies made in power to add to York and his earlier foes. York was no less wealthy and well-born than in 1450, if somewhat tarnished by fading memories of Dartford. He was the critic of the existing regime for those who wanted change and were enemies of Somerset. His frighteningly radical programme of 1450 was no longer current. Almost certainly, there was a fourth candidate, in Exeter, whose title was certainly superior to that of Somerset who, like the Nevilles, was descended from Gaunt's mistress and eventual third wife. Exeter's was a partisan case, that threatened defeat for Cromwell and the Nevilles; his credit must have suffered from Cromwell's petition; its passage exposed his limited support. No chronicle writes of the claims of Margaret, Somerset or Exeter. Yet the Lords hesitated before endorsing York. If no longer a potential dynastic rival, he was decidedly not the man to whom King Henry would have confided his power, as York's excuse for his absence from the Garter chapter on 11 May confirms:

> That the Sovereign had for some time been angry with him, and therefore he durst not come nearer, for fear if he did so, of giving unnecessarily an Occasion of greater Offence, whereby the King being out of Order (which God avoid he said) his Resentment and perhaps his Distemper might gain ground.[9]

York had enemies too. And so the decision was postponed.

Cardinal Kemp died on Friday 22 March. Next day an authoritative commission of twelve peers was instructed to consult the king, Warwick among them. Finding Henry still incapacitated, 'to their grete sorow and disconfort', they reported back on Monday. On Wednesday 27 March York was appointed Lord Protector 'for as long as it may please the king'. It was a solemn, indeed awesome, appointment, especially if it proved *not* to please the king or actions had later to be accounted for. Hence York wanted both the clearest definition of powers and the maximum support and sharing of responsibility. Without these, he said, he would not act. He did not claim, as in 1450, that he could do it all himself, but took the role not out of presumption, but 'onely of the due and humble obeissaunce that I owe to doo to the king our most dredde and soverain lord'. At his request, the Lords defined his powers as defence not government, assigned him revenues, and nominated a council, all of which was enshrined, for greater security, in an act of parliament. He was not to be governor of the king, tutor of the young prince, or regent. The formal patent specified that he would hold office during pleasure until Prince Edward reached years of discretion and became protector instead.[10]

Choices of new bishops were made and Salisbury was appointed chancellor, all by the old council, Warwick being present.[11] On 2 April the new council

9   Anstis, i. 151–2.
10   *RP* v. 242–3.
11   *RP* v. 449–50.

assembled for the first time. If York wished to share his responsibility with them, they were decidedly reluctant to take it on, and imposed several conditions. They wanted the rate for the job, each according to his rank, with some guarantee that it would be actually paid. They recommended that the government's financial position and necessary expenses should be declared to the Commons, so that they could not be held responsible for the dire situation later on, and said they were acting only for the good of the king and the country. With memories of Tailbois's murderous assault, Cromwell asked to come and go in safety. Each was asked directly by Salisbury as chancellor to serve and each sought to exculpate himself on grounds of health and other duties, which were scrupulously recorded; nevertheless each was persuaded to act. Their excuses were a convenient means of evading critical decisions. Even Warwick, who wanted the position, pleaded that he was 'yonge of age' – still only 25 – 'and yonger of discrecyon and wysdome, so that was unable [incapable]' to act. 'Notwithstanding he wold with right good-wyll doo that wiche was in his poure.'[12]

York's new appointments were appropriate: Salisbury as chancellor had ample experience for his new role. The council was balanced between the various estates. It contained the archbishop of York, four bishops, and the dean of St Severin's at Bordeaux. Apart from the protector and chancellor, there were two other dukes (Buckingham and Norfolk), four other earls, both viscounts, three barons, a knight and an esquire. 'It was, in fair', observed Virgoe, 'a council representative both of official activity and experience and of most of the interests of the English nobility'.[13] But the appointments were not balanced politically. Salisbury was York's brother-in-law. York as chief councillor was ever-present, but no place was found for his rivals the queen, for Somerset, or Exeter, or even for the king's half-brothers. This was the council to do York's will. No wonder Viscount Beaumont, the queen's chamberlain, felt isolated and anticipated the disagreements with some trepidation. Reserving his services to her, he reminded councillors of a standing order allowing free speech 'without any displeasure, indignacyon or wrothe of any other person for his sayinge'.[14]

If the new regime was to secure consent, it needed to be better balanced: hence the prompt addition of Sudeley, Dudley and Stourton, barons of relatively little weight associated with the court, and Thomas Bourchier Bishop of Ely as archbishop-designate.[15] Doubtless all 22 councillors wished to share in the happy task of creating the Prince of Wales and investing the infant with the gold circlet on his head, the gold ring on his finger, and the gold rod for which they commissioned themselves on 13 April.[16] Most council business, even during the protectorate, was humdrum routine. Those attending to it were predominantly

---

12   Griffiths, *King & Country*, 317–19.
13   Virgoe, 'Composition', 151.
14   Griffiths, *King & Country*, 319.
15   Ibid. 315. These may have always been intended, but unable to attend the meeting of 2 April, ibid. 315.
16   *CPR 1452–61*, 171.

ministers, churchmen and administrators, not lay magnates. About half the councillors attended each meeting.[17] Those present at parliament had been so few that on 28 February fines had been instituted for absentee peers. The turnouts at great councils in June/July and October/November were also very poor; in these cases, doubtless, because decisions had to be made and responsibility taken. Most knights absented themselves from the Garter chapter, some pleading sickness; perhaps they did not want to make elections for which they could later be held responsible? Even Warwick's father Salisbury pleaded bad feet that prevented him from walking or riding.[18]

The new protector was the saviour to provide direction to government and cope with pressures both at home and abroad. He, his chancellor, and council did fill the vacuum. Routine decision-making resumed, letters being warranted on occasion by York's own signet,[19] and firm action was taken, as we shall see, both to condemn lawlessness and to impose order. If nothing could be done to recover Normandy and Gascony, action was taken to save Calais and to protect the coast against French raids. York himself succeeded Somerset as captain of Calais and four earls headed by Salisbury were appointed keepers of the sea. The Commons refused to vote new taxes and there was to be no act of resumption, perhaps because the last one had been so effective: as we have seen, the duke sought some accommodation with the court, none of whom were treated like Somerset. There was no purge. If there was no new money, what there was could be better used. It was applied to the obvious priorities, by appropriation to Calais and household, to which serious economies were at length made in November:[20] a year after the king's malady became known.

As a reforming programme, it is not impressive, and it is not obviously compatible with other aspects of a regime which served the self-interest of the duke and his principal allies. The new chancellor, archbishop (Thomas Bourchier), and bishop of Ely (William Grey) were York's relatives. So was Warwick's youngest brother George, who was promised the next bishopric. York himself was again lieutenant of Ireland and took on as captain of Calais the principal military command from Somerset. He was authorized to retain eighty individuals on behalf of the crown. Salisbury was keeper of the seas for three years in lieu of Exeter, hereditary admiral of England, and was assigned the whole tunnage and poundage in support, to which was added the constableship of Portchester Castle in November.[21] It is probably at this point that Warwick recovered possession of the Channel Isles, adding it to his chamberlainship of the Exchequer.[22] Already joint wardens of the West March for twenty years, operable from 12 December 1453, the two Neville earls surrendered their patent and renewed for another

17 Virgoe, 'Composition', 151, 159.
18 Anstis, i. 151–2.
19 Johnson, *York*, 143n.
20 Wolffe, *Henry VI*, 281–5.
21 *CPR 1452–61*, 208.
22 He wrote to Nanfan as lord on 11 February 1455, BL Royal MS 17 B xlvii, f. 165v. No grant seems to exist.

Plate 1 The Neville matriarch Joan Beaufort Countess of Westmorland and daughters at prayer, from the Neville Hours. The daughters, who include three duchesses, are identifiable from the coats of arms beneath. (*Paris, Bibliothèque Nationale, MS Latin 1158, f.28v*)

Plate 2 Warwick's parents Richard Neville and Alice Montagu as Earl and Countess of Salisbury. Note the Neville saltire with a label of cadency. (*British Library, MS Loan 90, p.221 / in the collection of the Duke of Buccleuch and Queensberry, KT*)

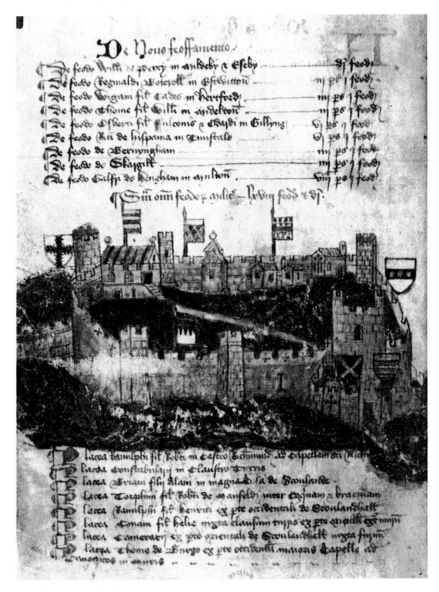

Plate 3   Richmond Castle. The banners identify those tenants responsible for guarding particular defences. The Neville saltire appears on the great tower to the right. (*British Library, MS Cotton Faustina BVIII, f.85v*)

Plate 4 Bear and ragged staff from a gold ring supposedly taken from Warwick's body at Barnet. (*Geoffrey Wheeler*)

Plate 5 The Neville screen, Durham Cathedral. (*RCHME, © Crown copyright*)

Plate 6 The south–west corner of Guyscliff Chapel. Note the massive rock-hewn statue of the Giant Guy. (*RCHME,* © *Crown copyright*)

Plate 7   Guy's Tower, Warwick Castle, with the barbican and gatehouse beyond.
(*RCHME, © Crown copyright*)

Plate 8 Warwick as a mourner from the monument of his father-in-law Richard Beauchamp Earl of Warwick at the Beauchamp Chapel, Warwick. (*Geoffrey Wheeler*)

Plate 9 Muzzled bears and ragged staves from the entrance to the Beauchamp Chapel, Warwick. (*RCHME*, © *Crown copyright*)

Plate 10   Warwick's seal as Lord of Glamorgan. The reverse depicts his wife's coat of arms supported by a muzzled bear and surmounted by a swan crest. On the obverse Warwick is a mounted knight; note his coronet with swan crest. His shield bears his own Neville saltire with a label. (*Geoffrey Wheeler*)

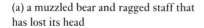

(a) a muzzled bear and ragged staff that   (b) a muzzled bear
has lost its head

Plate 11   Two cheap lead badges of the type distributed wholesale to Warwick's retainers (© *British Museum*)

twenty years from June, this time for £1,250 a year rather than the £983 Salisbury had accepted in 1443; £80 was now secured on the Carlisle feefarm,[23] late of lord Poynings, a more certain, convenient and locally prestigious source. How could this conform to York's drive for economy? There is also a case for arguing that it was their personal interests that motivated York's drive for public order rather than any abstract notion of justice. It is 'difficult to believe', as Johnson has said, 'that it was in the best interests of the nation that the earl of Salisbury should hold the great seal.'[24] It suited Warwick.

However widespread the support for York's appointment and however representative the council, York found few magnates prepared to commit themselves and fewer yet on whom he could depend. Norfolk and Cromwell were both inactive: perhaps we should take more seriously the duke's 'inffirmytye withe the wiche he is manye tymes vexed' as explanation for his inconvenient absences at key moments? Devon was a violent liability. None of these attended many council meetings or were added to commissions of the peace like York and the two Neville earls. Warwick, hitherto JP only for Warwickshire, joined another twelve commissions: for Worcestershire and Staffordshire on 22 April 1454, Gloucestershire, Nottinghamshire, Derbyshire, Leicestershire and (as befitted the marcher warden) Cumberland and Westmorland on 21–29 May, the West Riding of Yorkshire on 1 June and North Riding on 11 July, for Northamptonshire on 4 December, and Herefordshire on 19 February 1455.[25] This does not mean that Warwick had political designs on all these areas, as has sometimes been suggested from a single county perspective.[26] Far from it. Henceforth he could participate in their affairs, if he so wished and had the time, for he visited few of these counties and apparently attended no sessions. He rendered his provincial services principally through commissions of oyer and terminer.

However much the composition of the council assuaged the hostility of queen and court, it does not mean that the new regime could do as it wished. York was not able to destroy Somerset, as he had hoped. This was not because of a failure to bring him to trial, nor because Norfolk failed to prosecute his case. It does seem likely that the duke avoided bringing the case to parliament, which he could not control, and instead took it to successive great councils. The principal evidence here is a petition by Norfolk himself which comes from a late stage in proceedings. Norfolk had presented his articles, which focused on the loss of Lancastrian France, and Somerset had been arrested (23 November 1453). Somerset had answered the charges and offered evidence in support, which his accuser rejected as 'falseness and lesynges', and Norfolk had made his replication, which proved his case to his own satisfaction and those 'knowyng how justice owyth to be ministred'. The judgement that he requested of the Lords

23   Storey, 'Wardens', 605–6; Johnson, *York*, 145.
24   Johnson, *York*, 135.
25   *CPR 1452–61*, 663, 666–70, 672–7, 680–3.
26   Castor, 'Walter Blount', 22–3.

had not however materialized, 'whereoff y am so hevy that y may no lenger beere it'. Some peers thought exception should be made due to Somerset's lineage, which Norfolk saw as an excuse ('dissimulacion'), and detracted from the deterrent value of justice to future offenders; others, he thought, hoped to be bribed by Somerset; yet others considered that the charges 'ben but cases of trespass' not treason; and yet more argued the case for general reconciliation – 'universell peas' – not vengeance. There was no consensus in his favour to destroy a royal duke who had been the king's favourite and who had been exonerated several times by the king himself. This stage most likely occurred in July, for surely the second issue – whether the offences constituted treason – justified York's suggestion that it be referred to the judges. On 18 July York had to plead inadequate attendance to prevent Somerset from being released on bail. Following the departure for York of himself and Warwick, those remaining relieved Northumberland of the judicial proceedings that the duke himself had gone to continue! Though amazed by this conclusion, Norfolk apparently recognized that he could not secure an acceptable verdict under English law. Changing his tack, therefore, and citing foreign parallels, he asked that Somerset should be tried for his French offences under French law, that commissions of inquiry be held into the evidence, and that his original appeal should be enacted. Should his case again fail to prevail, he asked for a patent of discharge and threatened to make the failure of justice known. This, surely, was at the great council of 28 October, at which he was ordered to present (surely re-present?) his charges, the last occasion when it could have been heard, and resulted in neither Somerset's conviction nor Norfolk's discharge nor its exemplification. Again poorly attended, the trial was put off.[27] If the charges themselves related to service in France, York's main aim, as in 1450, was to destroy the principal obstacle in his way.

Nor did the protectorate achieve instant acceptance from the governed. York spent his whole protectorate struggling to secure the practical implementation of his captaincy of Calais, without success. The garrison mutinied for their pay and much effort was spent finding the funds to satisfy them. Somerset's lieutenants, lords Welles and Rivers, remained in possession and the duke continued to be excluded. The leading gentry in Derbyshire denounced Walter Blount as a traitor and sacked his house at Elvaston in May; perhaps this was because Blount was associated with the royal household; more probably he was already allied to York and hence to 'the illegitimate accroachment of royal power by a partisan faction'.[28]

More seriously yet, York's son-in-law Exeter – probably the protector's hopeful if unrealistic rival – thought himself more properly protector. Reading between the formulaic and partisan lines of indictments, Exeter apparently distinguished between the government and the duchy of Lancaster, to which he

---

27 Griffiths, *Henry VI*, 721; Johnson, *York*, 91–2, 143–4, 152–3; *PL* ii. 290–2. Norfolk's absences on some days does not *necessarily* mean he was absent on those when his appeal was heard.
28 Castor, 'Walter Blount', 31.

felt as next heir he should be custodian; not those without such claims.[29] There was a problem of respect and recognition for the protectorate, that King Henry himself with all his personal inadequacies had never experienced. This was aggravated by the factional nature of the regime. There was no place on the council for Exeter and Somerset, York's defeated rivals. Salisbury as chancellor was ever-present, but, in the context of the Percy–Neville feud, not Northumberland, Poynings, Egremont or Clifford. Warwick was there, but not his Beauchamp and Despenser rivals. Cromwell, one party in the Ampthill dispute, was there; Exeter was not. Council membership thus threatened to reverse the old division between ins and outs and harden it by identifying the protectorate with one faction in the principal feuds and by shutting out the others. So did the protector's own policy of enforcement.

York was appointed on 28 March. Perhaps it was not long afterwards that the protector, chancellor, treasurer, primate and Viscount Bourchier imposed a settlement on the Mountford dispute. York's son-in-law and enemy Exeter had made extensive military preparations in the far corners of the land by 8 May, when York commanded him to report his reasons and future intentions for decision by the council.[30] There was concern about disorders in Derbyshire and the North by 10–11 May, when the council wrote stern summonses to Exeter, Northumberland, Egremont and leading gentry.[31] All were ignored: so much for the new statute threatening such offenders with forfeiture! Quite what was intended by Exeter and Egremont is uncertain, though large forces were assembled at York and Spofforth and marched to Skipton (28 May) towards Lancashire, for their preparations were disrupted by York's rapid and decisive action: 'and hearing of the approach of the Duke of York they fled.' Assemblies in Lancashire were suppressed and others dispersed. Perhaps the lesser rebels were unwilling to resist royal authority and thus make themselves into traitors. Exeter had taken sanctuary at Westminster by 8 June, whence he was removed on 23 July to Salisbury's custody at Pontefract; Egremont disappeared. Between 15 and 26 June York and Warwick sat in judgement at York on the Percy–Neville feud and Exeter's rebellion, taking a systematically anti-Percy line. Unlike sessions after Dartford, which sought to minimize a genuine rebellion, indictments in this case sought to maximize the offence. York and Warwick had moved on by 1 July to Derby to hold sessions on the Derbyshire disturbances.[32]

29   This interprets KB 9/149/4/27, which is discussed in Storey, *Lancaster*, 124–32; Griffiths, *King & Country*, 344–6; T. B. Pugh, 'Richard Duke of York and the Rebellion of Henry, Duke of Exeter in May 1454', *HR* lxiii (1990), 248–62; Payling, 'Ampthill Dispute', 900–2.
30   C. Rawcliffe, 'Richard, Duke of York, the King's "Obeisant" Liegeman: A New Source for the Protectorates of 1454 and 1455', *HR* lx (1987), 238–9, as corrected by Pugh, 'Exeter's Rebellion', 256; cf. also Griffiths, *Henry VI*, 765n (125).
31   Griffiths, *King & Country*, 342.
32   Griffiths, *King & Country*, 350; *Henry VI*, 738; Storey, *Lancaster*, 146–7; KB 9/11 & 12; see also *York City Chamberlain's Account Rolls*, ed. R. B. Dobson (Surtees Soc. cxlii, 1980), 94–5.

Meantime the great officers Salisbury and Worcester conducted affairs in London, including the early stages of a great council. York and Warwick arrived late and left early. Back at York for sessions on 3 August, Warwick was at Middleham on the 20th, probably with his father, who carried the great seal with him to Middleham, Sheriff Hutton and Barnard Castle throughout August and September.[33] Both presumably returned to Westminster for York's great council in late October. Both were present on 13 November to approve a new ordinance for the royal household.[34]

Whatever else York's campaign in the North achieved, it did not bring peace. The sessions if anything inflamed the Percies. Chancellor and councillors were alarmed by the disturbances. The climax was another skirmish about 1 November, when Egremont was captured by Warwick's younger brothers at Stamford Bridge near York. Arraigned at York on 4 November, he was sentenced to punitive damages to the Nevilles that he could never hope to pay.[35] As Cromwell had recovered Ampthill once again and Warwick the exchequer chamberlainship, all the feuds had been settled in favour of York's allies. Justice, as always, was less important than order.

5.2   The First Battle of St Albans 1455

York was protector during the pleasure of a king who, at his appointment, could express neither pleasure nor any other sentiment. The king's malady proved not to be permanent. He recovered his faculties in the winter of 1454–5 and no longer required a protector. Having signed his last recorded council minute on 30 December, York left office in late January, probably unwillingly. Why else should he have insisted that more than the king's will was needed to terminate his second protectorate? Somerset may have been freed on 20 January and the removal of Exeter from Pontefract to Wallingford was ordered on 3 February. The strict conditions including exclusion from the royal presence that were attached to Somerset's formal release on bail on 5 February were relaxed at another great council at Greenwich on 4 March. Somerset reported that he had been imprisoned for a year and ten weeks 'without any reasonable Ground or laweful Processe' and declared his willingness to 'Answer and do all thyng that a trewe Knight owith to do according to Law and Knighthood': an invitation to trial by battle that neither York nor Norfolk took up! To this the king responded by recognizing 'his true and feithfull liegeaunce', 'willing it were known and understood that he so taketh him'. Henry intended this to be the last word on the subject. Henceforth York, who was present, could not legitimately charge Somerset with treason. Somerset was restored as captain of Calais and apparently resumed his central role in royal decision-making.[36] Any remaining issues

33   KB 9/149/1/27; *Paston L & P* ii. 100; Pollard, *North-Eastern England*, 260.
34   *POPC* vi. 233.
35   Griffiths, *King & Country*, 353–4.
36   Griffiths, *Henry VI*, 739–40; *Foedera*, v. i. 61–2; *Benet's Chron.* 212–13.

between him and York were again regarded as private and were to be settled by arbitration by 20 June. Both dukes promised under bonds of 20,000 marks (£13,666.33) to keep the peace towards each other pending the award.[37] Salisbury was replaced as chancellor on 7 March by Archbishop Bourchier and Worcester as treasurer by Wiltshire on the 16th. Cromwell ceased to be chamberlain of the household about the same time.

Historians have been highly critical of Henry's actions in these months, which threatened York and his Neville allies with ruin. To deprive Salisbury of the constableship of Portchester was victimization. The acquittal of Somerset was a 'rebuff' and gave 'the direct lie' to Norfolk. It was in any case unwise. A neutral figure like Buckingham should have been preferred as principal councillor. Henry was indecisive, ambivalent, dilatory and lethargic. His actions forced the Yorkists into a pre-emptive strike: they pointed the way directly to the first battle of St Albans.[38]

These judgements are unfair on Henry VI. Perhaps he was ungrateful to York for his services whilst he himself was incapacitated. An adult king needed no protector and was entitled to rule. He must have been astonished to find incarcerated the two dukes most closely related to the royal house. He was bound to reiterate his earlier satisfaction with Somerset's loyalty. Decisions that overturned his own were bound to be abrogated and officials who disobeyed him were liable to dismissal. Neither York, who *may* have resigned because of the release of Somerset, nor Salisbury, who *may* have left because of that of Exeter, could legitimately thwart the king's will. Moreover the king's rapid intervention in Somerset's case and his determination to settle any remaining issues contrast favourably with Somerset's lengthy imprisonment and repeated adjournments during York's protectorate. Remember that Norfolk had found no consensus among the Lords against Somerset. As he did not attend the crucial meetings affecting Somerset, his continued objections and rejection of the king's decision were decidedly unreasonable. It was one of the essential functions of a king to impose peace on his greatest subjects. Henry's decisions were measured and moderate. He acted not of his own arbitrary will, but with an impressive display of public consultation and consent, meeting a series of great councils at Westminster on 4 February, at Greenwich on 4 March, perhaps another at Westminster on 14–18 February, to which the Yorkist lords allegedly were not invited, and, prospectively, a fuller assembly with county representatives at Leicester on 21 May.

Historians have attached great significance to the Leicester venue as one where Henry VI was stronger than York and have seen his choice as anticipating his withdrawal from London to the Midlands from 1456. Admittedly Leicester was a centre of the Lancastrian estates, but Henry was already partial to locations

---

37 *Foedera* v.i. 61–2.
38 Storey, *Lancaster*, 159–61; Wolffe, *Henry VI*, 286; Griffiths, *Henry VI*, 239–41; Johnson, *York*, 153–5. Unless otherwise stated the rest of this section is based on C. A. J. Armstrong, 'Politics and the Battle of St Albans, 1455', *England, France & Burgundy in the 15th Century* (1983), 1–72.

outside London (e.g. Reading) and especially in the Midlands, where Leicester and Coventry had already hosted great councils and parliamentary sessions. If the Leicester great council was to feature the final settlement of York with Somerset on the declaration of the arbitration award, it was not likely to repeat York's public humiliation at Dartford, still less his destruction. We know better of arbitration than that. A formal public reconciliation like the Loveday of 1458 was far more likely. In return for the dismissal of his charges against Somerset, York would be protected from punishment, vengeance and damages to Somerset for his sufferings over the past eighteen months.

York may possibly have believed the language of common profit that he uttered in 1455, but it was new to the Nevilles, whose reasons for originally joining him and for remaining with him were essentially personal. It was not the public good that prompted the duke and earls to obstruct Henry's full resumption of power and the release of the two dukes. York wanted government for himself. It is doubtful whether any other substitute for Somerset could have satisfied him: subsequent favourites were also opposed. The two Neville earls had committed themselves more than any other magnates to the protectorate and stood to lose most, not least because they had exploited their opportunities to their personal advantage and the disadvantage of others. They could not withdraw from politics without repercussions. They saw the two Lancastrian dukes as their enemies and had given them good cause to become such. If Exeter was not important in any area significant to the Nevilles, his allies the Percies were. Any reinvestigation of the Percy–Neville feud was bound to be less favourable to the Nevilles than the judicial sessions of the previous year. Somerset could reasonably be expected in time to reopen both the Beauchamp and Despenser disputes. They had grounds for concern, but not alarm. They were wrong to reject the king's decisions and to reopen issues yet again that he had closed. They were even more blameworthy in resorting to force, particularly to force against the king, which transgressed the fundamental rules of political behaviour and constituted treason. And they also deliberately rejected the ties of kinship that bound them to their cousin the king, the brothers, brothers-in-law, uncles, nephews and cousins at court.

The preliminaries to this coup are not documented by judicial records because the rebels won. There were no judicial sessions. The precise form that they took was determined by the summons of the Leicester council on 16–17 April. After receipt of their writs considerable pre-planning was required. Between 3,000 and 7,000 were deployed at St Albans by three magnates, none of them particularly powerful in that region; they were also supplied, since no looting or foraging is reported. Very little is known of the composition of this force. One important element consisted of the borderers or 'marchmen' observed by the chroniclers: 600 northerners led by Salisbury's retainer Sir Robert Ogle of Bothal (Northumb.) played a key role.[39] As in 1450, 1452 and 1460, York most probably called out his Welsh retainers: Lord Grey of Powys may have been in his con-

39   *PL* iii. 32.

tingent. Warwick was also powerful in Wales. At the council on 11 February, Warwick was absent on 4 March. He was at Warwick on 12 April and 17 May and recruited there.[40] Humphrey Stafford of Grafton, as in 1450, was probably one of his men. Since York, Salisbury and Warwick were at Royston (Herts.) on 20 May and at Salisbury's town of Ware (Herts.) next day, their contingents cannot have met up significantly earlier, if they did at all. Possibly the various retinues, as opposed to their lords, were only combined at St Albans on the eve or day of the battle.

The first record that we have of the government's response to these manoeuvres is an urgent summons sent to Coventry on 18 May to send a contingent to St Albans; other letters were surely sent simultaneously to the offending lords. Privy seal letters probably preceded those under the great seal ordered on 19 May, which restricted York to a company of 200 and Norfolk, Salisbury and Warwick to 160 each. Presumably all these were preceded by the deputation of the Earl of Worcester, Bishop Boulers, and the prior of St John of Jerusalem, who were sent to summon them – a clear sign that they were known to be disaffected – and who were apparently detained by York to maintain secrecy about his movements and intentions. Perhaps because of these disturbances, the king's departure for Leicester was delayed until 21 May, the day the council was due to commence. Doubtless some lords absent from the battle were already at Leicester; others were not far from St Albans when the battle began. With Henry on leaving London were the Bishop of Carlisle, thirteen lay peers, and about 2,000 others. He overnighted at Watford. It would have been possible at this point for him to withdraw and thus avoid encountering the Yorkists, temporarily at least, as Somerset recommended. Instead, on the advice of Buckingham, to whom he had transferred command, he proceeded to St Albans, where – to his surprise – the Yorkists were already waiting for him. That was on Thursday 22 May at 7 a.m.

There followed three hours of negotiation via heralds and perhaps also by letter, which were conducted on the king's side by Buckingham and for the rebels by York alone. These apparently began with instructions via Somerset and Buckingham to York to disband and withdraw, which York did not obey, supposedly because they did not come directly from the king. Failing this, Buckingham asked him at least to withdraw to Barnet or Hatfield and to nominate 'a man of estate' – a magnate – to undertake substantive negotiations. York wanted a reply to petitions that had been delivered earlier by Salisbury's brother Lord Fauconberg. When it emerged that the king had not seen them, possibly because they had only been delivered in the early hours of the morning by York's confessor, Buckingham agreed to show them to the king and obtain his reply. York insisted on a response, which probably had to be favourable, without further delay and declared himself unwilling to accept promises. Henry did not answer, which probably means that he reserved his response to articles that he

40 BL Royal MS 17Bxlvii, f. 165v; Chatwin, 'Documents of St Mary's Church, Warwick', 4–5; Worcs. CRO 989/11 m. 1.

had only just received: 'Le Roy sadvisera' in parliamentary jargon. Henry revealed once again his refusal to be coerced. York was being unreasonable; he was trying to dictate terms by force. The victors' official version of events, the *Stow Relation*, states that they were threatened with the penalties of treason – death and forfeiture – if they attacked. This was not strictly accurate, but Buckingham's careful reminder that the king was present and his banner displayed amounted to the same thing. Buckingham stated that those with him were engaged in defending the king not any particular individual, e.g. Somerset. He invoked his kinship to all the parties and in particular to his nephew Norfolk, whom he supposed to be present and the one most susceptible to persuasion. At this point, the Yorkists attacked; Warwick may have attacked before the negotiations were over.

The king's best protection against attack was his special semi-divine status: for anyone to attempt to kill or even speak against him or to confront him with his banner displayed was treason. Henry was present and his standard was flying at St Albans: though, hidden behind the houses, it may not have been visible to many. Failing that protection, the two sides were ill-matched. All sources agree that the king's force was smaller, about 2,000. It was made up of people who had not expected to fight and were probably not equipped for it, including domestic servants and chancery clerks. York's force was larger, expecting and equipped to fight, and included, the sources testify, substantial numbers of hardened borderers accustomed to war. The comments of Abbot Whetehamstede of St Albans on the martial qualities of the northerners and the effeminacy (or civilian character?) of the king's forces has therefore some validity. Evidently the Yorkists also included archers and artillery that could injure from afar: the king and the more important of the wounded were hit by arrows in the face, shoulders and hand, Buckingham no less than three times. The royal force was on the defensive, in the town, which was not walled or gated. It was strung out along the main North–South thoroughfare, in Holiwell Street to the south, the market place in the centre, and St Peter's Street to the north; the king and his banner were in Holiwell Street. Failing to force an entry down St Peter's Street, which was barricaded and defended by Lord Clifford, Warwick led an attack across the gardens through the houses in Holiwell Street, blowing trumpets and shouting his warcry 'À Warwick! À Warwick!' This caused enough distraction for the barriers across the street to be penetrated. A key episode was Ogle's capture of the market square,[41] which punched a hole through the royal army and divided it into two halves. Somerset was killed, fighting valiantly, together with Northumberland, Clifford, and about fifty others. The king, Buckingham, Stafford, Dorset and Sudeley were slightly wounded. The possessions of the defeated were looted. 'And when the said lordes were dead, the battle was ceased', observes a Yorkist source. Presumably many of the royal party escaped over the fields to the west. His banner abandoned and himself slightly wounded in the neck, Henry took refuge in the abbey itself, where he was found by the Yorkists.

41   *PL* iii. 30.

The events are clear enough, but it is not easy now to identify precisely what York intended. We have neither his 'peticions, requestes et demandes', nor any of the inquiries, warnings, summonses, commands and prohibitions that the government surely sent him in the days before the battle. What we do have is the rebels' point of view – or, rather, their successive points of view[42] – in the form either of their propaganda or sources based upon it, which were designed to conceal the truth. Furthermore the battle itself, which York honestly hoped to avoid, changed the situation and made redundant demands, arguments and evidence that had applied earlier. What we have are principally explanations and justifications constructed by the victors with the benefit of hindsight. Their view prevailed. No Lancastrian version made its way into the chronicles.

Any insurrection was treasonable in fifteenth-century terms, however restricted its objectives. This particular rebellion had limited aims. York and the Neville earls did not seek to depose Henry VI; their consistent protestations to this effect may be accepted. At all stages they pronounced themselves his true liegemen. What they were engaged in was a coup d'état, much like those of 1450 and 1452, that were designed to change the king's government, his principal counsellors, especially Somerset, but also others unnamed. Perhaps there was a list as in 1450, on which from later evidence it seems likely that the Nevilles' northern enemies Lord Clifford and Sir Ralph Percy were included. To ensure they did retire, they were to be destroyed, executed;[43] in Somerset's case probably by convicting him of the treason alleged by Norfolk, as *Benet's Chronicle* explicitly states.[44] Somerset, remember, was brother-in-law to Warwick and cousin to them all. The rebels were able to persuade themselves that they were fighting Somerset not the king. We can be sure that the rebel articles contained more than this, but not what else they sought. Probably the expectation was that York and his principal allies would take Somerset's place, in pursuit of Henry's 'plesire, the honour, prosperite and wele of oure said Soveraine Lord, his said land and people' and 'the good publique, restfull and politique rule and governaunce' of the same. Only thus, surely, could they have restored their advantage over their private rivals? Ideally these aims were to be achieved peacefully, those offending being surrendered to them and perhaps even remanded pending a form of trial, which was to be conceded by the king to avoid 'any inconvenience' – a euphemism for the violent achievement of the same ends with the overwhelming armed force that they had accumulated. If such inconvenience ensued, it would be the fault of those about the king.[45] The lengthy negotiations on the morning of the battle were intended by York to render the use of force unnecessary.

---

42 I intend to discuss this and what follows at greater length elsewhere.
43 *PL* iii. 29.
44 *Benet's Chron.* 213; see also Whetehamstede, i. 167; T. Gascoigne, *Loci e Libro Veritatum*, ed. J. E. T. Rogers (Oxford, 1891), 203–4.
45 In 1459 the Yorkists later claimed such mortality to be 'casual' or accidental and not their fault.

The ideology, objectives and strategy of 1455 were thus very similar to York's earlier coups, but the differences are much more striking. This time their intentions were not advertised by appealing to public opinion, but were concealed, as they sought to take the government by surprise and thus avert effective countermeasures. It was not popular supporters, but their own retainers, who supplied them with the necessary manpower. The propaganda that they did distribute – their letters to the chancellor and king of 20–21 May – were designed not to inform, but to deceive. In them the three magnates asserted their loyalty, their commitment to the welfare of the king and the commonweal, their intention to come to the king and attend on his person to the Leicester council. They explained that they needed their forces as protection for themselves against their enemies about the king and they warned him against taking seriously those enemies about who doubted their intentions.[46] These letters were designed to reassure – wrongly – that they did not intend violence or treason: not just the king, government and perhaps potential opponents, who might otherwise have opposed them, but perhaps also their supporters too, who had no desire to fight the king or to commit treason. These assurances were obviously untrue. They need to be set alongside other instances of straightforward dishonesty: their reuse of the strange notion of loyalty that York had renounced in 1452, when his oath had specifically excluded the 'weye of feete'; and York's bond to keep the peace towards Somerset. In the first case he pleaded duress and doubtless would have done the same in the second. The success of such letters is perhaps shown in the fact that Buckingham, right up to the moment of battle, could not believe that York actually meant to attack and that some of the royal troops, who evidently shared his belief, had not put their armour on. Finally these two letters contained a threat of violence more muted than on previous occasions, when it had not been implemented, but much clearer on the morning of the battle. This time the king was to exercise no veto over legislation as in 1450, nor could he be sure as at Dartford that his opponents would not dare to fight him.

The crucial change from a semi-constitutional protest to a determined and decisive exercise in force has been credited to the Neville earls, most probably correctly. They had already shed blood in the North. The management of the whole campaign was much more direct than on York's previous coups. The Nevilles alone were prepared to couple their names with York both in his letters, unlike any other lords in his company or sympathizers like Norfolk, and in reports on the battle from which the names of all other participants were omitted. They attached their names to a tradition of protest associated with York that was potentially treasonable the moment they called out their men. The rebels of 1455 were more ruthless than York had ever been. They were the first to resort to violence and to the deliberate elimination of opponents. They attacked even when the king's banner was displayed. Their reckless reliance on ordnance and archery, which they wisely omitted from their official narrative, reveals them willing to risk killing Henry himself; far from being disastrous, this would have made Prince Edward king and ensured a prolonged protectorate that they could

46   *PL* iii. 24.

dominate. If York wished to dispose of Somerset, so did they. It was they who had an interest in the deaths of Northumberland and Clifford, if these were by design and not mere accidents. They surely suggested blaming Sir Ralph Percy for what happened. From Warwick's angle, the risks were justified by the results.

5.3   York's Second Protectorate 1455–6

The *Dijon Relation* reports that York removed the king to safety in the abbey before the fighting was over.[47] Duke and earls then went to the king, knelt before him, protested that they were humble liegemen, declared that they had been fighting not him but traitors, and had never intended to hurt him personally. They begged for grace and forgiveness. Henry was a prisoner in their power and had no choice. He accepted them as true liegemen and asked them to stop fighting, at which York proclaimed, in the king's name, that fighting should cease. It did. 'Thanks be to God', wrote the Yorkist narrator. Next morning they all travelled together to London, arriving in the evening, and processed through the city, Salisbury and York on either hand of the king and Warwick bearing his sword point uppermost in front. Henry stayed at the bishop's palace with all due solemnity and agreed to hold a parliament on 9 July.

The first Yorkist narrative, the Stonor version of the *Stow Relation*, may have been composed on Saturday 26 May or even Friday 25th for public distribution. Already concerned with reconciliation, it seeks to present an interpretation of the battle at variance with what actually happened. The emphasis was on the loyalty throughout of the Yorkists, from their initial protestations through to the ceremonies just described. They had requested the punishment of those unnamed who had deserved death but the king had declined to do justice. The battle itself occurred because they had to fight when the king 'in his own words' threatened them with forfeiture for treason and they were desperate: a clumsy explanation, but the best they could manage in a short time. For, with Somerset dead, there was no need to mention the long-term causes or issues that were divisive, like their demand for his execution or their own articles. The *Stow Relation* did not even mention the negotiations, which indicated that bloodshed could have been averted, or that messages had been concealed from the king, which would have required criticism of Buckingham with whom they hoped to deal. Relatively little is made of the battle, which is not actually well-recorded: there are no credits for distinguished conduct and no specific reference to the Yorkists' own casualties. Still frightened of treason charges, the *Stow Relation* avoided identifying even the three Yorkist commanders in the earliest Stonor version.[48] Wider approval was foreshadowed in the promise of a parliament, which was summoned on Saturday 26 May: the earliest possible opportunity. The regime's legitimacy was reinforced by the royal crown-wearing in St Paul's on Sunday, Whitsunday. It

47   The next six paras are based on Armstrong, 'Politics and the Battle of St Albans', 1–72.
48   *PL* iii. 25–9.

was important to stress that Henry was still an effective king and that no usurpation of his power had occurred. Anxious that only their version of events should be current, the new regime issued a proclamation forbidding discussion of the battle.

Updated versions of the *Stow Relation* were available over the weekend and early the next week. Already by Sunday, however, plans were changing. First of all, a decision was made to place the blame on particular individuals, on the dead Clifford and the living Sir Ralph Percy, Sir Thomas Tresham, Thomas Thorpe and William Joseph, as stated in the *Fastolf Relation* of 27 May.[49] *Pace* Armstrong, they were not selected because they did not matter. The presence of Clifford and Percy can be explained by their role in the Percy–Neville feud: they were there at the Nevilles' behest. Thorpe had prepared articles against the duke in 1454: he was to have no further opportunity. It had been Thorpe, Tresham and Joseph who had proposed a guard at Windsor to safeguard the insane king. The pursuit of Thorpe and Tresham into the second and perhaps third session of the ensuing parliament by the Yorkists, who were determined on their utter ruin, demonstrates that it was not their *insignificance* that prompted their choice. They were courtiers committed to Somerset, suspicious of York, and *dangerous*. They may therefore have been the survivors of a list of 'traitors' and enemies in the articles York submitted before the fighting who were actually at the battle. Here the *Fastolf Relation* anticipates the *Parliamentary Pardon* enacted in July that blamed the whole affair on Somerset, Thorpe and Joseph, who had misled the king – who accepted that he was deceived – and caused him to attack the Yorkists. The act alleged that they had earlier concealed from him the letters of 20–21 May and thus the 'trouthe' of the Yorkist lords, who were declared not to be at fault for any of the events.[50]

The Yorkist lords could not condemn those who defended the king in line with their allegiance. In the parallel instance at Dartford at this very same session, they cancelled the penalties against those who rebelled, but had also to recognize that those on the king's side (like Salisbury and Warwick) had acted only 'as thaire duetee was by thaire allegiaunce'.[51] Placing the blame on three scapegoats, who concealed the loyal intentions of the Yorkists, enabled both those who rebelled and those who fought for the king to be right: an essential requirement if wounds were to be healed and the Yorkists were to be accepted back as loyal subjects by their peers.

To emphasise the point, to continue the process of reconciliation, and to prevent any coups against themselves, a declared objective of the new parliament was

> to sette a parfite love and rest amonge the Lordes of this lande to thentent
> that they mowe drawe directly togidres in oon union and accorde, in that

49   *Vale's Bk.* 190–3; *PL* iii. 25–30.
50   *RP* v. 280–3.
51   *RP* v. 329.

they may be sowne to the honour, prosperite and welfare of the Kyng oure Soveraine Lord, and the politique and restful rule and governaunce of this lande and people.

Hence the formal renewals of allegiance sworn by every peer present; those absent were to swear later.[52] The Yorkists needed to heal the breaches in unity that they had themselves created and to harness for their leadership the respect due to the king. Hence they tried to come to terms with Buckingham, Wiltshire, the new Lord Clifford, and probably the new Duke of Somerset. On 31 July there was a general pardon to which even Exeter, Egremont and Sir Richard Percy were admitted.[53]

The *Stow Relation* made no popular appeal. However misguided, popular opinion had been dangerously hostile to Somerset and still viewed York most favourably, because, one chronicle says, he loved the people. Probably, therefore, York deliberately associated himself with Humphrey Duke of Gloucester ahead of the opening of parliament, which rehabilitated the duke and declared that he had died a true liegeman.[54] The parallel with York himself was obvious. When parliament opened, there was a renewed emphasis on reform, eight topics being identified for action. One was the peace among lords treated above. Another four dealt with the finances of the household, the defence of Calais and Berwick, the keeping of the seas, and disorder in Wales. On each of these committees of peers were established to prepare legislation.[55] The Commons were encouraged to prepare reforming proposals.

Up to a point, the Yorkists were successful. Devon, Fauconberg and Berners, who had been with the king at St Albans, joined them also at once, yet the Yorkists remained a mere fraction of the Lords, who had effectively rejected the views of the majority by attacking the king when accompanied by a quarter of the lay peerage. They themselves were vulnerable to counterattack by the other peers and their armed retinues, at Leicester or approaching St Albans. They had created new enemies by their victory – the Percies, Beauforts and Cliffords now had extra grounds to be vengeful! – and their old enemies had not all disappeared. In July and again in February 1456 they feared assassination or a counter-coup, though fortunately, as was conceded on the second occasion, there was no obvious leader to undertake it. It was perhaps for this reason that in June they moved the king, queen and prince away from London to Hertford Castle; it was probably on this occasion that Queen Margaret went hunting in Salisbury's park at Ware. York lodged at Ware friary, Salisbury at Sir Andrew Ogard's splendid Rye House, and Warwick himself at Sir William Oldhall's new mansion at Hunsdon.[56] Nobody attempted a counter-coup. Political debate was postponed

---

52   *RP* v. 279–80, 283–4.
53   Johnson, *York*, 165–6.
54   *RP* v. 335.
55   *RP* v. 279–8.
56   *PL* ii. 32; *Letters of Queen Margaret of Anjou*, ed. C. Munro (Camden Soc., lxxxvi, 1863).

to the new parliament, where an impressive display of legitimacy and unity was staged. It was Henry VI who opened parliament in person (9 July), received oaths of allegiance in person (24 July), and prorogued parliament (31 July).[57] The Commons, too, were certainly more inclined to reform and less favourable to the court than their immediate predecessors.

But the victors of St Albans did not get all their own way. They found the conditions set by Wiltshire to be unacceptable. Henry, the new Duke of Somerset and still a minor, who had been badly wounded at St Albans, was not conciliatory, and was placed in Warwick's custody. Exeter was imprisoned at Wallingford and Dudley in the Tower.[58] No chances were taken. Six of the triers of petitions for England, Ireland, Wales and Scotland were their adherents: York himself, Salisbury, Warwick, Viscount Bourchier, Fauconberg and Cromwell; Pembroke was the only exception. Little more than half of the peerage attended. None of the Yorkists were triers of Gascon petitions,[59] which were less politically sensitive. In this context, therefore, it was unfortunate that the most striking event of the session, on 17 July, was a furious row in the king's presence between Warwick and Cromwell:

> in somuch as the Lord Cromwell wold have excused hym self of all the steryng or moevyng of the male journey of Seynt Albones; of the which excuse makyng, my Lord Warrewikke had knolege, and in haste wasse with the Kyng, and sware by his oath that the Lord Cromwell said not trouth but that he was begynner of all that journey at Seynt Albones; and so betwene my said ij. Lords of Warrewikke and Cromwell ther is that at this day grete grugyng, in somoch as the Erle of Shrouesbury hath loged hym at the hospitall of Seynt James, beside the Mewes, be the Lord Cromwell desire, for his sauf gard.[60]

At the very least, given the continuing effort to place responsibility on Somerset, Thorpe and Joseph, this was unfortunate. It is also difficult to see how it could be true, unless Warwick was harking back to Cromwell's breach of unity among the Lords in 1450 that opened the way to Suffolk's impeachment and the disasters that followed. It is not clear whether it is for this reason, ten days into the session, that the men of York, Salisbury and Warwick were going armed and in armour and that the three lords came to Westminster and went home daily in barges full of weapons. Presumably they feared an ambush. It is not clear from whom. All others were ordered to go unarmed. The Yorkists did get their *Parliamentary Pardon* enacted, though even among the Commons 'mony a man groged full sore nowe it is passed'.[61] They also secured acts annulling the con-

---

57   *RP* v. 278, 282–3.
58   Griffiths, *Henry VI*, 747; *PL* iii. 33.
59   *RP* v. 279; J. S. Roskell, 'The Problem of the Attendance of Lords at Medieval Parliaments', *Parliament and Politics in Late Medieval England* (3 vols, 1981–3), i. II. 194.
60   *PL* iii. 44.
61   Ibid.

victions of Oldhall and Devereux, both retainers of Warwick as well as York, and the resumption against those at Dartford, and the passage of a further act compensating Thomas Young for his imprisonment in 1451. Following the prorogation, a great council was continued until at least 6 August.

Scarcely had the battle ceased on 22 May when the fruits of victory were being distributed. These were principally Somerset's offices. York took the constable-ship of England. This time it was Warwick who was appointed captain of Calais, by Whitsunday itself, indenting at the August great council. Like York, he had to wait to get in, until April 1456. Wisely he secured parliamentary recognition that he was not liable for its loss before he secured effective possession.[62] His other principal gain was in Wales, where on 31 May he was appointed steward and constable of both Monmouth and the Three Castles (Grosmont, Skenfrith and White Castle).[63] Taken alongside a proviso reserving the reversion of St Briavels and the Forest of Dean on the deaths of lords Sudeley and Beauchamp of Powicke, this grant consolidated his power in the triangle marked by Glamorgan, Abergavenny and Tewkesbury. The lordship and hundred of Barton by Bristol were also exempted from resumption.[64] In redemption of the promise of the previous year, Warwick's youngest brother George, though under age, was appointed to the bishopric of Exeter. Salisbury became chief steward of the North Parts of the duchy of Lancaster, but the loss of his £80 annuity from the Carlisle feefarm and of the castle, honour and feefarm of Richmond was confirmed.[65] That they lost anything suggests that the desire for economy was sincere.

Rewards were almost entirely confined to the relatively small group of Nevilles and Bourchiers on whom York could rely. Norfolk was nowhere to be seen. Devon, initially associated with the victors, rapidly became an embarrassment that required the government's firmest actions. There was little more committed support for the new regime than for York's first protectorate. Archbishop Bourchier was retained as chancellor and his brother Viscount Bourchier was appointed treasurer. In addition to Salisbury, it was now Warwick himself and Salisbury's next brother Fauconberg who were among the most assiduous councillors.[66] After his sojourn at Hunsdon, Warwick was at his castle of Hanley in Worcestershire on 28 June, returning to attend council at Westminster on 4 July and the opening of parliament on 9 July. He was again a trier of petitions, sitting on York's committees on Calais and Berwick and, as a marcher lord, on Wales. He took the oath on 24 July and attended the great council at Westminster on 6 August. He was at Hanley once again on 2 September.[67] No doubt it was as

62   *Paston L & P* ii. 116; G. L. Harriss, 'The Struggle for Calais: An Aspect of the Struggle between Lancaster and York', *EHR* lxxv (1960), 41, 44, 46; *RP* v. 309, 341.
63   R. Somerville, *History of the Duchy of Lancaster*, i (1953), 648.
64   *RP* v. 309.
65   Ibid.
66   Virgoe, 'Composition', 153.
67   Worcs. RO 989/111 m. 1; E 28/86/22; *RP* v. 278–80, 282–3; *Rous Roll*, no. 62; *POPC* vi. 257; E 28/86/34.

captain of Calais that he was consulted about negotiations with the French Duke of Alençon.[68] On 28 October he, York and Salisbury were to fetch from Hertford to London the king, who was sick again.[69] Warwick was at the council on 10 November that appointed York as lieutenant to reopen parliament next day, on the 12th and the 15th, sat on the committee to settle the details of York's powers as protector, and attended the royal council at Westminster almost daily both before and after the dissolution on 13 December. He was probably one of the lords spiritual and temporal that were vetting provisos of resumption at this time.[70]

During the first session of parliament, from 9–31 July, the Yorkist lords were concerned primarily to exculpate themselves for their rebellion and to secure acceptance of their authority. Controversial legislation was introduced but apparently not pressed. During the second session, it seems, they wanted both to consolidate their power and to penalize their opponents. To achieve these ends they needed more authority, for York to be protector once again. They had not succeeded in overawing their fellow peers, nor indeed the king. Whilst it is not altogether clear when such events occurred, a considerable number of radical Commons bills approved by the Lords were vetoed by the king. These included the initial bill to destroy Thorpe and Tresham by resuming their grants and imprisoning them for twelve years. It was therefore fortunate that the king was ill again, though it is clear that he was never as incapacitated as before; he insisted on being informed about matters affecting 'the honour, wurship and suertee of his moost noble persone'.[71] On 12 November 1455, the day after the reopening of parliament, there was a Commons delegation to the Lords led not by the Speaker, but by Walter Burley, a retainer of the duke. He asked that an able person be appointed protector, both as the addressee of petitions and to deal with the revival of private war in the West Country between Devon and Bonville. The Lords agreed to consider it. Three days later Burley returned to repeat his request and again on the 17th. The Lords reluctantly accepted that a protector was needed, each being asked individually, and agreed that York was the only possible candidate. The limitations to his power were as before. He was to rule with the council until Prince Edward was of age. York agreed to the same conditions as before, adding an additional salary, a down-payment, and, potentially crucially, the condition that he could be dismissed only by the king in parliament.[72] This could have given him greater security of tenure had King Henry recovered when parliament was not in session.

Having failed to secure the destruction of Thorpe and Joseph at the previous session, the Yorkist lords introduced two further bills to similar effect. Their fees and annuities were indeed resumed. First among the articles presented to the first

68 Johnson, *York*, 171.
69 *Paston L & P* ii. 127.
70 *RP* v. 287; *POPC* vi. 267, 272, 274–5, 278, 285; E 28/86/8–10, 12–13, 16, 18, 23–4, 26–9; B. P. Wolffe, *The Royal Demesne in English History* (1973), 139.
71 *RP* v. 290.
72 *RP* v. 284–7.

session and passed to a committee was 'to establish an ordinate and substantial for the king's honourable household'. Hence a new appropriation of revenues to it and hence also the draconian act of resumption. Despite heavy taxation, Henry VI was 'indetted in such outrageous somez, as be not easy to be paid' and yet had an unimpressive household to the diminishing of his worship and prosperity. A further act of resumption was the answer. This owed much to financial considerations, but it also served political purposes. Even as introduced in July, before it was sharpened by the Commons, the bill was draconian. It sought not only to remove many fees and annuities of courtiers – at last the effective action that York had wanted for so long! – but to curb the royal family as well. The bill vesting the Prince of Wales with his estates restricted his income to that appropriate to a child, the rest being assigned to the royal household. The bill placed a ceiling on the income of the queen. It resumed the lands still in trust for the performance of the wills of Henry IV and Henry V, the endowments of King Henry's two colleges of Eton and King's, and, particularly vindictive, the lands of the king's two Tudor half-brothers. Any provisos were to be approved by the Commons themselves.[73]

As with the trial of Somerset, York had once again gone too far for the Lords, who objected strongly to the bill of resumption. King Henry had recovered by 9 February, when the third session of parliament opened. York and Warwick appeared with 300 men, 'all jakked and in brigantiens', but for which, it was rumoured, the duke would have been dismissed. The connection between him and the resumption was clear. 'The resumpsion, men truste, shall forthe, and my Lordes of Yorkes first power of protectorship stande, and elles not, &c.' No other magnate had attended the opening.[74] If York had ever enjoyed general support, he had lost it. He pressed for the resumption and, too fearful to stop it, the Lords appealed to the king as the sole authority superior to the duke and able to prevent it. That was on 25 February, when the king formally entered parliament and took back his authority in exact accordance with the terms of York's appointment.[75] He rejected the oversight of the Commons over provisos, allowed provisos to the duchy of Lancaster trusts, the queen, his brothers and many other individuals. It was probably also he who rejected a second act imprisoning and fining Thorpe and Joseph and a variety of Commons measures resuming grants of franchises and wardships and taking action against oppressive royal officers.

73   *RP* v. 300–20. This is discussed in Wolffe, *Henry VI*, 297–8.
75   *RP* v. 321.

6

Countdown to
Civil War 1456–9

6.1 Towards Reconciliation

York's Second Protectorate collapsed. It had required pressure from the Commons to impose it even on those lords willing to attend parliament and his exercise of power thereafter had been partisan and unacceptable. Rejection by the Lords exposed the Yorkists as a faction and denied their claim to political consensus. They were never to recover it. They were no longer needed. There was no Somerset to upset the political equilibrium. Somerset's death indeed removed most of the disruptive issues of the early 1450s: the York–Somerset feud, the pursuit of traitors, and recriminations about the loss of Lancastrian France. International pressures had diminished. England lacked the financial and military resources for reconquest. The threat of a French invasion had receded. The case for reform had been much reduced by changes in personnel and an effective act of resumption. The most acrimonious feuds, between the Percies and Nevilles, over the Warwick inheritance and Ampthill, had been decisively settled. Moreover the resumption of royal rule was much less abrupt and complete. Henry VI was willing to forgive the battle of St Albans at which he himself had been wounded. He retained York's services, no longer as protector, but as chief councillor. He made no immediate change to his ministers. Each Yorkist magnate received small favours from him. He even continued and completed the complex negotiations to quell mutiny in Calais, to defray the enormous arrears in the garrison's wages, to provide for their payment in future, and to admit Warwick as captain. Warwick was free to take up office from April 1456.[1]

Warwick attended council on 2 March 1456, but by 5 May he was at Warwick,

---

1 Harriss, 'Struggle', 44–7. The commissioners included Fauconberg, Sir Edmund Mulsho, Osbert Mountford, Richard Whetehill and John Proud, ibid. 46n.

where he apparently remained until the opening of another great council at Westminster on 7 June attended by York, Salisbury and only one other lay peer. Warwick was there on 3 and 8 July.[2] Thereafter he could have visited Calais.[3] The aggressive posture of James II brought York to Sandal Castle (Yorks.), whence on 26 July he wrote defiantly to the Scottish king, apparently as Henry's representative.[4] Most probably Salisbury as warden of the West March also went northwards. There was nothing suspicious about their departures. Each was attending to his official duties.

Unfortunately this apparent return to normality and to consensus politics was not to last. It was not the fault of the Yorkists. They did not repeat their coup at St Albans. Henry's actions created no legitimate grievances and aroused no fears to justify another pre-emptive strike. Instead he treated the Yorkists as trusted and favoured members of the political nation and even the ruling regime. That this happy situation ceased and that tensions returned was not their fault.

The transformation is usually dated to the king's removal from Westminster to the Midlands in mid-August 1456, a move that became semi-permanent and was accompanied by a reversion to partisan politics. Most modern historians have followed contemporary chroniclers, all Yorkists, in blaming the change on Queen Margaret of Anjou. Now a mature and strong-minded woman, Margaret fomented division. Inevitably she had at heart the interests not just of her husband the king, but also those of their infant son Prince Edward. Her prime objective of protecting and continuing the family dynasty was naturally shared by the royal household and courtiers. After Henry first went mad, in 1454, she had sought the regency for herself, unavailingly. Twice since then the protectorate had been bestowed on York, who had tried to eliminate, curb and dispossess those most committed to her cause, and had not stopped at using force. Not surprisingly Margaret regarded the duke askance. She wanted to limit his influence and identified in his actions malign intentions that perhaps did not exist. 'That the fundamental intention of Margaret . . . was the outright destruction of those who had engaged in treasonable activity by accroaching the royal power', observes Dr Gross, 'there is, of course, no doubt.'[5]

This 'rash and despotic queen . . . carried him [Henry VI] off' to the Midlands about 17 August.[6] She and the prince had been there since May. Henceforth Henry resided at the Lancaster castles of Kenilworth (Warw.) or Leicester or at local religious houses, seldom ventured south, abandoned the regularization of his finances, lived from hand to mouth, and left much of his kingdom to itself. For Dr Wolffe, Henry's move 'marked the end of normal political life'.[7] The

---

2 *Paston L & P* ii. 143, 148; E 28/86/40, 42, 44.

3 Harriss, 'Struggle', 46. Warwick's letter from London to Burford corporation (Oxon.) of 5 Aug. probably belongs to this year, *HMC Var. Coll.* i. 49.

4 Griffiths, *Henry VI*, 772–3. Lancaster herald was sent by king and council to assist him in dealing with James II, E 403/807 m. 8.

5 A. Gross, *The Dissolution of the Lancastrian Kingship* (Stamford, 1996), 47.

6 Wolffe, *Henry VI*, 302.

7 Ibid. 309.

ministry inherited from the protectorate was replaced at the Coventry great council of September/October 1456, when Waynflete and Shrewsbury succeeded the Bourchier brothers as chancellor and treasurer. Using her dominance over king, prince and her own dower, Margaret constructed a regional hegemony in North Wales, the palatinates of Lancaster and Chester, and the North Midlands. Her connection of the white swan reveals her 'prepared, if not eager, for war'. By the autumn of 1456, observes Professor Griffiths, there was a committed regime:[8] committed to the Lancastrian dynasty at its most narrow interpretation, to its sectional benefits rather than the realm as a whole. Margaret could count on the support of such lesser royals as the king's half-brothers, Somerset, Exeter, and even Devon, whose victory over Bonville was allowed to stand and whose heir married the queen's cousin Marie of Maine in 1458.[9]

Such an interpretation made the eventual civil war inevitable.[10] But such judgements depend unduly on hindsight, on the knowledge that civil war *did* eventually break out, and interpret each earlier friction as heightening the tension that exploded into conflict. It follows those chroniclers, predominantly Yorkists, who read back into 1456–8 the circumstances of 1459, when the Yorkist lords were indeed excluded, and of 1461, when Margaret did indeed take charge. Her role in these years should not be interpreted in terms of Stodeley's observation of 1454 without rather more contemporary substantiation than Thomas Gascoigne, whose brief comment is demonstrably wrong in detail.[11] The politics of 1456–9 need not be seen in this way. For two years at least both king and Yorkists were determined to resist any escalation in political conflict. If there were differences, they were resolved or were not allowed to colour the whole political climate. If King Henry did in practice spend much of his time in the Midlands, that was the result not his intention. In September 1457 he returned to Westminster to hold a series of politically charged great councils. He did not remove to the Midlands because London was too turbulent for him to remain – indeed he remained in the London area when problems became acute – and there is no proof at this point that he avoided parliament because it might be hijacked by York. If Margaret was a partisan force in politics, she was not in control. The king was always more than a mere figurehead, more than a puppet, and he was capable of decisive interventions. If he held no parliament, he met regularly with his Lords at a series of great councils. He was not personally hostile to the Yorkists and remained temperamentally inclined towards peace and reconciliation. For tensions and crises to arise there needed to be appropriate occasions. Old grievances revived and new ones emerged.

Old grievances were the backcloth to political events. It had been one of York's considerable successes to quell private feuds, but his achievement was not permanent because his settlements were one-sided and self-interested. Neither the

8   Gross, *Dissolution*, 58; Griffiths, *Henry VI*, 774.
9   Griffiths, *Henry VI*, 802.
10   Storey, *Lancaster*, 177.
11   Gascoigne, *Loci e Libro Veritatum*, 204.

Beauchamp sisters nor George Neville of Bergavenny accepted Warwick's right to the whole of the Beauchamp and Despenser inheritances. Margaret, the second Beauchamp sister, was occupying Drayton Basset on 19 December 1456, when she promised to save harmless Henry Skernard who had delivered £160 'receyued of the lyuelode of the Erldome of Warrewyk the whiche we the said Countesse and our coparcioners claymen to be departed as our enheritances'.[12] Roos, eldest son of her sister Eleanor, was among those who sought to seize Warwick by force.[13] It was to Warwick's advantage that his own brother Thomas held the other chamberlainship of the exchequer with Cromwell's other coheir.[14] Warwick clung on to all the Despenser lands even after George proved his age on 25 July 1457 and his consequent licence to enter on the 30th.[15] The resentment of the Percies and their retainers at their sentences, especially Egremont's punitive fines, were fed by the slow process that brought them all eventually to the court of King's Bench. Egremont himself escaped from prison in November 1456 and remained at large, presumably harboured by his Percy kinsfolk. Such differences may lie behind some of the sporadic violence of these years. They remained latent and were revived in 1459, when opportunity offered.

Far more dangerous were the new grievances that the Yorkists themselves had created. The king may have forgiven them and parliament whitewashed them for St Albans, but others had not and were not to be denied vengeance. The Yorkist victory cost the lives of Somerset, Northumberland and Clifford. The Yorkists denied responsibility, as was necessary to acquit themselves of the imputation of treason, and their attribution of blame dishonoured Somerset and the other victims. Friendly overtures by the Yorkists to the late peers' heirs and to others such as Wiltshire had been rebuffed. The heirs of the dead lords, the new Duke of Somerset, Earl of Northumberland, and Lord Clifford, now wanted revenge for their fathers' deaths. They were not particular whether by constitutional trial or by assassination. They were especially hostile to Warwick. They ignored those Yorkist adherents who had not fought or were not known to have fought in the battle, such as the Bourchiers and Grey of Powys. If York and the Neville earls had wished to pursue their separate political ways, to dissolve what had begun as a temporary alliance of mutual self-interest now it had outlasted its usefulness, their vendetta with the victims of St Albans prevented them. At least until the formal reconciliation of 1458, self-defence preserved the alliance of York, Salisbury and Warwick and served to make it permanent. It was this feud that made normal politics increasingly impossible. And significantly the avengers allied themselves to the court.

A clash between Warwick and Beaumont in May 1456 was probably merely a rumour. More substantial were disturbances in Wales inspired by York during

12 *Sir Christopher Hatton's Book of Seals*, ed. L. C. Loyd and D. M. Stenton (Northants Rec. Soc. xv, 1950), no. 229.
13 Griffiths, *Henry VI*, 809.
14 C 81/1465/1. The other coheir was Humphrey Bourchier, son of Lord Bourchier, E 159/232 recorda Easter 34 Hen. VI rot. 3(3)d.
15 C 139/162/17/1–2; *CPR 1452–61*, 358; E 401/836.

the summer. As protector he had countered the disorders of the notorious Gruffydd ap Nicholas by appointing himself constable of Carmarthen and Aberystwyth in the southern principality. He had been unable to take possession, but had not been officially replaced when Richmond, evidently with royal cognizance, took the offensive against Gruffydd. A private army was despatched from Herefordshire on 10 August 1456 to enforce York's right. It seized Richmond himself, both castles, their archives, and the seal of the chamberlain of South Wales. The commanders were York's long-standing retainers Devereux and Herbert, who now commissioned themselves to hold the great sessions in South Wales: an action which went rather beyond the widest interpretation of York's legal rights. Their subsequent offences extended into the marches. Obviously York was implicated.[16] That the government once again blamed York's agents rather than the duke himself explains the resentful but obscure verses attached to the five dead dogs left outside York's London residence on the night of 19 September.[17]

It may be that it was actually this insurrection immediately preceding it that prompted Henry's departure to the Midlands. No government could ignore a private war on such a scale or in such defiance of its own wishes. Action was taken at the next great council at Coventry in late September and early October. It was this assembly that witnessed the replacement of the Bourchier brothers as chancellor and treasurer by Waynflete and Shrewsbury. There is no supporting evidence that it was the queen who 'made' Shrewsbury or 'inserted' Lawrence Bothe as keeper of the privy seal.[18] Warwick attended, apparently commuting from nearby Warwick, where he was on 30 October and 16 November, and where he received the king, who joined him and his countess in making offerings at St Mary's.[19] Perhaps they visited the temporary tomb of the king's late governor the countess's father and must certainly have witnessed the progress of the Beauchamp Chapel. York's relations with the king were reportedly friendly, those with the queen rather less so, and those with others unnamed decidedly hostile. The latter wished to 'distress' the duke at his departure, but were prevented by Buckingham.[20]

Warwick was not preoccupied by high politics. He attended the wedding of his brother John to Isabel Ingoldsthorpe at Canterbury on 25 April 1457. Archbishop Bourchier was the celebrant. Sole daughter of the late Sir Edmund Ingoldsthorpe and hence a modest heiress, Isabel was potentially coheiress

16   Storey, *Lancaster*, 178–9; Johnson, *York*, 176; Griffiths, *King & Country*, 213.

17   Johnson, *York*, 177–8; Robbins, *Hist. Poems*, 189–90, 355; Griffiths, *King & Country*, 214; A. Herbert, 'Herefordshire 1413–61: Some Aspects of Society and Public Order', *Patronage, The Crown and the Provinces in Later Medieval England*, ed. R. A. Griffiths (Gloucester, 1981), 103–22.

18   Watts, *Henry VI*, 335; Gross, *Dissolution*, 49n. Bothe and Waynflete were appropriately qualified clerics, the latter being the king's rather than the queen's man; Shrewsbury was a magnate. Compare the more measured judgement of Griffiths, *Henry VI*, 773 & n.

19   Worcs. RO 989/112; Warwick RO CR 26/4, f. 69.

20   Johnson, *York*, 177.

through her mother Joyce Tiptoft of the earldom of Worcester; hence Worcester himself 'broght about the marriage'. Although Isabel was over fourteen and hence of age, the queen insisted on payment for her marriage, subject to any subsequent ruling that adjudged it unnecessary. The down payment is not known: John bound himself to £1,000 in ten instalments and his parents settled eight Montagu manors on them in jointure in 1458.[21]

John's marriage immediately preceded Warwick's departure for Calais, where he was to spend much of the next two years. He remained joint warden of the West March at a salary of £1,250. Unlike their unfortunate counterparts in the East, who built up enormous arrears, the Nevilles' salaries were appropriated to feefarms and other sources that ensured regular payment and were not due from the exchequer. Fortunately, since what little was due there was seldom paid. Some of these revenues were actually assigned to Warwick's brother Sir Thomas Neville as their lieutenant on 1 September 1457 to pay his annual salary of 500 marks (£333.33),[22] which left them considerably in credit. It was not strictly profit since such unknown other costs as fortifications and retaining were not borne by the lieutenant.

In the spring Henry presided in person over sessions of oyer and terminer at Hereford that once again imposed exemplary retribution on York's retainers in his heartland. Herbert and Devereux again suffered brief periods of imprisonment. York was compensated with an annuity for dismissal from his constableships.[23] Such treatment was not unreasonable. It did not justify the Yorkists absenting themselves from the council. 'The gret princes of the lond wer nat called to Counceil bot sett A-Parte,' observed one contemporary chronicle.[24] Actually, all seem to have been assiduous in attending great councils and were not excluded from any before autumn 1459. Virtually nothing is known of attendance at the regular council in these years and Warwick had good reason to be absent in Calais for much of the time. Hence his absence from the extraordinary commissions in fourteen southern and midland counties appointed in July 1457. That York and Salisbury were also omitted is indicative of royal displeasure, but this is a relative term. It was a very mild disfavour that did not prevent the renewal of York's patent as lieutenant of Ireland at the same time, six months before the expiry of his previous term. Nor did it prevent the king and council from turning to Warwick to command a naval force in October following the French raid on Sandwich and developing it in December into a three-year appointment as keeper of the seas. Warwick was the regime's front line against France.

If not excluded from political influence or self-advancement, this was a bad

21   *Paston L & P* ii. 172; *CCR 1454–61*, 300–1; *Pedes Finium for the County of Somerset, Henry IV to Henry VI* (Somerset Rec. Soc. xxiii, 1906), 205; CP 25(1)/293/73/426; see also *RP* v. 387–8. Her relief was paid 3 October 1457, E 401/853 m. 1.
22   Madox, *Formulare Anglicanum*, 102–3; *pace* Summerson, *Medieval Carlisle*, 443.
23   Storey, *Lancaster*, 181.
24   *The Brut*, 527.

time for the Nevilles. Following the death of Edmund Tudor and the succession of his infant son as earl of Richmond, the stewardship of Richmondshire that Salisbury had coveted was granted to Humphrey Neville of Brancepeth (Dur.), a cadet of the senior, Westmorland, line. Similarly on 8 July Warwick's uncle Robert Neville Bishop of Durham died. His successor was to be the queen's client and keeper of the privy seal, Lawrence Bothe, who was to prefer the senior house of Neville as officeholders to the junior branch. Moreover Warwick's loss of the Channel Isles was again confirmed on 8 October 1457 with the ten-year appointment as governor of John Nanfan, admittedly Warwick's own chosen deputy.[25]

It was the 'grutche and wrath' of the victims of St Albans against the victors that was the cause of the 'grave and dangerous dissension' that paralysed political life and preoccupied the government in the autumn and winter of 1457-8. Hence the great council that met at Westminster from 12 October to 29 November 1457 'to set aside such variances as be betwixt divers lords' and which both York and Salisbury attended. Nothing is known of the proceedings, which do not seem to have been very successful: in November Exeter, Somerset, Shrewsbury and Roos tried to seize Warwick, but found him well-accompanied and 'durst [not] countre with him for he was named and taken in all places for the moost corageous and manliest knight lyvyng'. Hence presumably the deployment of royal troops around London, at Whetstone and Hornsey Park to the north, Hounslow to the west, and Southwark to the south. In December there may have been another attempt on the life of York himself at Coventry.[26] No wonder the king decided on a supreme effort at reconciliation the following year. 'And sith it is soo that as yet we have not fully concluded', the summons runs, so that our people remain in jeopardy, the lords were summoned to a further council on 26 January 'to sette apon such variaunce as been betwixt divers lordes of this our reame'.[27]

Once again the auguries were not favourable. All the principal parties did eventually appear, but they were as prepared for war as peace. So alarmingly large were their retinues that there was a real danger of conflict if mediation faltered or opportunity arose. Hence the Lord Mayor kept a force of 5,000 men in readiness to maintain the peace. Accounts differ on precise numbers, but not on the scale of the retinues. Exeter and Somerset brought 800 men and Northumberland, Egremont and Clifford another 1,500, who were accommodated between Temple Bar and Westminster, to the west of the City, from which the mayor excluded them 'because they came agaynst the pease' and intending to fight York. The Yorkists in contrast were allowed to lodge in their usual residences within the City: York at Baynards Castle, Salisbury at le Erber, and Warwick at Greyfriars. York may have brought as many as 400 men including 140 horsemen, and Salisbury 500 including 80 knights and squires, which were somewhat

25   *DKR* xlviii (1887), 424.
26   Griffiths, *Henry VI*, 799, 805; *Six Town Chronicles*, 144.
27   *POPC* vi. 291-5. The following discussion of the Loveday is particularly indebted to Johnson, *York*, 180 ff.

unconvincingly claimed by sympathizers to be their normal households and 'thinking none harme'. Warwick was reported to be held up by contrary winds on 4 February and arrived from Calais only on the 14th. He made an impressive and rather expensive show with a company of 600 men clad in red jackets with ragged staves embroidered on chest and back. No more than a fraction can have been members of his Calais crews.[28] Warwick's arrival signalled the start of serious negotiations.

Henry was committed to peace. He opened proceedings on 27 January 1458 by addressing the assembly in person on the dangers of dissension between lords.[29] He wanted a peaceful and permanent end to feuding. So, most likely, did the Yorkists. Their enemies may not have done. They had no choice, however, for the king required them to proceed to arbitration. Arbitration was an established mechanism of resolving disputes that entailed independent investigation of the grievances, arguments and evidence of both parties by a panel of arbiters acceptable to both sides, and the imposition of an award that settled the issues. Such awards were always compromises. They were also enforceable at the common law. In this case the king himself was to make the award. To ensure that the result was indeed acceptable to all and stuck, Henry was willing to devote the whole council session to the matter and to allow negotiations more like those between sovereign states. First the judges and then the bishops acted as mediators whilst he removed himself to Berkhamsted Castle (Herts.), which was reasonably accessible. Exeter, Somerset, Egremont and Clifford visited him there about 1 March,[30] presumably to influence the result: probably unsuccessfully. That Henry was not in their pocket is shown by the decision to confirm Warwick as keeper of the seas to the considerable offence of Exeter as hereditary Lord Admiral, who was compensated with £1,000 from the hanaper. It was a month into discussions, on 5 March, before several parties bound themselves to keep the peace until Michaelmas.[31] We can only guess at the stages along the route of what was evidently a protracted, difficult and latterly intensive set of negotiations that the victims of 1455 probably did not wish to succeed. The award refers to the examination of evidence from both sides, consultations with both parties, the hearings of grievances and the substances of controversies, their responses, and depositions. We need to recall this when considering the deceptively slender conclusion. On this occasion, unlike 1452 and 1455, persistence paid off and negotiations were brought to a successful conclusion.

The original award is missing from the close roll where supposedly it was enrolled; only a damaged exemplification survives. It is in English. The Latin version in Whetehamstede's *Register* was probably the abbot's own translation. The award is an impressively long and thorough document. The king desired a settlement, it says, 'for the tranquillity and conservation of his realms and

28   *PL* iii. 125; Kingsford, *Lond. Chrons.* 168; *Davies Chron.* 77.
29   Whetehamstede, i. 295–7.
30   *Paston L & P* ii. 533.
31   Johnson, *York*, 182.

territories and against external threats' – for foreign powers rejoiced in English divisions! – and 'for sane direction and rule at home'. The award tackled the 'controversies and differences . . . caused principally by a certain siege and attack before this time at the town of St Albans'. Henry recognized the Yorkist lords always to have been faithful lieges. The two parties dropped their differences and stopped their lawsuits. The Yorkists were to endow a chantry with income of £45 a year for the souls of those killed at St Albans. York was to pay the Dowager-Duchess of Somerset 2,500 marks (£1,666.66) and the new duke another 2,500 marks; Warwick was to compensate Clifford with 1,000 marks (£666.33). In each case payment was to be made by reassigning royal debts. Salisbury was to forgo the fines due from Egremont. He was also to return the obligations of knights, esquires, tenants and servants of Northumberland and Egremont arising from the Percy–Neville feud. The sheriffs of London were released from penalties for Egremont's escape and Egremont himself was bound to keep the peace towards Salisbury for ten years. And should there be any further disagreements between the servants and tenants, they were to be settled by the two chief justices. Resort to mediation, the courts and the judges were ordained for other kinds of dispute. The whole was to take effect within two years.[32]

Apparently the victims had still looked for vengeance rather than compromise as late as 9 March, when Warwick was warned, but he had insisted on attending the council. 'He wolle to Westmynster on the morow maugre them all'.[33] It was to exert his personal influence rather than merely to rubber-stamp the agreement that the king returned to Westminster on the 16th.[34] On 23 March all parties sealed bonds to abide the king's award. York was bound in £10,000, Salisbury and Warwick each in £8,000, Salisbury's bond also committing his younger sons, towards Somerset's widow Eleanor, the new duke and his brothers and sisters, the new earl of Northumberland and his brothers Egremont, Sir Ralph and Richard Percy, all of whom sealed equally impressive recognizances, and their servants and tenants.[35] If they did not comply with the award, these enormous sums would be due and payment could be enforced by the courts. Those paying would be ruined. The penalties were a formidable incentive to all the parties to keep the terms. Of course none of them would have sealed the bonds if the terms had been unknown or unacceptable. This must be an occasion when the details of the verdict had been negotiated in advance. The award was not imposed with royal authority from on high, but was a compromise that they had all agreed.

However it was not merely a series of legalistic settlements of specific differences. The package needed to be seen as a whole and as a mechanism for reconciliation and fresh beginnings. It was intended to set the contending parties at amity. As the ballad commissioned on the occasion states:

32 Bl Cotton Ch. xvi. 71; Whetehamstede, i. 298; Watts, *Henry* VI, 343n. For the assignments, see C 81/1468/46.
33 *Six Town Chronicles*, 160.
34 Johnson, *York*, 183.
35 *CCR 1454–61*, 292–3, 306.

Love hath put out malicious gouernaunce,
In euery place both fre & bonde
In Yorke, in Somerset, as I vnderstonde,
In Warrewik also is love & charite,
In Sarisbury eke, in Northumbrelande,
That euery man may reioise in concord and unite.[36]

And on 25 March, the feast of the Annunciation of the Blessed Virgin Mary or Lady Day, the king and queen, the reconciled parties, the negotiators, lords spiritual and temporal consecrated the agreement by solemnly processing to St Paul's and celebrated mass there. York walked alongside the queen, Salisbury walked beside Somerset, Warwick with Exeter, and the king wore his crown. 'Rejoise, Anglond, our lordes accorded to be.'[37] The poet captures the euphoria of the moment.

Modern historians have attached little weight to the accord. Henry VI was pathetic and at best well-meaning. The Loveday was a charade that failed. The participants cannot have been sincere, for the feud soon resumed and escalated and civil war lay only eighteen months away. More detailed research has revealed that the Yorkist concessions were limited. Far from actually making payments to the victims, they only handed over tallies that were worthless to them in the current state of public finances. York indeed managed to exchange them for licences to ship wool that may have made him £5,000.[38] The accord pandered to Henry's wishes. Kings had the right to impose settlements and Christians had a duty to seek reconciliation. The Yorkists could not be seen to disagree.

Such an interpretation, however, is anachronistic and rationalizes the Loveday in the light of later events. It was not just the writer of the ballad that praised the accord, but also all the Yorkist chroniclers who were aware of the end result.[39] They did not underestimate Henry's achievement or minimize the difficulties that were overcome en route. Nor should we. Remember how earlier attempts at arbitration in 1452 and 1455 had foundered, apparently because York and Somerset were irreconcilable. No accord could have been achieved in 1458 if both parties had been set against it. Remember how much divided the parties on this occasion. Blood had been spilt. The Yorkist lords claimed to have been acting at St Albans as loyal subjects in the king's interests against traitors. They had been in the right and all the blame rested with Somerset, Thorpe and Joseph. Moreover they had an act of parliament to back them up. Their immunity from punishment and their honour depended on maintaining this stance. As for their opponents, the victors were rebels, traitors and murderers whom they wished to see punished and destroyed. There was little common ground on which to build.

36   Robbins, *Hist. Poems*, 194–6 at 194.
37   Ibid. 104.
38   E.g. Johnson, *York*, 184.
39   E.g. *Davies Chron.* 77–8; *Gregory's Chron.* 203. Peace and reconciliation can never be criticized.

Without abandoning their claims to loyalty and justification, the Yorkists were induced to accept that they had been responsible for the deaths of Somerset, Northumberland and Clifford. They agreed to contribute to the good of their souls – though they may well have preferred them damned! – and to make meaningful compensation to the victims. The surrendered tallies were worth more to the recipients who enjoyed royal favour than to the Yorkists. Whilst the verdict against Egremont stood, the Yorkists had to accept that the fines designed to destroy him were excessive. Egremont was allowed free, but curbed by bonds to keep the peace. And they themselves had to forget the attempted arrests, ambushes and murders to which they had been subjected. Yet it is not really true that all the concessions were made by the Yorkists, still less, as recently suggested, that it was 'a triumph for their enemies'.[40] The heirs of the victims were obliged to accept their fathers' killers as loyal subjects and abandon plans for revenge. The chantry at St Albans was for the souls of all the fallen on both sides. And the penalties against their rivals were symbolic rather than punitive.

Historians have also denigrated the Loveday because it came too late; it was confined to 'the limited issue of atonement and compensation for the principals who had suffered injury or death at St Albans'; it was an 'evasion of the real issues'; it did not address the real problems. Who was to rule – Margaret or York? Perhaps Henry did not see the problem. What about reform, financial retrenchment, and international affairs? Did not the award ignore 'the entire public dimension', 'the misgovernment of the realm, the misleading of the king, the unavailability of justice', that St Albans had been fought about?[41] Such charges are misconceived. The quarrel of victors and victims was paralysing politics as completely as that between York and Somerset had done. All parties accepted that the king had a right to rule. All had an interest in peace. Warwick and the other Yorkist subjects knew themselves to be isolated. They could not expect to control the administration again or to win any conflict. Warwick himself really wanted the accord and was prepared to take considerable personal risks in pursuit of agreement. It offered an end to the tension and crises that threatened their lives and futures and the opportunity to return to the normal life and career of great magnates. It wiped away the unfortunate legacy of York's two protectorates and offered them a fresh start. It was because he saw the accord was to his advantage that Salisbury had an exemplification made of it.[42] As late as 11 February 1459 the Yorkists abode by the requirement to amortize land to St Albans for the souls of the victims.[43] Only the accord offered them hope of a peaceful future.

For the king and the public it offered hope also. Peace at home, as the Loveday ballad says, offers the prospect of good governance, wealth and

---

40   E.g. Griffiths, *Henry VI*, 807; Watts, *Henry VI*, 344.
41   Watts, *Henry VI*, 343; see also Griffiths, *Henry VI*, 805; Johnson, *York*, 179–80, 184–5; Gross, *Dissolution*, 46.
42   BL Cotton Ch. xvi, no. 71.
43   *CCR 1454–61*, 369.

prosperity. With peace restored at home, it was now possible to turn to international affairs:

> Rejoise, and thanke God for euermore,
> For now shal encrese thi consolacion;
> Oure enemnyes quaken & dreden ful sore,
> That peas is made there was diuision.
> Whiche to them is gret confusion.

'Ffraunce and Britayn repente shul thei,' continues the ballad.[44] Peace at home offered scope for warfare abroad. Actually this was not seriously considered. Peace at home instead offered the means to peace abroad. In May overtures were made to France and Burgundy for a cessation of hostilities: for a truce cemented by marriages involving Prince Edward and the offspring of the rival dukes of Somerset and York. With an end to war, there could be an end to war expenditure. Calais could be reduced to its peacetime establishment and cost. The seas need not be kept. Resources would be freed to restore royal credit. Trade and hence customs revenues could revive. We cannot show that Henry's government had such a vision, but if it did the reconciliation of the warring factions was a prerequisite and had to be attempted.

Initially the Loveday did bring peace at home. The serenity of a ballad *On the Ship or Poop* of January 1459 documents how much committed support the government now enjoyed. Henry himself was 'the noble ship of good tree'. His son was the mast, his step-brother Pembroke the mainyard, the Lancastrian dukes of Somerset and Exeter were the rudder and the light, and Buckingham was the stay. Devon, Grey of Ruthin and Beauchamp were the shrouds, Northumberland the sail, Roos, Clifford and Egremont the bonnets, Shrewsbury and Wiltshire the topmasts, and Beaumont, Welles and Rivers the anchors. Altogether the poet lists as king's men three dukes, five earls, a viscount, and seven barons, totalling sixteen; a third of the parliamentary peerage and more of the higher ranks, were identified with the king. 'Now is oure shype dressed in hys kynde', says the poet, celebrating the unity of the Lancastrian regime and his kindred. They include victims of the Neville–Percy feud and St Albans. Whilst guarding against the 'waves bothe wilde & wode' and 'ragged rokkes', it ends with a call for unity. St George is the lodestar

> To strengthe oure kynge and england ryght,
> And felle our fomenus [foemen's] pryde . . .
> Whos[o] loue it not, God make hym blynde
> In peynes to abide.

If foemen sound foreign, what follows seems to warn off domestic opposition. Moreover Prince Edward replaced another mast,

---

44 Robbins, *Hist. Poems*, 194–5.

Crased it was, it my[ght]t not last;
Now hath he one that wold not brest –
The old leyde on side.[45]

The prince made Lord Protector York unnecessary.

Yet there was no aggression to the ballad, which is not directed against anyone. At least initially the Loveday ended domestic strife. King Henry deserved the confidence of the overwhelming majority of the lords that he enjoyed in the great councils of 1456–9 and the ensuing civil wars. Ironically it was the self-confidence of the Yorkists, now reconciled with their enemies, that was to contribute to the eventual breakdown.

6.2   Captain of Calais and the Keeper of the Seas

Warwick was valuable to Lord Protector York as a great magnate committed to his cause who brought with him substantial military resources, the resolution and daring to deploy them, and a capacity and willingness for administrative work both at the centre and in the localities that Norfolk, for example, lacked. An additional use was found for the earl during York's Second Protectorate that launched his career in several different directions. After St Albans it was Warwick who succeeded Somerset as captain of Calais, which led in due course to his appointment as keeper of the seas (1457), to his involvement in continental diplomacy, and, in 1460, to his appointment as warden of the Cinque Ports. Military, naval, diplomatic and international dimensions were developed to his career that were denied, after 1453, to most of his noble contemporaries. Even within England, Warwick's attention was increasingly focused on the South-East and south coast, far from the centres of his estates. In the short term he was at Calais for much of the time that the government was in Coventry and the Midlands; in the medium term his command of Calais and the navy were crucial in the crises of 1459–61; and, in the longer term, the national and international character of his career after 1461 was established.

Calais was the last remaining English possession in France. The Hundred Years War did not end in 1453 with the final loss of Gascony as the history books say. That was merely when the active campaigning stopped. It ended when the English accepted their expulsion as final, which lay far in the future, perhaps in the reign of Henry VIII. English monarchs continued to title themselves kings and queens of France for another 300 years. Nobody in Warwick's lifetime undertook a thoroughgoing strategic review of the post-Hundred Years War situation. Neither side saw 1453 as the end. The French expected further counter-attacks and the English feared the besieging of Calais and even the

---

45   Robbins, *Hist. Poems*, 191–3. The dates 1458 old style and dominical letter G coincide in the first three months of 1459. It must precede the arrest of Exeter on 31 Jan. 1459.

invasion of England itself. As we have seen, Henry VI had neither the financial nor the military means to launch and sustain an assault on France; no English government after 1453 was capable of such an initiative. Yet his rival Charles VII was constantly advised that invasion was imminent and suspected collusion among his new subjects. When the Duke of Alençon was arrested in 1456 and tried for treason in 1458, it was on charges of inviting English intervention. Charles declined to join the Scots in a two-pronged attack on England in January 1457 because his enlarged dominions brought new responsibilities as well as new resources. He now had longer frontiers and coastlines to defend.[46] By the time Warwick took up the captaincy neither monarch was going to take the offensive. Each was committed to a defensive strategy. Each would have welcomed a re-laxation of tension, a reversion to peacetime establishments, and a reduction in military expenditure. Neither recognized this, however. Minor raids and clashes were interpreted as forerunners of full-scale conflict by councillors and servicemen on the spot, among them Warwick.[47] One wonders how far this was deliberate – a means to maintain a high profile and to take priority in supply.

Calais had a symbolic importance quite out of proportion to its military value. It had been a national crisis calling for supreme efforts when it was threatened in 1436. Viewed dispassionately, Calais was a financial burden without com-pensations, but after the national humiliation of 1449–53, it could not be allowed to fall. Neither Somerset, nor York, nor indeed Warwick dared to lose it. Even in peacetime the Calais garrison was much larger than other English military establishments. It was maintained on a war footing throughout the 1450s and indeed enhanced with a 'crew' attendant on the captain about 1451 and a further 300 men when Warwick took office. The colony was a major item of public expenditure and its support was one of the most intractable problems for Henry VI's embarrassed regime. It remained the principal military command of the English crown.

English Calais consisted of the port itself, about twenty miles of coast, and it extended six miles inland. Calais town had a population of about 5,000, most of whom were either members of the garrison, which fluctuated from about 800 to 1,000, or their dependants. Vestiges of the walls remain, but the castle has dis-appeared. To the east lay the low-lying districts of Oye and Mark, to the west the hillier county of Guines. None of the other settlements were more than villages. There were garrisons for Calais town and castle, for Rysbank tower, and for the castles of Hammes and Guines. The whole was an enclave within the dominions of the Duke of Burgundy. Border raiding was continuous. Apart from its role as a military outpost, Calais was commercially important as the staple-town of the merchants of the Staple, who had a monopoly of the export in English wool for the Flemish cloth industry. Although the wool trade was in decline, the staplers remained politically influential and still commanded formidable resources. They

46   M. G. A. Vale, *Charles VII* (1974), 60.
47   E.g. *Letters of the 15th and 16th Centuries from the Archives of Southampton*, ed. R. C. Anderson (Southampton Rec. Soc., xxii, 1921), 12–13.

were committed to the continuance of English Calais and it was only by tapping their resources that its status could be maintained.[48]

Following the loss of Normandy, Somerset became captain of Calais, then York. Duke Richard however was never able to make his appointment effective and Somerset's officers remained in command. Henry VI was chronically incapable of paying either the current wages or the outstanding arrears of the garrison, who understandably made satisfaction of their entitlements a condition for York's admission. Following Warwick's own appointment in 1455, there were lengthy negotiations to settle the financial issues between the government, the garrison and the staplers, for whom Calais was an essential commercial base and who alone had the interest and resources to provide the funds necessary for a settlement. The wages due were eventually computed at the enormous total of £65,444 16s. 9¾d. By agreement of February 1456 the whole sum was paid by the Staple, in cash or in wool, on the security of obligations already advanced and of the 'Calais part' of the customs; the garrison were pardoned their offences; and Warwick was at last admitted as captain. This was in July 1456: fifteen months after his original appointment and nearly a year since 4 August 1455, when he had indented for the office. He had already been granting licences to fishermen.[49]

It is no longer historically fashionable to regard the 'struggle for Calais' as a power-struggle between Lancaster and York; its importance in that context comes later. York regarded himself as a superior commander to Somerset and hence initially as the best person to occupy England's premier fortress. By mid-1455 he was willing to surrender his pretensions. He had other offices and responsibilities, as protector and as lieutenant of Ireland, and was seriously embarrassed by debts accrued in France and Ireland and by the thousands of pounds of unrealizable tallies with which the crown had reimbursed him. Now he appreciated how much personal attention the captaincy demanded that a revolutionary leader like himself could not spare. York did not need another drain on his financial resources. Moreover a reward and a role was needed for Warwick commensurate with his services. Mere retention of the Warwick inheritance was to be taken for granted. The captaincy of Calais was Warwick's share of the spoils of war.

We must presume that in 1455 Warwick wanted the captaincy. His acceptance of and presumably his request for the post implies existing military aspirations arising perhaps from a chivalric education and fed in his teens by military action on the northern borders and possibly even in France. When Cade's Rebellion broke out, Warwick was allegedly bound for foreign service. Warlike inclinations and an appreciation of the political uses of military force are revealed by the formidable retinues that he deployed in 1450, 1452 and 1458, by his aggression in Glamorgan and the North in 1453, and by his decisive intervention at the first battle of St Albans. Most probably he saw the captaincy as a means to military

48   J. R. Rainey, 'The Defense of Calais 1436–77' (PhD thesis, Rutgers Univ., 1987), 4–10.
49   Harriss, 'Calais', 41, 45–8; SC 8/28/1392.

action and distinction and to the profits of war. He is unlikely to have appreciated its essentially defensive role or the sheer commitment in time and money that it demanded.

Compared to his immediate predecessors, Warwick was lucky. He did not find a garrison that was actively mutinous and owed several years of arrears of pay. He did not come to the post heavily indebted and embittered by non-payment. In the absence of other evidence, he appears solvent, with at best short-term cash-flow difficulties that were easily dispelled by warrants to officers with cash in hand.[50] His debts to the crown as lessee and custodian and the debts of the government to him as a royal councillor were scarcely significant. Almost uniquely in Henry VI's regime Warwick received his first quarter's pay of £1,742 2s. 4d. in advance and a further £788 13s. 4d. for the extra 300 men he was to take with him. So too with the garrison. Their arrears were cleared; their future pay was guaranteed by the staplers; and the latter were assured of re-payment by strict appropriations of the customs. Perhaps Warwick, the garrison, and the staplers believed this. In practice, inevitably, the government failed to honour the agreement, first selling licences of exemption from the customs and then applying some of the revenues to the royal household. Out of the total wages of £13,550 a year, over £7,000 a year was unpaid by the treasurer of Calais in 1456-7 and 1457-8 and altogether £37,160 was due by 1461. The victualler also received insufficient for his needs.[51] Yet this was not directly Warwick's problem. It was not his job to pay the soldiers. With cash in hand, it took time for them to become mutinous and in the interim he found other sources of finance. Warwick's piratical exploits may have been primarily a money-raising exercise.

The garrison was pardoned on 1 May 1456 and 'soon afterwards [writes Harriss] the earl of Warwick, with his strengthened retinue, marched in to take command'.[52] If so, he did not stay there long, for he was at the king's great councils in July, the autumn, and probably the spring of 1457. It was Sir Robert Chamberlain whom the City sent with 500 men to safeguard Calais at its own expense in October 1456. Warwick was at Calais on 1 December 1456. His appointment of William Chamber rector of Olney as receiver-general of all his lands in England and Wales on 20 January 1457 anticipates a protracted stay in Calais.[53] Probably it was not until May 1457, after John's marriage, accompanied by 'a fayr ffellaushipp' that he, his countess and Fauconberg took up residence, which none of his immediate predecessors had done.[54] Perhaps he was no longer comfortable in Warwick under the eyes of the court. Most probably he saw a potential in Calais that he wished to exploit. A siege of the town was considered imminent. 'The Erle of Warwyk', it was reported on 1 May 1457, 'hath had the folk of Caunterbury and Sandwych before hym, and thanked hem of her gode

50   E.g. BL MS Royal 17Bxlvii, f. 165v.
51   Harriss, 'Calais', 45, 49.
52   Ibid. 46; E 101/71/4/936.
53   Six Town Chronicles, 145; Warwicks. RO CR 1886/ EM2; BL Lansdowne Ch. 163.
54   Brut, 524; Anstis, i. 161.

hertes and vytaillyng of Calix and prayeth hem of contynuance.'[55] It was like a royal audience and a royal commendation. Between midsummer 1457 and midsummer 1458 Warwick was at Calais for 267 days. In spite of the king's great councils and his responsibilities as keeper of the seas, Warwick was absent with one knight and twelve mounted archers from his crew for only ninety-eight days.[56]

Most captains of Calais were great magnates and most regarded the office as a sinecure, to be performed *in absentia*. Warwick did not. He resided in person, at least initially, and he ran it as directly as possible, delegating some responsibility temporarily, but declining to appoint permanent lieutenants like those of Somerset's whom he found. Several of these, such as Lords Rivers, Stourton and Welles, and the treasurer Sir Gervase Clifton, were closely committed to Somerset. Clifton was not immediately replaced. Sir Thomas Findern, lieutenant of Guines, and Sir John Marny, lieutenant of Hammes, were retained. Warwick himself kept Calais castle and Rysbank tower nominally under his own control.[57] Although not formally appointed, his militarily distinguished uncle Fauconberg was effectively his deputy from at least May 1457; another valued adviser if not officeholder was the Gascon Gailliard Lord Duras. Warwick used York's councillor Sir Edmund Mulsho as marshal until his death in 1458, when he borrowed Walter Blount of Elvaston (Derbys.) in his stead.[58] Most of the next level of officials held patents from the king and remained, such as the victualler, gunners, bailiffs and beadles, master mason, plumber and carpenter. Little can be known of the rank and file of soldiery in the absence of muster rolls and only sparse protections. That a merchant of Southampton, inhabitants of Faversham and Little Wenham (Suff.), and a chandler of Coventry had safe conducts tells us very little.[59] The government had assured the garrison that no dismissals were envisaged. Since Warwick was authorized to bring a further 20 mounted men-at-arms, 20 mounted archers, and 260 foot archers in addition to the crew already attendant on him,[60] we may guess (but not demonstrate) that he selected them from those he knew and trusted. No wonder that Warwick could take significant numbers for use elsewhere without endangering the colony and that loyalty was felt towards him personally.

There was no siege of Calais in 1457, but considerable conflict in the county of Guines is recorded in the treasurer's account. Expenditure increased from £263 to £600. Revenue fell sharply because no cranage or cambage could be collected from the vills of Merkyn, Froyton, Arderne and Bonynges because of war damage. Similarly Morlot de Renty on the Burgundian side disbursed compensation for a house destroyed by the daily English raids.[61] Such conflict

---

55 *Paston L & P* ii. 172.
56 E 101/195/7; see also E 403/810 sub 14 May, 15 July.
57 Harriss, 'Calais', 47.
58 Ellis, *Original Letters*, ii (1), 125–6.
59 *CPR 1452–61*, 267, 330, 467.
60 Rainey, 'Defense of Calais', 115–16.
61 Ibid. 93–4n.

was endemic on all marches and did not result from Warwick's arrival, although he was to take a more aggressive line that generated profit for the garrison, increased costs for the crown, and irritated Calais's neighbour Burgundy, with whom England was supposedly at peace. Warwick was expected to prevent conflict and correct infractions of the truce. Resolution of grievances and the cessation of English raids were a high priority for Philip the Good, Duke of Burgundy, who supposed that the English were incited to raid his territories by France. There was a conference of the marches at Ardre in December 1456 to January 1457. Following Warwick's arrival, Duke Philip corresponded several times with Warwick in January/February 1457; Warwick responded in February with a gift of an Irish pony to Philip's heir Charles the Bold, Count of Charolais. In April Henry VI commissioned Warwick to settle disputes. Hence in July 1457 he met Burgundian representatives between Oye and Mark. They were Anthony, Grand Bastard of Burgundy, and John of Burgundy, Count of Estampes. Fearful of treachery from the French, Estampes declined to dismount, so formal overtures were conducted from the saddle, but the Grand Bastard joined Warwick in a splendid banquet. The detailed negotiations were conducted by subordinates. Although the earl laboured hard for peace, so Chastellain reports, the other English diplomats were uncompromising. They declined to remedy the wrongs the English had committed and demanded full compensation for their grievances. When the Burgundians referred back to Duke Philip at Hesdin, he decided that concessions must be made at the next conference at St Omer and Calais in October. The duke's subjects were sacrificed to prevent any escalation of conflict with England.[62] The resultant truce covered conditions on land, not at sea, where Warwick if anything encouraged piracy.

Reiving and days of the march were nothing new to the son of a Scottish warden of marches, but border fighting on the European continent may have introduced Warwick to aspects of warfare with which he was unfamiliar. He learnt his lessons well, for amongst his English contemporaries it was he who appreciated best both the tactical use of artillery and the strategic role of seapower. Artillery was a commonplace both to the Calais garrison and its enemies. The king maintained at least 135 guns in Calais in the 1450s, both ordnance and handguns, and the victualler's accounts testify to prodigious expenditure in gunpowder, saltpetre, gunstones and burst guns. Calais was a port that was garrisoned and supplied by sea. A captain of Calais was much involved in the issuing of safe conducts, inquiries into piracy, and impressing of ships. Warwick's indenture made him responsible for shipping and reshipping himself to and fro at his own expense. We do not know what arrangements he made – was it at this stage that Warwick became a ship-owner? – but he must have made them. We cannot tell how familiar sea transport and naval warfare already were

62 M. R. Thielemans, *Bourgogne et l'Angleterre* (Brussels, 1966), 368n, 369; G. Chastellain, *Oeuvres*, ed. Kervyn de Lettenhove (8 vols, Brussels, 1863–5), ii. 338. It is not clear whether it was another Irish pony that Warwick reportedly gave Philip the Good also in 1457, R. Vaughan, *Philip the Good* (1970), 343.

to him: had he ever visited his jointure at Swainstown on the Isle of Wight, his Channel Isles where he was commissioned to suppress piracy in 1451, or had he assisted in fulfilment of his father's commission as one of the keepers of the seas in 1454? How far had Warwick proceeded by 1457 along the route that made him the second largest English ship-owner in the 1460s with perhaps eleven ships of 2,300 tons worth about £3,000?[63]

Warwick was the obvious choice for a naval command following the French raid on Sandwich on 24 August 1457. Commanded by Pierre de Brezé, seneschal of Normandy, and in numbers variously estimated from 2,000 to 15,000 men, the French attacked at dawn by both land and sea, sacked the town, and carried off many prisoners in spite of an effective counter-attack by Sir Thomas Kyriel lieutenant warden of the Cinque Ports as they withdrew.[64] Was this the occasion when a message from Warwick in Calais reached Lydd via Dover that 'the Frenchmen will come hither'? As a response to English piracy, which it probably was, the raid on Sandwich was a failure, for few ships were taken and hence it failed to curb piracy. To English opinion, however, it was a national disgrace comparable to the loss of France itself. It revived the threat of invasion and demanded urgent countermeasures. Three months later Norwich still feared a further descent and for several more years such apprehension was a potent political force, albeit generally unwarranted. On 3 October 1457 the king and great council appointed Warwick to go to sea with an armed force against the king's enemies. £3,000 voted in 1453 for maritime defence was claimed and ships were commandeered. Warwick simply had most immediate access to the ships and manpower. Such an emergency measure, taken ahead of agreement on all the aspects normally covered by an indenture, did not necessitate a permanent appointment, but it obviously made one more likely. On 26 November Warwick indented as keeper of the seas for three years from the previous March on the same terms as in 1454. His appointment was confirmed and regularized by three patents of 27 December 1457.[65]

Warwick was commissioned by the king to keep the seas 'for the resistance of his enemies and repressing of their malice'. He was to operate to the 'comfort and relief of his subgettes, frendes, allies' and those covered by English safe conducts and do 'to the kynges ennemyes all the hurt adnoyssaunce' possible by land and by sea. He was not to molest those on his own side and was to prevent piracy by others. He could issue his own safe conducts, such as that for two years of 1459 to the *Marie* of Bayonne.[66] He was to comport himself after the forms of war and

63   G. V. Scammell, 'Shipowning in England *c.* 1450–1550', *TRHS* 5th ser. xii (1962), 111.
64   *The Brut*, 524; *Three 15th-Cent. Chrons.* 71; C. Vallet de Viriville, *Histoire de Charles VII*, iii (Paris, 1863), 392–3; for the next sentence see HMC *6th Rep.* 521.
65   C. de la Roncière, *Histoire de la Marine Française* ii (Paris, 1900), 293; Vallet de Viriville, *Charles VII*, iii. 397; *Foedera* xi. 406; *CCR 1454–61*, 240; *CPR 1452–61*, 390, 413; E 403/812 m. 3; E 101/71/4/938; see also *CCR 1454–61*, 240. A copy of the indenture is BL Harl. Ch. 54C17. These are the sources of the next para.
66   *Great Red Book of Bristol* ii (Bristol Rec. Soc. viii, 1938), 76–7.

the law of arms: thus specifically he was to have a third of the spoils of his men and the crown a third of the thirds. To fulfil his objectives, he was required to recruit 3,000, 4,000 or 5,000 men 'armed and arraied for the war entyndyng upon the sea' and shipping as expedient. In return, he was to have all the receipts of the tunnage and poundage from all ports except Sandwich and Southampton, which were appropriated to other uses, and £1,000 a year from the Lancaster enfeoffments. Money was to be paid to him direct by the customers by indentures without recourse to the exchequer. He was even allowed to nominate the customers himself and did so: hence John Otter became collector of the customs of London and on 1 July 1458 Henry Auger at Chichester and William Nesfield at Poole.[67] He could keep any goods that he lawfully seized. He was thus offered complete assurance of reimbursement of his costs at a time when the crown's existing debtors had very little hope of payment. Should funds not be forthcoming or, more realistically, if the crown should again reassign the revenues, Warwick was offered the (not very promising) recompense at the receipt of the exchequer or allowed to withdraw from office without penalty. Less than three months later when the duchy revenues had not materialized he invoked this clause and secured an emergency payment of £500 in cash refundable from the hanaper.[68]

Unfortunately Warwick's indenture specifically released him from rendering any account, so we have no data revealing how he raised the ships and crews required or whether indeed he did. The five ships of the forecastle, three carvels and four pinnaces at his command in May 1458 surely fell well short of what his indenture envisaged.[69] John Nanfan, his governor of the Channel Isles, his retainer Richard Clapham, his customer Henry Auger, and John Paston stand out among those commissioned to impress men and purvey stores. From at least 20 April 1458 he could call on the only remaining royal ship, the *Grace Dieu* of 1446, master John Paynter, which was apparently at Bristol and required repairing, munitioning and manning at his own expense.[70] No other commissions are recorded in 1458. Masters and mariners were to be impressed and supplies seized in 1459, but not ships. Does this mean that the rest of Warwick's fleet was made up of his own ships and those of volunteers? Some, no doubt, were ships from Calais and perhaps even crewed by the Calais garrison; others hailed from the Cinque Ports. Lydd paid the expenses of divers men going to Dover to join Warwick at sea.[71] Yet others were ships of Dartmouth, Plymouth and Fowey, C. L. Kingsford's nursery of West Country seamen and notorious centres of

67 *CFR 1452–61*, 199, 217.
68 *POPC* vi. 294. On 1 Feb. Exeter, as Lord Admiral, was understandably displeased by Warwick's commission; he was compensated with £1,000 about 15 Mar., *Paston L & P* ii. 532; *PL* iii. 127.
69 *Paston L & P* ii. 340.
70 *CPR 1452–61*, 439, 494; R. C. Anderson, 'The Grace de Dieu of 1446–86', *EHR* xxxiv (1919), 585.
71 HMC *6th. Rep.* 522.

piracy.[72] With control of the customs, Warwick could pay them, but naval service was high risk. Probably they served for profit, which determined the kind of service that Warwick's navy undertook. At their request and in view of the high price of wheat, he secured a safe conduct for three Gascon, Norman and Breton ships to trade with south-western ports.

On 4 March 1458 the royal council believed that the French fleet was at sea and wanted Warwick to meet it. The *Grace Dieu* was to serve under him, it was reported on 20 April.[73] Again, on 7 September, Lord Chancellor Waynflete had heard tidings from Normandy that the French intended to repeat their Sandwich exploit. The lords had been alerted and ordnance had been sent to Southampton castle.[74] Nothing materialized. On 10 March 1459 Warwick was again planning to send a fleet to sea under his own command or that of his lieutenant.[75] We do not know what Warwick did to the French. Probably not very much. Did he avoid them? His activities in that quarter did not attract attention from the chroniclers and are not recorded among the public records. We cannot tell whether Warwick was successful in sweeping the French from his seas. It seems unlikely that he cleared the Channel of English pirates, since it was surely in response to them that neutral shipping took to sailing in convoy.

Piracy was nothing new. There was plenty before Warwick became keeper or indeed captain of Calais. As early as 22 November 1455 it was reported that two fishing vessels licensed by him had been captured by English pirates.[76] Some of the Calais garrison were also pirates: were the lengthy vacations of the treasurer's accounts sometimes a euphemism for piratical cruises? On 4 March 1457 Warwick himself, the mayor of Calais, and four Hanseatic merchants were commissioned to arrest Andrew Trollope, a member of the Calais garrison, and bring him before the council for seizing Hanseatic cloth that had paid the customs from the *Julian* of Blakeney, an English vessel of Lord Roos, and pillaging it off the Norwegian coast. It seems unlikely that they did, for it was allegedly on the earl's own orders that on 10 March 1457 Trollope and two other Calais soldiers had seized three ships containing wool worth £4,000 at Tilbury Ferry and bore them off to Calais, where captains and crews were dismissed and the cargoes and ships dispersed. If they were preying on those exempted by the king from the Staple, their action would be popular, though illegal, with staplers, London merchants and residents of Calais. On 24 and 28 April 1458 Warwick was among those commissioned to inquire into piracy against friendly Burgundian shipping by vessels from Calais: the *St Barbara* of Dordrecht with an English-owned cargo was carried off to Calais and despoiled and the *Cristofre* of Campe en route from Holland to Prussia was taken to Newcastle upon Tyne, where ship and cargo were sold. On 3 and 7 May Warwick was again commissioned to inquire into the

---

72   C 81/1472/19; C. L. Kingsford, *Prejudice and Promise in Fifteenth Century England* (1925), 82ff.
73   *CPR 1452–61*, 439.
74   *Southampton Letters*, 12–13.
75   *CPR 1452–61*, 494.
76   Ibid. 300.

seizures of the *James* and *Marie* of Spain by the pirates of Fauconberg in contravention of safe conducts and to make restitution.[77] Calais was alive with piracy,
Warwick's officers being as active as anyone else, and the king's commissions
came perilously close to asking Warwick to investigate himself. He did not
respect the neutrality or safe conducts of the Spanish, Hanse, Burgundians or
Genoese.

We know this because of Warwick's attacks on three foreign squadrons in the
summer of 1458. The first, on Trinity Monday (28 May), was a Spanish fleet of
22 sail, including no less than 16 great ships of the forecastle. Spying them from
Calais and with the clear alternative to leave them alone, he embarked with a mere
five ships of the forecastle, three carvels and four pinnaces. Far from being bold
or dashing, this was foolhardy and could easily have led to disaster. Eighty of
Warwick's men were killed and another 200 captured. The battle was hand-to-
hand, ebbed to and fro, and lasted for six hours. Right at the start John
Jerningham of Somerleyton (Suff.) and twenty-three others boarded a 300-ton
ship, struggled to overcome the crew, were captured when the enemy boarded
back, and were later freed in exchange for captured Spaniards. Altogether
Warwick took six prizes and sank six. 'And as men sayne', reported Jerningham,
'there was not so gret a batayle upon the sea this xl winter.' Warwick was not
satisfied: back at Calais on 1 June, Jerningham reported that 'my lord hathe sent
for more schippis, and lyke to fyzthe to-gedyr agayne in haste'. But the other ten
Spanish ships escaped.[78]

Emboldened by this experience, Warwick assailed another friendly squadron,
this time the Hanseatic fleet of seventeen hulks on its return from La Rochelle.
Since they were friendly with England, the Hanse complained to the king, who
appointed a commission of inquiry into the sea battle between Warwick and his
retinue and the men of Lübeck, to sit at Rochester and report back in August.
Probably by then – and certainly by 7 September – Warwick had attacked a
flotilla of two Genoese carracks and three Spanish great ships, capturing all
except for one of the Spaniards.[79] With complaints from friendly powers and
demands for restitution flooding in and international relations in a flux, it is no
wonder that the government mooted replacing Warwick as captain of Calais in
the winter of 1458–9.

Warwick's victories were clearly profitable. His share must have gone a considerable distance towards financing the costs of the fleet itself, for which of
course he was separately paid, and his service in Calais, for which reimbursement
was delayed. The spoils may have compensated members of the Calais garrison

77   Ibid. 103, 348, 436, 438, 441; Kingsford, *London Chrons.* 168–9; E 159/233 Easter
Recorda 35 Hen. VI rot. 12; Kendall, *Warwick*, 41–2; see also Rainey, 'Defense of Calais',
198n.
78   *PL & P* ii. 340; Roncière, *Marine Française*, ii. 294.
79   *Three 15th Cent. Chrons.* 71; M. M. Postan and E. Power, *Studies in English Trade in
the Fifteenth Century* (1966), 130–2; *Hansisches Urkundenbuch*, ed. W. Stein, viii (Leipzig,
1899), 480, 486; *Six Town Chronicles*, 147; Whetehamstede, i. 330–1; see also *Southampton
Letters*, 12.

in his ships and made naval service desirable to other mariners from whom such convoys were otherwise immune. Profit alone may explain his actions. There were other advantages. Customs revenues lost by licences of exemption were recouped. Exemptions were disliked by those who paid customs. So, too, were the Genoese in the aftermath of their notorious attack on the Bristol merchant Robert Sturmy in the Mediterranean in 1457. Thus Warwick's victories earned him popularity and renown: with his own men; with London merchants and staplers; with public opinion; and with chroniclers unaccustomed to any sort of success. As it was the government that had issued exemptions and that rescinded its embargo on the Genoese in August 1458, Warwick was applauded for opposing royal policy. Hence, it has been argued, the support of London for the Yorkist lords in 1459–61.[80] That Warwick had vanquished friends and neutrals was a side issue, for were they not all foreigners? The same prejudice explains attacks on Flemings and Lombards in London in 1457–8. But Warwick's exploits in 1458 do mark a change in practice, for was there not a Bay fleet to attack every year? His irresponsible aggression contributed to political breakdown in England.

6.3 The Opportunity Missed

It is notorious that the Loveday of St Paul's did not deliver enduring peace. By the summer of 1459 the Yorkist lords had lost the trust of the crown. Political violence returned. The countdown to civil war had resumed. Why this occurred is not easy to say. Of course the parties to the Loveday had doubts. They had to prove their sincerity by their conduct. But all had so much to gain. York, Salisbury and Warwick could resume their normal roles confident in their own security. The government could look to peace abroad and relative solvency. And even for those in receipt of royal favour, it was worth more under conditions of domestic harmony. Nor is the collision of regional hegemonies the answer. None of their major feuds revived. Lancastrian consolidation in North Wales and the West Midlands did not overtly clash with the local hegemonies of York and Warwick. Whatever the rhetoric of the Yorkists, one crucial difference in the summer of 1459 was that their quarrel was no longer with other noblemen, but with the king. King Henry himself lost patience with them. One new factor was certainly disagreement on international and maritime affairs. For them Warwick was largely responsible.

The Loveday enabled Henry VI to resume diplomatic relations with France that had officially ceased in 1449. What Henry had in mind was a long truce rather than a final peace. His model was the treaty of Tours of 1444 that had resulted in his own marriage, which he evidently did not see as the disaster that most modern historians perceive. English public opinion was not yet ready to

---

80   P. Nightingale, *A Medieval Mercantile Community* (1995), 507–12; J. L. Bolton, 'The City of London 1456–61', *London Journal* xii (1986), 14, 17–20.

acknowledge decisive defeat by France. He proposed the marriage of his heir Prince Edward and sons of York and Somerset to three French princesses. York had sought to marry his heir to a daughter of France a decade earlier and his own daughter to Charles the Bold, only son of Philip of Burgundy, in 1453–4. A match between Somerset and a Scottish princess was mooted.[81] York and Somerset were eligible to European eyes and were willing to be pawns in such diplomatic games. Such proposals assumed and reinforced the restoration of domestic peace. Henry's agents justifiably claimed the backing not only of the king and court, but of York, Norfolk and the Neville earls. An Anglo-French peace was compatible with continued amity towards Burgundy, though it is not certain that this is what Henry intended. Apparently he had still not forgiven Duke Philip for deserting him at the Congress of Arras in 1435![82] Moreover Charles VII was sympathetic. A year earlier he had declined to join in a Scottish attack on England and had waxed eloquent on the financial strain of maintaining defences along 450 leagues of coast from Bayonne to Picardy against enemies who knew the lie of the land as well as he and needed only six hours' favourable wind for the crossing.[83] For him, too, a cessation of hostilities would reduce financial strains; perhaps, as his enemies suspected, it would free him to attack Burgundy, which was harbouring his recalcitrant dauphin, the future Louis XI; perhaps, as he stated more than once, he could then assist crusaders against the Turk.

The fly in the ointment was the Yorkist lords. They interpreted the Loveday as a fresh start, that restored them to favour. Warwick received assignments from the exchequer for his long overdue pay as a royal councillor. York returned many bad tallies dating back to his time in Ireland and obtained substitutes. They continued to co-operate with one another – there was interchange of personnel and Warwick kept in closer touch with the developments in the North – and they were emboldened to act as a particularly forceful pressure group. Reconciliation for them entailed their restoration to political influence and a say, even a decisive say, in the making of policy. No longer defensive, they were self-confident, even aggressive. We have seen evidence of this in Warwick's maritime exploits in the summer of 1458. Nowhere is this more apparent than in international relations.

The Yorkists wanted to share in the making of England's foreign policy. They also wanted to shape it. They were unwilling to be bound by the government's assessment of national interests. They did not perceive that independent foreign policies were the prerogative of sovereign states. Warwick's use of sea-power itself determined national alignments. Moreover York resumed diplomatic manoeuvres of his own. When protector, he had still favoured an aggressive policy towards France, seeing an alliance with the Duke of Alençon as a means to resume the land war; in 1458, with Alençon in custody and about to be tried, this was no longer practical. As protector he had proposed his eldest son Edward as husband for Charles VII's daughter Madeleine. Secret proposals on his behalf

81   A. I. Dunlop, *Life and Times of James Kennedy, Bishop of St Andrews* (1950), 172.
82   M. R. Thielemans, *Bourgogne et l'Angleterre* (Brussels, 1966), 371.
83   Vale, *Charles VII*, 125.

were made on 23 May 1458 to King Charles at Montrichard, several months ahead of direct contacts between the English and French governments; the French proceeded no further because it was dishonourable to treat with a mere subject.[84] Warwick meantime appeared sympathetic to Burgundy. Subsequently the Yorkists committed themselves to Burgundy and undermined any *rapprochement* with France. Warwick's naval activity and their secret diplomacy was designed to align England with Burgundy against France: whether with a view to a resumption of war or merely the creation of a balance of power.

As a treaty would cut the Calais garrison drastically and remove the need for keeping the seas, possibly Warwick was selfishly seeking to perpetuate his appointments and maximize their value by obstructing peace. Certainly his activities forced the government to spend more on defence and postponed indefinitely its financial recovery. The Yorkists damaged England's diplomatic standing abroad, firstly by sending out ambiguous messages to her neighbours and secondly by scuppering the king's initiatives. Apparently it was at this stage that they struck up understandings abroad that helped them through the crises of 1459–61.

Henry VI's peace policy had been unpopular in the 1430s and 1440s, and doubtless there still remained a climate of opinion in England committed to the Hundred Years War as late as 1458. Hence the English made their first tentative approaches under cover of existing negotiations about border disputes in Calais. Warwick himself remained until May 1458 in London preparing the fleet for another summer of action: another reason for the French to wish to come to terms. Maybe he also attended the jousts between the king's and queen's men by the Tower and at Greenwich that followed the Loveday, at which Henry Duke of Somerset and Lord Rivers's son Anthony Wydeville distinguished themselves. Certainly Warwick was among those who on 9 May stood bail for his uncle Fauconberg, who had been imprisoned for some unknown matter – perhaps arising from the various commissions against piracy? – and was now released on condition that he appeared in chancery in October: when Fauconberg appeared, the case was dismissed. The other sureties were Warwick's brother Thomas, Buckingham and Bourchier. Warwick left London on 9 May, marching his retinue through the City at the king's request to overawe those citizens and lawyers who were tempted to resume their recent riots. This was en route for Canterbury, where he arrived in time for vespers on the 10th, on the way to Calais. From Canterbury he was in company with Richard Beauchamp, Bishop of Salisbury.[85]

Earl and bishop were the highest-ranking of twenty-two ambassadors nominated on 14 May to discuss infringements of the truce with Burgundy. They comprised Warwick, his two brothers, Viscount Bourchier and his brother and a son, and several doctors of law. The composition suggests that the Yorkists had

---

84   Scofield, i. 28n.

85   *Six Town Chronicles*, 146. On 15 May pursuant to a writ of 5 May he was paid £258 17s. 1d. cash as backpay from 1455 as a royal councillor, E 403/814 m. 2.

a hand in their selection. On 27 May Philip the Good commissioned a similarly prestigious embassy headed by the Count of Estampes, the bishop of Toul, and the marshal of Burgundy, who arrived soon after Warwick's victory over the Spaniards. They too seem unduly prestigious for dealing with routine border infractions. A secret letter from Duke Philip to Warwick implies that other issues were also to be raised. Probably it was at this time that Bishop Beauchamp spoke off the record to Morice Doulcereau, agent of Pierre de Brezé on behalf of Queen Margaret. He asked Doulcereau to get De Brezé to ask King Charles to resume diplomatic contacts with a view to a 'bonne paix': a treaty with France, he apparently said, was even preferable to one with Burgundy, in whom the queen no longer had any confidence. French and Burgundian responses to these overtures were sufficiently promising for the appointment of further ambassadors to treat with France and Burgundy on 29 August 1458.[86]

By the autumn of 1458 Warwick's naval depredations had put the government under considerable pressure. It took time for Spanish and Genoese complaints to their governments to produce representations to Henry VI, but the Hanse were quicker. On 31 July Rivers, Kyriel, doctors of law and others were commissioned to hold an inquiry into Warwick's battle with the friendly Hanse at Rochester on 9 August.[87] They can hardly have found in his favour, yet the Hanse obtained no satisfaction. Perhaps it was in response to Warwick's aggression that a further French raid by land and sea on the pattern of Sandwich was expected in September 1458 and afterwards. If so, Warwick's conduct ran directly counter to government policy. The king had intended to return to the North, by which probably the Midlands was meant, but a range of issues kept him near to London. It also prevented Waynflete, who was also bishop of Winchester, from visiting Hampshire to see good rule there, to attend to his own business, and for a holiday. The lords were told to remain in the south 'to thentent that yf any grete and sodayn cause falle that the lords shall mowe hastily be assembled and take such direcc[i]on of addresse therinne as shal be for the seurtee wele and hono[u]r of the kinge and his Reaume'. Another great council that was summoned on 26 August to Westminster on 11 October had a rather specialized membership that points to military and diplomatic business: though less than half the bishops and lay magnates were summoned, York, Salisbury, Warwick and Sir John Wenlock were included. The summons speaks of matters 'as concerne specially oure honeure & worship, the welfare of this oure lande and subgittes'. The issues that touched the government on 7 September, the chancellor wrote, were the anticipated French attack, treasonable collusion suspected at Southampton, continued friction between the citizens and men of law in London, and 'the matier concernyng the Jannayes [Genoese]' and 'the takyng of the Shippes of lubyck [Lubeck]' as causes for the change in plan.[88]

---

86   *Stone's Chron.*, 73; *Foedera* v.i. 80; *Paston L & P* ii. 340; Chastellain, *Oeuvres*, iii. 428; Scofield, i. 24–5, Thielemans, *Bourgogne et l'Angleterre*, 371–2.

87   *CPR 1452–61*, 443; *Foedera*, v.i. 82.

88   *Southampton Letters*, 12–13; *POPC* vi. 297.

Warwick's maritime exploits were thus a matter of official concern. It was certainly damaging to the king's 'honeure & worship' that his ships were attacking neutral and friendly shipping and it was surely intolerable that Warwick was determining foreign relations in this way. It was also in blatant contravention of his indenture of appointment as keeper of the seas. Probably Warwick did not intend responding to a summons to what was likely to be a disciplinary hearing. Still at Calais on 23 September, he was at his new house at Collyweston in Northamptonshire on 7 October, whence he wrote to York to ask for the services of his servant Walter Blount as marshal of Calais in succession to Mulsho, who had just died. Whilst decidedly reluctant, for he had uses for Blount himself, York agreed to second him to Warwick for one year only. That was in a letter of 17 October dated at Montgomery, so York was also missing the great council.[89] From Northamptonshire Warwick journeyed to Yorkshire, perhaps to meet his parents and to inquire into the keeping of the marches, of which he was still warden, at a time of unstable relations with the Scots. It was there shortly before 30 October that the king's servant William Say reached him with letters of privy seal from the king 'for divers special causes and matters in the same letters contained that concern the said lord king and council'. What was probably a further summons to the great council was presumably ignored since soon before 6 November John Moody, another royal messenger, served further letters of privy seal on him.[90] Warwick apparently responded, for it was most probably on 9 November when leaving a council session that he was embroiled in a fight in Westminster Hall that nearly cost him his life; an alternative date soon after Candlemas (2 February 1459) does not fit. Escaping by water in his barge, presumably to Greyfriars, he proceeded the same day to Warwick, and then, with the king's permission, returned to Calais. He thus avoided being held to account for his captaincy of Calais and keeping of the seas.

This was an important episode that made a big impression on Warwick. He repeatedly harked back to it and the fact that nobody was punished. Henceforward he distrusted the court and became irreconcilable. His experience may have prevented the events of the next summer from ending peacefully. All the chronicles present the same version of events. It was one of Warwick's retainers who struck the first blow, against a royal servant: itself an offence against the king, in the verge of whose household it occurred, and against the central courts that sat in the hall. The dispute escalated alarmingly: as cooks thronged from the royal kitchens armed with spits and pestles. Warwick's meinie was hard-pressed and suffered serious casualties. He required the intervention of other lords at the council to help him hack his way to his barge. Warwick regarded it as a deliberate assassination attempt, which at first sight seems unlikely: the menial status and improvised weaponry of his opponents militates against it, though it indicates that hostility was running high towards him in the royal household. However Friar Brackley later wanted Warwick reminding of the role in the fight 'at Westminster wharf' of Sir Thomas Tuddenham: formerly

---

89   Ellis, *Original Letters*, ii (1), 125–6.
90   E 403/817 mm. 3, 4.

Suffolk's notorious agent in East Anglia, now a noted courtier and keeper of the great wardrobe, and shortly to be treasurer of the household. If Tuddenham was involved, Warwick had justice in his sinister slant on events. As Warwick's man started it, the queen was justified in blaming Warwick and wanting him punished, but Henry would not allow it.[91] In the alienation of the earl from the court, this was a decisive moment.

Meanwhile informal negotiations were under way with Burgundy and France. The English ambassadors for what was still a low-level mission were Sir John Wenlock and Louis Galet from Calais, two of the lesser members of the May embassy. As her former chamberlain, Wenlock evidently still enjoyed the queen's confidence; after St Albans, however, he had been York's choice as Speaker and his conduct on this mission shows him to be committed to the Yorkists. Wenlock and Galet visited the Burgundian court and reached an understanding with the duchess. Evidently they proposed matches between Prince Edward, York's son and Somerset to the daughters of Charles the Bold, the Dukes of Bourbon and Guelders. Next they went under a safe conduct of 31 October delivered by Doulcereau and presumably procured by De Brezé, who was one of the French negotiators. Peace was agreed to be desirable, the marriages to be an appropriate means, and a truce was a necessary preliminary. Before proceeding further Charles wished to see conditions favourable to a final peace and ambassadors with enough powers. What made a 'paix finale' was likely to prove a sticking point. Modern historians have varyingly interpreted Charles's response as promising or evasion. Certainly it invited more formal negotiations through a more high-powered embassy.

France and Burgundy were unhappy to commit themselves to such an informal embassy and were uncertain whether it really represented the wishes of both the government and the Yorkist lords. They wanted assurances that any agreements were deliverable. Charles despatched his herald Maine to establish the real situation; probably it is his report to which we are indebted. Their suspicions were justified by Wenlock's subsequent behaviour. Returning to Calais, he supplied the Burgundians with a transcript of his understanding with the French, stated that he would inform them in advance of Maine king-at-arms's findings, and added that the French were more eager than the English for an agreement to forestall any hostile intervention by the English in the event of war with Burgundy. He urged Burgundy to keep hold of the dauphin: an action that was sure to prevent a *rapprochement* with France. Evidently Wenlock was currying favour with the Burgundians to prevent any reconciliation between them and France. That this information was then transmitted to Charles VII the following spring must have undermined Anglo-French relations.[92] Not that this

91 *The Brut*, 526; *Davies Chron.* 78; Kingsford, *London Chrons.* 169; *Paston L & P* ii. 214; *Six Town Chrons.* 146, which states that 'Warwyk should have be comyt to the law, but he wisely purveid a remedy therfor'; see also Waurin v. 272. In Dec. 1456 Sir John Neville had a tense confrontation with Somerset in London, Griffiths, *Henry VI*, 800.
92 Kendall, *Warwick*, 45–6; Griffiths, *Henry VI*, 816–17; Watts, *Henry VI*, 313–15. The basic source for all these is Stevenson, i. 361–77.

would have upset Wenlock, had he known, for on his return he reported to King Henry that the French were ready to attack; hence the appointment of new commissions of array for the counties from Cornwall to Lincolnshire on 15 February; hence also preparations on 7–10 March for Warwick's fleet to put to sea.[93]

The great council of January 1459 was ended by the arrest of the Duke of Exeter for striking a lawyer in Westminster Hall.[94] Another was summoned for 2 April to hear appeals for a crusade from a Byzantine knight and from the papal nuncio for a delegation to the General Council of the Church at Mantua. 'And it has been remarked how very few of the lords were at the court of the said king', observed a continental diplomat. An air of consensus and contentment with the government, illustrated by the ballad *On the Ship or Poop*, enticed few lords to attend. Hence the nuncio actually made his address at Coventry, to which the king withdrew on 23 May, and the impressive English delegation was commissioned only in July following another great council known to have met at Coventry after midsummer.[95]

The diplomatic report that is our best source at this stage is summarizing the situation as it appeared in February or perhaps as late as April 1459. Maine herald, the probable author, was still in England angling for safe conducts on 16 March. The report reveals that Exeter's disruption of the assembly was fortunate for Warwick, as it was notorious that he would otherwise have been relieved of the captaincy of Calais. Perhaps Warwick's own ships made him indispensable as keeper of the seas, in which role, shorn of his independent base, he would be easier to control and discipline? Warwick reportedly said that he would serve out the remaining six years of his contract and declared, somewhat implausibly, that he would rather give up his lands in England than the captaincy![96] The young Warwick was apparently prone to such impetuous statements: others were made about Alençon in 1455, Cromwell in 1456, and at Towton in 1461! *Davies' Chronicle* states that a privy seal letter of dismissal was sent to the earl, who rejected it, stating incorrectly that he had been appointed by parliament and, also wrongly, that he could only be removed by it. Perhaps significantly on 26 January 1459 Master Richard Fisher, Warwick's secretary, took the precaution of registering the earl's indenture as keeper of the seas in the exchequer.[97] Neither of Warwick's reported responses could have been made to the king in person or to the great council in session without leading to the earl's arrest. It therefore seems that he did not attend either of the great councils early in 1459 and remained

93   Roncière, *Marine Française*, ii. 294; G. Du Fresne de Beaucourt, *Histoire de Charles VII* (Paris, 1881), vi. 263.

94   Stevenson, i. 367–8.

95   *POPC* vi. 298–9; E 403/817 mm. 7–8; see also C. Head, 'Pius II and the Wars of the Roses', *Archivum Historiae Pontificiae* vii (1) (1970), 143–4; Whetehamstede, i. 335–6; *Foedera* v.ii. 84.

96   Stevenson, i. 368–9; Beaucourt, *Charles VII*, vi. 263.

97   *Davies Chron.* 78–9; E 159/235 commissiones 37 Hen. VI; *Hansisches Urkundenbuch*, viii. 486.

instead in Calais. He was certainly there on 2 April. How could the court oust from a fortress *overseas* the man who controlled the seas?

Had the government been aware of the diplomatic shenanigans of the Yorkist lords, they would have incurred the gravest displeasure, but there is nothing concrete to suggest that they came to official notice. They were not mentioned among the charges later laid against them. Warwick's piracy the previous year seems to have lost him royal confidence and his refusal to surrender Calais constituted rebellion. If modern historians have recently been convinced by a report that Sir Thomas Harrington committed himself to Salisbury and York on 1 November 1458, they have been too bold. The information comes from a declaration of trust cited in an inheritance dispute after 1485 relating to an enfeoffment in a different year: hardly a reliable source.[98] The event is more credible than the date. The Yorkists did not renege on the Loveday: they made the first annual payment of £45 towards their victims' chantry at St Albans Abbey by 11 February. That same day Warwick secured new assignments for bad tallies of £40 3s. 7d., in March royal commissioners were preparing his fleet, and even on 22 June he and his father were assigned £9 5s. as wardens of the West March. These are not 'measures which amounted to a deliberate harrying of the lords', nor a cause for a definitive rupture. We know the queen was not seeking their destruction.[99] The real root of the break is hinted at in a letter of 7 March from Salisbury to John Bromley, Prior of Arbury, traditionally dated to 1455, but actually attributable to 1459.

The letter relates to a time when Salisbury was in London, the queen was at such a distance that communication was by post, and when the prior was intermediary. Since Arbury is an extremely small priory to the north of Coventry, that suggests that the queen was at Kenilworth, Coventry, or thereabouts. York and Warwick were not immediately to hand. And the royal council, of which Salisbury was conspicuously not a member, was also in London. This does not fit 1453, 1454, 1455, 1456, 1457 or 1458, but does fit 1459. Salisbury was out of favour with the queen and had been trying to redeem himself with the prior as intermediary. His most recent assurances had been well received by her. Moreover, Salisbury reported, she had written to the lords of the council in pursuit of 'rest and unitee' and on terms that pleased him and would please also 'al thos whoome the matiere of the said blessed lettres touchen'. . . . Were they his associates or his enemies? Even as one source of disagreement dissolved, the prior had informed him of new charges by those of 'ryght hie estates' against him, York, and Warwick. We do not know what these were. If true, they were to their 'grete rebuke' and probably treasonable, since Salisbury hastily denied that 'I never ymagined, thought, ore saied eny suche matere or eny thing like therunto in my dayes'. He did not believe that York or Warwick had either, but doubtless

---

98   T. D. Whittaker, *History & Antiquities of Richmondshire*, ii. 167, quoted e.g. in Pollard, 'Northern retainers', 52; idem, *North-Eastern England*, 269. There is no inquisition or will for Sir Thomas.

99   *CCR 1454–61*, 369; *CPR 1452–61*, 494; E 401/863, sub 9 Feb.; Scofield, *Edward IV*, i 30n; E 403/819 m. 4.

they would deny it themselves. The letter ends by asking the prior to deny the charges on his behalf and assuring him of his own patronage.[100]

What new charge had suddenly been made against all three lords? Was it their dabblings in foreign policy? Had they been among those suggesting that Prince Edward was a bastard? Had they been planning a further coup? We cannot tell. There are no indictments and nothing in the 1459 act of attainder casts any direct light. However, all three lords are again linked. Most probably Salisbury's rebuttal was unsuccessful. Evidently he left London before the crusader's reception and was probably in the North when he made his will on 10 May. Some uprising was presumably feared on 26 April, when several East Anglian squires were summoned by privy seals to Leicester on 10 May with as many men as they could make defensibly arrayed prepared for two months service. And on 7 May 3,000 bowstaves and sheaves of arrows were ordered to the Tower 'considering the enemies on every side approaching us, as well upon the sea *as upon the land'*. Whilst that could allude to the anticipated French invasion or the Scottish assault on Roxburgh, it implies that the enemy were co-operating with English traitors. Most probably it relates to fears of another insurrection by the Yorkist lords in England and from Calais that prefigured what actually happened in September. If so, it did not immediately materialize. There is no direct evidence that anything actually happened. No uprising was alleged by the Lancastrians in the *Somnium Vigilantis* or the 1459 act of attainder. Salisbury's will, far from prefiguring a treasonable rebellion, presumed a peaceful death and an heir eligible to succeed him.[101]

About 23 May 1459 Henry VI returned to the Midlands and convened another great council at Coventry soon after midsummer (24 June). As usual, many lords were probably absent beside Archbishop Bourchier, York, Warwick and Salisbury, the Bishops of Ely (William Grey) and Exeter (George Neville), the Earl of Arundel and Viscount Bourchier; yet, according to *Benet's Chronicle*, all these were indicted by the counsel of the queen 'at Coventry'. Apart from the Yorkist lords themselves, the two Bourchiers, and Warwick's brother George, both Grey and Arundel had strong Yorkist connections, the bishop as York's kinsman and appointee and Arundel as husband to Warwick's sister Joan. The implication is that they did not attend because they knew they would be charged with something. They were charged; it does not follow from *Benet's Chronicle* that they were yet convicted. No formal action against them, such as summonses or arrests, are recorded in the royal records, but then the council and privy seal records and issue rolls all fail us at this point. Most probably, in the light of the Yorkists' complaints to the king in September, aspersions were cast on their allegiance, charges were made regarding earlier events that were covered by earlier pardons much as in the 1459 attainder itself, and articles now lost were laid against them, perhaps for trial at a later council.

---

100   J. H. Flemming, *England under the Lancastrians* (1921), 128–9.
101   Stevenson, ii.ii 511; *Testamenta Eboracensia* ii. ed. J. Raine (Surtees Soc. xxx, 1855), 239–46.

These deductions make sense of comments below later attributed by Abbot Whetehamstede to Warwick. They are also compatible with a great council at Coventry discussed in the 1459 act of attainder; regrettably the relevant passage is undated and states firmly (in apparent contradiction of *Benet's Chronicle*) that York and Warwick were present. Benet can however be read as implying that they were present, perhaps later, perhaps in response to the letter (summons?) sent to Warwick at Calais on 7 July mentioned on the issue rolls.[102] In the chronological sequence of charges against York, this one follows the Loveday of March 1458, after which the June 1459 assembly is the only Coventry great council. The passage cannot relate to earlier sessions at Coventry in spring 1457, since Warwick was absent, nor that of autumn 1456, when York departed on good terms with the king and it was Buckingham who was himself aggrieved at the dismissal from office of his Bourchier half-brothers.[103] In the session described in the attainder Buckingham was York's prime accuser and the Bourchiers themselves were accused. On 20 July 1459 at Coventry livery of dower worth up to £600 a year was granted to Buckingham's second son Henry and the latter's new wife Margaret Beaufort Dowager-Countess of Richmond.[104] It was not until 25 July that the Mantua delegation was commissioned. June/July 1459 thus appears the most probable date. Our source for this event is no more precise than the 1459 attainder's treatment of the Dartford and St Albans episodes, which can each refer to only one occasion, and expects them to be as familiar to its audience as those other occasions. The great council produced two formal acts that were originally appended to the 1459 act, but which have since been lost.

The scene opens with 'dyvers rehercels by your Chaunceller of Englond in youre moost high presence made to the seid Duc of York' in person. Next

> The Duc of Buckingham, on the bihalf of the Lordes Temporell, reherced full notably to make the seid Duc of York to understonde of what demeanyng he had bene, and lete hym witte that he had no thyng to lene to, sauf oonly your Grace, as more playnly is conteyned in an Acte therof made.

This was a formal process that resulted in a formal act of the great council. It sounds as though Lord Chancellor Waynflete laid charges against York (and indeed Warwick) for the Lords to judge, that York was convicted, and that Buckingham, perhaps as steward of England, pronounced the verdict. The king, always over-merciful, remitted the sentence. Next Buckingham and the Lords begged the king on their knees not to show any more clemency to York, but instead that

102   Benet's Chron. 223; E 403/819 mm. 5, 6 (7 July). Expenses for delivering most summonses to the great council at Coventry were attributed to 2 July, ibid. m. 5.
103   *The Coventry Leet Book*, ii, ed. M. D. Harris (EETS 102, 1908), 297–8; Wolffe, *Henry VI*, 310; Griffiths, *Henry VI*, 773–4, 801; Johnson, *York*, 179; J. R. Lander, *Government and Community: England 1450–1509* (1976), 199.
104   *CPR 1452–61*, 504; *POPC* v. 302. Note that on 25 July Salisbury was not included on an embassy to the Scots, *Foedera* v.ii. 85.

seyng the grete Jupartie for youre moost noble persone, and also the Lordes
so often charged, and inquietyng so often the grete parte of your Realme,
that it shuld not lyke You to shewe the seid Duc of York, nor noon other
herafter, [your] grace, if they attempted eftsones to do the contrary to
youre Roiall estate, or inquietyng of youre Realme and the Lordes therof,
but to be punyshed after their deserte, and have as they deserved, aswell
for the suerte of You, Soverayne Lord, as the generall suertee of all youre
Lordes and people.

To which the king replied 'that Ye wuld so doo'. The message was clear: no clemency for new offences. The words 'so often' reveal that York was charged with
the whole series of his coups. The articles sound like a preview of the 1459 act of
attainder itself. That what precipitated the charges was a further attempted coup
is suggested by a second enactment against the 'weye of feete'. Any lord feeling
himself aggrieved should henceforth complain to the king and seek redress
through the courts and 'noon otherwise' . . .

Remember that York's oath at St Paul's after his insurrection at Dartford had
specifically outlawed 'the weye of feete'. It was the same oath that he was required
to take again, *John Vale's Book* records, because it was still appropriate.[105] York
swore on the Bible to observe the act and signed it. Warwick, who was also
present, 'swore and signed the same Acte'. He also took another oath and offered
surety that he signed with his own hand and sealed with his seal: probably a bond
for good behaviour quite possibly secured by sureties from third parties. That
Warwick subscribed and took the oath indicates that he was also covered by the
charges: at this point the act of attainder was concerned only with York. Salisbury
may have been occupied with the Scots in the North, where the king despatched
messages both in May and July.

The Coventry assembly was a very public humiliation for the Yorkist lords,
whose coups d'état, which they still regarded as loyal demonstrations, were
labelled as treason not only by their peers, but also by their king. They were given
one more last chance. Because they were pardoned and had submitted they were
allowed to go free and retain their appointments, such as Warwick's captaincy of
Calais. They withdrew, York to Ludlow, Salisbury to Middleham, and Warwick
to Calais. Even Henry's mercy proved misplaced, for the Yorkists resented their
treatment, were aggrieved that past matters covered by royal pardons had been
raked up against them again, and rejected the verdict. They perjured themselves
even as they swore their oaths, as they doubtless considered under duress, and
planned at once on a further resort to force.

From this point there are two different interpretations of events, each partisan
and propagandist. The Lancastrian version is that stated in the tract called the
Somnium Vigilantis and the act of attainder later that same year. It presents the
Yorkists as deliberate conspirators and traitors. Having withdrawn to their
estates, they planned a rapid advance from Calais by Warwick to take the king by

105   *RP* v. 347; *Vale's Bk.* 193–4.

surprise at Kenilworth. They could then 'sodenly have fulfilled their traiterous entent', which was the destruction of the king, royal family, and those lords prepared to die for the king. To what end?

> In so moche that by Robert Radclif, oon of the felauship of the seid Duc of York, and Erles of Warrewyk and Salesbury, it was confessed at his dying, that both the Coroune of Englond and Duchie of Lancastre they wold have translated at their wille and pleasure.[106]

York was after the throne. He failed because their actions were anticipated, the king himself turned out against them and attracted a larger force, and because their followers would not fight the king once they knew that this was what they were doing.

There is no Lancastrian version of events dating from the time of the rebellion itself. We know nothing directly of the king's proclamations, overtures, or responses to Yorkist correspondence, which does not mean, as some historians have suggested, that such utterances were not made. In the longer term, then and later, the Yorkists won the propaganda war. We have lost most of this Yorkist literature. We still have the manifesto issued by Warwick as he advanced from Calais to London, a letter in *Davies' Chronicle* that the Yorkist lords in Ludlow sent to the king in Leominster which refers to earlier exchanges, and a record of their response in Whetehamstede's *Register* to a royal offer of pardon. Their version also colours almost all the chronicles, which apply it not merely to this crisis, but use it as framework for events since 1456. The Yorkists presented themselves as loyal subjects, the king's 'loveres', who sought to clear their names against unjust accusations and to reform the government for the common good. They sought an audience with the king to explain themselves and came in force to protect themselves since none of his pardons nor safe conducts could guarantee their safety. Instead they were attacked by malicious enemies who kept the truth from the king and hoped for a share of the Yorkists' forfeited property. If any violence ensued, it was not the fault of them, but their enemies. Much of this is reminiscent of earlier Yorkist coups, on which this one was evidently modelled, which does not mean that it was not what they themselves believed. Most chroniclers swallowed it.

6.4 Rout

The Yorkist uprising occurred in September, but with three such distant bases as Calais, Middleham and Ludlow it required considerable prior co-ordination. Allegedly there was plotting in London on 4 July by Sir William Oldhall and Thomas Vaughan, York's retainers, by Warwick's mother at Middleham on

---

106 *RP* v. 348–9. This was also the charge in 1460, C. L. Scofield, 'The Capture of Lord Rivers and Sir Anthony Woodville, 19 January 1460', *EHR* xxxvii (1922), 255.

1 August, and by the bailiff of Bawtry later the same month.[107] The manifesto issued by Warwick discloses a plan that required agreement considerably ante-dating both his arrival in London about 20 September and the battle of Blore Heath (23 September). The Lancastrians had good grounds for declaring the plot to have been precogitated long before. Probably it was at the Coventry great council itself and certainly not long after that the Yorkist lords decided to resort once again to arms. Once again their stated objective was an audience to put their case to the king: a captive king. This was a euphemism for another coup d'état that placed them in control of the administration.

The manifesto justifies the uprising. Although unattributed, it is couched in the first person plural ('wee'), and thus speaks for all three Yorkist lords. That it is unsigned and anticipated help from 'lordis of like disposicion' indicates their confidence in the support of some other peers. Once again it was a loyal protes-tation on behalf of the king's 'loveres' that claimed the moral high ground by promoting the interests of commonwealth and king. It appealed five times to God's authority: to his laws, his knowledge, grace and mercy. There was no preamble to a comprehensive indictment of the regime under five heads, of which the fifth was that the king did not know how bad things were. It was therefore feasible and justifiable to draw them forcibly to his attention. 'Seying these mischefes so parelous', the authors intend 'with lordis of like disposicion' to seek an audience with the king 'as lowly as we canne' to inform him of the real situa-tion and to obtain remedies for mischiefs, punishment of those responsible according to their deserts, and good government for his 'loveres'. England's trade, law and order, wealth, prosperity and international standing would thereby be restored to their former levels. Whilst offering their services 'aboute the kinges most noble persone and ther to be assistente yif it be his pleasir', the Yorkists promised not to take on the rule themselves nor to act for their own profit or private revenge. It was the king on 'thadvice of the grete lordes of his blood' whom they envisaged actually undertaking the reforms.

Nobody, surely, could object to such a programme, for England was certainly in a parlous state, the manifesto explains, and hence was not respected by her neighbours. The law was not properly observed, all kinds of crimes being committed, condoned and left unpunished. In particular insufficient regard was paid to the king's person, laws and commandments, 'to his presence, in his coun-sele, ne to the lordes spirituelx or temporelx in his counseill, ne to his iuges or officeres in his lawe setting inexecucion of the same et cetera'. Surely here Warwick was referring directly to the attack on him at the great council at Westminster the previous autumn? Henry was so impoverished that he could not maintain his estate even by resorting to 'unlefull meanes deceyvably and ageinste all Goddis lawe' that either hurt merchants – for example, by not paying debts and by selling exemptions from customs – or the poor from whom foodstuffs were requisitioned without payment. This was no fault of the king himself, who was as graciously concerned for the common weal as any Christian monarch, but

---

107   *RP* v. 349. I have relied for the course of events on A. Goodman, *The Wars of the Roses* (1981), 26–30.

of his covetous councillors, of the 'uttireste malice ageins such as God knowithe beene the verreye loveres of the said common wele'.[108]

This manifesto is shorter and less substantial than those of earlier years and overlaps little in content. Here are no denunciations of treason, nothing about Duke Humphrey or the loss of France, which were all out of date. No evil councillors are named. No solutions are proposed. It is deliberately unfair to the government in its denunciation of contemporary problems. If crime was a problem, so it had been throughout the reign; if aristocratic feuding was at fault, all such feuds had been stilled; and anyway the Yorkists were as responsible as any. Far from aristocratic feuds escalating, each in turn was terminated, admittedly not always justly, and none remained in progress when civil war broke out. If the king's finances were notoriously parlous, this was no longer because of his extravagance, for his household had been curtailed and there had been an effective resumption of his grants, but because he had insufficient money to meet his commitments. The debts of the Hundred Years War remained unpaid and unpayable. Richard II's income approaching £120,000 had dwindled to a third by the late 1450s. The most regular source of income, the customs, was appropriated to defence – to Calais, to the keeping of the seas, and to the defence of the marches towards Scotland – and some at least of his limited landed resources were similarly applied. And yet they did not suffice. The Yorkists knew this: Warwick after all, as captain of Calais, keeper of the seas, and joint-warden of the West March, was receiving much of what royal revenues there were. What else was there for the king to call on? When the Yorkists complained that Henry was 'soo unmesurable and outerageously spoiled and robbed from his lyvelodes and possessions perteyning therunto', they knew perfectly well that the only way resumption of royal grants could bring in more was by stretching the scope to expropriate the queen, the prince and the king's brothers, and thus pass beyond those limits that parliament had found unacceptable in 1456. Nobody was grossly enriching themselves at the king's expense in 1459 except, perhaps, Warwick himself.

The proposed remedies are equally disingenuous. It may be that the Yorkist lords had been denied a right of reply at the Coventry great council, but their views had long been known and heard. Whenever available, they and other great lords of the king's blood had been summoned to the frequent great councils up to and including the three in 1459. It was the verdict of the Lords that they now rejected. Only in the last nine months had they themselves stopped attending. Their promises now to leave reform to the king and the great lords of his blood and avoid private quarrels struck the right notes, for the Yorkists had their private enemies and threats of vengeance could be expected to generate more, but they are hardly convincing. Who were these evil councillors who were to be punished? Which royal princes were to be consulted, since obviously Somerset, Exeter, the king's half brother Pembroke, or even Buckingham were not to be included? Who was to manage the king? Given Henry's clear opposition to them

108 *Vale's Bk.* 208–10.

and the 'weye of feete' at the Coventry great council, was not there to be another protectorate or at least a further Yorkist domination of the government? Despite the accusation in the subsequent act of attainder, the Yorkist lords did not speak of deposition, only of loyalty and respect. Of course their language might have changed had they achieved a higher degree of success. If they could get an audience with the king and overawe him with their retainers, the Yorkists were confident of again securing control.

The manifesto, in short, was an exercise in publicity that used constitutionally appropriate language rather than a serious declaration of Yorkist intentions. It does not build on earlier manifestos or those aspects specifically associated in the past and future with York himself, and the topical allusions concerned Warwick most closely. It may not even have been distributed widely, for too much of it seems aimed at a specifically mercantile and London-based audience. All this suggests that it was Warwick's first essay in manifesto-writing, prepared with the Yorkists' agreed objectives in mind, but devised by Warwick himself. Maybe it was designed merely to get Warwick into London where the surviving copy ended up. It was meant to disarm opposition and perhaps win popular support rather than to recruit supporters. There is no specific appeal for support and Warwick's movements were too rapid in 1459 to permit serious recruitment. The idealistic and public-spirited tone of the manifesto, in short, was merely a veneer to the insurrection of a clique. Although following so closely on the Coventry council and stimulated by it, the rebellion was not born of desperation. Had not the Yorkist lords been awarded a last chance to accept the rules of the political game and take their place among the constitutional players? Had they not been allowed to retain their great offices, their military commands, and their existing royal offices? Admittedly the Coventry verdict limited them to their legal entitlements in their various feuds and required them to accept the right of the government to rule. Both were unacceptable to them. The three Yorkist lords were determined to replace the ruling regime with themselves, to rule once again in the king's name, and to destroy their enemies, both public and private. They hoped for support from others. But they were prepared to go it alone, to rely once again on the use of force, and to hazard everything on the gamble of another coup d'état.

Warwick crossed from Calais with a force of five hundred that included members of the Calais garrison led by Trollope and Blount, master porter and marshal of Calais. They overnighted on 20/21 September in London, probably where Wenlock and Colt joined them, and proceeded forthwith to Warwickshire. This was part of a three-pronged campaign. Salisbury was to bring the northerners. York assembled men from the Welsh marches. Warwick's march and use of the Calais garrison was to surprise the court, so the Lancastrians later claimed.[109] It seems unlikely. No march through London and the heart of the kingdom could be concealed; Henry knew of it before the earl was at hand. Moreover Warwick was later on the scene than his father. It could be that he was

109   *RP* v. 348.

delayed by contrary winds, as in 1458; possibly York and Salisbury were to act first and Warwick was to catch up later; and most probably all three were to meet up somewhat later, perhaps at Worcester or at Warwick, and seize the king together. They must have counted on Warwick's West Midlanders. Remember that they hoped for a bloodless coup, not a trial of strength or civil war. Hence Warwick brought only a select elite sufficient to overawe a king when taken by surprise. Salisbury may have been near full-strength – the Lancastrian act of attainder speaks of 5,000 men – but the Yorkist chroniclers indicate a more modest company that was outnumbered by a fragment of the royal forces at Blore Heath. We know only that Salisbury brought his sons Thomas and John, Sir John Conyers steward of Middleham, the Lancashire knight Sir Thomas Harrington, William brother of Lord Stanley, the Cumbrian squire Thomas Parre, and the Yorkshireman Sir James Pickering and Thomas Meryng of Tong.[110] The Yorkists' precise plans are obscured by effective royal countermeasures that diverted Salisbury through Cheshire, brought him prematurely to battle, and made it impossible for Warwick to recruit in his heartland, so close to Kenilworth and Coventry, or even pass through it safely. He was lucky to miss Somerset at Coleshill on 21 September. The property of such retainers as Richard Clapham and the Hugfords was plundered.[111]

King Henry knew in advance of Salisbury's preparations in the North and of his progress southwards from Middleham. He therefore proceeded in force to Nottingham, which caused the earl to divert westwards, and then shadowed Salisbury through Staffordshire, driving him through Cheshire on his way to Ludlow. There, at Blore Heath near Market Drayton on the road from Newcastle-under-Lyme to Shrewsbury, Salisbury was intercepted by a some- what larger local detachment commanded by Lords Audley and Dudley; the queen had a larger force to the north-west and the king was a little further away to the north-east. Salisbury wished to avoid fighting and parleyed. He could have withdrawn his forces or disbanded them without penalty. Since he was de- termined to link up with York, he had to fight. It was a fateful decision. The battle took place on 23 September. The hard-fought encounter was duly won, Audley being killed and Dudley captured. Salisbury's own force suffered casualties: both his sons Thomas and John were wounded and sent home, but were unfortunately captured by the Lancastrians at Acton Bridge near Tarporley (Ches.) soon after- wards. Salisbury was able to continue to Ludlow to join York, who had arrayed the men of the marches including, once again, Devereux.

Fighting had been no part of the Yorkist plan: 'hit was not thare entent, but happeth casually and ayenst thar wyll'.[112] It was to have serious repercussions. The battle demonstrated Salisbury's rebellious intentions and caused the king to

110   *RP* v. 349.
111   KB 9/313/57. They repeatedly complained about such unjust treatment, *Davies Chron.* 83, 89.
112   J. P. Gilson, 'A Defence of the Proscription of the Yorkists in 1459', *EHR* xxvi (1911), 516.

proclaim those involved to be traitors.[113] That discouraged others from joining, most notably Warwick's own brother-in-law Stanley, husband of his sister Eleanor and the most powerful magnate in north-west England. Once again the three Yorkist lords failed to find 'lordis of like disposicion' to join them. Sympathizers and those who shared some of their grievances, such as the Bourchier peers, again failed to commit themselves. The Yorkists' final appeal to the king was once again in the names only of York, Salisbury and Warwick. Denunciation as traitors also rendered unreliable those already recruited, none of whom had been told that treason was intended and whom the king conceded had been 'blynded' by the blandishments of their lords.[114] Warwick's contingent from Calais may have specifically requested and secured prior assurances that they were not being led against the king.[115]

The element of surprise was lost. Whilst Warwick did evade Somerset and joined his father and uncle, they were henceforth isolated – Clinton and Grey of Powys being the only peers to join them[116] – and on the defensive. They could not add substantially to their forces, for the king barred access to most of the kingdom, whilst the longer the confrontation lasted the more lords, retainers and 'naked men' (county levies) joined him. The Yorkists advanced from Ludlow through Worcester, where they faced the king's army in battle array, and then withdrew successively to Warwick's town of Tewkesbury, across the Severn to Ludlow, and thence to nearby Ludford, where they made their final stand. They drew up their forces above the River Teme in a defensive position, which they fortified additionally with carts, guns and obstacles. They fired on the king's forces 'aswell at youre most Roiall persone as at youre Lordes and people with You than and there being': clear treason. To embolden their men, that treason was not an issue, they proclaimed that the king was dead and even celebrated mass for his soul. Henry, unfortunately, showed himself to be alive, promised pardons to those who submitted, and thus induced Trollope's crucial Calais contingent to desert on the night of 12/13 October. The Yorkist leadership abandoned their army during the night. Warwick, Salisbury and York's eldest son fled to Calais, York and his next son Rutland to Ireland. Henry had rightly based his strategy on the unwillingness of the Yorkist rank-and-file to face him: on his moral authority, which incorporated the duty of allegiance that overrode other loyalties, the dread due to God's representative, and the horror with which treason was regarded. He wrongly expected Yorkist commanders would retrieve their desperate situation by submitting.

It is not clear how early the Yorkists wrote to the king to tell him that they sought the prosperity and advancement of him and the common weal. Henry refused to meet them, we may deduce, unless they laid down their arms and came as obedient subjects. Next they prepared an indenture testifying to their loyalty

113   RP v. 348.
114   Ibid.; cf. Foedera v.i. 97.
115   Gregory's Chron. 205.
116   Davies Chron. 81–3.

before independent witnesses in Worcester Cathedral, and consecrated it by taking communion at the hands of the notable canonist Master William Lyndwood. This process (so reminiscent of 1452) could be expected to appeal to the pious king and demonstrated, so they claimed, their loyalty and good intentions. They sent him one part of the indenture through an intermediary, the prior of Worcester. When this failed to secure the desired response, they certified the indenture to the king again by the hand of Garter king of arms. In a final letter of 10 October, which they sent from Ludlow to the king at Leominster, they made a direct appeal to him in person, whom they rightly saw as more open to persuasion and reconciliation than those about him. All they asked, so they said, was to make their complaints to their sovereign in surety: safe from arrest and violence? They were loyal subjects, they said, who had eschewed any effusion of blood – the dead of Blore Heath, by implication, had been the aggressors – and they would fight only if they had no choice. Their obligation as loyal subjects to submit unconditionally to royal authority was not regarded as an option. Nevertheless, so they complained, they had been unjustly accused of disloyalty and their tenants had been unlawfully despoiled. Their opponents were actuated by greed for a share of their estates. They urged Henry to accept their protestations of loyalty as set out in their Worcester indenture and not to allow himself to be influenced by their enemies, who coveted their lands and cared not for the effusion of Christian blood.[117]

Their appeal sounds reasonable. It was designed to touch both the king and those around him and has impressed some modern historians, who strangely perceive the Yorkists seeking a negotiated settlement rather than continuing their defiance. It failed. It contained no recognition that the Yorkists as subjects were engaged in rebellion or in treason. They expected their case to be conceded as well as heard and they were confident that it would be conceded once heard. Again they thought that they could mould King Henry as they wished. But it was too late and misjudged the king. By 10 October Henry was too strong to offer them what they were seeking and replied that he would see them on the field of battle. Judging from Waurin, the Yorkist line once again was that their missives were kept from the king and that others were in command, but this time Henry was not the tool in the hands of evil councillors that they portrayed. It was he himself who had declared at the Coventry great council that he would no longer tolerate the use of force and who promised to punish future offenders according to their deserts. Henry now took the lead in the repression. He had already made them a most generous offer of terms that guaranteed them their lives and property.

Henry was a merciful man and a most remarkable conciliator. There can surely have been few if any English kings who had been so prepared to let bygones be bygones, who had placed such emphasis on reconciliation, and who was so ready to work with those who had offended him. Faced with the incorrigible insurrections of the Yorkists and the verdict against them of the Lords at the Coventry

117   Waurin, 275.

great council, he had forgiven them, though for the last time. Following yet another attempted Yorkist coup, he was prepared to negotiate – hence the presence with the Yorkists of Garter king of arms – and offered to pardon them yet again. This was at Worcester in the person of Bishop Beauchamp. Whetehamstede reports that Henry not only offered them their lives, liberty, and property, but also to receive them once again as his dear kin and to treat them with the same favour as before.[118]. The offer excluded those who had already been proclaimed as traitors for the battle of Blore Heath, presumably Salisbury, his younger sons, Harrington and Stanley. This may have been crucial – Salisbury cannot have liked it and Warwick could have lost his Neville inheritance – but they could reasonably hope for further clemency later. For York and Warwick a return to the *status quo ante* without penalty was surely better than any defeated rebel could reasonably expect. Amazingly the time-limit of six days for acceptance of this pardon was allowed to expire. Again, on the eve of Ludford, Henry offered pardons of life and limb to all who submitted; those who accepted recovered their lands soon after. In between, the summonses for a new parliament, issued on 9 October, a day before the Leominster letter and two days before Ludford, are as likely to have assured the Yorkists of a public hearing as threatened them with destruction.[119] And as we shall see, even when the Yorkists were attainted, King Henry explicitly reserved the right to forgive and restore those attainted without further recourse to parliament.[120]

These were generous terms that deny any justice to the Yorkists' claim that they were driven to extremes by desperation arising from harsh treatment. However, they make no concessions to the Yorkists' persistent and passionate, if irrational and unacceptable, belief, that they were loyal and that their coup did not contradict their oaths. They were right and everybody else was wrong. Further insight into their mentality is offered by Abbot Whetehamstede's report of a speech by Warwick which, though Latinized, literary and embroidered, rings several bells. Warwick gave three reasons. First of all, he said, they had learnt that the king's pardons even when confirmed by parliament provided no protection. Here is surely a reference to their indictment at Coventry on charges covered by pardons and which had even, in the case of St Albans, been confirmed by parliament. Secondly, because those about the king did not observe his commands. They were men without prudence and counsel who needed reforming. The Yorkists, it seemed, would not accept a pardon that did not remove the current government and, by implication, replace its members with themselves! They would only cease their rebellion if they secured the objective for which they had rebelled! And thirdly, Warwick stated, they refused because the pardon offered them no real protection at great councils and parliaments, as Warwick himself could testify from his own experience when attending a great

---

118   Whetehamstede, i. 339.
119   S. J. Payling, 'The Coventry Parliament of 1459: a Privy Seal Writ concerning the Election of Knights of the Shire', *HR* lx (1987), 349–52; see also Griffiths, *Henry VI*, 823; Watts, *Henry VI*, 352n.
120   *RP*, v. 350.

council at Westminster to which he had been summoned by writ of privy seal and when counselling the king. This was a reference to the incident in November 1458.[121]

Whetehamstede's account is consistent with the stance of the Yorkists presented somewhat later in the *Somnium Vigilantis*. it explains what is otherwise inexplicable: why Warwick and the others rejected Henry's offer. All three, it seems, no longer had any confidence in the king's promises. Warwick, it seems, was finally disillusioned by the attack on him in Westminster Hall; for his father and uncle, it was their trial at Coventry on old forgiven charges that was conclusive. Hence they rejected the lifeline that the king offered them. The time for conciliation had passed. It was all or nothing now. They had passed imperceptibly from coups d'état, taking over the existing government, to civil war. They had rejected the consensus of the Lords at Coventry and now they rejected the military logic of their position. Their defiance threatened them with death and ruin. When Trollope deserted, they could still have made their peace and secured pardons, as so many of their leading followers did, but they did not seek them. That they did not, that they accepted the inevitable attainder that followed, surely means that even as they fled they intended to renew the struggle and to secure more than they had been offered. Even in defeat and flight, the Yorkist lords were already committed to seizing power by force once again. That was a mutual understanding before they fled. Probably they already hoped to achieve their objectives peacefully, by playing once again on Henry's clemency, from a position of strength.

121 Whetehamstede, i. 339–41.

7

Fortune's First Wheel
1459–61

7.1 *Reculer pour mieux sauter*

The rout at Ludford was one of the lowest points in Warwick's career. It was succeeded with extraordinary speed by a peak. From defeat and disgrace the Yorkists bounced back. Within a year York was protector for a third time. Warwick was the principal architect of this achievement. By now he overshadowed his ageing father, the teenaged Earl of March, and even York himself. His command of Calais and mastery of the seas first secured Calais and then made it into a springboard for invasion; it was probably he who devised the strategy and prepared the propaganda for the Yorkist riposte; he who commanded the invasion of Kent and the attack on the king's army at Northampton; and it was certainly he who was everywhere securing the new Yorkist regime. Warwick occurs planning, consulting, orating and persuading, pressing always for the bolder course and carrying it through to triumphant success. Warwick was a splendid military commander, a chivalric hero, and a statesman of international renown. He was worthy of the throne itself. Or so he seems. For Warwick's new-found eminence, so modern historians have come to realize, owes much to the admiration and eulogies of Waurin.[1] Whilst true, this is not entirely fair. Much of what Waurin says is supported by other sources. Rebel propaganda eulogized all the exiled lords. Other Yorkist chronicles also give Warwick the dominant role. Other witnesses wrote in just as exaggerated language at the time, not from hindsight: the papal legate, two anonymous correspondents, and Friar Brackley. If there was a time when Warwick was indeed 'an overmighty subject' and 'an idol of the multitude', it was in 1460.

Yet when the Yorkist lords fled so shamefully from Ludford, they did not attempt to hold out on any of their estates in England and Wales, as they could

1 E.g. Johnson, *York*, 213.

have done: several of their castles in Wales resisted after Ludford.[2] Instead they fled overseas, where they were secure from capture and could perhaps recoup their military resources. Ireland, where York was lieutenant, the greatest land-holder, and a former resident, was a logical destination. Warwick too may have intended going to Ireland. Was it mere accident that the two parties were separated and that Warwick's mother went to Ireland whilst his father ended up in Calais? Calais was where Warwick arrived. York's company was the larger. With him was his second son, the 16-year-old Edmund Earl of Rutland.[3] Warwick was accompanied by his father, Wenlock, Colt, Sir James Pickering and York's eldest son Edward Earl of March, the future Edward IV. That March was separated from York suggests that already it was considered essential to keep at large a representative of the house of York as an alternative claimant to the crown.

Though separated geographically, there were now four Yorkist lords: York himself, 'manly and mygtfulle' and 'of gret substaunce', who 'rideth and rulethe withe ryalle reputation'; the prudent Salisbury, royal, wise and undefeated; Warwick, the renowned warrior; and March, the 'Rose' of Rouen, fresh, prudent and 'manly-hede', 'trewe in euery tryall', and 'comyn of blode ryall'.[4] Now aged seventeen, March features in Yorkist poetry and manifestos alike.

Warwick travelled to the coast and took ship. His embarkation could have been from South Wales,[5] but was probably not. What lord of Glamorgan in South Wales could need to borrow the 220 nobles ($£76.66$) to buy a small ship (a balinger)? More probably he embarked in North Devon, the home country of his companion John Dynham, who allegedly put up the money. Later Edward IV was to refund $£84$ to Dynham's mother Joan for her costs.[6] They hired a crew, apparently a master and three seamen, pretending to embark for Bristol, and then revealed that they were sailing westwards. To this the crew disconcertingly responded that they did not know the way which, in Waurin's words, much abashed Salisbury and the others! As keeper of the seas Warwick had some relevant experience, albeit as an admiral with master mariners to handle his vessels, so now he took command, swearing by God and St George that he would carry them all to a port of safety. Ireland was accessible, but Warwick took them instead to Guernsey, one of his former possessions which he may well have previously visited and where the governor was Nanfan, his trusted retainer. Nanfan's garrison of 130 archers was probably on Jersey. The fugitives stayed there 'to refresh themselves' and await favourable winds, before proceeding up the Channel eastwards to Calais, which they entered on 2 November 1459 by a postern gate: presumably in case the town was already in Lancastrian hands. There they were well-received by Fauconberg and by the Countess Anne, who had heard of their flight and feared the worst. At once the fugitives gave thanks

2 Ibid. 194.
3 The fullest list is in ibid. 199n.
4 Robbins, *Hist. Poems*, 219–21.
5 Waurin, 277; Johnson, *York*, 195.
6 Waurin, 277–8; Kingsford, *London Chrons.* 171; E 403/824 m. 2.

for their deliverance at the shrine of Notre Dame de St Pierre by Calais (Newnham Bridge), returning to disappoint the herald announcing Somerset's impending takeover as captain.[7]

No battle occurred at Ludford on 13 October. The Yorkist army was leaderless. The Lancastrians pillaged Ludlow. No doubt some of the deserted Yorkists fled. If some were hanged,[8] they were few, for we know nothing of them. Traitors uncovered later were indeed tried and executed. Most of the rebels submitted, were pardoned and fined.[9] Since very few formal patents of pardon were issued and no list of payments survives, we cannot know the composition of the Yorkist army. A handful of more serious offenders like Devereux were pardoned their lives, but forfeited their property and were scheduled for attainder at the forthcoming parliament. For those who would not make their peace, the penalties of treason inevitably followed; their property was treated as forfeit even ahead of parliament.

For unrepentant traitors the government's model was Oldhall's attainder of 1453. Attainder was a development of the doctrine of treason applied to earlier traitors. When Warwick's great-grandfather John Earl of Salisbury and his countess's grandfather Thomas Lord Despenser died as rebels in 1400, they had forfeited only those lands that they held in fee simple and in trust; those entailed on their heirs were protected and subsequently many such heirs were restored to the remainder also. Now treason was presented as so horrible and shameful that the blood of traitors was corrupted – *attainted* – so that not only were their lands forfeit, but they could not be inherited by their heirs even if entailed on them. The parliament that met at Coventry on 20 November 1459 attainted York, Warwick's parents, himself and his younger brothers, William Stanley, two younger sons of Viscount Bourchier, and twelve others.[10]

The act honoured any claims existing before the attainder, so that the rebels' rivals could take advantage of the situation. Thus Lawrence Bothe Bishop of Durham seized Warwick's lordship of Barnard Castle, which his predecessors had claimed since 1293, and legitimized his action with a proviso to the act of attainder.[11] Similarly the Beauchamp half-sisters reasserted their rights. They secured parliamentary approval for an inquisition for Worcestershire of 1446 missing from chancery. On 8 May 1460 the Countess Margaret and the Duchess Eleanor secured the custody of Warwick's quarter share of the Beauchamp inheritance: their grant implies it had indeed been divided in four and that they had a quarter each. On 26 May Eleanor was also granted the keeping of Salwarpe and Droitwich which, by implication, were not subject to such division.[12]

7   *Gregory's Chron.*, 205–6; Waurin, 278–9.
8   Scofield, i. 36–7.
9   Ibid. i. 37 & n; Whetehamstede, i. 343–4; cf. Radcliffe's confession in *RP* v. 349.
10   *RP* v. 347–9.
11   A. J. Pollard, 'The Crown and the County Palatine of Durham 1437–94', *The North of England in the Age of Richard III* (1996), 78–9; M. A. Hicks, 'The Forfeiture of Barnard Castle to the Bishop of Durham in 1459', *Northern History* xxxiii (1997), 223–31.
12   *RP* v. 344; *CFR 1452–61*, 268, 272.

Far from being the Parliament of Devils, as the Yorkists were to dub it, the proscription of the Yorkists was limited and the result of 'mature deliberation' by the Lords.[13] There is no factual account of the debate, but two fragmentary surviving tracts indicate that even now the decision to punish rather than pardon was not automatic and that parliament vacillated between Justice and Mercy. The so-called *Somnium Vigilantis* is an anti-Yorkist dialogue. The Yorkists were 'lordis of tyme passed', reputed as traitors, and victims of 'pretens forysfactures' even before our text begins with a Lancastrian peroration urging rigorous punishment in the interests of 'universalle quyet', 'youre syngulere welth' and 'the generall consolacion of alle this contre'. The formal verdict was yet to be pronounced and sentence declared. By the time of the second tract the Yorkists were condemned, presumably in earlier sections on the prosecution and defence case. What is preserved in Whetehamstede's *Register* in elaborate literary Latin, perhaps translated and adorned by the abbot himself, is the replication of Justice and the mediation of Mercy, who, unhistorically, wins.[14] A replication contains no substantial data.[15]

This latter treatise presents the Yorkists, again unhistorically, as contrite and repentant, whereas the *Somnium* reveals them to be defiant and arguing on lines consistent both with Warwick's reported speech at Worcester and their later utterances. In the *Somnium* the spokesman of the Yorkists was unapologetic and justified their insurrection by their good motives and the poor governance that still required reform. He urged unity against foreign enemies for which Yorkist services are essential. Moreover they could not be destroyed, 'consyderynge thar powere and that thay have frendis in this lande and shall have who so ever says nay'. They will be driven to desperation if condemned. This is rather more than a muted threat! Like the act of attainder itself, the winning Lancastrian case presents the Yorkists as incorrigible, three times rebels and 'of a pure malice and longtyme precogitat wykednes'. The time for mercy was past. The Yorkists' claim to pursuit of the common good is dismissed: as subverting the office of the king; dishonest – if successful, 'Trow ye thay will have procured the commone welth?'; and far outweighed by the mortality at Blore Heath and by the 'extorcions . . . injuries and oppression' for which they were responsible. 'Who made hem juges?' They have broken their oaths so often that they cannot be trusted and if pardoned will merely offend again, to the jeopardy of all. If they can be kept out, keep them out. Probably they exaggerate their power. The French umpire found strongly against them: he urged the enriching of the king's

13 *RP* v. 350 quoted by J. C. Wedgwood, *History of Parliament* (2 vols, 1936–8), i. 244n. The next two paras are based on Gilson, 'Defence', 512–25; Whetehamstede, i. 346–56; M. L. Kekewich, 'The Attainder of the Yorkists in 1459: Two Contemporary Accounts', *BIHR* lv (1982), 25–34; see also J. G. Bellamy, *The Law of Treason in England in the Later Middle Ages* (1970), 201–4.
14 Whetehamstede, i. 346–56. I do not accept that Whetehamstede's underlying tract commences before the debate in 1459 or that the Yorkist case in the *Somnium* was surly or inadequate, Kekewich, 27, 31.
15 Ibid. 33.

supporters, that all unite against the Yorkists, who threaten all, and that spreaders of rumours be put to death.

It is interesting that there was debate about what appears an open and shut case. The decision to attaint was made in full awareness that the Yorkists were untamed, capable of continued resistance and even retaliation, and that any who opposed them were at risk. Moreover the Yorkists still had 'lordis of lyke disposicion' and 'frendis' who had not rebelled. Among those who swore allegiance to the king were many of their kinsfolk: the three brothers Bourchier, the archbishop, viscount, and Lord Berners; Bishop Grey; Salisbury's brother Bergavenny and brother-in-law Buckingham, his son Bishop Neville, his nephews Norfolk, Northumberland and Egremont, cousins, retainers, and supporters. If efforts to save two Bourchiers were unsuccessful, by later standards there were not many forfeitures. Many others almost as guilty could have been added: thus John Otter, Warwick usher of the exchequer, and Master Richard Fisher, the earl's secretary, were candidates for attainder, but were reprieved. King Henry refused his assent to the attainder of Grey of Powys and Devereux, attached a proviso to the main act that allowed him to forgive those attainted at will, and rejected a separate bill against Lord Stanley.[16] Some rebels had already been forgiven. Others were soon to recover their property.

The possessions of the attainted were forfeited and passed to the king. Royal patents and private grants by those attainted to people in the rebel armies were resumed and though less easily identifiable were again supposedly at the king's disposal.[17] Notoriously over-generous, Henry was expected to disperse these estates in lavish grants to his favourites – the French umpire of the *Somnium* even urged it – but actually he did not. No grants of land were made, though offices held by the Yorkist lords and offices on their estates were indeed redistributed to those whom the king trusted, though not in most cases at once. The estates were kept in hand and on 12/14 December were arranged in receiverships, whose accounts were subsequently enrolled on the foreign accounts of the exchequer. Anticipating the enlarged Yorkist crown estate, Henry VI's ministers – specifically the maligned Lord Treasurer Wiltshire, perhaps on advice of Chief Justice Fortescue? – planned to keep such lands in hand to enhance the king's revenues. Payments were assigned from them.[18] Whatever the designs of royal favourites, they did not secure shares of these forfeitures. The Yorkists were wrong to claim in 1459 that their enemies sought their destruction to secure their lands and in 1460 that this was the motive behind the 1459 act of attainder.[19] Even untrue, it made good propaganda.

Henry had created no vested interests to be dispossessed or to demand compensation if those attainted were restored. He was open to offers. Had Warwick and the other Yorkist lords been truly contrite and submitted, they too

16   *Paston L & P* ii. 188; *RP* v. 346–50, 370; Whetehamstede, i. 356.
17   *RP* v. 366.
18   Griffiths, *Henry VI*, 826.
19   *Davies Chron.* 82, 89.

could have been forgiven. It is not true, as some historians have supposed, that the Yorkist lords could only secure their restoration by another coup.[20] They sought so much more than mere restoration.

Initially the regime did not know where the Yorkists had gone or where it should locate its forces to guard against new insurrections. Its authority was not immediately accepted. In February and March 1460 York's castle of Denbigh and lordships of Usk and Caerleon and Warwick's lordships of Glamorgan and Abergavenny were still recalcitrant.[21] In time all resistance was quelled. Although Henry could now draw on forfeitures for resources, it took time to accrue revenues, and the costs of measures against the Yorkists proved beyond his immediate means. It was nevertheless a disastrous error to allow the Yorkist lords three weeks' grace to reach Calais.

It was Warwick at Calais who took the lead in Yorkist operations over the next nine months. Initially he was far from secure. Trollope's desertion had exposed the fundamental loyalty to Henry VI of at least some of the garrison, many of whom had also served under previous captains and lieutenants. All were surly at being virtually unpaid since Warwick took office in 1456. The Staple depended on good relations with England and its neighbours and was potentially seriously affected by the English ban on trade with Calais proclaimed by the Coventry parliament.[22] When Henry Duke of Somerset approached with a substantial force early in November 1459, he was fired on from Calais itself and from Rysbank tower, and hence failed to gain admittance. At Trollope's suggestion he landed instead at Wissault (Scales Cliff) and was admitted to the castle of Guines on the promise of payment of the garrison: he had 200 marks (£133.33) with him. Apparently he also secured Hammes. Although impeded by the immediate loss of Roos and Audley, troops, ships and munitions to the enemy, Somerset skirmished or 'bykerd togidres sondry tymes' with the garrison of Calais itself, many of whom, at this juncture, deserted to him. Warwick was obliged to provide armed escorts for traders and suppliers. Somerset's efforts culminated in a full-scale assault on 23 April, which was repulsed at Newnham Bridge.[23]

To recapture Calais, Somerset really needed supplies, reinforcements and command of the sea. These issues were tackled by three patents of 10/11 December 1459. William Scot was commissioned to raise ships crewed with 200 men-at-arms specifically to protect English fishermen and the town of Winchelsea. Buckingham as warden of the Cinque Ports was directed to secure against capture Warwick's former ships, still lying at anchor at Sandwich, at the time of 'le Sprynge' tides. Rivers and others were ordered to take the muster of

20   E.g. A. J. Pollard, *The Wars of the Roses* (Basingstoke, 1988), 25; Watts, *Henry VI*, 352.

21   Griffiths, *Henry VI*, 829; *CPR 1452–61*, 574, 578.

22   Postan and Power, *Studies in English Trade*, 316–17.

23   Kingsford, *London Chrons.* 170; Waurin, 279–82. Somerset was confirmed as captain of Calais for 12 years on 31 Jan. 1460, *DKR* 48 (1887), 441. Trollope was appointed bailiff of Guines in compensation for property lost at Calais, *CPR 1452–61*, 553.

the soldiers who were to take the sea with Sir Gervase Clifton, still nominally treasurer of Calais.[24]

Warwick quickly sought diplomatic recognition, both to protect Calais against foreign attack and to win international support for his restoration. The English truce with Burgundy expired in November and on the 26th Henry appointed eleven ambassadors (among them Sir John Marny captain of Hammes, Osbert Mountford, and William Overy) to negotiate an extension. They were too late. Warwick had already reached an understanding with Philip. Discussions were held with the marshal of Burgundy at Gravelines in November and with Charolais marshal-at-arms, who was at Calais from 5 November to 5 December. A three-month truce was concluded between the duke and the Yorkists.[25] Warwick also wooed the papal legate Francesco Coppini, Bishop of Terni, convinced him of the injustice done to the Yorkist earls and the righteousness of their cause, and persuaded him to intervene on their behalf.[26] At Bruges it was also believed that the Yorkists were colluding with the Scots against Henry VI.[27]

Warwick was not content to be defensive. When Somerset's ships fell into his hands, he personally interrogated the crews, identified those formerly of the garrison who had deserted him at Ludford, and executed them.[28] Presumably it was also he who persuaded Audley to change sides: amazingly, since it had been his father who had been killed at Blore Heath. The Calais garrison were discouraged from disloyalty towards him. Warwick launched raids across Burgundian territory into France in search of supplies and other plunder. He resumed his attacks on French, Castilian and Genoese shipping and continued to grant (sell?) safe conducts to foreigners. Booty from the raids and piracy and munitions intended for Somerset helped compensate for the lack of official supplies from England. On 16 March the Yorkists captured a shipment of pay for the garrison of Guines. Unofficial supplies were apparently forthcoming, as parliament's ban on English trade could not be made effective and was even infringed by the crown.[29] It had alienated the staplers, who were even more adversely affected by the government's declaration of a monopoly on the wool trade in May, and it aligned them definitely with Warwick. Allegedly they advanced him £18,000:[30] presumably including £3,580 that we know he 'chevisshed' (borrowed at interest).[31] Such loans financed his expedition to Ireland and probably also his invasion of England. The staplers were an influential group of London merchants. Once ashore and again short of money, the

24   *CPR 1452–61*, 555–6.
25   C 76/142 m. 13; Thielemans, *Bourgogne et l'Angleterre*, 375; C. L. Kingsford, 'The Earl of Warwick at Calais in 1460', *EHR* xxxvii (1922), 546.
26   *CSPM* i. 21.
27   See below pp.181.
28   Waurin, 280–2.
29   *Three 15th-Cent. Chrons.* 73; Waurin, 280–2; Postan and Power, 317.
30   Postan and Power, 318.
31   DL 37/32/79; M. K. Jones, 'Edward IV, the Earl of Warwick, and the Yorkist Claim to the Throne', *HR* lxx (1997), 343, 352.

Yorkists were able to borrow from the City corporation, livery companies and citizens.

It was inside information that prompted Warwick to launch a combined operation against Sandwich on 15 January 1460 that was conspicuously more successful than that of De Brezé three years earlier. A force somewhat smaller than that of Rivers, allegedly 700 strong and commanded by Dynham, Wenlock and Clapham, attacked at dawn over the dunes and from the sea. Rivers, his spouse and son, and all Warwick's former ships were carried off captive to Calais. The one exception was the unseaworthy *Grace Dieu*, which was stripped of all its equipment even including the cannons, presumably by the raiders.[32] Dynham's victory was exploited as a morale booster: once at Calais, Rivers and his son were paraded in public by the light of 160 torches and were reprimanded and humiliated as parvenus by the three Yorkist earls in a ceremony that stressed their own allegiance, royal blood and noble lineages.[33]

Fearful that this raid foreshadowed an immediate invasion, the crown arrayed the coastal counties and organized naval defences. In February Sir Baldwin Fulford indented to raise a naval force for three months and in March Lord Admiral Exeter was commissioned to raise another fleet. Lord Treasurer Wiltshire also provided a small squadron.[34] As Warwick had now recovered the core of what had been his fleet as keeper of the seas, these commanders were obliged to impress different ships unfamiliar with naval service. Genoese carracks were hired and an unavailing bid was made for the Venetian galleys. Since the government could not finance all these squadrons adequately, they were not particularly effective. They drained Henry's coffers and stretched his credit without achieving anything substantial. Warwick was not brought to battle nor were his operations impeded. Such efforts were also premature: by June, when Warwick invaded, Fulford's commission had expired and Exeter's fleet had mutinied. Besides all this, the crown was obliged to establish control in Wales and prepare for invasion from Ireland. On 20 May it expected the Yorkists to return with French support and on 23 June, when invasion was imminent, a proclamation reminded subjects that support of traitors was itself treason under the statute of 1352 and ordered them to prepare themselves for defence.[35]

By February 1460 Yorkist Calais was safe from any immediate threat from land and sea and its captain could be spared. York had also established himself at the head of the Irish government; Rutland was his chancellor. This was known to the Yorkists at Calais. They had even received letters from Duke Richard via the London vintner Thomas Dessford, whom they had had released from custody at Ostend.[36] What use was to be made of Calais was not something to be

32 Scofield, i. 51–2.
33 Ibid. i. 51–2; 'The Capture of Lord Rivers and Sir Anthony Woodville on 19th January 1460', *EHR* xxxviii (1922), 253–5.
34 Griffiths, *Henry VI*, 857, 862; *DKR* 48 (1887), 440, 443; *POPC* vi. 513–17.
35 *CPR 1454–61*, 409, 415–16.
36 Scofield, i. 59.

left to correspondence. Hence it was agreed that Warwick should visit the duke 'to take his advice how thei shold entre in-to England ageyn': as the most naval-minded, he was the obvious choice. The Gascon Duras was apparently his 'captain and admiral' and Pickering went too. This was Warwick's 'great journey to Ireland'. Warwick was later to secure repayment of £3,580 from Edward IV that he had borrowed to spend on his 'navyre', particularly on this expedition. The outward journey was unchallenged and Warwick was able to seize merchant vessels as he went, which subsequently spawned chancery suits among aggrieved merchants. Thus he commandeered both the balinger *Mary* of Bristol and the *Julian* of Fowey; the latter had a safe conduct to trade with France and was left by Warwick as transport for the Duke of York. Warwick was at Waterford with York and twenty-six ships on 16 March and the next day, St Patrick's Day, they landed and were received by the citizens with pomp and ceremony. It was during his stay that he and York determined on their next moves.[37] We may safely presume that Warwick's invasion of Kent in June and the line taken in his prop-aganda were decided in Ireland. We may safely deduce that they decided *not* to co-ordinate their invasions.

Warwick stayed throughout the session of the Irish parliament and returned to Calais late in May. On his return he confronted Exeter's fleet, which was lying in wait for his return where he had to pass. Waurin tells us that Warwick, 'who was very wise and imaginative', always posted a carvel in the van to scout ahead of his main force. The carvel *La Toucque* duly saw Exeter's ships, reported back to Warwick, and identified them by consultation with a fishing boat. There was time for Warwick to avoid Exeter. The earl preferred to fight. He consulted the masters of his ships, who reached the same conclusion. He encouraged his men with hopes of victory. Knowing what lay ahead, he re-arranged his squadron in close formation challenging battle, as he had against the Castilians in 1458, and sailed boldly towards the larger fleet, which may have consisted of fourteen ships and 1,500 men headed by the *Grace Dieu*. Exeter was less experienced and less prepared than Warwick and his crews were of dubious value, both because unpaid and because allegedly sympathetic to Warwick. Accordingly he avoided battle, taking refuge in Dartmouth. Warwick did not attack: wisely, for he could not afford the losses; according to Waurin, because he lacked victuals; perhaps also and significantly, in the somewhat ambiguous words of Davies's *English Chronicle*, because of Exeter's royal blood.[38] Warwick was able to continue to Calais, where he was received joyously, not least by his countess.[39]

The inhabitants of Calais were still plagued by the Duke of Somerset. Fearing that other loyal subjects were being suborned by the Yorkists, the government at last authorized Somerset to pardon any who submitted except Fauconberg,

37   *The Brut*, 529; Scofield, *Edward IV*, i. 59; *Great Red Book of Bristol*, iii (Bristol Rec. Soc. xvi, 1951), 20; DL 37/32/79; C 1/27/383, 440, 471.
38   *The Brut*, 529; *Annales*, 772; Waurin, 288–9.
39   Waurin, 289–90.

Dynham, Anson, Galet, Whetehill, and two others. That was on 5 June 1460 and was too late.[40] Meantime a rather smaller relief force was being prepared at Sandwich by Osbert Mountford, a former member of the garrison and recently royal ambassador to Burgundy. On his return Warwick was presented with demands to root out Somerset. He persuaded the complainants that the invasion of England was a preferable option.[41] Accordingly Fauconberg was launched against Sandwich on 24 June. Mountford made a stouter defence than Rivers, though with the same result. Dynham was badly wounded by a ball from a bombard. Mountford was captured and taken to Calais, where Warwick allowed his shipmen to execute him and two others.[42] Sandwich was secured as bridge-head for the Yorkist invasion of the English mainland.

7.2   Warwick's Triumph

Warwick, Salisbury and March landed at Sandwich on 26 June 1460. They declared their objective to be the remedy of the ills that beset the commonwealth and their remedy the reform of the government, in particular the removal of the king's evil councillors, whom this time they named as Shrewsbury, Wiltshire and Beaumont; later they added Buckingham, 'the which was hye and fat of greese' from profiteering at royal expense. The time had come (*Tempus* ys come) for revenge, one poem ominously declared: to destroy falsehood, eradicate weeds from the corn and cut back briars from the trees. Once again they wanted an audience with the king to put their points to him.[43] Initially their forces must have been small, more probably hundreds rather than the 2,000 stated by Waurin, but they expanded rapidly to perhaps 20,000 on their advance via Canterbury to London.[44] The inhabitants of Kent flocked to join them, even those commissioned to resist them, including the two resident peers Bergavenny and Cobham. Lords Scales, Hungerford, and others had been deputed to hold London against them, but the corporation, proud of its autonomy, rejected their assistance and they retired to the Tower. The corporation itself was divided. There was strong support for the Yorkists among the populace. After some hesitation, the Yorkists were admitted to the City amidst scenes of popular delight. They were greeted by two Yorkist bishops, Grey of Ely and Warwick's brother of Exeter, each with their own armed retinue, thirteen of whom were unfortunately crushed in the crowd. The Yorkist earls went in procession to St Paul's, where the convocation of Canterbury had been sitting for some weeks. Warwick told the assembled clergy, mayor and aldermen that they had come to remedy 'mysreule and myscheues'. They had been expelled from the king's presence and

---

40   C 76/142 no. 8. A grant was made of property forfeited by Galet, *CPR 1452-61*, 585.
41   Waurin, 290-1.
42   *Three 15th-Cent. Chrons.* 73; *Annales*, 772.
43   *Davies Chron.* 86-90, 93; Robbins, *Hist. Poems*, 209, 211.
44   *Annales*, 772.

denied an audience to refute 'suche fals accusacions layde ayens them'. They solemnly renewed their oaths of allegiance.[45]

The loss of London was a grievous and unexpected blow for Henry. His strategy was defensive. For nine months since Ludford the regime had guarded against further Yorkist insurgency, which could have fallen almost anywhere. They needed to watch for invasion by York from Ireland into Wales, Lancashire, or even the south-western peninsula; against a Scottish invasion; against insurrection by the Neville affinity in Richmondshire and other parts of the North; and against threats to East Anglia and the south coast posed by both Warwick and, supposedly, the French. Those deputed to resist York were fully committed and *hors de combat* whether the duke came or not. When it was clear where Warwick was coming, on 23 June, King Henry had ordered the south-eastern shires to resist him;[46] subsequently he summoned his supporters in the North to join him at Northampton. They took time to mobilize and concentrate: longer certainly than the mere fortnight that it took Warwick to proceed from the bridgehead at Sandwich to the battlefield at Northampton. He knew the importance of speed. The king's forces took up a defensive position in a curve of the River Nene near Northampton, which they fortified with ditches, guns and obstacles that should have sufficed against direct attack. Probably they also anticipated, wrongly, that the Yorkists would be as unwilling to confront the king as in 1459.

Having taken London, they deputed Salisbury, Cobham and Wenlock to hold it and to blockade the Tower, whilst Warwick and March pressed on rapidly to the king. Warwick had the popular support and March represented York, whereas Salisbury, so far from the Neville powerhouse in the North, could expect to attract few retainers. Warwick and March took five bishops, five barons, and Viscount Bourchier. Was it the attainder of his sons after Ludford that had transformed the viscount from a Yorkist sympathizer into a companion at arms? Without more concrete evidence, their army presumably consisted of a core of Calais professionals, a few retainers, and a host of 'naked men'; there is no evidence of many Neville or York retainers. Proceeding via St Albans and Dunstable, the Yorkists ranged their forces in front of the king on 10 July. Three times they sought an audience to explain the evils of his government and to request a remedy, initially by the medium of Bishop Beauchamp and latterly through Warwick herald. Warwick even offered to come on his own provided that his safety was guaranteed by hostages. The king's spokesperson, again Buckingham, rejected their overtures. In contrast to similar discussions at St Albans in 1455, he no longer accepted Yorkist protestations of loyalty and realized that nothing less than complete capitulation to Yorkist demands could avert conflict. He may also have feared both that the king would be too easily persuaded by Warwick of the latter's good intentions and that he himself would be among the evil councillors to be punished. It is hard to accept that the Yorkist ultimatum

---

45   *Three 15th-Cent. Chrons.* 74; *Davies Chron.* 94–5; *Annales*, 772–3.
46   *CPR 1454–61*, 415–16.

reveals a 'patent willingness to negotiate'![47] Buckingham told Warwick herald that if the earl came, he would die. Warwick responded that he would speak to the king by 2 p.m. or die on the field.[48] He had grounds for self-confidence since Grey of Ruthin on the Lancastrian side had already assured him of his intended treachery.[49]

The Yorkist forces were arranged in three battles commanded by Warwick and March with the veteran Fauconberg in the van. They attacked all along the line, enveloping the king's smaller forces, which were prevented by wet conditions from using their cannon, and were helped over the barriers from the Lancastrian side by Grey of Ruthin on the royalist right wing. The battle was quickly over with perhaps only 300 slain. Before attacking, Warwick had ordered the commons to be spared and the aristocrats killed. He can have wished for the death of none more than Buckingham, Shrewsbury, Beaumont and Egremont, the 'curre Dogges', all of whom were slain. The king was captured.[50]

There is no sign that the Yorkists considered killing or deposing the king.

> But the hunt [king] he [Warwick] saued from harme that day,
> He thouzht neuer other in all his mynde.[51]

Without pausing, they modelled their conduct on the successful precedent of 1455. They wanted to legitimize their treasonable attack on the king and their defiance of his banner displayed. For that they needed to mobilize Henry's authority on their behalf. Once again Henry was treated with the utmost outward respect. They assured him that they had not been fighting him, but merely their own malicious enemies. They were seeking only the good of the king and realm like true liegemen. At once he accepted them as such. Letters in his name issued under their aegis declare their condemnation of the previous year to be malicious and scandalous and repute the Yorkists to be loyal subjects. The day after the battle, as in 1455, the Yorkist lords took mass with the king, this time at the nearby abbey of St Mary-in-the-Meadows (Delapré Abbey). Three days were spent in Northampton, where Buckingham was honourably buried at the Greyfriars and the others at St John's Hospital. Since Buckingham was half-brother of Bourchier, brother-in-law of Fauconberg, and uncle of Warwick and March, since Beaumont was married to Warwick and March's aunt and Fauconberg's sister Katherine, and since Egremont was first cousin of the two earls, some show of sorrow was *de rigueur*; maybe there was some genuine regret as well. At dawn on the fourth day they took mass and set off for London, where they arrived on 16 July. They were met with 'myche ryalte' by Archbishop

47   As stated in Watts, *Henry VI*, 356–7.
48   *Davies Chron.* 96–7.
49   R. I. Jack, 'A Quincentenary: The Battle of Northampton, July 11th 1460', *Northamptonshire Past and Present* iii (1960), 21–5, esp. 23.
50   A. Goodman, *The Wars of the Roses* (1981), 37–8; *Davies Chron.* 97. The reference to 'curre Dogges' in the verses alludes back to the five dogs insult to York in 1456.
51   Robbins, *Hist. Poems*, 212.

Bourchier, the papal legate, and the Earl of Salisbury, who escorted them in procession into the City. On the precedent of 1455, the victors were again prominent: March rode beside the king and Warwick, his head bare, in front, with the king's sword point uppermost. Again Henry was lodged in the bishop of London's palace, Warwick at Blackfriars and March at Baynards Castle. On 17 July they proceeded solemnly through the City to St Paul's, where they celebrated a mass in honour of Jesus.[52] As after St Albans, the new regime was to be confirmed by parliament, which was summoned on 20 July.[53] A third Yorkist protectorate was probably the intended outcome.

The Yorkist coup d'état was successful. There remained three deficiencies: the Tower and Guines still held out; the queen, prince and other Lancastrians in the North, in Wales, and the West had not yet acknowledged defeat and submitted; and foreign intervention could yet overcome their achievement.

The Tower soon fell. It was not victualled for a long siege, supplies were severed by land and water, for Warwick's ships commanded the Thames, and considerable damage was caused by artillery firing over the river. Accordingly, on 18 July, the commanders agreed terms for capitulation that spared themselves and exposed the others to punishment. Even on release, they were not safe, for the populace wanted revenge for the casualties they had caused in the City. Scales sought sanctuary at Westminster Abbey, but was seized as he travelled on the Thames by Warwick's shipmen, who killed him and cast his body naked in the churchyard of the priory of St Mary Overy (now Southwark Cathedral). Since he was a war-hero and godfather to March, there was genuine regret at his death. Warwick and March attended his funeral the same day at the priory. Immediately afterwards Warwick ordered a stop to such violence.[54] Hungerford was licensed to go abroad on pilgrimage.[55] It was tacitly conceded that the original garrison had been acting on royal instructions and the king's behalf. Sir Thomas Browne and others who had broken through the Yorkist cordon into the Tower on 10 July, with the mistaken intention of prolonging the siege, were tried for treason at the Guildhall before Warwick, Bourchier, the Lord Mayor and judges on 22–3 July. Browne was charged with treason and rebellion against the king, with seeking to destroy the true lords of his blood, and with waging war against the king's lieges in London by shooting wildfire and other weapons into the City to the destruction of houses and the deaths of nine named individuals. Browne and five servants of the Duke of Exeter, hereditary constable of the Tower, were convicted and executed. So too, soon after, was John Archer, one of the duke's councillors. As a Milanese observer remarked, 'it is not thought that he [Warwick] will stay his hand, but will put to death all those who have acted against him'.[56] It is hardly surprising such executions were popular. The best way

52   Ibid. 212–14; *Davies Chron.* 97–8; *Three 15th-Cent. Chrons.* 74. It is not significant that Henry was not lodged at Westminster, *pace* Watts, *Henry VI*, 357n.
53   Whetehamstede, i. 375.
54   Waurin, 304; *Annales*, 773–4; *Three 15th-Cent. Chrons.* 74.
55   C 76/142 m. 6.
56   E 163/8/10; *Annales*, 773; *CSPM* i. 27.

to consolidate the new regime was to eliminate its opponents, by killing them or imprisoning them – the Bishop of Hereford was gaoled at Warwick Castle[57] – or to terrify them into submission. One wonders what attainders the Yorkists planned for their forthcoming parliament.

As Warwick had promised at Calais, his successful invasion isolated Somerset. Guines could no longer expect to be relieved. Now they were in control of the government machine the Yorkists were able to instruct him in the king's name to surrender the castle to Warwick. Warwick returned to Calais, where he was reunited with his countess and mother and was nobly received by the town's patricians, bourgeois and soldiers, whom he thanked for guarding the colony so well against his enemies. Next day (8 August) he met Somerset himself at St Pierre. Having kissed, Somerset promised not to fight the earl again, and was allowed to retire with Roos and Trollope to Dieppe. Whetehill took over at Guines.[58] Somerset's capitulation also restored peace at sea and enabled commerce to resume between England, Calais and Burgundy. That was what the merchants of the Staple had paid for.

That left unreconciled those in the North, Wales and West Country who had not accepted the verdict of Northampton, who absented themselves from parliament when it met, and who refused to accept its decisions. Defiance had not persisted during York's earlier protectorates. Most important of the irreconcilables were the queen and prince, who legitimately identified themselves with the future of the dynasty and appealed to those loyal to it. Margaret had not been at Northampton. After many vicissitudes, she brought her son in January 1461 to the North, where they found natural allies in the Percy and Clifford foes of the Nevilles, who had made themselves masters of the whole region. They did not relinquish control of Salisbury's estates and Yorkist sympathizers in the region had to toe their line. Similarly Pembroke remained in control in Wales despite ignoring government mandates to the contrary. So too in the West Country. It was an important concentration of forces in December 1460 when Somerset, Exeter and Devon took their retainers from the south-west to join the queen in the North. She also looked for help in Scotland:[59] dynastic interests prevailed over national interests. Against opponents, who rejected the verdict of battle and the manipulation of royal and parliamentary authority, the Yorkists must employ force. No doubt, as on many previous occasions, many lesser men would be disarmed by the Yorkists' claim to represent royal authority.

The Yorkist invasion had enjoyed widespread international backing. Duke Philip, the Dauphin Louis, Duke Francesco Sforza of Milan and Pope Pius II were all sympathetic; Yorkists were also suspected of encouraging James II's aggression on the northern frontier. Actually he was merely anti-English, regardless of faction, and his death in August before Roxburgh was as advantageous to the Yorkists as the Lancastrians. Philip and Louis were pleased with the Yorkist

57   *Davies Chron.* 97.
58   *Annales*, 774; Waurin, 306–7; *DKR* 48 (1887), 443.
59   Griffiths, *Henry VI*, 866, 869–70.

successes. Their support implied hostility from Charles VII and Philip's heir Charles the Bold. The Dauphin's emissary Seigneur de la Barde was well received by Warwick in September. The Yorkists sought to maximize Coppini's usefulness by praising him to the pope, recommending his promotion to the cardinalate, even licensing him to accept an English bishopric. The Burgundian emissary to Scotland Lord Gruthuyse thwarted Margaret of Anjou's attempts to ally with the Dowager-Queen Mary of Guelders. It took the Lancastrian victory at Wakefield to bring about an agreement of the two queens at Lincluden College near Dumfries and an understanding that may have included a marriage alliance between Prince Edward and Princess Mary of Scotland.[60]

The Yorkists soon nominated more sympathetic ministers. On 25 July it was Warwick's own brother George Bishop of Exeter who succeeded Archbishop Bourchier as chancellor. Viscount Bourchier resumed the treasurership and Robert Stillington replaced Lawrence Bothe as keeper of the privy seal. Warwick's veteran feoffee Beauchamp of Powicke remained steward of the household, but Warwick's younger brother John became chamberlain with control over access to the king and considerable say over who served about him. Warwick's Welsh retainer Sir Walter Scull succeeded Tuddenham as treasurer of the household. There were considerable changes among the lower ranks. In November Wenlock became chief butler of England, Dynham chancellor of Ireland, and Fauconberg and Blount respectively lieutenant and treasurer of Calais.[61]

It was a partisan regime and narrowly based. Apart from the three earls, Viscount Bourchier and Fauconberg, the only lay lords present at the transfer of the great seal and with the king at Canterbury were the four barons Beauchamp, Cobham, Grey of Ruthin and Scrope of Bolton.[62] There were no new faces: the adherence of Scrope of Bolton is unsurprising for a Richmondshire baron whose wife Joan was sister of Warwick's own brother-in-law FitzHugh. The familiar signatures of Archbishop Bourchier, Bishops Grey and Neville, the two Neville earls, Stanley, Dudley and Wenlock appear on a council minute of 11 November; only Lord Stourton was new.[63] Attendance at the session of parliament in between was probably not much better. When the Lancaster feoffees were re-constituted on 7 October to include Salisbury, Warwick, Bishop Neville, Grey of Ruthin and Beauchamp of Powicke for the first time, the only new peer was Warwick's brother-in-law William Earl of Arundel.[64] Not a feoffee, but nevertheless a highly significant recruit, was John Duke of Norfolk, the white lion of the political poems.

It is difficult to accept that the new Yorkist regime was sincerely committed

---

60   Scofield, i. 112–16, 134; C. Head, 'Pius II and the Wars of the Roses', *Archivum Historiae Pontificae* vii (1970), 158; M. A. Hicks, 'A Minute of the Lancastrian Council at York, 20 January 1461', *Northern History*, xxxii (1999).

61   Griffiths, *Henry VI*, 864; *CCR 1454–61*, 455–6; E 403/820 m. 2.

62   *POPC* vi. 362–3; *Stone's Chron.*, 81.

63   *POPC* vi. 387.

64   Somerville, *Duchy of Lancaster*, i. 212–13.

to reform since it neither retrenched nor introduced reforms to parliament. There was no new source of income. No attempt was made to secure a parliamentary grant of taxation. No act of resumption was proposed. Whilst the lands of the queen and prince were indeed resumed, as the Yorkists had wanted in 1455–6, it was only to endow the new protector and his sons to a lavish level perhaps exceeding the anticipated yield. Instead the regime relied on repeated loans totalling £11,000 from the City corporation between 4 July 1460 and 7 April 1461, £1,500 from three City livery companies and doubtless similar sums from others unrecorded, and at least £7,000 from ministers and officials in September; other sums were lent to the Neville earls, such as £100 lent to Warwick by the mercers' company.[65] The customs were appropriated neither to the royal household nor the most deserving and long-standing debtors, but to the staplers, Warwick's financiers, to those willing to lend to the regime, always on good security, and to Warwick himself as keeper of the seas. He now secured the whole subsidy, including that from Southampton and Sandwich that had been withheld in 1457.[66]

The new regime was more greedy for royal patronage and assets than the maligned Lancastrian favourites. Obviously the Yorkists resumed possession of their estates and indeed their offices: Warwick was reappointed governor of the Channel Isles on 8 August. On 8 October officers at Middleham and Ware (Herts.) were ordered to pay arrears to Salisbury and those at Penrith, Wressle and Pontefract were instructed to surrender control. These were probably merely the most recalcitrant.[67] On 1 December Salisbury joined his heir with him in new grants of the chief stewardship of the North Parts of the Duchy of Lancaster and of the duchy lands in Lancashire and Cheshire. He himself became great chamberlain of England, chief steward of the South Parts with Warwick (1 December) and keeper of the royal mews jointly with his son Thomas (22 August), who was appointed constable and steward of the Lancaster honour of Bolingbroke (20 October) and steward of Boston (Lincs.) as well. Warwick's range of interests emerges from these new duchy stewardships and his new role of feoffee, which gave him a dominant place in duchy administration especially in the North-West. He enhanced his authority in the Channel by adding the wardenship of the Cinque Ports and the governorship of the Channel Isles to the captaincy of Calais and by securing a further three-year term as keeper of the seas. On 18 November he extended his Midlands influence northwards by accruing the offices of constable, steward and master forester of the Lancaster honours of Tutbury (Staffs.), Duffield (Derbys.), and Leicester and the stewardship of Castle Donington (Leics.). And on 4 November on the sureties of Sir Walter Wrottesley and John Hay he was granted the keeping of the marcher lordships of Newport, Hay, Huntington, Brecon and Goodrich in the minorities of

65   C. M. Barron, 'London and the Crown 1451–61', *The Crown and Local Communities in England and France in the Fifteenth Century*, ed. J. R. L. Highfield and R. I. Jeffs (Gloucester, 1981), 97, 107–8.
66   *CCR 1454–61*, 474.
67   C 76/142 m. 6; *POPC* vi. 506; *CPR 1452–61*, 647, 649.

the heirs of Buckingham and Shrewsbury.[68] Was he already viewing the young duke and earl as eligible suitors for his daughters? On 8 February 1461 he was elected knight of the Garter.[69] What is clear is that he was enhancing his possessions and authority on all fronts and amassing what had formerly been divided between the queen, Buckingham, Shrewsbury, Wiltshire and Beaumont. Since his brothers were respectively chancellor and household chamberlain, this was decidedly a Neville-dominated regime. It was during these months that the foundation was laid for the rule of the Nevilles in the early years of Edward IV.

Warwick now overshadowed his father and uncle, his brothers, and his cousin of March. It was he who combined rank, experience and energy. He dominated the new regime. 'The government of the country', a Milanese observed in July, 'will remain in the hands of Warwick. . . . Everything is in Warwick's power and the war is at an end and he has done marvellous things. God grant him grace to keep the country in peace and unity.'[70] Friar Brackley asked that God preserve Warwick, his father and brothers. 'Yf owt come to my Lord Warwik but good, fare weel ye, fare well I, and al our frendys, for be the weye of my sowle this lond were vttirly on-done, as God forbede. . . .'[71] Warwick was now the principal Neville and the whole country was lost without him.

Warwick was everywhere and did everything. After the sessions in the London Guildhall on 22–23 July, he witnessed the transfer of the great seal to his brother at the bishop of London's palace on the 25th. There followed a lightning visit to Warwick on 28 July. On 2 August he reached Canterbury for evensong in company with the king, the papal legate, March, Salisbury, Bishop Neville and two Bourchiers. The archbishop and the prior of Christ Church were their hosts. There was a solemn procession on the morrow. Patents were sealed restoring Warwick's possession of Guines and the Channel Isles. Though the king remained at Canterbury for another fortnight, Warwick sped to Calais, sealing his agreement with Somerset on the 8th, feasted those who loved him both there and at Sandwich. His wife, mother and Wydeville prisoners accompanied him. Warwick caught up with the king at Greenwich on the 19th and shared in his grand reception in London, where the mayor, bourgeois and merchants came to him in his lodgings to thank him for the great benefits that he had performed and was still doing daily. It was at London on 24 August that the three Yorkist earls issued a safe conduct to John Davy of Bridgewater.[72]

Thereafter Warwick's movements are less certain. Waurin gives a lengthy account that is difficult to locate either chronologically or geographically. It

---

68   Somerville, *History of the Duchy of Lancaster*, i. 212–13n, 421, 429, 493, 540, 542, 576, 583; *CPR 1454–61*, 474, 589, 627, 642, 646; *CFR 1452–61*, 287–8.
69   Anstis, i. 168.
70   *CSPM* i. 27.
71   *Paston L & P* ii. 210.
72   *POPC* vi. 362–3; Barron, 'London & Crown', 97–8; BL Egerton Roll 8542 m. 3; *Stone's Chron.* 81; *DKR* 48 (1887), 443; Waurin, 307–8; G. Baskerville, 'A Latin Chronicle of 1460', *EHR* xxviii (1913), 126; *Bridgewater Borough Archives 1445–68*, ed. T. B. Dilks (Somerset Rec. Soc. lx, 1948), no. 615.

seems improbable that he went at once to Warwick since Waurin records him and his countess moving around, on pilgrimage to Walsingham, and shadow-boxing with Northumberland, perhaps in Lincolnshire, near the residence of his kinsman Richard Welles, Lord Willoughby who allegedly warned him against starting a war ahead of parliament. Thence he travelled via 'Fil' to 'Lislefil', most probably Lichfield in Staffordshire, whence Anne proceeded to Warwick.[73] Warwick himself met up with York at Shrewsbury, where they celebrated and spent 'four days between them devising their affairs'. The duke went on to Ludlow and the earl to Warwick.[74] All this may have been in fulfilment of (and hence subsequent to) a commission of 8 September to Warwick to arrest rebels in the ten Midland counties of Oxford, Gloucester, Shropshire, Worcester, Warwick, Leicester, Northampton, Rutland, Derbyshire and Staffordshire.[75] It was probably at Warwick that he was so well received by the local lords and ladies, who nevertheless 'complained to him of the great evils and damages done to them by the Duke of Somerset, who had pillaged, robbed and destroyed their vills and castles and taken any places of the earl' the previous autumn.[76] Certainly he was there on 28 September, when he issued a warrant of payment for supply of bullocks to the household by the grazier Benet Lee. The following day he visited Walford Parva in the south of the county, where he was one of the feoffees who leased land there to Thomas and Emma Ingram. Next day he and John Greville, Thomas Ferrers, Thomas Hugford, Richard Hotoft, Thomas Broughton and Thomas Walgrave, the first four at least being retainers, presided at quarter sessions, at which several of those who had wasted their lands the previous year were indicted. We know of four such indictments because much later they were moved to the court of King's Bench by writ of *certiorari*. Probably there were others that were not. He was back at Westminster for the opening of parliament on 7 October, when he was again a trier of petitions.[77]

The new regime was not in control of the provinces and depended for its authority on possession of the king, which offered none of the guarantees needed against reprisals. In 1455 York's tenure as protector had been secured by parliamentary authority, which allegedly Warwick had also claimed for his captaincy of Calais. It had not sufficed. King Henry had relieved York of office in parliament in 1456 exactly as ordained in his terms of appointment. Parliamentary authority for York as protector was surely the least that was sought on 20 July, when parliament was summoned. Perhaps something even more permanent was envisaged. Three preliminaries were essential. First of all, the king's authority and approval were required, which was assured by his opening of parliament in person in his full regalia. Secondly, the Yorkist lords had to be released from the sentence of the previous parliament. This was done in an act stating the acts of the Coventry parliament to have been 'synysterly and importunely laboured . . .

73 Waurin, 309–10.
74 Waurin, 310.
75 *CPR 1452–61*, 647.
76 Waurin, 309.
77 BL Egerton Roll 8541 m. 3; Add. Ch. 54950; KB 9/313/57; *RP* v. 373.

[by] dyvers seditious and evil disposed persones' with designs on the victims' property and approved by an improperly elected house of Commons. Friar Brackley reported that the Yorkists intended to wreak revenge on the authors of the act of attainder against them.[78] Thirdly, a change in government needed to be shown to be necessary. This was apparently the work of Lord Chancellor Neville, whose opening sermon recited the bad government and losses in France of the previous regime and promised remedies. His text from Joel II.16, 'Gather the people, sanctify the congregation', has been interpreted as presaging resistance to Queen Margaret's northern army.[79] Actually she was not there yet.[80] It points rather to a display of unity and a commitment to the liberties of the church. The Yorkist *Verses on the Battle of Northampton* looked forward to the restoration of unity. If Warwick intended to reconcile himself with those opposed to him, as Friar Brackley feared,[81] it would have been a statesmanlike act. That matters did not proceed exactly as planned was because York had his own agenda.

That Warwick left the *Julian* of Fowey in Ireland in May to transport York to the mainland may indicate that the duke was expected to cross to England soon. He did not. Yorkist verses of late July looked forward to the return of 'the mayster of this game', Richard Duke of York. On 9 August royal letters to Pembroke in Wales ordered York to be received as 'our approved and true liegeman and noo traitor, our true subget and noo rebell, our right feithful frend and noon ennemye'. Commissions issued by the London government to him on 22 and 26 August wrongly presumed his availability for service in Yorkshire.[82] It was not until 8/9 September that he landed at the Wirral, having bypassed North Wales, where royal servants had sought to impede his progress in 1449–50 and where Queen Margaret's supporters were poised to do the same. Once ashore, the duke took over a month to reach London, perhaps fulfilling various errands from the government on his way. His slow and stately progress is reminiscent of that of 1450, when he was concerned to show himself and to win support. From Chester (13 September) he passed via Shrewsbury – obviously before 28 September! – to Ludlow, Hereford and Gloucester, where he was on 2 October, and thence to Abingdon, Barnet, and eventually Westminster, where he arrived on 10 October.[83] He was late once again: again by design.

When he landed, with just a few men, York was conspicuously wearing the York family livery of silver and blue and the badge of the falcon and fetterlock that was so potent in the marches of Wales. He had his sword borne before before him point uppermost to the sound of trumpet fanfares. Latterly he was accompanied by a banner bearing the royal arms unquartered with those of others

---

78 *Paston L & P* ii. 210.
79 Waurin, 313; Johnson, *York*, 218–19.
80 A. I. Dunlop, *The Life & Times of James Kennedy, Bishop of St Andrews* (1950), 215.
81 *Paston L & P* ii. 221.
82 *POPC* vi. 303; Robbins, *Hist. Poems*, 215; *CPR 1452–61*, 608, 610.
83 Johnson, *York*, 212; Scofield, i. 101; Jones and Walker, 'Private Contracts', 164–5; *Gregory's Chron.* 208.

and without the label that distinguished a cadet line. Almost immediately after his landing he had ceased to use the regnal year in dating documents. Several indentures of retainer dated at Gloucester on 2 October promised him the loyalty of those retained without the customary reservation of overriding allegiance to the king.[84] Increasingly York interpreted his royal blood as arising not through his paternal York line, but through his maternal Mortimer ancestors from Lionel Duke of Clarence, a son of Edward III senior to John of Gaunt, the ancestor of the Lancastrian kings. He considered himself entitled to the throne and perceived in the Yorkist victory the opportunity for him to make his claims good. It was a logical next step that had been anticipated by some observers in July and August and, if Waurin is to be believed, had been urged by his Welsh retainers.[85] On Friday 10 October he arrived at Westminster with a powerful retinue of 800 'horses and men harnessed': was he trying to overawe parliament, as he had in 1450, 1454 and 1456? Entering the House of Lords, his sword borne point uppermost, he laid his hand upon the throne to claim the crown and turned his face towards the people.

> And ther under the cloth of estate stondyng, he gave them knowliche that he purposed nat to ley daune his swerde but to challenge his right . . . and purposed that no man shuld haue denye[d] the croune fro his hed.[86]

This was the signal for the assembled peers to acclaim him as king. They did not. After an awkward pause, the primate asked him whether he wished to see the king, to which the duke responded that the king should rather wish to see him. He lodged himself in the king's chambers, Henry VI himself removing elsewhere in the palace under guards appointed by York. If Waurin is correct, York had hoped to be crowned on the Monday following, St Edward's Day, when the king would normally have appeared crowned; a 'great multitude of pepill drew thedir' to see who did wear the crown, but no king appeared. York found that he had to win over the Lords. A formal submission of his case was submitted to the Lords on Thursday 16 October, which outlined the duke's descent through his mother Anne Mortimer from Lionel Duke of Clarence and its superiority to that of the Lancastrian kings. His claim was based entirely on hereditary right. Whilst the Lords were reluctant to take any such action, they agreed that York's claim like any other petition deserved consideration. As at other critical moments, they were anxious to shrug off responsibility for such a momentous decision: on to the king himself, who failed to stamp out speculation with his authority, which, by implication, he could have done. Instead Henry rather feebly asked them to find objections to York's title. And on to the judges and then the royal law officers, who all stated that the matter at issue was beyond their learning.

---

84 Johnson, *York*, 216; Waurin, 311–12. For what follows, see esp. Johnson, *York*, 213–18; Whetehamstede, i. 376–84.

85 Johnson, *York*, 214.

86 Ibid.

Reluctantly therefore the Lords debated the subject themselves on Wednesday 22 October: each was to speak freely without fear of penalties. They came up with five objections: the oaths of allegiance that they had sworn to Henry VI as king; the acts of parliament that had settled the crown on the Lancastrian line; the descent of the crown by entail; York's use of the arms of York rather than Clarence; and Henry IV's claim that he was king by inheritance not by conquest. York responded that he was king by divine law and that this superseded any oaths by himself or the Lords; that he had borne the arms of York (rather than Clarence) for reasons well known to everyone; and that the other objections all arose from deficiencies in Henry IV's title and were superseded by his own hereditary claims. No public response was made by the Lords. Naturally they were sympathetic to claims based on the practice of primogeniture, which allowed inheritance through females and by which they held their own titles and

Table 7.1   The House of York's Title to the Crown 1460–1

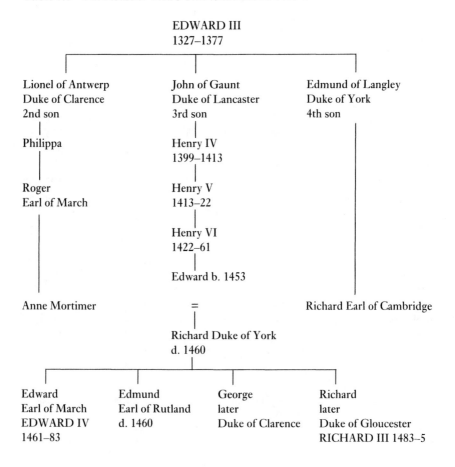

estates: all Warwick's current estates and hereditary expectations, except his Neville patrimony, were derived through the female line. They were not convinced by York's specious arguments that they could set aside their oaths to the king, which all had so recently renewed, whether at the Coventry parliament of the previous year or before convocation in July. They were not willing to set aside an adult king, the third of his dynasty, who had reigned over them for thirty-eight years and was definitely not willing to stand aside. Abbot Whetehamstede, who was present, testifies to the dismay of the lords.[87]

Not many peers attended the crucial discussions. The most active opponents of the regime, such as the dukes of Somerset and Exeter, had not responded to their summonses; others failed to attend at all or absented themselves from the crucial sessions.[88] Their absences cast doubt on the authority and validity of any decisions. Probably most of those present were spiritual peers; archbishops, bishops, abbots and priors, who carried little political clout. They were reluctant as a group to consent to York's demands. Lord Chancellor Neville guided their deliberations, but there is little evidence that he directed them either in York's favour or against.

What happened in parliament, however, may have mattered least. It was there that decisions were formally registered that were reached elsewhere. Waurin's account is more informal and personal. It emphasizes that York had not only to combat the reluctance of the Lords, but the active hostility of the Yorkist earls. Salisbury was offended by the king's eviction and protested to Warwick. Since Archbishop Bourchier was frightened of York's retainers, it was Warwick himself in company with his brother Thomas who took barge to the palace of Westminster and told the duke to his face that the deposition of the king was unacceptable to both Lords and people. There was a furious row, in which Rutland took his father's side and March temporized. Pope Pius II also reports that Warwick opposed York's claim.[89] Warwick knew how important assurances of loyalty had been for the Yorkist victory. The Yorkist lords at Calais had repeatedly given assurances of loyalty for themselves and York: to Coppini; in their manifestos; at the London convocation; to the king himself at Northampton; and at St Paul's. The verses issued after Northampton had proclaimed that they had never considered not being loyal and culminated in an appeal to the Trinity on behalf of both the king and the peace of the realm.[90] It was not possible to draw back without appearing to perjure themselves, even if York himself, as Abbot Whetehamstede mistakenly supposed, had papal absolution from his oath.[91] There were too many, such as the Church, the Bourchiers, and the people, who would be alienated by the deposition of the king. Those whom York had sought to retain by indentures without reserving allegiance to King Henry had declined to seal their contracts. Whetehamstede records popular anger at the duke's

87 Whetehamstede, i. 380–1.
88 *Annales*, 774.
89 Waurin, 314–15; Head, 'Pius II', 160.
90 *Davies Chron.* 86, 89, 95, 97; *CSPM* i. 24; Robbins, *Hist. Poems*, 210–15.
91 Whetehamstede, i. 383–4.

presumption. Representations may have been made to Warwick by the corporation of London and others.[92]

Waurin then tells a complex story of embassies and negotiations that commences at least one week early and most probably belongs after the public exchange reached impasse. Other sources record that many of the peers and perhaps others too undertook the substantive discussions at Blackfriars, where Warwick was residing. This was surely after York had formalized his claim. It was Warwick who took the lead in the discussions. On 21 October Margaret Paston wrote of a 'gret talkyng in this contre of the desyr of my lorde of York. The pepylle report full worchepfully of my lord of Warwyk.'[93]

After a fortnight of discussion, it was Warwick again who devised a compromise that was acceptable to all. 'Wherein my lorde of Warwik', observed someone at the time, 'be ha[ve]d him soo that [h]is fame is lik to be of great memory.'[94] The *Act of Accord* of 31 October mirrored and was perhaps modelled on the treaty of Troyes of 1420. Henry VI remained on the throne. Although the Lords concluded that York's hereditary claim could not be defeated, he had to abandon his immediate hopes of the crown. The immediate issue settled, Henry abandoned his son and recognized York and his issue to be his heirs. Meantime York was to be protector for life. He was assigned 10,000 marks (£6,666.66) for life, March 4,000 marks (£2,666.66) and Rutland 1,000 marks (£666.66) from the principality of Wales, duchy of Cornwall and county of Chester. Not much retrenchment there. As a sign of concord, King Henry wore his crown in procession to a solemn service at St Paul's. Among the peers in his company, Warwick bore the sword in front and March the train behind. At the ensuing banquet, Warwick's younger brother Sir John Neville was appointed chamberlain of the royal household.

So much effort was devoted to the dynastic issue that the parliamentary session achieved little else. The acts of the Coventry parliament were revoked, but no new attainders, if intended, or reforms were introduced or passed. The customs were appropriated to the repayment of the government's debts to the merchant staplers. It was York's task to secure submission from Henry VI's consort, son and other peers to the new regime. Warwick's duty, once again, was the keeping of the seas, to which he was reappointed on 17 December.[95] And in return for their services to the duke, his Neville allies had once again added to their offices wherever they had interests.

---

92   Jones and Walker, 'Private Contracts', 164–5, 165n; Whetehamstede, i. 377–80; see also Kingsford, *London Chrons.* 171; Waurin, 314.
93   *Paston L & P* i. 259.
94   Johnson, *York*, 214.
95   *CPR 1452–61*, 642.

7.3 The Ideology of Reform

The year from Ludford to York's Third Protectorate witnessed one of the most remarkable recoveries of political fortunes. The fugitives of Ludford had been exposed not only as traitors but as cowards, who had shamefully deserted their followers and left them to their fate. York had even abandoned his duchess and younger children to his enemies. It should have been difficult indeed, one might suppose, for the Yorkist lords to redeem their honour and retrieve the trust of their deserted retainers. Nine months later, in a remarkable reversal, they were in political control, and a year later York was protector for a third time.

Once victorious, as we have seen, the Yorkists reproduced the successful precedent of 1455, but neither the St Albans nor the Ludford campaigns was the model for Warwick's successful invasion. The Yorkists received more military support from other lesser peers than on previous occasions, but they made little use of their own bastard feudal retinues. The principal estates, concentrations of retainers, and hence the centres of power of Warwick, Salisbury, Fauconberg and March were far away from their Kentish bridgehead – in the West Midlands, the North, Wales and East Anglia – and initially at least they were scarcely tapped. Command of the sea enabled the Yorkists to land anywhere along the long coast-line from the south-west to Henry IV's own point of disembarkation on the Humber. They chose instead – surely *Warwick* chose instead? – to land in Kent, where none of them were significant landholders, though Warwick had commercial and maritime contacts as captain of Calais and keeper of the seas. Whilst York had tried unsuccessfully to raise revolt in Kent in 1452, it was Warwick who knew the current mood. He had marched unopposed through Kent and London only the previous autumn. What they launched was a popular rebellion. It was their capacity to mobilize public opinion that made their victory possible.

The debacle at Ludford may have left its mark. With that experience, York's Welsh retainers, Salisbury's northerners, and Warwick's West Midlanders might reasonably refuse another insurrection against the king. They may have needed to be reassured of the loyalty and legality of their cause before turning out for their lords again. As in 1456 and 1459, the Yorkists were backed by only a handful of the Lords, most of whom were staunchly loyal if also, it appears, out of touch with popular sentiment. Instead the Yorkists sought to exploit the long-standing Kentish grievances expressed by Jack Cade, repressed but not forgotten, and the apparently unquenched if unjustifiable hostility of the populace to successive royal governments, on both of which Warwick was updated through his contacts with the Cinque Ports. They also enlisted the Londoners, both oligarchs and populace, who approved of Warwick's support of English trade and admired his attacks on foreign shipping. They secured the support of the Church. They appealed to English patriotism. And they made a more sustained effort to present themselves as champions of the common good. The Yorkist campaign of 1460 was a popular uprising focused and directed by the great nobility.

The chosen strategy carried high risks. Warwick was required to metamorphose from great magnate into popular demagogue. He had to allow popular violence and revenge without prejudicing public order or alienating the propertied majority. Of course, the strategy worked, in the South-East. It does not appear to have had any impact elsewhere. The popularity of the Yorkists may have been only regional in scope: the North, the West Country and the Midlands were unsubdued. In the autumn the Yorkists were to whip up southern fears of the wild northerners against Queen Margaret. At the end of the year it was the northern commons who hated Salisbury enough to lynch him.

The Yorkists mobilized their target audience by carefully focused propaganda. It did not have to be true, as the Lancastrian speaker in the *Somnium* shrewdly observed.[96] We know that the Yorkists corresponded with England from abroad, though we do not have what they wrote or know for certain what it said. We may also deduce that they heard the government's replies and had incorporated their own ripostes in their manifestos. Some elements of propaganda in the chronicles do not derive from any surviving Yorkist poems and manifestos. Rumour and innuendo were rife. How much of this was fostered by the Yorkists? Were they behind smears too dangerous to acknowledge? Even before the Yorkists invoked the threat of a French invasion in their manifesto, the government feared it and diverted precious resources to obstruct it, for example by preparing Caister Castle in Norfolk:[97] was this because of disinformation from the Yorkists, as in 1458-9? Foreign threats had been invoked by the Yorkist apologist in the *Somnium Vigilantis* and were to be again against Queen Margaret,[98] admittedly with some justification. If the kingdom was in a dreadful state, as the Yorkists again alleged, surely it was not because the queen ruled all – a treasonable allegation which the Yorkists never specifically made – with the support of covetous evil councillors? Queen Margaret was said to be an adulteress and her son Prince Edward, the heir apparent, was not the king's son, but a bastard. The Yorkist verses posted on the gates at Canterbury referred, not too opaquely, to 'fals wedlock' and 'fals heyres'.[99] It was thus possible to separate allegiance to the king from commitment to his line.

The Yorkist lords were amazingly successful in evading the treason of which they stood convicted. Nowhere did they admit their disloyalty or rebellion, the justice of the verdict against them or the legitimacy of the Coventry parliament. They had been condemned unjustly and the first act of their new Yorkist parliament was to declare its predecessor illegitimate and void. It was the losing argument of the Yorkist apologist in the *Somnium Vigilantis* that prevailed, not the winning Lancastrian case. In the *Somnium* their uprising in 1459 had been justified because directed to the common good, to the reform of the government, and to 'the perempsion of such persones the whiche were odious to God and to the peple for thaire mysreule'. Far from deserving punishment, the Yorkist lords

96   Gilson, 'Defence', 521.
97   *CCR 1454–61*, 409.
98   Gilson, 'Defence', 515; *Davies Chron.* 87–8.
99   D. McCulloch and E. D. Jones, 'Lancastrian Politics, the French War, and the Rise of the Popular Element', *Speculum* lviii (1983), 130; note also the reference to March as 'conceived in wedlock' in the *Verses on the Yorkist Lords*.

merited thanks and reward.[100] When they invaded in 1460, they claimed that it was 'for the rizt of England' that they 'haue sufferd moche wo' and 'alle Englonde is be-holden to them'. York was compared to God's unworthy servant Job, 'whom Sathan not cesethe to be sette at care and disdeyne'. Warwick was reported to have complained to the king at Northampton that 'we haue be put in gret hevynesse'. They had 'never entendid to be otherwyse than feythfull and trew liege men to the king'; nor had York himself,

> Whom treason ne falshod neuer dyd shame,
> But euer obedient to his sovereigne;
> Falsehod euer-more put hym in blame,
> And lay awayte hym to have sleigne.

They had been constantly summoned, denied access and then destroyed. Their punishment had not been approved by the king.[101] The sentence against them was unusual, cruel and exceptional: one chronicle harked on the novel word *atteyntid*.[102] Evidently the new doctrine of attainder took time to catch on and did not easily overcome existing belief in the sanctity of inheritance. Sympathy for them may have attracted other lords to their camp. It certainly explains the adherence of Bergavenny to his brothers Salisbury and Fauconberg and nephew Warwick. At such times shared lineage counted for more than inheritance disputes, such as the Despenser one between Bergavenny's son and Warwick. Similarly the government's repression of treason in Ludlow and at Newbury, the latter the result of judicial sessions, were inflated into tyrannical reigns of terror. Not only does the 1460 manifesto allude to Newbury and to James Earl of Wiltshire, the principal commissioner, but the story found its way into the chronicles including that of the Burgundian Waurin.[103] A kingdom divided against itself, a poet observed, 'shall be desolate'.[104] Poets eulogized the Yorkist lords. England really needed them back at the political helm.

As captain of Calais, keeper of the seas, and on the march from Calais to the Midlands via London, Warwick had rediscovered and revived a crucial feature to his advantage: the popularity of the Yorkist lords and especially of the earl himself with the sailors and traders of the Cinque Ports and London. They were 'suche as stoden gretely in the fauuoure of the peple', asserted the Yorkist speaker in the *Somnium Vigilantis*, which his Lancastrian counterpart belittled rather than denied directly.[105] The chroniclers need to be treated with caution because they were biased towards the Yorkists and were influenced by the massive support that the earls actually secured. 'For it was sayde that alle Kent favoured and supported

100   Gilson, 'Defence', 515.
101   Robbins, *Hist. Poems*, 209, 213, 215, 219; *Davies Chron.* 93; *Three 15th-Cent. Chrons.* 72; *Foedera* v. ii. 97.
102   *Three 15th-Cent. Chrons.* 169; see also *Gregory's Chron.*, 120.
103   Waurin, 270.
104   Robbins, *Hist. Poems*, 208.
105   Gilson, 'Defence', 515, 521.

them and sothe it was', remarks the *English Chronicle*.[106] Yet it has a point. When Somerset landed at Guines, it was not pure accident that three of his ships entered Calais harbour and surrendered to Warwick. The crews favoured the earl. He let them go free. The men of Sandwich kept Warwick informed of the progress of countermeasures against him. Three times seamen deserted the king to join him. Londoners supplied him with munitions. Men crossed from England to join him at Calais.[107] As *The Brut* repeatedly observes, they all acted of their own 'fre wil'.[108] Warwick was able to receive complaints from England and incorporated them in his manifesto. And it was presumably Kentish sympathizers who supplied him with a copy of Jack Cade's own manifesto.

The ground had been prepared for a popular appeal and there were receptive minds close at hand when the Yorkists invaded. The Yorkists issued several bills, of which two are known to us directly; there are also several propagandist poems which surely emanated from them as well. Altogether we have eight pieces which, in their present forms, were designed for different audiences at different times; they may well have been reissued and adapted to other unknown occasions as well. They are unlikely to be all that once existed. These are:

1   the Yorkist apology in the *Somnium Vigilantis* of November 1459, which anticipates much later Yorkist propaganda;[109]
2   certainly antedating the Yorkist invasion, the 72 lines that Sir Frederick Madden dubbed *Verses on the Yorkist Lords*;[110]
3   the letter of the Yorkist earls to the papal nuncio Coppini, 25 June 1460;[111]
4   a recycled manifesto of Jack Cade, which obviously corresponded to Kentish grievances current a decade before, and of use primarily at the landing in Kent;[112]
5   eleven stanzas totalling 88 lines addressed to the 'To the ryghte Worshypfulle Cite of Caunterbury' and attached to the gates ahead of the arrival of the Yorkist lords;[113]
6   a wholly new manifesto addressed to Archbishop Bourchier, who was known to be in London, and the commons, dated about 3 July 1460;[114]
7   'A Poem on the Battle of Northampton' of 20 stanzas of 160 lines, composed after the death of Lord Scales on 18 July: Warwick features as the Bear and March as the Bearward;[115]
8   rumours against northerners disseminated by Richard Duke of York in

106   *Davies Chron.* 84.
107   *Three 15th-Cent. Chrons.* 73; *The Brut*, 528; *Annales*, 772; Waurin, 280–2.
108   *The Brut*, 528.
109   Gilson, 'Defence', 512–26, esp. 514–16.
110   Robbins, *Hist. Poems*, 218–21.
111   Ellis, *Original Letters*, 3 ser. i. 85–7.
112   *Vale's Bk.* 210–12.
113   *Davies Chron.* 91–4, repr. in Robbins, *Hist. Poems*, 207–10.
114   *Davies Chron.*, 86–90.
115   Robbins, *Hist. Poems*, 210–15.

the South which Queen Margaret and Prince Edward sought to rebut to the City of London in December 1460.[116]

All were loyal protestations that declared the rebels' commitment to the king. The *Verses on the Yorkist Lords* declares their objective to be to

> Destroy treson, & make a tryalle,
> Of hem that be fauty, & hurten fulle sore,
> For the wylle of [Henry], kyng most ryalle,
> That is the most purpose that we labor for.[117]

Cade's manifesto looks to remedies from the king. The City of Canterbury verses seek the advancement of:

> Harry oure souerayne and most Crystyne kyng.[118]

The new manifesto praises Henry VI and invokes Henry V, 'your fader of precious memory' with approval, whilst the Northampton stanzas stress the loyalty of the victors to the king.[119]

All Yorkist propaganda promoted the common good. The earliest verses were directed against treason and its perpetrators. The reissued Cade manifesto was not one of the early ones that dealt with sectional Kentish grievances, such as the jurisdiction of the lieutenant of Dover, but one that had recast Kentish ills into general complaints of wider appeal. England was no longer the kingdom of God, the Canterbury verses complain, but the realm of Satan, where false wedlock, perjury, heresies, unjust disinheritance, falsehood and treason abounded and where the king was impoverished. The new manifesto envisaged a king who favours God's church, who can maintain an honourable household and live honourably and worthily like other Christian princes, who dispenses good justice, *and* who leaves a proper livelihood for his subjects.

Inevitably it is the manifestos that go into most detail. Both are much more wide-ranging and general than that of 1459, which was a model known to the new author, who reshaped its conclusion, but was otherwise deliberately rejected. Both are in the third person rather than the first person plural. Gone are the topical and personal elements of 1459, such as the damage to trade and free access to the royal council; and other current issues of more general application are substituted, such as new taxes and compulsory military service. The core remains the clauses on law and order, royal finance, evil counsel, and the ignorance of the king. There are no significant changes here in what were evidently perennial

---

116 *Vale's Bk.* 142–3. These were the letters read to the City corporation on 2 December, Corporation of London RO, London Jnl. 6, ff. 279–80.
117 Robbins, *Hist. Poems*, 220–1. Though the only surviving texts say 'Edward', ibid. 279, they only make sense if at composition Henry was meant.
118 *Davies Chron.* 92.
119 Ibid. 87–9.

beliefs. The new manifesto makes more explicit the demand that the king should live of his own; topical references to new tallages are added and the evil counsellors are accused of peculating them. Shrewsbury, Wiltshire and Beaumont had despoiled the king to their own profit and now 'procede to the hangyng and drawyng of men by tyranny': surely a reference to Newbury? Most significantly the manifesto takes a longer timespan. It brings the issue of the treasonable loss of France up to date by relating it to attempts to suborn the wild Irish and continental princes against Yorkist Ireland and Calais. It even accuses the king's counsellors of intending a sell-out of England altogether. Back comes Duke Humphrey, that model of loyal and maltreated service represented in 1460 by York, Salisbury and Warwick. These additions and the reference to Ireland betray the role as draughtsman of York himself, who redeployed old charges still current to new effect. Nothing has got better since 1450. The issues of 1450 and Cade's old manifesto remained current. York's repeated 'unquieting' of the realm complained of at Coventry the previous year was justified by the continuation of the evils against which he had complained. The tables had been turned on his critics.[120]

Both manifestos are as unreasonable and deliberately misleading as Warwick's the previous year. Many of the strictures made above against the 1459 manifesto apply equally to these. Everywhere is the presumption that the king's undeniable poverty was due to profiteering by his favourites. The new tallages, peculation of fines by the treasurer, and acquisitions of forfeited property complained of are almost invisible to modern historians and pale beside the salaries and offices that York and his allies awarded themselves. If Henry VI needed extra money, compulsory military service and foreign co-operation, was it not because of the rebellion of the Yorkists and were they not necessary? Had they not destabilized the kingdom? The attainder at Coventry was enacted by common assent of parliament and the tribunal at Newbury had proceeded by strict legal form. The Yorkists themselves were much more ruthless towards their opponents. The new manifesto depicted things as they were or appeared to observers to be. Its skill as always – and this is a particularly adroit example of the genre – was to feed on justifiable dissatisfactions with the state of the commonwealth and to focus them in the desired direction. The fault was with the king's evil counsellors. Again, as Paul Johnson remarked, is it credible that there were so many evil counsellors, so that new ones always replaced each old one? Where did Henry find them? The remedy for all these evils lay with the Yorkist lords. This time, more wisely, there were no protestations of what *they* would and would not do.

One major difference in 1460 was that the Church was on the Yorkists' side and gave them the moral initiative. Warwick had foreseen the potential value of such backing. He had prepared the ground carefully, by cultivating and then enrolling the papal legate on their side. Bishop Coppini was a lightweight, a cleric of little judgement and much self-importance, who allowed himself to become embroiled in English politics and foolishly took sides. As early as March 1460 he

120 *Vale's Bk.* 210–12; *Davies Chron.* 86–94.

had met with Warwick, presumably at Calais, had been impressed by him, and acted on his advice. On 25 June, on the eve of their invasion, the Yorkist lords had written to him at length in Latin. They had recited the injustices to which York and themselves had been subjected and had besought his justice and intercession. They were about to invade England not to damage, but to promote the honour and glory of the king. They swore to God Almighty and to Coppini as legate that they were loyal, faithful and devoted both to the king and to the Holy See and promised that they would do their uttermost for the faith, for the Church, and for the defence of Christendom against the Turks. They assured him of York's compliance. They ended by urging him to accompany them.[121]

If not strictly truthful – none of them ever showed any serious intent in becoming crusaders! – the letter struck the right note. Coppini accompanied or followed the earls to England and to London, where he was on 3 July. He was rumoured (probably unjustly) to have offered remission of sins to the Yorkists and excommunicated supporters of Queen Margaret. He was induced on 4 July at London to write at length to Henry VI in their support. After exhorting the Yorkists to peace and obedience, so he reported, 'they gave me a written pledge that they were disposed to devotion and obedience to your Majesty and to do all in their power for the conservation and augmentation of your honour and the good of your realm'. The Yorkists wanted an audience and 'to be received into their former state and favour', from which they claimed to have been removed by the craft of their opponents. At their request and to spare bloodshed, Coppini had crossed the Channel with them. They were now willing to do whatever he proposed for the good of king and kingdom and in particular

> certain things contained in documents under their own seals and oaths, which they handed over, and which I am confident your Serenity would approve after viewing them with a tranquil and open mind, as they tend to the honour and glory of your lordship, the public exaltation of the realm, and the honour and advantage of princes and lords.

This sounds more concrete than the Yorkist manifestos. To complete his partisan commitment to the Yorkist cause, Coppini reported how his work had been impeded by 'some who professed themselves devoted to your Majesty and are not'. He even accepted as reasonable the Yorkist claims that they must come armed to any audience![122] What a gift Coppini was to Warwick! How potentially useful he was when dealing with a king so easily influenced and as religious-minded as Henry VI! And how actually useful the legate was to be in Warwick's dealings with the English Church.

The Verses on the Yorkist Lords culminate in an appeal to Christ himself that the Yorkist lords persist in their intent 'To the pleasaunce of God and the welfare of vs alle'.[123] The Canterbury verses, which contain numerous scriptural and

121   Ellis, *Original Letters*, 3 ser. i. 85–8.
122   Ibid. 3 ser. i. 89–97.
123   Robbins, *Hist. Poems*, 221.

liturgical allusions and Latin tags, ask Jesus himself to restore York, who is compared to Job, and end three verses with the Latin refrain 'Glory, Laud and Honour to you Christ, Redeemer, King'![124] The new manifesto, like that of 1459, makes frequent reference to God, invokes him and the saints as witnesses, presents a model of a Christian prince and twice judges evils as contrary to 'Goddys and mannys lawe'. The first clause laments 'the grete oppressyon, extorsion, robry, murther, and other vyolencys doone to Goddys churche, and to his mynystres therof, ayens Goddys and mannes law'. It is addressed not just to the commons, but to Archbishop Bourchier, primate of all England and diocesan bishop of much of Kent.[125] On arriving at Canterbury, the Yorkist lords entered the feretory of the cathedral and removed the cross of St Thomas (Becket) of Canterbury, the most revered of saints throughout England and especially in Kent. It was borne before the rebels like the banner of St Cuthbert in northern England. Proceeding to St Paul's Cathedral in the company of Coppini on Saturday 5 July, the Yorkists found the recipient of their manifesto Archbishop Bourchier, the kinsman and sympathizer of the Yorkist peers, presiding over a meeting of the convocation of Canterbury. Convocation contained several sympathetic bishops and was also at odds with the regime that had allowed the clergy to be molested by secular courts, the 'oppressyons' cited in the Yorkist manifesto. With 'alle the convocation and innumerable people standing about', Warwick was permitted to put the partisan Yorkist case. As in 1452 and 1455, this time on the cross of Canterbury and in the presence of convocation, the Yorkist lords solemnly swore 'that they had [n]euer bore vntrue feythe and lygeaunce to the kinges person, wyllyng no more hurt to hym than to theyr own persone'. Also that same day Coppini declared that he had with him papal bulls requesting the restoration of the Yorkist lords, the excommunication of their opponents, and the absolution of Yorkist sympathizers from any punishment or blame.[126]

The Yorkists took Coppini and the bishops with them to Northampton. Coppini claimed to be authorized to mediate for peace. Bishop Beauchamp's efforts at mediation were rejected by Buckingham as partisan. Not surprisingly, two bishops were embarrassed and joined the king; others had been with him throughout. Coppini committed himself further:

> [He] raised the standard of the Church of Rome and, on the ground that they were to do battle against the enemies of the Faith, he granted plenary remission of sins to those who were to fight on the side of the Earl of Warwick. He likewise pronounced anathema on their enemies, exhibiting before the camp an Apostolic letter which was believed to contain this

124 *Davies Chron.* 93.
125 Ibid. 86–90.
126 Ibid. 94–5; *Stone's Chron.*, 79–80; R. L. Storey, 'Episcopal King-Makers in the Fifteenth Century', *The Church, Patronage and Politics in 15th Century England*, ed. R. B. Dobson (Gloucester, 1984), 87; G. Baskerville, 'A London Chronicle of 1460', *EHR* xxviii (1913), 125.

formula though in reality its contents were quite different. . . . [He also] forbade burial to those who died in battle.[127]

The battle won, as we have seen, the sacraments and processions of the Church sanctioned the Yorkist victory. 'If God be with vs, who is vs a-gayne?', demanded the poet. Henry VI is made to give thanks to God and St Thomas.

> Blessed be God in trinite,
> Ffadir & Son & holygoste,
> Whiche kepithe his servauntes in aduersite,
> & wold not suffre theyme to be lose.
> As thou art lord of mightes moste,
> Saue the king & his ryalte,
> And illumyn him with the holygoste,
> His reme to set in perfyt charite. Amen.[128]

The Yorkists were fulfilling God's wishes. Divine authority was invoked in support of Henry VI himself and the restoration of domestic peace. The text chosen for the chancellor's opening sermon to parliament hinted at the remedy of ecclesiastical grievances.

Loyalty remained a central theme. In 1459 the Yorkists' protestations of loyalty may have inhibited them. In 1460 such considerations were not allowed to hold them back. Nobody taking the Yorkist side could have expected them to achieve their objectives without violence. The Yorkist lords regarded themselves as loyal and rejected the sentence against them. How dare anyone presume to make such charges against princes of their blood? How could they be traitors? So runs the argument of the Yorkist apologist of the *Somnium Vigilantis*. Were they not lords of 'olde ancetrie of gret myght and strengt'?[129] This note of incredulity and indeed much else emerges in William Paston's famous description of Lord Rivers's uncomfortable interview with his captors at Calais in January 1460:

> there my lord of Salesbury reheted hym, callyng hym knaves son that he schuld be so rude to calle hym and these other lordys traytours, for they schull be found the Kyngys treue liege men whan he schuld be found a traytour &c. And my lord of Warrewyk reheted hym and seyd that his fader was but a squyer and broute up wyth King Herry the vte, and sethen hym-self made by maryage and also made lord, and that it was not his parte to have swyche langage of lordys beyng of the Kyngys blood. And my lord of Marche rehetyd hym jn lyke wyse, and Ser Antony [Wydeville] was reheted for his langage of all iij lordys jn lyke wyse.[130]

127 Head, 'Pius II', 156–7, 173.
128 Robbins, *Hist. Poems*, 215.
129 Gilson, 'Defence', 515.
130 *Paston L & P* i. 162; see also Waurin, 284.

The Yorkists' lengthy pedigrees and royal descent were far superior to those merely associated relatively recently with Henry VI, *created* – we would say of merit! – rather than born into the peerage, and married into the European aristocracy. They were not just ingenuous in claiming that their attainder in 1459 was the craft of their enemies, which we know not to be true. They were not accusing evil councillors merely because they could not legitimately attack the king without committing treason. It had to be so. Men of our lineage could not be traitors. The 'weye of feete' when they took it was not treasonable, but was compatible with the public good and did not break their oaths of allegiance.

Hence those who stood against them were the traitors. It was not possible to have an honest difference of political opinion or to believe their opponents loyal and well-meaning, if perhaps mistaken. Critics, opponents, rivals were all traitors. When the Irish parliament recognized York as lieutenant, it threatened with attainder those who opposed him. Accordingly York executed William Overy, now representative of the Earl of Wiltshire, whom King Henry had just appointed lieutenant of Ireland in York's lieu and who was therefore rightfully the king's representative.[131] So, too, at Calais, Warwick executed members of the garrison who had deserted him and later Mountford too.[132] They were traitors to him and therefore to the crown. At Northampton, like St Albans but unlike Ludford, the Yorkists did not hold back from attacking when the royal banner was displayed. Those killed, whom they regarded as their particular enemies, were surely those whom they most wished to eliminate. Several were slain, unnecessarily, in their tents. The garrison of the Tower were judicially murdered as traitors although they had certainly been fighting for the king. In 1460, in short, no holds were barred. Those who stood in the way of the Yorkists were traitors and killed, both as an example to others and to ensure that they could cause no further trouble. Terror was an important element in this Yorkist coup. No wonder that Wiltshire fled abroad. Fearful of sharing the fates of Moleyns and Aiscough, two bishops murdered by the populace in 1450, Waynflete surrendered the great seal on 7 July. That same day he, Bishop Bothe, and the Bishop of Hereford secured general pardons from the king.[133] Royal pardons and holy orders were no protection against the mob. Indeed Hereford was imprisoned in Warwick Castle. Warwick was a far more ruthless politician than his uncle of York. Had he been king at the Coventry great council of 1459, rebels such as the Yorkist lords would not have escaped his grasp and would have received no last chance!

The notion of loyalty that the Yorkist lords subscribed to allowed them almost a free hand in what they did. However, it was genuine enough. They were consistent in their respect to the office of the king. Those summoned to their support were

131   Scofield, i. 46.
132   Waurin, 281.
133   *CPR 1452–61*, 599; *POPC* vi. 361.

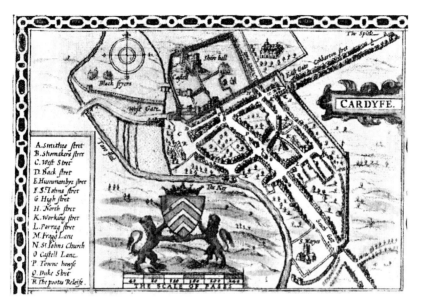

Plate 12 Cardiff, the principal town of Warwick's lordship of Glamorgan, from the early seventeenth-century map of John Speed. (*Peter Jacobs*)

Plate 13 Following the Yorkist discomfiture at Ludford in 1459, Henry VI sits in triumph (*left*) whilst the future Edward IV and other Yorkist lords embark for Calais (*right*). (*British Library, MS Harley 7353*)

Plate 14 The east end of Tewkesbury Abbey refashioned by Hugh Despenser the Younger and encircled by the tombs of the founder and other de Clares and Despenser patrons. Note, front left, the splendid chantry of Warwick's mother-in-law Isabel Despenser. (*RCHME,* © *Crown copyright*)

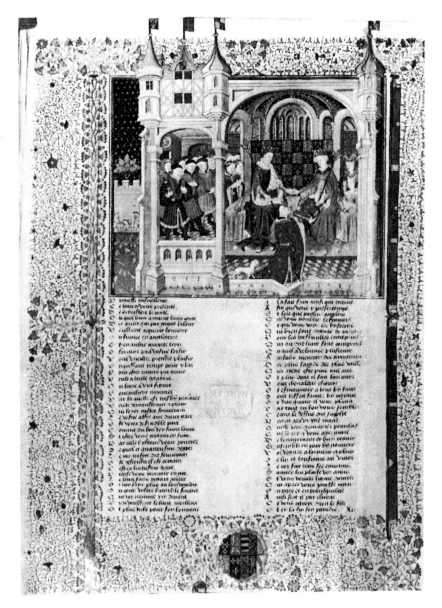

Plate 15 A court scene. Warwick's brother-in-law John Talbot Earl of Shrewsbury presents a book to King Henry VI and Queen Margaret of Anjou. (*British Library, MS Royal E VI, f.2v*)

Plate 16 Bisham Priory, the Salisbury mausoleum where Warwick, his parents and brothers were buried. (*British Library, MS Loan 90, p.188 / in the collection of the Duke of Buccleuch and Queensberry, KT*)

Plate 17 Reconstruction of Middleham Castle showing the large windows of the extra residential storey to the keep perhaps added by Warwick. Note how stone-built ancillary buildings have encroached on the original courtyard. (*English Heritage; drawing by Terry Ball*)

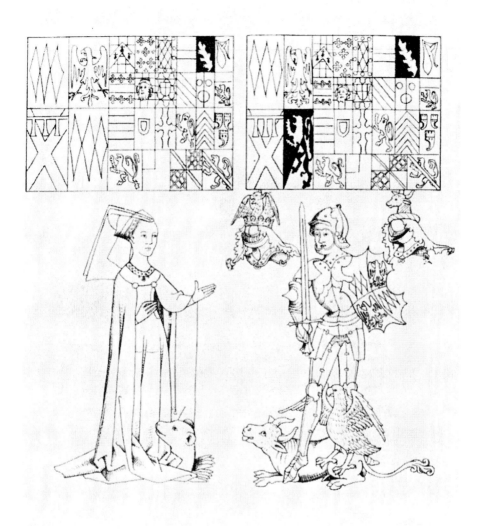

Plate 18   Warwick and the Countess Anne from John Rous's Roll of the Earls of Warwick. (*Peter Jacobs*)

Plate 19 Warwick's sole surviving book, a luxury Burgundian copy of *L'Enseignement de la vraie noblesse*. Note his arms encircled with the Garter at the bottom and a continental version of the bear and ragged staff to the right. (*Geneva, Bibliothèque publique et universitaire, MS français 166, f.3*)

Plate 20 King Louis XI
of France. (*National
Portrait Gallery, London*)

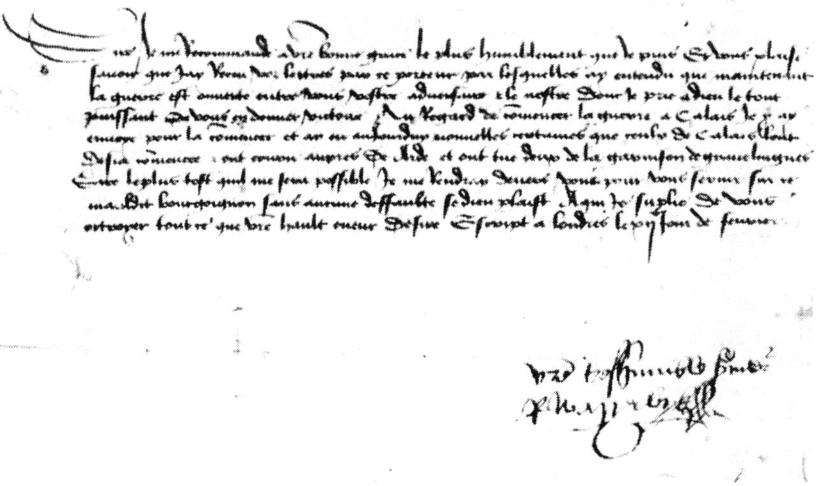

Plate 21 Letter of 12 February 1471 in French signed by Warwick promising King
Louis XI that he has ordered the Calais garrison to commence hostilities against
Burgundy forthwith. (*British Library / Geoffrey Wheeler*)

Plate 22 The Battle of Barnet. Edward IV (*centre*) leads the royal army to victory. Warwick and his men, recognizable from the ragged staves on their backs, flee to the right. (*Besançon, Bibliothèques et archives municipales, MS 1168, f.2*)

doyng alwey the dewte of ligeaunce in oure persone to oure souuerayne
lorde, to hys estate, prerogatyf, and preemynence, and to thassuerte of hys
most noble persone vnto we haue euer be and wylle be as trew as any of his
subgettes alyve.[134]

At Calais, in their manifestos, at St Paul's, before the battle, immediately afterwards, and on procession into London the Yorkists stressed that they had ever
been loyal and still were. Their commitment was repeatedly confirmed by oaths
sworn as publicly as possible and sanctioned by the Church. It was King Henry
who presided at the opening of the new parliament. Their respect related both
to the office and the person of the king himself. If Henry was malleable and as
easily manipulated when in their hands as by his erstwhile favourites, yet he was
not personally at fault: 'swiche ys himself a[s] noble, as vertous, as ryghtewys,
and blyssed of dysposicione, as eny prince erthely . . . [and] nother assentyng ne
knowyng' what was done in his name.[135] Similarly Warwick's manifesto of the
previous year had observed that 'our soveraigne lorde of his blessed conversacion
ys of his owne noble disposicion as gracieuxle aplied to the seid commone wele
and to the reformyng of these premisses as ene prince cristen'.[136] Does not this
go far beyond exculpating the king and blaming others? Is not the use of the
word 'blessed' in both manifestos remarkable? Were not the Yorkist lords on both
occasions paying tribute to King Henry's very special piety, to the saintly character dwelt on by his acquaintance John Blacman and identifiable as a model of
the new devotional piety?[137] It is evidence that Henry's saintliness and goodness
were already accepted even by his regime's critics during his first reign. Charges
of evil governance could not be laid against a man who was so conspicuously
good. It was not just the law of treason that placed him above criticism. This need
not prevent the Yorkists taking power. The familiar image of the realm as body
politic features in the Latin refrain of the Canterbury ballad: 'The head of all is
weary and the heart of all deserving'.[138] The Northampton verses make Henry
admit that the 'curre Dogges' made him act as he did although they sought to do
him mischief.[139] If the king was weary and easily led, should not the Yorkist lords
rule on his behalf? Did not such propaganda pave the way for a third, enduring,
protectorate? It was also incompatible with Henry's deposition and York's
succession.

Undoubtedly the Yorkists resented their treatment in 1459. They considered
their conduct to have been justifiable and loyal. No more in 1460 than on previous

---

134   *Davies Chron.* 89–90.

135   Ibid.

136   *Vale's Bk.* 209.

137   R. Lovatt, 'A Collector of Apocryphal Anecdotes: John Blacman Revisited',
Property and Politics: Essays in Later Medieval English History, ed. A. J. Pollard
(Gloucester, 1984), 174.

138   *Davies Chron.* 91–2. Johnson identifies the text, but differs in his analysis, Johnson,
York, 203–4.

139   Robbins, *Hist. Poems*, 213.

occasions did they adopt a defensive tone, seek to rebut charges against themselves and thus inadvertently give them currency. Instead they took the offensive, presenting a positive vision and blackening others. It was this message that mobilized the public opinion that secured them victory. The ideology of reform was a potent appeal to popular opinion combined with reassurance that nothing revolutionary was intended. The Yorkists appealed to accepted notions of good governance and denounced obvious evils to which all could subscribe. They combined a long-term view – the notoriety of the ills besetting England and the incorrigibility of the king's evil councillors – with more immediate novelties that refreshed the more hackneyed grievances. That the message was effective mattered more than its truth. They were short on solutions: there is no proof of any. Whilst appealing to the public good, they sought primarily to recover both the possessions that they had lost in 1459 *and* the political ascendancy that they had so briefly enjoyed in 1454–6. The Neville regime benefited the Nevilles most. Their professions of allegiance enabled loyal critics to join them and made it difficult for mere loyalists to oppose them. How could one object to the good of king *and* commonwealth?

7.4   From Abyss to Victory

York's claim to the throne was an error of judgement and a crucial turning point. It cost him his life, plunged the country into civil war, and shed an ocean of blood. Was it York's error alone or was Warwick also at fault? Surely York's conduct since his landing anticipated what was to follow? Moreover, so Johnson has argued, Warwick's visit to York at Shrewsbury enabled the two to finalize arrangements which may even have been planned when they were in Ireland. York's actions were interpreted in this way, at least in retrospect, Jones has shown.[140] None of these arguments are conclusive. The other Yorkists are hardly likely to have known of York's revised dating formulae and new-style indentures and may not have recognized the implications. His stately progress had precedents in earlier years when he did *not* claim the crown. Was he trying to avoid the other Yorkist lords? Even the use of the royal arms, like the stress on his 'yssew royale' in the new manifesto and the *Verses on the Yorkist Lords*, could have been the necessary preliminary to claiming the protectorate ahead of other royal princes; in both cases they were accompanied by protestations of loyalty. Waurin claims that Warwick knew nothing of York's claim in advance. Both he and Pope Pius II reported the earl's objections. Most significant is the absence of any stage-management for York's claim. The Lords were not prepared for his usurpation. There was no acclamation: not even by the Nevilles. There was no pressure from the Commons as in 1455. The king had not been prepared – no abdication had been arranged, as in 1399 – and he was allowed and even

---

140   Johnson, *York*, 211–12; Jones, 'Edward IV, Warwick and the Yorkist Claim', 348–50. The Count of Foix, Archibald Whitelaw and Edward IV were all writing *after* the dynastic revolution of 1461.

invited to object. If the Yorkist peers had known and approved of York's choice, Henry would not have opened parliament in person. Such matters need not have been left to chance. The victory at Northampton had caused Duke Richard to change his views. Now was the time to sweep away his pathetic cousin, with whom he no longer had any patience, and to take his right. Wrongly he expected his allies to think likewise.

Yet there is an interpretation that squares the circle and removes the apparent contradictions. All the Yorkist professions of loyalty were directed at the king, none to the prince. Already in July it was rumoured 'that they will make a son of the Duke of York king and that they will pass over the king's son, as they are beginning to say that he is not the king's son'.[141] Prince Edward could be set aside. To establish his rights as heir presumptive of King Henry over the Holland, Beaufort and Stafford lines, York needed to establish his Mortimer claim. Up until his entry to the Lords all his reported actions contributed to this. What Warwick and his fellow Yorkists wanted was the duke's recognition as heir to the throne and his appointment as protector during Henry's life: the eventual *Accord* in fact. Commons and Lords could support that, but not the king's deposition. Whilst to contemporary thinking Henry's madness could have been regarded as a malady of the body politic as Gross has shown,[142] this was not stated in Yorkist propaganda and conflicted with the saintly image described above. For York to present himself to parliament as 'principall physician' with the prescription to extirpate 'the rote and botome of this long festered cankar' was to demonstrate that he was out of touch.[143] Lacking support even from his own side, York was obliged to withdraw and complex negotiations were needed to attain the objective that his fellow Yorkists had always sought and that earlier had seemed assured.

Hence York was forced into a humiliating retreat. He had revealed the ambitions for the throne that some already suspected, exposed himself to charges of disloyalty and perjury, and appeared an obstacle to concord and compromise even to those at parliament. It was not York who was credited with the *Accord*. Those Lords who consented were all to some degree Yorkist sympathizers; else they would not have been present. Only Rutland concurred with York's claim to the crown. Some Lords backed a Yorkist government; a few had fought at Northampton; and others, probably, were prepared to acquiesce. Several who attended the chapter of the Garter or otherwise co-operated with the new regime were later to oppose it. We do not know how many lay peers attended the parliamentary session and agreed to the *Accord*; probably not many.[144] The *Accord* itself was never actually enacted into law by parliament: could the Commons not be prevailed upon to consent? York's Third Protectorate, like his Second in 1455,

141   *CSPM* i. 27.
142   Gross, *Dissolution*, 15–17.
143   C. Rawcliffe, *Medicine and Society in Late Medieval England* (Stroud, 1995), 46. The speech may not however be authentic, since Rawcliffe's source for a speech mentioned by nobody else is the mid-Tudor chronicle of Edward Hall.
144   The best assessment is now Watts, *Henry VI*, 359n.

was established by a minority of sympathetic Lords who nevertheless needed intimidating with overwhelming force.

As on earlier occasions, in 1454 and 1456, those opposed to the Yorkists failed to appear. Among the absentees were the sons of Buckingham, Shrewsbury and Beaumont, who could reasonably have wanted revenge for their fathers' deaths. Also missing were the queen and prince, the dukes of Exeter and Somerset, the five earls of Northumberland, Westmorland, Pembroke, Wiltshire and Devon, one viscount, and many barons. The Yorkist regime may have ruled the South and Midlands, but it did not control the West Country, Wales or the North. Its opponents were prepared for violence – according to Waurin, Northumberland had tried to ambush Warwick in August[145] – but there was no civil war as yet. Parliamentary elections were held all over the kingdom and those elected duly attended parliament. Despite the blood that had been shed at and since Northampton, the Yorkists could reasonably hope that as on previous occasions parliamentary authority would prevail and political opponents would accept the new protectorate.

York's attempted usurpation had changed all that. The title that the Lords at Westminster accepted as irrefutable was unacceptable to the queen, to her son, and to other members of the royal family, some with their own claims, such as Exeter, Somerset, the king's half-brother Pembroke, or Sir Henry Stafford, new husband of Margaret Beaufort. Whatever the face-saving formulae, York could no longer be credited with the loyalty that he had earlier asserted. His claim to be acting with the king's consent was thrown into doubt: was Henry a free agent? The parliamentary unanimity that might have given the moral ascendancy was missing. York had alienated people loyal to Henry VI and had inflamed his own enemies. For them, far from being a compromise, the *Accord* was a declaration of war.

The duke's action offered propagandist opportunities to the Lancastrians, who did not hesitate to write to the corporation of London and no doubt other towns to exploit them. It made more credible the claims of Queen Margaret and her son that Duke Richard had *long* secretly (and treasonably) imagined the destruction of the king, that his assertions that he had never intended harm to the king when rebelling were false, that he had killed divers lords of malice not for the public good, and that he had lately sought the crown contrary not only to his allegiance but also to 'divers solempne othes of his owne offre made uncompelled or constraigned'. They were able to thank the corporation for thwarting York's intended usurpation. And Prince Edward declared his intent 'to thenlarging of my lord' (of releasing the king) 'at such tyme aswe shalbe disposed'. If not acted on immediately, these letters were nevertheless read to the City corporation to which they were addressed and were recorded in the City journal.[146] They were not dismissed out of hand. However, as we shall see, the Lancastrians failed to make the most of their propaganda opportunity, were quickly driven on

---

145   Waurin, 309.
146   *Vale's Bk.*, 142–3; Corp. of London RO, London Jnl. 6, ff. 279–80.

the defensive, and were unable to win many of their potential sympathizers still in the South to their cause.

Of course there were those who applauded the new regime. Among them apparently was the aged chronicler John Hardyng, whose verses on York as potential ruler and references to his 'regalitie' can belong only to this time. He looked forward to

> Howe ye shall rule your subiectes, while ye lyve,
> In lawe, and peace, and all tranquyllite
> Whiche ben the floures of all regalyite.

Apart from aliens, York needed to watch against divisions at home.[147] York was indeed determined to enforce his authority in the provinces, but did not appreciate that its opponents were now as ruthless and merciless as the Yorkists were themselves. He expected his opponents to respect the authority of king, protector and parliament, to melt away and submit as Exeter's men had done in 1454 and the Yorkists themselves did at Ludford the previous year. He did not anticipate that their opponents were now engaging in proper strategic planning and colluding with foreign powers, nor did he expect them really to sacrifice national interests to those of the house of Lancaster. The Yorkists expected them to avoid bloodshed at all costs, as on previous occasions, and they expected them to honour their words. Hence they failed to mobilize their forces fully and indeed divided them. Warwick, Norfolk, Arundel and the Bourchiers were left behind with the king and government, when on 9 December 1460 March was despatched to establish control of Wales and York and Salisbury proceeded northwards to sort out the queen, the Percies and other northerners, and to relieve their own beleaguered tenants and retainers. On 16 December Warwick's retainer Sir Geoffrey Gate was despatched to the Isle of Wight, where he quickly overcame Somerset's brother Edmund Beaufort and his sixty-one men. The Earl of March was to be as similarly successful in Wales.[148]

Yet the greatest threat was in the North, where Queen Margaret had assembled almost all branches of the Lancastrian royal family and where she enjoyed the support of almost the whole regional nobility. Somerset, Exeter and Devon had joined her. She could draw on the justifiable hostility towards the junior house of Neville fomented by the Percy–Neville feud, by the partisan anti-Percy verdicts of the resulting judicial commissions, and by the deaths of the second Earl of Northumberland, Lord Clifford, and Lord Egremont at St Albans and Northampton. She also sought to make common cause against a common enemy with the Scots. If Salisbury himself was missing from the Lancastrian councils and army, his allies FitzHugh and Greystoke were not able to absent themselves, and the Earl of Westmorland and Lord Neville were representatives of the senior line.[149] Salisbury's forfeiture in 1459 had allowed

---

147 *Hardyng's Chronicle*, ed. H. Ellis (1812), 16, 155, 179.
148 Scofield, i. 118–20.
149 *Annales*, 775; see also Hicks, 'An Alternative Government'.

local rivals to recover, to assert control over his own estates, and to neutralize the famous Neville connection. Late in 1460 the North was Lancastrian.

Though York's duchy took its name from a northern county and though Salisbury and Warwick were themselves northerners by birth and inclination, it is indicative of how opportunist was Yorkist propaganda that the Yorkists now blackened the northern character of Margaret's regime. The 'same fals traitour', complained Prince Edward, 'hathe nowe late sowen amongis you and many othir of my lordis trewe liegemen . . . that we shuld entende to make assembles of grete nombre of straungeres that wolde purpose to dispoile and robbe you and thayme of yor goodes and uttirly to distruye you and thayme for evur mo'. Queen and prince denied the slander in letters read to the City aldermen on 2 December.[150] Long before the Lancastrians came southwards, the Yorkists were concerned to whip up fear and regional animosity against them in the South, evidently to re-inforce the commitment towards themselves of southerners and Londoners against their factional and dynastic rivals. We have no direct evidence that such slanders were circulating in the North. Instead of exploiting to the full the prop-aganda initiative that York's failed usurpation offered, queen and prince were obliged to defend themselves against these charges in their letters, and found their freedom of action inhibited next year when they did indeed proceed southwards.

York and Salisbury took with them only a small force since, as prominent northern magnates, they had many local followers to count upon. They were unable to make contact. Instead they found themselves isolated at York's small castle of Sandal near Wakefield by much more numerous foes. Allegedly Sir Andrew Trollope used ragged staves to make his forces appear as supporters of Warwick. When rashly counter-attacking, York and Salisbury were easily defeated on 31 December. York himself, his son Rutland, Warwick's father Salisbury, brother Thomas, brother-in-law William Lord Harrington, the Neville knights Parre, Radford and Harrington, and Harrow, captain of the Londoners, were among those killed or executed. It was now the Lancastrians' opportunity for revenge. Salisbury had initially been spared, but was lynched by the commons at Pontefract: 'the commune peple of the cuntre loued him nat'. However popular the Nevilles were in the South, they had as committed opponents as supporters in the North.[151]

The death of so many kinsmen was certainly a severe blow to the Yorkist leadership and encouraged further opposition, such as that of Thomas Daniel at Castle Rising (Norf.), but the Yorkists were unwilling to concede defeat. York's son Edward Earl of March succeeded not only to his father's duchy, but also to his protectorate and his status as heir to Henry VI. Henceforth he styled himself as 'verrey heir'. Theoretically, for he was far away in Wales. Initially it was more important that in London Warwick was 'like another Caesar'.[152] He may have had private doubts, as he told Antonio de la Torre[153] – he seems to have found it easier

---

150 *Vale's Bk.* 142–3; see also Goodman, *Wars of the Roses*, 44; *POPC* vi. 307–10.
151 *Davies Chron.* 107; *Annales*, 772.
152 *CSPM* i. 46.
153 Scofield, i. 130–1.

to confide in foreigners – but he took command and acted defiantly and reso-
lutely. He wrote at once to the pope, dauphin, dukes of Burgundy and Milan
assuring them that the defeat would soon be reversed.[154] On 5 January he and
other lords secured a further 2,000 marks (£1,333.66) in loan from the City. On
the 8th the mercers' company agreed to lend Henry VI a further 500 marks
(£333.66) for the benefit of king and commonwealth and specifically 'to the hasty
spede of Erle of Warwik vnto the North Contre with his puissance'.[155] On
13 January Philip the Good replied. A troop of Burgundian handgunners was
despatched under the command of Seigneur de la Barde.[156] Warwick again
induced Coppini to intervene: he wrote indirectly to Queen Margaret offering
his mediation in negotiations and asserting his authority – had the Lancastrians
questioned that he was a true legate? – though he was not to live up to renewed
promises to Warwick to give papal support to his cause in battle.[157] Parliament
met again and adjourned without any legislation. The earl is reported to have
regarded Somerset's involvement with the Lancastrians as a breach of the
promise that he had made to him at Newnham Bridge.[158] He expected others to
adhere more strictly to their promises than he did himself.

If Warwick ever intended counter-attacking into the North, where he had
succeeded to his father's Neville estates and wardenry, he thought better of it.
There was no need, as Margaret's army advanced southwards. Coppini advised
a defensive strategy.[159] This was sensible, for the Lancastrians had not the access
to taxation and loans of the Yorkists and could not remain in the field indefinitely,
but a kingdom could not be won without fighting. The Yorkists in London determined instead on an offensive strategy and defensive tactics. They resolved
on a pitched battle on ground of their choosing near St Albans. Norfolk led one
column via Barnet and Warwick himself the other with 'grete ordnance' via his
mother's town of Ware. Small detachments were placed at Dunstable and in
St Albans itself, but the main force was aligned to the east of St Albans astride
the two roads down which the Lancastrians must approach from Luton. The
chosen site was formidably entrenched. The chronicler Gregory speaks of pali-
sades with loopholes, nets with nails, caltrops, and Burgundian handgunners
besides the more conventional artillery. London lent the money for bows, arrows
and bowstaves. The best of contemporary military science was on the Yorkist
side. Perhaps it would make up for inadequacies in the troops themselves, which
as in 1460 consisted of 'grete multitude of commons' from Kent, Essex and East
Anglia with at best a leaven of seasoned professionals and aristocratic retainers;
Warwick's Midlanders and Welshmen were probably absent. The intention was
that the Lancastrians should attack and be shot to pieces by the Yorkists, as in

154   Ibid. i. 129–30.
155   Barron, 'London and Crown', 103; *Acts of Court of the Mercers' Company 1453–1547*,
ed. L. Lyell and F. D. Walney (Cambridge, 1936), 48, 51–8.
156   Scofield, i. 131, 141; ii. 159–60.
157   Ibid. i. 132–3; Head, 'Pius II', 163–6, at 163.
158   Waurin, 327.
159   *CSPM* i. 41.

the English victories at Crécy, Poitiers and Agincourt and the triumph of the French cannons at Châtillon only seven years before. Historians have probably been correct in ascribing responsibility for these dispositions to Warwick as the most experienced of the Yorkist commanders and the most interested in military innovations.[160]

Perhaps Warwick's tactics were misguided and inflexible, but the Lancastrians manoeuvred with speed and audacity. Once at Luton, they traversed rapidly westwards to Dunstable and thence by night to St Albans, where they arrived unexpectedly on 17 February and exposed the Yorkist right wing. Warwick had to change his alignment, abandoning his carefully prepared defensive position, and his army lost cohesion. The earl himself responded aggressively enough, leading his forces to St Albans, but finding them isolated, he first withdrew, failed to secure the king, and then fled. The chronicler Gregory reports on the ineffectiveness of the new-fangled mounted pikemen and handgunners, who were blinded by the smoke from their own weapons.[161] The desertion of Lovelace's Kentishmen may have added to the confusion, but was not as decisive as the Yorkists understandably claimed. It was surely Yorkist propaganda that attached weight to his revelation of the (lack of) Yorkist plans and that claimed that he had been suborned with money.[162] Much of the Yorkist army melted away without fighting. Most of the leaders escaped, though Bonville and Kyriel, two of their new knights of the Garter, were taken and executed. Warwick's own brother John was again captured, but was spared for fear of reprisals against Somerset's brother Edmund.[163] The king was the prize of the victors. And several peers present at the January parliament – among them Anthony Wydeville Lord Scales – now followed Henry into the Lancastrian army.

So complete was the Lancastrian victory that Norfolk, Warwick and Arundel made no attempt to hold London, which they wrote off as lost. They could not effectively resist the Lancastrian army. But Margaret wanted the City's support as well as its compliance and hence temporized, seeking to reassure the authorities of the peaceful and law-abiding intentions of her army. Her case, which was already undermined by regional animosity,[164] had been weakened by her wasting of Yorkist property on her way southwards and by the sacking of St Albans in defiance of King Henry's own order for peace. Coppini's despatches attributed a cruelty to Margaret's northerners that he had somehow overlooked in Warwick.[165] The City corporation were conciliatory, organizing the despatch of a convoy of victuals, which was despoiled by their rather less accommodating populace.[166] Margaret's opportunity passed. Warwick, at least, did not see all as

160   E.g. Goodman, *Wars of the Roses*, 45.
161   *Gregory's Chron.* 213.
162   Waurin, 327, 329.
163   Scofield, i. 144.
164   Whetehamstede, i. 388–401; *Ingulph's Chronicle of the Abbey of Croyland*, ed. H. T. Riley (1854), 421–3.
165   *CSPM* i. 39.
166   Scofield, i. 146.

lost and joined up with York's son Edward, now himself duke of York, fresh from his victory at Mortimer's Cross on 3 February over Pembroke, Wiltshire and the Welsh Lancastrians. This was in Oxfordshire, either at Chipping Norton or at Warwick's own town of Burford. Thence the two earls marched to London, where they were admitted on 27 February.[167] The Lancastrians withdrew to the North.

The Lancastrian victory had removed the legal justification for the Yorkist regime. York had ruled in Henry VI's name and supposedly with his authority. Now that Henry was in their hands, the Lancastrians had gained and the Yorkists had lost the right to act in his name. Queen Margaret could not accept Edward Duke of York as heir presumptive. Once again the Yorkists were traitors doomed to destruction. Perhaps they could have submitted and made their peace: if the Lancastrians were still willing to forgive; if the Yorkists would abandon their aspirations for power; and if either could trust the other's intentions for the future. Perhaps Warwick had a real choice. The third preferred alternative was to increase the stakes, to convert Edward into King Edward, and thus to legitimize the deposition of Henry VI. It was a desperate and outrageous gamble. It was desperation that caused Warwick to promote Edward's candidacy for the crown only five months after thwarting that of his father. It could convince only those willing to be convinced. Securing consent among Yorkist partisans was relatively easy; it was far less easy to make Edward's title effective when most people still recognized King Henry and when Edward's usurpation drove loyalists from passivity into outright opposition. Many more noblemen fought for Henry VI at the battles of Ferrybridge and Towton on 28–29 March 1461 than on any previous occasion and the Lancastrian army contained peers such as Scales who had attended parliament at Westminster in January.[168]

Edward IV's accession was orchestrated with a skill completely lacking from his father's botched usurpation of the previous year. Someone undertook considerable research into accessions and coronations – remember that there had been none for thirty years! It is unlikely to have been Warwick. Was it his brother George, Lord Chancellor and Bishop of Exeter? Certainly it was George who first broached Edward's title in a sermon on Sunday 1 March. He detailed the offences of Henry VI and in particular how he had reneged on the *Accord* by joining the Lancastrians and how Edward's superior title should now take effect. This was at St John's Fields – to an audience several thousand strong of committed supporters – soldiers, retainers and Londoners – who could be trusted to acclaim him as king. The captains then visited Edward at Baynards Castle and asked him to take the crown. On 3 March a great council elected him as king. This was a politically committed assembly even less representative than the autumn parliament: apart from the Archbishop of Canterbury, Bishops Neville and Beauchamp, and only two great magnates in Norfolk and Warwick, mention is made only of the decidedly minor aristocrats, the titular Lord

---

167   Ibid. i. 149 & n.
168   Cf. C. F. Richmond, 'The Nobility and the Wars of the Roses', *Nottingham Medieval Studies* 21 (1977), 71–85; Watts, *Henry VI*, 359n, 361n.

FitzWalter, Herbert and Devereux. Next morning, 4 March, Edward processed through the City to St Paul's, where the *Te Deum* was sung and Bishop Neville preached another sermon setting out Edward's title and refuting possible objections. His sermon ended with further popular acclamation. King Edward then removed to Westminster Hall and entered the court of chancery, where he took his oath in the presence of the Lords. After donning the cap of estate and rich robe, he moved into the court of King's Bench elsewhere in the hall, sat on the throne in signification that he had taken possession of the realm, and declared his title himself. Acclamation followed and again he swore an oath, surely this time the coronation oath. Finally he proceeded to Westminster Abbey, where he made offerings at several altars, received St Edward's sceptre, sat on a specially prepared throne, heard another *Te Deum*, received the homage of the lords, and again declared his title in person. Edward's succession was thus consecrated by ceremonies of great solemnity that mimicked the election by parliament and the coronation that could not be undertaken in the time and presumably convinced his supporters of his legitimacy.[169]

The new king's proclamation of 6 March built on the long-standing grievances of the Yorkist manifestos. It reiterated many of the old charges against Henry VI's regime: the loss of France, of which he was true inheritor, the decay of trade and justice, the self-interest of rulers, and Henry's own broken oath. He and his supporters were denounced as rebels, whose conduct towards the Church, property and women was compared to that of Saracens. Altogether twenty-two Lancastrians were excluded from pardon, none of them peers or northerners – clearly Edward wanted to win over the powerful if he could! – and none of the obvious enemies of Warwick himself except FitzHarry and Trollope.[170]

'Warwick . . . has made a new king of the son of the Duke of York', remarked Coppini.[171] Such an interpretation sorely understates the contribution of Edward himself – not least because of the speeches that the nineteen-year-old monarch uttered in person. Nor should we ignore that it was the work of a small, partisan, and self-interested faction.[172] The legitimacy that Edward's accession bestowed on the regime assisted it to secure support. London advanced another £3,333.66 and possibly even £5,333.66 on 4–7 March.[173] The new king's brother-in-law John Duke of Suffolk was one of several magnates to join his cause and who enabled the Yorkists to raise their largest army, little smaller and ultimately superior to that of Henry VI. Recruitment began at once. Norfolk departed on 5 March for East Anglia and Warwick 'with a grete puissance' on the 7th for the Midlands. There he had to compete with the bastard of Exeter, representative of the Lancastrian court that had centred on Coventry and Kenilworth, and won.

169   C. A. J. Armstrong, 'The Inauguration Ceremonies of the Yorkist Kings and their Title to the Throne', *England, France and Burgundy in the Fifteenth Century* (1983), 73ff.
170   Scofield, i. 156.
171   *CSPM* i. 69.
172   J. R. Lander, *Crown and Nobility 1450–1509* (1976), 104.
173   Barron, 'London and Crown', 104.

The bastard himself, who had participated in his father Salisbury's death, was executed by Warwick at Coventry, whose corporation sent forty men with the earl to support Edward IV. Thence Warwick travelled via Lichfield to Doncaster where he joined the king.[174] Fauconberg led the Yorkist vanguard from London on 11 March and King Edward himself followed on the 13th in a progress northwards via Newark and Nottingham that was deliberately slow to permit further recruitment. To the men of London and the Home Counties, Edward's own Welsh borderers, and Norfolk's East Anglians were added contingents summoned from many towns and the Midlanders recruited by Warwick himself. He rendezvoused with the new king at Doncaster about 27 March. Perhaps only Neville and other Yorkist supporters in Lancastrian-dominated territory were excluded.

Meanwhile Queen Margaret had mobilized the northerners, including certain Yorkist sympathizers on the wrong side of the territorial divide. She also commanded the West Country levies of Somerset, Exeter and Devon, which were presumably a select elite rather than at full strength, and probably attenuated by a winter's service without pay, victuals and munitions. After St Albans it had been perhaps a crucial mistake to withdraw to Yorkshire and thus concede the Lancastrian heartlands to such as Warwick, both weakening her own forces and strengthening those of her adversaries.[175] The greater size of her army was not in proportion to the much larger share of the peerage who supported her.

On 28 March the Yorkists forced a crossing of the Aire at Ferrybridge after beating off an attack by Clifford, who was killed; so was the Yorkist FitzWalter, whilst Warwick himself suffered a slight arrow wound in the leg. This was a prelude to the full-scale battle at Towton next day, when Edward attacked the Lancastrian army and destroyed it. Warwick was fully engaged. There are two stories, both probably apocryphal, about his role. In one, recorded by the French chronicler Du Clercq, the earl dispensed with his horse and vowed to fight to the death.[176] Warwick's vow appealed to post-medieval historians and romantic artists. Neither did he flee. As so often, Edward IV's boldness more than compensated for his smaller numbers.

174   Scofield, *Edward IV*, i. 157–62; Goodman, *Wars of the Roses*, 50.
175   Goodman, *Wars of the Roses*, 50.
176   J. du Clercq, *Mémoires de la règne de Philippe le Bon, Duc de Bourgogne* (Brussels, 1835–6), iii. 118. For what follows, see e.g. Liverpool City Art Gallery.

8

The Rule of the
Nevilles 1461–7

8.1 The First Family

Apart from the brief period of York's final protectorate, it had been Warwick who
had directed the Yorkist regime from the battle of Northampton until King
Edward's accession. He had relied principally on his own kinsmen and retainers.
This pattern continued for the next few years. Although often remote on the
Scottish marches, Warwick was widely perceived as the dominant figure of
the new regime, by foreigners, East Anglians, suitors and chroniclers alike.
Perhaps mistakenly. His actions, utterances and opinions were rapidly reported
at the French, Burgundian and even Milanese courts. His brother George,
Bishop of Exeter, remained chancellor until 1467. His uncle William Lord
Fauconberg, newly created Earl of Kent and lavishly endowed with West
Country forfeitures, remained his nephew's valued lieutenant in the North and
at sea until his death in 1463 when Warwick's third brother John, now lord
Montagu, was allowed to take his place. Warwick's erstwhile brother-in-law John
Tiptoft, Earl of Worcester, was as welcome a recruit to the earl as he was to the
king, who appointed him Lord Treasurer in 1461. Many Neville clients secured
promotion in royal service. Thus Henry Sotehill and Thomas Colt, both in
Warwick's service since 1449 and still deputizing for him as chamberlain of the
exchequer and chief steward of the North Parts, became royal councillor and
king's attorney respectively.[1]

The key post of king's chamberlain, which controlled access to the king's
person, went to the new baron William Lord Hastings, whose family had served
the house of York over three generations and who may have been a childhood

---

1   J. C. Wedgwood, *History of Parliament 1439–1509* (2 vols, 1936–8), *Biographies*, 209;
E 403/822 sub 21 Jun. 1461; R. Somerville, *History of the Duchy of Lancaster*, i (1953), 425.

friend of the king. Hastings was soon attached to the Nevilles by his marriage to Warwick's widowed sister Katherine Bonville; the endowment he received for his barony was supplemented by other forfeitures specifically settled on them jointly that made him the principal magnate in Leicestershire; and the stewardships and constableship of Leicester and Castle Donington that passed to him were more probably surrendered willingly by Warwick than wrested from him. In 1468 Warwick was to appoint Hastings as his own steward in Leicestershire.[2] Hastings was one of several royal servants who initially identified themselves with Warwick and the Nevilles, the dominant faction. Others were William Herbert, now Lord Herbert, and Walter Devereux, Lord Ferrers of Chartley, in Wales, both long-standing family retainers as well as retainers of the house of York. Another was Sir Walter Blount, whose elevation to the treasurership of England in 1464 and to the peerage as Lord Mountjoy was agreeable to the earl and perhaps even at his prompting; his replacement as treasurer in 1466 was reportedly to 'the great secret displeasure of the earl of Warwick and the magnates of the realm'.[3] There was no contradiction between service to the king and to the earl.

The pre-eminence of the Nevilles was reflected in their grants. Every Yorkist regime from 1454 had brought rewards to Salisbury and his sons. At first these continued, pending the inevitable review by a usurping king of the patronage of his unreconciled predecessor, and in the event almost all were retained. The king had to be asked, however, and henceforth it was to him that gratitude was due. Warwick remained captain of Calais, keeper of the seas, constable of Dover and warden of the Cinque Ports. He instantly became the king's lieutenant in the North and admiral of England. On 5 May he secured royal confirmation of all offices and custodies that he had held jointly with his father or brothers, the offices for life and the custodies for twenty years.[4] At that stage he is unlikely to have known what they all were except the most important: the great chamberlainship of England, the wardenship of the West March, the chief stewardships of the duchy of Lancaster North and South, other duchy offices, and the custody of Egremont were all comprehended in this grant. When Edward was at Middleham with Warwick and Chancellor Neville on 5–7 May 1461, he approved a shopping list of nine requests including some of those above, but adding the mastership of the royal mews that Salisbury had enjoyed, the custody of Lord Latimer and his lands, the keeping of the lordships of Goodrich and Urchenfield (Heref.) during the minority of the Earl of Shrewsbury, and the offices of steward, master forester, and parker of Feckenham (Warw.) that Duke Henry had possessed. A patent for his new foundation at St William's College at York was added four days later.[5] Perhaps Warwick was requesting at this stage not all

---

2   *CPR 1461–7*, 103–4; Somerville, i. 564, 568; HMC *Hastings* i. 302; *pace* C. D. Ross, *Edward IV* (1974), 71.

3   *Annales*, 788. Did Warwick surrender the stewardship of High Peak (Derbys.) to Mountjoy before the honour was granted to Clarence in 1464?

4   *CPR* 1461–7, 95.

5   Ibid. 45, 47, 71; *CFR 1461–71*, 37–8.

that he wanted, but everything of which he was precisely informed. Perhaps also there were limits to what even he could have. Yet more grants followed as rewards for good service, persistence in researching what the king had to give, and frequent requests.

What these early patents demonstrate is the Nevilles' determination – and Warwick's in particular – to hang on to whatever they already possessed and to amplify it. Warwick abandoned or downgraded none of his interests, but sought to develop them all. Dover and the Cinque Ports were the logical extension and complement of Calais and the keepership of the seas; the Stafford marcher lordships were complementary and indeed interspersed with Glamorgan, Abergavenny and Elvell that he held in his wife's right and Monmouth and the Three Castles of which he was steward; and in the North, where he was already warden of all marches and lieutenant, another shopping list filled the gaps in his range of duchy of Lancaster offices. That was in December 1461, when he was pardoned all offences including illegal entries to land, and licensed to enter the whole of his countess's Despenser inheritance. On 5 April 1462 he re-indented for Calais, Hammes and Guines, for the West Marches, and for the keeping of the seas. On the 27th he secured his first batch of forfeited property. Much of this comprised Percy and Clifford holdings in Yorkshire and Cumberland that were obviously complementary to his own inheritance, but additionally he secured a further manor in Newport Pagnell (Bucks.), More End in Northamptonshire, and two properties in Warwickshire that rounded off his existing holdings.[6] Even where he was relatively weak, in the East Midlands, he looked to strengthen himself, and he was prepared to act as good lord everywhere.

The value attached to Warwick's good lordship emerges most obviously in his much more frequent (and ill-documented) activity as feoffee (trustee), recipient of chattels, executor and arbiter. Any continuing responsibilities as feoffee to Richard Duke of York, Sir Robert Danby, Sir Baldwin Mountford, Sir Henry Bedford, Master John Somerset and Thomas Ferrers endured after 1461, even after death, in certain cases for many years. He was acting additionally for Sibyl Rythe of Alton (Hants) and Brian Brouns of Holburne (Berks.) in 1461, for John Hancocks of Aston Cantelowe (Warw.) in 1465, for Alice Duchess of Suffolk and the Kentishman John Squery junior in 1466, apparently for Stephen Scrope in 1467, for Anna daughter of John Thorpe, and for John atte Wood, Sir Edward Grey of Groby, and Sir William Parre in 1468. Gifts of chattels, most probably a means of escaping liability for debt, were made to the earl by William Bereshyn in 1464, by Thomas Middleton of Middleham, Thomas Scarborough of Knaresborough (Yorks.), and William Groser of London and by the London broker John Bell in 1466, and by William Joce merchant of Bristol in 1467. He was supervisor of the wills of Anne Duchess of Exeter in 1458, John Duke of Norfolk in 1461 and (as my 'magnificent and most powerful lord') of Katherine, the widow of Roger Tempest, in 1468. Most probably it was as murderers of Richard Earl of Salisbury that Sir William Plumpton and Sir George Darell were

6 *CPR 1461–7*, 186, 189.

each bound in £1,000 to Alice Countess of Salisbury to abide the award of her and her three sons on 31 May 1461. Warwick was arbiter in the bullion case of Giles Bruyce in 1468, in the Harrington inheritance dispute that same year, and for John Crosby alderman of London in 1471.[7] The list is cursory and incomplete and could be much longer. Obviously he was not active in every case or, indeed, ever in the daily grind of administering trusts and executing wills. That was not why he was in demand. That he features so frequently, often for individuals with whom he had little prior contact from areas where he was not a major landholder and who merely wanted his name to deter rivals, is a further mark of his prestige. That was what was sought.

Such roles inevitably required more of his good lordship and drew him into disputes. Inevitably: that was why good lords were sought. It could have degenerated into the undiscriminating support of those with access to him, encouraging self-help, litigiousness, and the maintenance of dubious cases. In 1464 the earl and Lord Hastings accepted enfeoffment from Thomas Foljambe of Walton to protect his lands from Sir William Plumpton. About the same time Warwick was enfeoffed by Edmund Rous with the disputed manor of East Lexham. In or after 1467 the earl, his brother George, and Edward Gower sued in chancery against Thomas Belknap vintner of London as feoffees of Anna Thorpe. In 1465 he ordered Sir William Plumpton to leave Spencers Close in Knaresborough unmolested in the hands of Thomas Scarborough, whose feoffee he was, pending arbitration.[8] When Roger Radcliff questioned John Felbridge's title to certain land, he 'laboured to me dayly by my lordes commandement off Warwick', and the earl insisted on the inspection of Felbridge's title by Chief Baron Illingworth and other of his council. This was a patron worth having! Radcliff defaulted, leaving Felbridge free to sell. Similarly Warwick was satisfied that property at Attlebridge had rightly descended to Roger Taverham clerk, who warned John Paston off, and the widowed Elizabeth Mountford hoped that reliable information on the validity of her title to East Lexham would cause Warwick to withdraw his backing as feoffee from her rival Edmund Rous. She expected Paston to intercede with Warwick, 'the qwech is your good lord'. 'I pray yow to gete me his good lordship,' asked the troubled Thomas Denys, a veteran of the earl's battles of Northampton and Wakefield, shortly before his murder. In the Pastons' own Fastolf inheritance dispute it was recommended in May 1461 that the Pastons should persuade Warwick to 'meve that the Kyng or hym-sylf

---

7 *CCR 1454–61*, 186, 324; *1461–8*, 90–1, 93, 135, 323, 369–70, 375, 382, 441, 449; *1468–76*, nos. 136, 278, 335; *CPR 1461–7*, 112; *1467–77*, no. 1206; *RP* v. 634–5; HMC *9th Rep.* ix. 270–1; iv. 461; *Testamenta Vetusta*, ed. N. H. Nicolas (1826), i. 293; *Testamenta Eboracensia*, iii, ed. J. Raine (Surtees Soc. xlv, 1864), 170; *A Descriptive Catalogue of Ancient Deeds*, 6 vols (1890–1915), i. C17; iii. 4251–3; *Plumpton L & P* 37; E 326/B6800, B10787; G. Wrottesley, 'Extracts from the Plea Rolls', *Staffs. Hist. Collections* ns. vi.i. (1903), 130.
8 C 1/39/33; *Collectanea Topographica et Genealogica*, i. 347–8; *The Plumpton Correspondence*, ed. T. Stapleton (Camden Soc. iv, 1839), xciv; *CCR 1468–76*, no. 676; *Plumpton L & P* 37.

or my lord Chawmbyrleyn [Hastings] or som othyr wytty men may take a rewle betwexe you and youre adversaryes'. It did not happen. In 1464 it was Warwick who was to persuade the king to grant a licence to found Caister College for the substantial inducement of £100. Again, nothing happened. Nor indeed was the row between Warwick and his brother George with the Duke of Norfolk in the king's chamber more successful. George did not take up residence as he had threatened in Caister castle and Warwick did not challenge Norfolk on his own ground or resort to force.[9]

Indeed, he never seems to have done so. Few if any of these connections are adequately documented. Nevertheless Warwick's notion of good lordship in his client's just cause, it seems, was to pressurize and seek a solution compatible with the legal title, rather than to support the fraud and violence that he was prepared to use himself. Perhaps he had too many links with both sides, with the dukes of Norfolk and Suffolk, ever to commit himself wholeheartedly to the Pastons. East Anglia was far from the focus of his interests. It could be the complexity of the issues or the desire to offend neither his retainers Sir James Harrington and Sir John Huddleston nor his brother-in-law Lord Stanley that prevented him making an award on the wardships of Anne and Elizabeth Harrington. What matters is that no award was made.[10] Similarly he is to be found supporting both Yorkist grantees and dispossessed Lancastrians. Such conduct makes his exercise of good lordship responsible and restrained. By imposing limitations on his own power and influence, it also rendered him less than overmighty.

Several individuals wanted him to exercise his influence with the king on their behalf; so did monasteries and corporations. Others wanted him to pass information to the king.[11] Warwick had unfettered access and seems on occasions capable of persuading Edward against his own preferences. In 1465 Warwick in person presented several provisos of exemption to the act of resumption to the king in his chamber and secured his signature.[12] In a handful of cases we know that he secured grants for others: for Geoffrey Walsh in 1461; and in 1463 for Sir Walter Scull, who was granted the next presentation to the deanery of Wallingford jointly with himself that resulted in Leysan Geoffery's institution by 1469.[13] Probably there were many others, for neither patents nor warrants at this time commonly record at whose instance they were granted, a commonplace practice 150 years earlier. Thus the grant of the forfeited manor of Loxton (Som.) to his councillor Edward Grey in 1461 and of twenty oaks from Kenilworth to Warwick herald in 1464 may have been his doing.[14] Others came from him directly, such as deputyships of Lancaster and Calais offices, the posts of usher

---

9   *Paston L & P* i. 322–3, 388–9; C. F. Richmond, *The Paston Family in the Fifteenth Century: The First Phase* (Cambridge, 1991), 156; *Fastolf's Will* (Cambridge, 1996), 120, 126.

10   *CCR 1468–76*, no. 136.

11   *Paston L & P* ii. 273.

12   C 76/145 m. 14; C 81/792/1096; C 49/55/32, /60/2.

13   *CPR 1461–7*, 215; *1467–77*, 160.

14   DL 37/33/91; *CPR 1461–7* 111.

and clerk to the Warwick chamberlain of the exchequer, and duchy leases granted in his capacity as chief steward to Thomas Colt of the tolls of the bridge of Ware (Herts.) and to Sir James Harrington.[15] As warden of the West March, keeper of the seas and captain of Calais he had much employment and profit to offer to soldiers, merchants and suppliers that the protections that he authorized allow us only to glimpse. Not demonstrably, but most probably, Warwick was the best avenue to royal favour and royal patronage in the early and mid-1460s. And not just royal favour: on 12 February 1462 he solicited Windsor college for appointment as steward of Richard Lovell, 'a man right learned and of good fame reputation and hability' just as he earlier petitioned Dame Elizabeth Woodhill's hand in marriage for his protégé.[16]

Important though such influence was to Warwick, valuable in enhancing both his authority and his income, it was supplementary to the hereditary estates that underpinned his power. Even disregarding his attainder in 1459, these were not altogether secure. Lawrence Bothe, Bishop of Durham, was to renew his challenge to the earl's tenure of Barnard Castle, for which he had a good case, even daring to plead it against the earl and before the king in 1462. The service of an earl of Warwick, as always, outweighed that of the bishop, particularly such a redoubtable earl and a bishop of such dubious antecedents and loyalty, so Warwick's tenure was confirmed.[17]

More serious, perhaps, was the challenge of his countess's half-sisters to the Beauchamp inheritance. All four still occasionally presented to livings together.[18] Once again he was decidedly in the ascendant and they were in retreat. Eleanor Duchess of Somerset, the second sister, was not allowed control even of her own estates lest she should help her sons Roos and Somerset, still committed Lancastrians. The third sister, Elizabeth Lady Latimer, was still stymied by the madness of her husband and by Warwick's custody of his person and his lands. Margaret Countess of Shrewsbury, the eldest, also widowed, was politically isolated. Eventually, in 1466, they settled for eight scattered manors, a price that Warwick willingly paid for security from challenge for his daughters after his death. No agreement was reached about the Beauchamp trust, whose lands were contested by the coheirs in 1478–85. Warwick's final concord of 1449 was at last completed: failing his issue, it recognized that Margaret's senior line should have Warwick itself and other Warwickshire estates.[19] This provision was fulfilled by the succession in 1547 of Margaret's great-great-grandson John Dudley as earl of Warwick. The splendid tombs of John's sons Ambrose Earl of Warwick and Robert Earl of Leicester are in the Beauchamp Chapel of Margaret's father.

15   E 210/D2617; E 315/50/132.

16   BL MS Harl. 787, f.2.

17   Hicks, 'Barnard Castle', 225; A. J. Pollard, 'St Cuthbert and the Hog', *Kings and Nobles in the Late Middle Ages*, ed. R. A. Griffiths and J. W. Sherborne (Gloucester, 1986), 110.

18   *Register of Thomas Bekynton, Bishop of Bath and Wells 1443–65*, ed. H. C. Maxwell-Lyte and M. C. B. Dawes (Somerset Rec. Soc. xlix, 1934), no. 1617.

19   Hicks, *Richard III*, 324; *Warwickshire Fines*, no. 2683.

The challenge to the Despenser inheritance was more acute, since Warwick's cousin George Neville of Bergavenny was indisputably of age, well-connected, and already a substantial magnate in his own right. An act of the 1461 parliament revoking the forfeiture of Thomas Lord Despenser (d. 1400) set aside the inquisitions under which George claimed and entitled Warwick's countess to the whole inheritance as sole sister of the whole blood of Duke Henry. A proviso of exemption in favour of George, which Warwick himself had exemplified on 30 January 1462, merely reserved the former's title should Anne's line die out. The Countess Anne was licensed to enter the whole inheritance on 12 December 1461.[20] The act also confirmed Warwick's tenure of the fee simple Despenser lands held under a patent of 1414 that should have escheated on Duke Henry's death in 1446 as Warwick had evidently realized, but nobody else had. Henceforth, therefore, Warwick was assured of the whole of his wife's two inheritances, though George did not forget his Despenser aspirations and indeed revived them both in 1470 and in 1484.

Actually justice was done to Warwick by the parliamentary resettlement of the Despenser inheritance since, as we have seen, George should not have been found to be coheir in the inquisitions of 1450–1. Whether Lords and Commons realized what they were doing is doubtful, for the act purported to reverse the sentence of forfeiture for treason against the king's grandfather Richard Earl of Cambridge in 1415. His promotion of the Mortimer claim, henceforth to be seen as rightful rather than treasonable, was also extended at Warwick's request to his wife's grandfather Thomas Lord Despenser and his own great-grandfather John Earl of Salisbury, the rebels of 1400. In each case it was claimed that the lands had been lost to their heirs by forfeiture, but in neither case was this strictly true. The concealed impact of the Despenser reversal has already been discussed. In the Salisbury instance, it not only strengthened the Nevilles' right to the earldom, which should really have escheated in 1428–9, but enabled them to recover properties in Wiltshire, Somerset and Dorset that had actually escheated then. The manors of Amesbury, Winterbourne Earls and Canford (Dors.) had been bought by Cardinal Beaufort, Canford had passed to his nephew Somerset, and the remainder had been used to endow his enlargement of the hospital of noble poverty of St Cross near Winchester. This act enabled Warwick to recover these estates, worth several hundred pounds a year, and forced the hospital sharply and permanently to curtail the number of Beaufort brothers at his great-uncle's foundation. An uneasy conscience is suggested by his supposed, unfulfilled, intention to endow a similar almshouse at Guyscliff with the proceeds.[21]

The Montagu–Holland inheritance belonged to Warwick's mother the Dowager-Countess Alice, who was licensed on 5 July 1461 to enter all the estates of her father to which she was heiress, all those she held jointly with her late

20   M. A. Hicks, 'An Escheat Concealed: The Despenser Estate in Hampshire 1400–61', *Hampshire Studies* liii, 183–9 (1998), forthcoming; E 159/239 rec. Trin. 1 Edw. IV m. 13d; *CPR 1461–7*, 119.
21   Hicks, *Richard III*, 359–60; *Rous Roll*, no. 59.

husband (principally Sheriff Hutton), and any other lands held in fee simple. These only passed to Warwick on her death, some time before 9 December 1462, when Warwick was licensed to enter her lands and after which he described himself as Earl of Warwick *and Salisbury*.[22] Few others did. They still called him Warwick and so usually did he, signing himself 'R. Warrewyk' and employing a Warwick rather than a Salisbury herald. It was Warwick not Salisbury that was the premier earldom and that gave him precedence over all other earls. From this point on and allowing for a thousand pounds of forfeited lands a year, Warwick's estates alone may have been worth up to £7,000 a year, which was certainly much more than any contemporary subject. There were besides his royal offices, which the Frenchman Philippe de Commines guesstimated at 80,000 crowns (about £16,500) a year.[23] Whilst undoubtedly an exaggeration and ignoring the salaries of deputies and other overheads, a quarter of that sum would have given the earl a ceiling of £12,000 in total. That is about twice those of York and Buckingham, the richest magnates of the previous decade, and over half of that of John of Gaunt. Where York and Buckingham, moreoever, had financial difficulties, living above their income and owed large sums by the crown, Warwick appears not to have had such problems. Without accounts, we have to guess; a few unpaid debts are known, most notably his failure to pay the instalments due on Collyweston to Cromwell's executors, but we have no evidence of financial embarrassments.

Warwick's finances enabled him to cut a figure on the European stage where the great continental feudatories generally commanded far larger resources than their English counterparts. He could afford to captain Calais, keep the seas, guard the West March, and go on embassy with little expectation of immediate payment by an impoverished king. Large sums could be raised when needed. He did not stint on splendour when on embassy, he developed and maintained his own ordnance and navy, he patronized the church. Had we the evidence, he might be shown to have been spending on building, jewelry, books and furnishings like his contemporaries. We know relatively little of his retaining, except that it was remarkable. Of Henry Duke of Buckingham in 1483, John Rous observed that 'so many men had not worn the same badge since the time of Richard Neville, earl of Warwick'.[24] We have no lists of members of his household, no ordinances nor accounts, yet his lavish housekeeping was legendary:

> The which Erle was evyr hadd In Grete ffavour of the commonys of thys land, By Reson of the excedyng howsold which he dayly kepid In alle Cuntrees where evyr he sojournyd or laye; and when he cam to london he held such a howse that vj Oxyn were etyn at a Brekefast, and every tavern was fful of his mete, ffor whoo had any acqueyntaunce In that hows, he

22   *CPR 1461–7*, 215–16; see also e.g. *Plumpton L & P* 37.
23   P. de Commines, *Mémoires*, ed. J. Calmette and G. Durville (3 vols, Paris, 1923–5), i. 191–2.
24   J. M. W. Bean, *From Lord to Patron* (Manchester, 1989), 178.

shuld have hadd as moch sodyn & Rost as he myght cary upon a long daggar. . . .[25]

If not exaggerated, such conspicuous consumption was not mere vain display, but was calculated to impress, to maintain and indeed stimulate the popular support that Warwick prized and might have a use for again. Perhaps it did: however the degree of public support for him again in 1469–71 cannot be explained purely by his hospitality. Nobody, however rich, could have been so open-handed everywhere or without ulterior motive. There were three celebrations of the Nevilles' pre-eminence.

The Countess Alice was buried in the Salisbury mausoleum of Bisham Priory in Buckinghamshire. It had been there, beside previous earls of Salisbury, that her husband wished to be buried, in a certain place already agreed with the prior.[26] Salisbury and his son Thomas, both victims of Wakefield, were re-interred with her in the priory with ceremonial so magnificent that it was recorded by heralds as the model for the funeral of an earl. The author may have been John Waters, Chester herald and formerly Warwick herald, who participated in the proceedings. The remains of Salisbury and Sir Thomas had been removed from the gates of York after Towton. Now they were placed in coffins on a chariot drawn by six horses, one with trappings of the arms of St George and the others draped in black. On Monday 14 February 1463 the cortège was joined by Warwick himself, who rode behind with Montagu to his right and Latimer's son Henry on his left, sixteen knights and squires on either side. Received at the west front by Bishop Neville, the Bishop of St Asaph, and two mitred abbots, the coffins were carried to the choir in a procession that included the dukes of Clarence and Suffolk, the earls of Warwick and Worcester, lords Montagu, Hastings and FitzHugh, their spouses, many other knights and squires. Alice's coffin was already in the sanctuary lying on a hearse, both it and the adjoining parclose screens being draped in white. Salisbury's coffin was placed above and Thomas's below on a second hearse to the west, both hearse and screens being hung with a black cloth. The service for the dead was held. Garter and Clarenceux Kings-of-Arms, Windsor, Chester and many other heralds were in attendance. Next morning there was a high mass, followed by presentation of the earl's arms, shield, sword, helm, and even his war-horse, which was brought through the nave to the entrance of the choir, by offerings of money and baldekine cloth, and by the actual interment. We cannot tell whether the tomb was already surmounted by the earl's alabaster monument, now defaced and displaced at Burghclere.[27]

---

25 *Great Chron.* 207.
26 *Testamenta Eboracensia*, ii. 242–3.
27 P. W. Hammond, 'The Funeral of Richard Neville, Earl of Salisbury', *The Ricardian* 87 (1983), 410–16; P. Routh, 'Richard Neville, Earl of Salisbury: The Burghfield Effigy', loc. cit. 417–23; *Collection of Ordinances of the Royal Household* (Soc. Antiquaries, 1790), 131–3; W. E. Hampton, *Memorials of the Wars of the Roses: A Biographical Guide* (Upminster, 1979), no. 5.

Table 8.1 The Salisbury Celebrations at Bisham 1463

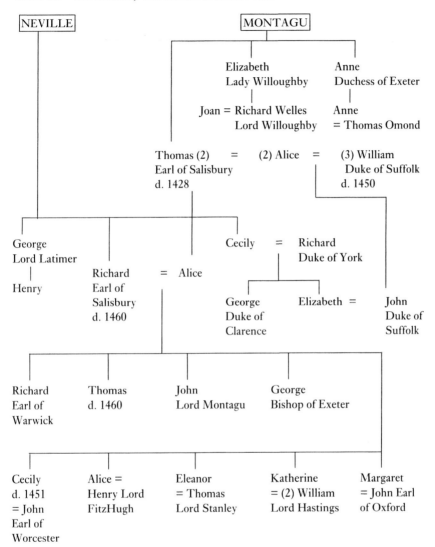

The significance of the event is somewhat ambiguous. On the one hand it was the funeral of an earl of Salisbury and the last of the Montagus among their ancestors. That aspect is celebrated in the first surviving version of the Salisbury Roll most probably revised for this occasion. It contains a view of Bisham Priory. From Richard I and Affrica Lady of Man it depicts fifty figures splendid with their coats of arms, often husbands and wives in pairs, culminating appropriately in the earls and countesses of Salisbury and Warwick, Sir Thomas Neville and

Lady Willoughby. An interest in heraldry, lineage and ceremonial that unites the Roll with the funeral narrative surely derives from the patron of both, presumably Warwick himself. Some of the oddities of the Roll, the inclusion of obsolete collateral branches and the omission of Warwick's own sisters, all peeresses, perhaps indicate hasty preparation following Alice's death and the absence of her sons on military duty in the North. If complete, the Roll appears merely to update an earlier exemplar, distinguished though the illuminator may have been.[28]

The narrative, in contrast, depicts both a Neville and a national reunion. Sir Henry Neville of Latimer, so prominent in proceedings, had no Montagu or Salisbury ancestry, but he was currently the Neville male heir after Montagu and was Warwick's constable at Middleham. Incidentally he was also son of Elizabeth, the third Beauchamp coheir. Warwick was heir to all his father's arms. It was his father's membership of the Garter, the arms of St George, that was singled out and it was the royal dukes of Clarence and Suffolk, neither Nevilles nor Montagus, who took precedence. If the intention was to emphasize the family's national importance, the attendance was somewhat disappointing, for none of the most desirable constituencies were present in force. Where was the king, the late earl's sisters of Buckingham, Norfolk, Northumberland and York, where his sons-in-law Arundel and Stanley, where his daughter-in-law Maud Lady Willoughby, Warwick's own countess and daughters? But such disappointments were relative. Even the king could not indulge his father's memory on a comparable scale for another thirteen years.

Next year, as we shall see, a grateful king elevated Montagu to an earldom and promoted Bishop Neville to the archbishopric of York. It was a mark of his personal pride and that of his family that his enthronement feast was also the most splendid of those recorded and, like Salisbury's reinterment, has become legendary. Held in September 1465 at the archbishop's palace at York, it was attended by over 2,000 people who were regaled on the most lavish scale. They included 8 bishops, 18 heads of religious houses, the royal dukes of Suffolk and Gloucester, 6 earls, 7 barons, 18 knights, 69 esquires, and 33 judges, serjeants, and lawyers. The dean and chapter of York Minster, the mayor of the Calais Staple, and the mayor and aldermen of York were included. Warwick was steward, his brother Northumberland was treasurer, Hastings was controller, Lord Willoughby was carver, the late duke of Buckingham's son John Stafford was cupbearer, and Lords Greystoke and Neville were keepers of the cupboard. Three prominent retainers, Fauconberg's son-in-law Sir Richard Strangways, Sir Walter Wrottesley, and Sir John Malliverer were respectively sewer, marshal and pantler. Apart from thirteen tables in the hall, chief, second and great chambers, 412 lesser men were fed in the lower hall and 400 servants in the gallery. Warwick's family were prominent. Apart from his mother's stepmother Alice Duchess of Suffolk, his two brothers, his sisters of Oxford, FitzHugh, Stanley and Hastings with their husbands, his countess was in the second chamber and

28   A. Payne, 'The Salisbury Roll of Arms, c.1463', *England in the Fifteenth Century*, ed. D. Williams (Woodbridge, 1987), 187–98, esp. 197.

Table 8.2 The Nevilles in the North in the 1460s

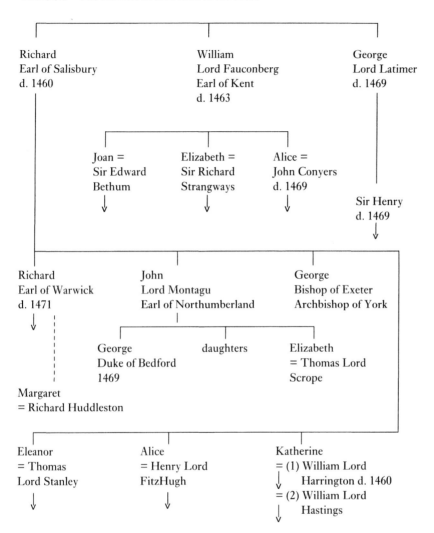

his two daughters in the great chamber. Apart from his brother of Northumberland and brothers-in-law of FitzHugh and Stanley, the northern peerage was represented by the Earl of Westmorland, Lords Scrope, Dacre and Ogle. Though very much a Neville celebration, the enthronement of the arch-bishop was an occasion that attracted all northerners, regardless of faction.[29]

29 J. Leland, *De rebus britannicis collectanea*, ed. T. Hearne (Oxford, 1770), vi. 2–4. Warwick was at Topcliffe on 19 September, *Plumpton L & P* 37.

The third set of remarkable ceremonies relates to the wedding of Warwick's eldest daughter Isabel to the king's brother, once heir apparent and still heir male, George Duke of Clarence. It was preceded by the commissioning of Warwick's 'great ship', the *Trinity*. So remarkable was this that John Stone included it in his chronicle. It happened at Sandwich on 12 June 1469, Trinity Sunday. A service of blessing 'with the greatest solemnity' held on board was conducted by Archbishop Neville in the presence of Warwick himself, Clarence, Bishop Kemp of London, Lord Wenlock, Sir Walter Wrottesley and Sir John Guildford. Mass was sung by a choir including the prior, three monks, and boys of Canterbury cathedral priory. The ensuing banquet lasted from the second to the fifth hour.[30] Regrettably there is no narrative of the wedding, surely no less magnificent, at Calais castle on 11 July 1469. We know that it was conducted by the archbishop in the presence of the Earl and Countess of Warwick, the earls of Shrewsbury and Oxford, five knights of the Garter presumably including Wenlock, Harcourt and Duras, 'and many other lordes and ladies and wurshipfull knightes, well accompanied with wise and discreet esquires, in right great numbyr, to the laude presinge of God, and to the honoure and wurship of the world'. Such attendance is all the more surprising given that the king opposed the match and was con-spicuously absent. The need to ensure that its validity could not be impugned perhaps explains the addition of this memorandum to Clarence's new household book.[31] Unfortunately there was to be no baptism of the earl's first grandson, Clarence's son, who less than a year later was born and buried at sea off Calais, and the earl was to miss both the weddings of his second daughter Anne to royal princes.

Earthly glories, of course, are always sure to fade. Mortality lies just around the corner. Even Warwick needed to think of the future, of his line and of his soul. Hence on 14 June 1463 he was licensed to enfeoff lands worth £1,000 a year for the performance of his will and the payment of his debts; immediately after his victory in the North gave him time to arrange his affairs.[32] We lack the insight that a will or foundation deeds might have given to his piety. We have en-countered his oaths by the saints, the conventional dedication of his ships to saints and the quite unconventional blessing of the *Trinity*, and his reverence for St George. He secured the usual papal dispensations for a portable altar and plenary remission of sins in the hour of death in 1467–9.[33] He continued to do his duty by his predecessors, his wife's parents Earl Richard Beauchamp and the Countess Isabel Despenser. It was only in 1462 that Warwick secured the licence to appropriate Goldcliff Priory in Wales to Isabel's chantry in Tewkesbury Abbey.[34] Work on the Beauchamp Chapel and at Guyscliff continued. Again, it was Warwick who on 1 June 1463, a fortnight before the enfeoffment to the use of his will, secured licences to alienate property worth £8 to Tewkesbury for a

30   *Stone's Chron.*, 109–10.
31   *Collection of Ordinances*, 98.
32   *CPR 1461–7*, 270.
33   *CPL 1458–71*, 593, 614, 704.
34   *CPR 1461–7*, 93; but see also ibid. *1467–77*, 67.

chantry, £13 6s. 8d. to Elmeley College for an additional priest, and £40 to Warwick College for another chantry for the soul of Earl Richard Beauchamp. The total fine paid was £75 7s. Evidently settling accounts on earth was much on his mind. However, it was only in 1469 that the three manors of Baginton, Wolverton (Warw.) and Preston Capes (Northants) were conveyed in fulfilment of the licence to the Beauchamp Chapel. The consecration itself was deferred until 1475.[35] Though he was a co-founder of the college of St William at York in 1461, he may have been more of a figurehead.[36] More significant surely, because more personal, was the licence of 18 June 1465 to appropriate 10 marks-worth of land a year to 'Therle of Warrewyks Chaunterie' of one chaplain celebrating at St Mary's altar 'according to his ordinance' in his wife's church of Olney in Buckinghamshire for the souls of themselves and the king. Regrettably we lack the ordinance. And, as we have seen, he allegedly intended an almshouse of noble poverty for superannuated retainers attached to Guyscliff and burial in the Beauchamp Chapel.[37] Whatever Warwick promised, it was not fulfilled. Actually he was buried at Bisham.

The glories were due to fade also for rather more prosaic reasons. The union of the Beauchamp, Despenser, Salisbury and Neville inheritances was destined to be ephemeral for Warwick (and, indeed, all his brothers) failed to maintain their line. Daughters they produced in plenty, but no sons. Warwick's second and last daughter Anne was born in 1456 and it was surely apparent soon after that there was to be no son. His death without issue was a contingency to be seriously considered on 14 June 1463. At that point, however, he surely expected the Beauchamp, Despenser and Salisbury lands to descend in the female line, to be divided between his two daughters and their issue. The Neville patrimony was entailed in the male line: on Warwick's death, it would pass to his brother John, with remainder if he had no son to Latimer's son Henry: was not he being groomed as prospective heir at Bisham? In 1463 John had no son. How important Warwick regarded the birth of George Neville, Montagu's son, on 22 February 1465 is shown by the splendid match he arranged for him to the Exeter heiress and his disappointment when the bride went elsewhere in 1466![38] What Warwick's reflections on these points were are suggested by the titles by which he held his grants of forfeited estates. Those bestowed in 1462 were held in fee simple: they could descend to his daughters, but they could also be alienated, for the good of his soul, to his brother or another. Those received in 1465 were to himself and the heirs of his body and would thus pass to his daughters.[39] Perhaps this indicates that a prospective son-in-law was already interested in northern properties so complementary as Barnard Castle to Richmond, Helmsley and Spofforth which Clarence already held?

35   Ibid. *1467–77*, 295–6; Hicks, *Richard III*, 343.
36   See below p. 237.
37   *CPR 1461–7*, 462; *CPL 1458–71*, 322–4; *Rous Roll*, no. 57.
38   *Annales*, 786.
39   *CPR 1461–7*, 186, 189, 434–5.

Probably Warwick would have liked to be a duke. He liked being premier earl. His pride in his lineage, love of ceremony and heraldry are all well attested. The title of duke was the only honour of Duke Henry that he had failed to attain. In retrospect his absence from Edward's coronation, where the king's brothers were created dukes and two others were made earls, was a mistake. Warwick was ambitious. Their lineage, their wealth, and the scale of the inheritance they carried with them made his heirs worthy of the highest rank. Nothing less than a duke would do. Even for his bastard daughter Margaret Neville, Warwick was prepared to provide a portion of £200, the manor of Halle (Norf.) and property in Richmondshire for her marriage to Richard, son of Sir John Huddleston of Millom, on 12 June 1464.[40] He matched his niece Alice FitzHugh to Francis Lord Lovell. For his last unmarried sister Margaret he secured John de Vere, son and brother of traitors, whom he probably helped to recover his family earldom of Oxford. Warwick's eldest legitimate daughter Isabel was old enough for Oxford or Lovell, but he bestowed their hands elsewhere, because he was looking higher for her. Was it with a view to a match with Henry Stafford Duke of Buckingham that Warwick sought the custody of Hay, Huntington, Brecon and Newport, so complementary to his own and his daughters' marcher lordships? Why else should the wedding of the young duke to Katherine Wydeville in 1465 be to his 'great secret displeasure' whereas the simultaneous marriage of his nephew Maltravers to another Wydeville was not?[41] Why was he so upset at the overturning of the somewhat premature match of his infant nephew George to Anne heiress of the Duke of Exeter in 1466? Why indeed did Warwick defer Isabel's espousals for several years after the king forbade the banns for her and his brother of Clarence? Did he also consider Clarence's brother Gloucester for his other daughter Anne? There were partners enough of appropriate rank and indeed some heirs and heiresses of modest fortune that did not take his fancy. If Warwick's vast accumulation of estates was to be divided, he wanted for his heirs even higher rank and perhaps no less in fortune. Such aspirations came to conflict with those of a king for whom his brother's hand was a diplomatic pawn and who had his own ideas of degree. Just as Edward apparently thought his sisters-in-law deserved nothing less than an earl and endowed his brothers at four times the minimum for a duke, so he made dukes only of his three sons and his intended son-in-law. This was the king, remember, whose sumptuary law of 1483 set the royal family above mere dukes. From this clash of stations emerged Warwick content with nothing less for his daughters than the crown itself.

8.2   The Pacification of the North

The Nevilles earned their rewards by continuous and strenuous service. Though Towton was the bloodiest battle of the Wars of the Roses and witnessed the

40   Bodl. MS. Dodsworth, 41, f. 113v; SC 6/1085/20.
41   *Annales*, 783.

highest mortality among the commanders on the losing side, it was not decisive. It reinforced Edward's hold on the Midlands and the South, but left the North and Wales unsubdued. Almost the whole Lancastrian royal family survived. So did many other noblemen and gentry who did not accept their cause to be irretrievably lost. Henry VI, Queen Margaret, Prince Edward, Somerset, Exeter, Roos and Hungerford escaped. Now that they had been ousted, they received that active support from the Scots and French that had been denied to them hitherto. However libellous had been the earlier charges of the Yorkists of treasonable alliances with the ancient enemy of France, from 1461, to Margaret at least, the Scots and French were the lesser foes. Scottish support was bought by her surrender of Berwick to the Scots as early as 25 April 1461; almost equally early the Channel Isles were granted to the Frenchman Pierre de Brezé; and French support was bought on 23 June 1462 at Chinon with the promise of Calais should it fall into her hands. With international backing, the Lancastrians were a formidable threat to the periphery of the realm, where long borders were exposed to attack by land and sea. International recognition of the new regime was slow in coming. The French threatened Warwick's town of Calais, where Hammes still held out, and the seas of which he was keeper. They captured Mont Orgueil and the six westernmost parishes of Jersey of which he claimed to be lord; they had to be left in control until 1468.[42] Repeatedly they brought reinforcements by sea to revive Lancastrian resistance in Wales, where Warwick's countess held marcher lordships, and in the North, where his Neville patrimony lay. Warwick was the obvious man to take the lead in every sector, starting, logically, with the North; it was not his plan to stay there. That was what happened. It took him three years to pacify the North; three years that distracted him from priorities elsewhere.

During the 1450s the Nevilles of Middleham had dominated the North and had prevailed over the Percies, the principal other northern house. The Nevilles' own defeat in 1459 deprived their connection of its natural leaders and left their own lands and retainers exposed to their enemies. This did not change after Northampton and York's recognition as heir to the throne, for the North fell into Margaret's sphere of influence. Most of the northern nobility joined the Lancastrians: a meeting of the queen's council in January 1461 was attended by the earls of Northumberland and Westmorland, Clifford, Dacre, FitzHugh, Greystoke, Neville, Roos and Scrope.[43] In 1447 Greystoke had been formally retained by Salisbury.[44] FitzHugh was Warwick's near-neighbour, retainer and brother-in-law, the husband of his sister Alice. That neither fought for King Henry at Towton and that both were received into Edward's allegiance could not immediately allay doubts about their fidelity and reliability. Warwick succeeded Salisbury in the North. The simultaneous death of his next brother Thomas, already his lieutenant in the West March, elevated the third brother John Lord

---

42   Scofield, i. 161, 176, 179, 251; Waurin-Dupont, iii. 177.
43   BN MS 20488 f. 23.
44   Jones and Walker, 'Private Contracts', 157–8.

Montagu to that status. Warwick and Montagu needed to recover their estates, to rebuild their connection, and win back their retainers' confidence. They had also to supplant their Lancastrian rivals. Though so many northern peers had been slain – Northumberland, Egremont, Clifford, Dacre and Westmorland's heir Neville – there still remained ample Percies, Cliffords, Dacres and Nevilles of Brancepeth and plenty of aggrieved retainers to carry on fighting. Roos was an irreconcilable Lancastrian. The loyalties of Bishop Bothe of Durham and the Earl of Westmorland were suspect. The Neville brothers faced an uphill and frustrating task in repressing the Scottish, French and Lancastrian incursions that repeatedly assailed the East March, the former domain of their rivals the Percies, whose allegiance to the English crown could not be relied upon.

Warwick succeeded to all his father's estates except for Sheriff Hutton and the handful of other properties held in trust for his mother.[45] To his wife's castle of Barnard, which the king confirmed to him despite Bothe's claims,[46] he now added Middleham and Penrith. Formerly joint officer with his father, he was now sole warden of the West Marches, sole chief forester North of the Trent, and sole chief steward of the North Parts of the duchy of Lancaster. He also succeeded to his father's custody of Snape and the other Latimer lands[47] and could draw also on his uncle William's Yorkshire barony of Fauconberg. He added a large share of the forfeited estates of the Percies and Cliffords both in Cumbria, where they had been the principal landholders, and north-west Yorkshire. The castles of Brougham in Cumberland and Topcliffe in Yorkshire in 1462 and that of Cockermouth in 1465 reinforced his holdings where they were weakest and strengthened them where they were strong. Moreover from 15 December 1461, if not earlier, he was also steward of Blackburn and master forester of Bowland (Lancs.), steward, constable and master forester of the honours of Pontefract and Knaresborough, steward and master forester of Pickering, most of which Lancaster offices had formerly been held by his father.[48]

Warwick succeeded to more than his father's power in the North, for Salisbury's resources and authority had always been balanced by those of the Percies. Initially his authority was latent rather than real. Many of his father's most trusted friends and allies had temporized with and perhaps even collaborated with the Lancastrians. They had not suffered significant casualties. As a Neville and a northerner, Warwick already knew his father's principal allies and was content to rely on them. To his uncle William and his brother John, he added Sir Robert Ogle of Bothal (Northumb.) and Sir Thomas Lumley, who were both elevated to the peerage; Ogle, the bailiff and lieutenant of Tynedale, was appointed warden of the East March, whereas Warwick was warden in the west.[49]

45   *Testamenta Eboracensia* ii. 242; *CPR 1461–7*, 15.
46   Hicks, 'Barnard Castle', 225. In January 1462 the prior of Durham confirmed Bothe's grant to him, Durham Chapter Reg. Parv. 3, f. 110.
47   Somerville, i. 422, 493; C 81/783/167; *CPR 1461–7*, 71, 95; DL 37/34/33–5.
48   *CPR* 1461–7, 186, 189, 434–5; Somerville, i. 507, 514–15, 518, 524–5, 534; DL 37/34/35.
49   R. L. Storey, 'The Wardens of the Marches of England towards Scotland

Warwick's marriage of his bastard daughter Margaret to Richard Huddleston of Millom, son and heir of Sir John,[50] not only provided for her, but bound another trusted retainer more closely to himself. The earl continued the annuities granted by his father payable from the lordship of Middleham and doubtless other un-documented lordships too. Whilst the level of annuities that he was paying there in 1465–6 was markedly less than the Percys' and comparable to his father's in the 1450s,[51] he was probably paying more in total from a substantially larger estate. He was recruiting new retainers from the start and feeing them from Middleham and elsewhere. Others were appointed deputies to the earl in one of his many offices: this was true for example of Sir Thomas Gargrave in 1463 and Henry Sotehill in 1465 as steward of Pontefract and Walter Calverley as constable of Pontefract and Pickering in 1464.[52] No less than seven indentures of retainer were contracted in 1461–2, all apparently with an eye to defence of the borders: he was deliberately recruiting men who would not otherwise be in his service. Sir John Trafford was a Lancashireman. Another five were men of the West March, who were more naturally attached to the Cliffords, Dacres and Percies, and were thus formally detached from their former allegiance and bound to himself. Another, John Faucon gunner, was an expert in the ordnance required at Carlisle. Most of these indentured retainers were feed from Penrith or Warwick's lands in Westmorland. It was from Penrith that Thomas Hutton of Hutton John was to draw the 5-mark fee he was granted on 20 August.[53]

The Nevilles identified themselves with the North and needed to present themselves as its natural patrons. Warwick joined Bishop Bothe on his knees at Edward's departure from Durham cathedral priory on 22 April 1461 to solicit the king's repayment of loans made by the priory to their Lancastrian enemies. 'Priour, I will be youre goode lorde', said the king, 'and I shall remember your bill', though it was thirteen years or more before he fulfilled his promise.[54] Only a fortnight later, on 11 May 1461, Warwick and Bishop Neville were licensed to found a college for the chantry priests of York Minster in fulfilment of a scheme first mooted in 1414 and nourished by George when prebendary of Masham. The new college was to have a provost and was licensed to acquire lands worth £100 a year. Dedicated to St William at York and actually never so generously endowed, it was housed in a two-storeyed quadrangle of stone and half-timbered

---

1377–1489', *EHR* lxxii (1957), 614 & n. Warwick's new West March indenture of Feb. 1462 for 20 years from 4 Mar. 1461 slightly extended his previous term from 1474 to 1481, ibid. 614 & n.

50   Bodl. MS Dodsworth 41, f. 113v.

51   Bean, *From Lord to Patron*, 168; Pollard, 'Northern Retainers', 64–5; SC 6/1085/20 m. 11.

52   Somerville, i. 425, 514–15; DL 37/33/66.

53   Jones and Walker, 'Private Contracts', 167–8, 171; C. H. Hunter Blair, 'Two Letters for Hutton John, near Penrith, Cumberland', *Archaeologia Aeliana* 4th ser. xxxix (1961), plate xxxiv.

54   *Priory of Hexham*, ed. J. Raine (Surtees Soc. xliv, 1863), ciii.

buildings under construction in 1465–7 that still survives.[55] Richard Clervaux of Croft, although apparently not formally retained by the lords of Middleham and if anything a collaborator with the Lancastrians in 1459–61, nevertheless turned to the earl when he wanted exemption from border service and it was the latter's intercession that secured the necessary signet letter of immunity from the king.[56] Even though on the Lancastrian side at Towton and fortunate to redeem himself, Sir William Plumpton entered Warwick's service and emerged to his own local advantage as the earl's steward of Spofforth and deputy-steward at Knaresborough.[57]

After Towton, Edward IV (and probably Warwick) had spent Easter (5 April) at York. Warwick was at Middleham on the 20th, where he retained the Cumberland esquire Roland Vaux for life, and was with the king on the 22nd at Durham. Edward was at Newcastle on 1 May and with the earl at Middleham on 5–7 May and at York on the 10–11th.[58] On 10 May Warwick was appointed to commissions to array seven counties, including the three northernmost shires, three Yorkshire Ridings and three parts of Lincolnshire, and on 13 May he headed a commission of fifteen to arrest and pardon rebels in the North Riding. On his departure for his coronation, Edward 'left behind him the Earl of Warwick to have the oversight and governance there'. To the wardenship of the West Marches, which Warwick already held, the king had added that of the East with the title of lieutenant as early as 20 April. Probably Ogle continued as deputy.[59] It proved to be no sinecure. On 12 June an army of Lancastrians and Scots invaded the West March, burnt the suburbs of Carlisle, invested and took the city, 'the key of the West marches of England'. Montagu, apparently acting as his brother's lieutenant, quickly raised the siege, allegedly killing 6,000 Scots. Warwick himself arrived by 24 June, when he retained Faucon as gunner, to serve at Carlisle with his man.[60] East of the Pennines matters were much worse. Roxburgh had fallen to the Scots in August 1460 and Berwick itself was handed over to them in April 1461, when an attack on Norham was threatened. There was actually no Yorkist presence in the Percy country north of Tynemouth and Newcastle, where Lumley and Kent had garrisons, and all the major castles remained in hostile hands. On 26 June Lord Roos, William Tailbois, the lord of Tynedale, and other prominent northerners raised revolt both at Ryton south-west of Newcastle and at Brancepeth, a senior Neville castle just south-west of Durham. Each was quickly quashed, the latter by Bishop Bothe,[61] but Warwick

---

55   *CPR 1461–7*, 47; RCHME, *Inventory of Historical Monuments in the City of York*, v, *The Centre* (1981), 62–3, 65–6.

56   Pollard, 'Richmondshire Community', 54–5.

57   *Plumpton L & P* 6–7; *CPR 1452–61*, 177.

58   Scofield, i. 174–5; *CPR 1461–7*, 45; *Ingulph's Chronicle of the Abbey of Croyland*, ed. H. T. Riley (1854), 426.

59   *CPR 1461–7*, 30, 561–2, 563–5, 569; *The Brut*, 533.

60   *RP* v. 478; Scofield, *Edward IV*, i. 183; Jones and Walker, 'Private Contracts', 167–8; Summerson, *Medieval Carlisle*, 446–8.

61   *RP* v. 478; Ross, *Edward IV*, 46.

was also required. He was advanced 500 marks on 28 July, formally commissioned as warden of the East and Middle Marches on 31 July and to negotiate alone with the Scots on 2 August.[62] From Middleham on 20 August he proceeded to Northumberland, where the Percy castle of Alnwick fell on 13 September and the coastal stronghold of Dunstanburgh by the end of the month.[63] In November and December he attended Edward IV's crucial first parliament at Westminster.

Warwick's absence, of course, meant that others had to take the lead elsewhere. Hammes was blockaded by his Calais officers, Duras, Whetehill and Blount, and eventually fell next year; fortunately King Charles VII respected Philip the Good's refusal of free passage across his territory to attack the colony.[64] Warwick was unavailable to resist De Brezé's invasion of the Channel Isles or Pembroke and Exeter's campaign in Wales. Apart from his wife's lordships of Glamorgan, Abergavenny and Elvell, the earl was custodian of several Stafford and Lancaster lordships. Though commissioned with others to array the marcher and southwestern shires on 12 August 1461, he was quite unable to participate. That same day William Lord Herbert was commissioned to recover Monmouth and the Three Castles and supplanted the earl as steward.[65] By May 1462 Herbert had captured everywhere except Harlech Castle, which was to hold out until 1468.

Warwick came south for the opening of Edward's first parliament on 6 November 1461. Doubtless he heard his brother George's opening sermon and the protestations as Speaker of his own retainer Sir James Strangways. He himself attended the Lords every day bar one from 28 November to 11 December. He was again a trier of petitions and more important, on 3 December, he was appointed steward of England temporarily for the purpose of pronouncing sentence on Henry VI and the other Lancastrians for offences dating from Wakefield almost to the present day. He was exempted from the act of resumption and, as we have seen, he benefited from the revocation of the sentences against Cambridge (1415), Salisbury and Despenser (1401). He secured a general pardon, a licence to enter the whole Despenser estate, and a comprehensive list of offices in the duchy of Lancaster.[66]

The earl was in London on 11 January 1462, when he wrote to the Duke of Milan, and on 13 February, when he was commissioned to keep the sea for a further three years at £1,000 a year. He was reappointed captain of Calais and was granted the proceeds of the subsidy and aulnage in support.[67] From London Warwick proceeded to Sandwich and Dover, where he held his Shepway court as warden of the Cinque Ports on 27 February and received lavish gifts from the

62   *Rot. Scot.* i. 402; E 404/72/1/32; Scofield, *Edward IV*, i. 184, 190.

63   Scofield, i. 204; Goodman, *Wars of the Roses*, 57.

64   Scofield, i. 205, 254.

65   DL 37/30/16, 216; see also C. Richmond, 'The Nobility and the Wars of the Roses 1459–61', *NMS* xxi (1977), 86.

66   *CPR 1461–7*, 89, 119; C 81/788/623; *The Fane Fragment of the Lords Journal*, ed. W. H. Dunham (New Haven, Conn., 1935), 3–28.

67   Scofield, i. 234; J. Calmette and G. Perinelle, *Louis XI et l'Angleterre* (Paris, 1930), 14n, 264–5.

corporation of Rye,[68] and apparently made a lightning visit to Calais. He was back with the king by 5 March and was probably engaged in preparing his fleet, for which he was commissioned to array Hampshire on 18 March and which was scheduled to sail against France on 1 May. He may also have considered attending a peace conference at Valenciennes. It was not to be, however, as northern affairs called and took longer than anticipated to settle. Warwick had foreseen this on 15 February, when he had appointed William Lord Say to captain and govern his 'navagia' in his absence, but actually it was Warwick's uncle Kent who took command and successfully raided Conquet and the Île de Rhé.[69] The garrison of Calais, again mutinous, would harken only to the king or earl; in the earl's absence it was the king who acted.[70]

The rapid reduction of the northern Lancastrians had proved illusory. It was hard to pacify a shire so accustomed as Northumberland to war and so well furnished with castles, peles and lesser fortifications, so divided by liberties, so traditionally committed to his Percy enemies, and where it was so easy for enemies based in Scotland to attack and retreat across the border by land and sea. During the winter of 1461–2 Tailbois took Alnwick and Sir Humphrey Dacre recovered his family seat of Naworth near Carlisle.[71] Troublesome though such incursions were to the Yorkists, they posed no direct threat to the regime and offered the Lancastrians no immediate hope of recovering the realm. Both sides, indeed, saw them in the context of wider international alignments. Indeed the Scots were divided. The queen-dowager, who headed the regency for the young James III, was far from committed to the Lancastrians, though the influential James Kennedy Bishop of St Andrews was 'pro-French by conviction' and hence strongly Lancastrian. The alliances that Edward concluded with the Earl of Ross and Lord of the Isles on 17 March 1462, surely on Warwick's advice, whilst no threat to the queen, would distract and disarm Mary of Guelders and discourage her from supporting the Lancastrians. Edward was to come north himself, but was not required.[72]

On 7 March, before departing, Warwick had indented with Robert Perrot. Probably he proceeded via Warwick to Lichfield, where he was on 5 April, and thence presumably up the west coast via Carlisle to Dumfries to meet Mary of Guelders. He offered her an alliance reinforced by three matches, one matching herself with King Edward, but unsuccessfully, allegedly because of the hostile intervention of Bishop Kennedy, Margaret of Anjou's ally. Warwick stepped up the pressure. This was still in April. Failing to secure the co-operation that he

---

68   Scofield, i. 238, 241, 244n; East Sussex RO Rye Borough Recs. 60/2 m. 94-d; see also *Calendar of the Black & White Books of the Cinque Ports 1431–1955*, ed. F. Hull (1966), 43.
69   Scofield, i. 248, 255, 258; Bodl. MS. Dugdale 18, f. 59v; G. Vaesen, *Lettres de Louis XI*, ii (SHF ccxlviii, Paris, 1890), 68.
70   Scofield, i. 256.
71   Ross, *Edward IV*, 47–8.
72   Vallet de Viriville, *Charles VII*, iii. 463; Dunlop, *Kennedy*, 224–5; N. Macdougall, *James III: A Political History* (Edinburgh, 1982), 53, 59; Scofield, i. 244.

sought, he retired to York, where he left his countess, and thence to Middleham, where on 26–28 April he retained Thomas Blenkinsop, Robert Warcop, Thomas Sandford and Christopher Lancaster.[73] Presumably they shared in his raid over the border which culminated in the capture of an unnamed Scottish castle; Edward's client Ross ravaged Atholl. The Scots returned to the negotiating table. Warwick led another English delegation at Carlisle, where an extremely short truce running only to 24 August was concluded. The Scots were divided on the proper course of action. Perhaps Warwick also was insincere and playing for time; the freedom from Scottish intervention gained by the truce was enough to restore control as complete as the previous autumn. Montagu captured Naworth from Dacre and on 30–31 July Alnwick fell to Warwick's brother-in-law Lord Hastings and Sir Ralph Grey.[74] Whilst the terms offered allowed opponents to fight another day, they also materially shortened campaigns at the very extreme of English lines of communication and supply.

A second diet, to extend the truce, did not happen,[75] presumably because Margaret returned with reinforcements. Though neither the French nor Burgundians committed themselves to her, she landed in Northumberland on 25 October 1462 with the veteran De Brezé 'best warrer of that time' and 800 Frenchmen in 40 ships. The imposing castles of Alnwick, Bamburgh, Dunstanburgh and Warkworth fell again into her hands – they lacked the provisions for a siege – but this time the local populace failed to join her. When the news reached London, Edward commissioned Warwick to take charge again and determined this time to follow with 'a mighty powair to thentent tentre into Scotland for the subduyng of your adversaries there' and presumably to capture Berwick. Edward was accompanied by most of the English nobility on leaving London on 3 November. By the 30th he was at Durham and stayed there for Christmas. Alarmed by their approach, Margaret garrisoned the castles and on 13 November withdrew her field army by sea. Unfortunately it was wrecked on Lindisfarne, 400 Frenchmen being captured, and Margaret herself was lucky to escape.[76]

Warwick's letter from Newcastle of about this time reveals his appreciation of the realities of border warfare. He doubted that Edward had the resources to campaign in Scotland. Numbers were not everything and indeed aggravated the difficulties. An army in Scotland could not live off the land; it had to be supplied by sea and victuals must be sent ahead of it. It required munitions:

73   E 101/71/5/940–4, 946; *York Chamberlain's Accounts*, 110; *Annales*, 779; Scofield, i. 244n; Jones and Walker, 'Private Contracts', 169–71; F. W. Ragg, 'Helton, Flechan Askham and Sandford of Askham', *TCWAS* n.s. xxi (1921), 186–7.

74   Dunlop, *Kennedy*, 229–30; Macdougall, *James III*, 60; Ross, *Edward IV*, 49; Scofield, i. 248–9; *Vale's Bk.* 144; *Paston L & P* ii. 279, 284–5; *Annales*, 779; *York Chamberlains' Accounts*, 111; SC 6/1085/20 m. 11.

75   *Vale's Bk.* 144.

76   *Annales*, 780; Ross, *Edward IV*, 50; Scofield, i. 261–4; *Paston L & P* i. 522; *CPR 1461–7*, 231.

sufficient stuff of all maner artillerie, that is to saye grete gunnes for betyng of places and othre gunnes for the [battle]felde, suffycient powdre, stones and al othre stuff for the same, grete quantitie of bowes, arows, stringes, speres and all othre habilementes of werre, sufficient nombre of men for ordinaunce as gonners and othre.

Was Warwick's understanding of the importance of logistics, of seapower, and of the role of combined operations ever more clearly expressed? Whilst welcoming Edward's participation, which was good for morale, he and the other 'lordes and men of reputation in thise parties' respectfully submitted that it would be better for Edward not to come until he could bring such resources.[77]

It was in this spirit, we may suppose, that Warwick took command when Edward was laid low at Durham with measles. No invasion was launched against Scotland. Some magnates and troops were left with the king and at Newcastle, and the three principal castles with their substantial garrisons were invested by two other earls and four barons. Warwick had men enough, it was reported, though the ordnance was at Newcastle. Probably it was not employed for fear of damaging fortifications that they hoped to reuse. Instead the garrisons were starved out: Bamburgh and Dunstanburgh on 26–27 December and Alnwick on 6 January 1463. Alnwick was besieged by Kent and Scales, Bamburgh by Montagu and Ogle, and Dunstanburgh by Worcester and Grey. Warwick, the king's lieutenant, Wenlock, Grey of Codnor and Cromwell based themselves at Warkworth Castle, presumably in the comfortable polygonal tower-house of the Percies. Daily Warwick undertook the arduous sixty-mile circuit of the besiegers. He saw it as his task to keep them supplied, so it was reported on 11 December, the day after an armoured convoy of ordnance and victuals was brought through hostile terrain from Newcastle under the escort of the Duke of Norfolk.[78]

When the castles capitulated, Pembroke and Roos were allowed to withdraw to Scotland, whilst Somerset, Percy and others were granted their lives and were received into Edward's allegiance. Percy was even appointed constable of Bamburgh and Dunstanburgh. Such leniency proved to be misplaced and Edward IV has been much criticized for it. However Warwick had been interested in terms for Somerset the previous September[79] and it must have been he who negotiated the terms. Whilst no doubt he wanted the defectors to be sincere and considered a Percy the most respected commander in Percy country, there were other good reasons for the compromise. It was difficult to conduct sieges in the northern winter. Foodstuffs were short for besiegers as well as besieged; far from maximizing his forces, Warwick had quite enough men to supply. Moreover he wanted a hasty conclusion, before the oft-threatened relief approach. The Scots had failed to appear as forecast before 11 December, when they promised to arrive on the 19th but did not, and on the 28th King Edward

---

77   *Vale's Bk.* 171–2.
78   *Paston L & P* i. 523.
79   Ibid. ii. 286.

knew of yet another such assurance to the Alnwick garrison.[80] A Franco Scottish-Lancastrian army led by De Brezé and the Earl of Angus did indeed materialize on 5 January; Angus had been retained by Henry VI in November.[81] Warwick did not intercept them, for which he has been much criticized, but instead fortified his camp. Such defensive tactics, so well tried during the Hundred Years War, were his normal response as an army commander: the boldest of strategists, he was a cautious tactician, who rated (and probably overrated) the defensive potential of his artillery very highly. Warwick cannot have wished to be caught between garrison and army. As contemporaries claimed, he may have been reluctant to commit his weather-beaten and probably unhealthy troops, 'greved with cold and rayne that thei had no coreage to feght', to battle with a larger and fresher army. 'And they may have been wise', observed pseudo-Worcestre, 'as there might have been destroyed all the nobility of the lords of England'. Whether he expected to be attacked or not, Warwick was doubtless surprised that the garrison preferred evacuation to reinforcement and that Angus resisted De Brezé's urgings to engage. He may well have had domestic considerations in mind; however he was certainly strong enough to fight.[82] Whatever the reasons, Warwick's enemies abandoned the castles and Yorkist control was again restored over Northumberland. It was a formidable military achievement.

The capitulation of the castles enabled Edward and indeed Warwick to retire southwards. Both were at Middleham again on 17 January 1463; on the 30th Warwick feed Sir Richard Redman and yet another Harrington from the lordship.[83] Warwick attended his parents' funeral at Bisham on 14/15 February, the royal council at Westminster on 5 and 7 March, granted an annuity in London on the 18th, and witnessed the opening of another parliament at Westminster on the 29th, when he was again a trier of petitions.[84] Foreign affairs were scheduled for the summer, but again northern affairs intervened. The peaceful intermission was disappointingly brief. All three castles reverted to the Lancastrians, for Sir Ralph Percy carried Bamburgh and Dunstanburgh to the enemy and Grey, disappointed not to be captain of Alnwick, betrayed it.

His uncle of Kent, formerly Fauconberg, who may have been Warwick's lieutenant in the East March, died at Durham on 9 January 1463.[85] Some reshaping of command was essential. Some may already have occurred since FitzHugh, Warwick's brother-in-law and future lieutenant of the West March, first served as commissioner of array for Cumberland in December 1462. Montagu, who had proved himself, became warden of the East and Middle Marches in succession to Warwick, who remained in charge in the West. Warwick and Stanley, another

80   Ibid. i. 523; *Priory of Hexham*, cvii.

81   Goodman, *War of the Roses*, 131.

82   *Warkworth's Chron.* 2; *Annales*, 781; *Priory of Hexham*, cvii; Dunlop, *Kennedy*, 232; Macdougall, *James III*, 60.

83   Pollard, 'Richmondshire Gentry', 54; SC 6/1085/20 m. 11.

84   *Select Cases before the King's Council 1243–1482*, ed. I. S. Leadam and J. F. Baldwin (Selden Soc. xxxv, 1918), 114; E 28/90/21, 23; *CPR 1476–85*, 379; *RP* v. 496.

85   *Priory of Hexham*, lxi; *GEC* v. 205.

brother-in-law, set off northwards on 3 June, immediately after Whitsun.[86] Montagu, who was on the spot, staved off a threat to Newcastle and captured four French ships, including the carvel of the count of Eu. The castle blockaded by De Brezé and Grey that Montagu relieved was evidently Norham; it was known at Boulogne by 15 July that they had withdrawn ahead of Warwick's arrival at Newcastle with 'tout grosse puissance de gens'. [87]

Whether King Edward believed it or not, he told the mayor of London that Queen Margaret had conceded to the Scots at Edinburgh the seven northern counties (sheriffwickes), many English benefices including the archbishopric of Canterbury for James Kennedy, and that she had committed England to the 'Auld Alliance' of France and Scotland, 'the which we purpos to resiste with Goddes grace and arredie us therto'. Although this lurid account was intended to secure a loan,[88] the fact that Angus was offered a dukedom gives some credence to the story; moreover Edward really did intend campaigning himself. At midsummer he commandeered all the ships of London and the Cinque Ports to scour the northern seas. A plea for taxation from the convocation of Canterbury on 15 July quoted a warning from Warwick of future descents on Norham. £240 sent to the earl was borrowed on the security of the tax:[89] a paltry sum but all the king could manage.

Warwick foresaw a full-scale invasion. 'Please hit the same to witte', he wrote on 11 July from Middleham, 'yt I knowe for certein that the Scottez, the kynges auncien grete enemyes, with his traitours and rebellez, have entred this land with grete puissance, entendyng to do therto and to the inhabitantez of ye same, all the hurt and damage that thay can ymagine'.

Apart from raising his own Yorkshiremen and unleashing Douglas on the West March, Warwick instructed Archbishop Bothe to array the northern clergy at Durham on the 15th. A muster of the clergy was a fairly desperate step, so it seems that Hastings was correct in supposing Warwick to be dependent on local resources only.[90] It was not until the 26th that the invasion was launched from Berwick on Norham, 'comprising the whole power of the kingdom garnished with great artillery' and led by both kings (James III and Henry VI) and by De Brezé. Without waiting for Edward IV, Warwick dashed boldly forward in three battles, those of himself, his brother and the clergy of the province of York, but made no contact with the enemy, who fled in disarray 'for fear of his coming . . . to their great shame and villainy and dishonour'. So great was their fear of Warwick! Hastings was not boasting on 7 August when he wrote that 'the noble and valiant lord' had made 'la plus grande journee' for many years and had followed it up into Scotland where he wasted the countryside, destroyed

86   Summerson, *Medieval Carlisle*, 462; Scofield, i. 288; Storey, 'Wardens', 615 & n.

87   Waurin-Dupont, iii. 160, 162–3; *Registrum Thome Bourgchier Cantuariensis Archiepiscopi 1454–86*, ed. F. R. H. Du Boulay (Canterbury & York Soc. liv, 1957), 101.

88   *Vale's Bk.* 148–9.

89   *Chronicles of London*, ed. C. L. Kingsford (1905), 178; *Reg. Bourgchier*, 101; E 404/72/3/70,/71,/74.

90   *Priory of Hexham*, cviii; *Testamenta Eboracensia*, ii. 242n; Scofield, ii. 461.

fortresses, and took prisoners, mainly Scots but including the Frenchman Robert of Avranches. News from the other side recorded his penetration an improbable sixty-three miles and that no castle, village or house had been spared. Even Kennedy appreciated the need to treat.[91]

Thoroughly discomforted, Queen Margaret sailed as early as 31 July from Bamburgh to the continent to impede the peace negotiations that Warwick also should have been attending. He had repeatedly deferred his departure. This was not because his triumph presaged another supreme effort against the Northumbrian castles. The necessary resources were lacking. Though Edward still anticipated being at Newcastle on 13 September, he did not arrive. Warwick's fleet paraded futilely along the coast. Following the omission of the Scots from an Anglo-French truce in October, negotiations resumed. They led at length on 9 December at York to a ten-month truce with Scotland and agreement on a full-scale Anglo-Scottish conference at Newcastle in March. Meantime the English were not to support Douglas, nor the Scots the Lancastrians.[92] Three days before Warwick had received the custody of the temporalities of the bishopric of Carlisle during its vacancy.

Though the castles still held out, the Lancastrians were left to their own resources. Warwick turned his attention to peace-keeping and diplomacy in the Midlands and London. There was widespread fear of treason after Christmas. Warwick was nominated to judicial commissions in eight counties on 25 January 1464 and to another twelve on 8 February. He was at Coventry on 10 January 1464 and sat in session with Worcester, Dudley, Hastings, Rivers and Wenlock later the same month. Presumably it was now that he, his countess and the king made offerings at St Mary's Warwick. On 3, 8 and 11 February Worcester, Rivers and himself were holding sessions of oyer and terminer at Gloucester.[93] Protracted discussions with French ambassadors in London lasted until April, the time fixed for definitive negotiations in the North with the Scots. Warwick indeed was among ten commissioners named to treat with the Scots on 5 April, but his brother, the chancellor, preceded him. Perhaps Warwick had set off by 29 April, when he and Montagu were exempted from the Garter chapter because they 'were guarding the northern borders of the kingdom, by the king's command, that they might gallantly oppose rebels and enemies, if they attempted to make an invasion'. Warwick was at York on 5 May with Archbishop Bothe to prorogue parliament.[94]

Meanwhile Montagu won the northern war. The Lancastrians had overrun

---

91   Scofield, ii. 461–2; K. Bittman, 'La campagne lancastrienne de 1463', *Revue Belge de Philologie et d'Histoire* xxvi (1948), 1058–83, esp. 1082–3; *Three 15th-Cent. Chrons.* 177; Calmette and Perinelle, 31.
92   Scofield, i. 310–11.
93   *CPR 1461–7*, 303–4; Scofield, i. 317–19n; *Coventry Leet Book*, ii. 325–6; Ross, *Edward IV*, 57; KB 9/33/10d, 49; Warwicks. RO CR 26/4, f. 69.
94   *CPR 1461–7*, 325; *RP* v. 315, 500; Anstis, i. 178; *Rot. Scot.* i. 410–11; *Foedera* v.ii. 514. The other ambassadors were Greystoke, Ogle, Kent, Strangways, Constable; earlier also Thornton and Goldwell.

Northumberland. To Bamburgh, Dunstanburgh and Alnwick, they had added Bywell, where King Henry himself was staying, Langley and Hexham, all on the Tyne, and even Skipton in Yorkshire. To convey the Scottish ambassadors to the intended Anglo-Scottish peace conference required an armed escort, which the Lancastrians attacked on 25 April at Hedgeley Moor. Montagu won the skirmish in which Percy, significantly, was killed. Though actually very few in number, the Lancastrians foolishly confronted Montagu in the open near Hexham on 15 May. Their army was destroyed and almost all their remaining leaders were killed or executed, Somerset, Roos, Hungerford, Findern and Tailbois almost at once. Henry VI was so nearly captured that his bycocket (coronet) fell into Yorkist hands.[95]

Montagu delivered it to the king at Pontefract on the 19th. On the 24th all three Neville brothers were at St Leonard's Hospital at York when the great seal was returned to George. On the 27th, at the archbishop's palace, Edward rewarded Montagu by elevating him to the earldom of Northumberland and granted him forfeited Percy lands worth about £1,000 a year in that shire. On 1 June 1464 Edward concluded a fifteen-year truce with Scotland.[96] Next day the Scottish envoys mysteriously bound themselves on pain of £1,000 to Warwick that Sir Roos of Haukehede knight of Scotland 'shall entre his body within the iron gate of the castle of Middleham' or other place appointed by the earl by 30 November next.[97]

The last Lancastrians remained to be mopped up. On 11 June 1464 both Neville earls were commissioned with others to reduce the Northumberland castles. They were authorized to agree terms with the garrisons, Sir Ralph Grey and Sir Humphrey Neville of Brancepeth only excepted. Each was also directed to redress infringements of the truce within his wardenry.[98] Bombards brought by sea to Northumberland could now be deployed since there was no immediate need for the castles to be defensible. On 23 June, when Warwick appeared before Alnwick 'with the puissance', it was surrendered on terms; so too was Dunstanburgh next day. On 25 June he blockaded Bamburgh, which Grey intended to defend. Chester herald, formerly Warwick herald, and the current Warwick herald Davy Griffith directed the rebels to surrender forthwith. And all those

> disposed to receyve the Kynges grace, my said Lord of Warrewike, the Kinges lieutenant, and my Lorde of Northumbreland, Wardeyn of the marches, grauntith the Kyng['s] grace and pardon, body, lyvelodes,

95 Scofield, i. 329–30, 333–4; *Three 15th-Cent. Chrons.* 178–9; *Annales*, 782; *Priory of Hexham*, lviii–lx; DL 37/33/66.
96 *London Chrons.* 178; *CPR 1461–7*, 295–6; *Foedera* xi. 517, 524–5.
97 BL Add. MS. 15644, f.9.
98 *Foedera* v.ii. 124; *Rot. Scot.* i. 413; *CPR 1461–7*, 342–3. His fellow mediators were FitzHugh, Greystoke, Huddleston, Sir William Parre, Christopher Conyers, and Master Roger Kelingale. There was no overlap with Montagu's commissioners.

> reservyng ij. persones, is understoude, Sir Humfrey Neville and Sir Rauf Grey, thoo twen to be oute of the Kinges grace, without any redempcion.

Not surprisingly Grey rejected the offer and determined to fight. After warning him of God's wrath for the ensuing bloodshed and of the Neville earls' intent to prosecute the siege for seven years if need be, the heralds threatened the execution of one man for every cannon shot: King Edward still wanted his castle back undamaged! The king's great guns *Newcastle* and *London* and a brass gun opened fire, shooting right through the walls and dislodging masonry, some of which fell on Grey in his chamber and disabled him. Whether or not an assault followed, the garrison yielded and handed Grey over to the besiegers. Thence he was conveyed to the king at Doncaster, where on 10 July he was tried according to the law of arms, sentenced to degradation from knighthood, and was executed.[99] Following these elaborate rituals, Warwick proceeded via Middleham (20 July) to Lochmaben Stone near Dumfries in the West March on 23 July to redress infractions of the truce.[100] On 12 December 1465 Warwick was one of the commissioners at Newcastle who further prolonged the truce until 1519.[101] King Edward contented himself with what he had recovered. Retrieving Roxburgh and Berwick was unattainable.

Now that the North was pacified, Warwick was free – at last – to turn to other matters and to visit his other estates. He was never to spend as much time in the North again. It remained the source of his most trusted retainers and Middleham, it appears, was his favourite residence. It was actually only in 1465 that he accrued the Percy honour of Cockermouth and the Percy third of Egremont, making two-thirds in all, of which he had the custody earlier in year. With the hereditary shrievalty of Cumberland, they made his hold on the West March even more overwhelming. In 1465 he was to add the forfeited lands of Lord Neville in Sowerby to his own. A regrant of the chief justiciarship of the northern forests on 21 November 1466 appropriated particular local revenues to the emoluments; similar progress was made in appropriating the additional revenues he had secured for the wardenship, now worth £1,250 in peacetime rather than the £983 of 1443.[102] Ironically now the borders were secure, there was less need for Warwick to be there; his rule was exercised through intermediaries, in particular FitzHugh as lieutenant and Richard Salkeld as constable of Carlisle. Like his father and grandfather before him, Warwick was developing his inheritance step by step. So, too, was his brother John, Earl of Northumberland, who in 1466 succeeded to the constableships of Pontefract and Knaresborough, more probably by surrender than by ousting his brother.[103]

---

99   *Annales*, 783; *Priory of Hexham*, cxi; *Warkworth's Chron.* 37–9.

100 E 315/50/132; *Foedera* v.ii. 124.

101 *Foedera*, v.ii. 136.

102 *CPR 1461–71*, 45, 241; C 81/1633/102; *CPR 1461–7*, 422, 540; C. Arnold, 'Commission of the Peace for the West Riding of Yorkshire 1437–1509', *Property & Politics: Essays in Later Medieval History*, ed. A. J. Pollard (Gloucester, 1984), 136.

103 Somerville, i. 524.

The enthronement of the third brother George as archbishop sealed the Neville dominance of the North.

8.3   Changing Priorities

The events of 1461–4 forced the problems of the North, his northern estates and northern retainers to the front of Warwick's attention, rather than preoccupying him. The earl was actively interested in diplomacy, corresponding with pope and foreign rulers. He oversaw those deputizing for him elsewhere. He was appointed to commissions in the West Midlands, London and the South-East, and the West Country. His royal grants included a refund in 1463 of £3,580 spent on his ships on his 'great journey to Ireland' in 1460 and 100 oaks for his park of Canford in 1464.[104] He was solicited for his good lordship by suitors from everywhere. Important though Yorkshire and the borders were to him, it was not solely northerners whom he trusted with his last will or who were his most prominent councillors.

During the 1450s Calais had offered Warwick a degree of maritime, military and diplomatic independence to be enjoyed nowhere else. That continued. It was there in 1469, effectively outside Edward's reach, that his daughter was married. However Warwick could not be at Calais in the early 1460s. He had to rely on his officials there – Duras the marshal, Blount the treasurer, and Whetehill the controller – to reduce Hammes and manage day-to-day affairs. The victualler's accounts for 1461–2 record the phenomenal consumption of guns (3), gunpowder (1120 lb), 998 gunstones, 122 bows, 3 crossbows, 8,370 crossbow bolts, and 85 lances for the reduction of Hammes, and the smaller but nevertheless considerable quantities used on the Lancastrian side.[105] This time Warwick indented separately for Calais, Hammes, Guines and Rysbank and was thus free to appoint his own deputies.[106] Whetehill became lieutenant of Guines; also active in diplomacy, he corresponded directly with Louis XI. By 1466 Warwick's former household steward Otwel Worsley was lieutenant of Calais town and of Rysbank Tower. Sir Geoffrey Gate, governor of the Isle of Wight 1461–6, succeeded Duras as marshal. The principal officers in a commission of 1468 were Warwick, his lieutenant Wenlock, the treasurer and stapler John Thirsk, Duras, Worsley, Richard and Adrian Whetehill.[107] There was no peace dividend at Calais, so close to the mutually hostile French and Burgundians, and Edward IV had as much difficulty as Henry VI in meeting the wages and staving off the mutiny that was again imminent in September/October 1462.[108] A further assumption of responsibility by the staplers resolved the crisis, but deprived

104   DL 37/32/79; DL 37/33/45.
105   Rainey, 'Defense of Calais', 91n, 92; Goodman, *Wars of the Roses*, 56 & n3.
106   E 101/71/5/941–5.
107   E 101/96/2 mm. 31–2; E 101/196/8 esp. f. 114-v; E 404/72/1/107; *CPR 1467–77*, 290; SC 1/57/104.
108   *Paston L & P* ii. 287.

historians of the most detailed particular accounts. Warwick was described as 'our good lord' in a letter of 4 June 1467 from the mercers of London to William Caxton, their governor in Calais.[109] The personal commitment of the garrison to Warwick was reiterated in 1470–1.

Warwick issued a comprehensive set of ordinances for the colony on 26 July 1466. They promoted 'the plaisir of god and oure seid sovereigne lord and for the assured governaunce & prosperite of the seid towne & marche in fourme folowyng' with a view 'to the sure gode & politique governaunce & defense of the towne'. Most of the nine clauses relate to crime, which covered sanctuarymen and treason, retaining and discipline. It is the fifth ordinance, which is particularly strongly expressed, that offers most insight perhaps into a frontier garrison town and also to Warwick's own sentiments 'Where it is to drede the most emynent peryll of the town' and to the displeasure of God that 'thabhominable and common adulteries' of the married and unmarried abound, therefore they must cease, on pain of the stopping of wages for the man and of expulsion of the woman, which all officers were to enforce on pain of answering at the day of judgement in co-operation with the archbishop's commissary.[110] A similar commitment to Calais emerges in the papal licence of 1465 to Warwick and Duras of seven years' indulgence for those visiting and giving alms to the church of St Nicholas and chapel of Christ Jesus to which they were devoted at Easter and Corpus Christi.[111]

The wardenship of the Cinque Ports was the natural complement to Calais and the keeping of the sea. Sandwich was the main port for Calais, the route that trade, munitions, supplies and ambassadors normally took, and the base for the English navy. Both the ports themselves and their Kentish hinterland, including the regional capital of Canterbury, provided the necessary manpower, ships and mercantile expertise. Town records contain much Cinque Port business, relatively little about Warwick himself. Normally absent, he appointed deputies. In 1462 his former household steward Otwel Worsley was lieutenant-warden and was resident; John Greenford was steward of Dover castle in 1464; and later the Kentishman Sir John Guildford was lieutenant.[112] As warden Warwick was appointed to commissions of array, oyer and terminer, the peace and inquiry in Kent. Presumably he tendered his oath of office at the Shepway Court scheduled for 27 February 1462 and received his 100-mark (£66.66) gift; certainly Sandwich incurred considerable expense on that occasion. In 1464 a special session of the Brodhull asked Warwick's deputy-constable of Dover to petition the earl to move the king to confirm their charters. Sandwich spent £5 4s. 7½d. on victuals, including thirty-four gallons of wine and the spices to make hypocras, and two dozen capons for the earl and his entourage on two occasions in 1465–6, and a further £1 8d. on the earl and his entourage on two later occasions.[113] Their gifts also chart his movements in 1469.

109　*Mercers' Company Acts*, 284.
110　C 76/149 m. 14, transcribed in Rainey, 'Defense of Calais', appx. 2.
111　*CPL 1458–71*, 403.
112　*Cinque Port Books*, 44, 51.
113　Ibid. 44, 59; Maidstone, Centre for Kentish Studies, Sa F/At 5 mm. 6–7.

Meantime Warwick was maintaining and developing his own private fleet. His 'great ship' was with Thomas Anger at Beverley in April 1461 and 'bribers' were recorded to be illicitly requisitioning ships and supplies at Yarmouth under the pretext they were for him. On 11 July 1461 the exchequer was ordered to pay him £1,956 10s. for keeping the sea and in August his men were refitting the *Grace Dieu*, which supported the Welsh campaign that autumn. Warwick's formal commission as keeper of the seas was for three years from November 1461 at £1,000 a year,[114] but it was his uncle Kent who commanded the raids on Conquet and Île de Rhé, which caused extensive damage and raised substantial ransoms. He also captured fifty of a combined French, Breton and Spanish fleet of sixty sail, including twelve great ships. Warwick's ships the *Trinity* and *Mary Grace* were in the van.[115]

For further expeditions in 1462–4 Warwick provided the following ships:

Name	Tunnage	Master
Trinity	350	John Porter
Mary Grace	240	William Fetherston
Mary Clift or *Cliff*	280	Thomas Phillip
Christopher Warwick		John Hartlepool
George	140	Thomas William
Christopher		Richard George
Katherine Warwick	220	Richard Strange
Mary Warwick [*Grete Marie*]	500	William Thomas
Giles	240	
Mary Richardson	80	

The *Jesus Warwick*, master John Ball, was recorded carrying wine at Fowey in 1465–6. On the basis of the stated tunnages of 2,170 for nine of these eleven ships, Dr Scammell assessed Warwick's total tunnages at 2,300, second only among contemporary ship-owners to the 3,000 tons of William Canynges of Bristol. The capital value, at £1 5s. ton, would be £2,900.[116] Doubtless they required refitting and supplying just as much as the *Grace Dieu* notoriously did. Ship-owning and privateering were expensive and risky. Warwick's own *Trinity* and *Mary Clift* were seriously damaged in 1462, and the *Trinity* was captured by St Malo pirates in 1465, though possibly returned on Louis XI's command because under safe conduct and carrying supplies to Calais for Warwick's embassy to France.[117] A new *Trinity* was ceremoniously commissioned on 12 June 1469 at Sandwich and based at Southampton. It may have been the ship that was built and fitted out for the earl at Newport by John Colt and Richard Port the purser sometime before

114   *Paston L & P* i. 520; *CPR 1461–7*, 38; *Foedera* xi. 488–9; E 404/72/1/15.
115   *Paston L & P* ii. 286.
116   *CPR 1461–7*, 204, 302; E 122/144/3 rot. 2 m. 2; C 81/1378/16; Scammell, 'Shipowning in England', 110–11.
117   *Paston L & P* ii. 286–7; Vaesen, *Lettres de Louis XI*, ii. 195; Calmette and Perinelle, 56n.

22 November 1469.[118] Warwick also drew on his own officials and therefore presumably his estates to munition and provision in 1461, when the familiar names of John Otter and his estate officials Daniel Sheldon, Walter Mymmes and John Luthington were employed.[119] Though only the *Jesus Warwick* occurs in customs accounts, others were also used for trading. Warwick's commission expired in November 1464 and there were long truces before then. On 30 August 1464 the earl, John Otter and William Kelsy were licensed to send stated tunnages to trade at Bordeaux; Otter had also secured another such licence to help him pay his 9½-month ransom from Normandy. Next year the same three, Henry Auger and Nicholas Faunt of Canterbury were licensed to ship merchandise to France, Normandy and Acquitaine for fourteen months, subject to payment of customs. Again on 3 August 1466 Warwick, Robert Pudsey and John Defford were licensed to trade to France and Spain with the *Mary Clift*.[120] Warwick persisted with privateering: in 1468 the mayor of Canterbury paid £4 'to conduct soldiers to the assistance of the earl of Warwick against the great fleet of France, being in the sea called the Downs by Sandwich', and in 1468–9, perhaps on the same occasion, the corporation of Sandwich assisted the earl in capturing a French ship called *Columbes* near the Downs.[121] His fleet remained a potent and committed force in 1470–1, when the *Margaret* and *Ellen* are also recorded.[122]

Warwick's bastard feudal connection is obscure. We can hardly glimpse the largest concentrations of manpower: in his household, though some were paid from Warwick in 1451–2 and Middleham in 1465–6; at Calais, though one muster roll for Rysbank survives;[123] or in the Carlisle garrison. Very few estate accounts survive. It is apparent that he had not one such connection, but several rooted in different areas, with those he trusted most superimposed on top. If Whetehill, Duras and Faunt were prominent in the South-East, the Throckmortons, Hugfords, Mountfords and Burdets in the West Midlands, the Conyers, Huddlestons and Metcalfes in the North, and Wenlock, Colt and Whetehill in diplomacy, few of these were included among the household, council or feoffees who co-ordinated his affairs. The ten men named as Warwick's feoffees in 1463, who ought also probably to be regarded as his executors, had a pronounced northern character;[124] however several had undertaken their service for him since 1449 outside their region of origin. There were only two peers, only one cleric – his brother Bishop Neville – and one magnate, his ex-brother-in-law Worcester. His other brother Montagu and his other brothers-in-law Arundel, Oxford, Hastings, Stanley and FitzHugh were omitted.

---

118 *Stone's Chron.*, 109–10; Warwicks. RO CR 1998/J2/177.
119 *CPR 1461–7*, 38.
120 C 76/148 m. 6; C 76/147 m. 15; C 76/150 m. 17.
121 'Interim Report on Work carried out in 1988 by the Canterbury Archaeological Trust', *Archaeologia Cantiana* cvi (1988), 158; HMC *9th Rep.* i. 141.
122 *CPR 1467–77*, 250.
123 BL Add. Roll 46555; Warwicks. RO Warwick Castle MS 491 m. 6; SC 6/1085/20.
124 *CPR 1461–7*, 270.

Strangely, since demonstrably they were on good terms with Warwick and were deployed by him in positions of trust. Stanley, for example, resided for thirteen days at Middleham in 1465–6 and FitzHugh was Warwick's lieutenant of the West March.[125] Two other feoffees, Sir James Strangways and Thomas Witham, were long-standing Neville retainers and executors of his father.[126] There were two judges: Sir Robert Danby, to whom Warwick had been a feoffee in 1453, and Sir John Markham. The three knights were Strangways, Blount, in turn Warwick's marshal and treasurer of Calais, and Sir Walter Wrottesley of Wrottesley (Staffs.), already undersheriff of Worcestershire in 1451, sheriff of Glamorgan in the 1460s, and to be Warwick chamberlain of the exchequer from 1467.[127] The four esquires – Colt, who died in 1467, Sotehill, Witham and Kelsy – were long-standing administrators of northern extraction. Warwick's choice of secretary after Master Richard Fisher's death was his distant cousin Robert Neville from the West Riding.[128] The three councillors despatched to Glamorgan in 1469 were Wrottesley, the Ferrers of Groby cadet Sir Edward Grey of Astley (Warw.), and the veteran Sir Walter Scull of Holt (Heref.), whose service dated back to the 1430s and who was estates steward in Worcestershire.[129]

Warwick deployed such people widely. William Kelsy was renewing rentals from Canford (Dors.) to Hanley Castle (Worcs.) in the 1460s; Otwel Worsley served in his household, the Cinque Ports and Calais; and John Otter, ultimately from Uskelf in Yorkshire and Warwick usher of the exchequer from 1451, cited seven aliases in his pardon of 1471.[130] The West Midlander Thomas Throckmorton was receiver-general of Glamorgan in 1469 where the Geordie John Colt was building the ship.[131] Both the Colts, Otter, Wrottesley, Blount and Gate served the earl at Calais, which was perhaps the earl's principal source of salaried employment and required a constant inflow of genteel soldiers. Other Nevilles and Otters, West Midlanders and Kentishmen feature among the thirty-four geographically diverse members of the garrison pardoned in 1471.[132]

These were the foundations for a change of focus after 1464, after the pacification of the North and in the light of the king's marriage. No longer lieutenant of the North, he remained warden of the West March. Middleham remained his favourite residence and northerners were among his most valued retainers. Henceforth, however, he was as often in Warwick, London and

125 Jones and Walker, 'Private Contracts', 156–7, *Testamenta Eboracensia* ii. 242–3; J. S. Roskell, 'Sir James Strangways of West Harlsey and Whorlton', *Parliament and Politics* (3 vols, 1981–3), i. 12.279–306.

126 SC 6/1085/20; Bodl. MS Dodsworth 18, f. 41.

127 CP 25(1)/83/56/74; *CPR 1452–61*, 49; Wedgwood, *Hist. Parl. Biographies*, 974.

128 Calmette and Perinelle, 64; Wedgwood, *Hist. Parl Biog.* 627.

129 Wedgwood, *Hist. Parl. Biog.* 773–4; Stratford, Shakespeare Birthplace Trust, DR 5/2870 m. 2; BRL 422751; Warwicks CR 1998/J2/177.

130 DL 29/644/19445 mm. 1–d, 2; *CPR 1467–77*, 291; Warwick RO CR 1998/J2/177. Warwick remitted all actions to Otter 1 Feb. 1465, BL Add. Ch. 74449.

131 Warwicks. CR 1998/J2/177.

132 *CPR 1467–77*, 290–2.

Calais, and for the next two years it was diplomacy that occupied much of his time.

Throughout the summer of 1464, Warwick had been intending to attend a conference with Louis XI and Duke Philip and was still expected into October, but the king's marriage required revision of the objectives of English foreign policy, so he did not come. Warwick visited the Cinque Ports in November 1464, when the corporation of Sandwich feasted him, Kelsy and company at Deal, and journeyed thence to Warwick by 22 November. Four days later he was at York proroguing parliament with his brother Northumberland and Greystoke. Back at Coventry on 10 January 1465 and acting as a feoffee, he attended the parliamentary session at Westminster commencing on the 16th, and delivered provisos signed with the king's hand in his chamber to the clerk in the parliament chamber on 14 and 16 March. He left London for Calais on 11 May, conducted negotiations with Burgundy at Boulogne and the French at Calais, and returned to London on 22 July.[133] Two days later he met those escorting the captured Henry VI at Islington, had his feet humiliatingly tied under his horse, and brought him with maximum publicity through Cheapside to the Tower.[134] There could be no better demonstration of the completeness of the Yorkist victory and the shame attached to Lancastrianism. Two days later he sealed his new ordinances regulating the garrison of Calais. Still in London on 31 July, on 14, 17 and 31 August he was holding judicial sessions at Warwick. The offerings made at St Mary's Warwick by the earl and countess, his brothers-in-law Hastings and FitzHugh, and the king's brother Richard Duke of Gloucester who was living in his household probably date from September, shortly before all proceeded to Cawood for Archbishop Neville's enthronement at which he was steward. He was at Topcliffe on 19 September and on 12 December he was at Newcastle negotiating with the Scots.[135]

When Edward IV's first child and heiress presumptive was born on 11 February, Warwick was her godfather. Probably he was also the most powerful earl whom the Hungarian Leo Rozmital saw presiding over the churching of the queen.[136] On 6 May payment was ordered to cover six weeks' negotiations overseas, spent in Calais, St Omer and Boulogne. At Warwick on 30 July, he was continually at Middleham until at least 14 October, when he appointed FitzHugh to be lieutenant of the West March. He was at London with 300 horse on 6 November and spent Christmas 1466 at Coventry.[137]

---

133   Centre for Kentish Studies, SA/At 5 m. 6; *RP* v. 315; C 49/55/32; C 49/60/2; C 49/58/16; *Selected List of the Charters and Evidence Belonging to the Corporation of Coventry* (1871), 13.

134   E 404/73/1/69; *Annales*, 785.

135   KB 9/334/123, 124; KB 9/313/26; Warwicks. RO CR 26/4 f. 69; Devon, *Issues*, 490; SC 6/1085/20 m. 11; *Plumpton L & P* 37; *Foedera* v.ii. 136.

136   *Annales*, 785; *Travels of Leo Rozmital*, ed. M. Letts (Hakluyt Soc. 2nd ser. cviii, 1957), 46–7.

137   KB 9/334/118–19; G. M. Coles, 'The Lordship of Middleham', Liverpool MA thesis 1961, 290; Bodl. MS Dugdale 18, f. 41.

1467 was another arduous diplomatic year. At Westminster on 17 February 1467, he negotiated with ambassadors from France first in London and then in France. He and an entourage of 200 embarked with them for Honfleur from Sandwich on 28 May. He was received with great honour, Louis sparing no pains and expense to impress and win over the English envoys. As he proceeded up the Seine, the towns along the way presented him with their keys, and Louis himself, with great condescension, came five leagues to meet him at La Bouille on 6 June. They made a grand entry to Rouen via the Quai St Eloy, proceeding through the streets accompanied by the crosses and banners of every parish and all the city clergy clad in copes to Notre Dame cathedral, where the earl made offerings. Warwick was lodged in the Dominican friary. Whereas Warwick had brought English dogs as gifts, Louis responded with gold and silver plate, bestowing a gold cup worth 2,000 livres on the earl, showering money on his steward, herald, trumpeters, and even his grooms and pages. The English were allowed a free choice of fine Rouen textiles and all their expenses were paid.[138] Never had the earl encountered such respect and munificence!

Though Warwick had twelve days of Louis's undivided attention, the conference was cut short by the death of Philip the Good. The earl departed from Rouen on 16 June and from Honfleur on 23 June, arriving back in London on 1 July.[139] In his absence, however, not only had he missed the whole of the opening session of parliament, but also on 8 June the dismissal of his brother Archbishop Neville as chancellor. Coinciding with Warwick's absence and the tournament of the queen's brother Anthony Lord Scales with Anthony Grand Bastard of Burgundy, it was a coup d'état comparable to Richard II's declaration of age in 1389 and Gloucester's assumption of the protectorate in 1483. The dominance of the Nevilles had ended. An era of Anglo-Burgundian alliance had begun.

138   *Plumpton L & P* 38; Waurin-Dupont, iii. 190; *Plumpton Correspondence*, 17.
139   PSO 1/71/56; Scofield, i. 413–15; *Annales*, 787; J. de Roye, *Journal*, ed. B. de Mandrot (SHF cclxx, 1894), i. 170–2.

9

Dropping the Pilot 1467–9

9.1 Growing Apart

The Nevilles' pacification of the North was a major achievement that secured Edward's throne. Henceforth defence was no longer the priority. Ironically the Nevilles' victory made them dispensable. Not at once, however. For several years Warwick was to be as busy as an ambassador and his brother as chancellor as before. If the archbishop's dismissal was a turning point, it need not have generated the conflict that was to follow. It was not without bitterness and malice on the king's side, perhaps because the Nevilles had presumed too much, had taken him for granted, had even thwarted and overridden his wishes. Nor was it accepted as decisive or irreversible by the Nevilles. To locate the breach in 1467 does not tell us when it originated or why.

Edward was always king, Warwick his subordinate. Hence the deferential submission in his letters to Edward's right to decide and to disregard his own advice.[1] Although Edward was frequently prepared to direct his own campaigns, he never did, because his subordinates managed alone, because he had other distractions, and once because he was ill. Edward was a good delegator and allowed his officers to attract the applause. Warwick was credited with the pacification of the North and Warwick was the man with whom outsiders thought they had to deal. The king grappled with depleted finances, matching ends to means, and strove to meet the bills in an *ad hoc* manner akin to Henry VI. It was therefore Edward also in 1469 who was held responsible for the failure of his first reign to improve radically on that of his Lancastrian predecessor.

That Warwick was in charge was widely believed. To Bishop Kennedy he was the 'conduiseur' of the kingdom of England under King Edward; Warwick, observed an Italian, 'seems to be everything in this kingdom', and for Louis XI

1   *Vale's Bk.* 171–2.

in 1467 he was 'le plus grant et puissant seigneur dudit royne d'Angleterre'. It was believed even by Warwick's own entourage: 'there are at present two chiefs in England, of which Monsieur de Warwick is one, and they forget the name of the other'.[2] The joke was not wholly a joke. Similarly it was Hastings of all people, the king's own chamberlain, who applauded Warwick's victory in 1463 and reported that the king was busy hunting.[3] Though writing for diplomatic effect, his letter conforms with Edward's secret and irresponsible marriage in 1464, when Warwick and Montagu were engaged in the North, and which even Hastings did not suspect. If Hastings underestimated his master, it is no wonder than continental diplomats and chroniclers did likewise and that Commines painted the portrait of licentious indolence that was accepted until quite recently![4]

Warwick could obtain from the king whatever he wanted. So it appears from the succession of patents for himself, his brothers and clients, his preference at the exchequer of an impoverished king, and his share in the dispersal of the forfeited estates that Edward had hoped to retain as a source of income. That Edward's first patent roll was the largest of the reign does not reflect excessive liberality so much as the number of vacancies to be filled after a contested dynastic revolution. Nor was it initially lavish. Much remained to be given away at the end of 1461. It was only from 1464 that the combination of over-generous provisions for his two brothers and his new family of in-laws exhausted the fund of forfeitures and forced Edward to alienate parts of the duchy of Lancaster and even the county of Chester to endow his queen and the royal dukes. Even more years were to pass before the aspirations of his new favourites came into conflict with the old. Warwick, it seems, could persuade the king. That the royal visit to Middleham on 5–7 May 1461 produced such a flurry of grants suggests that Warwick could persuade the king to give him whatever he pleased. But four days later on 11 May, though still exposed to the earl's powerful presence and that of his brother, but no longer a guest in his baronial hall, Edward changed his mind. Though Warwick was to retain most of what he sought, the custody of the lordship at Newport was transferred to Herbert, who also on 7 September was appointed steward of all the other Stafford lordships of which Warwick theoretically remained custodian. Herbert had already supplanted Warwick as steward elsewhere.[5] Edward had determined that it was Herbert who was to pacify Wales. Though undoubtedly disappointing to Warwick, to say that this 'action sparked off eight years rivalry between the two men' is grossly to overstate.[6] At this stage

2   *Three 15th-Cent. Chrons.* 176; Scofield, *Edward IV*, i. 310; Vaesen, *Lettres de Louis XI*, iii. 155; Waurin-Dupont, iii. 184; *CSPM* i. 100.

3   Scofield, ii. 461–2; for what follows see *New Dictionary of National Biography*, sub Elizabeth.

4   As discussed in Lander, *Crown and Nobility*, 161–2.

5   Pugh, *Glamorgan County History*, 197–8; *Marcher Lordships of South Wales 1415–1536*, ed. T. B. Pugh (Cardiff, 1963), 240; Somerville, i. 648.

6   G. Williams, *Recovery, Reorientation, and Reformation: Wales 1415–1642* (Oxford, 1987), 203.

Warwick was infinitely the more eminent, powerful, and more influential at court. Though he still had aspirations in Wales and still had a role there, he never found the time. There is no evidence that he ever visited any of his marcher lordships or offices again. Edward's priorities were Warwick's too.

Nor is this all. When totting up the Nevilles' rewards and finding Warwick 'excessively greedy',[7] Professor Ross underplayed the number that merely continued from the previous reign and how long Warwick had to wait, for example, for any forfeitures. The king's two brothers were endowed before the earl and much more generously. First Gloucester and then Clarence were given the honour of Richmond, overlord of Middleham, which the Nevilles had coveted for so long; it was Clarence also who was granted the Percy estates in Craven and in Northumberland, admittedly nominally.[8] Warwick's uncle Kent received more lands than Warwick in 1461 and so later from 1464 did his brother of Northumberland, the new queen and her kin. The grants of land to Warwick, though substantial, were not excessive, either in comparison to what others received or in relation to his services. The earl still had to approach his acquisitions piecemeal, step by step, from custody to grant to enlargement, just as his forebears had done.

Moreover, there were disappointments. The rule of Wales has been discussed. The earl was indeed highly honoured, appointed at once to the rule of the North with the unprecedented title of lieutenant, and he always styled himself in his letters both great chamberlain of England and captain of Calais. In 1461 and 1465 he acted as steward of England, supplanting the king's own brother-in-law John Duke of Suffolk, who had officiated at the coronation.[9] But Warwick was not the duke he probably wished to be. Nor was he admiral of England as again he wished to be. Exeter, the hereditary admiral, was a committed Lancastrian who forfeited the office. Probably Warwick was appointed to succeed him by word of mouth, not formal patent, since he used the title and the admiralty court was held in his name, but in February 1462 he indented only as keeper of seas for a fixed term that expired in 1464. It was his uncle William Earl of Kent who was appointed Lord Admiral on 30 July 1462 during pleasure and the king's brother Richard Duke of Gloucester who instantly supplanted him on 12 August following. In 1468 it was the queen's brother Anthony Lord Scales who was appointed keeper of the seas. Only in 1470 was Warwick again required and only in 1471 did he become Lord Admiral.[10]

Of course, there were frictions. There are in any relationship. But these occurred in a context where the king's interests were also those of the Nevilles and where many of the Nevilles' interests were those of the king. In retrospect, the Nevilles always had more to gain from working with the king and submitting

7   C. D. Ross, *Edward IV* (1974), 71.
8   *CPR 1461–7*, 212–13. He did not receive the revenues until 1464 or seisin until 1466.
9   Ibid. 89. Though appointed steward again on 8 March 1465 to pronounce sentence on traitors in parliament, it was Clarence who was steward for the queen's coronation, ibid. 451; *The Coronation of Elizabeth Woodville*, ed. G. Smith (1935), 14.
10 *CPR 1461–7*, 195, 197; *1467–77*, 109, 233; *Foedera v.i.* 110.

to his authority, as was their duty as loyal subjects, rather than seeking to overawe and oppose him. The ways parted because Edward developed his own policies and found the regal authority to assert himself. In this context, his chosen advisers, those who shared his ends and helped achieve them, were not the Nevilles, but the Wydevilles.

It is often said stated that Warwick objected to the advancement of the Wydevilles because they had been Lancastrian in 1461. So they had been: the queen's first husband, Sir John Grey, had indeed fallen in the field against Warwick at the second battle of St Albans. This may be a factor in Warwick's disapproval. More certainly in 1460 he had regarded Rivers and his son Anthony Wydeville as parvenus, socially inferior to him, and hence also to the king, but he was not a diehard anti-Lancastrian. If on occasion he insisted on the attainder and execution of enemies such as Browne and requested their possessions, yet he also saved some like Plumpton from forfeiture, allowed others like Somerset to make their peace on generous terms, and enabled yet more to be fully restored. Just as Durham priory wanted repayment of debts due from some Lancastrians[11] and London creditors were tied unwillingly to others, so too Warwick was bound inescapably to them as surety, feoffee and kinsman. It was his pressing interest as surety ultimately liable for the refund of the loans contracted in 1458 to pay the ransom of Robert Lord Hungerford and Moleyns, still due after the latter's forfeiture, that forced him to support the latter's grandmother in her struggle to save the family inheritance from such trusted Yorkists as Dynham and Gloucester. Similarly it was a distant kinship to Anne Hankford, a niece of Thomas Earl of Salisbury, that prompted the earl and chancellor to act as custodians of her lands on 14 May 1463 during the life of her attainted husband Thomas Ormond.[12] As in previous generations, it was a Neville marriage – to Warwick's sister Margaret! – that probably averted the forfeiture of the de Vere inheritance, again to Gloucester's potential loss.

That the breakdown is generally dated to Edward's Wydeville marriage is not merely the perception of modern historians, but was widely believed at the time. It was not so. Warwick was disappointed, even dismayed, as he himself reported,[13] but he was not humiliated by public promises about Edward's marriage that he could not keep. He was not actually in France as once supposed.[14] He recognized at once that he must make the best of the king's choice. It was Warwick himself on Michaelmas Day 1464 who conducted his new queen into Reading Abbey, who stood godfather to her eldest daughter and presided at her churching. He missed her coronation, where Clarence stood steward, because he was on a mission abroad. He made no recorded objection to the Wydeville

11 *Priory of Hexham*, cii–civ.
12 *CPR 1461–7*, 265, 283–4; *1467–77*, 36; *Descriptive Catalogue of Berkeley Castle*, ed. I. H. Jeayes, 191; see also *Testamenta Vetusta*, ed. N. H. Nicolas (1826), ii. 293; Payne, 'Salisbury Roll', 197.
13 Scofield, i. 355.
14 A. L. Brown and B. Webster, 'The Movements of the Earl of Warwick's in the Summer of 1464 – A Correction', *EHR* lxxxi (1966), 80–2.

marriage of his nephew Maltravers, son of his sister Joan Countess of Arundel, so precipitately concluded at Reading in October 1464; nor indeed to the pairing of other sisters of the queen to Essex's heir William Bourchier, Herbert's heir and namesake William Herbert, or to Anthony Grey of Ruthin, though all were eligible spouses for his own daughters. That he objected to the Buckingham and Exeter matches, as we have seen, had highly specific reasons; his disapproval of the creation of the younger Herbert as lord Dunster presumably arose because he, like Clarence, was backing the restoration of the Luttrells, kinsfolk of Clarence's clients the Courtenays of Powderham.[15] Such frictions mattered, but once past, did not lead to breakdown.

The frustration of Isabel's match to Clarence was different, not least because the duke remained unmarried despite Edward's diplomatic manoeuvres. The king's prohibition was not respected. That earl and chancellor worked for a papal dispensation, ultimately secretly and successfully, was not the cause of the breach. Nor indeed were the matrimonial aspirations of Herbert for his daughters, directed towards the restoration of the Percy and Tudor heirs designated as their husbands, which threatened not just the possessions of Clarence and the Nevilles in the North, but to erect anew a rival to the Nevilles' regional hegemony.[16] These were aggravating factors, that assumed a greater importance because attainable once the rupture had occurred; they were not its cause.

Of course Edward's marriage was a symbol of his capacity for independence from all his advisers. It was rather the differences in foreign policy that the authoritative Crowland continuator saw as the key issue:

> At this time emissaries were sent to England from Flanders seeking the Lady Margaret, King Edward's sister, as a wife for the Lord Charles, eldest son of Philip, duke of Burgundy (the father being still being alive). The marriage took place and was solemnised in the following July, 1467 [recte 1468]. Richard Neville, earl of Warwick, who for some years had appeared to favour the French as against the Burgundian faction, was deeply offended. . . . It is my belief that this was the real cause of dissension between the king and the earl rather than the marriage between the king and Queen Elizabeth. . . .[17]

Yet this is often placed too early. It is far from obvious that Warwick was identified with a pro-French policy as early as 1464. Similarly it cannot have been until Buckingham was married elsewhere and Clarence's majority, both in 1466, that the matching of Warwick's daughters became acute.

When the Yorkists invaded England in 1460 and overthrew the Lancastrians, it was with the covert – and then, in 1461, with the overt – support of Philip the Good and the Dauphin Louis, who was in refuge at his court. This ran counter

---

15   *Annales*, 783–6; J. R. Lander, *Crown and Nobility 1450–1509* (1976), 110–13.

16   Hicks, *Clarence*, 31–2.

17   *Crowland Chronicle Continuations 1459–86*, ed. N. Pronay and J. Cox (1986), 115.

to the wishes of Duke Philip's son and heir, Charles the Bold, who was sympathetic to his distant and legitimate relatives, the Lancastrians. The root of Warwick's antipathy towards Charles, reported by the Crowland continuator, originated in the fears of both the earl and his king in 1462–3 at the prospect of Charles's succession to Duke Philip.[18] The Yorkist victory was also unwelcome to the dauphin's father Charles VII, who provided more open support after the Lancastrian defeat, and the Scots. King Charles's death in 1461 may have appeared at first to offer hope of a united pro-Yorkist Franco-Burgundian front, but in his new role as King Louis XI the former dauphin adopted his father's policy. Louis was to prove, if anything, more hostile to Burgundy. He was open to approaches from both parties, unwilling to commit himself clearly to either, and practised a subtle diplomacy of dissimulation, double-dealing and disinformation that considered every possibility, however impractical, and which at least twice, in 1465 and 1468, brought him to the edge of disaster. King Louis came to regard Warwick as the key pawn in his chess-game; he cultivated him when he could and fêted his subordinates when he could not. Warwick's whole career in the 1460s was presented by Kendall through the subtle twists and turns of Louis's diplomacy and derived from the king's own utterances, sometimes perhaps informative, but often deliberately made to his agents or Milanese ambassadors and intended to mislead their own correspondents.[19]

Actually foreign affairs bulked less large in Warwick's career. That the insights acquired before 1461 remained relevant thereafter was because of repeated threats to Calais, the garrison's proximity to both France and Burgundy, and the use of maritime power as a coercive instrument of diplomacy. The solution to Lancastrian insurrection in the North was diplomatic. Warwick maintained his own independent correspondence with foreign potentates and was regarded by both them and Edward as a key intermediary. Early in the reign, he and King Edward were of one mind, often writing parallel letters to the same recipients,[20] and using the same intermediaries: Warwick herald, Thomas Colt, the earl's secretary Robert Neville, Master Thomas Kent, Wenlock, Hastings, Galet and Whetehill. Their common objective was to secure the regime by denying support and refuge to the Lancastrians, which they sought to achieve through a combination of diplomacy and seapower. Unsuccessfully. In 1461, when the Yorkists offered both French and Scots their principal prize, King Edward's own hand in marriage, Charles VII declined, unwilling to commit himself so irrevocably to a fledgling dynasty. Next year King Louis found Margaret's offer of Calais too alluring, a decision which Kent's maritime depredations caused him to regret. Louis was temperamentally unprepared to close any diplomatic door. In the event, rather than easing the pacification of the North, substantive diplomacy followed the Nevilles' victory there.

18   Ibid.; *Mémoires de Philippe de Commynes*, ed. E. Dupont, iii (SHF, 1847), 201–2.
19   Kendall, *Warwick*, parts III and IV. Unless otherwise stated, this section is based on ibid.; Scofield, i; Ross, *Edward IV*; Calmette and Perinelle; M. R. Thielemans, *Bourgogne et Angleterre* (Brussels, 1966), *passim*.
20   Vaesen, *Lettres de Louis XI*, ii. 38.

Until then Warwick's diplomatic role was limited by commitments elsewhere. He had been unavailable in 1462 both for the intended conference with Burgundy at Valenciennes and to command the fleet. The French envoy La Barde had to seek him in York. 1463 was the year of the conference at St Omer of England, France and Burgundy arranged for midsummer by the good offices of Duke Philip. It was abortive because Warwick, the key figure, could not come; he repeatedly deferred and never arrived. It was left on 3 October to his brother Bishop Neville to conclude a truce on land, that required Louis to abandon the Lancastrians, and to fix another conference at St Omer in April to agree a truce at sea. By this time, however, convinced that the Yorkists had come to stay, Louis wished to commit them to his anti-Burgundian coalition to be secured by the marriage of his sister-in-law Bona of Savoy to King Edward. An exchange of correspondence brought Louis's envoy Lannoy early to England, where he was initially ill-received: the French king's secretary Guillaume Cousinot was among the Lancastrians at Bamburgh and a French assault on Calais was suspected. It was Warwick who brought Lannoy safely to London on 21 March 1464, who was commissioned to treat with him on the 28th, and who negotiated the truce at sea on 12 April. Obviously more substantial issues were discussed. Also on 12 April, Edward commissioned Warwick and Wenlock to treat for peace with both France and Burgundy. At this stage that was what he wanted, whereas Lannoy and Louis sought an alliance with England against Burgundy. Though Warwick again was in the North, Wenlock and Whetehill were able to attend the postponed diet in late June and early July. King Louis introduced Bona to Wenlock, who agreed to urge her case with Edward. Warwick herald was also sympathetic. Louis still expected Warwick to materialize later, in October 1464.

That Warwick's agents favoured Bona probably does reflect the views of their master. But he was by no means committed. The truce at sea was a necessity that someone had to settle and in which Warwick had an obvious interest. On 3 May 1464, even after concluding the truce, Lannoy warned Louis that something would have to be done to satisfy the English over Cousinot, *especially Warwick*.[21] Certainly no French match had been fully negotiated at September 1464, when the Reading council demanded of Edward his decision whether to proceed further. If Edward had to marry, he did not have to marry Bona. It is striking that one chronicler supposed that Warwick was backing a Scottish candidate and another refuted a Spanish one. Edward probably still had an eligible alternative in Isabella of Castile, sister of King Henry IV, a possibility broached earlier in the year and later considered for Clarence. We should not read too much in Isabella's later complaints to Richard III about her rejection by his brother since all candidates were ruled out by Edward's marriage to Elizabeth Wydeville![22] Even without that obstacle, an acceptable marriage treaty with France still had to be

21   BN MS 6960, f. 616.
22   *Letters and Papers illustrative of Richard III and Henry VII*, ed. J. Gairdner (2 vols, Rolls ser. 1861–3), i. 31; *Chronicles of the White Rose of York* (1843), 15; *Great Chron.* 202; *Crowland Continuations*, 115. Note that Isabella's marriage to Clarence or Gloucester was still possible on 6 Jul. 1467, Scofield, i. 428.

devised. It is however strange that Edward is never blamed for throwing away the princely dowry so vital for his finances.

Edward's policy was subtly changing. His initial objectives were obsolete. He was no longer so weak that he needed to bind himself to France. Now, secondly, he sought peace with all parties. He wished to avoid reinforcing his most formidable and predatory neighbour, France, and in January 1465 was to agree to supply troops to Brittany to preserve its autonomy. Perhaps it was now that Warwick refused Montagu's services as commander because he was still needed in the North? By 1468 Edward had moved further to a third position, had constructed a coalition against Louis with a view to making good his nominal kingship of France. Perhaps such aspirations were always there, but were shelved as impractical. Neither he nor Warwick had ever considered ceding Calais for dynastic advantage. This third policy required Edward to suspend any remaining doubts about Charles the Bold, just as the latter, rather ostentatiously, had to swallow his objections and recognize an English alliance as the price of his survival. Since Duke Philip and his son were diametrically opposed in 1461 and had to be treated separately up until the duke's death in 1467, it was not that Edward remained constant to his original ally. And Warwick? Warwick, it appears, did not overcome his distaste for Charles, perhaps on direct acquaintance. He did come to commit himself to a pro-French foreign policy. If Louis courted and flattered him and Warwick's subordinates succumbed to his charms, it seems that any courting happened after Warwick had made up his mind. It need not follow that Warwick was equally susceptible and that pandering to his *amour propre* made him easy to manage. The earl may well have felt that it was best to ally with England's most powerful neighbour and to recognize that the English claim to France was unenforceable. We cannot know. It is impossible to say whether he ever considered that Edward should renounce the crown of France. No circumstances demanded an *aggressive* alliance either with France or Burgundy.

On 8 March 1465 Warwick was conservator of the truce with Brittany and on the 28th was commissioned to treat with Charles's representative Jacques de Luxembourg. The earl, Hastings, Master Pierre Taster Dean of St Severin's, and Master Thomas Kent spent six weeks at Calais, apart from four days at Boulogne treating directly with Charles the Bold. Nothing substantive resulted, not apparently because Warwick wanted an agreement with France, but because Charles was still inclined to the Lancastrians.[23] Under further commissions of 8 May, Warwick and Hastings were abroad from 11 May to 22 July. Ten-month truces with France by land and sea were concluded, Louis agreeing not to aid the Lancastrians and Edward not to back Burgundy and Brittany against France.[24] Further negotiations may have been delayed and were ultimately interrupted by the War of the Public Weal, the conspiracy of French feudatories against Louis that culminated in the drawn battle of Montlhéry on 16 July 1465. Louis soon

23   As suggested by Scofield, *Edward IV*, i. 379; *CPR 1461–7*, 451; *Foedera* v.ii. 129.
24   *Annales*, 784; E 404/73/1/69.

emerged unscathed, but a further conference at St Omer in October did not happen.

What broke the deadlock, in retrospect, was the death of Charles's consort Isabel de Bourbon in September 1465, since this enabled and perhaps prompted him to propose the marriage of himself to Edward's unmarried sister Margaret of York. On 22 March 1466 Warwick led those commissioned to treat for a commercial treaty with Burgundy, to treat with Charles for his marriage to Margaret and for that of his daughter Mary to Clarence, and to treat with the French also.[25] Warwick, it seems, was unenthusiastic. The most substantial achievement was a further prolongation of the French truces to March 1468. Louis, however, was induced to offer a choice of partners in a draft treaty in which Louis himself would pay the dowry.[26] Both negotiations were pursued over the next year. Charles had no interest in Clarence and wanted a firm defensive alliance with England if he was to marry Margaret. A Burgundian match was clearly Edward's preferred option. The French alternative, strongly preferred by Warwick whom Louis now saw as his partisan, was firmed up into marriage and a pension of 40,000 crowns (*c.*£8,000); what Louis told the Milanese duke, that there were to be three marriages involving Margaret, Clarence and Gloucester, Edward's renunciation of the French throne and a joint war of partition against Burgundy, was probably Louis's wish-list rather than what he could agree even with Warwick. The more realistic motive of averting the marriage of Charles with Margaret was stated in his letters of 28 May 1467 to his subjects.[27] Though Warwick carried on, pressing a case that the king had decided against, Margaret herself accepted the match in October 1467 and the wedding itself was on 3 July 1468.

9.2 Rising Tensions 1467–9

To change the chancellor usually had few repercussions for either politics or policy. The archbishop's dismissal symbolized the end of the Nevilles' dominance of government, marked a change in the direction of Edward's regime, and signalled a decisive change in foreign policy. All three were blows for Warwick. Coming at a time when he was negotiating abroad, they were a humiliation. Thanks to pseudo-Worcestre, we know of a chain of earlier events 'to the great secret displeasure of the earl of Warwick'; clearly there were counterparts for the king, who took this opportunity also to resume lands from both earl and archbishop.[28] Not much, but enough to indicate that he was master, a warning to them to toe the party line. Far from stilling factional strife within the government, his

25 *Foedera*, v.ii. 138–9.
26 Scofield, i. 406 quoting BN 20488, f. 22.
27 Scofield, i. 412; *CSPM* i. 118–20; *Annales*, 788; Vaesen, *Lettres de Louis XI*, iii. 144; see also ibid. iii. 155 (13 Jan. 1467)
28 *Annales*, 786.

actions heightened tension, for neither Neville brother accepted their exclusion or the king's authority.

We lack the contemporary testimony to chart this escalation that exists for the previous decade. As in the 1450s, there evidently were interchanges of letters and schedules of charges. Instead we have the laconic notes of the chronicler pseudo-Worcestre, the correspondence and comments of the French king, and a very few hard facts.

On returning to England to find his brother and his own diplomatic efforts so decisively rejected, Warwick was obliged to hang around for six weeks in London, Windsor and Canterbury until the high-level French embassy that he had brought with him could embark empty-handed from Sandwich in mid-August 1467. From thence he retired to his Yorkshire estates, where given time, perhaps, he could have reconciled himself to the new and unpalatable situation. Time, however, was not allowed to him, and only two years later his relations with the king had degenerated to the verge of civil war.

Even after Edward had committed himself, Warwick still advocated a pro-French foreign policy. News of a meeting between King Louis and Duke Charles in January 1468, which threatened to thwart Edward's policy, was said to be the best possible news for him.[29] He refused to be a guarantor of Margaret of York's dowry. Those against the French alliance, notably the Wydevilles, were regarded as enemies. Other events inflamed the situation. When the king learnt in the autumn of the earl's secret plans to marry his eldest daughter to his brother of Clarence, he was understandably annoyed. To veto it and stop the papal dispensation was nevertheless an extreme step, that struck at the legitimate aspirations of all parties. We do not know Edward's reasons. If the king thought higher for his brother, it was offensive to Warwick; if he wanted Clarence as a diplomatic pawn, it was offensive to the duke; and if he feared to strengthen the earl, his action served to make him into the threat that he wished to dispel. The resumption of some lands of the earl and the archbishop, a reminder of royal power, created a legitimate grievance; especially if also resumed were the Channel Isles, part of the inheritance from Duke Henry, which Edward tactlessly bestowed on Scales in 1468.[30] Again, it may have been merely a cruel joke on 18 September to send to Archbishop Neville papal notification of the cardinal's hat for his counterpart at Canterbury that he had sought for himself, but it was ill-timed and misdirected. The earl was at Warwick on 25 September 1467, when he retained Robert Cuny esquire for life, and absented himself from the great council of Kingston upon Thames on 1 October at which Princess Margaret engaged herself to Charles the Bold. Tension between king and earl explains why, when in October Lord Herbert captured a Lancastrian in Wales who implicated Warwick and maliciously sent him to Edward, the king took the charge seriously and summoned Warwick from Middleham to answer the allegation in person. It also explains why, sensing an attempt to destroy him, the earl refused to come

29   Waurin-Dupont, 190.
30   Scofield i. 479.

even when promised a safe conduct. Realizing in time how perilously events were escalating, Edward wisely forwarded the accuser to Sheriff Hutton to the earl, who exculpated himself without difficulty.[31] On 12 December the king signed Warwick's warrant of repayment for expenses of £1,573 13s. 4d. for his two embassies, cross-Channel shipping, and conveyance of the French ambassadors from London to the coast.[32]

Unfortunately, the relaxation of tension was brief indeed. Warwick was not directly involved in the murder of Roger Vernon in Derbyshire, the latest reprisal in a lengthy feud, but he was indirectly as the Vernons' lord, as ally of Clarence, Shrewsbury and Mountjoy against Henry Lord Grey of Codnor and the Vernons' other enemies. Edward had to intervene.[33] Another summons to the earl to come to Coventry despatched about Epiphany (6 January 1468) met with a brusque refusal, 'tout court', from the earl and his council. He could not come whilst his enemies, the Wydevilles, Herbert and Audley, were at court. So wrote the Franco-Scottish emissary William Monypenny, Sieur de Concressault, to King Louis on 16 January 1468. Warwick was behind the sacking of Rivers's house at the Mote, Maidstone, the poaching of his deer and the pillaging of the contents, and behind a popular movement in the provinces, which Monypenny located in 'Suffolchier' and attributed to one Robin, who assured the earl of their support when required. The earl himself withdrew northwards, so Monypenny wrote, to consult with his brother Northumberland with a view to defending himself militarily against a royal strike. There was widespread hostility to the king's advisers and favourites and extensive support for Warwick.[34] In March 1468 the earl's progress was accompanied by cries of 'À Warwick! À Warwick!'[35] Perhaps it was at this stage that, according to Warkworth, the earl was recruiting retainers to make himself stronger.[36]

Although Monypenny may have misinterpreted events at a distance, this is unlikely. Why else would King Edward have rewarded Archbishop Neville by returning his resumed properties when he brought about a *rapprochement*? By mediation of friends, the archbishop and Rivers met at Nottingham, as a result of which the former escorted Warwick to Coventry where he was formerly reconciled with Herbert, Stafford and Audley, though not yet Rivers or Scales.[37] 'And in this mayers tyme', reports the *Great Chronicle*, 'many murmurous talys Ran in the Cite atwene therle of warwyk & the Quenys blood'.[38] Probably his brother John reacted strongly against rebellion and both Warwick's brothers pulled him back from the brink. It was on 2 April that Warwick appointed his

31 *Annales*, 788; Jones and Walker, 'Private Contracts', 172.
32 E 404/73/3/73a & 73b.
33 *Annales*, 788; *CCR 1468–76*, nos. 93–5; M. A. Hicks, 'The 1468 Statute of Livery', *HR*, lxiv (1991), 16–20.
34 Scofield, i. 451–2, 474, 475–7; Waurin-Dupont, 193–5.
35 P. Morice, *Mémoires pour servir de preuve à l'histoire de Bretagne* (Paris, 1746), ii. 160.
36 *Warkworth's Chron.* 3–4.
37 *Annales*, 789.
38 *Great Chron.* 207.

brother-in-law Hastings as his steward in Leicestershire, Rutland and Northamptonshire; he had need of the intercession of the king's chamberlain. Northumberland was with him at Warwick Castle on 3 May.[39] Outwardly, at least, he was reconciled with the king. He was in London on 10 and 18 June and escorted Margaret of York on her wedding journey as far as Margate on 1 July, returning to London to try traitors, find in favour of the claim to petercorn of St Leonard's Hospital at York, and, with his brothers, rule against the Hanse and order the seizure of their ships. As Ross remarks, there is plenty of evidence of the Nevilles at court. It was in the king's chamber in the autumn that Warwick and the archbishop had a furious row with the Duke of Norfolk.[40] Warwick's known movements reveal him at Walden in Essex on 16 September, at Warwick about Michaelmas, at Collyweston on 30 October, at Waltham Abbey with Clarence and Shrewsbury finalizing the duke's household ordinance on 9 December, and at Warwick on the 16th.[41] On 20 December the two Neville earls, Sir John Howard, and one George Willerby leased all mines of silver, gold and lead north of Trent for forty years and on 24 April 1469 the earl secured the necessary mortmain licences for the Beauchamp Chapel, Warwick.[42]

These are evidence of renewed favour towards the Nevilles, but not of their return to dominance. Their hopes were disappointed. Hopes that the archbishop would resume his chancellorship were dashed.[43] The king's foreign policy prevailed, though the earl continued to object and obstruct in practice. Warwick and Clarence kept machinating for a papal dispensation. 'And yett thei were acorded diverse tymes', wrote Warkworth with hindsight, 'but thei nevere loffyd togedere aftere'.[44] Yet Warwick's brother John was different. Now earl of Northumberland, he was happy with his lot, loyal and quick to crush rebellion. In the spring of 1469, it appears, Edward agreed in principle to the marriage of John's son George Neville to Princess Elizabeth:[45] a match that would have bound him yet more closely to the crown, offered a splendid future to young George, and met one of Warwick's grievances. It was not Edward's intention, of course, that he himself would bear no sons and that Elizabeth of York would be his successor.

It was the prerogative of a king to decide his foreign policy. By June 1467 Edward already clearly had pro-Burgundian and anti-French preferences, which enjoyed the support of his Wydeville in-laws. He proceeded to conclude a marriage alliance between his sister Margaret and Charles the Bold, who was the

39   *HMC Hastings*, i. 302; C 81/818/2420.
40   *Annales*, 789–90; Ross, *Edward IV*, 120–2; *CPR 1467–77*, 131–2; *Collections for the History of Staffordshire* ns. vi.ii (1903), 223; *Excerpta Historica*, ed. S. Bentley (1831), 227–8.
41   PSO 1/48/2477; *Collection of Ordinances*, 86; Bodl. MS Dugdale 15, f. 73; BL Add. Ch. 30873.
42   *CPR 1467–77*, 132, 153.
43   *CSPM* i. 120.
44   *Warkworth's Chron.* 3–4.
45   *CSPM* i. 129.

most eligible widower in Europe. There was already a treaty of amity, which was supplemented, and other treaties were contracted of amity with Brittany, Denmark and Castile; others were sought with Aragon and even Armagnac.[46] Such alliances indicate the international recognition and respectability of the Yorkist dynasty now secure on the throne. To preserve the independence of Burgundy and Brittany and to prevent complete French dominance of the Channel coast were policies of which modern historians have generally approved. Edward's intention, however, was aggressive. Louis was to be encircled by his enemies, as Edward sought to reconstruct and reinforce the momentary coalition of the Public Weal. That he included in his treaty with Brittany provision for the transfer to himself of conquered royal demesne and for other conquests to be held of him reveals him reviving English claims to the crown of France. It was for this that he had been working, he informed parliament in May 1468, perhaps with hindsight, demanding and securing taxation for an invasion from a parliament that remained strongly anti-French.[47]

Historians have questioned whether Edward really intended to invade: was he not seeking rather to fight through his French feudatories? Was he perhaps seeking taxation for other purposes for which it would not have been granted, such as Margaret's dowry? If so, he deliberately misled his subjects, for whom his declared intention was unambiguous enough. Did he seek international renown, military glory, the recovery of France, to trade his French crown for territorial gains? Whichever he wanted, he seriously miscalculated, as Warwick was to point out.

Edward's policies had obvious disadvantages. To secure the Burgundian alliance, he had to suspend English statutes restricting Burgundian trade, but he was unable to persuade Charles to raise the Burgundian embargo on English cloth. For the marriage he had to provide an expensive trousseau and pay a dowry of 200,000 crowns (£41,666.66) over four years. The down payment of 50,000 crowns, a mere £10,416.22, strained his credit to the limit and was secured on parliamentary taxation; the remaining three instalments were due over the next three years. The fleet and expeditionary force commanded by Scales that he sent to Brittany in 1468 cost £18,000. Given his financial straits, still burdened by Henry VI's debts, how could Edward finance a full-scale continental war? Moreover Edward renounced not only the benefits of peace with his powerful neighbour, the marriage of his sister to the brother-in-law of the French king for which no dowry was payable, but also marriages for the other royal dukes, an alternative commercial treaty, a pension of 8,000 marks, a share of the Burgundian Netherlands, and the reference of his claims to Acquitaine and Normandy to papal arbitration.[48] Of course, such promises to prevent an Anglo-Burgundian alliance were unlikely to be fulfilled, but outright rejection had immediate and dangerous repercussions.

46   *RP* v. 622–3.
47   *RP* v. 572–3; *Annales*, 789; Scofield, i. 451–2.
48   Scofield, i. 412; *Annales*, 787.

Louis was alarmed. He was impelled to destabilize Edward, by despatching Jasper Tudor to North Wales and by fomenting Lancastrian conspiracy. Edward took such threats seriously, perhaps too seriously, both at home and when a non-existent invasion from Harfleur was supposedly threatened. Louis was stimulated to neutralize the other players. Far from a circle of steel, Edward's alliances proved weaker than he apparently supposed, certainly weaker than in 1465. His international partners had more limited objectives in mind than putting an Englishman on the throne of France. Louis extended his truce with Burgundy, removed his brother from the duchy of Normandy and placated him with more distant Guienne, knocked out Britanny, and made concessions to Burgundy. Ironically the treaty of Peronne forced on Louis on 14 October 1468 gave Charles the Bold what he wanted and removed Burgundy as an effective ally for Edward. The date for invasion was repeatedly put back: not in 1468, nor in 1469. And Edward, bereft of effective allies, found himself isolated, and anxious to treat.

Warwick recognized all this. He had a clearer appreciation of the realities of North European power politics. He realized how weak was England in relation to the great power that was France and how limited was the commitment of Edward's potential allies. Treaties with Denmark, Naples and Castile were of little military use. However popular an anti-French policy was, he realized that there was no hope, in the short term, of making good the English claim to France. Friendly relations with England's most powerful neighbour were desirable. Englishmen disliked foreigners. There was as much hostility to Flemings as to Frenchmen, Lombards and Scots. Whether Warwick was ready at this stage to ally with France in an aggressive war, which would surely also have been un-popular, is less certain. Meantime in pursuit of his alternative policy, Warwick continued his independent correspondence with King Louis, maintained contacts with those with access to Edward's secrets, and passed these on to Louis. Thus he assured Louis that England would not prevent his brother from being ousted from Normandy.[49] He also pressed his case: he declined to guarantee half Margaret's dowry as Edward requested.[50]

Warwick's continued opposition, therefore, can be argued to have been on principle and policy, on which he had preferable alternatives to offer. He was consistent. However, there was much more to his conduct than this.

First of all, there was a tendency to read Warwick's opposition on foreign policy and alienation as the basis for rebellion, treason, deposition. This was so even in 1464, when Louis stated to the Milanese ambassador that, in the event of a break between Warwick and Edward, he would back Warwick.[51] Louis's will-ingness to contemplate several alternative policies simultaneously meant that Warwick was encouraged to destabilize the Yorkist regime. On the basis that my enemy's enemy is my friend, it was logical for Margaret of Anjou's brother John

49   Ross, *Edward IV*, 107.
50   Scofield, i. 444.
51   Ibid. i. 355.

Duke of Calabria in February 1467 to suggest an alliance between his sister and Warwick; this may also have been proposed by Margaret's chancellor Sir John Fortescue in memoranda to the French king.[52] Such facile deductions were also made nearer to home. Two sources, *Hearne's Fragment* and Thomas Basin, indicate that Warwick's over-cordial reception by Louis in 1467 prompted suspicions of treason. Edward himself did not altogether rule such possibilities out.[53] The earl, like everyone else, had Lancastrian kinsmen and especially kinswomen, knew Lancastrians, and was potentially implicated in the Lancastrian plots uncovered in 1468–9: Thomas Porthaleyn, one of those charged in Cook's plot in mid-1468, had been an important Warwick administrator on the 1430s, 1440s and 1450s; John Hawkins was servant to Warwick's ally, Lord Wenlock; and his new brother-in-law the Earl of Oxford was arrested, allegedly 'confessed much thing', but was then acquitted.[54] Sir Thomas Hungerford, whose family Warwick had assisted to rehabilitate, was convicted for further treasons later in 1468 and was executed in January 1469.

Actually there is no evidence that Warwick himself ever seriously considered turning Lancastrian. Though Edward feared the worst, none of the plots that were uncovered indicated the Lancastrians to be more than isolated, predictable and easily identifiable individuals. The shock at Sir Thomas Cook's involvement was that he was so unexpected as a London alderman at the heart of the regime and a principal beneficiary from it. There was nobody more difficult for Lancastrians to reconcile with than their destroyer, the most ruthless and merciless of their opponents, and Warwick himself had too much to lose. To restore the Lancastrians must threaten the tenure of forfeited estates by himself and his family, challenge his local supremacy in the North, and raise up other rivals to his dominance of policy. A Lancastrian alliance was an admission that he had been wrong, which he would not willingly do: nothing suggests that he was a subtle or flexible negotiator. Could Warwick carry his retainers with him? Was it not the highest of high-risk strategies? Disagreement was not incompatible with loyalty and ought not to be equated with emnity. If such constitutional rectitude proved impractical, it was far preferable for Warwick to recover his dominance of the existing regime, ideally peacefully, alternatively by force. Control of Edward IV, then substitution of his brother Clarence, relegated cooperation with the Lancastrians to a distant third, the last resort, in 1470. There is no evidence to suppose that it ever rated higher before that.

However such charges had their uses. It was Herbert who despatched the Lancastrian envoy with his charges against Warwick to Edward. Although not involved in foreign policy and hence not initially regarded so seriously by Warwick, Herbert was the most ambitious and dangerous of the earl's opponents. From being a principal officer in Wales of Warwick *and* York, he had

---

52   Gross, *Dissolution*, 77–80; *CSPM* i. 117–18, 120.
53   T. Basin, *Histoire de Louis XI*, ed. C. Samaran (1966), i. 179; *Chrons. White Rose*, 237; *Annales*, 788.
54   *Annales*, 789–90; *Great Chron.* 204; *Plumpton L & P* 40; Hicks, *Richard III*, ch. 23.

made himself Edward's indispensable agent there and was rewarded, ultimately, on the fall of Harlech with the earldom of Pembroke in October 1468.
He had acquired a host of grants and offices, including the elevation in 1465 of
Raglan into a marcher lordship. Nor was his ambition confined to Wales. His
interest in Dunster has already been touched on. He also sought to extend his
authority by a series of marriages. According to the *Great Chronicle*, he solicited
the marriage for his son and heir of the heiress of Bonville and Harrington,
daughter of Warwick's sister Katherine and stepdaughter of Lord Hastings.
Warwick reportedly declined,[55] perhaps partly because Herbert was insufficient
in status and lineage. Instead Herbert bound his son to a Wydeville in 1467,
contracted alliances for other daughters to two royal wards Viscount Lisle and
Lord Grey of Powys, and projected yet further matches to Henry Tudor and
Henry Percy.[56] Tudor was heir apparent to the Lancastrian earl of Pembroke,
who was still influential in Wales. As son of Edmund Tudor, Earl of Richmond,
he was also heir to the resumed earldom, honour, lordship and castle of
Richmond. Percy was heir to the forfeited earldom of Northumberland. If
Pembroke had yet to obtain royal consent to marry them to his daughters, he
was nevertheless speculating on their restorations, a game that the Nevilles had
played so well and that his Wydeville alliance made much more feasible. He had
other arrears due to him like those he remitted for the marriages of Lisle and
Grey of Powys. Were Pembroke to succeed, the principal losers would be
Warwick, the Nevilles and Clarence, who would lose their Percy estates,
Richmond honour itself, the eastern wardenry, and their unchallenged dominance of the North.[57] And by 1468 it was Pembroke who had greater influence
with the king.

By the spring of 1469, therefore, Edward's foreign policy was in ruins.
Warwick could reasonably feel that he could do better. He had sound grounds
for hostility to the king's new favourites. So too did the king's next brother and
heir male, George Duke of Clarence, who had no desire for his hand to be
hawked around as a diplomatic pawn and who preferred instead to advance
himself by marrying Warwick's daughter Isabel, the greatest of English heiresses. It was also the best match that Warwick could arrange. That the marriage
was indeed concluded in the face of Edward's hostility, a dispensation being
secured secretly in Rome, was itself a political triumph for both parties. By
binding Warwick yet more closely to the house of York, it could have fostered
a *rapprochement* with the king. Actually, however, Warwick's thoughts dwelt
less on reconciliation than on revenge. The marriage was the foundation for an
immediate coup d'état: a pre-emptive strike. A rebellion in Yorkshire led by
one Robin of Redesdale, whose earlier insurrection had been easily crushed by
Warwick's brother John,[58] was not Lancastrian in origin but Neville. Hence

55   *Great Chron.* 208. The story is late. Was Cecily Bonville reserved for Montagu's son?
56   Hicks, *Clarence*, 38–9.
57   Ibid. 38–40.
58   Scofield, *Edward IV*, i. 488.

Edward underestimated it and his favourites were defeated and destroyed at Edgecote on 24 July 1469,[59] the king himself becoming Warwick's puppet. That the eventuality was not foreseen indicates that Warwick chose this course of action; it was not yet forced upon him.

9.3   Warwick's First Coup 1469

Edward IV's first reign had been a disappointment to his subjects. Such is the reasonable deduction from the rebellions of Robin of Holderness and Robin of Redesdale in the North and of the men of Kent in 1469 and the popular backing for the Readeption of Henry VI in 1470–1. There were real grievances and real dissatisfaction.[60] The removal of Henry VI had not proved to be the universal panacea. Financial solvency, law and order, the removal of corrupt favourites, international stature and, by implication, the recovery of English possessions in France had not materialized. Henry VI's debts remained unpaid and new ones were contracted. Corrupt new favourites succeeded the old. Edward IV moreover made rash promises that he could not keep. His assurance in 1467 that he would 'lyve vpon my nowne and not to charge my Subjettes but in grete and urgent causes' and his call to arms against France in 1468 had both been popular,[61] but the promised invasion came to nought and the taxes granted were diverted to ordinary expenses. The rebels complained of taxes and tributes.[62] His foreign policy collapsed. Already in 1468 Monypenny reported that people in London and throughout England were saying that those responsible for Edward's foreign policy should have their heads cut off.[63] In 1468 Warwick had identified Earl Rivers, his son Scales, Lords Herbert, Audley and Stafford of Southwick as his enemies at court. In 1469 the rebels added to these Rivers's wife Jacquetta Duchess of Bedford, another son Sir John Wydeville, and Sir John Fogge.[64] It was apparently at this time that one Woodhouse, a jester, appeared before the king in long boots and staff and explained that 'thorwth many Cuntrees of your Realm . . . the Ryvers been soo hie that I coude hardly scape thorw theym, But as I was fayn to serch the depth wyth this long staff': he meant by it, explained the chronicler, 'the grete Rule which the lord Ryvers & his blood bare that tyme withyn hys Realme'. Warkworth was not the only chronicler to agree.[65]

Such was also the message of the articles and petitions of the rebels of July

59   W. G. Lewis, 'The Exact Date of the Battle of Banbury, 1469', *BIHR* lv (1982), 194–6.

60   *Vale's Bk.*, 46.

61   *RP* v. 572, 622–3.

62   K. R. Dockray, 'The Yorkshire Rebellions of 1469', *The Ricardian* 83 (1983), 246–57, at 252.

63   Waurin-Dupont iii. 193.

64   *Vale's Bk.* 213; *Annales*, 788.

65   *Warkworth's Chron.* 48; *Great Chron.* 208.

1469.[66] They were concerned by the king's poverty, that thrust financial burdens on the people, and with the breakdown of justice, which arose whenever 'the seid Kings estraingid the gret lordis of thayre blood from thaire secrete Councelle' in favour of self-interested parvenus, 'seducious persones', who sought only 'theire singuler lucour' at royal and public expense. Such had been the three principal articles, the rebels claimed, behind the depositions of Edward II, Richard II and Henry VI. Now they applied once again. Whereas no king had been better endowed than Edward IV, his wealth was dispersed to his favourites 'above theire disertis and degrees. So that he may nat lyf honorably and mayntene his estate and charges ordinarie withinne this lond'. They had caused him to change the coinage, reduce his household, 'charge us his trewe commons and subgettis wyth suche gret imposicions and inordinate charges . . . [to] the utter empoverysshyng of us his treue Commons and subjettes', the enriching of themselves to the tune of 200,000 marks (£133,333.33), and the dread of anyone who incurred their malice. They had caused the king to misappropriate taxation, 'accordyng to the promyse that he made in his last parliament, openly wyth his owen mouthe unto us'. They had even spent ecclesiastical wealth collected for the crusade, thus threatening an interdict. They had committed all kinds of crime and encouraged crimes by their maintenance and had excluded from the royal council any 'true lordis of his blood' who might frustrate 'theyre fals and disceyvable purpos'. The offence of these 'seducious persones', not really treason at all, was what in early times was meant by accroachement of the king and the 'appec[h]yng' or diminishing of his estate.

Much of the tally of charges has the ring of truth. King Edward did indeed (wisely) reduce his household, at least below the size of Henry VI's. He did alienate crown, Lancaster and forfeited lands and did reward the Wydevilles and Herberts generously, in part from these sources. Among many financial expedients, he had resorted to recoinage, borrowing money without repayment, forced loans, tenths and taxes. And he did use tunnage and poundage for purposes other than the keeping of the sea and direct taxation for ordinary expenses. In principle, therefore, it is possible that he over-used purveyance and seized the goods of rich men from their executors. More specifically, what of the charge that financial motives lay behind the 'impechementes of treasounes to whom they owe any eville will; so that ther can be no man of worshippe or richesse . . . or any other honest persone, in surete of his lyf, lyvelode, or goodis'? Many suspected Lancastrians had been 'sent for', imprisoned or placed in protective custody, some tried, a handful convicted, some secured with bonds, others obliged to surrender their lands or wives' inheritances, fined, and even executed? In particular, there were the highly topical and notorious cases of Sir Thomas Cook, convicted the previous year only of misprision of treason (foreknowledge), who was fined £8,000 and pillaged by Rivers, Jacquetta and Fogge, and in 1469

66 *Warkworth's Chron.* 46–51, printed from Bodl. Ashmole Roll 33; another version, lacking the covering letter, is in *Vale's Bk.* 212–15. This is the source of the next four paras.

of the heir to the Courtenay earldom of Devon: 'Menne seyde the Lorde Stafforde of Southwyke was cause of the seyde Herry Curtenayes dethe, for he wolde be the Erle of Devynschyre, and so the Kynge made hym afterwarde. . . .'[67] Note that Rivers, the Duchess Jacquetta, Fogge and Stafford were all among those charged in the manifesto. As for the embezzlement of crusading revenues, might not this refer to the king's use of the priorate of St John's to provide for the young non-Hospitaller Sir John Wydeville? Note the appeal once again, here and elsewhere, to religious motives. Subsequent events substantiate the popular hostility to Rivers in Kent and Stafford in Somerset, their home countries where they had 'the rule'; Stafford was to be lynched by the men of Bridgwater.[68] Surely the author had also heard Edward speak with his own mouth at the Westminster Parliament of July 1467?

That such speculative questions need to be asked indicates the lack of precision of the articles. They are of general application, for general consumption and allegedly widely distributed, and do not specify a particular region. In so far as local grievances can be detected, they relate not to Yorkshire whence Robin of Redesdale hailed, but to Kent and London: hence the apparent allusions to Cook; the inclusion in Fogge of a Kentishman and keeper of the royal wardrobe; and the harking on the diversion of tunnage and poundage from the keeping of the seas. As in 1459–60, the grievances are those of the Cinque Ports, staplers and shipmen, who duly obeyed Warwick's summons. Others current in 1450–60, against the constable of Dover for example, are omitted, presumably irrelevant, because the current constable was Warwick himself.

What, then, were the remedies to 'the grete inconveniencis and mischeves that fall in this lond'? Not the king's deposition or even the threat of his deposition, the ominous warning that Miss Scofield perceived in the parallels drawn between him and his disastrous predecessors. The rebels stressed their loyalty. They were the

> trewe and feythefulle subjettes and commons of this land for the wele and surete of the Kyng our sovereigne lord and his heirs and the commonwele of this land, evir to be continued. For we take God to recorde we entende but only for the wele and surete of the Kyng oure sovereigne lord, And the common wele of this lond.

Theirs was another loyal rebellion. They sought the punishment of those named 'accordyng to their werkes and untrouthes' as an example to others; the appropriation of royal revenues to ordinary charges, so that the king could maintain his estate without taxation; the punishment of any seeking grants in contravention of this; the appropriation of tunnage and poundage to the keeping of the sea; and the observation of the laws of Edward III. Why rebel? Why not petition the king? Perhaps they had. The petitions do not say. King Edward, unlike King

---

67   *Warkworth's Chron.* 8.
68   Ibid. 7.

Henry, was presented not as ignorant but as ill-advised. The petitions were therefore addressed to the 'trewe lordis, spirituelle, and temporelle, to yeve assistence and aid in thys oure true and goodeley desyres'. It was such lords spiritual and temporal – Warwick, Clarence and Archbishop Neville – who received the petitions. Finding them

> resonabyll and profitable for the honoure and profite of oure seid sovereyn Lord and the commun wele of all this his realm, [they were] fully purposed with other lordis to shew the same to his good grace.

Hence they summoned supporters 'to accompayneye us thedir, with as many persones defensably arrayede as y[e] can make'. This was to be forceful petitioning: Edward was to be induced to concede by a display of force.

The articles and petitions existed and exist independently of the covering letter of the three lords. It is therefore possible, if highly unlikely, that the popular movement originated independently. Whenever the articles first circulated, the covering letter is dated 12 July, three days *after* the king wrote to Warwick, Clarence and Archbishop Neville about their misconduct. Whilst the articles draw on earlier precedents both of rebellions and manifestos, there is no reuse of past words or phrases, and they were not necessarily of Warwick's devising. He knew, of course, how unfair some charges were, how little choice Edward had, how much the Nevilles themselves had benefited from Edward's largesse, how inaccurate were some of the details, but it made good propaganda. It focused on popular grievances, 'wheche caused alle the people of this lond to grugge', rather than his own: it draws on popular xenophobia rather than arguing foreign policy; and it treats the counsel of great lords of the blood as good government itself rather than means to ends. Probably Warwick fomented popular insurrection; certainly he wished to exploit it, to destroy his own enemies – 'certeyne seducious persones', and pursue his own objectives; and a general manifesto served to enlist support everywhere.

As in 1460, the overwhelming numbers of a popular uprising were to be harnessed by a ruthless noble leadership. Rebellions in Yorkshire and the Midlands were to be supplemented by an invasion through Kent and London spearheaded by Calais and swelled by thousands of mariners, Kentishmen and Londoners. The latter are indistinct because it was the northerners who proved decisive. Warwick was however admitted both to Canterbury (18 July) and to London, whose corporation even made further loans to him. Was not popular discontent too good an opportunity for Warwick to miss? Had it not transformed a minority faction into an overwhelming majority in 1460? This time it was to prove disastrous for the earl. Up to this point, Warwick had been a loyal subject. He could accept Edward's authority, resign himself to an honourable if secondary role, abandon certain cherished lands and perhaps the unchallenged dominance of the North. He would retain, however, the far larger estates that made him the greatest of English magnates, his constellation of offices, an important if subordinate and honourable part in domestic affairs, and the leadership of English embassies abroad. His rebellion was treasonable in itself. It involved the arrest and imprisonment of the king. It may always have entailed and soon required further rebellions, depositions, civil wars, invasions, and usurpations ever more desperate that propelled him on the perilous course that destroyed him and his dynasty. It was his actions now that earned him the sobriquet 'the Kingmaker' – a title reluctantly earned; that overturned his renown amongst contemporaries; and that condemned him as a selfish egotist for posterity. He was insatiable.

Such analysis attributes a cynical and self-interested attitude to Warwick that has much to commend it. But as explanation it is not enough. Warwick was convinced that Edward's foreign policy was wrong. He sincerely believed that his alternative was in the public interest; so was his rule. He genuinely believed in government by those of ancient ancestry, the highest nobility, the king's natural councillors, not by parvenus, amongst whom in 1460 he had numbered the Wydevilles. We know of his inability to accommodate differences of opinion, his equation of disagreement with opposition and treason. He saw the rebellions of others as treason and those of himself as legitimate. There had been a sequence of minor disappointments that had left him feeling ill-used. He thought the king's favourites were ganging up on him and were out to destroy him or cut him down to size, as Herbert apparently was. Royal patronage to himself was the just reward for services rendered – admittedly, enormous services – and he nourished other legitimate expectations that were not being satisfied. And the risks that he took in 1469 – the risk of total destruction, which he of all men could calculate – demand faith in his sincerity of purpose.

Remember that many of Warwick's earlier historians saw him as consistent, not the king, who had not treated the earl with the respect that he deserved. It had been Warwick in 1459–60 who had taken over York's popular appeal and had harnessed it to decisive effect. Edward had also benefited. Since then Edward had lost that popular support. Warwick, however, had retained it. His very public opposition to the king's favourites and policies had distanced him from the popular grievances of 1469 and cleared him of complicity. He stood in 1469 for the same as a decade earlier and appeared in popular eyes as the consistent advocate of the common weal. So well had Warwick gauged the popular mood that he can be said to have represented it. That does not determine whether he sincerely stood for their interests, or cunningly manipulated them.

As in 1455, 1459 and 1460, most of the principal rebels concealed their identity: the covering letter was issued only in the names of Warwick, Clarence and Archbishop Neville. Even they, however, revealed their hand only on 12 July, when the rebellion in Kent was already under way and that in Yorkshire was far advanced. The Yorkshire rebellion was led by Warwick's Richmondshire connection: by his brother-in-law Lord FitzHugh, his cousins Sir Henry Neville of Latimer and Sir John Conyers, steward of Middleham, though the nominal leader was Robin of Redesdale.[69] Once again Warwick was to bring the Calais garrison to England and call out his West Midlanders. A multi-pronged campaign required careful planning and secrecy.

69   Dockray, 'Yorkshire Rebellions', 255.

It was preceded and concealed by two important ceremonies. Warwick's presence in the South-East could excite no surprise as he had business there to execute. In February he was commissioned to inquire into land tenure in the Calais Pale. It was he, not Gloucester or Scales, who was fitting out the fleet. He was personally engaged in negotiations with Burgundy at Ardres on 21 April and at St Omer on the 26th. He met and encouraged the chronicler Waurin, but lacked the time to be really helpful.[70] The dedication of the *Trinity* on 12 June has already been described. Secondly, Warwick's daughter Isabel was married to the king's brother Clarence at Calais on 11 July. A papal dispensation had been secured at last on 14 March and a licence from Cardinal Bourchier for George Neville to marry them at Calais on 30 June: the delay may account for some of the otherwise unexplained toing and froing by earl, duke and archbishop. Edward's continuing disapproval is implied by his absence, when he had intended to visit Calais; he cannot have been ignorant of what everyone else knew.

The marriage secured for Warwick a duke for his oldest daughter and determined the destination of one share of his inheritance, a small part of which was assigned as jointure. It also committed to him the king's brother and male heir, an ally who lent respectability to any insurrection or imposed ministry, his own resources, and bound to their cause those who attended the wedding in the teeth of Edward's hostility. They remained at Calais for five days, Clarence's honeymoon, after the wedding.[71] The northern sector of the rebellion had been unleashed much earlier, by 28 June at least when Warwick wrote to Coventry soliciting a band of soldiers for service with him and the king against the northern insurgents.[72]

From Edward's angle, of course, it looked like a marriage alliance *with* him, binding the Nevilles more tightly to him, rather than against him. Evidently he saw no connection with Robin of Redesdale's rising. Such revolts occurred frequently. The name, which had been used before and been easily crushed, had no Neville connotations; Redesdale was in Northumberland and thus implied Percy and Lancastrian origins that could be left to his northern officers. Warwick, as we have seen, was apparently mobilizing forces of repression from Coventry. Whilst preparing to go north if necessary, Edward went on pilgrimage to Bury St Edmunds, Walsingham and Norwich, before taking alarm and calling out the Welsh and West Country levies of Pembroke and Devon. By 9 July Edward had heard rumours of 'suech disposition towards us' of the three lords:[73] did he yet appreciate the connection between their actions in Kent and the northerners and the real character of the latter? The northerners took at least a month to travel from Richmondshire to Banbury, longer clearly than the Welsh and West Country levies with which Herbert and Stafford reacted. The underlying strategy is concealed. Were the king's forces to be lured northwards, leaving the

70   Scofield, i. 488; Gransden, *Historical Writing*, ii. 290.
71   Hicks, *Clarence*, 32–3.
72   Scofield, i. 494.
73   *PL* v. 35–6.

South exposed for Warwick to repeat the triumph of Northampton in 1460? Or were efforts being made to co-ordinate and amalgamate the various rebel forces? We do not know how close Warwick's own force proceeded from London towards the king.

What happened, however, is clear enough. Finding Edward's forces divided, the northerners fell on Pembroke's Welshmen at Edgecote on 24 July and destroyed them. Whether a popular element was involved, it was Warwick's Middleham connection that bore the brunt and won the victory. It paid a high price. Among the fallen were two of Warwick's nephews, a son of Lord FitzHugh and Sir Henry Neville of Latimer, the latter's brother-in-law Oliver Dudley, and John Conyers, son of the steward of Middleham and son-in-law of Fauconberg.[74] As on previous occasions, Warwick made sure that his enemies would cause no further trouble: Rivers, Pembroke and Devon, Sir John Wydeville, Sir Richard and Thomas Herbert were executed. The Duchess Jacquetta herself was appealed of sorcery by Warwick's retainer Thomas Wake. Only Scales, his younger brothers, Audley and Fogge, escaped. The king himself was arrested almost alone at Warwick's manor of Olney by Archbishop Neville and imprisoned first at Warwick, where he offered at the College, and then at Middleham.

It was 'the Earl of Warwick, as astute as ever was Ulysses', who stayed with Edward and directed the government from afar, the archbishop and duke taking the lead at court. Letters of instruction that were acted on survive among the chancery warrants from the earl to the council in London. The spoils of victory were distributed: Sir John Langstrother, preceptor of Balsall and now un-contested prior of St John, became treasurer in Rivers's place. Apart from another great duchy of Lancaster office, as supervisor and approver, Warwick was appointed on 17 August to be chief justice and chamberlain of South Wales, steward and constable of Cardigan and Carmarthen, late of the Earl of Pembroke. His brother-in-law Hastings was appointed his counterpart in North Wales.[75] Evidently Warwick thought Hastings was still his man.

Such were the arrangements in the short term. Warwick, however, was not content with them. Mere restraint was not enough. Like Richard Duke of York a decade earlier, he needed more secure long-term arrangements, the more so because Edward was vigorous and decisive where Henry VI had been merely passive and inept. Hence his decision to summon parliament, taken against advice.[76] One would like to know why: whether because a permanent transfer of power was opposed, because his capacity to control parliament was doubted, or because Warwick had deposition in mind? Surely at the very least Warwick intended a protectorate, from which he or Clarence as protectors could be dismissed only by parliament? Just possibly he may have been taking the more drastic course of deposing the king, as the Milanese ambassador supposed on

74 Dockray, 'Yorkshire Rebellions', 255; *Rous Roll*, no. 53; *Warkworth's Chron.* 7.
75 *CPR 1467–77*, 165; Somerville, *Duchy of Lancaster*, i. 422.
76 *CSPM* i. 132.

16 September?[77] Such an approach could exploit the rumours current in August 1469 that Edward IV himself was a bastard, the son of the Duchess Cecily and a franc archer called Blancborgne.[78] A charge of sorcery against Jacquetta, perhaps to explain Edward's infatuation with her daughter, could perhaps have been used to discredit Edward's marriage. Neither can be traced to the rebel lords. The precedents of 1460 are obvious. If so, it was surely Clarence, next brother of the king, who was to be advanced. We do not know. Probably Warwick's intentions were never revealed. Certainly they cannot have been, if deposition and usurpation was intended, for such plans were never made a charge against him, even by chroniclers. At a more mundane level, parliament could be induced to neutralize the Wydevilles and Herberts by resumption of their grants.

No parliament was held, because writs of supersedeas were issued. The rule of all English governments over the localities depended on consent, not force. Warwick, despite his victory, lacked that consent, the moral force that a legitimate king possessed. Thus John Duke of Norfolk's siege of Caister (Norf.), far from being halted by the intervention of the archbishop and Clarence, proceeded apace, Norfolk remarking that he would not desist for any duke in England. So, too, in the North, where the irreconcilable and incurably optimistic Humphrey Neville of Brancepeth saw another opening for a Lancastrian revolt. Neville's previous efforts had been quelled with ease, but not this time. Not apparently because more popular, but because Warwick's usual manpower would not serve. Edward had first to be exhibited in public and then allowed to release himself before Warwick was able to deal with Neville, definitively. An impressive escort of English nobility accompanied Edward into London about 10 October. Warwick, Clarence and the archbishop were not among them.[79]

77   Ibid.
78   Kendall, *Warwick*, 243.
79   Hicks, *Clarence*, 37–9.

Fortune's Second
Wheel 1470–1

10.1 Warwick's Second Coup 1470

It was Warwick's inability to rule with Edward in custody that resulted in the king's return to power. Failure for Warwick was not the same as defeat. The bases of his power, his connection, and his popularity remained. What happened next was not preordained. If the initiative had undoubtedly passed to the king, several courses of action were possible. Bereft of his former favourites, Edward could have remained as much a Neville puppet, though at liberty. This option he decisively rejected. Alternatively the king could have sought revenge on his erstwhile captors. That this was his initial objective is suggested by their exclusion from the capital, the hostile language of his household men, the omission of Warwick and Clarence from commissions of array of 29 October 1469, and the summons of the great council that met from 6 November.[1] What to do with the coup leaders must have been on the agenda. No revenge followed. The king's own language was always more favourable;[2] perhaps more diplomatic and non-committal. That so many attended the great council emphasized the loyalty of the Lords, their confidence in the king's government, and hence their disapproval of Warwick's coup. However loyal they might be, many among them were Warwick's own kin, friends and former allies, who did not wish to proceed to extremes. Edward lacked the strength to be certain of victory in a further civil war and the justification for provoking one. Even if he preferred revenge, Edward had to receive his captors back into his allegiance.

This was not automatic. Once excluded, the rebel lords needed to be reassured about their safety. Terms had to be negotiated for their readmittance

---

1 Scofield, i. 504–5; Hicks, *Clarence*, 41.
2 *Paston L & P* i. 410.

to allegiance. The Crowland continuator summarizes a complex (and un-documented) process:

> There were frequent missions and embassies going between the king and the disaffected lords. Eventually, on the appointed day, in the great chamber of Parliament, the duke of Clarence, the earl of Warwick and their supporters appeared before a Great Council of all the lords of the realm where peace was made and it was agreed that all disagreements should be abandoned.[3]

That was after 6 December. A general pardon covered all offences before Christmas. Warwick, Clarence and the archbishop shared in further council sessions in the New Year.[4]

Edward offered reconciliation from a position of strength. He was the rightful king and ruler. He reconstructed his regime first and then negotiated with Warwick, who had to accept the changes made. Warwick's brief regime was repudiated and the king's earlier policies resumed. Warwick's chancellor and treasurer were replaced, Anthony Wydeville returned to court as second earl Rivers, and Warwick lost the offices in Wales that he had bestowed on himself. After Christmas the sorcery trial against the Duchess Jacquetta was terminated by her acquittal. The king reaffirmed his foreign policy on 22 December by elevating Charles the Bold to the order of the Garter. He himself accepted that of the Golden Fleece (Toison d'Or). At home, the king's youngest brother Richard Duke of Gloucester emerged on to the political stage and was despatched to overawe Wales, with the guidance and backing of Herbert's brother-in-law Walter Devereux, Lord Ferrers of Chartley. The backing of the powerful Stafford influence was reinforced by the elevation of John Stafford to the earldom of Wiltshire. The release from the Tower on 27 October of Henry Percy, heir to the earldom of Northumberland, foreshadowed the restoration of the Percy earldom in the North and the dispossession of Warwick, Clarence, and Warwick's brother John. The latter indeed renounced his Percy forfeitures on 13 February.[5]

Though Warwick lost his immediate ill-gotten gains, he was allowed to retain the whole constellation of offices that he had accumulated earlier. But his power was to be curbed in many ways in the Neville heartlands of northern England whence the army of Edgecote had come. The impending restoration of Henry Percy involved the loss of extensive estates and income and, more important, the division of power both on the borders and in Yorkshire, where the Neville–Percy feud had been fought. The recent death of the mad Lord Latimer and, at Edgecote, of his eldest son Henry permitted the transfer of the Latimer estates

3   *Crowland Continuations*, 117.
4   Scofield, i. 505n, 506; *RP* vi. 232. The earl was at Warwick on 22 Nov., Warwicks. RO CR 1998/J2/177.
5   C 81/830/3022; Hicks, *Clarence*, 40–7.

from Warwick to the custody of Cardinal Bourchier during the minority of the infant heir. In the West March the first steps in the restoration of the Dacres followed on the elevation in 1468 of the queen's chancellor Edward Storey as bishop of Carlisle. And private negotiations for the transfer of custody of young Henry Tudor to his mother, another major Cumbrian landholder, and her second husband Sir Henry Stafford brought closer the restoration of the earldom of Richmond, to the material loss of Clarence and, in Richmondshire, of Warwick, who could expect, once again, another earl to take precedence over himself as premier earl.[6] Threats that were merely potential and which Warwick had sought to dispel by his summer rebellion now became actual.

Admittedly these uncompromising moves were tempered by others that were more conciliatory. Neither the new treasurer Bishop Grey of Ely nor the new constable, Gloucester rather than Rivers, nor Edward's employment of the Blounts and Staffords were objectionable to Warwick. Moreover on 6 November, ahead of any reconciliation, the king had formally betrothed his eldest daughter Elizabeth to Warwick's nephew George Neville, son of Warwick's brother John. George was created Duke of Bedford and John, somewhat later, became Marquis Montagu. This should have been the masterstroke that gave Warwick the royal match and ducal title that he had been seeking and offered his family and followers a route to royal favour other than through opposition. Warwick ought to have been disarmed, Clarence's pretensions countered, and the unity of the Nevilles broken.[7]

From Edward's angle, this was a carefully balanced package that offered Warwick forgiveness and security and recognized certain of his grievances, whilst denying him the rewards of rebellion, curbing his excessive ambitions, and clarifying his place as a subject. That Edward believed the reconciliation to be real emerged in the spring, when he assumed that the Lincolnshire uprising had merely local origins and even commissioned Warwick and Clarence to raise men to suppress it. It was a miscalculation that might have had serious consequences.

Desperation forced Warwick to release Edward. It signalled cohabitation once again of king and earl. Warwick cannot have considered all the ramifications. It was desperation also that forced him to come to terms in December. He had no choice except rebellion against king and great council which he could not win. In between, the earl's exclusion from court and council and Edward's apparent reluctance to receive him back can only have fostered his distrust, which Edward's terms did not allay and which Warwick must accept. In return for mere forgiveness for past offences, Warwick had to accept the confirmation of Herbert authority in Wales and the presence of the Wydevilles at court, the king's new appointments, the continuance of his Burgundian foreign policy, and the curbing of his own family's power in the North: perhaps their essential interests. Any hopes for a resumption of Neville influence on government and policy were firmly rebuffed. This was not a compromise and no security was offered by the

---

6   Scofield, i. 507n; Hicks, *Clarence*, 43–7, 50–1.
7   Hicks, *Clarence*, 48–9.

match of two children of three and five which Edward could (and did) break when he chose. No doubt Warwick feared that Edward would take vengeance when he could.

For that, Edward needed evidence of treason beyond that found inadequate by the autumn council. This was provided by the Lincolnshire rebellion of Sir Robert Welles of spring 1470. Was this rebellion fostered or even fomented by Edward in order to destroy his enemies as has recently been suggested?[8] It is hardly likely. After Edgecote, Edward must have doubted his own support and been wary of Warwick's. To encourage Warwick to recruit in his home country on the authority of a commission of array risked raising an uprising that he could not quell. How could Edward have anticipated that Warwick's own retainers would reject even a royal commission as evidence of the earl's legitimate intentions? There was greater security in denying the commission and seizing Clarence whilst he was in his power, just as he was to arrest Lord Welles. Originating as a private feud like others lately consumated at Caister (Norf.) and Nibley Green (Gloucs.), Welles's uprising apparently lacked a national dimension and occurred in a county from which Warwick was conspicuously absent. Whilst admitting our dependence on sources generated by the crown, such as the official *Chronicle*, royal proclamations and *The Confession of Sir Robert Welles*, which are indeed interrelated, we must reject the new conspiracy theory as oversubtle.

All the contemporary sources accept the involvement of Warwick and Clarence (especially Clarence) in the rebellion. Their participation within four months of making peace shows their reconciliation to have been insincere. There are striking resemblances with events in the summer of 1459. The rebellion took the familiar form of a popular uprising led by a 'great captain' (like Robin of Redesdale) that did not require their direct involvement and might have permitted their disengagement in the event of defeat. If the rebellion succeeded, Warwick could reap the benefits, and, if not, he could escape the consequences. He could also hope for royal authority to raise forces against the crown which were not forthcoming for avowed treason. The objective, as indicated by Sir Robert Welles's confession and the *Chronicle*, was surely to substitute Clarence, whom Warwick could manage, as king in place of Edward. Making his son-in-law into a king and his daughter Isabel into a queen was obviously attractive to Warwick, but it was surely the use that was to be made of control of government and fears of the alternative that impelled him into this momentous step. The bills hostile to him and Clarence posted in London in early February, perhaps by royal courtiers, were further causes for apprehension. Both duke and earl were also omitted from commissions of array on 2 March.[9]

As lord of the honour of Richmond, Clarence was a significant landholder in and around Boston. Some of his men were involved both in the rebellion and in

8   See P. Holland, 'The Lincolnshire Rebellion of March 1470', *EHR* ciii (1988), 851–69, esp. 863, 866–7, 869.
9   Ibid. 854, 866.

Table 10.1   Title to the Crown and the Succession 1470–1

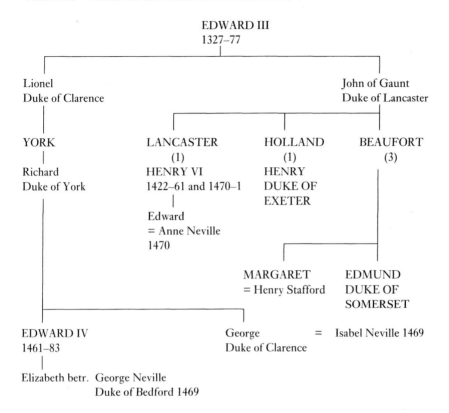

the earlier riot at Gainsborough in which the house of Thomas Burgh, a royal favourite, was demolished. Significantly, in Sir Thomas Dymmock and Sir Thomas Delalaunde, they included two brothers-in-law of Richard Lord Welles and Willoughby.[10] He was related to Warwick, and features on the Salisbury Roll; they may have had direct dealings in the 1450s when Warwick's brother Thomas was married to Maud, Dowager-Lady Willoughby and Lady Welles's step-mother. Welles was carver at Archbishop Neville's enthronement feast.[11] It was Lord Welles and his son Sir Robert who were prime movers in the Lincolnshire Rebellion. They had been recently restored (by Warwick's agency?) to the two baronies that they had forfeited as Lancastrians. It is tempting to see the riot as originating in the barring by Burgh of the Welles' return to their natural local

10   Hicks, *Clarence*, 54.
11   A. Payne, 'The Salisbury Roll of Arms c.1463', *England in the Fifteenth Century*, ed. D. Williams (Woodbridge, 1987), 197; see above p. 230.

ascendancy. Whether the riot occurred before or after 2 February and whether or not Warwick and Clarence were involved from the start has been much debated and is insoluble in the current state of the evidence. Certainly it caused King Edward to proceed on progress to Lincolnshire and enabled Sir Robert to play on popular fears about the king's intentions to enlist support. The Lincolnshire insurrection provided a focus for another many-sided rebellion, in which Warwick and Clarence intended deploying their West and North Midlanders, the men of Middleham and Lancashire. Warwick, it appears, counted for support on his brothers-in-law Stanley and FitzHugh.[12] He, Clarence and Clarence's friend Shrewsbury were to raise the West and North Midlands. Apparently Wales, Kent and Calais were not to be involved this time. Such multi-pronged uprisings were difficult to co-ordinate. What caused them to fail in this case was not merely Edward's fortunate interception of messengers and his decisive countermeasures, but Sir Robert's decision to fight ahead of meeting up with Warwick, the latter's difficulty in recruiting, and the unwillingness of the northerners to join him after his initial failure.[13]

Such factors nullified the success of the camouflage that initially concealed the real character and objectives of the uprising from the king. If Edward did not provoke the insurrection to expose Warwick, which seems incredible but true, we must accept that he did not recognize it for what it really was. Our principal sources give us the advantage of hindsight that contemporaries lacked. Whilst Edward knew of the Welles–Burgh feud, the actual uprising had the characteristics of the genuine popular rebellion with which he was familiar. Compared with his reaction to Robin of Redesdale the previous year, about which he was doubtless sensitive, Edward rather overinsured, going in person with many magnates and a large force. Doubtless he was relieved to accept assistance from Warwick and Clarence.

Most probably Warwick spent Christmas at Warwick, where he was on 16 January 1470, but he was at Westminster by the 20th, when he shared in the exoneration of the Duchess Jacquetta of sorcery.[14] In or before early March he returned to Warwick, where he was on the 10th, having agreed in advance to bring his retinue to join Edward at an agreed (but unknown) time and place.[15] Lord Welles meantime was at Hellowe (Lincs.), whence on 22 February he was summoned to London and pardoned on 6 March. Clarence meantime was in London, where he liaised with Welles and met up with the king (4–6 March), whose departure he thus delayed, whom he persuaded of his loyalty, and from whom he secured commissions of array against the Lincolnshire rebels for himself and Warwick. Unfortunately these covered only Warwickshire and Worcestershire, where even Warwick's retainers doubted his intentions, and

---

12 Hicks, *Clarence*, 55, 58–9.
13 'Chronicle of the Rebellion in Lincolnshire', ed. J. Nichols, *Camden Miscellany* i (1847), 6, 9, 11–12. The following account of the rebellion is based on ibid. *passim*; Hicks, *Clarence*, 52–61.
14 PSO 1/51/2360A; *RP* vi. 232.
15 PSO 1/51/2630A; 'Chron. Lincs.', 10.

thus neither Clarence's Tutbury estates nor Warwick's Yorkshire connection. The commissions secured, Clarence joined the earl at Warwick. As Edward's impressive entourage was more than a match for Welles's popular levies, their plan was to deter the king from attacking Welles's forces as they drifted westwards until he joined up with them near Leicester at which point, crucially, Edward could be surprised by Welles and themselves. They wrote both to Welles and to the king with this object in mind. But Edward learnt of Sir Robert's participation and threatened to execute his father, so that the former attacked on his own. Inevitably he was defeated at Empingham (Losecote Field) on 12 March. Once captured, he revealed the involvement of duke and earl, which, if the *Lincolnshire Chronicle* is to be believed, had already been revealed by cries of 'À Clarence! À Clarence! À Warrewik!', by the participation of men in Clarence's livery, and by the discovery of a casket of incriminating papers 'redy to be shewed'. The king's instruction next day to Warwick and Clarence to disband and come to him 'with convenient nombre for thaire astates' was thus designed to bring them into his power rather than indicating the naive ignorance of their role depicted in the *Chronicle*.

Still too weak to fight on their own and indeed still at Coventry, Warwick and Clarence promised to do as he asked, but proceeded instead via Burton-on-Trent and Derby, through Clarence's Tutbury and Duffield estates, to Warwick's town of Chesterfield and Shrewsbury's Sheffield, recruiting all the time and intending to join up with Warwick's North Yorkshiremen. Though they sent [John] Rufford and Henry Wrottesley to assure the king of their loyal intentions, Edward sent them a sterner summons on 17 March on pain of their allegiance and threatened military action against them. Recording their illegal recruitment, 'noo mencion made of us', which he was inclined to forget, he wrote of activities 'contrarie to naturall kyndenes and dutie of allegiance . . . of grete poise' committed against him.

> And that is to calle you to your declaracion on the same, and to receyve you therunto, if ye wolle com as fittethe a liege man to com to his soveraigne lorde in humble wise. And if ye soo doo, indifference and equite shall [be] by us remembred, and soo as no resonable man goodly disposed shall mowe thinke but that we shall entrete you according to your nyghenes of oure blood and oure lawez.

They might bring fitting escorts to put their case and to receive their just deserts. In so far as Warwick and Clarence were prepared to temporize, they wanted safe conducts secured by mutual oaths – thus impugning the king's honesty and honour! – and pardons for their men. Securely ascendant, affronted by their dishonesty and presumption, and backed by his own council of war, Edward insisted on them submitting without preconditions. Whilst he wished them to have proved their innocence, yet should they be unable to do so, he would take account of their close kinship, 'his old love and affeccion' towards them, and temper 'rightwisseness with favour and pite'. No doubt Edward considered this as far as he could go. For Warwick and Clarence, execution and attainder remained possibilities which they would not risk. So deep had their distrust become! After looking first to the North-West, where Stanley and others declined to join a losing cause, they fled southwards: to Bristol; to Exeter (3 April), which they relieved from a siege by the Courtenays of Bocannoc; and to Clarence's town of Dartmouth (9 April), whence many of Warwick's shipmen came. There they embarked for exile.[16] Edward had won: in the short term.

When Warwick turned northwards, he still intended to fight. When he turned southwards, he knew that he would not be strong enough and already had flight overseas in mind. He chose not to make a stand at Warwick, where he would have been starved out, he declined to raise Wales, and neither he nor Clarence were particularly strong in the far west. Rumours that Clarence was to proceed to Ireland proved groundless. Their flight was not precipitate, but deliberate. Warwick was accompanied by his artillery as far as Bristol. He picked up his countess and daughter on the way. Flight was not his sole thought. Already, it appears, Warwick was planning to repeat his success of 1459–60, to retire to Calais, mobilize his fleet and diplomatic contacts, with a view to future invasions or more probably negotiation from strength. Edward, his fellow rebel of a decade earlier, realized this and was able to send his own agents to thwart the earl both at Calais and at Southampton. But he was unable to deny Warwick his fleet or his diplomatic contacts, and in England the earl's bastard feudal connection remained almost intact. Among over sixty partisans whose arrest Edward ordered, most of them Clarence's or Welles's men, a mere handful were Warwick's adherents. Among them were his three councillors Sir Walter Wrottesley, Sir Edward Grey and Sir Geoffrey Gate; the Midlanders Thomas Stafford of Grafton and Richard Clapham; the northerners Robert Strangways, John Conyers, two Huddlestons and three Otters.[17] The rest remained untouched. Whilst Edward was constitutionally correct in his summonses to Warwick and had good cause to doubt whether the earl could ever be trusted again, he was unwise to be so unyielding. At this juncture, might not Warwick have given up even the wardenship of the West March, captaincy of Calais, and the keeping of the seas for life and lands? Instead he was to demonstrate again just how dangerous he was.

10.2   Warwick as Kingmaker

In 1470 Warwick had no need to borrow to buy a balinger. His departure from Dartmouth was more deliberate. He took several ships and quickly added numerous prizes. If his followers were few, at the least they ran into scores and perhaps into hundreds. His plan seems to have been the same as in 1459: to retrieve his fleet, base himself in Calais, and launch an invasion from there on England, presumably through Kent. Unfortunately Edward's memories of that

16   'Chron. Lincs.', 13–15; Hicks, *Clarence*, 52–61; Holland, 854–61; Goodman, *Wars of the Roses*, 73.
17   *CPR 1467–77*, 218.

earlier triumph reminded him how to frustrate any repetition. He denied Warwick the breathing space of a decade earlier. Edward prepared seaward defences, ordered the seizure of Warwick's ships, and sent orders to the Cinque Ports, Calais and Southampton to oppose the earl. One of his agents wiped out the humiliations suffered on that previous occasion. Warwick deputed his councillor Sir Geoffrey Gate, formerly governor of the Isle of Wight, to remove the earl's own ship the *Trinity* from Southampton. Anthony Earl Rivers was ready for him. The cutting-out party was more than repelled. Gate lost ships, men, and his own liberty. More than twenty captives were tried as traitors and condemned to death by the Earl of Worcester as Lord Constable, of whom Richard Clapham and some lesser men were executed. At Worcester's initiative, they were also impaled. Gate himself was spared. Moving on to Calais with about thirty ships, Warwick found not only that Edward's messenger had preceded him, but that the marshal, Lord Duras, already an exile from his original Gascon homeland, was determined to obey Edward's orders. Calais Castle may have adhered to Warwick. The earl was driven away by gunfire and his first grandson was born and died at sea. Even though Wenlock was more sympathetic, sending wine out to the duchess, Warwick could not gain admittance. Soon after he was joined by his nephew Thomas Neville, bastard of his late uncle Fauconberg, who commanded some of the earl's own ships and was joint commander of Edward's fleet. They preyed on neutral shipping, whether Spanish, Dutch, English or Hanseatic, and on 20 April captured about forty Burgundian and some Breton merchantmen. 'In the memory of man, the people of the Low Countries had never suffered such a disaster from pirates.' Some of these were subsequently lost to Edward's other commander Lord Howard and another fourteen to Rivers and Hans Voetken in a lively conflict in which 500–600 mariners were slain. Vanquished once again, if yet unbowed, Warwick took refuge with eighty ships about 1 May in the Seine estuary at Honfleur and Harfleur.[18] From this nadir, Warwick was to return in triumph, as Kingmaker to Henry VI, who resumed his reign or Readeption from Michaelmas (29 September) 1470.

What were Warwick's intentions after these setbacks? Doubtless they were the same as a decade before, the obvious precedent, when Calais had been the impregnable base where he had awaited the right moment. Piracy kept his men occupied and raised their spirits, kept them supplied, and provided the rewards they expected. It was a reversion to his youth when his maritime exploits had made his name internationally feared. If piracy was a necessity at this juncture, it was also a short-term expedient. His fleet alone was not going to win back what he had lost. Few if any were great ships of the forecastle. Without Calais, he had no base, without which no ships could survive for long. That could only be provided by Ireland or France. Clarence was lieutenant of Ireland, which was under consideration as a refuge on 18 April,[19] but was rejected. France was more promising: in the event, Normandy was to fill the role of Calais in 1459–60. In

---

18   Scofield i. 519 20; *Hansisches Urkundenbuch*, ed. W. Stein (Leipzig, 1899–1907), 663n; C. de la Roncière, *Histoire de la Marine Française*, ii (1900), 340.
19   Calmette and Perinelle, 311–12.

1470 France was at peace with England and Burgundy. Warwick's future depended on changing that. Therefore he needed to exploit his one asset, seapower, in the exercise of which he had no rival, to secure what he did want: restoration to his lands and influence in England and even the overthrow of Edward IV.

Warwick's maritime exploits exerted military, political and diplomatic pressure on the three principal northern states: England, France and Burgundy. He forced King Edward to keep his own fleet in being at considerable cost and might have forced him to treat, though actually Edward obdurately declined to negotiate from strength. He provoked Edward's ally Charles the Bold, whose subjects suffered most from his depredations. Charles considered his brother-in-law was dangerously underestimating Warwick. When Edward sought to reinforce Calais in July, which the incumbent garrisons prevented, and appointed Rivers as governor over Wenlock's head (11 June), it was Charles who intervened, granting a pension to Wenlock and securing oaths of allegiance from him and the garrison. Charles appreciated that Calais was not really secure, realized Warwick's potential for destabilizing relations with France, and recognized the continuing threat that he posed to Edward.[20] Hence he raised a fleet which he despatched against Warwick and exerted diplomatic pressure on France. Piracy was Warwick's route to break the amity between Burgundy and France, which had to be done if he was to return to England. Always unfriendly towards Charles the Bold and committed in the long term to his destruction, it was Louis XI alone who could shelter Warwick from storms and the Burgundian fleet and mobilize the resources necessary for a new invasion of England. By taking refuge in France, Warwick offered alluring possibilities to Louis, who harboured him, and thus raised the tensions between France and Burgundy. It was as an instrument against Burgundy that Louis backed Warwick's invasion of England.

Perhaps Warwick saw and planned this far ahead during the three weeks between his embarkation from England and arrival in France. We cannot easily tell, since we have only the largely retrospective observations of contemporaries from which to deduce. What is clear from the moment that he arrived in France is that he perceived the need to cajole, persuade and even coerce Louis if he was to obtain what he wanted. There were three preliminary objectives to be achieved. First of all, Warwick must be allowed to remain in France; he must be neither expelled nor surrendered; nor must he be merely harboured in internal exile as Queen Margaret of Anjou had been. Secondly, he needed Louis to commit himself to a full-scale invasion of England. Warwick was looking at reconquest, not mere revictualling and despatch as an irritant against England like so many puny Lancastrian flotillas in the past and like Oxford in 1472–3. That meant that he must resist being secreted where he was less embarrassing to Louis, that Louis must receive him in public, that tensions with Burgundy must

---

20 Scofield, i. 520–1; Vaesen, *Lettres de Louis XI*, iv. 350–1; G. Chastellain, *Oeuvres*, ed. K. de Lettenhove (Brussels 1863–5), v. 458; Commines, *Mémoires*, ed. Calmette and Durville, 197.

be fanned, and that adequate resources must be extracted from the French. And thirdly, since Louis was no charity, Warwick needed to demonstrate that he was worth backing and had better prospects of success than before. That was where his alliance with the Lancastrians fitted in, an alliance of 'alluring possibilities' that appealed to the universal spider that was Louis XI. Warwick achieved all these ends and Louis too fulfilled his wildest dreams, yet it was not the most harmonious of alliances. Obstacles posed by Louis himself were amongst the most important to be overcome.

Louis's jubilation on 3 April at Warwick's rumoured victory[21] understandably gave way to disappointment and a lack of confidence in the earl. Nevertheless, albeit unwillingly, Louis allowed Warwick to stay at Honfleur, rather than expelling him at once, as Duke Charles demanded as early as 5 May. Warwick's depredations on Burgundian shipping had shown him to be Charles's enemy and hence Louis's too; to harbour him was to breach the treaty of Peronne. So, too, the duke wrote to the Parlement of Paris, to bring extra pressure on Louis, and followed it up with numerous further protests throughout the summer. By their deeds and words Warwick and Clarence declared themselves to be his enemies, the duke wrote on 25 May, noting that despite Louis's promises three Burgundian ships remained to be returned. Other French notables objected, such as Queen Elizabeth Wydeville's uncle the count of St Pol, who was also constable of France. So moreover did Duke Francis II of Brittany, who had agreed a treaty of mutual assistance with Burgundy only on 19 April and whom Louis feared the most. Chastellain was not alone in denouncing the exiles as ancient enemies of France, plunderers without shame, traitors, cowards and without honour.[22]

Anticipating this reaction, Louis had told Warwick right at the start (12 May) that he could not receive him. Warwick must remove himself from Burgundian eyes, to the Channel Isles, where he had been lord, whence he could visit Cherbourg or Granvelle on the Cotentin peninsula under pretence of revictualling. A secret meeting with Louis could then be arranged. Warwick declined to entertain this dangerous proposal, which would have reduced his nuisance value and political leverage and removed him also from Louis's vision. He stayed where he was. By 19 May Louis had, reluctantly, conceded that point, but still wanted the fugitives to move to other ports. Some of the ships and men did indeed move to Barfleur in the Cotentin on 29 June, when the admiral of France himself was about to go there to oversee arrangements. This may have been when the English fleet was required elsewhere to counter a Hanseatic threat, but en route ten vessels were nevertheless lost. By 8 July Warwick himself was at nearby Valognes, where his wife and daughters were lodged. Following his stay at Angers on 24

21   *CSPM* i. 135–6.
22   Scofield, *Edward IV*, i. 522ff.; P. de Commines, *Mémoires*, ed. L. de Fresnoy (1747), iii. 121, 132–3; *CSPM* i. 136–7; U. Plancher, *Histoire Générale et Particulière de Bourgogne*, iv (1781), cclxi–cclxxxiii; BN MS 6977, f. 68-v, 73. For what follows, see Chastellain, *Oeuvres*, v. 463.

July/4 August with Louis and Margaret, the earl remained continuously in the Cotentin, at Carentan, Valognes and Barfleur, until he sailed from La Hogue on 9 September.[23] At Honfleur there remained at least some ships, certainly including that of the admiral of France.

Louis found Warwick's presence embarrassing and wanted it to be a purely temporary interlude. As early as 17 May, so the Milanese ambassador reported, Louis was urging Warwick 'by every means in his power' to embark for England. He had sent offers of warships and troops. 'Accordingly it is believed that he will return soon.' . . .[24] Many of Louis's letters to his principal agent Jean de Bourré Sieur Duplessis press the necessity for Warwick's speedy departure. Thus on 22 June he asked Bourré to put it to Warwick gently, as in his own interests. How could it be? To this Warwick presumably responded that he could not go until he had agreed the treaty with Queen Margaret and seen their offspring married, since on 3 July, when they were expected to meet at Le Mans, Louis thought that this would remove any justification for further delays. Louis saw Warwick's reply as a pretext, which it may have become in part. Originally Warwick had planned to be in England by early August and was eventually prepared to manage without Margaret if no agreement could be reached, but he also wanted to prepare an expedition capable of conquering England whereas Louis, as he confided to Bourré on 22 June, saw it as a distraction for Edward.[25] Why waste money, time and foreign policy on something that was going to fail?

Warwick's very presence committed Louis more than he wished. The king did receive the Countess of Warwick and her daughters and was genuinely concerned about their safety. He was also obliged to deploy his own forces, two great ships, and build fortifications to protect the earl's squadron.[26] From the start Warwick used the Seine as a base for further piracy: the Bastard of Fauconberg seized a further fifteen or sixteen Dutch ships; even a carvel of the admiral of France, one of Louis's intermediaries, was used on 23 May to cries of 'À Warwick! À Warwick!' to raid the Burgundian base at Sluys, where yet another ship was destroyed.[27] Though Louis did have some ships handed back and offered compensation for others, he was apparently powerless to prevent further seizures or the sale of the prizes and their cargoes in France.[28] Not surprisingly, since the aim was to inflame Franco-Burgundian relations. Such provocation caused Duke Charles on 11 June to mobilize a large multi-national fleet including 6,000 troops commanded by the Lords Veere and Gruthuyse. After meeting up with Rivers's own English squadron, it raided Harfleur on 2 July and subsequently St Vaast-la-Hogue, destroying several vessels, before anchoring first to blockade the Seine

23   Scofield, i. 525–6; Vaesen, *Lettres de Louis XI*, iv. 110–14, 349–50; Roncière, *Marine Française*, 344; J. de Roye, *Journal*, ed. B. de Mandrot (Paris, 1894), i. 238–9.
24   *CSPM* i. 136.
25   Vaesen, *Lettres de Louis XI*, iv. 121–3, 128, 349; BN MS 6977, f. 173, 20486, 20490.
26   Vaesen, *Lettres de Louis XI*, iv. 112, 114.
27   Scofield, i. 526; Roncière, *Marine Française*, 341.
28   BN MSS 20490, f. 91; 6977, f. 26–v; 20485, f. 101; 20486, ff. 6, 8; Vaesen, *Lettres*, iv. 112; *CSPM* i. 140.

and then, from 29 August, Barfleur. There were English and Burgundian land-ings, on one occasion repelled by francs archers, to the war-cry 'Vive Bourgogne et Roi Edward!'[29] The reprisals Warwick had unleashed were apparently more than he could cope with without Louis's support; it is striking that unlike 1460 no raids were launched on the English coast! The ships that he had captured, though numerous, were probably small and/or mercantile rather than military and poorly provided with cannon, and his fellow exiles and Fauconberg's shipmen especially after casualties must have been stretched to crew them all. Charles had also seized all French goods within his dominions, it was reported on 20 July, when Louis intended not to reciprocate. Louis was trying to restrain Warwick's corsairs, whilst simultaneously preparing himself for war with Burgundy.[30] The king found himself propelled willy-nilly towards the war that Warwick wanted and which, only two months earlier, had been thought to be highly improbable. Gradually, however, it was the effective prosecution of such a war in the event of Warwick's success that became Louis's prime objective.

Another reason why Louis had wanted peace was allegedly because he had no money. He did not want to spend much on Warwick, but he allegedly promised 50,000 crowns (£10,416.66) about 17 May and *The Maner and Guyding* speaks of 66,000.[31] Whilst there are many references to payments, it is not clear whether they came out of this sum, though ultimately he was to spend much more, certainly more than he wished. Louis's surviving correspondence to Bourré stresses his determination to restrict payments and to curb what he regarded as Warwick's importunate demands, if necessary by such cheap stratagems as moving further away and lying about how much cash he had with him. Ironically Louis's prevarications may have delayed Warwick's departure and increased his costs. The requests that are recorded, however, seem reasonable and relate to expenses actually incurred, for artillery, horses, ships or pay. A largely illegible muster roll lists an impressive number of names. Warwick had 190 brigandines, 80 bows and 300 quivers at Rouen and another 400 bows and 1,000 quivers at Paris on 13 August. The receiver-general of Normandy supplied 200 lances and 2,000 crossbow cords and conveyed them from Rouen to Harfleur at a total cost of £68 18*s.* 4*d.* tournois. Warwick's requests from the Cotentin were supported by Louis's own officers, such as Tanguy de Chastel, who were on the spot and saw the need. They knew the king's concern to save money, but Warwick's seamen would mutiny, desert and certainly not fight if they were not paid. Warwick wrote briskly but persuasively to Bourré. He tried to speed payment by sending quittances in advance.[32] Remember that logistics were Warwick's forte. He was determined that the fleet should be properly equipped and manned and so, at Louis's expense and despite his wishes, it seems to have been. *The Maner*

29   Scofield, i. 526; Roncière, *Marine Française*, 344.
30   *CSPM* i. 136.
31   Ibid. i. 137; *Vale's Bk.* 218.
32   Calmette and Perinelle, 315–16; BN MSS 6977, f. 197-v; 20486, f. 26; 20487, f. 19; 20490, ff. 12, 52.

and Guyding speaks of 2,000 francs archers, but apart from the two great ships of the admiral and vice-admiral of France which accompanied the invasion, there is no other evidence to suggest that it was other than a purely English force.

Similarly on 12 May Louis could not meet Warwick openly, though he would meet him secretly at Mont St Michel on pilgrimage. By the 19th he was prepared to receive him at Vaujous near Tours, still secretly.[33] When Warwick and Clarence did visit him at Amboise on 8 June, their reception could not have been more public and welcoming. Not only did Louis send notables to meet them, advancing a distance towards them and introducing his queen, but he had lengthy discussions with them, visited them daily in their chambers, fêted and entertained them. On 12 June they departed to their ships. Warwick was still at Honfleur on 29 June.[34] The earl's subsequent stay with the king on 24 July/4 August at Angers was just as public. Warwick forced the king to make his commitment to the earl, the Lancastrian alliance and the invasion as binding as was possible for such a slippery schemer. Louis's international standing was involved and hence, too, inevitably his purse.

The alliance between Warwick and the Lancastrians was already envisaged on 12 May, when Louis reported that he had already sent for Queen Margaret and her son, the topic evidently broached, and on 17 May it was expected that the prince would accompany Warwick to England.[35] Probably it had been suggested by the earl, who certainly made no objections. Louis was enthusiastic, though still prepared for Warwick to go before any agreement was concluded. The notion had been floated several times before by the Lancastrians and was supported by them now. Perhaps this was what Margaret and her son Prince Edward had in mind in the letter they wrote from St Mihiel in Bar on 1 May in the light of Warwick's flight to the Hanseatic League at Lubeck seeking support against their mutual enemy King Edward IV. A memorandum in favour by Margaret's chancellor Fortescue arguing that the treaty be cemented by marrying her son Edward of Lancaster to Anne Neville may be their contribution to the treaty. The match is first mentioned on 2 June.[36] What Margaret had to offer was principally legitimacy – the legitimacy that Warwick and Clarence had so conspicuously lacked and which they placed first in their new proclamation. Henry VI was an anointed king of nearly fifty years' standing and the succession was assured by his son. The support of the Lancastrian exiles, though significant, and of Lancastrians in England, though important, was perhaps secondary. How many still remained after countless executions and a decade of Yorkist rule? Hence Jasper Tudor, Earl

33 Vaesen, *Lettres de Louis XI*, iv. 111, 113.
34 *CSPM* i. 138–9.
35 Ibid. i. 136.
36 Ibid. i. 138; *Hanserecesse von 1431–1476*, ed. G. von der Ropp, vi, 277–8. The memorandum in BN MS 6964, f. 27, printed in T. Fortescue, *Family of Fortescue* (1880), 80–2, is discussed in Hicks, *Clarence*, 65n, 68, and Gross, *Dissolution*, 75–9, at 79, which date it respectively to 1470 and 1468. Whilst obviously Fortescue composed the treatises over time, the reference to Warwick's daughter in the singular points decisively to a date after Isabel's marriage to Clarence in May 1469.

of Pembroke, half-brother of King Henry and still a power in Wales, was to sail with Warwick and was joined in his proclamation. What Warwick offered, of course, was his reputation, direction, experience, contacts, popularity, and the participation of his retainers and allies in England. And Louis as the third party possessed the resources to carry it through.

Though the advantages of the agreement were so obvious to all, it was not concluded at once. Not all the parties were together at the same time. Warwick and Louis may have hoped to settle it at Amboise early in June, but Margaret had still not set off from Lorraine on the 7th, when an urgent summons was sent to her, and she was not to arrive until 22 June.[37] She may have been considering other options. Warwick also may have had alternative plans, since there is a manifesto from him and Clarence that makes no mention of the Lancastrians and a rebellion was launched in Yorkshire ahead of any agreement. It seems that he hoped to be gone a month or more before he actually sailed. Queen Margaret, who had so much to give, wanted to assure herself of the benefits – a genuine and binding commitment from Warwick – and to minimize the risks. To avoid recriminations Louis settled the main terms with both parties, perhaps no easy task, before bringing them together at Angers, where queen and earl were reconciled immediately. If Margaret played hard to get, therefore, as stated in several quarters, it was probably earlier rather than, as depicted by Warwick's propaganda tract *The Maner and Guyding*, at Angers itself. This presents Margaret arguing against this alliance on three grounds: an alliance with him could alienate some of her supporters, which was probably true; Edward IV was offering the hand of Elizabeth of York to Edward of Lancaster, which is unsubstantiated and if true was tentative and left open such major issues as what would happen should Edward IV bear a son; and that she could conquer England from Lancastrian resources alone, which was frankly incredible. These arguments were designed, perhaps, to strengthen her hand in negotiations and to give her the high moral ground. So too was her assertion that she could not in honour pardon Warwick, which both Basin and Chastellain elaborated: she had suffered great injuries, many at Warwick's hands; the charge that she had conceived her son in adultery rankled most. Warwick was obliged to defend himself for his actions in 1459–61. Whilst admitting that he was prime mover in her sufferings, he claimed that he had acted under duress and 'that thereinne he had not donne but that a noble man outraged and dispeired oughte to have doone'. He was required to sue on bended knee to the queen, who condescended to pardon him, King Louis acting as surety, and was bound also to the most solemn oaths of allegiance taken on the true cross in Notre Dame cathedral at Angers. She and Louis also had oaths to take. *The Maner and Guyding* also depicts her refusing to marry her son to Anne Neville, thus making her compliance into a bigger concession.[38]

37   BN MS 6758, f. 44v; *CSPM* i. 139. For what follows, see *Vale's Bk.* 218–19.
38   T. Basin, *Histoire de Louis XI*, ed. C. Samaran, ii (Classiques 27, 1963), 16–18; Chastellain, *Oeuvres*, v. 467–8; see also *CSPM* i. 140; *Vale's Bk.* 217–18.

The Maner and Guyding portrays Warwick as the initiator of the treaty, who secured a good deal against the odds, and overriding an unreasonable queen; if his retainers were to follow him this time, it was important not to be seen as desperate, unprincipled and grasping at straws. Margaret, also, needed to show her supporters in France and at home that she had not given in too easily. Both parties needed as binding security for themselves and their followers as they could obtain. There were to be no recriminations: 'for the deedis passed nevur here aftir to make reproche'. Complete trust remained impossible. It was for this reason, apparently, because she was unwilling to consign her son to Warwick's care, that Margaret refused to allow him to join the invasion. Even Louis could not change her mind.[39] Whilst this was clearly disappointing to Warwick, who had counted on the prince's presence and had to explain away his absence, it was quite sensible. Prince Edward's death would spell the end of the Lancastrian cause and was a risk that need not be taken. Similarly the agreement that the Lancastrians struck with Louis guaranteed that in the event of failure they and indeed King Henry could return to France; not that Louis could be expected to honour such promises.

What Margaret may well have been 'right dificyle' about were the details: of government and restorations, what Warwick's men could keep and what they must give up, which were potentially explosive issues and which were set out 'in thappoyntemente', now lost.[40] Just as Warwick had left the main terms to Louis, so now, it seems, he took no action to protect the interests of his retainers. How could he protect them against the restitution of forfeited property to new-found Lancastrian allies? Perhaps he also failed to obtain all he had wanted for himself. On future government, *The Maner and Guyding* states that 'after the recovere of the reaume of Englande . . . [Warwick] holden and advouched for king and the prince for regente and gouvernour of the seid reaume'.[41] For historians such as the present author this has been interpreted as meaning that Warwick would rule in their name. Though an adult, Henry VI was not to be allowed to rule and Warwick did indeed become king's lieutenant.[42] But that is not actually what it says. Might it not mean merely that immediately after the reconquest Warwick would rule until such time as the prince arrived? As we shall see, the prince did indeed supersede Warwick as lieutenant. Fortescue's undated memorandum apparently spoke of Warwick living 'in security' and having 'the principal role in government of the kingdom', not necessarily the protectorship. The somewhat idealistic proposals by Fortescue forwarded to Warwick by Prince Edward envisage the king's power being restrained by a council of twenty-four including a mere four lords temporal;[43] no mention is made therein of a president, protector or lieutenant. If Warwick was unable to safeguard his adherents, it may be because he could not achieve rule himself. Perhaps the ambiguous sentence in

39   *CSPM* i. 139–41.
40   *Vale's Bk.* 215–18, *pace* ibid. 48.
41   Ibid. 217.
42   Hicks, *Clarence*, 68.
43   *Vale's Bk.* 222–5.

The Maner and Guyding was intended to suggest to his supporters more than he had actually achieved.

This was not a treaty between two principal parties, but three. King Louis, as honest broker and paymaster, maximized his own benefits, which earl and queen were desperate enough to concede. His course was smoothed by their honourable treatment: thus the young prince of Wales stood sponsor to Louis's own son and heir the future Charles VIII at his christening on 30 June. The key element, an offensive alliance against Burgundy, was probably settled by 30 July, when a more limited entente was confirmed by Louis's brother Charles Duke of Guienne.[44] Even as Louis sought to appease the Burgundians' immediate grievances, the necessary price of peace should Warwick fail, he was reassuring Francis II of his good intentions towards Brittany and was planning the immediate attack by land and sea that he did indeed launch as soon as Warwick was successful. For Louis, Warwick's conquest of England became merely part of his struggle against Burgundy, albeit the crucial prerequisite.

For such a policy to succeed, the expedition had to be properly prepared, as Warwick perceived and Louis did not. Warwick was in no hurry. Ultimately he knew that Louis possessed the resources necessary and used the additional costs of delay to extract the necessary funds. He wanted to go when the time was ripe. That meant when his treaties with Margaret and Louis had been finalized and formalized. Whatever was proposed in May and roughed out in June and however soon he may originally have hoped to complete them, it was not until 22 July that Warwick and Margaret were formally accorded at Angers and 25 July that their offspring were betrothed in the cathedral; after that Warwick need not wait for the marriage which ran into short-term (but superable) problems of consanguinity.[45] The time was also ripe when it was safe to sail. That was not until 9 September. That a storm had scattered the Anglo-Burgundian blockaders was not mere luck, for no fifteenth-century fleet could remain at sea indefinitely, but it was nevertheless essential. A third necessity was that his allies in England had been primed to rebel as he invaded. They were prepared. It was more likely the continuing blockade and delays in finalizing the Lancastrian alliance rather than contrary winds that delayed the earl's departure beyond 'the appointed day' and caused the Richmondshire uprising led by Lord FitzHugh to occur prematurely and to be easily repressed. That 'appointed day', we may deduce, was before 5 August 1470,[46] probably late in July.

What had been achieved was a diplomatic revolution which duly delivered a dynastic revolution. Warwick could justifiably claim the principal credit and was certainly a principal beneficiary. He was to return to England, to be restored to

---

44   Basin, *Louis XI*, ii. 25–9; *Lettres de Rois, Reines et autres personnages des cours de France et d'Angleterre*, ed. J. Champollion-Figeac, ii (Paris, 1847), 488–91.

45   Scofield, i. 530n; Hicks, *Clarence*, 69–70. On 29 June Warwick was not prepared to leave prior to the marriage, Vaesen, *Lettres de Louis XI*, iv. 349–50.

46   A. J. Pollard, 'Lord FitzHugh's Rising in 1470', *BIHR* lii (1979), 170–5; Waurin, v. 607; Goodman, *Wars of the Roses*, 74. Pollard overlooked Waurin's reference which, however, wrongly states that [FitzHugh] was executed.

his titles, estates and offices, and was apparently to take command of a government committed to his own policies. His future was assured by the marriage
of his youngest daughter to the crown prince, who could be expected to make
her queen. Not that this was without cost. Warwick had to swallow his pride,
renounce his principal achievement in dethroning Henry VI, and publicly
apologize and submit to Queen Margaret. Though he had made a very
similar public commitment to King Edward only six months before, Warwick
was later to recognize this one as binding with fatal consequences for himself.[47]
He was never to experience Margaret's superiority in practice as she never
returned to reign in his lifetime. Lands unspecified would also have to be surrendered. These concessions pale beside the losses to be expected by his son-in-law
Clarence, who must renounce his immediate pretensions to the crown and
abandon his siblings, and those allies and retainers including Clarence who had
benefited from Lancastrian forfeitures. Understandably *The Maner and Guyding*
made no specific reference to these. Clarence was to have the duchy of York. If
he was recognized as heir in reversion to the crown failing Henry's issue, as
Warkworth says, nobody else thought it worthy of remark.[48] Warwick's restoration and favour at court, the principal gains to be anticipated, were less
substantial. It was their former enemies, the Lancastrians, who were to benefit.
In other areas, too, Warwick had focused on essentials and made concessions less
important to him. Neither he nor Louis bothered much with the commercial
treaty that Fortescue thought so important.[49] It was agreed to delay Prince
Edward's passage to England until after victory was achieved; he came too late.
A thirty-year alliance with France without abandoning the English claim to the
crown or possession of Calais may have been sensible, though Warwick wisely
concealed it from English eyes. His own proclamations made much of Edward's
dependence on foreigners. But it was Warwick's concession to Louis that war
with Burgundy should begin at once that precipitated Edward IV's own invasion.
If far from inevitable, the collapse of the new regime was foreshadowed in its
origins.

10.3   From Triumph to Disaster 1470–1

The success of the invasion was astonishing. Without any fighting, Henry VI was
re-placed on his throne and Edward IV himself was exiled. Seapower once again
gave Warwick the strategic initiative, supported this time by a range of support,
real and potential, that King Edward found baffling and against which he was
unable to guard. 'Seeing that almost all his partisans were deserting him and
joining up with his enemies', observed Thomas Basin, Edward 'could not tell
with certainty whom he must guard against' and 'judged it most opportune to

47   *The Arrivall*, 12.
48   *Vale's Bk.* 217–18; *Warkworth's Chron.* 10.
49   *Fortescue Family*, 82.
50   Basin, *Louis XI*, ii. 50–1.

take flight.' . . .[50] He could not distinguish his friends from his enemies. It was a supposed ally, Warwick's brother John Marquis Montagu, with troops recruited on Edward's behalf, whose defection was the decisive blow.

This was the supreme achievement of Warwick's life, though unintended. A gradual escalation carried him far beyond his objectives in 1469. To be a Kingmaker was a remarkable distinction, though one reluctantly attained and aspired to never.

A vital change in the autumn of 1470 from the spring was that Warwick could rely on his retainers. Not to support the earl's treason was very different from condoning his dispossession. Edward adamantly declined to treat. Worcester's executions and impalements may have offended contemporaries other than chroniclers. More important, the rebels' estates were seized as forfeit, the revenues paid to the crown, annuities granted out of them, and some new appointments were made, most notably to Lord Treasurer and Constable Worcester himself as lieutenant of Ireland in succession to Clarence, as Warwick chamberlain of the exchequer, and as weigher of Southampton. Worcester was conspicuously acquisitive. In the short run it appears that Edward was to use these forfeitures to re-endow the crown, as had been tried in 1459–61 and was to be again from 1478. Some disputed properties were conceded to loyal rivals, such as Barnard Castle (Dur.) to Bishop Bothe, 100-marks jointure in four of Clarence's manors to the Dowager-Countess of Wiltshire, and property of Sir Edward Grey and Sir George Vere to the Lisle coheirs. Hastings's brother Richard was allowed to become Baron Welles. George Neville of Abergavenny was again licensed to enter his Despenser inheritance. Notably missing from this list was Warwick's brother John Marquis Montagu, male heir of the Neville patrimony. Not only had he been deprived of the earldom of Northumberland in return for a marquisate and Courtenay lands of equal value in the far west, an exchange that he compared to a '[mag]pies nest', but he was apparently to be deprived of what he doubtless regarded as the hereditary expectations of himself and his son, his Neville patrimony.[51] Edward learnt from his error: in 1471 Clarence was granted admission to Warwick's lands immediately after his father-in-law's death. If Montagu's defection was therefore predictable, if unsuspected by the king, the invocation of Henry VI's authority gave a moral legitimacy to the earl's cause that had been lacking in the spring.

Warwick's Lincolnshire campaign had failed to achieve the coalition of interests and areas that had been so successful in 1460 and 1469. No use was made of the military and maritime resources of Calais and Kent, any genuinely popular support was confined to Lincolnshire itself, and his own retainers failed him. As in 1459, they doubted his loyalty. Without them, he could not exploit Edward's initial misdiagnosis of the uprising. Warwick's second campaign of 1470 remedied these deficiencies. Seapower enabled him to strike anywhere; his point of disembarkation was unpredictable. Moreover the substantial range of

---

51 *Warkworth's Chron.*, 4, 10–11; *CPR 1467–77*, 205, 207, 211; DURH 3/48/5; E 28/90/22d; PSO 1/34/1784, /1786; C 81/831/3069, /3071.

places where Warwick, Clarence and Oxford could look for support – Kent, Essex, south Wales, the West Midlands and the North – was complemented by others in the West Country, north Wales and Cheshire where Lancastrians such as Margaret herself, Pembroke, Somerset and Devon had been strong. Was there any district without concealed Lancastrians? After a decade of repression how could their numbers be gauged? The substantial size of the expeditionary force made it immune to immediate defeat from mere local levies. Add to this Warwick's appeal for popular support and Edward could only wait and see. Having guarded against obvious dangers, such as a landing in Kent or a renewed uprising in Yorkshire, it was sensible to wait at York and then Nottingham with his field army until the invasion had occurred and events clarified themselves.

There are some other indications of a carefully planned ideological offensive supplementing the meticulous preparations in France. Four surviving manifestos, copies of which ended up in London, were tailored to different audiences. Others are implied or can be deduced. If there were verses too, none survive. Such preparation was essential to explain the extraordinary speed and scale of Warwick's recruitment on landing.

Even before agreement with Margaret and the invasion itself, the exiles appealed for popular support. Their letter 'to the commones of Englande' could date from before the treaty of Angers; it makes no reference to King Henry. It resembles earlier manifestos of 1459, 1460 and 1469, but does not derive directly from them; most probably because the exiles had no copies to hand. It was posted on the standard in Cheapside, on London Bridge and churches in London, and elsewhere in England. It was another loyal manifesto that sought to exploit popular disillusionment with the government. Warwick and Clarence protested at their disinheritance and estrangement 'from the londe and naturall place of our births' (though Clarence was born in Dublin), not because of their own faults, but 'for the trewe hertis, tendir zelis, lovis and affeccions that God knoweth we have evur borne and entende tafore all thinges erthly to the wele of the crowne and thavauncyng of the commen weele of Englonde and for reproving of falsehod and oppression of the poore peopull'. . . . King Edward was not held personally responsible. There is no hint here of deposition. Remember that if Clarence was to have supplanted him earlier in the year, the rebels never went public; only the king proclaimed it. The culprits were once again the king's favourites, this time unnamed, again 'such certeyne coveitous and sedicious personnes . . . about thastate roiall of the reaume', who were out for their own benefit 'to the grete hurte, enpoverisshing and the utter destruccion of you'. The realm, moreover, was to be alienated to and governed by 'strangeres and outewarde nacions', by which was evidently meant the Wydevilles' Burgundian kin: an issue surely current, if at all, only in the mercantile and shipping circles of London and the Cinque Ports? Taking a stand on 'olde custumes' against 'new lawes' and committing themselves to the crown and commonwealth, the two magnates pledged themselves in the name of God, the Virgin, and St George to chastise the evil councillors, restore justice and end the 'thraldome of outewarde nacions'. Lord Mayor Lee reportedly tore down such bills to prevent them being 'openly knowne ner seen to the commones', not wholly successfully.[52]

There are no surviving examples of specifically Lancastrian letters sent to particular Lancastrians or of the correspondence of Warwick with his connection, who assured him of their support.[53] We do however possess in *The Maner and Guyding* a treatise from Warwick to those existing supporters of himself, Clarence and Oxford for whom his future, that of his daughter, and their own futures counted for more than dynastic principle. Reading between the lines, they were as concerned about their own pardons for creating the Yorkist regime, their own access to royal favour, and their tenure of Lancastrian forfeitures as Warwick was himself. It dates from between 4 August, 'which day he departed from Aungiers', and his embarkation on 9 September, for it refers to actions that Warwick 'yit dotthe'. Presumably it was sent to inform and reassure either ahead of the invasion or actually at the time. It presents the treaty of Angers as the fulfilment of Warwick's objectives. Henry VI was to be restored, Edward having been silently supplanted. Warwick himself was to rule, his position much strengthened by alliance with King Henry, and guaranteed by the match between their children. His followers were reassured by Margaret's pardon to the earl, sealed by her most solemn oath, and by her acceptance of the earl as a faithful liegeman. Clarence and Warwick were to retain their lands. King Louis features as honest broker, surety and supplier of ships, money and men. Whilst the latter were welcome, Warwick was conducting an *English* invasion.[54] To an English audience to be enflamed by Edward's dependence on the Burgundians, it would have been counterproductive to mention the invaders' own commitments to King Louis, the subservience of their foreign policy to the French, and the silent abandonment of the English claim to France.

A second rebel manifesto followed the treaty of Angers. It is quite different. It said little specific about the 'great mischevus, oppressions and . . . inordinat abusiones' and promises no specific reforms beyond 'perpetuell peax and prosperite and commone weele'. Nothing was said of evil councillors, though capital enemies were to be punished. The focus was dynastic. The first and longest of the three articles concentrated on the legitimacy of Henry VI as king compared with 'his grete rebell and enemye Edward, late erle of Marche' and hence of his 'verrey trewe feithfull cousines, subgiettes and liegemen' Clarence, Pembroke, Warwick and Oxford by authority delegated by Queen Margaret and Prince Edward. What Lancastrians wanted to hear could also appeal to the erstwhile Yorkists covered by the general pardon in clause 2 for past offences against King Henry. The chronicler Warkworth reports the support of 'the more parte of peple', who had grudged 'bycause of his fals lordes and nevere of hym', and were disillusioned with Edward's failure to deliver 'grete prosperite and reste'.[55]

52   *Vale's Bk.* 218–19.
53   Ibid. 218.
54   Ibid. 215–18.
55   Ibid. 220–1; *Warkworth's Chron.* 51.

Clause 3 summoned all the king's new subjects to assist in his restoration on pain of forfeiture. Most probably it was after the invasion had landed and to avoid alienating local people that four additional clauses regulated offences against the Church and women, violence among the troops and billeting.[56] There are also two protections for the sanctuaries of Westminster and St Martin's le Grand, where prominent Yorkists had taken refuge, and, on 26 October from Clarence alone, for Walter Lord Mountjoy.[57]

Warwick's multi-pronged strategy was again intended to surprise. A rising in Richmondshire was to be expected, but happened prematurely, so that it was suppressed ahead of the main invasion, though Edward IV understandably kept his eye on it. Once again there were rebels in Kent, who pillaged Southwark, but this time Warwick chose not to land there. Instead on 13 September he disembarked in the far west, at Exmouth, Dartmouth and Plymouth. The removal of Stafford of Southwick made for weak opposition. They recruited 'a grete peple' there,[58] perhaps of Courtenay of Bocannoc and Beaufort affiliations though aspirants to the duchy of Somerset and earldom of Devon were absent, and certainly of Lancastrian sympathies. They proceeded thence via Bristol, where they picked up the artillery and baggage Warwick had abandoned six months earlier,[59] through the heart of Warwick's West Midlands estates to Coventry, where, the *Coventry Leet Book* reports, they were 30,000 strong. Within three days, wrote Jean de Roye, he had 60,000 men-at-arms: even more than the 50,000 promised in *The Maner and Guyding*![60] Warwick's publicity and organization must have been excellent. Whilst doubtless exaggerating, this indicates an impressive force: as well as the invaders, West Countrymen, the Warwick connection, and probably Clarence's North Midlanders, they had been joined by Shrewsbury and Stanley,[61] presumably the Midlanders and men of Lancashire, Cheshire and Derbyshire, where their principal estates lay. King Edward at Nottingham, in contrast, recruited few, too few to risk a battle even ahead of Montagu's betrayal, as Warkworth, Basin, Waurin and Crowland all agree.[62] Given that the quality was probably low, it was as important for Warwick to deny Edward manpower as to recruit his own. With his brother Gloucester, Hastings, Howard, Say and Duras, Edward embarked from Kings Lynn on 29 September and arrived at The Hague on 11 October. On 6 October King Henry was ceremonially removed from the Tower to resume his reign: his second reign or Readeption, which however he dated from Michaelmas. Escorted principally by his veteran courtiers Waynflete and Sudeley, he was accompanied by Archbishop Neville, Clarence, the earls of Warwick and Shrewsbury, and

56   *Vale's Bk.* 221.
57   Ibid. 222; Ellis, *Original Letters*, ii.i. 139–40.
58   *Warkworth's Chron.* 10; see also 'muche pepull', *Coventry Leet Bk.* 358.
59   Roye, *Journal*, i. 245.
60   *Coventry Leet Bk.* 358–9; Roye, *Journal*, i. 245–6; *Vale's Bk.* 218.
61   Waurin, v. 611; *Coventry Leet Bk.* 359.
62   Ibid. 355–9; *Warkworth's Chron.* 11; *Crowland Continuations*, 121; Basin, *Louis XI*, ii. 50–1; Waurin, v. 611.

by Stanley;[63] Oxford arrived later and his half brother Pembroke was in Wales.

This was not a large turnout of noblemen and consisted predominantly of known supporters of Warwick and Clarence. Such prominent Lancastrians as Exeter and Devon returned only in February. A victory so rapid, complete and bloodless was as glorious as the Crowland continuator observed,[64] but it left Edward's supporters undefeated. Only Warwick's erstwhile brother-in-law Worcester, notorious as the bloodthirsty beheader and impaler of Lancastrians and of Clapham, was 'juged by such lawe as he dyde to other menne' by Oxford, son and brother of two former victims, and was duly executed.[65] A few obvious targets had taken sanctuary, such the queen, her mother and the chancellor, but most of Edward IV's nobility, household and county elites remained in place. They had been denied the chance to fight the invaders and now submitted. Parliament also did their bidding. But the new regime had constantly to work with people who constituted a considerable security problem. Like Warwick himself, King Edward had taken refuge with a friendly power, Burgundy, whence he and his small following hoped to return.

Though Henry was to reign, others were to rule, as envisaged even at Angers. Warwick as king's lieutenant dominated the political scene pending the return of Margaret and her son. Though often expected, from November onwards, the queen only arrived at Harfleur on 24 March and was then delayed for seventeen days by contrary winds. The capacity of her and Warwick to work together was never tested. Nor, indeed, does it seem likely that the conciliar control of patronage favoured by Sir John Fortescue was fully implemented, though certainly the council was active and Henry's initiative was confined to clerical appointments. Several warrants explicitly invoked the authority of Warwick alone or in conjunction with Clarence and the archbishop. Warwick received several minor favours, such as the presentation to a prebend at St Stephen's Chapel Westminster, but he also paid over a thousand pounds towards household expenses.

There was some genuine sharing of office. The great offices went primarily to Warwick's faction: Archbishop Neville was again chancellor and Langstrother again treasurer, as in 1469, but the keeper of the privy seal was Margaret's former chancellor John Hales Bishop of Lichfield and the secretary was Clarence's own servant Piers Courtenay. The household was dominated by two long-standing (and formerly attainted) Lancastrians in Sir Henry Lewis as governor, a new post, and Sir Richard Turnstall (chamberlain); Oxford was steward, the treasurer John Delves transferred from the same office in Clarence's own household, and the keeper of the wardrobe was the former London alderman and

---

63   *Warkworth's Chron.* 11; *Coventry Leet Bk.* 358–9; *English Historical Documents 1327–1485*, ed. A. R. Myers (1969), 306–7. For what follows, see Westminster Abbey MS 12183, f. 18.

64   *Crowland Continuations*, 123.

65   *Warkworth's Chron.* 13.

Lancastrian plotter Sir John Plummer.[66] Until the queen and prince returned, the regime was bound to appear a revival of the Neville rule rejected the previous autumn.

As early as 15 October a new parliament was summoned to meet at Westminster. There were to be two short sessions, 26 November–December 1470 and January/February 1471. Its task was obvious: to confirm the change of king and to settle the succession; to proscribe those who accompanied Edward into exile; to reverse the sentences against erstwhile Lancastrians; and to confirm the terms of the treaty of Angers. The outline has to be so bald because the parliament roll was destroyed by Edward IV on his return and very little can be known for certain. There is much now lost that we need to know. If there was a general reversal of attainders, as the chronicler Warkworth supposed,[67] a general dispossession of the lands and offices of the loyal Yorkists surely followed. At this point the cracks that the treaty of Angers papered over reappeared. If Warkworth is correct in stating that Clarence was recognized as heir in reversion should Prince Edward die, then it was at the expense of long-standing Beaufort and Holland claimants. Such a distant prospect mattered less than possession of the duchy of York, promised in *The Maner and Guyding*, a title which he never used and therefore probably failed to secure. He had to give up lands of the duchy of Lancaster, revested in the Lancastrian dynasty, including his principal seat of Tutbury (Staffs.), but retained Richmond against the king's own nephew at some political cost.[68] On the other hand, Henry Percy had committed no offence to justify dispossession of his earldom and estates in favour of Montagu who, indeed, lost his Courtenay compensation to the restored Courtenay Earl of Devon. Not everyone could be satisfied. Reversals of attainders, in whole or in part, revived old enmities and partly explain the divisions that emerged on Edward's return. Not only did Clarence decide his interests were best served by the restoration of Edward IV and of what he had previously had, but leading Lancastrians were to consider, mistakenly, their cause to be strengthened by Warwick's fall.[69]

Warwick also failed to win a lasting protectorate for himself. On 27 March 1471 Prince Edward himself was appointed the king's lieutenant.[70] This may always have been intended. It may however have been a desperate ploy to demonstrate that the new regime was more than their own faction, to appease Lancastrians, and to maximize their appeal to them. Unquestionably Warwick wanted the queen and prince over sooner; her absence was not his wish. When in Burgundy the dukes of Somerset and Exeter were unenthusiastic about Warwick;[71] when back in England in February 1471 it is not surprising that they questioned and resented the Angers settlement. Warwick really needed Margaret

66 Hicks, *Clarence*, 78; *CPR 1467–77*, 232, 244; Myers, *English Historical Documents*, 306.
67 *Warkworth's Chron.* 12–13.
68 Hicks, *Clarence*, 83–5.
69 *The Arrivall*, 23.
70 *Foedera*, v.ii. 194.
71 Scofield, i. 556, 562. Prince Edward apparently married Anne Neville at Amboise on

and her son if unity was to be maintained.

Security had to be high on the new regime's priorities. In its favour was a genuine popularity among the commons, of which there is evidence in the West Country, North and Kent. 'All contemporary sources emphasize that popular sympathy had swung to Warwick.'[72] This was acknowledged even by the Yorkist paean of triumph after Barnet and Tewkesbury:

Yett the pepull ben blynde, they will not understonde.
Stryve not with the pepull, ne the werkys of his honde,
And thanke hym hertelyn it pleaseth hym so to doo;
And lett us say, 'Good Lorde, ever thy will be doo.[73]

Hence perhaps the large numbers that turned out for Warwick in 1471. Apart from his own northerners and midlanders, most of whom probably turned out for him, he had only limited support among the nobility and gentry that did not grow. Chastellain reports on Edward's confidence that 'great part of the nobles of England, covertly and all the time, held him in favour'.[74] It is striking that Sir Henry Stafford, who sought favours from the new regime and was one of its royal family, nevertheless fought against it and that Sir James Harrington and Sir William Parre, two Cumbrians whom Edward had frightened into obedience in 1470, were to join him voluntarily in 1471.[75] Whatever their original affiliations, the ruling elite had participated for ten years in Yorkist rule and its favours, which were now to be withdrawn or curtailed. They may have felt a genuine distaste for the domination once again of the Neville faction. Though shipmen, Kentishmen and the London *canaille* apparently appreciated opportunities to pillage foreigners of all kinds, the Calais staplers and London elite enthused neither about a break with Burgundy nor closer commercial ties with France.

The Readeption relied on very few individuals and Warwick at times appeared a one-man band. 'The king was a subject there and ordered like a crowned calf,' Chastellain observed, admittedly with virulent exaggeration, but not without justice. 'And the subject was then the governor and dictator of the realm and did everything! Such government was there in London and not much better in Calais.'[76] Warwick dominated parliament and conducted foreign policy. He himself was to fetch Queen Margaret in person in December and late February. He was to command the army against Burgundy. As energetic as ever, in practice he lacked the time. When in Warwickshire in January, it was Clarence who took his place in London.[77] Both magnates resumed their former offices, leaving

72 Ross, *Edward IV*, 153–4.
73 Wright, *Political Poems*, ii. 272–3.
74 Chastellain, *Oeuvres*, v. 465.
75 Hicks, *Clarence*, 84–5; 'Chron. Lincs.', 15–16; *The Arrivall*, 7; see also Ross, *Edward IV*, 158.
76 Hicks, *Clarence*, 83; 'Chron. Lincs.', 14. Warwick was at Warwick on 17 Jan. 1471, E 404/74/22, 28/3 & 12/5/1482.
77 Chastellain, *Oeuvres*, v. 490.

nothing for their new allies.

Warwick was issuing protections and safe conducts as admiral and engaging in piracy and trade from the moment of his return. Having recovered possession of those ships seized by King Edward, he admitted the *Trinity, Margaret, Christopher* and *Elyne* into his fleet as early as 27 October; the *Katherine Warwick*, which followed on 10 December, unfortunately became a Dutch prize. The earl was paid £2,000 for an army of ships to fetch the queen on 17 December and was recruiting in the Cinque Ports for this on 21 January. Imagine how disastrous it would have been had she and her son been intercepted! The fleet maintained itself by piracy against foreigners of all types. The Bastard of Fauconberg, Warwick's overall captain, is recorded capturing Portuguese shipping. Such behaviour, whilst popular with the shipmen and helping to finance the fleet itself, was questionable in a government. In particular such depredations may explain why Hansard ships helped convey Edward to England, their nominal enemy, and how he slipped through the English blockade at a time when it was preoccupied by Breton and Hanseatic squadrons seeking reprisals.[78]

Warwick also reasserted his authority in Calais. Suddenly everyone was again wearing the ragged staff (*le rave-stoc*). He put in extra men by 8 October, increasing the crew (his personal guard) to 500.[79]

Warwick was appointed justice of the peace in every county. In December and January Montagu, once again warden of the East March, was commissioned to array the North; Clarence, Warwick, Oxford and Scrope of Bolton to array in East Anglia and the East Midlands; and Clarence, Pembroke and Warwick in Wales. How few magnates Warwick thought that he could trust! 'Never had commissions of array for defence been placed in the hands of so few'.[80] He was apparently unwilling to rely on Shrewsbury, Stanley and Devon. Another tactic was to remove suspect notables from their home country: thus Norfolk was removed from East Anglia and leading gentry were summoned then by writs of privy seal, some being incarcerated and bound under sureties.[81] This proved a highly effective countermeasure on Edward's landing; it contrasts with the complete ineffectiveness of Edward's defences in 1470. Terror and frightfulness also had their place. What holds were barred for the man who eliminated in Worcester his brother-in-law, long-standing patron, friend and ally, feoffee and executor? When Edward landed, relatively few noblemen and gentlemen joined him in the early stages; more were willing to back his claim to his duchy than to the crown. However much the Readeption enjoyed popular support, it had relatively little among the aristocracy. No wonder Warwick hesitated to commit

78   Scofield, i. 558–9, 564–5; Myers, *English Historical Documents*, 306; *CPR 1467–77*, 250; C 1/49/45; Maidstone, Centre for Kentish Studies, MS Sa/Ac1 m. 199; Ross, *Edward IV*, 161–1; see also Sa/Ac1 m. 199; Ross, *Edward IV*, 161–1; see also C. F. Richmond, 'Fauconberg's Kentish Rising of May 1471', *EHR* lxxxv (1970), 675–6.
79   Commines, *Mémoires*, ed. Dupont, iii. 271–2; Rainey, 'The Defense of Calais', 116n; Chastellain, *Oeuvres*, v. 488; see also *DKR* xlviii (1887), 448–9.
80   Ross, *Edward IV*, 157; *CPR 1467–77*, 251–2.
81   *The Arrivall*, 2.

everything to battle! It was better to be sure.

As Edward IV had found, the best way to secure a regime was not by defeating invaders or intercepting them at sea, but by denying them any refuge from which to launch attacks through treaties with neighbouring countries. Edward's obvious ally was his brother-in-law Charles the Bold, with whom he had taken refuge. Charles, however, wanted peace. His credence for Philippe de Commines on 8 October was to declare his love of England, illustrated by his marriage to Margaret of York, his desire for continuing trade, and his pleasure at the restoration of King Henry VI, since he himself was of Lancastrian descent. Four days later he protested to the English chancellor and council at reinforcements to Calais, which were unwarranted on security grounds and which he hoped were not for use against him in time of truce. He had no part in the quarrels of England, but merely wanted friendship, he wrote in his own hand and sealed with his oath of St George. Charles declined to meet Edward until December and never *publicly* committed himself to his return.[82] Charles was alarmed, of course, that French support for the invasion was directed against himself, as Louis certainly intended. The treaty of Angers had provided for a thirty-year Anglo–French truce and probably also a formal alliance.[83] Commines found that Louis had banned trade with Burgundy on 8 October. On 28 November Louis concluded a treaty with the young Prince Edward committing himself to war with Duke Charles until Burgundy was conquered, neither side being entitled to make peace without the other.[84]

This was the main objective of the mission Louis despatched to England with instructions dated 13 November. The five ambassadors were headed by Louis de Harcourt, Bishop of Bayeux, Tanguy de Chastel, and William Monypenny. They were to congratulate Henry VI on his restoration and to stress his debt to Warwick, in whom Louis had the greatest confidence: it was clearly in *his* interest that Warwick was in control! They were to point out the services the French had rendered to him and Louis's willingness to abide by the terms of Angers. Their real business was to conclude an aggressive alliance against Burgundy in which neither side was to make peace until it was conquered. They might treat about the partition of Charles's territories, offering Warwick himself Holland and Zeeland, and about expenses. Louis would attack the duchy and county of Burgundy. They were to offer a choice of strategies for the English army and to fix the day when fighting would commence. Delay was to be prevented, but they were to agree whatever Warwick wanted. They also sought details of Burgundian negotiations in breach of the treaty of Peronne, for it was on that basis on 6 December that Louis and the princes of the blood released themselves from the

82   Plancher, *Bourgogne*, iv. clxxxix; Commines, *Mémoires*, ed. Dupont, iii. 271–2; ed. Calmette and Durville, 208.
83   Vaesen, *Lettres de Louis XI*, iv. 123–5; Champollion-Figeac, *Lettres*, ii. 488–91; L. Visser-Fuchs, 'Edward IV's *Memoir on Paper* to Charles Duke of Burgundy: The So-called "Short Version of *The Arrivall*"', *NMS* xxxvi (1992), 168–70; see also the observation of Basin, *Louis XI*, i. 24–7.
84   Plancher, *Bourgogne*, cccii; Basin, *Louis XI*, ii. 24n–9.

terms of the treaty. War was declared on 4 January 1471. The ambassadors had to negotiate not only with Warwick, but also the English parliament, which would have to vote taxation for the war. They had a formal audience with King Henry on 19 December 1470.[85]

Although there was disquiet among the mercantile community, which Louis did his unsuccessful best to disarm, Monypenny reported favourable progress on 19 January 1471. Negotiations were almost complete on 6 February. Harcourt assured Louis that there would be no peace between England and King Edward and that a ten-year truce and unbreakable alliance against Burgundy had been agreed as he required. From other sources we know that negotiations for a permanent Anglo-French peace were approved. Today, the bishop wrote, Warwick has sent orders to Calais to start fighting on the agreed strategy: evidently the earl preferred to campaign separately. The fleet would put to sea by the stipulated day. A further 2,000–3,000 men would be despatched as reinforcements in 10–12 days and a further army of 8,000–10,000 would follow under Warwick's own command as soon as possible. 'Sire I promise you,' Warwick added in his own hand in a French postscript, that everything in this letter will be performed, 'for it is all that I desire.' A week later he wrote again, wishing Louis victory, and assuring him that the garrison of Calais had actually started fighting, advancing to Gravelines. 'As soon as I possibly can, I will come to you to serve you against this accursed Burgundian without any default, please God, to whom I pray to grant you all that your heart desires'.[86] *Accursed* was what Louis thought and wanted to hear; but Warwick's own disagreement and dislike for Charles, as for Rivers and Worcester before him, was also now extreme. Warwick was personally in control of foreign policy and was fulfilling personal undertakings to King Louis. To Louis his value was precisely that he acknowledged such obligations and carried them through, however herculean. The formal appointment of English ambassadors on 13 February was followed on the 16th by the conclusion of the truce and arrangement of a future conference on a final peace.[87]

Initially, at least, the fighting was small-scale, with only two of the garrison of Gravelines reported dead on 13 February and all fighting being confined to the immediate locality. Led by Sir John Benstead, forays were made against Marquise, Wymel, Harlow and Wissant (whose inhabitants sheltered in the church), and there was considerable expenditure on munitions. Money was being raised at Coventry for recruitment of a field army on 22 February.[88] Far from distracting attention from domestic problems, an aggressive war was likely to be a financial strain which the government could not sustain[89] and would remove

85 Waurin-Dupont, iii. 196–204; Commines, *Mémoires*, ed. Fresnoy, iii. 68–71, 154–5.
86 Calmette and Perinelle, 323–5; Scofield, i. 560–2; Myers, *Eng. Hist. Docs.*, 307, transl. from A. R. Myers, *Crown, Household, and Parliament in Fifteenth-Century England* (1985), 320.
87 *DKR* xlv (1884), 333; xlviii (1887), 448; C 76/144 m. 30.
88 Myers, *Crown, Household & Parliament*, 320; *Coventry Leet Bk.* 362; Rainey, 'Defense of Calais', 97, 103.
89 Ross, *Edward IV*, 159; Commines, *Mémoires*, ed. Calmette and Durville, 210.

from England those on whom the new regime most relied. Might it not be as unpopular as Edward's alternative? We cannot know how far the promises of manpower were honoured; Commines's estimate of 4,000 men is an exaggeration; Warwick himself was not able to cross and on 11 April, quite improperly, Louis agreed a truce with Burgundy.[90] An Anglo-French war against Burgundy compelled Charles from self-interest secretly to back Edward, which perhaps he always intended, in the hope at the least of diverting English attention and at the most of dislodging the new regime. This was on a much smaller scale than Louis' the previous year, but with as complete success. Whatever commitments Warwick and Margaret had given to Louis at Angers, it was contrary to English interests to fulfil them before their regime was secure. Nor was it in Louis's interests. Haste lost him everything. Whilst Warwick had long favoured an alliance with France rather than Burgundy, his sense of obligation and service to Louis and his hostility to Duke Charles now led him seriously astray. This war was therefore a major factor in his fall.

Although a mistaken foreign policy impelled Charles to assist in Edward's return and though the Readeption regime was itself divided, it does not follow at all that a counter-revolution was bound to succeed. Edward returned with only three ships and 1,000 men,[91] far less than the invaders of the previous year, and initially was ill-received. His was ultimately to be the victory of a better general with smaller forces over superior but divided enemies. Whatever the end result, the threat that he posed assisted Duke Charles by dislocating the Readeption government, which virtually ceased operating in March, and preventing English intervention abroad.

Successfully if inadvertently evading Warwick's fleet, Edward landed at Cromer, close to the Scales estate of Middleton, but was deterred by Oxford's defensive countermeasures and disembarked instead on 14 March at Ravenspur on the Yorkshire side of the Humber, where Montagu was in command. Warwick's Richmondshire retinue had proved too strong for the Percy Earl of Northumberland the previous August. There was no spontaneous outburst of support or hostility for the Readeption. That he landed in Percy country, having previously corresponded with Northumberland, meant in practice that the earl was able to restrain his Lancastrian-inclined followers rather than provide direct help. Fortunately Edward appeared willing to compromise. He would settle for the duchy of York, to which his title was unquestionable, rather than the crown. That ruse was popular. It secured him admission to York and recruits even from those who did not want him as king. It even impressed his enemies, so that Montagu at Pontefract could not persuade his men to attack and permitted Edward to pass by. Having evaded Montagu's northern forces, the king proceeded southwards, recruiting all the time, and arrived on 29 March at

90   BN MS 3887, f. 100; it is unlikely that England's military contribution was more than nominal.
91   Ross, *Edward IV*, 160n.
92   *The Arrivall*, 2–9; Visser-Fuchs, 'Edward IV's *Memoir*', 210–13.

Coventry.[92]

Warwick himself was at Warwick by 25 March, when he informed his retainer Henry Vernon of Edward's landing with a force of Flemings, Easterlings and Danes not exceeding 2,000 and of his inability to recruit from the country. Vernon was summoned to Coventry with as many men as he could make 'as my verray singuler trust is in you and I mowe doo thing to youre wele and worship herafter'. Though it did not work in this case, he remembered the personal touch in his postscript: 'Henry, I praye you fayle not now as ever I may do for you.'[93] It was therefore at Coventry that Warwick assembled his army, which may well have been swollen by those recruited for war against Burgundy, and he was still there on Edward's arrival. Basing himself at the earl's own town of Warwick, Edward offered battle on three consecutive days. Warwick, however, remained within the city walls.

Therein lay Warwick's undoing. He was not a coward as Edward supposedly thought,[94] but he was too cautious to be a successful field commander. If he was never in the position of 1470 where victory was assured, he was never to be so strongly placed again. Edward was unwilling to attack the earl in his preferred defensive position and Warwick refused to fight on equal terms. This was not stalemate, for it conceded to Edward the initiative both morally and militarily. The army that was available to Warwick, comprising only his northern and midland supporters, was nevertheless larger than Edward's. Was it not better to fight while he had that advantage than wait for reinforcements that might be countered by those of the king? But Warwick hoped to place the battle beyond doubt. He waited to be joined by Exeter, Beaumont and Oxford, whom Edward had out-pointed but not defeated at Newark. He was waiting also for Clarence, whose letters of encouragement reported his approach from the south-west. Once united, Warwick hoped to attack the king with their combined forces; ironically the duke defected to the king. Delay was to Warwick's advantage; though the king encamped at the earl's town of Warwick, presumably being excluded from the castle, his shortage of victuals meant that he could not remain. A manly man in chivalric parlance rather than devil-may-care, Warwick could live with the cheap aspersions of Yorkist propaganda. War was too important to leave to chance. If he was not sure to win, like Wellington, he would not fight. Challenged to battle again on 5 April, he again declined.[95]

Given all that had passed, it is surprising to find that negotiations occurred between the two parties at Coventry. Feelers were supposedly put out on the earl's behalf, which prompted Edward, anxious to avoid bloodshed, to offer the earl his life, the lives of his army, and 'dyvars othar fayre offars made hym, consythar his greet and haynows offenses'. This implies that Warwick was willing to abandon his Lancastrian allies and dishonour his promises of the previous year. Did Warwick foresee the conflicts within the Readeption outlined above and was he forestalling them by a further change of sides? Was his victory of the previous

93   *HMC Rutland*, i. 3–4.
94   *The Arrivall*, 9; Wright, *Political Poems*, ii. 273; Chastellain, *Oeuvres*, v. 465.
95   *The Arrivall*, 9–13.

year and the whole Readeption merely strengthening his hand in negotiations with King Edward? Invigorating though such speculation is, it rests on insecure foundations. Our sole authority is *The Arrivall*, Edward IV's own retrospective propaganda.[96] If such contacts did indeed occur, may it not be that Warwick offered Edward the duchy of York under King Henry VI? Further offers were made later at the instance of Clarence, who did not want his father-in-law destroyed, but these too were rejected: we may speculate, as *The Arrivall* does, whether this was because distrust ran too deep, because of the solemn engagements given to the Lancastrians, or for other reasons.[97]

Following Edward's departure from Coventry, Warwick may have hoped to catch him between his army and the walls of London, but he found his hold on the capital to be weaker than he had supposed. Far from holding the city or joining the earl, the Lancastrian Duke of Somerset and Earl of Devon left it on 8 April to meet Queen Margaret in the West Country: surely the most disastrous strategic error? The populace could not be relied upon in Warwick's absence. Hence Archbishop Neville, who was left to defend the city, proved unable to persuade the Londoners to keep King Edward out. He lacked the confidence in his brother to continue resistance and reached the best deal for himself with Edward that he could. He failed to withdraw King Henry to safety, either in the Tower or at Calais. When London was yielded into Edward's hands, so too was Henry VI. Warwick's failure to fight at Coventry deprived him of the military initiative, Clarence's defection passed it to King Edward, and the fall of London enabled the latter to defeat his enemies in detail.

Even at this juncture, Edward may have been weaker than the combined opposition but they could not unite. Throughout the 1471 campaign, Pembroke was in Wales and missed all the action. Warwick's Calais garrison and the Bastard of Fauconberg's shipmen could not be brought to bear until too late. The leading West Country Lancastrians, Somerset and Devon, made no attempt to join the earl, waiting instead for Queen Margaret and suffering separate defeat and death at Tewkesbury. Thus it was Warwick's army alone that Edward attacked on Easter morning, 14 April 1471, not far from Barnet in Hertfordshire. Advancing from London on the Saturday, Edward pushed back the earl's advance riders and dislodged an advance guard from Barnet itself. Probably Warwick's forces were still the larger. Again he ranged his army on the defensive, though his flanks could not be secured, and protected them with cannon. He planned again that his foes would destroy themselves attacking his guns as at Châtillon. His cannon were fired all night before the battle: ineffectively, because of the lie of the land. They gave away his precise dispositions. After such a night it is hard to understand the Crowland continuator's claim that Warwick sought to take Edward by surprise by an attack on Easter Day! It was Edward who attacked before dawn, when the poor visibility was to his advantage and contributed to confusion in his enemies' ranks. When Montagu turned his flank, his success was concealed from Edward's army and he came to blows instead with Oxford from his own side. It was a hard-

96 Ibid. 9.
97 Ibid. 12.

fought battle with many casualties.

Once the result was clear, Warwick attempted to escape on horseback, perhaps, as *The Arrivall* suggests elsewhere, hoping to escape to Calais and to fight another day. Had he survived, still popular and with his shipmen and garrison intact, he might yet have contrived a further transformation. This time he failed. Boxed into a wood from which there was no escape, he was slain. His body was stripped and robbed: his seal is in the British Library; perhaps it is his gold ring that belongs to Liverpool City Museums. If Edward sought to save him, it was surely for exemplary execution rather than any gentler motives. The bodies of Warwick and his brother Montagu, who was also slain, were displayed at St Paul's as proof that they were definitively dead.[98] There was to be no myth of his survival, no hopes of his return. He was still only forty-two years old.

---

98 *Hanserecesse*, ii. 416.

11

Terminus

Man proposes, oftimes in veyn,
But God disposes, the boke telleth pleyn.[1]

Edward's victory was God-given. It was also a surprise, as the ballad after Barnet, even before Tewkesbury, authentically records. Edward had won against the odds, in defiance of public opinion: 'Turn again, ye commons, & drede your king' was the refrain. Warwick had blown it. Warwick died not as a power-hungry and turbulent baron seeking only his own advancement, but representing public opinion. He stood for the expression of popular grievances and for a popular mood that was larger and more enduring than himself. He was still trusted by the commons to deliver the remedy. Warwick was the man in the ballad who proposed. In control and with the majority behind him, he had contrived to lose. However militarily brilliant in other contexts, Warwick was not Edward's equal on the field of battle.

Defeat did not make Warwick wrong. Edward's second reign, like his first, commenced with his victory over the majority. That Edward was to die peacefully in his bed twelve years later cannot conceal that ten weeks only were needed to overthrow his heir. The successful usurper attacked the record of Edward's second regime in terms reminiscent of 1469–70 and found a receptive chord. If Warwick was Richard III's model, as has been suggested, it was a recipe that worked because the problems of the 1450s and the 1460s remained unresolved, at least in the eyes of the commons. The Wars of the Roses did not end in 1471, still less on the battlefield of Barnet.

Edward's Barnet ballad is more than a celebration. It is an appeal, to unity, to allegiance. For 'right many wer and [still are] towardes him [Warwick], and for

---

1   Robbins, *Hist. Poems*, 226–7. This is the source of this section.

that entent returnyd and waged with hym', explains *The Arrivall*.[2] For the
commons and many others, there was no longer a cause to fight for:

> *Conuertimini* [Turn again], and leue your opinion,
> And sey *Credo* [I believe], hy woll noon other-wyse be;
> For he ys gon that louyd dyuision [obviously Warwick]
> *Mortuus est* [He is dead], ther can noman hym se. . . .

Return to your allegiance in the interests of reconciliation. It is God's will. That
was the ballad's message. Some listened. Some of Warwick's supporters did make
their peace after Barnet. Their loyalty was to Warwick, not Henry VI. Others did
not. Wenlock fought and died at Tewkesbury. Oxford was still at arms in 1473.
The Bastard of Fauconberg, Warwick's shipmen, Nicholas Faunt of Canterbury
and the Kentishmen fought on even after Tewkesbury and tried to carry London
with them. The Richmondshire connection considered a further uprising.

For Barnet was not the end of the Readeption. It was a stunning blow, but not
in itself conclusive. Another four weeks were to pass until the Lancastrian cause
was finally destroyed at Tewkesbury, where Warwick's second son-in-law Prince
Edward was slain. Henry VI died soon after and Margaret languished as a prisoner and exile for the rest of her days. Yet fourteen years on, it was Edward's
own dynasty that was supplanted.

> 'Allas!' may he syng that causyd all thys. . . .

Barnet ended Warwick's life. It was not the end of his line. It was his other
son-in-law Clarence, husband of his daughter Isabel, who was allowed to enter
her inheritance immediately after the battle. Clarence's son was to become earl
of Warwick and his daughter countess of Salisbury. Subsequently Warwick's
widowed daughter Anne remarried the king's other brother Richard Duke of
Gloucester. Warwick's ambition of ducal status for them was achieved; for Anne,
a crown followed. Nor was it the end of Warwick's retainers. They were a prize
that was coveted. When the two dukes divided his estates, they divided also his
connection, which they nurtured as the basis of their own power. Both followed
Warwick as overmighty subjects, and the younger, Richard, usurped the crown,
with the same disastrous consequences as Warwick's own kingmaking. It was his
northern, Neville, Middleham connection on which he relied as king. Barnet was
admittedly a disaster for Warwick's countess, who lost her husband, her inheritance and her independence. Whatever their rights, none of the junior house
of Neville – John's son George, later the Latimer and Bergavenny lines – were
ever to recover their northern patrimony.

Hume and Lytton were wrong. Warwick was not the last of the barons. There
were to be further overmighty subjects and idols of the multitude for whom he
may have been an inspiration. Warwick was also an innovator in many ways, some

2   *The Arrivall*, 21.

without a sequel. If no future magnate was to deploy seapower or to commit the Calais garrison in domestic power politics, it was because Warwick's example was remembered, feared, and guarded against. Others were to appeal directly to public opinion and to peddle public grievances as the cloak for their own private ends. Moreover Barnet was not the end of the Warwick legend. We have already remarked the admiring place surprisingly reserved for Warwick in so many subsequent histories. If never revived as the focus for future revolts or canonized, Warwick remains a household name: much more so than either of his kings.

Select Bibliography

(a)   Manuscript Sources

Bibliothèque Nationale, Paris, fonds français

Bodleian Library, Oxford
    Ashmole, Dugdale, Dodsworth, Lyell, Rawlinson MSS; Top Glouc.d.2

British Library, London
    Additional, Cotton, Harleian, Loan, Royal, Sloane MSS
    Additional, Cotton, Egerton Charters & Rolls, Lansdowne Charters

Corporation of London Record Office
    Journals 6, 7

Exeter, Devon Record Office
    Diocesan Records, Chanter MS 722

Maidstone, Centre for Kentish Studies
    MSS of corporations of New Romney and Sandwich

Public Records Office, London
    Chancery: early chancery proceedings (C 1); miscellanea (C 47); parliamentary and
        council proceedings (C 49); Charter Rolls (C 53); pardon rolls (C 67); treaty rolls
        (C 76), warrants for the great seal (C 81); inquisitions *post mortem* (C 139, C 140)

    Common Pleas: feet of fines, series 1 (CP 25(1)); de banco rolls (CP 40)

    Duchy of Lancaster: ministers' accounts (DL 29), chancery rolls (DL 37)

Exchequer, Treasury of Receipt: council and privy seal (E 28); receipt rolls (E 401); issue rolls (E 403); warrants for issue (E 404)

Exchequer, King's remembrancer: various accounts (E 101), particular customs accounts (E 122), inventories (E 154), memoranda rolls (E 159), miscellanea (E 163)

Exchequer, Lord Treasurer's Remembrancer: foreign accounts (E 364), memoranda rolls (E 368)

Exchequer, Augmentations Office: miscellaneous books (E 315); ancient deeds, series B (E 326)

King's Bench: ancient indictments (KB 9); coram rege rolls (KB 27); controlment rolls (KB 29)

Prerogative Court of Canterbury, Probate Registers: PROB 11.

Privy Seal Office, warrants for the privy seal, series 1 (PSO 1)

Special Collections: ancient correspondence (SC 1); court rolls (SC 2); ministers' accounts (SC 6); ancient petitions (SC 8); rentals and surveys, rolls (SC 11)

Warwickshire Record Office
Warwick Castle MSS
Coughton Court MSS (CR 1998)
Warwick College MSS (CR 26)

Worcestershire Record Office
Elmeley Castle Accounts

A fuller list is published in M. A. Hicks, *False, Fleeting, Perjur'd Clarence* (1st edn 1980), 248–55.

(b) Printed Primary Sources

Acts of Court of the Mercer's Company, ed. Lyell, L., and Watney, F. D., 1936.

'Accounts of the Rectory of Cardiff and some other Possessions of the Abbey of Tewkesbury in Glamorgan 1449–50', ed. Rees, W., *South Wales and Monmouth Record Society* ii, 1950.

Basin, T., *Histoire de Charles VII*, ed. Samaran, C., Paris, 1933–4; *Louis XI*, Paris, 1963.

Basin, T., *Histoire des règnes de Charles VII et Louis XI*, 4 vols, Société de l'Histoire de France, ed. Quicherat, J., Paris, 1855–9.

The Beauchamp Cartulary 1100–1268, ed. Mason, E., Pipe Roll Society new ser. xliii, 1980.

The Brut or the Chronicles of England, ed. Brie, F. W. D., ii, Early English Text Society original ser. cxxxvi, 1908.

Bulwer-Lytton, E. G. E. L., *The Last of the Barons* (3 vols, 1843).

Calendar of the Black and White Books of the Cinque Ports 1432–1955, ed. Hull, F., 1966.

Calendar of Charter Rolls, vi, *1427–1516*, 1927.

Calendar of the Close Rolls 1422–76 (8 vols, 1933–53).

Calendar of Documents relating to Scotland, ed. Bain, J., iv, Edinburgh, 1884.

Calendar of Entries in the Papal Registers relating to Great Britain and Ireland, 4 vols, ed. Bliss, W. H., and Twemlow, J. A., 1893–1957.

Calendar of the Fine Rolls 1422–71, 6 vols, 1935–49.

Calendar of the Patent Rolls 1422–77, 8 vols, 1897–1910.

Calendar of State Papers and Manuscripts relating to English Affairs existing in the Archives and Collections of Milan, i, ed. Hinds, A. B., 1913.

Calendar of State Papers and Manuscripts relating to English Affairs existing in the Archives and Collections of Venice, ed. Brown, R., 1864.

Calendarium Inquisitionum post mortem sive escaetarum, ed. Caley, J., and Bayley, J., Record Commission iv, 1828.

Cartae et alia munimenta quae ad Glamorgancie pertinent, ed. Clark, G. T., 5 vols, Cardiff, 1910.

The Cely Letters 1472–88, ed. Hanham, A., Early English Text Society, Oxford, 1975.

Chartier, J., *Chronique de Charles VII*, ed. Vallet de Viriville, A., Paris, 1858.

Chastellain, G. de, *Oeuvres*, ed. de Lettenhove, K., 8 vols, Académie Royale de Belgique, Brussels, 1863–5.

'Chronicle of the Rebellion in Lincolnshire', ed. Nichols, J., *Camden Miscellany* i, 1847.

Chronicles of the White Rose of York, ed. Giles, J. A., 1845.

Chatwin, P. B., 'Documents of "Warwick the Kingmaker" in the Possession of St Mary's Church, Warwick', *Transactions of the Birmingham Archaeological Society* lix, 1938.

'Chronicle of John Stone', ed. Searle, W. G., Cambridge Antiquarian Society, octavo ser. xxxiv, 1902.

Chronicles of London, ed. Kingsford, C. L., 1905.

Collection of Ordinances and Regulations for the Government of the Royal Household, Society of Antiquaries, 1790.

Commines, P. de, *Mémoires*, ed. Calmette, J., and Durville, G., Les Classiques de l'Histoire de France au moyen âge, Paris, 1924–5.

Commines, P. de, *Mémoires*, ed. Dupont, E. L. M. E., Société de l'Histoire de France, Paris, 1840–7.

Commines, P. de, *Mémoires*, ed. Fresnoy, L. de, Paris, 1747.

Commines, P. de, *Mémoires*, ed. Mandrot, B. de, 2 vols, Paris, 1901–3.

The Coronation of Elizabeth Woodville, ed. Smith, G., 1935.

Coventry Leet Book or Mayor's Register, ed. Harris, M. D., Early English Text Society original ser. 134–5. 138, 146, 1907–13.

The Crowland Chronicle Continuations 1459–86, ed. Pronay, N., and Cox, J. C., Gloucester, 1986.

'A Defence of the Proscription of the Yorkists', ed. Gilson, J. P., *English Historical Review* xxvi, 1911.

A Descriptive Catalogue of Ancient Deeds, 6 vols, 1890–1915.

A Descriptive Catalogue of the Berkeley Castle Manuscripts, ed. Jeayes, I. H., 1892.

Devon, F., *Issues of the Exchequer*, 1837.

Drucker, L., *Feet of Fines for Warwickshire*, Dugdale Society xviii, 1943.

Du Clercq, J., *Mémoires sur le règne de Philippe le Bon, Duc de Bourgogne*, ed. Reiffenberg, Brussels, 1835–6.

Dugdale, W., *Antiquities of Warwickshire*, ed. Thomas, W., 2 vols., 1730.

Dugdale, W., *Baronage of England*, 2 vols, 1675.

Dugdale, W., *Monasticon Anglicanum*, ed. Caley, J., and others, 1817–30.

An English Chronicle of the Reign of Richard II, Henry IV, Henry V, and Henry VI, ed. Davies, J. S., Camden Society lxiv, 1856.

English Historical Documents, iv, *1327–1485*, ed. Myers, A. R., 1969.

Escouchy, M. d', *Chronique*, ed. Beaucourt, G. du Fresne de, Paris, 1863–4.

Excerpta Historica, ed. Bentley, S., 1831.

The Fane Fragment of the 1461 Lords Journal, ed. Dunham, W. H., Yale, 1935.

Foedera, conventiones, literae et cujuscunque generis Acta Publica, ed. Rymer, T., v, vi, 1745.

Formulare Anglicanum, ed. Madox, T., London, 1702.

Fortescue, T., *The Family of Fortescue*, 1880.

Gascoigne, T., *Loci e Libro Veritatis*, ed. Rogers, J. E. T., Oxford, 1881.

The Great Chronicle of London, ed. Thomas, A. H., and Thornley, I. D., 1938.

The Great Red Book of Bristol, ed. Veale, E. W. W., 5 vols, Bristol Record Society, 1931–53.

Habington, T., *A Survey of Worcestershire*, ed. Amphlett, J., 2 vols, Worcestershire Historical Society ii, 1899.

Hall's Chronicle, ed. Ellis, H., 1809.

Handbook to the Maude Roll, ed. Wall, A., Auckland, 1919.

Hanserecesse von 1431–1476, ed. von der Ropp, G., Leipzig, 1888–92.

Hansisches Urkundenbuch, ed. Stein, W., viii–x, Leipzig, 1899–1907.

Hardyng, J., *Chronicle*, ed. Ellis, H., London, 1812.

'Historiae Croylandensis Continuatio', *Rerum Anglicarum Scriptores Veterum*, ed. Fulman, W., Oxford, 1684.

Historiae Dunelmensis Scriptores Tres, ed. Raine, J., Surtees Society ix, 1839.

Historical Manuscripts Commission *Reports*.

Historical Poems of the Fourteenth and Fifteenth Centuries, ed. Robbins, R. H., New York, 1959.

Historie of the Arrivall of Edward IV in England and the Finall Recouerye of his Kingdomes from Henry VI, ed. Bruce, J., Camden Society i, 1838.

Historical Collections of a Citizen of London, ed. Gairdner, J., Camden Society new ser. xvii, 1876.

Ingulph's Chronicle of the Abbey of Croyland, ed. Riley, H. T., 1854.

'John Benet's Chronicle for the Years 1400–62', ed. Harriss, G. L., and M. A., *Camden Miscellany* xxiv, 1972.

Leland, J., *De rebus brittanicis collectanea*, ed. Hearne, T., 6 vols, Oxford, 1770.

'A Letter from the "Kingmaker"', ed. Bloom, J. H., *Notes and Queries* 12th ser. v, 1919.

Letters and Papers illustrative of Richard III and Henry VI, ed. Gairdner, J., 2 vols, Rolls Series, 1861–3.

Letters and Papers illustrative of the Wars of the English in France during the Reign of King Henry VI, ed. Stevenson, J., 3 vols, Rolls Series, 1864.

Lettres de Louis XI, roi de France, ed. Vaesen, J., and Charavay, E., Paris, 1883–1909.

Lettres de Rois, Reines, et autres personnages des cours de France et de l'Angleterre, ed. Champollion-Figeac, J., 2 vols, Paris, 1847.

List of Sheriffs, Public Record Office Lists and Indexes ix.

Major, J., *Historia Maioris Britannia*, Lodoco Badia, 1521.

Major, J., *History of Greater Britain*, ed. Constable, A., Scottish Hist. Soc., 1892.

Marche, O. de la, *Mémoires*, ed. Beaune, H., and Arbaumont, J. d', 4 vols, Société de l'Histoire de France, 1883–8.

Marcher Lordships of South Wales, ed. Pugh, T. B., Cardiff, 1963.

Memorials of the Most Noble Order of the Garter, ed. Beltz, G. F., 1841.

Ministers' Accounts of the Warwickshire Estates of the Duke of Clarence 1479–80, ed. Hilton, R. H., Dugdale Soc. xxi, 1952.

Mirror for Magistrates, ed. Campbell, L. B., 1938.

Original Letters illustrative of English History, ed. Ellis, H., 11 vols in 3 ser., London, 1824–46.

The Paston Letters AD *1422–1509*, ed. Gairdner, J., 6 vols, London, 1904.

Paston Letters and Papers of the Fifteenth Century, ed. Davis, N., 2 vols, Oxford, 1971–6.

Plumpton Letters and Papers, ed. Kirby, J., Camden 5th ser. iv, 1997.

The Plumpton Correspondence, ed. Stapleton, T., Camden Society iv, 1839.

'Political Poems of the Reigns of Henry VI and Edward IV', ed. Madden, F., *Archaeologia* xxix, 1842.

Political Poems and Songs relating to English History, ed. Wright, T., ii, Rolls Series, London, 1861.

Politics in the Fifteenth Century: John Vale's Book, ed. Kekewich, M. L., Richmond, C. F., Sutton, A. F., Visser-Fuchs, L., and Watts, J. L., 1996.

The Priory of Hexham, ed. Raine, J., 2 vols, Surtees Society xliv, xlvi, 1864–5.

Proceedings and Ordinances of the Privy Council of England, ed. Nicolas, N. H., 6 vols, London, 1834–7.

The Pageant of Richard Beauchamp Earl of Warwick, ed. St John Hope, W. H., and Viscount Dillon, 1908.

'Private Indentures for Life Service in Peace and War', ed. Jones, M., and Walker, S., *Camden Miscellany* 5th ser. iii, 1994.

Register of the Most Noble Order of the Garter, ed. Anstis, J., 2 vols, London, 1724.

Register of Thomas Bekyngton, Bishop of Bath and Wells 1443–65, ed. Maxwell-Lyte, H. C., and Dawes, M. C. B., Somerset Record Society xlix, 1934.

Registrum Honoris de Richmond, ed. Gale, R., 1722.

Registrum Thome Bourgchier, 1454–86, ed. Du Boulay, F. R. H., Canterbury and York Society liv, 1955–7.

Reports of the Deputy Keepers of the Public Record Office xliv (1883); xlviii (1887).

Reports from the Lords Committees on the Dignity of a Peer, v, 1829.

Rolls of Parliament, ed. Strachey, J., and others, Record Commission, v, vi, 1777.

Rotuli Scotiae, ed. Macpherson, D., and others, 2 vols, Record Commission, 1814–19.

Rous, J., *The Rous Roll*, ed. Courthorpe, W. H., 1859.

Roye, J. de, *Journal*, ed. Mandrot, B. de, 2 vols, Paris, 1894–6.

Sir Christopher Hatton's Book of Seals, ed. Loyd, L. C. and Stenton, D. M., Northamptonshire Record Society xv, 1950.

Six Town Chronicles of England, ed. Flenley, R., Oxford, 1911.

Stonor Letters and Papers of the Fifteenth Century, ed. Kingsford, C. L., 2 vols, Camden 3rd ser., 1919; Camden Miscellany xiii, 1924.

Testamenta Eboracensia, ed. Raine, J., ii–iv, Surtees Society xxxx, xlv, lxxxix, 1855–69.

Testamenta Vetusta, ed. Nicolas, N. H., i, 1826.

Three Books of Polydore Vergil's English History, ed. Ellis, H., Camden Soc. xxxix, 1844.

Three Fifteenth Century Chronicles, ed. Gairdner, J., Camden Society n.s.xxviii, 1880.

Vergil, P., *Historia Angliae 1555*, repr. 1972.

Visser-Fuchs, L., 'Edward IV's *Memoire on Paper* to Charles, Duke of Burgundy: The so-called "Short Version of the *Arrivall*"', *Nottingham Medieval Studies* xxxvi, 1992.

Warkworth, J., *Chronicle of the First Thirteen Years of the Reign of King Edward IV*, ed. Halliwell, J. O., Camden Soc. vi, 1839.

Waurin, J. de, *Anchiennes Chroniques de l'engleterre*, ed. Dupont, E. L. M. E., Société de l'Histoire de France, Paris, 1858–63.

Waurin, J. de, *Recueil des Chroniques et anchiennes istoires de la Grant Bretaigne*, ed. Hardy, W., and E. L. C. P., Rolls Series v, 1891.

Whetehamstede, J., *Registrum*, ed. Riley, H. T., 2 vols, Rolls Series, 1872–3.

Worcestre, W., *Itineraries*, ed. Harvey, J. H., Oxford, 1969.

York City Chamberlains' Account Rolls, ed. Dobson, R. B., Surtees Society cxcii, 1980.

(c) Secondary Sources

Anderson, R. C., 'The Grace de Dieu of 1446–86', *English Historical Review* xxxiv, 1919.

Armstrong, C. A. J., *England, France and Burgundy*, London, 1983.

Arnold, C., 'Commission of the Peace for the West Riding of Yorkshire 1437–1509', *Property and Politics: Essays in Later Medieval English History*, ed. Pollard, A. J., Gloucester, 1984.

Baldwin, J. F., *The King's Council in England during the Middle Ages*, Oxford, 1913.

Barron, C. M., 'London and the Crown 1451–61', *The Crown and Local Communities in England and France in the Fifteenth Century*, ed. Highfield, J. R. L., and Jeffs, R. I., Gloucester, 1981.

Baskerville, G., 'A London Chronicle of 1460', *English Historical Review* xxviii, 1913.

Bean, J. M. W., *The Estates of the Percy Family 1416–1537*, 1958.

Bean, J. M. W., 'The Financial Position of Richard, Duke of York', *War and Government in the Middle Ages*, ed. Gillingham, J., and Holt, J. C., 1984.

Bean, J. M. W., *From Lord to Patron*, Manchester, 1989.

Beaucourt, G. du Fresne de, *Histoire de Charles VII*, 6 vols, Paris, 1881–91.

Bellamy, J. G., *The Law of Treason in England in the Later Middle Ages*, Cambridge, 1970.

Birch, W. de Gray, *History of Neath Abbey*, Neath, 1902.

Birch, W. de Gray, *History of Margam Abbey*, 1897.

Bittman, K., 'La campagne Lancastrienne de 1463', *Revue Belge de Philologie et d'Histoire* xxvi, 1948.

Blair, C. H. Hunter, 'Two Letters Patent for Hutton John, near Penrith, Cumberland', *Archaeologia Aeliana* 4th series xxxix, 1961.

Bolton, J. L., 'The City of London 1456–61', *London Journal* xii, 1986.

Brown, A. L., *The Governance of Late Medieval England 1272–1461*, 1989.

Brown, A. L., 'The Movements of the Earl of Warwick in the Summer of 1464 – A Correction', *English Historical Review* lxxxi, 1966.

Calmette, J., and Perinelle, G., *Louis XI et L'Angleterre*, Paris 1930.

Carpenter, M. C., 'The Duke of Clarence and the Midlands: A Study in the Interplay of Local and National Politics', *Midland History* xi, 1986.

Carpenter, M. C., 'The Beauchamp Affinity: A Study of Bastard Feudalism at Work', *English Historical Review* xcv, 1980.

Carpenter, M. C., *Locality and Polity: A Study of Warwickshire Landed Society 1401–99*, Cambridge, 1992.

Carpenter, M. C., 'Sir Thomas Malory and Fifteenth-Century Local Politics', *Bulletin of the Institute of Historical Research* liii, 1980.

Castor, H. R., 'New Evidence on the Grant of Duchy of Lancaster Office to Henry Beauchamp, Earl of Warwick, in 1444', *Historical Research* lxviii, 1995.

Castor, H. R., '"Walter Blount was gone to serve Traitours": The Sack of Elvaston and the Politics of the North Midlands in 1454', *Midland History* xix, 1994.

Chrimes, S. B., Ross, C. D., and Griffiths, R. A. (eds), *Fifteenth-century England, 1399–1509: Studies in Politics and Society*, Manchester, 1972.

Couper, H. S., 'Millom Castle and the Huddlestons', *Transactions of the Cumberland and Westmorland Archaeological Society* xxiv, 1924.

Dobson, R. B., *The Church and Society in the Medieval North of England*, London, 1996.

Dobson, R. B. (ed.), *The Church, Patronage and Politics in 15th-Century England*, Gloucester, 1984.

Dobson, R. B., *Durham Priory 1400–1450*, Cambridge, 1974.

Dockray, K. R., 'The Yorkshire Rebellions of 1469', *The Ricardian* 83, 1983.

Dunham, W. H., *Lord Hastings' Indentured Retainers 1461–83*, Transactions of the Connecticut Academy of Arts and Sciences, xxxix, New Haven, 1955.

Dunlop, A. I., *The Life and Times of James Kennedy, Bishop of St Andrews*, Edinburgh, 1950.

Dunning, R. W., 'Thomas, Lord Dacre and the West March towards Scotland, 1435', *Bulletin of the Institute of Historical Research* xliv, 1968.

Dyer, C., 'A Small Landowner in the Fifteenth Century', *Midland History*, i, 1972.

Edwards, A. J. G., 'The Manuscripts and Texts of the Second Version of John Hardyng's Chronicle', in *England in the Fifteenth Century*, ed. Williams, D., Woodbridge, 1987.

Emden, A. B., *A Biographical Register of the University of Cambridge to AD 1500*, Cambridge, 1963.

Emden, A. B., *A Biographical Register of the University of Oxford to AD 1500*, 3 vols, Oxford, 1957–9.

Ferguson, J. T., *English Diplomacy 1422–61*, Oxford, 1972.

Flemming, J. H., *England under the Lancastrians*, 1921.

Gairdner, J., *The Houses of Lancaster and York*, 1874.

Gibbs, V., et al., *Complete Peerage of England, Scotland, Ireland and the United Kingdom*, 13 vols, 1910–59.

Goodman, A., *The Wars of the Roses: Military Activity and English Society 1452–97*, 1981.

Gransden, A., *Historical Writing in England*, ii, 1982.

Gray, H. L., 'The Income Tax of 1436', *English Historical Review* xlviii, 1936.

Griffiths, R. A., *Conquerors and Conquered*, Cardiff, 1993.

Griffiths, R. A., 'Duke Richard of York's Intentions in 1450 and the Origins of the Wars of the Roses', *Journal of Medieval History* i, 1976; repr. in *King and Country*.

Griffiths, R. A., 'The Hazards of Civil War: The Case of the Mountford Family', *Midland History* v, 1981; repr. in *King and Country*.

Griffiths, R. A., *King and Country: England and Wales in the Fifteenth Century*, 1991.

Griffiths, R. A., 'The King's Council and the First Protectorate of the Duke of York 1450–4', *English Historical Review* xcix, 1984; repr. in *King and Country*.

Griffiths, R. A., 'Local Rivalries and National Politics: the Percies, the Nevilles and the Duke of Exeter, 1452–55', *Speculum* xliii (1968); repr. in *King and Country*.

Griffiths, R. A. (ed.), *Patronage, the Crown, and the Provinces in Later Medieval England*, Gloucester, 1981.

Griffiths, R. A. (ed.), *The Principality of Wales in the Later Middle Ages*, i, *South Wales 1277–1536*, Cardiff, 1972.

Griffiths, R. A., *The Reign of King Henry VI*, 1981.

Griffiths, R. A., 'The Sense of Dynasty in the Reign of Henry VI', *Patronage, Pedigree and Power in Late Medieval England*, ed. Ross, C. D., Gloucester, 1979; repr. in *King and Country*.

Griffiths, R. A., 'The Winchester Session of the 1449 Parliament: A Further Comment', *Huntington Library Quarterly* xlii, 1979; repr. in *King and Country*.

Gross, A., *The Dissolution of the Lancastrian Kingship*, Stamford, 1996.

Hammond, P. W., 'The Funeral of Richard Neville, Earl of Salisbury', *The Ricardian* 87, 1983.

Hammond, P. W., *The Battles of Barnet and Tewkesbury*, Gloucester, 1990.

Harriss, G. L., *Cardinal Beaufort: A Study of Lancastrian Ascendancy and Decline*, Oxford, 1988.

Harriss, G. L., 'Marmaduke Lumley and the Exchequer Crisis of 1446–9', *Aspects of Medieval Government and Society*, ed. Rowe, J. G., Toronto, 1986.

Harriss, G. L., 'The Struggle for Calais: An Aspect of the Rivalry of Lancaster and York', *English Historical Review* lxxv, 1960.

Harvey, I. M. W., *Jack Cade's Rebellion of 1450*, Oxford, 1991.

Head, C., 'Pius II and the Wars of the Roses', *Archivum Historiae Pontificae* viii, 1970.

Herbert, A., 'Herefordshire 1413–61: Some Aspects of Society and Public Order', *Patronage, the Crown and the Provinces in Later Medieval England*, ed. Griffiths, R. A., Gloucester, 1981.

Hicks, M. A., 'A Minute of the Lancastrian Council at York, 20 January 1461', *Northern History* xxxv, 1999.

Hicks, M. A., *Bastard Feudalism*, London, 1995.

Hicks, M. A., 'The Beauchamp Trust 1439–1487', *Bulletin of the Institute of Historical Research* liv, 1981; repr. in *Richard III and his Rivals*.

Hicks, M. A., 'Between Majorities: The "Beauchamp Interregnum" 1439–49', *Historical Research*, lxxii (1998).

Hicks, M. A., 'Cement or Solvent? Kinship and Politics in the Fifteenth Century: The Case of the Nevilles', *History* lxxxiii, 1998.

Hicks, M. A., 'Descent, Partition and Extinction: The "Warwick Inheritance"', *Bulletin of the Institute of Historical Research* lii, 1979; repr. in *Richard III and his Rivals*.

Hicks, M. A., 'Edward IV, the Duke of Somerset, and Lancastrian Loyalism in the North', *Northern History* xxii, 1984, repr. in *Richard III and his Rivals*.

Hicks, M. A., 'An Escheat Concealed: The Despenser Estate in Hampshire 1400–61', *Proceedings of the Hampshire Field Club and Archaeological Society* liii, 1998.

Hicks, M. A., 'The Forfeiture of Barnard Castle to the Bishop of Durham, 1459,' *Northern History*, xxxiii, 1997.

Hicks, M. A., *False, Fleeting, Perjur'd Clarence: George Duke of Clarence 1449–78*, rev. edn., Bangor, 1992.

Hicks, M. A., 'The Neville earldom of Salisbury 1429–71', *Wiltshire Archaeological Magazine* 72/73, 1980; repr. in *Richard III and his Rivals*.

Hicks, M. A., *Richard III and his Rivals: Magnates and their Motives during the Wars of the Roses*, 1991.

Hicks, M. A., 'The 1468 Statute of Livery', *Historical Research* lxiv, 1991.

Highfield, J. R. L., and Jeffs, R. I., (eds), *The Crown and Local Communities in England and France in the Fifteenth Century*, Gloucester, 1981.

Holland, P., 'The Lincolnshire Rebellion of March 1470', *English Historical Review* ciii, 1988.

Jack, R. I., 'Entail and Descent: The Hastings Inheritance 1370–1436', *Bulletin of the Institute of Historical Research* xxxviii, 1965.

Jack, R. I., 'A Quincentenary: The Battle of Northampton, July 10th, 1460', *Northamptonshire Past and Present* iii (1), 1960.

Johnson, P. A., *Duke Richard of York 1411–1460*, Oxford, 1988.

Jones, M. K., 'Edward IV and the Beaufort Family: Conciliation in Early Yorkist Politics', *The Ricardian* 83, 1983.

Jones, M. K., 'Edward IV, the Earl of Warwick, and the Yorkist Claim to the Throne', *Historical Research* lxx, 1997.

Jones, M. K., 'Somerset, York and the Wars of the Roses', *English Historical Review* civ, 1989.

Keen, M. H., and Daniel, M. J., 'English Diplomacy and the Sack of Fougères in 1449', *History* lix, 1974.

Kekewich, M., 'The Attainder of the Yorkists in 1459: Two Contemporary Accounts', *Bulletin of the Institute of Historical Research* lv, 1982.

Kendall, P. M., *Louis XI*, 1971.

Kendall, P. M., *Warwick the Kingmaker*, 1957.

Kingsford, C. L., *English Historical Literature in the Fifteenth Century*, Oxford, 1913.

Kingsford, C. L., 'The Earl of Warwick at Calais in 1460', *English Historical Review* xxxvii, 1922.

Kingsford, C. L., 'The First Version of Hardyng's Chronicle', *English Historical Review* xxxvii, 1922.

Kingsford, C. L., *Prejudice and Promise in the Fifteenth Century*, 1926.

Lander, J. R., 'Attainder and Forfeiture 1453–1509', *Historical Journal* iv, 1961; repr. in *Crown and Nobility*.

Lander, J. R., *Crown and Nobility, 1450–1509*, 1976.

Lander, J. R., *Government and Community 1450–1509*, 1980.

Lander, J. R., 'Henry VI and the Duke of York's Second Protectorate', *Bulletin of the John Rylands Library* xliii, 1960; repr. in *Crown and Nobility*.

Lander, J. R., 'Marriage and Politics in the Fifteenth Century: The Nevilles and the Wydevilles', *Bulletin of the Institute of Historical Research* xxxvi, 1963; repr. in *Crown and Nobility*.

Lewis, W. G., 'The Exact Date of the Battle of Banbury, 1469', *Bulletin of the Institute of Historical Research* lv, 1982.

Lovatt, R., 'A Collector of Apocryphal Anecdotes: John Blacman Revisited', in *Property and Politics: Essays in Later Medieval English History*, ed. Pollard, A. J., Gloucester, 1984.

Lowry, M., 'John Rous and the Survival of the Neville Circle', *Viator* 19, 1988.

McCulloch, D., and Jones, E. D., 'Lancastrian Politics, the French War, and the Rise of the Popular Element', *Speculum* lviii, 1983.

Macdougall, N., *James III: A Political Study*, Edinburgh, 1982.

McFarlane, K. B., *England in the Fifteenth Century*, 1981.

McFarlane, K. B., *The Nobility of Later Medieval England*, Oxford, 1973.

Mason, E., 'Legends of the Beauchamps' Ancestors: the Use of Baronial Propaganda in Medieval England', *Journal of Medieval History* 10, 1984.

Morris, R. K., 'Tewkesbury Abbey – The Despenser Mausoleum', *Transactions of the Bristol and Gloucestershire Archaeological Society* xliii, 1987.

Myers, A. R., *Crown, Household and Parliament in Fifteenth-Century England*, 1983.

Nightingale, P., *A Medieval Mercantile Community*, London, 1995.

Oman, C., *Warwick the Kingmaker*, London, 1893.

Payling, S. J., 'The Coventry Parliament of 1459: A Privy Seal Writ concerning the Election of the Knights of the Shire', *Historical Research* lx, 1987.

Payling, S. J., 'The Ampthill Dispute: A Study in Aristocratic Lawlessness and the Breakdown of Lancastrian Government', *English Historical Review* civ, 1989.

Payne, A., 'The Salisbury Roll of Arms, 1463', *England in the Fifteenth Century*, ed. Williams, D., Woodbridge, 1987.

Pepin, P. B., '*Monasticon Anglicanum* and the History of Tewkesbury Abbey', *Transactions of the Bristol and Gloucestershire Archaeological Society* xxxviii, 1981.

Plancher, U., *Histoire Générale et Particulière de Bourgogne*, 4 vols, 1781.

Pollard, A. J., *John Talbot and the War in France 1427–53*, 1983.

Pollard, A. J., 'Lord FitzHugh's Rising in 1470', *Bulletin of the Institute of Historical Research* lii, 1979.

Pollard, A. J., *North-Eastern England during the Wars of the Roses*, Oxford, 1990.

Pollard, A. J., 'The Northern Retainers of Richard Nevill, Earl of Salisbury', *Northern History* xi, 1976.

Pollard, A. J. (ed.), *Property and Politics: Essays in Later Medieval English History*, Gloucester, 1984.

Pollard, A. J., 'Richard Clervaux of Croft: A North Riding Squire during the Fifteenth Century', *Yorkshire Archaeological Journal* 1, 1978.

Pollard, A. J., 'The Richmondshire Community of Gentry in the Fifteenth Century', *Patronage, Pedigree and Power in the Late Middle Ages*, ed. Ross, C. D., Gloucester, 1979.

Pollard, A. J., *The Wars of the Roses*, 1988.

Pollard, A. J. (ed.), *The Wars of the Roses*, 1995.

Pollard, A. J., and Britnell, R. (eds), *The McFarlane Legacy*, Stroud, 1995.

Postan, M. M., and Power, E., *Studies in English Trade in the Fifteenth Century*, 1968.

Pugh, T. B. (ed.), *The History of the County of Glamorgan*, iii, *The Middle Ages*, Cardiff, 1971.

Pugh, T. B., 'Richard, Duke of York and the Rebellion of Henry, Duke of Exeter, in May 1454', *Historical Research* lxiii, 1990.

Pugh, T. B., 'Richard Plantagenet (1411–60), Duke of York, as the King's Lieutenant in France and Ireland', *Aspects of Late Medieval Government and Society*, ed. Rowe, J. G., Toronto, 1986.

Ramsey, J. H., *Lancaster and York*, 2 vols, Oxford, 1892.

Rawcliffe, C., 'Richard Duke of York, the King's "Obeissant Liegeman": A New Source for the Protectorates of 1454 and 1455', *Bulletin of the Institute of Historical Research* lx, 1987.

Rawcliffe, C., *The Staffords, Earls of Stafford and Dukes of Buckingham 1394–1521*, Cambridge, 1978.

Richmond, C. F., 'English Naval Power in the Fifteenth Century', *History* lii, 1967.

Richmond, C. F., 'Fauconberg's Kentish Rising of May 1471', *English Historical Review* lxxxxv, 1970.

Richmond, C. F., 'The Nobility and the Wars of the Roses 1459–61', *Nottingham Medieval Studies* xxi, 1976.

Richmond, C. F., *The Paston Family in the Fifteenth Century: The First Phase*, Cambridge, 1991.

Richmond, C. F., *The Paston Family in the Fifteenth Century: Fastolf's Will*, Cambridge, 1996.

Roncière, C. de la, *Histoire de la Marine Française*, 2 vols, 1900.

Rosenthal, J. T., 'The Estates and Finances of Richard Duke of York', *Studies in Medieval & Renaissance History* ii, ed. Bowsky, W. M., Nebraska, 1965.

Roskell, J. S., *Parliament and Politics in Later Medieval England*, 3 vols, 1981–3.

Ross, C. D., *Edward IV*, 1974.

Ross, C. D., *The Estates and Finances of Richard Beauchamp, Earl of Warwick*, Dugdale Society occasional paper xii, 1956.

Ross, C. D. (ed.), *Patronage, Pedigree and Power in Later Medieval England*, Gloucester, 1979.

Rowe, J. G. (ed.), *Aspects of Late Medieval Government and Society*, Toronto, 1986.

Rowland, D., *Genealogical Account of the Most Noble House of Neville*, 1830.

Rowney, I. D., 'Government and Patronage in the Fifteenth Century: Staffordshire 1439–59', *Midland History* viii, 1983.

Scattergood, V. J., *Politics and Poetry in the Fifteenth Century*, 1972.

Scammell, G. V., 'Shipowning in England *c.*1450–1550', *Transactions of the Royal Historical Society* 5th ser. xii, 1962.

Scofield, C. L., 'The Capture of Lord Rivers and Sir Anthony Woodville, 19 January 1460', *English Historical Review* xxxviii, 1992.

Scofield, C. L., *The Life and Reign of Edward IV*, 2 vols, 1923.

Somerville, R., *History of the Duchy of Lancaster*, i, 1953.

Storey, R. L., *The End of the House of Lancaster*, 2nd edn, Gloucester, 1986.

Storey, R. L., 'Episcopal King-Makers in the Fifteenth Century', *The Church, Patronage and Politics in 15th-Century England*, ed. Dobson, R. B., Gloucester, 1984.

Storey, R. L., 'The Wardens of the Marches of England towards Scotland 1377–1489', *English Historical Review* lxxii, 1957.

Thielemans, M. R., *Bourgogne et Angleterre: Relations politiques et économiques entre les Pays-Bas bourguignons et l'Angleterre 1435–1467*, Brussels, 1966.

Thomson, J. A. F., ' "The Arrival of Edward IV" – The Development of the Text', *Speculum* xlvi, 1971.

Vale, M. G. A., *Charles VII*, 1974.

Vallet de Viriville, C., *Histoire de Charles VII*, vol. 3, Paris, 1865.

Vaughan, R., *Philip the Good*, 1970.

Vaughan, R., *Charles the Bold*, 1973.

Virgoe, R., 'The Composition of the King's Council 1437–61', *Bulletin of the Institute of Historical Research* xliii, 1970.

Virgoe, R., 'William Tailboys and Lord Cromwell: Crime and Politics in Lancastrian England', *Bulletin of the John Rylands Library* lv, 1973.

Watts, J. L., *Henry VI and the Politics of Kingship*, Cambridge, 1996.

Wedgwood, J. C., *History of Parliament 1439–1509*, 2 vols, London, 1936–8.

Whittaker, T. D., *An History of Richmondshire*, 2 vols, 1823.

Williams, D (ed), *England in the Fifteenth Century*, Woodbridge, 1987.

Wolffe, B. P., *Henry VI*, London, 1981.

Wolffe, B. P., *The Royal Demesne in English History*, London, 1971.

Wright, S. M., *The Derbyshire Gentry in the Fifteenth Century*, Derbyshire Record Society viii, 1983.

Index

Abbreviations: abp = archbishop; bp = bishop; c = count, countess; d = duke, duchess; da = daughter; e = earl; k = king; ld = lord; m = marquis; q = queen; s = son; v = viscount; w = wife.

Abergavenny (Wales), 13, 26–7, 34–5, 41–2, 45–6, 48–9, 53, 60, 63, 78, 84, 123, 173, 222, 239; *see also* Beauchamp, Richard *and* William; Neville, Edward *and* George
Aberystwyth (Wales), 130
Abingdon (Berks.), 186
Accord, Act of (1460), 190, 211–12, 217
Acquitaine, Guienne, Gascony (France), 69, 78–9, 87, 90, 138, 251, 267–8; *see also* Charles of France
Acton Bridge (Ches.), 163
Affrica, lady of Man, 10, 229
Aiscough, William, bp of Salisbury, 72, 200
Alençon (France), d of, 124, 139, 149, 154
Alnwick Castle (Northumb.), 240–3, 246
Alton (Hants.), 222
Amboise (France), 292–3, 302
Amesbury (Wilts.), 226
Ampthill (Beds.), dispute, 83, 85, 96, 111–12, 126
Anger, Thomas, 250
Angers (France), treaty of (1470), 292–3, 295, 298–9, 301–2, 305, 307

Angus, e of, *see* Douglas
Anne, q to Richard III, *see* Neville, Richard
Anson, Richard, 177
Anthony, bastard of Burgundy, 143, 254
ap Nicholas, Gruffydd, 130
ap Thomas, Sir William, 32; *see also* Herbert, William
Arbury, prior of, 155–6
Archer, John, 180
Ardres (France), 143, 276
Armstrong, C.A.J., 120
Arras (France), congress of, 149
Arrivall of Edward IV, 301, 308–10, 312
Arundel, William, e of Arundel, 24, 156, 182, 213, 216, 230, 251; Joan his w, 24, 156, 259; Thomas, e of Arundel, 35; Thomas, ld Maltravers, 234, 259
Atholl (Scot.), 241
attainders, 159, 170–2, 190, 193, 196
Attlebridge (Suff.), 223
Audley,
    James ld (d.1459), 156–8, 163, 174
    John ld (d.1490), 173–4, 265, 271, 277
Auger, Henry, 145, 251

Avranches (France), Robert of, 245
Axholme Priory (Lincs.), 81

Baginton (Warw.), 58, 233
Bainbridge (Yorks.), 20
Ball, John, 250
Bamburgh Castle (Northumb.), 241–3, 245–7, 261
Banbury (Oxon), 271; *see also* Edgecote
Barde, sr de la, 182, 215, 261
Barfleur (France), 289–90
Barnard Castle (Dur.), 22, 27–8, 33, 54, 67, 86, 112, 170, 225, 233, 236, 297
Barnet (Herts.), 186; battle (1471), 308–9; *see also plate 22*
Barton by Bristol (Glos.), 123
Basin, Thomas, 2, 269, 293, 300
bastards, *see* Burgundy, Exeter, Fauconberg, Neville
battles, *see* Barnet, Blore Heath, Châtillon, Edgecote, Empingham, Hedgeley Moor, Heworth, Hexham, Mortimer's Cross, Nibley Green, Northampton, St Albans, Stamford Bridge, Tewkesbury, Towton, Wakefield
Bayeux (France), bp of, *see* Harcourt
Beauchamp,
   Anne, c of Warwick (d.1492), 24, 27, 32, 38–9, 41, 43, 45–6, 49–51, 53n, 57, 61, 78, 82–3, 130, 141, 169, 181, 184, 225–6, 230, 235, 241, 245, 253, 286–9; depicted, *plate 18*; her husband, *see* Neville, Richard; *see also* Beauchamp inheritance, sisters, trust
   Anne, c of Warwick (d.1449), 25, 30–3, 35–6, 37n, 39, 46, 67, 77, 142–3
   Guy, e of Warwick, 56, 58
   Henry, d of Warwick, 17, 24, 27–8, 31–2, 34–5, 39–44, 48–51, 58, 60–1, 67, 76, 221, 226, 234, 264; his w Cecily Neville, 17, 24, 27–8, 32–4, 39, 48, 53, 77, 97
   John, d Beauchamp of Powicke, 32, 34–7, 51–2, 67, 69, 75, 77, 92, 123, 137, 182

Richard, e of Warwick (d.1439), 23–4, 26–9, 31, 33–4, 40, 50, 53–9, 130, 232–3; his *Pageant*, 58, 61; his tomb, *plates 8 and 9*; for his w, *see* Despenser, Isabel
Richard, ld Bergavenny and e of Worcester, 27, 35, 60; for his w, *see* Despenser
Richard, bp of Salisbury, 150–1, 166, 178, 198, 217
Thomas I, e of Warwick (d.1369), 40, 55–7; his sons, 58
Thomas II, e of Warwick (d.1401), 40, 56–7; his w Margaret, 57
William, e of Warwick (d.1298), 35
William, ld Bergavenny (d.1411), 26, 35; his w Joan, 26, 35, 42
Beauchamp arms, 57, *plate 18*; chapel, *see* Warwick college; family, 54; inheritance, 67, 114, 129, 233, *see also* Beaufort, Neville, Talbot; pedigree, 38; piety, 56; sisters, 37, 41, 51, 75, 77–8, 82, 128, 111, 170, 225, *see also* Beaufort, Neville, Talbot; trust, 32, 34, 50, 53, 62, 225;
Beaufort,
   Edmund, c of Mortain, d. of Somerset (d.1455), 26, 140; Beauchamp inheritance, 32, 37, 51, 71, 77–8, 84–5; in Normandy, 36–7, 69, 76; his quarrel with York, 71–4, 76, 109–10, 112–18; 120; dominates court (1450–3), 42, 69, 80, 83–4, 90; imprisoned and tried, 91, 93, 94, 97–112; death, 116; Eleanor Beauchamp his w, 27, 32, 76, 78, 129, 134, 170, 225; his children, 134, 137
   Edmund, d of Somerset (d.1471), 213, 216, 302, 309
   Henry, cardinal, 12, 15, 62, 66, 226
   Henry, e of Dorset and d of Somerset (d.1464), seeks revenge for father's death, 116, 121–2, 128–9; reconciled with Yorkists (1458), 132–3, 135–7, proposals for marriage, 149, 153; resists Yorkists (1459), 161, 163–4;

Beaufort, Henry *(continued)*
    besieges Calais, 170, 173, 176–7,
    181; supports Queen Margaret,
    184–5, 189, 194, 212, 215, 219;
    fights on after Towton, 225–6,
    235, 242; killed at Hexham, 248
    Joan, c of Westmorland, 12–14, 17,
    23–5
    John, e of Somerset (d.1410), 11, 15
    Margaret, c of Richmond, 15, 25, 70,
    82, 157, 212
    Thomas, d of Exeter, 15
Beaufort claim to crown, 211, 302; dukes
    of Somerset, 15, 19, 67; family, 70;
    lineage, 110
Beaumaris (Wales), 71
Beaumont,
    John v (d.1460), 93, 99, 129, 137, 177,
    179, 184, 196; his w Katherine
    Neville d of Norfolk, 179
    William v, 212, 308
Bedford, Sir Henry, 222
Belknap, Thomas, 223
Bell, John, 222
Benet's Chronicle, 117, 156–7
Bensted, Sir John, 306
Bereshyn, William, 222
Bergavenny, ld, *see* Abergavenny;
    Beauchamp, Richard and William;
    Neville, Edward and George
Berkeley Castle (Glos.), 46, 78, 83
Berkeley, James ld, 32, 46, 78
Berkeley–Lisle dispute, 32, 37, 46, 77–8,
    83; *see also* Nibley Green
Berkeswell (Warw.), 50, 56, 58, 89
Berkeswell, William, 32, 50, 56, 58, 62
Berkhamsted (Herts.), 45, 133
Berwick-upon-Tweed, 121, 123, 235, 238,
    241, 244, 247
Beverley (Yorks.), 250
Bisham Priory (Berks.), 10, 62, 228–30,
    233, 243; depiction, *plate 16*
Blackburn (Lancs.), 29, 236
Blacman, John, 209
Blenkinsop, Thomas, 241
Blore Heath (Staffs.), battle (1459), 160,
    163, 165–6, 174

Blount, Sir Walter, later d Mountjoy,
    110, 142, 152, 162, 182, 221 & n,
    239, 248, 252, 265, 281, 300
Bolingbroke (Lincs.), 183
Bona of Savoy, 261
Bonville,
    William ld Bonville, 25, 79, 93–4, 124,
    128, 216, 270
    William ld Harrington, 25, 214, 270;
    his da Cecily, 270; his w
    Katherine Neville, *see* Hastings
Bonville–Courtenay dispute, *see*
    Courtenay
Bordeaux (France), 90, 251
Bordesley Abbey (Warw.), 54, 56
Boston (Lincs.), 183, 282
Boteler,
    James, e of Wiltshire, 79, 84, 91–4, 113,
    121, 137, 172, 175, 177, 193, 196,
    212, 217; his w Eleanor, 297
    Ralph ld Sudeley, 34–7, 40, 51–2, 67,
    75, 77, 92, 99, 116, 123
    Thomas, 258; his w Anne Hankford,
    10, 258
Bothe,
    Lawrence, bp of Durham, 130&n, 132,
    170, 182, 200, 225, 236–8, 297
    William, abp of York, 89, 99, 244–5
Boulers, Reginald, bp of Hereford, 79,
    115
Boulogne (France), 244, 253, 262
Bourbon, d of, 153; da of, 153; Isabel de,
    d of Burgundy, 263
Bourchier,
    Henry v Bourchier, 83, 87, 92, 11,
    122–3, 128, 150, 156–7, 172,
    178–80, 182, 184; e of Essex, 259
    Humphrey ld Cromwell, 242
    John ld Berners, 121, 172
    Thomas, abp of Canterbury, 99, 100,
    111, 113, 123, 128, 130, 156–7,
    172, 179–81, 184, 187, 194, 198,
    200, 281; cardinal, 264, 276
    William, 259
Bourchier family, 70, 123, 129–30, 150,
    164, 170, 172, 189, 213
Bourre, Jean de, sr Duplessis, 290–1
Bowland (Lancs.), 29, 236

Brackley, friar, 152, 168, 184, 186
Brailes (Warw.), 40, 50, 63
Brancepeth (Dur.), 12, 16, 236, 238, 246;
   see also Neville
Brecon (Wales), 183, 234
Brewster,
   John the elder, 56, 58
   John the younger, 58
Breze, Pierre de, 144, 151, 153, 175, 235,
   239, 241, 243–4
Bridgewater (Soms.), 184, 273
Bristol, 169, 176, 222, 250, 286
Brittany, 262, 267–8; ships of, 287, 304
Broke, Edward, ld Cobham, 80, 177–8,
   182
Brome, John, 48, 51, 77
Bromley, John, prior of Arbury, 155–6
Brougham (Westmor.), 236
Broughton, Thomas, 185
Brouns, Brian, 222
Browne, Sir Thomas, 180, 258
Brut, chronicle, 194
Bruyce, Giles, 223
Bulmer, Anketil, 12
Burdet, Thomas, 50, 63
Burford (Oxon.), 217
Burgh, Sir Thomas, 283
Burghclere, 228
Burgundy (France), alliance with
   England, 254–5, 259–63, 266–8, 276,
   288–9, 295; bastard, *see* Anthony;
   dukes of, *see* Charles, Philip;
   dynastically uncommitted, 241, 248,
   253; helps overthrow the
   Readeption, 303, 305–8; negotiations
   with, 137, 143, 149–51, 174, 181,
   253; hists. of, 2, *see also* Chastellain;
   ships of, 287, 289; trade embargo,
   267
Burgundy, John of, c of Estampes, 143,
   151
Burley, Walter, 124
Burton-on-Trent (Staffs.), 285
Burwell (Lincs.), 88
Bury St Edmunds (Suff.), 73, 276
Buxhull, Sir Alan, 10
Bywell (Northumb.), 246

Cade, Jack, 45, 53, 65, 68, 70–1, 83, 140,
   191, 194–6
Caerleon (Wales), 173
Caister (Norf.), 192, 224, 278, 282
Calabria, *see* John
Calais (France), 126, 262; defence of, 26,
   79, 97, 100, 121, 161, 261; depiction,
   plate 13; garrison, 150, 153, *see also*
   officers; Warwick at, 44, 127, 131,
   133, 155, 157–8, 162, 169, 173–7,
   181, 184, 197, 200, 252–3, 262;
   Warwick's captaincy (1456–61),
   138–47, 154; retires to and invades
   from (1459–60), 168, 173–8, 181,
   189, 196, 199–200, 209; government
   of (1461–70), 239–40, 247–9, 260,
   276, 286; Lancastrian cession to
   France, 235; Warwick's excluded
   (1470), 287; rule (1470–1), 303–6,
   309–10, 312
officers of: 182, 224, 231; captains, 76,
   100, 112, 123–4, 126, 173n, 140,
   173n, 185, 222; lieutenants, *see*
   Fauconberg, Neville, Welles,
   Wenlock, Wydeville; marshalls,
   see Blount, Duras, Gate, Mulsho;
   master porter, *see* Trollope;
   mayor, 146; officers of, 139;
   treasurers, *see* Blount, Clifton,
   Thirsk; harbour, 194; *see also*
   Findern, Marny, Rivers, Welles,
   Whetehill
topography: 139; St Nicholas Church,
   249; Castle, 142, 287; Arderne,
   142; Bonynges, 132; Froyton, 142;
   Guines, 131, 142, 173–4, 180–1,
   182, 194, 248; Hammes, 139, 142,
   173–4, 235, 239, 248; Mark, 139,
   143; Merkyn, 142; Newnham
   Bridge, 170, 181, 215; Oye, 139,
   143; Rysbank tower, 139, 142,
   173, 248, 251; St Pierre, 170, 181;
   Wissault (Scales Cliff), 173
Calverley, Walter, 237
Canford (Dors.), 26, 226, 247, 252
Canterbury (Kent), 130, 141, 150, 177,
   184, 219, 192, 194–5, 264, 274;
   archbishopric, 244, *see also*

Canterbury, (Kent) *(continued)*
   Bourchier, Kemp; Becket's cross,
   198; convocation, 177, 189, 198, 244;
   mayor, 251; prior, 184, 232
Canynges, William, 250
Cardiff (Wales), 27, 44, 45, 49, 52, 59–61,
   81–2, 84–5, 89, *plate 12*
Cardigan (Wales), 277
Carlisle (Cumb.), 21, 23, 30, 76, 109, 123,
   238, 240–1, 247; bishops of, *see*
   Percy, Storey; temporalities, 245
Carmarthen (Wales), 130, 277
Carpenter, Christine, 51
Carte, Thomas, 4
Castile, relations with, 267–8; royal
   family, *see* Eleanor, Henry, Isabella;
   shipping of, 174, 176
Castle Donington (Leics.), 183, 221
Castle Rising (Norf.), 214
Caversham (Berks.), 58
Cawood Palace (Yorks.), 253
Caxton, William, 249
Chamber, William, 141
Chamberlain, Sir Robert, 141
chancellors of England, *see* Bourchier,
   Fortescue, Kemp, Neville,
   Stillington, Waynflete
Channel Isles, 39, 41, 44, 76, 81–2, 100,
   132, 144–5, 183–4, 235, 239, 264,
   289; governor of, *see* Nanfan; *see also*
   Guernsey, Jersey, Mont Orgueil
Charles VII, k of France, 139, 149–51,
   153, 182, 239, 260; his daughters,
   149; his sons, *see* Louis XI, Charles
Charles VIII, k of France, 295
Charles the Bold, c of Charolais, d of
   Burgundy (1467–77), 143, 149, 153,
   182, 259–60, 262–4, 267–8, 288–9,
   305–7; his daughter Mary, 263; his
   wives, 263, 266
Charles of France, d of Normandy and
   Guienne, 268, 295
Charlton, Sir Thomas, 96
Charolais, *see* Charles the Bold
Chastel, Tanguy de, 291, 305
Chastellain, Georges, 2, 143, 289, 293,
   303
Châtillon (France), battle, 90, 97, 216, 309

Chaucer, Geoffrey, 11; his daughter
   Alice, *see* Montagu, Pole
Cherbourg (France), 289
Cherhill (Wilts.), 48
Chester, 70–1, 186
Chesterfield (Derb.), 285
Chichester (Suss.), 145; bp, *see* Moleyns
Chinon (France), treaty, 235
Chipping Norton (Oxon.), 78, 217
Christope, of Campe, 146
Cinque Ports, 138, 144–5, 173, 183, 191,
   193, 222, 239, 244, 252–3, 273, 287,
   298, 304; warden, *see* Neville,
   Richard; lieutenants, *see* Guildford,
   Kyriel, Worsley; ports, *see* Deal,
   Dover, Lydd, Rye, Sandwich
Clapham, Richard, 51, 62, 145, 163, 175,
   286–7, 301
Clare, earls of Gloucester, 43, 54, 59–60;
   see also Joan of Acre
Clarence, dukes of, *see* George, Lionel,
   Thomas
Clarendon (Wilts.), 85
Claverdon (Warw.), 56
Clavering (Essex), 11n
Clercq, Jean Du, chronicler, 219
Clervaux, Richard, 238; genealogy, 17,
   18n, 19
Clifford,
   John ld (d.1455), 89, 91, 93, 111,
      116–17, 119–20, 129, 136
   John ld (d.1461), 121, 129, 132–4, 136,
      181, 213, 219, 235–6
Clifford family, 21, 236–7
Clifton, Sir Gervase, 142, 174
Cobham, *see* Broke
Cockermouth (Cumb.), 236, 247
Cokefield, Janet, 50
Colsehill (Warw.), 163; priory, 54
Collyweston (Northants.), 152, 227, 266
Colt,
   John, 250–2
   Thomas (d.1467), 22, 30, 39, 162, 220,
      225, 252, 260; Warwick
      chamberlain, 48–9, 62, 77
Columbes, 251
Combe Abbey, 52
Commander, Robert, 51

Commines, Philippe de, 227, 256, 305, 307

Conquet (France), 250

Constable, Sir Robert, 22, 245n

Conyers,
Sir Christopher, 22, 246n
Sir John, 163, 275, 286
John, 277

Conyers family, 22, 251

Cook, Sir Thomas, 272–3

Coppini, Francesco de, bp of Terni, 168, 174, 180, 182, 184, 189, 194, 196–8, 215–16, 218

Cotentin (France), 289–91

Courtenay,
Henry (d.1469), 273
John, e of Devon (d.1471), 301–2, 304, 309
Piers, 301
Thomas, e of Devon (d.1458), 79–81, 91, 94, 96, 109, 121, 123–4, 128
Thomas, e of Devon (d.1461), 128, 136, 181, 212, 219, 298; his w Marie of Maine, 128

Courtenay family, of Bocannoc, 286, 300; of Powderham, 259

Courtenay–Bonville dispute, 79, 83, 124, 128

Cousinot, Guillaume, 261

Coventry (Warw.), 54, 115, 132, 138, 142, 156, 163, 265, 276, 300, 306–9; corporation, 219; great councils at, 79–80, 114, 128, 130, 152, 157–8, 160, 165–7, 196, 200; parliament at, 170–3, 185–6, 189–90; Warwick at, 84, 219, 245, 253, 265, 285, 300, his countess at, 45, 49

Cowbridge (Wales), 59–60, 84–5

Cromer (Norf.), 307

Cromwell, Ralph ld (d.1456), 28n, 74, 77, 83, 85–8, 91, 94, 96, 98, 109, 111–13, 154; executors, 227; heirs, 129; *see also* Bourchier, Neville

Crosby, John, 223

Crosse, William, 50

Crowland continuator, 259 60, 280, 300–1, 309

Cuny, Robert, 264

Dacre,
Sir Humphrey, 240–1
Randal ld, 235
Sir Thomas, 22

Dacre family, 13, 20, 236–7, 281; *see also* Fiennes

Danby, Sir Robert, 22, 222, 252

Daniel,
Samuel, 4
Thomas, 41, 75, 214

Darell, Sir George, 222

Dartford (Kent), insurrection, 53, 80–2, 85, 120, 123, 157–8

Dartmouth (Devon), 145, 176, 286, 300

Davy, John, 184

Deal (Kent), 253

Defford, John, 251

Deighton, 30

Delves, John, 301

Denbigh (Wales), 71, 173

Denys, Thomas, 223

Derby, 111, 285

Despenser,
Isabel, c of Warwick and Worcester (d.1439), 27, 31, 34, 38, 60–1, 232
Richard ld (d.1414), 13, 35; his w Eleanor Neville c of Northumberland, 13
Thomas, ld Despenser and e of Gloucester (d.1400), 15, 59, 170, 226, 239

Despenser arms, 57; family, 59–60, 170; inheritance, 28, 32, 34, 39, 46, 49, 51, 53–4, 114, 129, 193, 222, 226, 233, 239, 297; mausoleum, *plate 14*; trust, 32, 34, 46, 49–53, 60–1, 67, 75, 77

Dessford, Thomas, 175

Devereux,
Sir Walter (d.1459), 35, 123, 130–1
Sir Walter, ld Ferrers of Chartley (d.1485), 63, 163, 170, 172, 218, 221, 280

Devon, e of, *see* Courtenay

Dieppe (France), 18

Doncaster (Yorks.), 219, 247

Dorset, e of, *see* Beaufort

Douglas,
  Archibald, e of Angus, 243–4
  James, e of Douglas, 244–5
Doulcereau, Morice, 151, 153
Dover (Kent), 144–5, 195, 221–2, 239, 273
Drayton Bassett (Staffs.), 51, 58, 129
Droitwich (Worc.), 170
Dudley,
  Ambrose, e of Warwick, 225
  John, ld Dudley, 84–5, 99, 122, 163, 182, 245
  John, e of Warwick, 225
  Oliver (d.1469), 57, 277
  Robert, e of Warwick, 225
Duffield, John, 50
Duffield honour (Derbys.), 31, 183, 285
Dumfries (Scot.), 182, 240, 247
Dunstable (Beds.), 178, 215–16
Dunstanburgh (Northumb.), 239, 241–3, 246
Dunster (Soms.), 259, 270
Duras, Gailliard ld, 142, 176, 232, 239, 248–9, 251, 287, 300
Durham, 238, 241–4; Cathedral, 12, *plate 5*; city, 23; Priory, 237, 258
Dynmock, Sir Thomas, 283
Dynham, John, 169, 175, 177, 182, 258; his mother Joan, 169

East Lexham (Suff.), 223
Edgecote (Oxon.), battle, 57, 271, 277, 280, 285
Edinburgh (Scot.), 244
Edmund, d of York, 11
Edmund, e of Rutland, 164, 169, 175, 189–91, 214
Edward I, 10, 96
Edward II, 11, 272
Edward III, 7, 10, 70, 96, 187, 273
Edward IV: lineage, 200, *see also* Mortimer; capacity, 277
  as e of March (1459–60): 1, flight to Calais, 164, 168–9, *plate 13*; successful invasion, 177–80, 184, 189–90, 192n, 199, 211, 213
  as d of York and protector: 214, 217, 307
  first reign (1461–70): 211, 223–4, 230,
233, 235, 237–9, 248, 255–6, 265, 269; usurpation 1, 217–20; coronation, 234; marriage and negotiations, 256, 258–62, 278; Burgundian foreign policy and alliance, 263–4, 266–8, 271, 281; finances, 267, 271–2; marriage negotiations, 256, 258–62, 278; lays claim to France, 267–8; Warwick's first coup (1469), 271–8; recovers, 278–97; uncompromising, 285–8; indictment of regime, 271–4, 311
  deposition: 1, 299; defeat and exile, 300, 302
  victorious return: 303–12
Edward of Lancaster, prince of Wales and heir to throne (1453–60), 90, 93, 96, 98–9, 118, 124, 127, 137, 149, 153, 156, 180–2, 190; set aside, 192; resists, 195; in exile, 211–12, 214, 235; reconciled to Warwick, 292–6, 299, 300–2; married, 302n; king's lieutenant, 302; treaty with France, 305; death, 312
Edward, d of York (d.1415), 70
Egremont (Cumb.), 30, 86, 247; ld, *see* Percy, Thomas
Eleanor of Castile, q of Edward I, 10
Elizabeth, q of Edward IV, 253, 257–9, 261, 301; her family, *see* Wydevilles; her first husband, *see* Grey
Elizabeth of York, 253, 266, 281–2, 293
Elmley Castle (Worcs.), 50, 54, 57–8, 233
Elvaston (Derby), 110, 142
Elvell (Wales), 27, 42, 222, 239
Empingham (Lincs.), battle (1470), 285
Estampes, c of, *see* Burgundy
Eton College (Berks.), 20, 67, 125
Eugenius IV, pope, 13
Ewelme (Oxon.), 37 & n
Ewyas Lacy (Wales), 27, 42, 46, 78, 84
Exeter (Devon), 286; bastard of, 218–19; bp of, *see* Neville; d of, *see* Holland
Exmouth (Devon), 300

Fabyan's Chronicle, 4

Fastolf dispute, 223–4, 278; *see also*
  Caister
Fastolf Relation, 120
Faucon, John, gunner, 237, 238
Fauconberg, Thomas, bastard of, 287,
  290–1, 304, 309, 312; ld, *see* Neville,
  William
Faunt, Nicolas, 251, 312
Feckenham (Worc.), 31, 44, 76, 82, 221
Ferrers, Thomas, 185, 222
Ferrers of Chartley, William ld, 44, 45,
  63; *see also* Devereux
Ferrers of Groby, ld, *see* Grey
Ferrybridge (Yorks.), battle, 217, 219
Fetherston, William, 250
feuds, *see* Ampthill, Beauchamp,
  Berkeley–Lisle, Courtenay–Bonville,
  Despenser, Fastolf, Mountford,
  Neville–Neville, Percy–Neville,
  Talbot–Lisle, Vernon–Blount
  disputes
Fiennes,
  James, ld Say, 67, 72, William 240
  Richard, ld Dacre, 231
Findern, Sir Thomas, 142, 246
Fisher, Richard, 154, 172, 252
FitzHamo, Robert, 59–61
FitzHarry, Thomas, 45, 46, 218
FitzHugh, Henry ld, 22, 25, 89, 91–2,
  182, 213, 228, 230–1, 235, 243, 246n,
  247, 251–3, 275, 284, 295; his w
  Alice Neville, 230, 235; his da, 234;
  his s, 277
FitzHugh family, 13, 19, 20
FitzWalter, John ld, 218–19
Flamstead (Herts.), 48
Flaxhale, Henry, 85
Fogge, Sir John, 271–3, 277
Foix, c of, 211
Foljambe, Thomas, 223
Fortescue, Sir John, 172, 269, 292 & n,
  294, 301
Fotheringhay (Northants.), 73
Fougeres (France), 36, 65–6, 68
Fowey (Devon), 145, 176, 186
France: wars against, 26, 29, 36–7, 44, 66,
  68, 72–3, 77; attempted
  rapprochement with (1458–9), 139,

148–51; threat from (1461–4),
  235–6, 248, 250; negotiations for
  alliance (1464–8), 254, 259–60;
  English claim to, 267; kings of, *see*
  Charles, Louis; trade with, 251;
  admiral of, 290, 292; *see also*
  Acquitaine, Normandy, Sandwich
Franceys, Maud, c of Salisbury, 10, 96
Francis II, d of Brittany, 289, 295
Francis, K.H., 1
Frank, William, 22
Franklin, Thomas, abbot of Tewkesbury,
  49
Fulford, Sir Baldwin, 175
Fulthorpe, 22

Gainford, Thomas, 1, 4
Gainsborough (Lincs.), 283
Gairdner, James, 5
Galet, Louis, 153, 177 & n, 260
Gargrave, Sir Thomas, 237
Gascoigne, Thomas, 128
Gate, Sir Geoffrey, 213, 248, 252, 286–7
Genoa, people of, 148, 151; ships of, 147,
  174, 175
Geoffrey, Leysan, 224
George, d of Clarence, 55, 58, 61, 66,
  221n, 228, 230, 232–4, 261 & n,
  263–6, 269, 274–86, 292, 297–304;
  his w Isabel Neville, 61, 232, 234,
  282, 287, 292n; his children, 232,
  312; d of York, 302
George, Richard, master, 250
Glamorgan (Wales), 27, 43, 44, 46,
  53 & n, 59, 84–5, 123, 140, 169, 173,
  222, 239, 252
Gloucester, 46, 186–7, 245; d of, *see*
  Humphrey, Richard, Thomas; e of,
  59, 60; *see also* Clare Despenser,
  Monthermer
Goldcliff Priory (Wales), 32, 61, 232
Goldwell, James, 245n
Goodrich (Here.), 183, 221
Gower, Edward, 223
Grace Dieu, 145–6, 175–6, 250
Grafton, 43, 44, 89
Granvelle (France), 289
Gravelines, 174, 306

Great Chronicle of London, 265, 270
great councils, 79–81, 90–2, 96, 112–13,
    123, 126, 128, 131–2, 144, 151, 152,
    154, 156–8, 160, 161, 165–6, 261,
    264, 279–80
Greenford, John, 249
Greewich (Kent), 112–13, 150, 184
Gregory's Chronicle, 215–16
Greville, John, 185
Grey,
    of Astley and Groby, Sir Edward, 222,
        224, 252, 286, 297
    of Chillingham, Sir Ralph, 241–4,
        246–7
    of Codnor, Henry ld, 242, 265
    of Groby, Sir John, 258; *see also*
        Elizabeth
    of Powys, John ld, 270
    of Powys, Richard ld, 114, 129, 164,
        172
    of Ruthin, Anthony, 259
    of Ruthin, Edmund ld, 83, 91, 179, 182
    William, bp of Ely, 100, 156, 172, 177,
        182, 281
Greystoke, Ralph ld, 20, 22, 213, 230,
    235, 245, 246n, 253
Griffith, Henry, 45
Griffiths, Davy, 246
Griffiths, R.A., 25, 64, 83, 87–8, 128
Groby, ld Ferrers of, *see* Grey
Grocer, William, 222
Grosmont castle (Mon.), 123; *see also*
    Three Castles
Gross, A., 127, 211
Gruthuyse, Louis ld, 182, 290
Guelders (Neths.), 153
Guernsey, 169; *see also* Channel Isles
Guildford, Sir John, 232, 248
Guyscliff, *see* Warwick

Habington,
    Thomas, 5
    William, 5n
Hadleigh (Essex), 67
Hague, The (Neths.), 300
Hales, John, bp of Lichfield, 301
Hall, Edward, 4, 211n
Halle (Norf.), 234

Hang, East and West (Yorks.),
    wapentakes, 20, 82
Hankford, Anne, 258; her family, 10
Hanley Castle (Worcs.), 54, 58, 123, 252
Hanseatic League, 146–7, 151, 267, 287,
    289, 292, 304; *see also* Lübeck
Hanslope (Bucks.), 27, 48, 57, 58
Harcourt,
    Louis de, bp of Bayeux, 305–6
    Sir Robert, 44, 52, 232
Hardyng, John, 213
Harfleur (France), 268, 287, 290–1, 301
Harington,
    Sir James, 224, 225, 303
    Thomas, 155 & n, 163, 166, 214
Harington family, 223–4, 243; inheritance
    dispute, 223–4
Harlech (Wales), 239, 270
Harriss, G.L., 141
Hartlepool, John, master, 250
Hastings, William ld, 220–1, 223–4, 228,
    230, 241, 244–5, 251, 253, 256, 260,
    262, 266, 270, 277, 300; his w
    Katherine Neville, 221, 230, 270
Hawarden (Wales), 25
Hawkhead, Sir Roos, 246
Hawkins, John, 273
Hay (Wales), 183, 234
Hay, John, 183
Hearne's Fragment, 269
Hedgeley Moor (Northumb.), battle, 246
Hellowe (Lincs.), 284
Helmsley (Yorks.), 233
Henry IV, of Castile, 261
Henry IV, of England, 8, 15, 20, 94, 125,
    188
Henry V, 9, 15, 36, 125, 195
Henry VI: character, 66–7, 195, 199, 209,
    277; court, *plate 15*
    first reign (1422–61): minority, 11, 23;
        Warwick inheritance, 33, 34,
        41–2, 45; government, 3, 160–1,
        172, 267, 271; allegiance to,
        121–2, 188, 197–200, 209–10, 213,
        293, 297; defence against York,
        68–9, 78–81, 83, 85, 88, 98;
        madness (1453–5), 90, 92–3, 98,
        112, 120, 126; recovery, 112–14;

captured at St Albans, 116–19; resumes control, 125–9; reconciles factions, 132–8; royal faction, 137–9; political recovery, 148–60; 1459 campaigns, 162–7, *plate 13*; merciful to Yorkists, 157–8, 165, 167, 172–3; 1460 campaign and capture, 177–84; defence of title, 187–90; third protectorate, 212–16; recovery, 148–60; deposition of, 1, 209–10, 217–19
resistance after 1461: 235, 243–4, 246; attainder, 239; capture, 253
readeption: 1, 271, 287, 294, 299–310; death, 312
royal family: see Beaufort, Holland, Richard, Stafford; his q, *see* Margaret of Anjou; his s, *see* Edward
heralds, 165–6, 174, 228, 246, 280; *see also* Maine, Warwick
Henry VIII, 138
Herbert,
  Sir Richard, 277
  Thomas, 277
  William (d.1469), sheriff of Glamorgan, 49, 84; raid (1456), 130, 131; ld Herbert, 218, 221, 239, 256, 259, 264–5, 269–71, 276–7; e of Pembroke, 270
  William, e of Pembroke, 259, 270
Hereford, 131, 186; bp of, *see* Boulers, Stanbury
Hertford, 121, 124
Hesdin (Belg.), 143
Heworth (Yorks.), battle, 87
Hexham (Northumb.), battle, 246
High Peak (Derb.), 221n
Holburne (Berks.), 222
Holland,
  Edmund, e of Kent (d.1408), 7; his sisters, 7, 11
  Henry, d of Exeter (d.1475), title to crown, 70, 94, 110–11, 302; Ampthill dispute, 83, 85, 88–9, 91, 93–4, 96, 98; rebels (1454), 110–12; political career, 121–2, 128, 132–3, 135, 137, 154, 161,

180–1, 189; resists Edward IV, 212–14, 219, 235, 239; supports Readeption, 301–2, 309; admiral, 100, 133, 175–6; his da Anne, 233–4, 259
  John, e of Huntingdon and d of Exeter (d.1400), 94; his w Elizabeth, sister of Henry IV, 94
  John, d of Exeter, 67; Anne, w of, 10, 222
Holland family, 7–8; inheritances, 11, 16, 226; pedigree, 8; title to crown, 302
Honfleur (France), 254, 287, 290, 292
Hoo, Thomas, 75
Hospitallers, *see* St John
Hotoft, Richard, 22, 185
Howard, Sir John ld, 266, 287, 300
Huddleston,
  Sir John of Millom, 224, 237, 246n
  Richard, 234, 237; his w Margaret Neville, 234, 237
Huddleston family, 251, 286
Hugford,
  John, 33
  Thomas, 33, 50, 62–3; 185; his family, 251
Hume, David, 4, 5, 312
Humphrey, d of Gloucester (d.1447), 18, 26, 34, 64–6, 70, 121, 161, 196
Hungerford,
  Robert ld (d.1464), 177, 180, 235, 246
  Sir Thomas (d.1469), 269
Hunsdon (Herts.), 121, 123
Huntington (Wales), 183, 234
Hutton, Thomas, of Hutton John, 237

Illingworth, Ralph, 223
Inglewood (Cumb.), 21
Ingoldsthorpe, Isabel, 25, 130, 131n; *see also* Neville
Ingram, Thomas, 185; his w Emma, 185
Ireland, 69, 71, 73, 83, 131, 164, 169, 174, 176, 178, 182, 186, 196, 210, 248, 286–7; lieutenants, *see* Boteler, James; George, Richard
Ireland, John, 22
Isabella of Castile, 261 & n
Isabella of France, q to Edward I, 7

Isles (Scot.), ld of the, 240

James of Spain, 147
James II, k of Scotland, 127, 181
James III, k of Scotland, 240, 244
Jerningham, John, 147
Jersey, 169, 235; *see also* Channel Isles
Joan of Acre, c of Gloucester, 10, 59, 96
Joce, William, 222
John of Gaunt, d of Lancaster, 14, 55, 70,
    187, 227; his w Katherine Swynford,
    15, 23, 98; their children, *see*
    Beaufort
John, d of Bedford, 20, 21, 36; his w
    Jacquetta, 20; *see also* Wydeville
John, d of Calabria, 268
John Vale's Book, 158
Johnson, Paul, 91, 109, 196, 209–10
Jones, M.K., 210
Joseph, William, 120, 122, 124–5, 135
Julian of Blakeney, 146; of Fowey, 176,
    186

Katherine, q of Henry V, 11, 82
Kelingale, Roger, 246n
Kelsy, William, 62, 251–3
Kemp,
    John, cardinal, 69, 97–8
    Thomas, bp of London, 232
Kendal (Westmor.), 21, 82, 86, 260
Kendall, P.M., 1, 5
Kenfig (Wales), 59
Kenilworth (Warw.), 45, 55, 59, 127, 159,
    163, 218, 224
Kennedy, James, bp of St Andrews, 240,
    244–5, 255
Kent, c of, 11; e of, *see* Holland, Edmund;
    Neville, William
Kent, Thomas, 245n, 260, 262
Kidwelly (Wales), 84
King's College, Cambridge, 69, 91, 93–4,
    97
Kingsford, C.L., 145
Kingston upon Thames (Surr.), 264
Knaresborough (Yorks.), 222–3, 236, 238,
    247
Knight, Thomas, bp of St Asaph, 228
Kyriel, Sir Thomas, 144, 151, 216

La Rochelle (France), 147
Langley castle (Northumb.), 246
Langstrother, John, prior of St John, 277,
    280–1, 300
Latimer, ld, *see* Neville, George and
    Henry
Leconfield (Yorks.), 89
Lee, Benet, 185
Leicester, 113–15, 118, 127, 156, 183,
    221, 285
Le Mans (France), 290
Leominster (Here.), 159, 165, 166
Lewis, Sir Henry, 301
Lichfield (Staffs.), 89, 185, 219, 240; bp
    of, *see* Hales
Lincoln Cathedral, 23
Lincolnshire Rebellion, 281–5
Lindisfarne (Northumb.), 241
Lionel, d of Clarence, 70, 187
Lisle inheritance, 28, 32, 34, 53n; *see also*
    Berkeley, Talbot
Llandaff (Wales), 49, 59
Llanwhit (Wales), 49
London, 53, 69, 71–2, 80–2, 89, 112–15,
    121, 124, 128, 145, 148, 151, 156,
    177–9, 193, 197, 215–17, 219, 241,
    244–5, 253–4, 261, 264–6, 275,
    277–8, 282, 284, 309
    corporation: 175, 177, 183–4, 190, 195,
        212, 215–16, 218, 275; livery
        companies, 175, 183; mayor,
        298–9; alderman, 249; sheriffs,
        134; customer, 145; *see also* staple
    people: Flemings and Lombards, 148;
        mercers, 249; mob, 303, 309
    topography: Baynard's Castle, 130, 132,
        180, 217; bishop's palace, 119,
        180, 184; Blacfriars, 73, 180, 190;
        Cheapside, 253, 298; City, 119,
        150, 177, 180, 209, 265;
        Greyfriars, 132, 152; Guildhall,
        180, 184; le Erber, 132; London
        Bridge, 298; St John's Fields, 217;
        St Paul's Cathedral, 80, 119, 135,
        158, 177, 180, 189–90, 198, 209,
        218; Temple Bar, 132; Tower, 74,
        91, 93, 122, 150, 156, 177–8, 180,

200, 253, 280, 300; *see also*
Southwark, Westminster
loans from, 175, 183, 215, 218, 275
Warwick at, 81, 112, 124, 162, 177–80,
213–15, 239, 243, 252–3, 261, 266,
300
Losecote Field (1470), battle, 285
Louis XI, as dauphin, 149, 153, 181–2,
259–60; as k of France, 5, 253–6,
260, 262–5, 267–9, 288–96, 299,
305–7; depiction, *plate 20*
Loveday at St Paul's, 132–8, 148, 150,
155, 157
Lovelace, Geoffrey, 49
Lovell,
Francis ld, 234
Richard, 225
Loxton (Soms.), 224
Lübeck (Germany), 147, 151, 292; *see also*
Hanseatic League
Lucy, Sir William, 87, 90
Ludford (Salop.), 164, 166, 168–70, 177,
200, 213
Ludlow (Salop.), 73, 83, 158–9, 163–5,
170, 185–6, 193
Lumley,
Marmaduke, bp of Carlisle, 21, 66
Thomas ld, 236, 238; family, 13
Luthington, John, 251
Luton (Beds.), 215–16
Luttrell family of Dunster, 259
Luxembourg, Jacques de, 262
Lydd (Kent), 144
Lytton, ld (E.G.E.L. Bulwer-Lytton), 5,
312

McFarlane, K.B., 5, 53n, 95
Maidstone (Kent), 265
Maine herald, 152, 154
Major, John, 3
Malliverer, Sir John, 230
Malory, Sir Thomas, 52, 81
Maltravers, ld, *see* Arundel
Maner and Guyding, 291–5, 299–300, 302
manifestos, 65, 68–73, 79, 114, 115, 118,
154, 158–62, 166–9, 177, 189, 192–8,
209–10, 218, 271–5, 282, 298–300
Mantua (Italy), council of, 154

Margam Abbey (Wales), 49; abbot, 49, 59,
60–1
Margaret of Anjou, q of Henry VI:
marriage, 23, 29; pregnant, 83; seeks
regency, 93–4, 97; political career
(1455–9), 121, 126, 128, 130–1, 135,
151, 153, 156; resists after
Northampton, 180–4, 186, 192, 195,
197; resists after Towton, 212–17,
219, 235, 240, 244–5, 260; reconciled
with Warwick, 288, 290–1, 299,
301–2; returns to England and
captured, 303–4, 309, 312
Margaret of York, d of Burgundy, 241,
259, 263–4, 266–9, 305
Margate (Kent), 266
Marie, of Bayonne, 144
Marie, of Spain, 147
Markham, Sir John, 252
Markyate priory, 54
Marny, Sir John, 142, 174
Mary of Guelders, q of Scotland, 182, 240
Mary of Scotland, 182
Mary of Bristol, 176
Mason, Emma, 58
Mereworth (Kent), 34, 41, 53n, 84
Meryng, Thomas, 163
Messenger, Richard, 49
Middleham (Yorks.), 158–9, 163, 222,
252, 284, 312; castle, 12, 18, 23, 24,
plate 17; constable, 230; lordship, 22,
183, 236–7, 251, 275, 277; town, 18;
Warwick at, 89, 112, 221, 238, 247,
264
Middleton (Norf.), 307
Middleton,
John, 22
Thomas, 8
Milan, d of, *see* Sforza; Milanese
correspondence, 180, 184, 220, 260,
268, 277, 290
Mirror of Magistrates, 1, 3, 5
Moleyns, Adam, bp of Chichester, 70, 72,
200
Monmouth, 84, 123, 222, 239
Mont Orgueil (Jersey), 235

Montagu,
    John, e of Salisbury (d.1400), 8, 170,
        226, 239
    Sir Richard, 11
    Thomas, e of Salisbury (d.1428), 7–9,
        11, 258; his sisters, 10; his w
        Alice, *see* Pole; his w Eleanor
        Holland, 7, 11; his daughters, 7,
        11; *see* Neville
    William, e of Salisbury, 7
Montagu family, 7, 10, 229; inheritance,
    226; *see also* Salisbury Roll
Montgomery (Wales), 152
Mothermer family, 10, 59
Monypenny, William, sr de Concressault,
    265, 305
Moody, John, 152
More End (Northants.), 222
Moreton Morell (Warw.), 50
Mortimer's Cross, battle, 217
Mountford,
    Sir Baldwin, 52, 222
    Sir Edmund, 52
    Osbert, 174, 177, 200; his w Elizabeth,
        223
    Sir William, 51–2
Mountford dispute, 51–2, 111; family,
    251
Mowbray,
    John, e marshall and d of Norfolk
        (d.1425), 13, 15; his w Katherine
        Neville, 13, 15
    John, d of Norfolk (d.1461), 73, 91, 93,
        99, 109–10, 113, 115–17, 123, 182,
        213, 215–18, 222
    John, d of Norfolk (d.1476), 224, 242,
        266, 278, 304
Mulsho, Sir Edmund, 142, 152
Musgrave, Richard, 22, 82
Mymmes, Walter, 251

Nanfan, John, 34, 49, 51, 62, 77, 82, 100n,
    132, 145, 169
Naworth Castle (Cumb.), 240–1
Neath (Wales), Abbey, 59–60; Abbot, 49
Nesfield, William, 145

Neville,
    Edward, ld Bergavenny, 13, 14, 18,
        26–7, 32–7, 42, 48, 78, 84, 172,
        177, 193; his w Elizabeth
        Beauchamp, 26–7, 32, 35
    George, ld Latimer (d.1469), 13, 14,
        18, 24, 77–8, 97, 225–8; his w
        Elizabeth Beauchamp, 27, 225,
        230
    George, later ld Bergavenny, 37, 42–3,
        48, 53, 61, 76, 78, 82, 84, 111, 128,
        193, 226, 297
    George, abp of York: youth, 12, 24; bp
        of Exeter, 100, 123, 156, 172, 177,
        182, 184, 186, 189, 224, 228, 237,
        251; abp, 199, 217–18, 220–1, 232,
        239; 245–7, 254–5, 259, 261,
        263–6; rebels, 273–8, 280–1, 283;
        supports Readeption, 300;
        enthronement, 230–1
    George, d of Bedford, 233, 266, 281–2,
        312
    Sir Henry of Latimer (d.1469), 17, 57,
        228, 233, 275, 277, 280
    Sir Humphrey, of Bracepeth, 246–7,
        278
    Sir John (d.1420), 8, 11, 13, 16
    John, ld Neville (d.1461), 213, 235–6,
        247
    John, ld Montagu and e of
        Northumberland (d.1471),
        marriage 24–5; early career,
        130–1, 141, 150, 153, 163, 166,
        184, 228; attainder (1459), 170;
        chamberlain of household, 182,
        190; captured again, 216; 220;
        created earl, 230–1, 246;
        dominates North, 233, 235, 238,
        241–7, 251, 253, 256–7, 262,
        265–6, 270, 280, 281; m Montagu,
        281; supports Readeption, 297,
        300–1, 302, 307, 312; killed at
        Barnet, 310
    Ralph, e of Westmorland (d.1425),
        13–16, 20, 86; his w Joan
        Beaufort, 13, 15–16, 29, *plate 1*

Ralph, e of Westmorland (d.1484), 8, 13, 16, 18, 21, 29, 89, 212–13, 231, 235–6

Ralph of Ousley, 16

Ralph, ld Neville, later e of Westmorland, 230

Richard, e of Salisbury (d.1460), 7, 10, 12–14; creation, 11; northern magnate, 15, 20–1, 24–8, 30, 33, 35–6, 40, 44, 53, 67, 74, 78–9, 81, 83, 87; warden of West March, 67, 100, 127, 131, 155; at Dartford (1452), 81–2; Percy feud, 85–90; supports York (1453–6), 91–125; chancellor, 98–9, 109, 11–13; at St Albans, 115–16, 118–20; Loveday, 132–8; treason charges (1459), 155–6; rebels (1459), 158–60, 162–7; attainder, 170; flees to Calais, 164, 169, 199; invades England, 178, 191; Neville regime, 184–6; great chamberlain and chief steward of North Parts, 183; opposes York's usurpation, 189; killed at Wakefield, 214, 218, 220; funeral, 228–30; depiction, *plate 2*; his w Alice Montagu, 10, 131, 159, 169, 181, 226, 228–30, *plate 2*; his children, 24, *plate 1*; *see also* Arundel, Beauchamp, Bonville, FitzHugh, Hastings, Stanley, Vere

Richard, e of Warwick and Salisbury (d.1471), the Kingmaker:

life: birth, 7; connections, 2–11, 15; marriage, 24, 26–9; knight, 29; e of Warwick, 30, 33–8, 49–50, 51–63, 67, 74–5, 77–8, *see also* Beauchamp, Despenser; premier earl, 44, 82–3, 227, 234, 281; K.G., 184; e of Salisbury, 227; aspires to dukedom, 234, 257; death, 310

principal offices: admiral, 221, 304; captain of Calais, 123–4, 126–7, 138–47, 152, 154, 161, 191, 193, 221–2, 225, 227, 239, 248–9, 257,

see also, Calais; chief steward of North Parts, 183, 221; great chamberlain, 257; hereditary sheriff of Cumberland, 24–7; keeper of seas, 131–3, 138, 144–8, 152, 154, 161, 183, 190–1, 193, 221–2, 225, 227, 257; lieutenant of England, 301; lieutenant of North, 221, 238, 242, 257; master of mews, 221; steward of England, 257n; warden of Cinque Ports, 138, 183, 221; warden of West March, 29, 100, 109, 131, 155, 161, 221–2, 225, 227, 252, 288

his connection: 49–52, 62–3, 81, 115–16, 123, 191, 222–5, 227–8, 236–41, 264, 312; his feoffees, 252–3; his secretary, *see* Fisher, Neville

his itinerary: *see* Calais, Coventry, London, Middleham, Warwick, Westminster

his arms, 15, 57, *plate 18*; badges, 58, 61, 74, 77, 214, 227, 304, *see also plates 9, 11, 18 and 22*; biographies, 1; book, 57, *plate 19*; council, 223, 265, *see also* Gate, Grey, Scull, Wrottesley; depictions, *plates 8 and 18*; letter, *plate 21*; piety, 232–3; propaganda, 160–2, 164–5, 191–9, 271–5, 298–300; ring, 61, 310, *plate 4*; seal, 310, *plate 10*; ships, 144–5, 154, 173–6, 232, 250–1, 286–92, 295, 299, 304, *see also Trinity*; vow, 219; warcry, 116, 265, 285, 290; will, 232

his w Anne, *see* Beauchamp; his daughters Isabel and Anne, 49, 63, 81, 230–2, 234, 259, 264, 286, 289–90, 292–3, 302, 312; his bastard Margaret, 234, 237; his heirs, 233

Robert, bp Salisbury & Durham (d.1457), 12–17, 33, 89, 92, 132

Robert, Warwick's secretary, 252, 260

Sir Thomas of Raby, 16

Sir Thomas (d.1460), 24, 49, 62, 82, 87–9, 129, 131, 150, 163, 166, 170,

Neville, Sir Thomas *(continued)*
183–4, 189, 189, 228–9, 235, 283;
his w Maud Stanhope Lady
Willoughby, 24, 283
William, ld Fauconberg, e of Kent
(d.1463), 13–14, 36–7, 91–2, 115,
121–2, 141–2, 147, 150, 169,
176–7, 179, 182, 184, 191, 193,
219–20, 235–6, 240, 242, 257; his
bastard Thomas, *see* Fauconberg
Neville family: 12–19, 193, 199–200, 210,
236, 246, 312; arms, 12, 15, 17, *plates
1 and 3*; churchmen, 12; earls, 94,
100, 114, 118, 129, 149, 182–4;
income, 19; inheritance, 233;
marriages, 13–16, 22, 24–9, 86,
130–1, 179, 184, 221, 232, 264, *plate
2*; Neville's Cross, battle, 13; Neville
Book of Hours, 13, *plate 1*;
Neville–Neville feud, 16–17, 29;
Neville screen, 12, *plate 5*; royal
lineage, 76
Newbury (Berks.), 193, 196
Newcastle-upon-Tyne, 146, 238, 241–2,
245, 247, 253
Newport (Wales), 183, 234, 250, 256
Newport Pagnell (Bucks.), 222
newsletters, 92–4, 116–17, 119–22, 282,
291–5, 309–10
Nibley Green (Glos.), 282; *see also*
Berkeley–Lisle dispute
Norham castle (Northumb.), 238, 244
Normandy: loss of, 64–6, 68–9, 72, 76–7,
79, 140, 144, 146, 267–8; trade, 251;
base for invasion (1470), 287
Norris, John, 33–4, 51, 75, 77
Northampton, battle (1460), 168, 178–9,
181, 186, 189, 191, 198, 200, 211,
220, 223
Northumberland, e of, *see* Percy, Henry
Norwich, 144, 276
Nottingham, 219, 265, 297, 300

oaths, 79–81, 121–2, 158, 188–9, 197,
209–10, 218, 285, 288, 293
Ogle, Sir Robert, later ld Ogle, 114, 116,
231, 236, 238, 242, 245n

Oldhall, Sir William, 69, 73, 121, 123,
159, 170
Olney (Bucks.), 141, 233, 277
Oman, Sir Charles, 1
Ormond, *see* Butler
Oseney Abbey (Oxon.), 54
Ostend (Belgium), 175
Otter,
John, 62, 145, 172, 251, 252 & n
Thomas, 62
Otter family, 286
Overy, William, 174, 200
Oxford, e of, *see* Vere

Pains Castle (Wales), 42
Paris (France), 291; parlement, 289
parliaments, 37, 43–4, 53, 66, 68–9, 73–5,
83, 96–8, 120, 122–5, 166, 170–3,
180–1, 185–9, 199, 209, 212, 218,
226, 239, 243, 245, 253–4, 267, 270,
277–8, 302–3, 306; speakers, *see*
Charlton, Oldhall, Strangways,
Thorpe, Wenlock
Parliamentary Pardon (1455), 120, 122
Parre,
Sir Thomas, 214
Sir William, 163, 222, 246n, 303
Paston,
John, 223–4; Margaret his w, 190
William, 199
Paston family, 65; letters, 65; *see also*
Fastolf
Paynter, John, master, 145
Pembroke, e of, *see* Herbert, William;
Tudor, Jasper
Penrith (Cumb.), 15, 16, 21, 183, 236–7
Percy,
Henry, e of Northumberland (d.1455),
13–15, 18, 21, 53, 85–6, 89, 91, 96,
110–11, 116, 119, 213; his w
Eleanor Neville, 35 & n, 37,
53 & n, 86, 230
Henry, ld Poynings and e of
Northumberland (d.1461), 76, 89,
91, 93, 96, 109, 129, 132, 134–7,
172, 185, 212–13, 235–6
Henry, e of Northumberland, 259, 270,
280, 302, 307

Sir Ralph, 117, 119–20, 134, 242, 246
Sir Richard, 96, 121, 134
Thomas, ld Egremont (d.1460), 86–9, 91, 93–4, 96, 111–12, 121, 129, 132–4, 136, 172, 179, 213, 236
William, bp of Carlisle, 86, 115
Percy family, 12, 94, 96, 129, 181, 213, 236, 240; forfeitures, 257, 280; Percy–Neville feud, 85–9, 111, 114, 120, 126, 134, 137, 213, 235, 280
Peronne, treaty of, 268, 289, 305
Perrot, Robert, 240
Petworth (Suss.), 89
Philip, Thomas, master, 250
Philip the Good, d of Burgundy (d.1467), 139, 143 & n, 149, 151, 174, 181–2, 215, 239, 253–4, 259–62
Pickering (Yorks.), 236–7
Pickering, Sir James, 163
Pius II, pope, 181–2, 189, 210, 215
Pleasance, William, 50
Plummer, Sir John, 301
Plumpton, Sir William, 222–3, 238, 258
Plymouth (Devon), 145
Pole,
    John de la, of Suffolk, 153, 218, 228, 230, 257
    William de la, e, m and d of Suffolk, 11–12, 18, 35–6, 44, 64–9, 75, 122; Alice Chaucer his w, 11, 75, 222, 230
political verse, 65, 74, 134–5, 137–8, 154, 169, 177, 179, 181, 186, 189, 192–5, 197–9, 303, 311–12
Pollard, A.J., 19, 58
Pont L'Arche (France), 36
Pontefract Castle (Yorks.), 29, 111–12, 183, 214, 236–7, 246–7
Poole (Dors.), 145; *see also* Canford
Popes, *see* Eugenius IV, Pius II; nuncio, *see* Coppini
Port, Richard, purser, 250
Portchester Castle (Hants.), 100, 113
Porter, John, master, 250
Porthaleyn, Thomas, 26–8, 49, 58, 62, 269
Power, Watkins, 57
Preston Capes (Northants.), 233

Proclamations, 175, 218, 282, 293
propaganda, 192, 194–5, 197, 212, 214, 216, 308; *see also* attainder, manifestos, newsletters, oaths, political verse, proclamations
protectorates, *see* Richard
Public Weal, War of, 262, 267

Queens of England, *see* Eleanor, Elizabeth, Isabella, Katherine, Margaret, Neville
Quyxley, John, 22

Raby Castle (Dur.), 12, 16, 23
Radcliff, Roger, 159, 223
Radford, Sir Henry, 214
Raine, James, 4
Rapin de Thoyras, P., 5
Raughton, Emma, anchoress, 56, 58
Raven, Margaret, 50
Ravenspur (Yorks.), 307
Rawcliffe, C., 211
Readeption, *see* Henry VI
Reading (Berks.), 83, 90, 258–9, 261
Redesdale, *see* Robin
Redman, Sir Richard, 243
Renty, Merlot de, 142
Rhé Île de (France), 240, 250
Richard I, 229
Richard II, 8, 11, 15, 254, 272
Richard III, 10, 55, 26, 311; as d of Gloucester, 18, 62, 230, 234, 253–4, 257–8, 261, 263, 276, 280–1, 300; for his consort Anne, *see* Neville, Richard
Richard, e of Cambridge, 15, 226, 239
Richard, d of York (d.1460), 131, 150, 169, 175–6
    lieutenant of Ireland, 69, 71, 83, 131, 140, 169, 175–6; captain of Calais, 140
    political career: political opposition (1450–3), 64, 69, 74–6, 83–4; Dartford campaign (1452), 79–81; returns to power (1453), 90–112; king's lieutenant, 96, 112; first protectorate (1454–5), 97–9, 109–13; attacks court at St Albans,

Richard, duke of York *(continued)*
114–19; second protectorate,
124–6, 138, 153, 185, 211;
quarrels, 126, 129–30; Loveday
(1458), 132–8; accused of treason
(1459), 155–9; rebels 158–67;
claims the crown, 186–90, 210–12;
third protectorate, 168, 180,
185–91, 194, 196, 209, 211, 213;
killed at Wakefield, 214
his w Cecily Neville, 13–14, 191, 230,
278; his offspring, 37, 149, 191; *see
also* Edmund, Edward, George,
Margaret, Richard
Richmond, C.F., 2
Richmond (Yorks.), 12, 18–19, 20, 276,
plate 3; e of, 10, 12, 14, 19, 20, *see
also* Tudor; honour, 15, 19, 67, 76,
233, 257, 270, 281–2, 302
Richmondshire connection, 20, 132, 276,
284, 295, 300, 307, 312
Ringwood (Hants.), 20
Robin, rebel, 265
of Holderness, 271
of Redesdale, 270–1, 274–6, 282
Rochester (Kent), 147, 151
Rody, Nicholas, 33, 50, 62
Roos,
Thomas ld (d.1430), 27, 36–7
Thomas ld (d.1464), 129, 132, 137,
146, 173, 181, 225, 235, 238, 242,
246
Ross, e of, 240–1
Ross, C.D., 28, 257
Ross-on-Wye (Here.), 84
Rouen (France), 23, 36, 68, 254, 291
Rous,
Edmund, 223
John, 3, 50, 55–9, 61–2, *205*, 227
William, 57
Roxburgh (Scot.), 156, 181, 247
Roye, Jean de, 266, 300
Royston, 115
Rozmital, Leo, 253
Rufford, John, 285
Rutland, e of, *see* Edmund
Rye (Suss.), 240
Rye House (Herts.), 121

Rythe, Sibyl, 222
Ryton (Dur.), 238

St Albans (Herts.), 45, 71, 73, 213; abbey,
61, 116; battles, 74, 81–2, 113–19,
121, 132, 134–5, 140, 153, 215–16,
258; chantry, 135–6, 155
St Asaph, bp of, *see* Knight
St Barbara of Dordrecht, 146
St Briavel's (Gloucs.), 31, 123
St John prior, 112, 273, 277; *see also*
Langstrother
St Malo (France), 250
St Omer (France), 143, 253, 261, 263, 276
St Pol, c of, 289
St Vaast La Hogue (France), 290
Salisbury, bp of, *see* Aiscough, William;
Beauchamp, Richard; Neville,
Robert; e of, *see* Montagu, John,
Thomas *and* William; Neville,
Richard
Salisbury Rolls, 9–12, 96, 229–30, 283,
plates 2 and 18
Salkeld, Richard, 247
Salwarpe (Worcs.), 24, 170
Sandal Castle (Yorks.), 127, 214
Sandford, Thomas, 241
Sandhutton (Yorks.), 89
Sandwich (Kent), 131, 141, 14–6, 151,
173, 177–8, 183, 194, 232, 239,
249–51, 254
Say, William, 152; ld, *see* Fiennes
Scales, Thomas ld, 177, 180, 194; *see also*
Wydeville, Anthony
Scammell, G., 250
Scarborough, Thomas, 222–3
Scot, William, 173
Scotland, 30, 139, 149, 158, 174, 178,
181–2, 235–6, 238–47, 253, 260, 268;
see also James, k of Scotland
Scull, Sir Walter, 224, 252
Scrope,
John ld Scrope of Bolton, 89, 91–2,
182, 231, 304; his w Joan
FitzHugh, 182
Stephen, 222
Thomas, ld Scrope of Masham, 235
Scrope family, 13, 19, 20

Sforza, Francesco de, d of Milan, 181, 215, 239, 263

Shakespeare, William, 1

Sheffield (Yorks.), 285

Sheldon, Daniel, 251

Sheriff Hutton (Yorks.), 12, 16, 23–4, 87–8, 112, 226, 236, 265

Sherston (Wilts.), 34, 51

ships, 144–7, 154, 173–6, 180, 186, 232, 244, 286–7; *see also* Neville

Shouldham Priory, 54

Shrewsbury, 70–1, 185–6, 210; e of, *see* Talbot

Skenfrith (Wales), 123; *see also* Three Castles

Skernard, Henry, 129

Skipton (Yorks.), 111, 246

Sluys (Belgium), 290

Sodbury (Glos.), 46, 77

Somerlane, Henry, 49

Somerset, John, 222; d of, *see* Beaufort

Somnium Vigilantis, 156, 158–9, 167, 171–2, 192–4, 199

Sotehill, Henry, 30, 39, 62, 220, 237, 252

Southampton (Hants.), 142, 145–6, 183, 250, 286–7

Southwark (Surr.), 132, 180

Sowerby (Yorks.), 86, 247

Spain, *see* Castille

Spofforth (Yorks.), 111, 233, 238

Stafford,
Fulk, of Clent, 85
Sir Henry, 157, 212, 303; his w Margaret Beaufort, 157, 212, 281
Henry, d of Buckingham (d.1483), 184, 212, 227, 234, 259; his w Katherine Wydeville, 234, 259
Humphrey, d of Buckingham (d.1460), 13–14, 17, 51–3, 70, 78, 81, 93–4, 96, 99, 113, 115–16, 118, 121, 130, 137, 150, 157, 161, 172–3, 177–9, 184, 227; his w Anne Neville, 13, 17
Humphrey, e of Stafford (d.1458), 116
Humphrey, of Grafton, the elder (d.1450), 43–5, 50, 52, 63; the younger, 115

Humphrey of Southwark, e of Devon (d.1469), 265, 271, 273, 276–7, 300
John, e of Wiltshire, 230, 280
Stafford lordships in Wales, 256; *see also* Brecon, Hay, Huntington, Newport,
Stafford-Harcourt dispute, 44, 52

Staindrop College (Dur.), 13, 23

Stamford Bridge (Yorks.), battle, 112

Stanbury, John, bp of Hereford, 181, 200

Stanhope, Maud, lady Willoughby, 24, 87–8, 230; *see also* Neville, Thomas

Stanley,
Thomas ld, 24, 163, 172, 182, 224, 230–1, 243–4, 251–2, 284, 300, 304; his w Eleanor Neville, 24, 164, 230
William, 163, 166, 170

Stanton Harcourt (Oxon.), 44

Stillington, Robert, bp of Bath, 182, 301

Stodeley, John, 89, 92–4, 128

Stokdale, Thomas, 22, 62

Stone, John, 232

Stony Stratford (Northants.), 71

Storey, Edward, bp of Carlisle, 281

Stourton, William ld, 99, 142, 182

Stow Relation, 116, 119–21

Strangways,
Sir James, 22, 239, 245n, 252
Sir Richard, 230
Robert, 286

Stubbs, William, bp of Oxford, 5

Sudeley, ld, see Boteler

Suffolk, d & e of, *see* Pole, John *and* William

Surienne, François de, 66

Sutton Coldfield (Warw.), 40, 56, 58

Swainstown (I of Wight), 29, 144

Tailbois, William, 74, 99, 238, 240, 246

Talbot,
John, e of Shrewsbury (d.1453), 18, 27, 32, 36–7, 40, 51, 76–9, 83, 90, 97, *203*; his w Margaret Beauchamp, 40, 44, 46, 51, 56, 77–8, 97, 129, 170, 225

Talbot *(continued)*
  John, e of Shrewsbury (d.1460), 32, 97,
    122, 128, 130 & n, 132, 137, 177,
    179, 196
  John, e of Shrewsbury (d.1473), 184,
    212, 221, 265–6, 284, 300, 304
  John, ld Lisle (d.1453), 32, 46, 78, 90,
    97
  Thomas, v Lisle (d.1470), 270
Talbot–Talbot feud, 97
Taster, Pierre, dean of St Severin's, 99,
    262
Tattershall (Lincs.), 87–9
Taunton (Soms.), 93
Taverham, Roger, 223
Tempest, Katherine w of Roger, 222
Tewkesbury (Glos.), 46, 52, 59–61, 77–8,
    82, 89, 123, 164; battle, 303, 311–12;
    chantries, 32, 34, 37n, 38, 60–2, 232,
    plate 14; chronicle, 26, 61
Thomas, d of Clarence, 11; d of
    Gloucester, 70, 96
Thomas, William, master, 250
Thornton, Roger, 245n
Thorpe,
  Anna da of John, 222–3
  Thomas, 83, 93, 96, 120, 122–3, 125,
    135
Three Castles (Wales), 84, 123, 222, 239
Threlkeld, Sir Henry, 22
Throckmorton,
  John (d.1445), 32, 48, 78
  Thomas, 77, 252
Tiptoft,
  John, e of Worcester (d.1470), 32, 37,
    39–40, 42, 92, 97, 111–13, 115,
    131, 220, 242, 245, 251, 297, 301,
    304, 306; his w Cecily Neville, 32,
    36; *see also* Beauchamp
  Joyce, 131; her inheritance, 25
Topcliffe (Yorks.), 86–7, 236, 253
Torre, Antonio de la, 214
Tosny family, 54, 57, 58
Toul, bp of, 151
Tours, treaty of, 36, 65, 148
Towton (Yorks.), battle, 154, 217, 219,
    228, 234–5, 238
Trafford, Sir John, 237

treasurers, *see* Blount, Boteler, Bourchier,
    Fiennes, Grey, Langstrother,
    Lumley, Talbot, Tiptoft
treaties, *see* Angers, Arras, Chinon,
    Peronne, Tours, Troyes
Tresham, Sir Thomas, 120, 123
Trinity, 232, 250–1, 276, 304
Trollope, Sir Andrew, 146, 162, 165, 167,
    173 & n, 181, 214, 218
Troyes, treaty, 190
Tuddenham, Sir John, 65, 152–3, 182
Tudor,
  Edmund, e of Richmond (d.1456), 25,
    82, 85–6, 93, 99, 125, 130, 132,
    270
  Henry, e of Richmond, 132;
    speculation on restoration, 259,
    270, 281, 302
  Jasper, e of Pembroke, 82, 85, 92–3, 99,
    122, 125, 137, 161, 181, 186, 212,
    217, 239, 242, 268, 270, 292–3,
    297, 299, 300, 304, 309
  Owen, 82
Tunstall,
  John, 22
  Sir Richard, 301
Tutbury (Staffs.), 31, 45, 183, 285, 302
Tuxforth (Notts.), 86, 93
Tynedale (Northumb.), 236, 238
Tynemouth (Northumb.), 238

Urchenfield (Wales), 221
Usk (Wales), 173

Valognes (France), 289–90
Vampage, John, 33, 75
Vaughan, Thomas, 159
Vaujous (France), 292
Vaux, Roland, 238
Veere, ld, 290
Venice, galleys, 175
Vere,
  Sir George, 287
  John, e of Oxford (d.1513), 230, 232,
    234, 269, 288, 297, 299–301, 304,
    307–9, 312; his w Margaret
    Neville, 230, 234, 251, 258

Vernon,
  Henry, 308
  Roger, 265
Vernon-Blount feud, 110, 265
Virgoe, Roger, 99
Voetken, Hans, 307

Wake, Thomas, 277
Wakefield (Yorks.), battle (1460), 182,
  215, 223, 228, 239
Walden (Essex), 266
Wales, 169, 173, 175, 178, 181, 183, 186,
  189, 191, 212–14, 217, 221, 235, 239,
  250, 256–7, 264, 268–70, 276, 277,
  284, 298, 304, 309; *see also*
  Abergavenny, Cardiff, Elvell,
  Glamorgan
Walford Parva (Warw.), 185
Walgrave, Thomas, 185
Wallingford (Berks.), 112, 122, 224
Walsh, Geoffrey, 224
Waltham Abbey (Essex), 266
Warcop, Robert, 241
Ware (Herts.), 22 & n, 115, 121, 183, 215,
  225
Warkworth Castle (Northumb.), 241–2
Warkworth, John, 265–6, 271, 291, 300,
  302
Warmington Priory, 54
Warwick, 27, 55, 33, 40, 49–50, 52, 54–5,
  200, 225, 266, 277; arms, 57, *plate 8*;
  topography, 54–5; college, 32–3,
  55–7, 61–2, 130, 239, 245, 253, 277;
  Beauchamp Chapel, 32, 56, 62, 130,
  225, 232–3; *plates 8 and 9*; and e of,
  see Beauchamp, Neville; Guy of,
  giant, 55, 58, *plates 6 and 7*;
  Guyscliff Chapel, 27, 32–3, 55, 58–9,
  62, 226, 232–3, *plate 6*; herald,
  178–9, 224, 227–8, 246, 260–1, *see*
  also Griffiths, Water; officers, 49–50;
  Wedgenock Park, 50, 56
Warwick at, 43–5, 49, 81, 84, 126, 130,
  184–5, 240, 245, 252–3, 264, 266,
  280, 284–5, 303n, 308
Water, John, 228
Waterford (Ire.), 175
Watford (Herts.), 115

Waurin, Jehan de, 165, 168, 176–7,
  184–5, 187, 190, 193, 210, 212, 276,
  300
Waynflete, William, bp of Winchester,
  92, 128, 130n, 146, 151, 157, 200,
  300
Welles,
  Leo ld (d.1461), 110, 137, 142
  Richard, ld Willoughby, later ld
    Welles, 185, 230, 282–5
  Sir Robert, 282–5
Welles–Burgh feud, 283–4
Weltden, Richard, 22
Wenham, Little (Suff.), 142
Wenlock, Sir John, 151, 153–4, 162, 169,
  175, 178, 182, 232, 242, 248, 251,
  260–1, 269, 287–8, 312
Wessington, John, 24
Westacre Priory, 54
Westminster (Middx.), 112–13, 127, 132,
  124, 160, 167, 180n, 185–7, 217;
  Abbey, 218; great council at, 279–80,
  Hall, 73, 152, 154, 167, 218;
  parliament at, 73, 273, 302;
  sanctuary, 300; St Stephen's Chapel,
  301; Warwick at, 239, 243, 253–4,
  280, 284
Whetehamstede, John, abbot of St
  Albans, 116, 133, 157, 159, 166–7,
  171, 189
Whetehill,
  Adrian, 248
  Richard, 177–81, 239, 248, 251, 260–1
White Castle (Wales), 123; *see also* Three
  Castles
Whitelaw, Archibald, 211
Wickwane (Glos.), 53n, 77
Wight, Isle of, 67, 248, 287
Willbery, George, 266
William, Thomas, 250
Willoughby family, 10, 11, 25; ld, *see*
  Welles
Wiltshire, e of, *see* Boteler, James
Windsor (Berks.), 90, 120, 225, 264
Winchester (Hants.), 37, 56, 62, 173, 226
Winterbourne Earls (Wilts.), 226
Witham, Thomas, 22, 252
Wodehill, Elizabeth, 225

Wolverton (Warw.), 233
Wood,
Helne, 50
John atte, 222
Worcester, 54, 164–8; e of, *see*
Beauchamp, Richard; Tiptoft, John
Worcestre, pseudo-, chronicler, 243,
263–4
Worsley, Otwell, 248–9, 252
Wressle (Yorks.), 88, 183
Wrottesley,
Henry, 285
Sir Walter, 183, 230, 232, 252, 286
Wydeville,
Sir Anthony, ld Scales and e Rivers
(d.1483), 150, 175, 184, 199,
216–17, 242, 254, 257–8, 264–5,
267, 271, 276, 280–1, 288
Sir John, 271, 274, 277

Richard, ld and e Rivers (d.1469), 110,
137, 142, 151, 173, 175, 177, 184,
199, 245, 258, 265, 274, 277, 281,
306; his w Jacquetta, d of Bedford,
175, 271–2, 274, 277–8, 280, 284,
301
Wydeville marriages, 234, 259, 270

Yardley (Worcs.), 50
Yarmouth (Norf.), 250
York, 86, 111–12, 28, 230, 245, 297; abp
of, *see* Bothe, Neville; abp's palace,
230, 246; anchoress, 56; d of, *see*
Edmund, Edward, George, Richard;
gates, 228; Minster, 230; provincial
clergy, 244; St Leonard's Hospital,
246, 266; St William's College, 23,
221, 233, 237–8; Warwick at, 112,
238, 240, 245–6, 253, 261;
Young, Thomas, 70, 76, 123